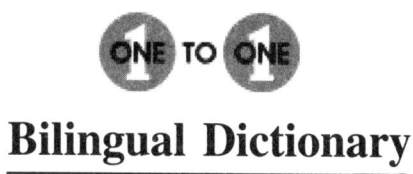

## Bilingual Dictionary

# English-Hindi
# Hindi-English
## Dictionary

Compiled by
**Sudhakar Chaturvedi**

ibs BOOKS (UK)

© Publishers

First Edition: 2011

ISBN : 978-1-905863-78-5

Published by
**ibs BOOKS (UK)**
55, Warren Street, London W1T 5NW (UK)
e-mail: indbooks@aol.com; starbooksuk@aol.com
www.starbooksuk.com

Printed in India at
Star Print-O-Bind, New Delhi-110020

# About this Dictionary

Developments in science and technology today have narrowed down distances between countries, and have made the world a small place. A person living thousands of miles away can learn and understand the culture and lifestyle of another country with ease and without travelling to that country. Languages play an important role as facilitators of communication in this respect.

Innumerable surveys have failed to determine the accurate number of languages spoken globally, though it is estimated that there may be more than 300 official languages around the world which have their own script. But majority of the world people speak and understand English, which is used as a medium to learn and translate other languages.

To promote such an understanding, **ibs BOOKS(UK)** has planned to bring out a series of bilingual dictionaries in which important English words have been translated into other languages. This publication is one of them.

This is a humble attempt to bring people of the world closer through the medium of language, and thus promote mutual understanding.

These dictionaries have been compiled and edited by teachers and scholars of relative languages.

## ibs BOOKS (UK)
London W1T 5NW (UK)

# Bilingual Dictionaries in this Series

| | |
|---|---|
| English-Arabic/Arabic-English | Rania-al-Qass |
| English-Bengali/Bengali-English | Amit Majumdar |
| English-Cantonese/Cantonese-English | Nisa Yang |
| English-Dari/Dari-English | Amir Khan |
| English-Farsi/Farsi-English | Maryam Zamankhani |
| English-Gujarati/Gujarati-English | Sujata Basaria |
| English-Hindi/Hindi-English | Sudhakar Chaturvedi |
| English-Hungarian/Hungarian-English | Lucy Mallows |
| English-Lithuanian/Lithuanian-English | Regina Kazakeviciute |
| English-Nepali/Nepali-English | Anil Mandal |
| English-Punjabi/Punjabi-English | Teja Singh Chatwal |
| English-Pashto/Pashto-English | Amir Khan |
| English-Polish/Polish-English | Magdalena Herok |
| English-Romanian/Romanian-English | Georgeta Laura Dutulescu |
| English-Somali/Somali-English | Ali Mohamud Omer |
| English-Tamil/Tamil-English | Sandhya Mahadevan |
| English-Turkish/Turkish-English | Nagme Yazgin |
| English-Urdu/Urdu-English | S.A Rahman |

**More languages in print**

# ibs BOOKS (UK)
London W1T 5NW (UK)

# ENGLISH-HINDI

# A

aback *adv.* भौचक्का bhauchakka

abandon *v.t.* त्याग देना tyag dena

abase *v.t.* अपमानित करना apmanit karna

abasement *n* अपमान apman

abash *v.t.* लज्जित करना lajjit karna

abate *v.t.* कम करना kam karna

abatement *n.* कमी kami

abbey *n.* ईसाई मठ isai math

abbreviate *v.t.* संक्षिप्त करना sankshipt karna

abbreviation *n* संक्षिप्तीकरण sankshiptikaran

abdicate *v.t,* त्यागना tyagna

abdication *n* पद-त्याग pad tyag

abdomen *n* पेट pet

abdominal *a.* पेट-संबंधी pet-sambandhi

abduct *v.t.* अपहरण करना apaharan karna

abduction *n* अपहरण apaharan

abed *adv.* बिस्तर पर bistar par

aberrance *n.* विचलित होना vichalit hona

abet *v.t.* उकसाना uksana

abetment *n.* उकसाव uksaav

abeyance *n.* ठहराव thahrav

abhor *v.t.* घृणा करना ghrina karna

abhorrence *n.* घृणा ghrina

abide *v.i* पालन करना palan karna

abiding *a* पालन करते हुए palan karte hue

ability *n* योग्यता yogyata

abject *a.* अधम adham

ablactate *v. t* दूध पिलाना dudh pilana

ablaze *adv.* जलता हुआ jalta hua

able *a* योग्य yogya

ablepsy *n* अन्धापन andha-pan

ablush *adv* लज्जित lajjit karna

abnegate *v. t* त्याग करना tyag karna

abnegation *n* त्याग tyag

abnormal *a* असामान्य asamanya

aboard *adv* नौका पर nauka par

abode *n* घर ghar

abolish *v.t* उन्मूलन करना unmulan karna

abolition *v* उन्मूलन unmulan

abominable *a* घिनौना ghinauna

aboriginal *a* मूल mul

aborigines *n. pl* मूल निवासी mul nivasi

abort *v.i* गर्भपात होना garbhpaat hona

abortion *n* गर्भपात garbhpaat

abortive *adv* निष्फल nishphal

about *adv* लगभग lagbhag

about *prep* विषय में vishay mein

above *adv* ऊपर upar

abreast *adv* बराबर में barabar mein

abridge *v.t* संक्षेप करना sankshep karna

abridgement *n* संक्षेप sankshep

abroad *adv* विदेश videsh

abrogate *v. t.* रद्द करना radd karna

abrupt *a* आकस्मिक aakasmik

abruption *n* एकाएक टूटना eka-ek tutna

abscond *v.i* फ़रार होना farar hona

absence *n* अनुपस्थिति anupasthiti

absent *a* अनुपस्थित anupasthit

absent *v.t* अनुपस्थित रखना anupasthit rakhna

absolute *a* पूर्ण purna

absolutely *adv* पूर्ण रूप से purna rup se

absolve *v.t* दोषमुक्त करना doshmukt karna

absonant *adj* न्याय विरुद्ध nyaya virudh

absorb *v.t* सोखना sokhna

abstain *v.i.* बचना bachna

abstract *a* अमूर्त amurt

abstract *n* सारांश saransh

abstract *v.t* अलग करना alag karna

abstraction *n.* मतिहीनता matihinta

absurd *a* मूर्खतापूर्ण murkhatapurn

absurd *adj* विवेकहीन vivekhin

absurdity *n* मूर्खता murkhata

abundance *n* प्रचुरता prachurta

abundant *a* प्रचुर prachur

abuse *v.t.* गाली देना gaali dena

abuse *n* अपशब्द apshabd

abusive *a* अपमानजनक apmanjanak

abut *v* मिलना milna

abuttal *n* मिलन स्थल milan sthal

abyss *n* रसातल rasatal

academic *a* विद्यामूलक vidyamulak

academy *n* अकादमी akadami

acarpous *adj.* बाँझ banjh

accede *v.t* मान लेना maan lena

accelerate *v.t* गति बढ़ाना gati barhana

acceleration *n* गतिवृद्धि gativridhi

accent *n* स्वर svar

accent *v.t* स्वरोच्चारण करना svarochaaran karna

accept *v.t.* स्वीकार करना sveekar karna

acceptable *a* प्रिय priya

acceptance *n* स्वीकृति svikriti

access पहुँच pahunch

access *n* प्रवेश pravesh

accession *n* सहमति sahamati

accessory *n* उपसाधन upsadhan

accident *n* दुर्घटना durghatna

accidental *a* आकस्मिक aakasmik

acclaim *v.t* जय जयकार करना jay jaykar karna

acclaim *n* जयकार jaykar

acclamation *n* प्रशंसा prashansa

accommodate *v.t* अनुकूल बनाना anukul banana

accommodation *n.* निवास nivas

accompaniment *n* संगत sangat

accompany *v.t.* साथ देना saath dena

accomplice *n* अपराध का साथी apradh ka saathi

accomplish *v.t.* पूर्ण करना purna karna

accomplished *a* पारंगत parangat

accomplishment *n.* निपुणता nipunta

accord *v.t.* सहमत करना sahamat karna

accord *n.* सहमति sahamati

accordingly *adv.* तद् नुसार tadanusar

account *n.* खाता khata

account *v.t.* विचार करना vichar karna

accountable *a* उत्तरदायी uttardayi

accountancy *n.* मुनीमी munimi

accountant *n.* मुनीम munim

accredit *v.t.* सच मानना sach manana

accrete *v.t.* साथ उगना sath ugna

accretion *n* क्रमिक वृद्धि kramik vridhi

accrue *v.i.* वृद्धि होना vridhi hona

accumulate *v.t.* बढ़ना badhna

accumulation *n* संग्रह sangreh

accuracy *n.* शुद्धता shudhata

accurate *a.* ठीक theek

accursed *a.* अभागा abhaga

accusation *n* आरोप aarop

accuse *v.t.* अपराधी ठहराना apradhi thaharana

accused *n.* अपराधी apradhi

accustom *v.t.* आदी बनाना aadi banana

accustomed *a.* आदी aadi

ace *n* ताश का इक्का taash ka ikka

acephalous *adj.* बिना सिर का bina sir ka

acetify *v.* सिरका बनाना sirka banana

ache *n.* पीड़ा peerha

ache *v.i.* पीड़ा होना peerha hona

achieve *v.t.* हासिल करना hasil karna

achievement *n.* सफलता safalta

achromatic *adj* बिना रंग का bina rang ka

acid *a* अम्ल amal

acid *n* तेज़ाब tezab

acidity *n.* अम्लता amlata

acknowledge *v.* धन्यवाद देना dhanyavad dena

acknowledgement *n.* रसीद raseed

acne *n* मुँहासा muhansa

acorn *n.* बलूत का फल balut ka phal

acoustic *a* ध्वनि-संबंधी dhvani sambandhi

acoustics *n.* ध्वनिशास्त्र dhvani shastra

acquaint *v.t.* परिचय कराना parichay karna

acquaintance *n.* परिचित व्यक्ति parichit vyakti

acquiesce *v.i.* राज़ी होना razi hona

acquiescence *n.* रज़ामंदी razamandi

acquire *v.t.* प्राप्त करना prapt karna

acquirement *n.* प्राप्ति prapti

acquisition *n.* अभिग्रहण abhigrahan

acquit *v.t.* निर्दोष घोषित करना nirdosh ghoshit karna

acquittal *n.* दोषमुक्ति या रिहाई doshmukti ya rihai

acre *n.* एकड़ acre

acreage *n.* एकड़ों में नाप ekarhon mein nap

acrimony *n* रूखापन rukhapan

acrobat *n.* कलाबाज़ kalabaz

across *adv.* आर-पार aar-paar

act *n.* कार्य karya

act *v.i.* अभिनय करना abhinay karna

acting *n.* अभिनय abhinay

action *n.* कार्य karya

activate *v.t.* शक्ति बढ़ाना shakti barhana

active *a.* चपल chapal

activity *n.* चपलता chapalta

actor *n.* अभिनेता abhineta

actress *n.* अभिनेत्री abhinetri

actual *a.* यथार्थ yatharth

actually *adv.* वस्तुत: vastuteh

acumen *n.* कुशाग्रता kushagrata

acute *a.* पैना paina

adage *n.* कहावत kahavat

adamant *a.* हठी hatthi

adapt *v.t.* अनुकूल बनाना anukul banana

adaptation *n.* अनुकूलन anukulan

add *v.t.* जोड़ना jorna

addict *v.t.* आदी होना aadi hona

addition *n.* जोड़ने की क्रिया jorhne ki kriya

additional *a.* अतिरिक्त atirikt

addle *adj* सड़ा हुआ sadha hua

address *v.t.* निवेदन करना sambhodan karna

address *n.* पता pata

addressee *n.* पत्र पाने वाला patra pane wala

adduce *v.t.* प्रस्तुत करना prastut karna

adept *n.* निपुण व्यक्ति nipun vyakti

adept *adj.* निपुण nipun

adequacy *n.* प्रचुरता prachurta

adequate *a.* पर्याप्त paryapt

adhere *v.i.* चिपकना chipakna

adhesion *n.* चिपकाव chipkav

adhesive *n.* चिपकाने वाला पदार्थ chipkane wala padarth

adhesive *a.* चिपकनेवाला chipakane wala

adieu *n.* विदाई vidayee

adieu *interj.* अलविदा alvida

adjacent *a.* समीपवर्ती samipvarti

adjective *n.* विशेषण visheshan

adjoin *v.t.* अगला होना agla hona

adjourn *v.t.* स्थगित करना sthagit karna

adjournment *n.* स्थगन sthagan

adjudge *v.t.* निर्णय करना nirnay karna

adjuration *n* शपथ shapath

adjust *v.t.* अनुकूलित करना anukulit karna

adjustment *n.* अनुकूलन anukulan

administer *v.t.* प्रबंध करना prabandh karna

administration *n.* प्रबंधन prabandhan

administrative *a.* प्रशासन-संबंधी prashasan-sambhandhi

administrator *n.* प्रशासक prashasak

admirable *a.* प्रशंसनीय prashansniya

admiral *n.* नौसेनाध्यक्ष nausena adhyaksha

admiration *n.* प्रशंसा prashansa

admire *v.t.* प्रशंसा करना prashansa karna

admissible *a.* स्वीकार्य svikarya

admission *n.* प्रवेश pravesh

admit स्वीकार करना svikar karna

admit *v.t.* प्रवेश की अनुमति देना pravesh ki anumati dena

admittance *n.* प्रवेश pravesh

admonish *v.t.* चेताना chetana

admonition *n.* चेतावनी chetavani

ado *n.* हलचल halchal

adolescence *n.* किशोरावस्था kishoravastha

adolescent *a.* किशोर kishor

adopt *v.t.* अपनाना apnana

adoption *n* अंगीकरण angikaran

adorable *a.* आराध्य aradhya

adoration *n.* आराधना aradhana

adore *v.t.* पूजा करना puja karna

adorn *v.t.* सजाना sajaana

adscript *n.* दास daas

adulation *n* चापलूसी chaplusi

adult *a* वयस्क vyasak

adult *n.* वयस्क व्यक्ति vyasak vyakti

adulterate *v.t.* मिलावट करना milavat karna

adulteration *n.* मिलावट milavat

adultery *n.* व्यभिचार vyabhichar

advance *v.t.* आगे बढ़ाना agay badhana

advance *n.* उधार udhaar

advancement *n.* प्रगति pragati

advantage *n.* लाभ labh

advantage *v.t.* लाभ पहुंचाना labh pahunchana

advantageous *a.* लाभदायक labhdayak

advent *n.* आगमन aagman

adventure *n* साहसिक कार्य sahasik karya

adventurous *a.* जोखिम से भरा jokhim se bhara

adverb *n.* क्रिया-विशेषण kriya-visheshan

adversary *n.* दुश्मन dushman

adverse *a* हानिकारक hanikarak

adversity *n.* दुर्भाग्य durbhagya

advertise *v.t.* विज्ञापन करना vigyapan karna

advertise *v.t.* घोषित करना ghoshit karna

advertisement *n* विज्ञापन vigyapan

advice *n* परामर्श paramarsh

advisable *a.* उचित uchit

advise *v.t.* परामर्श देना paramarsh dena

advocacy *n.* वकालत vakalat

advocacy *n.* पक्षपोषण pakshposhan

advocate *n* वकील vakil

advocate *v.t.* पक्षपोषित करना pakshposhit karna

aerial *a.* हवाई havayee

aerial *n.* एंटिना antenna

aeriform *adj.* वायु के समान vayu kay saman

aerodrome *n* हवाई अड्डा havayee adda

aeronautics *n.pl.* विमान चालन-विज्ञान viman chalan-vigyan

aeroplane *n.* हवाई जहाज़ havayee jahaz

aesthetics *n.pl.* सौंदर्यशास्त्र saundryashastra

aestival *adj* ग्रीष्म ऋतु सम्बन्धी grishma ritu sambandhi

afar *adv.* दूरी पर duri par

affable *a.* मिलनसार milansaar

affair *n.* मामला mamla

affect *v.t.* प्रभावित करना prabhavit karna

affectation *n* दिखावा dikhava

affection *n.* प्यार pyar

affectionate *a.* प्यारा pyara

affidavit *n* शपथपत्र shapathpatra

affiliation *n.* संपर्क sampark

affinity *n* समानता samanta

affirm *v.t.* दावे से कहना davay se kahana

affirmation *n* पुष्टिकरण pushtikaran

affirmative *a* सकारात्मक sakaratmak

affix *v.t.* चिपकाना chipkana

afflict *v.t.* सताना satana

affliction *n.* यातना yatna

affluence *n.* संपन्नता sampannata

affluent *a.* धनवान dhanvan

afford *v.t.* जुटाना jutana

afforest *v.t.* वन लगाना van lagana

affray *n* हंगामा hungama

affront *v.t.* अपमानित करना apmanit karna

affront *n* अपमान apman

afield *adv.* खेत में khet mein

aflame *adv.* आग पर aag par
afloat *adv.* बहता हुआ bahata hua
afoot *adv.* सक्रिय स्थिति में sakriya sthiti mein
afore *prep. & adv.* आगे aage
afore *prep. & adv.* सामने samney
afore *prep.* प्राचीन काल में prachin kaal mein
afraid *a.* भयभीत bhaybhith
afresh *adv.* नए सिरे से nayain sire se
after *prep.* के बाद में ke baad mein
after *adv* उसके बाद uske baad
after *conj.* उसके बाद जब uske baad jab
after *a* आगामी aagami
afterwards *adv.* बाद में baad mein
again *adv.* फिर से phir se
against *prep.* विरोध मे virodh mein
agamist *n* विवाह विरोधी vivah virodhi
agape *adv.,* मुंह खोले हुए munh kholay hue
age *n.* आयु ayu
aged *a.* वृद्ध vridh
agency *n.* शाखा shakha
agenda *n.* कार्यसूची karya suchi
agent *n* प्रतिनिधि pratinidhi
aggravate *v.t.* बिगाड़ना bigarhana
aggravation *n.* वृद्धि vridhi
aggregate *v.t.* संचित करना sanchit karna
aggression *n* आक्रमण akraman
aggressive *a.* क्रोधी krodhi
aggressor *n.* आक्रामक akramak
aggrieve *v.t.* पीड़ित करना peerhit karna
aghast *a.* आश्चर्यचकित aashcharyachakit
agile *a.* फुर्तीला phurtila
agility *n.* चपलता chapalta
agitate *v.t.* उत्तेजित करना uttejit karna
agitate *v.t.* हिलाना hilana
agitation *n* आंदोलन aandolan
aglow *adv.* चमकता हुआ chamakta hua
agnus *n* मेमना memna

ago *adv.* बहुत समय पहले bahut samay pahley
agog *adj.* गतिमान gatimaan
agonist *n* योद्धा yodha
agonize *v.t.* कष्ट देना kasht dena
agony *n.* यंत्रणा yantrana
agoraphobia *n.* भीड़ से डर लगना bheerh se dar lagna
agrarian *a.* भूमि-संबंधी bhumi-sambandhi
agree *v.i.* सहमत होना sahmat hona
agreeable *a.* सहमत sahamat
agreement *n.* सहमति sahamati
agricultural *a* कृषि-संबंधी krishi-sambandhi
agriculture *n* कृषि krishi
agriculturist *n.* किसान kisaan
agronomy *n.* ग्रामीण व्यवस्था gramin vyavastha
ague *n* बुखार bukhar
ahead *adv.* आगे aage
aid *n* सहायता sahayata
aid *n* सहायक sahayak
aid *v.t* सहायता देना sahayata dena
aigrette *n* सफेद सारस पक्षी saphed saras pakshi
ail *v.i.* बीमार होना beemar hona
ailment *n.* बीमारी beemari
aim *n.* लक्ष्य lakshya
aim *v.i.* लक्ष्य साधना lakshya sadhna
air *n* वायुमण्डल vayumandal
aircraft *n.* विमान viman
airy *n.* हवादार havadar
airy *a.* वायु-संबंधी vayu-sambandhi
ajar *adv.* अधखुला adhakhula
akin *a.* समान प्रकृति वाला saman prakarti vala
akin *n.* सगा saga
alacrity *n.* फुरती phurti
alarm *n* चेतावनी chetavani
alarm *v.t* खतरे की सूचना khatre ki suchana

albeit *conj.* हालांकि halanki

album *n.* चित्राधार chitradhar

albumen *n* अंडे की सफेदी ande ki saphedi

alchemy *n.* कीमियागीरी kimiyagiri

alcohol *n* मद्यसार madyasar

ale *n* शराब sharab

alert *a.* फुरतीला phurtila

alertness *n.* फुरतीलापन phurtilapan

algebra *n.* बीजगणित beejganit

alias *n.* उपनाम upnaam

alias *adv.* अन्यथा anayatha

alibi *n.* अन्यत्र उपस्थिति anyatra upasthit

alien *a.* अजनबी ajnabi

alienate *v.t.* पराया करना paraya karna

aliform *adj.* परदार pardar

alight *v.i.* नीचे आना neechay aana

align *v.t.* श्रेणीबद्ध करना shrenibadh karna

alignment *n.* सीध निर्धारण seedh nirdharan

alike *a.* समान saman

alike *adv* समान रूप से saman rup se

aliment *n.* पोषण poshan

alive *a* ज़िंदा zinda

alkali *n* पोटास potash

all *a.* समस्त samast

all *n.* सबकुछ sabkuchh

all *adv.* पूर्णतया purnataya

all *pron.* सब sab

allay *v.t.* शांत करना shant karna

allegation *n.* आरोपण aaropan

allege *v.t.* आरोपित करना aaropit karna

allegiance *n.* निष्ठा nistha

allegorical *a.* अन्योक्ति-संबंधी anyokti-sambandhi

allegory *n.* अन्योक्ति anyokti

allergy *n.* चिढ़ chidh

alleviate *v.t.* कम करना kam karna

alleviation *n.* कमी kami

alley *n.* गली gali

alliance *n.* संधि sandhi

alliteration *n.* अनुप्रास anupras

allocate *v.t.* निर्धारित करना nirdharit karna

allocation *n.* आवंटन aavantan

allot *v.t.* नियत करना niyat karna

allotment *n.* हिस्सा hissa

allow *v.t.* अनुमति देना anumati dena

allowance *n.* अनुमति anumati

alloy *n.* खोट khot

allude *v.i.* इंगित करना ingit karna

allure *v.t.* आकर्षित करना aakarshit karna

allurement *n* प्रलोभन pralobhan

allusion *n* संकेत sanket

allusive *a.* सांकेतिक sanketik

ally *v.t.* जोड़ना jorhna

ally *n.* मित्र mitr

almanac *n.* पंचांग panchang

almighty *a.* सर्वशक्तिमान sarvashaktiman

almost *adv.* करीब-करीब karib-karib

alms *n.* भिक्षा bhiksha

aloft *adv.* आकाश में aakash mein

alone *a.* अकेला akela

along *adv.* साथ में saath may

along *prep.* समानांतर samanantar

aloof *adv.* अलग alag

aloud *adv.* ऊँची आवाज़ में unchi awaz may

alp *n.* पर्वत की चोटी parvat ki choti

alpha *n* आरम्भ aarambh

alphabet *n.* वर्णमाला varnamala

alphabetical *a.* वर्णक्रमानुसारी varnakramanusari

already *adv.* पहले से pehle se

already *adv.* अब तक aab tak

also *adv.* साथ ही saath he

altar *n.* बलिवेदी balivedi

alter *v.t.* परिवर्तित करना parivartit karna

alteration *n* संशोधन sanshodhan

altercation *n.* झगड़ा jhagrha

alternate *a.* क्रम से होने वाला krama se hone wala

alternate *v.t.* आगे-पीछे करना aage-peeche karna

alternative *n.* विकल्प vikalp

alternative *a.* वैकल्पिक vaikalpik

although *conj.* यद्यपि yadyapi

altitude *n.* ऊँचाई uchayee

altogether *adv.* पूर्णरूप से purna rup se

aluminium *n.* अल्युमीनियम aluminium

always *adv* सर्वदा sarvada

am हूं hun

amalgam *n* मिश्रण mishran

amalgamate *v.t.* मिल जाना mil jana

amalgamation *n* मिश्रण mishran

amass *v.t.* एकत्र करना ekatra karna

amateur *n.* अव्यवसायी avyavyasayee

amaze *v.t.* विस्मित करना vismit karna

amazement *n.* विस्मय vismay

ambassador *n.* राजदूत rajdoot

amberite *n.* बिना धुऐं का बारूद bina dhuain ka barud

ambient *adj.* चारों ओर रहने वाला charon aur rahne wala

ambiguity *n.* संदिग्धता sandigadhata

ambiguous *a.* अनेकार्थी anekarthi

ambition *n.* महत्वाकांक्षा mahtvakansha

ambitious *a.* महत्वाकांक्षी mahtvakanshi

ambry *n.* भण्डार bhandar

ambulance *n.* रोगी-वाहन rogi-vahan

ambulate *v.t* इधर उधर घूमना idhar udhar ghumna

ambush *n.* घात ghat

ameliorate *v.t.* सुधरना sudharna

amelioration *n.* सुधार sudhar

amen *interj.* तथास्तु tatasthu

amenable *a* प्रतिसंवेदी pratisanvedi

amend *v.t.* संशोधन करना sanshodhan karna

amendment *n.* सुधार sudhar

amends *n.pl.* क्षतिपूर्ति kshatipurti

amiability *n.* सुशीलता sushilta

amiable *n.* सौम्य saumya

amiable *a.* प्रेमपात्र prempatra

amicable *adj.* मित्रभाव का mitrabhav ka

amid *prep.* दौरान dauran

amiss *adv.* अनुचित रूप में anuchit rup se

amity *n.* मित्रता mitrata

ammunition *n.* अस्त्र-शस्त्र astra-shastra

amnesty *n.* सर्वक्षमा sarvakshama

among *prep.* बीच में beech mein

amongst *prep.* बीच में beech mein

amoral *a.* नैतिकता-निरपेक्ष naitikta-nirpeksha

amorous *a.* प्रेमातुर prematur

amount *n* योग yog

amount *v.i* परिणाम होना parinam hona

amount *v.* बराबर होना barabar hona

amour *n* प्रेम prem

ampere *n* विद्युत् धारा की इकाई vidyut dhara ki ekayee

amphitheatre *n* रंगभूमि rang bhumi

ample *a.* प्रचुर prachur

amplification *n* प्रवर्धन pravardhan

amplifier *n* ध्वनिविस्तारक dhvanivistarak

amplify *v.t.* बढ़ाना badhana

amuck *adv.* पगलाकर paglakar

amulet *n.* ताबीज़ tabeez

amuse *v.t.* मनोरंजन करना manoranjan karna

amusement *n* मनोरंजन manoranjan

an *art* एक ek

anabaptism *n* दुबारा नामकरण dubara namakaran

anadem *n* माला mala

anaemia *n* खून की कमी khoon ki kami

anaesthesia *n* बेहोशी behoshi

analogous *a.* अनुरूप anurup

analogy *n.* अनुरूपता anurupta

analysis *n.* वाक्य-विग्रह vakya vigreh

analyst *n* विश्लेषणकर्ता vishleshan karta

analytical *a* विश्लेषणात्मक vishleshanaatmak

anamnesis *n* पूर्व जन्म का स्मरण purv janam ka smaran

anamorphous *adj* विकृत अंग वाला vicrit ang wala

anarchism *n.* अराजकतावाद arajkatavaad

anarchist *n* अराजकतावादी arajkatavaadi

anarchy *n* अराजकता arajakata

anatomy *n.* शरीर-रचना विज्ञान shareer rachna vigyan

ancestor *n.* पूर्वज purvaj

ancestral *a.* पैतृक petrak

ancestry *n.* वंशावली vanshavali

anchor *n.* लंगर langar

anchorage *n* लंगरशुल्क langar shulk

ancient *a.* प्राचीन prachin

ancon *n* कोहनी kohni

and *conj.* और aur

anecdote *n.* रूचिकर घटना ruchikar ghatna

anew *adv.* फिर phir

anfractuous *adj* पेचीला pechila

angel *n* देवदूत devdoot

anger *n.* क्रोध krodh

angina *n* गण्डमाला gandmala

angle *n* कोन kona

angry *a.* क्रोधित krodhit

anguish *n.* परिताप paritaap

angular *a.* कोण-संबंधी kon-sambandhi

animal *n.* प्राणी prani

animate *v.t.* जीवन युक्त करना jivan yukt karna

animate *a.* जीवित jeevit

animation *n* सजीवता sajivta

animosity *n* वैर vair

animus *n* द्वेष dwesh

aniseed *n* सौंफ का बीज saunf ka beej

ankle *n.* टखना takhna

anklet *n* नुपूर nupur

annalist *n.* इतिहासकार itihaascar

annals *n.pl.* वार्षिक वृत्तांत varshik vrintant

annectant *adj.* जोड़ने वाला jodne wala

annex *v.t.* अधिकार करना adhikar karna

annex *v.t.* संबद्ध करना sambadh karna

annexation *n* संयोजन sanyojan

annihilate *v.t.* नष्ट करना nasht karna

annihilation *n* ध्वंस dhvansh

anniversary *n.* जयंती jayanti

announce *v.t.* घोषणा करना ghoshna karna

announcement *n.* घोषणा ghoshna

annoy *v.t.* चिढ़ाना chiddhana

annoyance *n.* चिढ़, गुस्सा chiddh, gussa

annual *a.* वार्षिक varshik

annuity *n.* वार्षिक अनुदान varshik anudaan

annul *v.t.* रद्द करना radhya karna

annulet *n* छोटी अँगूठी choti anguthi

anoint *v.t.* मरहम लगाना maraham lagana

anomalous *a* अनियमित aniyamit

anomaly *n* नियम-विरोध niyam virodh

anon *adv.* शीघ्र shighra

anonymity *n.* अज्ञात होने की अवस्था agyat hone ki awastha

anonymity *n.* अनामता anamata

anonymous *a.* अनाम anaam

another *a* अन्य anya

answer *n* समाधान samadhaan

answerable *a.* उत्तरदायी uttardayi

ant *n* चींटी chhinti

antacid *adj.* अम्लत्व amlatv

antagonism *n* बैर bair

antagonist *n.* विपक्षी vipakshi

antagonize *v.t.* वैरी बनाना veri banana

Antarctic *a.* दक्षिणध्रुवीय dakshin dhruviya

ante nuptial *adj.* विवाह से पूर्व होने वाला vivah se purva hone wala

antecede *v.t.* समय से पूर्व घटित होना samay se purva ghatit hona

antecedent *n.* पूर्वगामी purvagami

antecedent *a.* पूर्ववर्ती purvavarti

antedate *n* स्थिर काल से पूर्व का समय sthir kaal se purve ka samay

antenatal *adj.* उत्पत्ति से पूर्व utpatti se purv

antennae *n.* एंटिना antenna

anthem *n* भजन bhajan

anthology *n.* चयनिका chayanika

anti-aircraft *a.* विमान-भेदी viman-bhedi

antic *n* अजीब कार्य अथवा व्यवहार ajib karya athawa bahawayar

anticipate *v.t.* पूर्वानुमान होना purvanuman hona

anticipation *n.* पूर्वानुमान purwaanuman

antidote *n.* विषमारक औषध wishmarak aushadhi

antinomy *n.* अधिकार विरोध adhikar virodh

antipathy *n.* विरोध virodh

antiphony *n.* प्रतिगान pratigan

antipodes *n.* प्रतिलोम pratilom

antiquarian *a.* पुरातत्व-विषयक puratatva-vishayak

antiquarian *n* पुरातत्ववेत्ता puratatvaveta

antiquated *a.* प्राचीन prachin

antique *a.* अप्रचलित aprachalit

antiquity *n.* प्राचीनकाल prachinkaal

antiseptic *n.* रोगाणुरोधक औषधि roganurodhak aushadhi

antiseptic *a.* रोगाणुरोधक roganurodhak

antitheist *n* नास्तिक nastik

antithesis *n.* विरोध virodh

antonym *n.* विलोम vilom

anus *n.* गुदा guda

anvil *n.* निहाई nihaye

anxiety *a* चिंता chinta

anxious *a.* चिंताजनक chintajanak

any *a.* कोई koi

any *adv.* किसी सीमा तक kisi seema tak

anyhow *adv.* किसी न किसी तरीके से kisi na kisi tarike se

apace *adv.* शीघ्रता से shigrahta se

apart *adv.* अलग से alag se

apartment *n.* कक्ष kaksh

apathy *n.* उदासीनता udasinta

ape *n* कपि kapi

ape *v.t.* अनुकरण करना anukaran karna

aperture *n.* छिद्र chhidra

apex *n.* शिखर shikhar

aphorism *n* वचन vachan

apiary *n.* मधुमक्खीपालन-स्थान madhumakhipaalan-sthan

apiculture *n.* मधुमक्खी-पालन madhumakhi-paalan

apish *a.* वानर-सदृश vanar-sadrish

apnoea *n* साँस की रुकावट saans ki rukawat

apologize *v.i.* खेद प्रकट करना khed prakat karna

apologue *n* उपदेशपूर्ण कहानी updeshpurna kahani

apology *n.* स्वदोष-स्वीकार svadosh svikar

apostle *n.* धर्मप्रचारक dharampracharak

apotheosis *n.* देवता तुल्य निर्माण devta tulya nirman

apparatus *n.* उपकरण upkaran

apparel *n.* वस्त्र vastr

apparel *v.t.* वस्त्र पहनना vastr pehnana

apparent *a.* प्रत्यक्ष pratyaksh

appeal *n.* अपील apeel

appeal *v.t.* विनती करना vinti karna

appear *v.i.* प्रतीत होना pratit hona

appearance *n* उदय uday

appease *v.t.* शांत करना shant karna

appellant *n.* अपीलकर्त्ता apeelkarta

append *v.t.* संलग्न करना sanlagna karna

appendage *n.* संलग्नक sanlaganak

appendicitis *n.* उपांत्रशूल upantrashool

appendix *n.* शेष संग्रह shesh sangreh

appendix *n.* परिशिष्ट parishisht

appetence *n.* अभिलाषा abhilasha

appetent *adj.* अति उत्सुक ati utsuk

appetite *n.* भूख bhukh
appetizer *n* क्षुधावर्धक वस्तु kshudhavardhak vastu
applaud *v.t.* प्रशंसा करना prashansa karna
applause *n.* प्रशंसा prashansa
apple *n.* सेब seb
appliance *n.* उपकरण upkaran
applicable *a.* प्रयोग योग्य prayog yogya
applicant *n.* प्रार्थी prarthi
application *n.* अनुप्रयोग anuprayog
apply *v.t.* लागू करना lagu karna
appoint *v.t.* नियुक्त करना niyukt karna
appointment *n.* नौकरी naukari
apportion *v.t.* बांटना bantana
apposite *adj* योग्य yogya
apposite *a.* संगत sangat
appositely *adv* उचित रीति से uchit riti se
appraise *v.t.* मूल्यांकन करना mulyankan karna
appreciable *a.* उल्लेखनीय ullekhaniya
appreciate *v.t.* मूल्यांकन करना mulyankan karna
appreciation *n.* प्रशंसा prashansa
apprehend *v.t.* डरना darna
apprehension *n.* आशंका ashanka
apprehensive *a.* आशंकित ashankit
apprentice *n.* प्रशिक्षु prashikshu
apprise *v.t.* सूचित करना suchit karna
approach *v.t.* पास पहुंचना paas pahunchana
approach *n.* आगमन aagman
approach *n.* विधि vidhi
approbate *v.t* अनुमोदन करना anumodan karna
approbation *n.* अनुमोदन anumodan
appropriate *v.t.* हड़प लेना harhap lena
appropriate *a.* उपयुक्त upyukt
appropriation *n.* स्वायत्ती करण svayattikaran
approval *n.* अनुमोदन anumodan

approve *v.t.* अनुमोदन करना anumodan karna
approximate *a.* समीप samip
appurtenance *n* लगाव lagav
apricot *n.* खूबानी khubani
apron *n.* पेटबंद pet band
apt *a.* योग्य yogya
aptitude *n.* औचित्य auchitya
Aquarius *n.* कुम्भ राशि kumbh rashi
aqueduct *n* नहर nahar
arable *adj* जुताई-योग्य भूमि jutayee-yogya bhumi
arbiter *n.* मध्यस्थ madhyastha
arbitrary *a.* निरंकुश nirankush
arbitrate *v.t.* मध्यस्थता करना madhyasthata karna
arbitration *n.* पंचफैसला panch faisla
arbitrator *n.* मध्यस्थ madhyasth
arc *n.* चाप chap
arch *n.* तोरण toran
arch *v.t.* मेहराबदार बनाना mehrabadaar banana
arch *a* प्रधान pradhan
archaic *a.* अप्रचलित aprachalit
archangel *n* प्रधान देवदूत pradhan devdut
archbishop *n.* प्रमुख पादरी pramukh padri
archer *n* धनुर्धर dhanrudhar
architect *n.* वास्तुकार vaastukar
architecture *n.* निर्माण शैली nirman shaili
archives *n.pl.* अभिलेखागार abhilekhagar
Arctic *n* उत्तरीध्रुव-संबंधी utaridhruva-sambandhi
ardent *a.* उत्साही utsahi
ardour *n.* जोश josh
arduous *a.* कठिन kathin
area *n.* भू-भाग bhu-bhag
area *n.* क्षेत्रफल kshetraphal
areca *n* सुपारी का वृक्ष supari ka vriksh
arena *n* अखाड़ा akharha
argil *n* एल्यूमिनियम aluminium

argue *n.* तर्क प्रस्तुत करना tark prastut karna

argue *v.t.* प्रमाणित करना pramaanit karna

argument *n.* वाद-विवाद vaad-vivad

arid *adj.* गरमी से झुलसा हुआ garmi se jhulsa hua

Aries *n* मेष राशि mesh rashi

aright *adv* उचित रीति से uchit riti se

aright *adv.* ठीक प्रकार से theek prakar se

arise *v.i.* ऊपर उठना upar uthana

aristocracy *n.* कुलीनतंत्र kulintantra

aristocrat *n.* कुलीन व्यक्ति kulin vyakti

arithmetic *n.* अंकगणित ankganit

arithmetical *a.* अंकगणित-संबंधी ankganit-sambandhi

ark *n* तिजोरी tijori

arm *n.* भुजा bhuja

arm *n.* हथियार hathiyaar

arm *v.t.* युद्ध के लिए तैयारी करना yudh ke liye taiyar karna

armada *n.* युद्धपोतों का बेड़ा yudhpoton ka berha

armament *n.* युद्ध-सामग्री yudh-saamagri

armistice *n.* युद्धविराम yudhviram

armlet *a* समुद्र की शाखा samudra ke shakha

armour *n.* कवच kavach

armoury *n.* शास्त्रागार shastragar

army *n.* सेना sena

around *prep.* चारों ओर chaaron aur

around *adv* आसपास aaspass

arouse *v.t.* क्रियाशील बनाना kriyashil banana

arraign *v.* दोष लगाना dosh lagana

arrange *v.t.* क्रम में रखना kram mein rakhna

arrangement *n.* क्रमस्थापन karmsthapan

arrant *n.* कुख्यात kukhyat

array *n.* क्रम kram

arrears *n.pl.* बकाया bakaya

arrest *v.t.* रोकना rokna

arrest *n.* गिरफ़्तारी giraphtari

arrival *n.* आगमन aagman

arrive *v.i.* पहुंचना pahunchana

arrogance *n.* घमंड ghamand

arrogant *adj.* घमंडी ghamandi

arrogant *a.* अक्खड़ akharh

arrow *n* तीर teer

arrowroot *n.* अरारोट aararot

arsenal *n.* आयुधागार aayudhagar

arsenic *n* संखिया sankhiya

arson *n* आगज़नी aagzani

art *n.* कुशलता kushalta

artery *n.* धमनी dhamni

artful *a.* चालाक chalak

arthritis *n* जोड़ों की सूजन jorhon ki sujan

artichoke *n.* चुकन्दर chukandar

article *n* लेख lekh

article *n.* वस्तु vastu

articulate *a.* स्पष्ट spasht

artifice *n.* साधन sadhan

artificial *a.* नकली nakali

artillery *n.* तोपखाना topkhana

artisan *n.* शिल्पी shilpi

artist *n.* कलाकार kalakar

artistic *a.* कलात्मक kalatamak

artless *a.* सीधा sidha

as *adv.* इस सीमा तक is seema tak

as *conj.* समान saman

as *pron.* जिसको jisko

asafoetida *n.* हींग hing

ascend *v.t.* ऊपर जाना upar jana

ascent *n.* चढ़ाई chadhayee

ascertain *v.t.* निश्चित करना nishchit karna

ascetic *n.* तपस्वी tapasvi

ascetic *a.* तपस्यापूर्ण tapasyapurna

ascribe *v.t.* आरोपित करना aropit karna

ash *n.* अवशेष avshesh

ashamed *a.* लज्जित lajjit

ashore *adv.* किनारे पर kinare par

aside *adv.* अलग alag

asinine *adj.* मूर्ख murkh

ask *v.t.* निवेदन करना nivden karna

ask *v.t.* पूछना poochhna

ask *v.t.* माँगना mangana

asleep *adv.* सोता हुआ sota hua

aspect *n.* आकृति aakriti

aspect *n.* पहलू pehlu

asperse *v.* निन्दा करना ninda karna

aspirant *n.* उच्चाकांक्षी व्यक्ति uchakankshi vyakti

aspiration *n.* अभिलाषा abhilasha

aspire *v.t.* महत्वाकांक्षा mahatvakanksha

ass *n.* गधा gadha

ass *n.* मूर्ख व्यक्ति murkh vyakti

assail *v.* आक्रमण करना akraman karna

assassin *n.* हत्यारा hatyara

assassinate *v.t.* हत्या करना hatya karna

assassination *n* हत्या hatya

assault *n.* धावा dhava

assault *v.t.* आक्रमण करना aakraman karna

assemble *v.t.* एकत्र करना ekatra karna

assembly *n.* मंडली mandali

assent *v.i.* सहमत होना sahamat hona

assent *n.* अनुमति anumati

assert *v.t.* दावा करना dava karna

assess *v.t.* अनुमान लगाना anuman lagana

assessment *n.* कर-निर्धारण kar-nirdharan

asset *n.* संपत्ति sampatti

assibilate *v.* सीत्कार सहित बोलना seetkaar sahith bholna

assign *v.t.* नियुक्त करना niyukt karna

assignee *n.* संपत्ति-भागी sampatti-bhagi

assimilate *v.i.* पचाना pachana

assimilate *v.* परिपाक करना paripak karna

assimilation *n* समीकरण samikaran

assist *v.t.* सहायता करना sahayata karna

assistance *n.* सहायता sahayata

assistant *n.* सहायक sahayak

associate *v.t.* संयुक्त करना sanyukt karna

associate *v.t.* साथ देना sath dena

associate *n.* साथी sathi

association *n.* संगति sangati

association *n.* घनिष्ठता ghanishtata

assoil *v.t.* पाप से मुक्त करना paap se mukt karna

assort *v.t.* वर्गीकरण करना vargikaran karna

assuage *v.t.* मृदु करना mridu karna

assume *v.t.* कल्पना करना kalpana karna

assumption *n.* पूर्व धारणा purva dharna

assumption *n.* मान्यता manyata

assurance *n.* प्रतिभूति pratibhuti

assure *v.t.* बीमा करना bima karna

astatic *adj.* अस्थिर asthir

asterisk *n.* तारक चिन्ह taarak chinha

asterism *n.* तीन तारों का चिन्ह teen taaron ka chinha

asteroid *adj.* एक छोटा तारा ek chota tara

asthma *n.* दमा dama

astir *adv.* गतिशील gatishil

astonish *v.t.* विस्मित करना vismit karna

astonishment *n.* विस्मय vismaya

astound *v.t* चकित करना chakit karna

astray *adv.,* पथभ्रष्ट pathbhrasht

astrologer *n.* ज्योतिषी jyotishi

astrology *n.* ज्योतिष jyotish

astronaut *n.* अंतरिक्ष- यात्री antriksh-yatri

astronomer *n.* खगोलशास्त्री khagolshastri

astronomy *n.* खगोलशास्त्र khagolshastra

asunder *adv.* अलग-अलग alag-alag

asylum *n* शरण-स्थल sharan-sthal

at *prep.* के पास ke paas

atheism *n* नास्तिकता nastikta

atheist *n* नास्तिक nastik

athirst *adj.* प्यासा pyasa

athlete *n.* क्रीड़ा-प्रतियागी krirha pratiyogi

athletic *a.* बलवान balwan

athletics *n.* खेलकूद khelkud

athwart *prep.* आर पार aar paar

atlas *n.* मानचित्रावली manchitrawali

atmosphere *n.* वायुमंडल vayumandal

atom *n.* परमाणु parmanu

atomic *a.* अणु-संबंधी anu-sambandhi

atone *v.i.* प्रायश्चित करना prayashchit karna

atonement *n.* प्रायश्चित prayashchit

atrocious *a.* भयंकर bhayankar

atrocity *n* नृशंसता nrishansata

attach *v.t.* जोड़ना jorna

attache *n.* दूतावास का अधिकारी dutavas ka adhikari

attachment *n.* संलग्न sanlagna

attachment *n.* लगाव lagav

attack *n.* हमला hamla

attack *v.t.* आलोचना करना alochana karna

attain *v.t.* हासिल करना hasil karna

attainment *n.* कौशल kaushal

attaint *v.t.* अपमानित करना apmaanit karna

attempt *v.t.* प्रयत्न करना prayatna karna

attempt *n.* प्रयास prayas

attend *v.t.* साथ होना sath hona

attendance *n.* उपस्थिति upasthith

attendant *n.* सेवक sevak

attention *n.* सावधान savdhan

attentive *a.* सतर्क satark

attest *v.t.* प्रमाणित करना pramanit karna

attire *n.* परिधान paridhan

attire *v.t.* वस्त्र पहनाना vastra pahanaana

attitude *n.* मुद्रा mudra

attorney *n.* प्रतिनिधि pratinidhi

attract *v.t.* आकर्षित करना aakarshit karna

attraction *n.* आकर्षक वस्तु aakarshan

attractive *a.* आकर्षक aakrashak

attribute *v.t.* आरोपित करना aaropit karna

attribute *n.* आंतरिक गुण aantrik gun

auction *n* नीलामी neelaami

auction *v.t.* नीलाम करना neelaam karna

audible *a* श्रव्य shravya

audience *n.* श्रोतागण shrotagan

audit *n.* अंकेक्षण ankekshan

audit *v.t.* अंकेक्षण करना ankekshan karna

auditive *adj.* श्रवण सम्बन्धी shravan sambandhi

auditor *n.* अंकेक्षक ankekshak

auditorium *n.* श्रोताकक्ष shrotakaksh

auger *n.* बरमा barma

aught *n.* कोई वस्तु koi wastu

augment *v.t.* बढ़ना badhana

augmentation *n.* वृद्धि vridhi

August *n.* अगस्त August

august *n* भव्य bhavya

aunt *n.* चाची chachi

auricle *n.* कानखोदनी kaan khodni

auricular *adj.* कान की आकृति का kaan ki aakriti ka

aurora *n* अरूणोदय arunodaya

auspicate *v.t.* अभिमंत्रित करना abhimantrit karna

auspice *n.* शकुन विचार shakun wichar

auspicious *a.* शुभसूचक shubhsuchak

austere *a.* सरल saral

authentic *a.* प्रामाणिक pramanik

author *n.* लेखक lekhak

authoritative *a.* आधिकारिक adhikarik

authority *n.* शक्ति या अधिकार shakti ya adhikar

authorize *v.t.* प्राधिकृत करना pradhikrit karna

autobiography *n.* आत्मकथा aatmakatha

autocracy *n* एकतंत्र ektantra

autocrat *n* निरंकुश शासक nerankush shasak

autocratic *a* निरंकुश nerankush

autograph *n.* हस्ताक्षर hastakshar

automatic *a.* अविवेचित avivechit

automobile *n.* मोटरकार motorcar

autonomous *a* स्वायत्त svayat

autumn *n.* पतझड़ patjharh

auxiliary *a.* सहायक sahayak
auxiliary *n.* सहायक क्रिया sahayak kriya
avail *v.t.* उपयोगी होना upyogi hona
available *a* पहुंच के अंदर pahunch ke andar
avarice *n.* लालसा lalsa
avenge *v.t.* प्रतिशोध लेना pratishodh lena
avenue *n.* मार्ग marg
average *n.* औसत ausat
average *a.* औसत दर्जे का ausat darjay ka
average *v.t.* माध्य निकालना madhya nikalna
averse *a.* विपरीत viparit
aversion *n.* घृणा ghrina
avert *v.t.* रोकना rokna
aviary *n.* चिड़ियाखाना chirhiyakhana
aviation *n.* विमानचालन vimanchalak
aviator *n.* विमानचालक vimanchalak
avid *adj.* उत्सुक utsuk
avidity *adv.* उत्कट इच्छा utkat ichcha
avidly *adv* उत्सुकता से utsukta se
avoid *v.t.* से बचना se bachna
avoidance *n.* बचाव bachav
avow *v.t.* घोषणा करना ghoshana karna
avulsion *n.* अलगाव algav
await *v.t.* आशा करना asha karna
awake *v.t.* सचेत होना sachait hona
awake *a* सचेत sachait
award *v.t.* प्रदान करना pradan karna
award *n.* पुरस्कार puraskaar
aware *a.* अवगत avgat
away *adv.* अलग alag
awe *n.* विस्मय vismaya
awful *a.* अति महान ati mahan
awhile *adv.* कुछ देर के लिए kuchh der ke liye
awkward *a.* नाज़ुक naajuk
axe *n.* कुल्हाड़ी kulharhi
axis *n.* अक्षरेखा aksharekha
axle *n.* धुरी dhuri

# B

babble *n.* बकवास bakwas
babble *v.i.* बकवास करना bakwas karna
babe *n.* बच्चा bachha
babel *n* बवाल bawal
baboon *n.* बड़ा बन्दर barha bandar
baby *n.* शिशु shishu
bachelor *n.* अविवाहित व्यक्ति avivahit vyakti
back *n.* पिछला भाग pichla bhag
back *adv.* पिछली तरफ़ pichli taraph
backbite *v.t.* चुगली खाना chugli khana
backbone *n.* आधार aadhar
background *n.* पृष्ठभूमि prishthbhumi
backhand *n.* बाईं ओर झुका हुआ लेख bayeen aur jhuka hua lekh
backslide *v.i.* पतित होना patit hona
backward *a.* पिछड़ा हुआ pichhra hua
backward *adv.* भूतकाल की ओर bhootkal ki aur
bacon *n.* शूकर- मांस shukar-mans
bacteria *n.* जीवाणु jewaanu
bad *a.* बुरा bura
bad *a.* गंभीर gambhir
badge *n.* बिल्ला billa
badger *n.* बिज्जू bijju
badly *adv.* बुरे प्रकार से bure prakar se
badminton *n.* बैडमिंटन badminton
baffle *v. t.* विफल कर देना vifal kar dena
bag *n.* थैला thaila
bag *v. i.* पकड़ना pakarhna
baggage *n.* यात्री- सामान yatri-saman
bagpipe *n.* मसक बाजा masak baja
bail *n.* ज़मानत zamanat
bailable *a.* जिसकी ज़मानत हो सके jiski zamanat ho sake
bailiff *n.* कारिंदा kaarinda

bait *n* प्रलोभन pralobhan
bait *v.t.* तंग करना tang karna
bake *v.t.* सेंकना senkna
baker *n.* नानबाई naanbaai
bakery *n* बेकरी bakery
balance *n.* संतुलन santulan
balance *v.t.* संतुलित करना santulit karna
balcony *n.* छज्जा chajja
bald *a.* गंजा ganja
bale *n.* गांठ gaanth
bale *v.t.* गांठ बनाना gaanth banana
baleen *n.* ह्वेल मछली की हड्डी whale machali ki haddi
baleful *a.* हानिकारक hanikarak
ball *n.* गेंद gend
ballad *n.* गाथा-गीत gatha-geet
ballet *sn.* बैले नृत्य belle nritya
balloon *n.* गुब्बारा gubbara
ballot *n.* मत पत्र mat patra
ballot *n* गुप्त मतदान gupt matdaan
balm *n.* मरहम marham
balsam *n.* गुलमेंहदी gulmehndi
bam *v.t.* धोखा देना dhoka dena
bamboo *n.* बांस bans
ban *n.* प्रतिबंध pratibandh
ban *v t* प्रतिबंधित करना pratibandhith karna
banal *a.* निम्नस्तरीय nimnastariya
banana *n.* केला kela
band *n.* पट्टी patti
bandage *v.t* पट्टी बांधना patti bandhana
bandit *n.* डाकू daku
bang *v.t.* धम से बंद करना dham se band karna
bang *n.* ज़ोरदार दस्तक jordar dastakh
bangle *n.* चूड़ी chudi
banish *v.t.* निर्वासित करना nirvasit karna
banishment *n.* निर्वासन nirvasan
banjo *n.* एक प्रकार का बाजा ek prakar ka baja

bank *n.* बैंक bank
bank *v.t.* आशा करना asha karna
banker *n.* बैंक-कर्मी bank-karmi
bankrupt *n.* दिवालिया deevaliya
bankruptcy *n.* दिवालियापन deevaliyapan
banner *n.* कपड़े पर लिखा संदेश kapde par likha sandesh
banquet *n.* दावत dawat
banquet *v.t.* दावत देना dawat dena
bantam *n.* नाटा पुरुष nata purush
banter *v.t.* मज़ाक उड़ाना mazak urhana
banter *n.* मज़ाक mazak
bantling *n.* बच्चा bachha
banyan *n.* बरगद bargad
baptism *n.* दीक्षा-स्नान diksha snan
baptize +*v.t.* दीक्षा-स्नान कराना diksha snan karna
bar *n.* बाधा baadha
bar *v.t* रोकना rokna
barbarian *a.* जंगली jangali
barbarian *n.* असभ्य व्यक्ति asabhya vyakti
barbarism *n.* असभ्यता asabhyata
barbarity *n* बर्बरता barbarta
barbarous *a.* असभ्य asabhya
barbed *a.* कांटेदार kantedar
barber *n.* हज्जाम hajjam
bard *n.* कवि kavi
bare *a.* खाली khali
bare *v.t.* नंगा करना nanga karna
barely *adv.* मुश्किल से mushkil se
bargain *n.* सौदा sauda
bargain *v.t.* सौदा करना sauda karna
barge *n.* नाव nav
bark *n.* छाल chhaal
bark *v.t.* भौंकना bhaunkna
barley *n.* जौ jau
barn *n.* कोठार kothar
barn *n.* पशुपाला pashupala
barometer *n* वायुदाबमापी wayudaabmapi

barrack *n.* सेनावास sainavas
barrage *n.* भारी गोलाबारी bhari golabari
barrator *ns.* अदलतिया adlatiya
barrel *n* पीपा pipa
barrel *n.* बंदूक की नाल banduk ke naal
barren *a.* अनुपजाऊ anupajau
barren *n* बांझ banjh
barricade *n.* बाधा badha
barrier *n.* अवरोध avrodh
barrister *n.* वकील vakil
barter *v.t.* अदला-बदली करना adla-badli karna
barter *n.* विनिमय vinimaya
basal *adj.* आधार सम्बन्धी adhar sambandhi
base *n.* आधार aadhar
base *v.t.* आधारित करना aadharit karna
baseless *a.* निर्मूल nirmul
basement *n.* तहखाना tahakhana
bashful *a.* संकोची sankochi
basic *a.* बुनियादी buniyadi
basil *n.* तुलसी tulsi
basin *n.* चिलमची chilamachi
basis *n.* मूलाधार muladhar
bask *v.i.* आनंद लेना anand lena
basket *n.* टोकरी tokari
bastard *n.* अवैध संतान awaidh santan
bastard *a* अवैध awaidh
bat *n* चमगादड़ chamgaadharh
bat *n* बल्ला balla
batch *n* घान dhaan
bath *n* स्नान snaan
bathe *v. t* स्नान करना snaan karna
baton *n* छड़ी chadi
batsman *n.* बल्लेबाज ballebaj
battalion *n* वाहिनी vahini
battery *n* तोपखाना topkhana
battle *n* युद्ध yudh
battle *v. i.* युद्ध लड़ना yudh ladna

bawl *n.i.* चिल्लाकर बोलना chilakar bolna
bay *n* खाड़ी kharhi
bayonet *n* संगीन sangin
be *v.t.* होना hona
beach *n* समुद्र-तट samudra tat
beacon *n* संकेतक sankaitak
bead *n* मनका manka
beadle *n.* गिरजे का पदाधिकारी girja ka padadhikari
beak *n* चोंच chonch
beaker *n* बीकर beekar
beam *n* किरण kiran
beam *v. i* चमकना chamakana
bean *n.* सेम same
bear *n* भालू bhalu
bear *v.t* ले जाना le jana
beard *n* दाढ़ी dadhi
bearing *n* आचरण aacharan
beast *n* पशु pashu
beastly *a* क्रूरतापूर्ण krurtapurna
beat *v.t.* पीटना peetna
beat *v. t.* पराजित करना parajit karna
beat *n* धड़कन dharkan
beautiful *a* सुंदर sundar
beautify *v. t* सजाना sajana
beauty *n* सौंदर्य saundariya
beaver *n* लोमचर्म lomcharm
because *conj.* क्योंकि kyonki
beck *n.* पहाड़ी नाला या नदी paharhi nala ya nadi
beckon *v.t.* संकेत करना sanket karna
beckon *v. t* इशारा करना ishara karna
become *v. i* हो जाना ho jana
becoming *a* उपयुक्त upyukt
bed *n* चारपाई charpai
bedding *n.* शयन सामग्री shayan saamagri
bedevil *v. t* सताना satana
bedight *v.t.* सजाना sajana
bed-time *n.* निद्रा का समय nindra ka samay

bee *n.* मधुमक्खी madhumakhi
beef *n* गोमांस gomans
beehive *n.* मधुमक्खी का घर madhumakhi ka ghar
beet *n* चुकंदर chukandar
beetle *n* भृंग bhring
befall *v. t* घटित होना ghatit hona
before *prep* के सामने ke saamney
before *adv.* सामने saamney
before *conj* इससे पहले कि is se pehle ki
beforehand *adv.* पहले ही pehle hi
befriend *v. t.* मित्र बनाना mitr banana
beg *v. t.* निवेदन करना nivedan karna
beget *v. t* जन्म देना janm dena
beggar *n* भिखारी bhikhari
begin *n* प्रारंभ करना prarambh karna
beginning *n.* प्रारंभ prarambh
begird *v.t.* घेरना gherna
beguile *v. t* मोहित करना mohit karna
behave *v. i.* आचरण करना aacharan karna
behaviour *n* आचरण aacharan
behead *v. t.* सिर काटना seer katna
behind *adv* पीछे की ओर peeche ki aur
behind *prep* से बाद में se baad mein
behold *v. t* ध्यान से देखना dhyan se dhekna
being *n* प्राणी prani
belabour *v. t* पीटना peetna
belated *adj.* देर से आने वाला der se aane wala
belch *v. t* डकार लेना dakaar lena
belch *n* डकार dakaar
belief *n.* विश्वास vishwas
belief *n.* आस्था astha
belief *n* धारणा dharna
believe *v. t* भरोसा रखना bharosa rakhna
bell *n* घंटा ghanta
belle *n* सुंदरी sundari
bellicose *a* लड़ाकू larhaku
belligerency *n* युद्धप्रियता yudhapriyata

belligerent *a* युद्धरत yudhrat
belligerent *n* युद्धरत राज्य yudhrat rajya
bellow *v. i* गरजना garjana
bellows *n.* धौंकनी dhaunkani
belly *n* पेट pet
belong *v. i* होना hona
belongings *n.* व्यक्तिगत माल-असबाब vyaktigat maal-asbaab
beloved *a* परमप्रिय parampriya
beloved *n* प्रियतम priyatam
below *adv* नीचे neechay
below *prep* से नीचे se neechay
belt *n* पट्टा patta
bemire *v. t* कीचड़ से गन्दा करना kicharh se ganda karna
bemuse *v. t* बुद्धिहीन करना budhihin karna
bench *n* अदालत adalat
bend *n* मोड़ morh
bend *v. t* हार मानना haar maanna
beneath *adv* नीचे neeche
beneath *prep* के नीचे ke neeche
benefaction *n.* उपकार upkaar
benefice *n* पादरी की वृत्ति padri ki vriti
beneficial *a* लाभकारी labhkari
benefit *n* लाभ labh
benefit *v. t.* लाभ पहुँचाना labh pahuchana
benevolence *n* कृपा kripa
benevolent *a* कृपालु kripalu
benign *adj* दयालु dayalu
benignly *adv* दयालुता से dayaluta se
benison *n* वरदान vardan
bent *n* रूझान rujhan
bequeath *v. t.* वसीयत में देना vasiyat mein dena
bereave *v. t.* वंचित करना vanchit karna
bereavement *n* वियोग viyog
berth *n* शायिका shayika
beside *prep.* के पास में ke paas mein
besides *prep* के अतिरिक्त ke atirikt

besides *adv* **साथ ही** saath he

besiege *v. t* **आक्रमण करना** akraman karna

beslaver *v. t* **चाटुकारी करना** chatukari karna

bestow *v. t* **प्रदान करना** pradan karna

bestrew *v. t* **छींटना** chintana

bet *v.i* **शर्त लगाना** shart lagana

bet *n* **शर्त** shart

betel *n* **पान** paan

betray *vt.* **विश्वासघात करना** vishvasghat karna

betray *v.t.* **प्रकट करना** prakat karna

betrayal *n* **विश्वासघात** vishvasghat

betroth *v. t* **वाग्दान करना** vaagdan

betrothal *n.* **वाग्दान** vaagdan

better *a* **पहले से अच्छा** pehle se acchha

better *adv.* **और अच्छे ढंग से** aur aache dhang se

better *v. t* **सुधारना** sudhaarna

betterment *n* **सुधार** sudhar

between *prep* **मध्य** madhya

beverage *n* **पेय** paye

bewail *v. t* **शोक मनाना** shok manana

beware *v.i.* **चौकस रहना** chaukas rehna

bewilder *v. t* **उलझन में डालना** uljhan may dalna

bewitch *v.t* **मोहित करना** mohit karna

beyond *prep.* **से ऊपर** se upar

beyond *adv.* **दूरी पर** duri par

bi *pref* **दोहरा** dohara

biangular *adj.* **दो कोण का** do kon ka

bias *n* **पक्षपात** pakshapat

bias *v. t* **पक्षपातपूर्ण बनाना** pakshapatpurna banana

biaxial *adj* **दो धुरा वाला** do dhura wala

bibber *n* **पियक्कड़** piyakkad

bible *n* **ईसाइयों की धर्म पुस्तक** isaiyon ki dharm pustak

bibliography +*n* **ग्रंथ-सूची** granth-suchi

biceps *n* **द्विशिर पेशी** dvishir peshi

bicker *v. t* **विवाद करना** vivad karna

bicycle *n.* **बाइसिकिल** bicycle

bid *v.t* **आदेश देना** adesh dena

bid *n* **प्रयत्न** prayatan

bidder *n* **दाँव या बाजी लगाने वाला** dav ya bazi lagane wala

bide *v. t* **सहना** sahana

biennial *adj* **दो साल में होने वाला** do saal mein hone wala

bier *n* **अरथी** arthi

big *a* **महान** mahan

bigamy *n* **द्विविवाह-प्रथा** dvivavah-pratha

bight *n* **छोटी खाड़ी** choti kharhi

bigot *n* **धर्मांध व्यक्ति** dharmandh vyakti

bigotry *n* **कट्टरता** kattarta

bile *n* **पित्त** pit

bilingual *a* **द्विभाषी** dvibhashi

bilk *v. t.* **धोखा देना** dhokha dena

bill *n* **बिल, प्रपायक** bill, prapayak

billion *n* **एक अरब** ek arab

billow *n* **लहर** lehar

billow *v.i* **लहराना** lehrana

bimonthly *adj.* **महीने में दो बार** maheene mein do bar

binary *adj* **दोहरा जोड़ा** dohara jorha

bind *v.t* **बांधना** baandhana

binding *a* **अनिवार्य** anivarya

binocular *n.* **दूरबीन** durbin

biographer *n* **जीवनी-लेखक** jeevani-lekhak

biography *n* **जीवनी** jeevani

biologist *n* **जीव विज्ञानी** jeev vigyani

biology *n* **जीव विज्ञान** jeev vigyan

biped *n* **द्विपाद** dvipad

birch *n.* **भोजपत्र** bhojpatra

bird *n* **पक्षी** panchi

birth *n.* **जन्म** janm

biscuit *n* **बिस्कुट** biscuit

bisect *v. t* **द्विविभाजित करना** dvivibhajit karna

**bisexual** *adj.* द्विलिंगीय dvilingiya
**bishop** *n* बिशप bishap
**bison** *n* जंगली साँड jangali sand
**bit** *n* टुकड़ा tukra
**bitch** *n* कुतिया kutiya
**bite** *v. t.* काटना kaatna
**bite** *n* काटने का घाव katne ka ghav
**bitter** *a* पीड़ादायक pirhadayak
**bi-weekly** *adj* अर्ध साप्ताहिक ardh saptahik
**bizarre** *adj* पागल pagal
**blab** *v. t. & i* भेद खोल देना bhed khol dena
**black** *adj.* काला kala
**black** *a* प्रकाश-रहित prakash-rahit
**blacken** *v. t.* काला करना kala karna
**blackmail** *n, v.t.* डरा कर वसूल करना dara kar vasul karna
**blacksmith** *n* लोहार lohar
**bladder** *n* मूत्राशय mutrashaya
**blade** *n.* पत्ती patti
**blain** *n* छाला chaala
**blame** *v. t* दोष लगाना dosh lagana
**blame** *n* दोष dosh
**blanch** *v. t. & i* भय से पीला पड़ जाना bhay se peela parh jana
**bland** *adj.* विनीत vineet
**blank** *a* कोरा kora
**blank** *n* रिक्त स्थान rikt sthan
**blanket** *n* कंबल kambal
**blare** *v. t* चिल्लाकर बोलना chilakar bolna
**blast** *n* धमाका dhamaka
**blast** *v.i* नष्ट करना nasht karna
**blaze** *n* चमक chamak
**blaze** *v.i* दहकना dahakana
**bleach** *v. t* सफेद करना saphed karana
**blear** *v. t* मन्द करना mand karna
**bleat** *n* मिमियाहट mimiyahat
**bleat** *v. i* मिमियाना mimiyana
**bleb** *n* फफोला phaphola
**bleed** *v. i* खून बहना khoon behna

**blemish** *n* दोष dosh
**blend** *v. t* मिलना milna
**blend** *n* मिश्रण mishran
**bless** *v. t* प्रदान करना pradaan karna
**blether** *v. i* बड़बड़ करना barhbarh karna
**blight** *n* पाला pala
**blind** *a* अंधा andha
**blindness** *n* अंधापन andhapan
**blink** *v. t. & i* टिमटिमाहट timtimahat
**bliss** *n* परमानंद parmanand
**blister** *n* फफोला phaphola
**bloc** *n* गुट gut
**block** *n* कुंदा kunda
**block** *v.t* अवरुद्घ करना avrudh karna
**blockade** *n* घेराबंदी gherabandi
**blockhead** *n* मूर्ख व्यक्ति murkh vyakti
**blood** *n* खून khun
**bloodshed** *n* रक्तपात raktapaat
**bloody** *a* निर्दय nirdaya
**bloom** *n* यौवन yauvan
**bloom** *v.i.* महकना mahakna
**blossom** *n* मंजरी manjari
**blossom** *v.i* खिलना khilna
**blot** *n.* दाग daag
**blot** *v. t* धब्बा लगाना dhabba lagana
**blouse** *n* ब्लाउज़ blouse
**blow** *v.i.* बजाना bajana
**blow** *n* झटका jhatka
**blue** *n* नीलवर्ण neelvarna
**blue** *a* आकाश-नील akash-neel
**bluff** *v. t* धोखा देना dhokha dena
**bluff** *n* धोखा dhokha
**blunder** *n* भारी भूल bhari bhul
**blunder** *v.i* भारी भूल करना bhari bhul karna
**blunt** *a* कुंद kund
**blur** *n* कलंक kalank
**blush** *n* झेंप jhenp
**blush** *v.i* झेंपना jhenpana
**boar** *n* सूअर suar

board *n.* तख्त takht
board *v.t.* सवार होना sawar hona

boarding *n* भोजन bhojan
boast *v.i* डींग मारना ding marna
boast *n* डींग ding
boat *v.i* नाव खेना nav khena
boat *n* नाव nav
bodice *n* चोली choli
bodily *adv.* सशरीर sasharir
bodily *a* शारीरिक sharirik
body *n* काया kaya
bodyguard *n.* अंगरक्षक angrakshak
bog *n* दलदल daldal
bog *v.i* फंस जाना phans jana
bogus *a* खोटा khota
boil *n* फोड़ा phorha
boil *v.i.* उबलना ubalna
****boiler *n* देग deg
bold *a.* निडर nidar
boldness *n* निर्भीकता nirbhikta
bolt *n* काबला kabla
bolt *v. t* सिटकनी लगाना sitakani lagana
bomb *n* बम bam
bomb *v. t* बम गिराना bam girana
bombard *v. t* बमबारी करना bambari karna
bombardment *n* बमबारी bambbari
bomber *n* बमवर्षक bambvarshak
bonafide *adv* सद् भावपूर्वक sad bhavpurwak
bonafide *a* सद् भावपूर्ण sad bhavpurna
bond *n* अनुबंध anubandh
bondage *n* दासता daasta
bone *n.* हड्डी haddi
bonfire *n* उत्सवाग्नि utsvaagni
bonnet *n* बोनिट bonnet
bonus *n* बोनस bonus
book *n* पुस्तक pustak
bookish *n.* पढ़ाक्कू padhaku

book-keeper *n* हिसाब करने वाला hisab karne wala
booklet *n* पुस्तिका pustika
book-seller *n* पुस्तक बेचने वाला pustak bechne wala
book-worm *n* पाठक paathak
boon *n* वरदान vardan
boor *n* किसान kisan
boost *n* सहारा sahara
boost *v. t* बढ़ावा देना badhava dena
boot *n* जूता joota
booth *n* मंडप mandap
booty *n* लूट का माल lut ka maal
booze *v. i* अधिक मदिरा पीना adhik madira peena
border *n* किनारी seemant
border *v.t* किनारी लगाना kinari lagana
bore *v. t* छेदना chedna
bore *n* छेद ched
born *v.* पैदा हुआ paida hua
born rich *adj.* जन्म का धनी janam ka dhani
borne *adj.* लाया हुआ laya hua
borrow *v. t* उधार लेना udhar lena
bosom *n* छाती chaati
boss *n* मालिक malik
botany *n* वनस्पति विज्ञान banaspati wigyan
botch *v. t* फोड़ा foda
both *a* दोनों dono
both *pron* दोनों लोग dono log
both *conj* समान रूप से saman rup se
bother *v. t* परेशान होना pareshan hona
botheration *n* झंझट jhanjhat
bottle *n* बोतल botal
bottom *n* तह teh
bough *n* शाखा shakha
bouncer *n* झूठा jhutha
bound *n.* सीमा seema
boundary *n* सीमारेखा seema rekha

bountiful *a* प्रचुर prachur
bounty *n* उपहार uphar
bouquet *n* गुलदस्ता guldasta
bout *n* बीमारी का दौरा bimari ka daura
bow *v. t* झुकना jhukana
bow *n* नमन naman
bow *n* धनुष dhanush
bowel *n.* आंतें aante
bower *n* कुंज kunj
bowl *n* कटोरा katora
bowl *v.i* गेंद फेंकना gend phenkna
box *n* संदूक sanduk
boxing *n* मुक्केबाज़ी mukkebazee
boy *n* बालक balak
boycott *v. t.* बहिष्कार करना bahiskar karna
boycott *n* बहिष्कार bahishkar
boyhood *n* लड़कपन larhakpan
brace *n* बढ़ाई का औज़ार badhai ka auzaar
bracelet *n* कंगन kangan
brag *v. i* डींग मारना ding marna
brag *n* डींग ding
brain *n* दिमाग़ demaag
brake *n* ब्रेक break
brake *v. t* ब्रेक लगाना break lagana
branch *n* शाखा shakha
brand *n.* व्यापारिक चिन्ह vyaparik chinh
brand *n* तलवार talwar
brandy *n* ब्रांडी brandi
brass *n.* पीतल peetal
brave *a* बहादुर bahadur
bravery *n* बहादुरी bahaduri
brawl *v. i. & n* विवाद vivad
bray *n* गधे की रेंक gadhe ki renk
bray *v. i* रेंकना renkna
breach *n* विच्छेद viched
bread *n* रोटी roti
breadth *n* चौड़ाई chaurhayee
break *v. t* नष्ट करना nasht karna
break *n* भंजन bhanjan
breakage *n* तोड़ने की क्रिया torhne ki kriya

breakdown *n* अचानक अवरोध achanak avrodh
breakfast *n* नाश्ता nashta
breakneck *n* बहुत तेज़ bahut tez
breast *n* छाती chhaati
breath *n* श्वसन shvasan
breathe *v. i.* सांस लेना sans lena
breeches *n.* जांघिया jhangiya
breed *v.t* पालन- पोषण करना palan-poshan karna
breed *n* जाति jati
breeze *n* समीर samir
breviary *n.* स्तोत्र संग्रह stotra sangreh
brevity *n* संक्षिप्तता sankshiptata
brew *v. t.* शराब बनाना sharab banana
brewery *n.* यवसुरा निर्माणशाला yavsura nirmansala
bribe *n* घूस ghoos
bribe *v. t.* रिश्वत देना rishvat dena
brick *n* ईंट eent
bride *n* दुलहन dulhan
bridegroom *n.* दुल्हा dulha
bridge *n* पुल pull
bridle *n* लगाम lagam
brief *a.* संक्षिप्त sankshipt
brigade *n.* वाहिनी vahini
brigadier *n* ब्रिगेडियर brigadier
bright *a* चमकदार chamakdaar
brighten *v. t* चमकाना chamkana
brilliance *n* चमक chamak
brilliant *a* प्रतिभाशाली pratibhashali
brim *n* मुख mukh
brine *n* खारा पानी khara pani
bring *v. t* लाना lana
brinjal *n* बैंगन baingan
brink *n.* कगार kagar
brisk *adj* चपल chapal
bristle *n* बाल baal
British *adj* अंग्रेज़ angrez
brittle *a.* टूटने-योग्य tutne-yogya

broad *a* चौड़ा chaurha

broadcast *n* प्रसारण prasaran

broadcast *v. t* प्रचारित करना pracharit karna

broaden *v. t. & i* चौड़ा करना या होना chaurha karna ya hona

brocade *n* ज़रीदार कपड़ा zaridar kapda

broccoli *n.* फूलगोभी phoolgobhi

brochure *n* छोटी पुस्तक chhoti pustak

brochure *n* विवरणिका vivranika

broker *n* दलाल dalal

bronze *n. & adj* काँसा kasha

brook *n.* छोटी नदी choti nadi

broom *n* झाड़ू jharhu

broth *n* शोरबा shorba

brothel *n* रंडी का घर randi ka ghar

brother *n* भाई bhai

brotherhood *n* भ्रातृत्व bhratritva

brow *n* भौंह bhaunh

brown *a* भूरा bhoora

brown *n* भूरा रंग bhoora rang

browse *n* नई पत्तियाँ nayee pattiyan

bruise *n* चोट chot

bruit *n* झूठी खबर jhuti khabhar

brush *n* सफ़ाई का ब्रश safai ka brush

brutal *a* निर्दय nirdaya

brute *n* पशु pashu

bubble *n* बुलबुला bulbula

bucket *n* बाल्टी balti

buckle *n* बकसुआ baksua

bud *n* कली kali

budge *v.t.* हिलना hilna

budget *n* कोष kosh

buff *n* घूँसा ghoonsa

buffalo *n.* भैंसा bhainsa

buffoon *n* मसखरा maskhara

bug *n.* खटमल khatmal

bugle *n* बिगुल bigul

build *v. t* निर्माण करना nirman karna

build *n* रचना rachna

building *n* इमारत imarat

bulb *n.* रोशनी वाला बल्ब roshni vala bulb

bulk *n* आकार aakar

bulky *a* भारी bhari

bull *n* सांड sand

bulldog *n* एक प्रकार का कुत्ता ek prakar ka kutta

bullet *n* गोली goli

bulletin *n* विज्ञप्ति vigyapati

bullock *n* बैल bell

bully *n* धौंसिया dhaunsiya

bully *v. t.* भयभीत करना bhaybhit karna

bulwark *n* कोट coat

bumpy *adj* उछाल वाला uchhal wala

bunch *n* गुच्छा guchha

bundle *n* पुलिंदा pulinda

bungalow *n* बंगला bangla

bungle *v. t* बिगाड़ना bigarhana

bungle *n* घपला ghapla

bunk *n* सोने के लिये पटरी sone ke liye patri

bunker *n* सेनावास senavas

bunting *n* कपड़े की सजावटी पट्टी kaparhe ki sajawat patti

buoyancy *n* हल्कापन halkapan

burden *n* बोझा bhojha

burden *v. t* लादना laadna

burdensome *a* कष्टकारी kashtakari

bureau *n.* मुहकमा muhakama

bureaucracy *n.* नौकरशाही naukarshahi

burglar *n* चोर chor

burglary *n* चोरी chori

burial *n* दफ़न dafan

burn *v. t* जलाना jalana

burn *n* जलने की चोट jalne ki chot

burrow *n* बिल bill

burst *v. i.* फोड़ना phorhna

burst *n* विस्फोट visphot

bury *v. t.* दफनाना dafnana

bus *n* बस bus

bush *n* झाड़ी jhaarhi

business *n* व्यापार vyapar
businessman *n* व्यापारी vyapari
bustle *v. t* जल्दी से काम करना jaldi se kam karna
busy *a* व्यस्त vyast
but *prep* उसके अतिरिक्त uske atirikt
but *conj.* किंतु kintu
butcher *n* कसाई kasayee
butcher *v. t* हत्या करना hatya karna
butter *n* मक्खन makhan
butter *v. t* मक्खन लगाना makhan lagana
butterfly *n* तितली titli
buttermilk *n* मट्ठा matha
button *n* बटन batan
button *v. t.* बटन लगाना batan lagana
buy *v. t.* खरीदना kharidana
buyer *n.* क्रेता kreta
buzz *v. i* गुंजन करना gunjan karna
buzz *n.* भिनभिनाहट bhinbhinahat
by *prep* दौरान dauran
by *adv* पास में paas mein
bye-bye *interj.* अलविदा alvida
by-election *n* उप-चुनाव up-chunav
bye-law *n* उपनियम upniyam
bypass *n* उपमार्ग upmarg
by-product *n* उपोत्पादन uptopadan
byre *n* गोशाला gaushala
byword *n* लोकोक्ति lokokti

cab *n.* टैक्सी taxi
cabaret *n.* नाच naach
cabbage *n.* बन्दगोभी bandgobhi
cabin *n.* कोठरी kothri
cabinet *n.* मंत्रि-मंडल mantri-mandal
cable *n.* डोरी rassa
cable *v. t.* समुद्रीतार से भेजना samudritar se bhejna

cache *n* गुप्त भंडार gupt bhandar
cachet *n* मोहर mohar
cackle *v. i* कूकना kukna
cactus *n.* नागफनी nagphani
cadet *n.* सैनिक छात्र sainik chhatra
cadge *v. i* भीख माँगते फिरना bheekh mangte phirna
cadmium *n* टीन समान धातु tin saman dhatu
cafe *n.* काफ़ीघर cafighar
cage *n.* पिंजरा pinjra
cain *n* हत्यारा hatyara
cake *n.* केक cake
calamity *n.* विपत्ति vipatti
calcium *n* चूने का तत्त्व chune ka tatva
calculate *v. t.* गणना करना ganana karna
calculation *n.* गणना ganana
calculator *n* गणना करने का यन्त्र ganana karn ka yantra
calendar *n.* पंचांग panchang
calf *n.* पिंडली pindali
calf *n.* बछड़ा bachhra
call *v. t.* पुकारना pukaarna
call *n.* पुकार pukaar
calligraphy *n* लिखावट likhavat
calling *v.* बुलाना bulana
callous *a.* कठोर kathor
callow *adj* अनुभवहीन anubhavhin
calm *n.* शांत shant
calm *v. t.* शांत करना shant karna
calm *n.* शांति shanti
calmative *adj* शान्ति लाने वाली shanti lane wali
calorie *n.* तापमान का माप taapman ka maap
calumniate *v. t.* निन्दा करना ninda karna
camel *n.* ऊँट unt
camera *n.* कैमरा camera
camp *n.* शिविर shivir
camp *v. i.* पड़ाव डालना parhav dalna

campaign *n.* आंदोलन andolan

camphor *n.* कपूर kapur

can *v. t.* डिब्बे में बंद करना dibbai mein band karna

can *v.* संभव होना sambhav hona

can *n.* डिब्बा dibba

canal *n.* नहर nahar

canard *n* कल्पित कथा kalpit katha

cancel *v. t.* रद्द करना radd karna

cancellation *n* रद्द radd

cancer *n.* कैंसर cancer

candid *a.* मासूम maasum

candidate *n.* परीक्षार्थी pariksharthi

candle *n.* मोमबत्ती mombatti

candour *n.* निष्कपटता nishkapatata

candy *n.* मिसरी misri

candy *v. t.* पागना paagana

cane *v. t.* बेंत से मारना bent se marna

cane *n.* बेंत bent

canister *n.* कनस्तर kanastar

cannon *n.* तोप top

canon *n.* तोप गोला top gola

canopy *n.* छतरी chhatri

canteen *n.* जलपान- गृह jalpan-greh

canter *n* कदम चाल kadam chal

canton *n* प्रदेश pradesh

cantonment *n.* छावनी chhavani

canvas *n.* चित्रकारी के लिए कपड़ा chitrakari ke liye kapda

canvass *v. t.* वोट मांगना vote mangana

cap *v. t.* टोपी पहनाना topi pahanana

cap *n.* टोपी topi

capability *n.* सामर्थ्य samarthya

capable *a.* योग्य yogya

capacious *a.* विशाल vishal

capacity *n.* क्षमता kshamta

cape *n.* अंतरीप antreep

capital *n.* राजधानी rajdhani

capital *n* पूंजी punji

capitalist *n.* पूंजीपति punjipati

caprice *n.* सनक sanak

capricious *a.* मनमौजी manmauji

Capricorn *n* मकर राशि makar rashi

capsicum *n* बड़ी लाल मिर्च barhi lal mirch

capsize *v. i.* उलट जाना ulat jana

capsular *adj* बीजकोष सम्बन्धी bijkosh sambandhi

captain *n.* कप्तान kaptan

captaincy *n.* कप्तानी kaptani

caption *n.* शीर्षक shirshak

captivate *v. t.* आकर्षित करना aakarashit karna

captive *a.* बंदी बना हुआ bandi bana hua

captive *n.* बंदी bandi

captivity *n.* बंदी दशा bandi dasha

capture *n.* बंदीकरण bandikaran

capture *v. t.* बंदी बनाना bandi banana

car *n.* गाड़ी garhi

carat *n.* स्वर्ण शुद्धता का माप svarn shuddhta ka map

caravan *n.* काफ़िला kaphila

carbon *n.* कार्बन carbon

card *n.* ताश का पत्ता taash ka patta

cardamom *n.* इलायची ilaychi

cardboard *n.* गत्ता gatta

cardiac *adjs* हृदय सम्बन्धी hriday sambandhi

cardinal *n.* बड़ा पादरी bara padri

cardinal *a.* प्रधान pradhan

care *n.* देख-रेख dekh-rekh

care *n.* चिंता chinta

career *n.* व्यवसाय vyvasaya

careful *a* सचेत sachait

careless *a.* असावधान asavdhan

caress *v. t.* पुचकारना puchkaarna

cargo *n.* पोतभार potbhar

caricature *n.* व्यंग्य-चित्र vyangya chitr

carious *adj* गला हुआ gala hua

carnage *n* संहार sanhar

carnival *n* आनन्द उत्सव anand utsav

carol *n* आनन्द का गीत anand ka geet
carpal *adj* कलाई संबंधी kalai sambandhi
carpenter *n.* बढ़ई barhayee
carpentry *n.* बढ़ईगीरी barhayeegiri
carpet *n.* कालीन kalin
carriage *n.* गाड़ी garhi
carrier *n.* वाहक vahak
carrot *n.* गाजर gajar
carry *v. t.* उठाना uthana
cart *n.* छकड़ा chakrha
cartage *n.* ढुलाई का काम dhulayee ka kam
cartoon *n.* कार्टून cartoon
cartridge *n.* कारतूस cartoos
carve *v. t.* मूर्ति का रूप देना murti ka rup dena
cascade *n.* जलप्रताप jalpratap
case *n.* संदूक sanduk
cash *v. t.* नगदी में बदलना nagadi mein badalna
cash *n.* नकद धन nagad dhan
cashier *n.* ख़ज़ांची khajanchi
casing *n.* ढकना dhakna
cask *n* पीपा pipa
casket *n* जवाहरात का बक्सा jawaharat ka baksa
cassette *n.* कैसिट cassette
cast *v. t.* ढालना dhalana
cast *n.* ढांचा dhancha
caste *n* जाति jati
castigate *v. t.* दंड देना dand dena
casting *n* धातु को गलाकर ढलाई dhatu ko galakar dhalayee
cast-iron *n* कान्ती लोहा kanti loha
castle *n.* दुर्ग durg
castor oil *n.* रेंडी का तेल redi ka tel
casual *a.* आकस्मिक aakasmik
casualty *n.* दुर्घटना durghatna
cat *n.* बिल्ली billi
catalogue *n.* सूचीपत्र suchipatra
cataract *n.* मोतियाबिंद motiyabind

catch *n.* धोखा dhokha
catch *v. t.* पकड़ना pakarna
categorical *a.* सुनिश्चित sunishchit
category *n.* श्रेणी shreni
caterpillar *n.* कीड़ा kirha
cathedral *n.* प्रधान गिरजाघर pradhan girjaghar
catholic *a.* इसाई धर्म का isaai dharm ka
cattle *n.* मवेशी maveshi
cauliflower *n.* फूलगोभी foolgobhi
causal *adj.* कारण बतलाने वाला kaaran batlanay wala
causality *n* कारणत्व karanatva
cause *v.t* कारण बनना kaaran banana
cause *n.* कारण kaaran
causeway *n* बाँध baandh
caustic *a.* तीखा teekha
caution *v. t.* चेतावनी देना chaitavani dena
caution *n.* चेतावनी chaitavani
cautious *a.* सतर्क satarkh
cavalry *n.* वख्तरबंद सेना vakhtarband sena
cave *n.* गुफ़ा gufa
cavern *n.* गुफ़ा gufa
cavil *v. t* दोष निकालना dosh nikalna
cavity *n.* गुहा guha
caw *v. i.* काँव-काँव करना kanw-kanw karna
caw *n.* काँव-काँव kanw-kanw
cease *v. i.* बंद करना band karna
ceaseless ~*a.* निरंतर nirantar
cedar *n.* देवदार का वृक्ष devdar ka vriksh
ceiling *n.* भीतरी छत bhitari chat
celebrate *v. t. & i.* उत्सव मनाना utsav manana
celebration *n.* उत्सव utsav
celebrity *n* प्रसिद्ध व्यक्ति prasiddh vyakti
celestial *adj.* दिव्य divya
celestial *adj* सुन्दर sundar
celibacy *n.* अविवाहित जीवन avivahit jeevan
cell *n.* कोठरी kothari

cellar *n* तहखाना tahakhana
cellular *adj* जालीदार jalidaar
cement *v. t.* जोड़ना jorhna
cement *n.* सीमेंट cement
cemetery *n.* कब्रिस्तान kabristan
cense *v. t* धूप देना dhup dena
censor *v. t.* निरीक्षण करना nirikshan karna
censor *n.* नियंत्रक niyantrak
censorious *adj* दोष निकालने वाला dosh nekalne wala
censure *n.* निंदा ninda
censure *v. t.* निंदा करना ninda karna
census *n.* जनगणना janganana
cent *n* सौ sau
centenarian *n* शतायु व्यक्ति shatayu vyakti
centenary *n.* सौ वर्ष का समय sau varsh ka samay
centennial *adj.* सौवीं वर्षगाँठ sauvin varshaganth
centigrade *a.* सौ अंशों में विभाजित sau anshon mein vibhajit
centipede *n.* कनखजूरा kankhajura
central *a.* केंद्रीय kendriya
centre *n* केंद्र kendra
centrifugal *adj.* केन्द्र से हट जाने वाली kendra se hat janai wala
centuple *n. & adj* सौगुना saugunna
century *n.* शतक shatak
ceramics *n* मिट्टी के पात्र mitti ke patra
cerated *adj.* मोम से ढँका हुआ mom se dhaka huya
cereal *a* अन्नमय annmaya
cereal *n.* अन्न ann
ceremonial *a.* समारोहपूर्ण samaarohapurna
ceremonious *a.* औपचारिक aupcharik
ceremony *n.* धर्मक्रिया dharmakriya
certain *a* निर्विवाद nirvivad
certainly *adv.* निःसंदेह nisandeh
certainty *n.* सत्य satya

certificate *n.* प्रमाण पत्र pramanpatra
certify *v. t.* प्रमाणित करना pramanit karna
cerumen *n* कान का खूँट kaan ka khunt
cesspool *n.* हौदी haudi
chain *n* बेड़ी bedhi
chair *n.* कुर्सी kursi
chair *n.* पद pad
chairman *n* सभापति sabhapati
chaise *n* आनन्द की सवारी anand ki savari
challenge *v. t.* चुनौती देना chunauti dena
challenge *n.* चुनौती chunauti
chamber *n.* सदन sadan
champion *n.* विजेता vijeta
champion *v. t.* समर्थन करना samarthan karna
chance *n.* संयोग sanyog
chancellor *n.* कुलाधिपति kuladhipati
chancery *n* प्रधान न्यायालय pradhan nyayalaya
change *n.* परिवर्तन parivartan
change *v. t.* बदल देना badal dena
channel *n* नाला nala
chant *n* भजन bhajan
chaos *n.* अव्यवस्था avyavastha
chaotic *adv.* अव्यवस्थित avayvasthit
chapel *n.* पूजास्थल pujasthal
chapter *n.* अध्याय adhyaya
character *n.* चरित्र charitra
charge *n.* धावा dhava
charge *v. t.* दोष देना dosh dena
chariot *n* रथ rath
charitable *a.* दानशील daanshil
charity *n.* दानी संस्था dani sanstha
charm *n.* आकर्षण aakarshan
charm *v. t.* आनंद देना anand dena
chart *n.* नक्शा naksha
charter *n* प्राधिकार pradhikar
chase *v. t.* पीछा करना pichha karna
chase *n.* पीछा pichha
chaste *a.* पवित्र pavitra

chastity *n.* शुद्धता shudhta
chat *n.* गपशप gapshap
chat *v. i.* बातचीत करना batchit karna
chatter *v. t.* बकवास करना bakvas karna
chauffeur *n.* कार-चालक kar-chalak
cheap *a* सस्ता sasta
cheapen *v. t.* सस्ता करना sasta karna
cheat *n.* ठग thag
cheat *v. t.* ठगना thagna
check *n* अवरोध avarodh
check *v. t.* जांचना janchana
checkmate *n* शहमात shahamat
cheek *n* गाल gaal
cheer *n.* प्रसन्नता prasannata
cheer *v. t.* जयजयकार करना jayjaykaar
karna
cheerful *a.* प्रसन्न prasann
cheerless *a* उदास udas
cheese *n.* पनीर panir
chemical *n.* रासायनिक पदार्थ rasayanik
padarth
chemical *a.* रसायन-संबंधी rasayan-
sambandhi
chemise *n* शमीज़ shamiz
chemist *n.* औषध-विक्रेता aushadh vikreta
chemistry *n.* रसायन-शास्त्र rasayan shastra
cheque *n.* चेक cheque
cherish *v. t.* पोसना poshana
cheroot *n* सिगार sigaar
chess *n.* शतरंज shatranj
chest *n* छाती chhati
chestnut *n.* पांगर paangar
chevalier *n* महावीर mahavir
chew *v. t* चबाना chabana
chicken *n.* चूजा chuja
chide *v. t.* डाँटना dantna
chief *a.* मुख्य mukhya
chieftain *n.* मुखिया mukhiya
child *n* बच्चा bachcha
childhood *n.* शैशव shaishav

childish *a.* बचकाना bachkana
chill *n.* ठंड thand
chilli *n.* लाल मिर्च lal mirch
chilly *a* ठंडा thanda
chimney *n.* चिमनी chimni
chimpanzee *n.* वनमानुष vanmaanush
chin *n.* ठोड़ी thorhi
chirp *v.i.* चींचीं करना chinchin karna
chirp *n* चींचीं chinchin
chisel *v. t.* छेनी से काटना chaine se katna
chisel *n* छेनी chaine
chit *n.* पर्ची parchi
chivalrous *a.* शौर्यवान shauryavan
chivalrous *a.* उदार udar
chivalry *n.* शिष्टता shishtata
chlorine *n* साँस घुटाने वाली एक गैस saans
ghutanai wali ek gas
chocolate *n* चोकोलेट chocolate
choice *n.* पसंद pasand
choir *n* गायक-मंडली gayak-mandali
choke *v. t.* गला घोंटना gala ghontna
cholera *n.* हैज़ा haija
choose *v. t.* चुनना chunana
chop *v. t* काटना katna
chord *n.* तार taar
choroid *n* आँख की झिल्ली aankh ki jhilli
chorus *n.* गायक-दल gayak-dal
Christ *n.* मसीहा masiha
Christendom *n.* ईसाई जगत isai jagat
Christian *n* ईसाई isai
Christian *a.* ईसाई धर्म-संबंधी isai dharma-
sambandhi
Christianity *n.* ईसाई धर्म isai dharma
Christmas *n* ईसा-जन्मोत्सव isa-
janmotasav
chrome *n* पीला रंग peela rang
chronic *a.* पुराना purana
chronicle *n.* इतिहास itihas
chronology *n.* कालक्रम kaalkram

chuckle v. i दबी हँसी हँसना dabi hansi hansna

chum n पुराना मित्र purana mitr

church n. गिरजाघर girjaghar

churchyard n. कब्रिस्तान kabristan

churl n गँवार ganvar

churn n. दूध का मटका dudh ka matka

churn v. t. & i. बिलोना bilona

cigar n. सिगार sigaar

cigarette n. सिगरेट cigrate

cinema n. सिनेमाघर cinemaghar

cinnabar n सिन्दूर sindur

cinnamon n दालचीनी daalchini

cipher, cypher n. शून्य का अंक shunya ka ank

circle n. वृत vrit

circle n. घेरा ghera

circuit n. परिधि paridhi

circular a गोल gol

circular n. परिपत्र paripatra

circulate v. i. प्रसारित करना prasarit karna

circulation n प्रसारण prasaran

circumference n. परिधि paridhi

circumspect adj. सावधान savdhan

circumstance n.pl. परिस्थिति paristithi

circumstance n घटना ghatna

circus n. सर्कस sarkas

cist n पत्थर का सन्दूक pathar ka sanduk

citadel n. दुर्ग durg

cite v. t अदालत में तलब करना adalat mein talab karna

citizen n नगर-निवासी nagar-nivasi

citizenship n नागरिकता naagrikta

citric adj. खटा khatta

city n नगर nagar

civic a नगर का nagar ka

civics n नागरिकशास्त्र naagrikshastra

civil a असैनिक asainik

civilian n असैनिक व्यक्ति asainik vyakti

civilization n. सभ्यता sabhyta

civilize v. t सभ्य बनाना sabhya banana

clack n. & v. i कर्कश शब्द karkash shabd

claim v. t दावा करना dava karna

claim n दावा dava

claimant n दावेदार davedar

clamber v. i कठिनता से चढ़ना kathinta se chadhna

clamour v. i. कोलाहल करना kolahal karna

clamour n कोलाहल kolahal

clamp n शिकंजा shikanja

clandestine adj. छिपा हुआ chhipa hua

clap v. i. ताली बजाना tali bajana

clap n कड़क karhak

clarification n स्पष्टीकरण spashtikaran

clarify v. t स्पष्ट करना spasht karna

clarion n. तुरही turahi

clarity n सफाई safaai

clash v. t. विरोध होना virodh hona

clash n. संघर्ष sangharsh

clasp n आलिंगन alingan

class n कक्षा kaksha

classic n उत्कृष्ट कृति utkrisht kriti

classic a उत्कृष्ट utkrisht

classical a प्राचीनकाल-संबंधी prachinkaal-sambandhi

classification n वर्गीकरण vargikaran

classify v. t वर्गीकृत करना vargikrit karna

clause n धारा dhara

claw n पंजा panja

clay n मिट्टी mitti

clean v. t साफ़ करना saaf rakhna

clean a. साफ़ saaf

cleanliness n स्वच्छता svachhata

cleanse v. t परिमार्जन करना parimarjan karna

clear a साफ़-सुथरा saaf-suthara

clear v. t साफ़ करना saaf karna

clearance n निकासी nikaasi

clearly adv स्पष्ट रूप से spasht rup se

cleft n दरार darar

clergy n पादरी paadri
clerical a याजकीय yaajkiya
clerk n लिपिक lipik
clever a. चतुर chatur
clew, clue n. सुराग़ suraag
click n. खटखट की आवाज़ khat-khat ki awaz
client n.. ग्राहक grahak
cliff n. खाड़ी चट्टान kharhi chattan
climate n. जलवायु jalwayu
climax n. शिखर shikhar
climb n. चढ़ाई chadhayee
climb v.i चड़ाई करना chadai karna
cling v. i. चिपटना chiptana
clinic n. चिकित्सालय chikitsalaya
clink n. कील keel
cloak n. चोग़ा choga
clock n. घड़ी gharhi
clod n. मूर्ख murkh
cloister n. मठ math
close a. घनिष्ट ghanisht
close v. t बंद करना band karna
close n. अंत aant
closet n. कोठरी kothari
closure n. समापन samapan
clot n. थक्का thakka
clot v. t थक्का बनाना thakka banana
cloth n कपड़ा kaprha
clothe v. t कपड़े पहनाना kaprhe pahnana
clothes n. परिधान paridhan
clothing n परिधान paridhan
cloud n. बादल baadal
cloudy a धुंधला dhundhala
clove n लवंग lavang
clown n विदूषक vidushak
club n मंडली mandali
clue n संकेत sanket
clumsy a अनाड़ी anari
cluster n गुच्छा guchha

cluster v. i. समूहबद्घ होना samuhbadh hona
clutch n चंगुल changul
clutter v. t चिल्लाकर दौड़ना chillakar dhaudna
coach n रेलगाड़ी का डिब्बा railgarhi ka dabba
coachman n गाड़ीवान gaarivaan
coal n कोयला koyla
coalition n मेल mail
coarse a घटिया ghatiya
coast n समुद्र-तट samudra-tat
coat n कोट coat
coating n रंग की तह rang ke the
coax v. t बहलाना behalana
cobbler n मोची mochi
cobra n विषैला साँप vishaila sanp
cobweb n मकड़ी का जाला makrhi ka jala
cocaine n कोकीन kokeen
cock n मुर्गा murga
cocker v. t दुलार करना dulaar karna
cockle v. i फूलना phulna
cock-pit n. वायुयान में चालक-कक्ष vayuyan mein chalak kaksha
cockroach n तिलचट्टा tilchatta
coconut n नारियल nariyal
code n संहिता sanhita
code n. संकेत लिपि sanket lipi
co-education n. सहशिक्षा sahashiksha
coefficient n. गुणक gunak
co-exist v. i सहवर्ती होना sahavarti hona
co-existence n सहअस्तित्व sah-astitva
coffee n कॉफ़ी के बीज़ coffee ke beej
coffin n ताबूत taabut
cog n पहिये का दाँता pahiye ka danta
cogent adj. प्रबल prabal
cognate adj सम्बन्धी sambandhi
cognizance n जानकारी jankaari
cohabit v. t सहवास करना sahawas karna
coherent a सुसंगत susangat

cohesive *adj* सहचारी sahchaari
coif *n* टोपी topi
coin *n* सिक्का sikka
coinage *n* सिक्का sikka
coincide *v.i.* संयोग sanyog
coincide *v. i* सहमत होना sahamat hona
coir *n* नारियल की जटा nariyal ki jata
cold *a* शीतल sheetal
cold *n* सर्दी sardi
collaborate *v. i* सहयोग करना sahayog karna
collaboration *n* सहयोग sahayog
collapse *v. i* एकाएक गिरना eka ek girna
collar *n* कॉलर kaular
colleague *n* सहकर्मी sahakarmi
collect *v. t* संग्रह करना sangreh karna
collection *n* संचित वस्तु sanchit vastu
collective *a* सामूहिक samuhik
collector *n* वसूल करनेवाला vasul karnewala
college *n* महाविद्यालय maha vidyalaya
collide *v. i.* भिड़ना bhirhna
collision *n* भिड़ंत bhirhant
collusion *n* दलबन्दी dalbandi
colon *n* अपूर्ण विराम apurna viram
colon *n* बड़ी अंतड़ी barhi antarhi
colonel *adj.* कर्नल karnal
colonial *a* औपनिवेशिक upniveshak
colony *n* उपनिवेश upnivesh
colour *v. t* रूप बदल देना rup badal dena
colour *n* रंग rang
column *n.* स्तंभ stambh
column *n* कॉलम kaalam
coma *n.* अचेतन अवस्था achetan avastha
comb *n* कंघा kangha
combat *n* संग्राम sangram
combat *v. t.* विरोध करना virodh karna
combatant *n* योद्धा yodha
combatant *a.* युद्घशील yudhshil
combination *n* संगठन sangathan

combine *v. t* मिल जाना mil jana
come *v. i.* आना aana
comedian *n.* हास्य अभिनेता hasya abhineta
comedy *n.* प्रहसन prahasan
comet *n* पुच्छलतारा puchaltara
comfit *n.* मिठाई mitthai
comfort *n.* आराम aaram
comfortable *a* आरामदायक aaramdayak
comic *n* हास्यरस की पत्रिका hasyaras ki patrika
comic *a* आनंदप्रद anandprad
comical *a* मज़ाकिया majakiya
comma *n* अल्पविराम चिह्न alpawiram chinah
command *n* आदेश aadesh
command *v. t* आदेश देना aadesh dena
commandant *n* सेनानायक sainanayak
commander *n* नायक nayak
commemorate *v. t.* कीर्तिमान होना kirtimaan hona
commemoration *n.* स्मरणोत्सव smaranotsava
commence *v. t* प्रांरभ करना prarambha karna
commencement *n* प्रारंभ prarambha
commend *v. t* प्रशंसा करना prashansa karna
commendable *a.* प्रशंसनीय prashansniya
commendation *n* प्रशंसा prashansa
comment *n* टिप्पणी tippani
comment *v. i* टिप्पणी करना tippni karna
commentary *n* टीका टिप्पणी tika-tippani
commentator *n* भाष्यकार bhashyakar
commerce *n* वाणिज्य wanijaya
commercial *a* व्यवसायिक vyavasayik
commiserate *v. t* दया करना daya karna
commission *n.* आयोग aayog
commissioner *n.* आयुक्त aayukt
commissure *n.* संयोजिका tantu bandh

commit *v. t.* प्रतिज्ञा करना pratigya karna
committee *n* समिति samiti
commodity *n.* माल maal
common *a.* साधारण saadharan
commoner *n.* सामान्य व्यक्ति samaniya vaykti
commonplace *a.* सामान्य samanya
commonwealth *n.* राष्ट्रमंडल rashtrmandal
commotion *n* शोरगुल shorgul
commove *v. t* उत्तेजित करना uttejet karna
communal *a* सांप्रदायिक sampradayik
commune *v. t* बातचीत करना baat-chit karna
communicate *v. t* सूचित करना suchit karna
communication *n.* सूचना suchna
communiqué *n.* सरकारी विज्ञप्ति sarkaari vigyapati
communism *n* साम्यवाद saamiyvad
community *n.* समाज samaaj
commute *v. t* अदल बदल करना adal badal karna
compact *a.* ठोस thos
compact *n.* संविदा sanvida
companion *n.* साथी sathi
company *n.* साथ saath
comparative *a* तुलनात्मक tulnaatmak
compare *v. t* तुलना करना tulna karna
comparison *n* मिलान milan
compartment *n.* रेलगाड़ी का डिब्बा rail garhi ka dibba
compass *n* परकार parkar
compassion *n* सहानुभूति sahanubhuti
compel *v. t* दबाव डालना dabav dalana
compensate *v.t* क्षतिपूर्ति करना kshatipurti karna
compensation *n* क्षतिपूर्ति kshatipurti
compete *v. i* प्रतिस्पर्धा करना pratispardha karna

competence *n* सामर्थ्य samarthya
competent *a.* समर्थ samarth
competition *n.* प्रतियोगिता pratiyogita
competitive *a* प्रतियोगी pratiyogi
compile *v. t* संग्रह करना sangrah karna
complacent *adj.* सन्तुष्ट santusht
complain *v. i* शिकायत करना shikayat karna
complaint *n.* शिकायत shikayat
complaisance *n.* भलमन्सी bhalmansi
complaisant *adj.* सुशील sushil
complement *n* पूरक purak
complementary *a* अनुपूरक anupurak
complete *a* पूर्ण purna
complete *v. t* पूरा करना pura karna
completion *adj.* पूर्ति purti
complex *a* जटिल jatil
complex *n* भवन समूह bhavan samuh
complexion *n* वर्ण warn
compliance *n.* आज्ञाकारिता aagyakarita
compliant *adj.* संकोची sankochi
complicate *v. t* उलझाना uljhana
complication *n.* उलझन uljhan
compliment *n.* प्रशंसा prashansa
compliment *v. t* प्रशंसा करना prashansa karna
comply *v. i* पालन करना palan karna
component *adj.* साधक saadhak
compose *v. t* शांत होना nirmit karna
composition *n* रचना rachna
compositor अक्षर योजक akshar yojak
compost *n* मिश्रित खाद mishrit khad
composure *n.* शान्ति shanti
compound *a* यौगिक yogik
compound *n* समास samaas
compound *n* अहाता ahaata
compound *v. i* मिलाना milaana
compounder *n.* औषधि बनाने वाला aushadhi banane wala
comprehend *v. t* समझना samajhna

comprehension *n* धारणा dharana

comprehensive *a* व्यापक vyapak

compress *v. t.* दबाना dabana

compromise *v. t* समझौता करना samjhota karna

compromise *n* समझौता samjhota

compulsion *n* बाध्यकरण badhyakaran

compulsory *a* अनिवार्य anivarya

compunction *n.* मनोव्यथ manovyath

computation *n.* गिनती ginti

compute *v.t.* लेखा करना lekha karna

comrade *n.* साथी sathi

concave *adj.* नतोदर natodar

conceal *v. t.* छिपाना chipana

concede *v.t.* अंगीकार करना angikar karna

conceit *n* घमण्ड ghamand

conceive *v. t* विचार करना vichaar karna

concentrate *v. t* केंद्रित करना kendrit karna

concentration *n.* एकाग्रता ekagrata

concept *n* संकल्पना sankalpana

conception *n* अवधारण avdharan

concern *v. t* चिंतित करना chintit karna

concern *n* चिंता chinta

concert *n.* संगीत गोष्ठी sangeet gosthi

concession *n* छूट chhoot

conch *n.* शंख shankh

conciliate *v.t.* शान्त करना shant karna

concise *a* संक्षिप्त sankshipt

conclude *v. t* समापन करना samapan karna

conclusion *n.* निर्णय nirnaya

conclusive *a* निर्णायक nirnayak

concoct *v. t* पकाना pakana

concoction *n.* मनगढ़ंत कहानी mangharant kahani

concord *n.* सामंजस्य samanjasya

concrete *a* ठोस thos

concrete *v. t* ठोस रूप देना thos rup dena

concubinage *n.* वेश्यापन veshyapan

concubine *n* उपपत्नी up patni

condemn *v. t.* निंदा करना ninda karna

condemnation *n* निंदा ninda

condense *v. t* गाढ़ा करना gaadha karna

condite *v.t.* अचार aachaar

condition *n* शर्त shart

conditional *a* प्रतिबंधात्मक pratibandhatmak

condole *v. i.* शोक प्रकट करना shok prakat karna

condolence *n* शोक shok

condone *n.* क्षमा प्रदान kshama pradan

conduct *n* आचार व्यवहार aachar vyavahar

conduct *v. t* नेतृत्व करना netritva karna

conductor *n* निर्देशक nirdeshak

cone *n.* शंकु shanku

confectioner *n* हलवाई halwai

confectionery *n* मिष्ठान गृह mishthan greha

confer *v. i* प्रदान करना pradan karna

conference *n* सभा sabha

confess *v. t.* स्वीकार करना svikar karna

confession *n* पाप स्वीकरण paap svikaran

confidant *n* विश्वासपात्र vishvaspatra

confide *v. i* गुप्त रूप से बताना gupt rup se batana

confidence *n* विश्वास vishvast

confident *a.* आश्वस्त ashvast

confidential *a.* गुप्त gupt

confine *v. t* कैद करना kaid karna

confinement *n.* कारावास karavas

confirm *v. t* पुष्टि करना pushti karna

confirmation *n* प्रमाणीकरण pramanikaran

confiscate *v. t* ज़ब्त करना jabt karna

confiscation *n.* ज़ब्ती zabti

conflict *n.* संघर्ष sangharsh

conflict *v. i* संघर्ष करना sangharsh karna

confluence *n* संगम sangam

confluent *adj.* बहता हुआ bahta hua

conformity *n.* समानता samanata

conformity *n.* अनुकूलता anukulta

confraternity *n.* भाईचारा bhaichara

confrontation *n.* विरोध virodh

confuse *v. t* अव्यवस्थित करना avyavasthit karna

confusion *n* अव्यवस्था avyavastha

confute *v.t.* झूठा सिद्घ करना jhuta sidh karna

conge *n.* विदाई vidayee

congenial *a* अनुकूल anukul

congratulate *v. t* बधाई देना badhai dena

congratulation *n* बधाई badhai

congress *n* सम्मेलन sammelan

conjecture *n* अनुमान anumaan

conjugal *a* वैवाहिक vaivahik

conjugate *v.t. & i.* विवाह करना vivah karna

conjunct *adj.* संयुक्त sanyukt

conjunctive *n.* आंख की झिल्ली aankh ki jhilli

conjuncture *n.* घटना ghatna

conjure *v.t.* अनुरोध करना anurodh karna

conjure *v.i.* जादू करना jadu karna

connect *v. t.* जोड़ना jorna

connection *n* संबंध sambandh

connivance *n.* आनाकानी anakani

conquer *v. t* जीतना jeetna

conquest *n* विजय vijay

conscience *n* विवेक vivek

conscious *a* सचेतन sachetan

consecrate *v.t.* प्रतिष्ठा करना pratistha karna

consecutive *adj.* लगातार laga-taar

consecutively *adv* क्रम से kram se

consensus *n.* अनुकूलता anukulta

consent *v. i* सहमत होना sahamat hona

consent *v.t.* स्वीकार करना svikar karna

consent *n.* सहमति sahamiti

consequence *n* परिणाम parinam

consequent *a* अनुगामी anugami

conservative *n* रूढ़िवादी व्यक्ति rurhivadi vyakti

conserve *v. t* सुरक्षित रखना surakshit rakhna

consider *v. t* विचार करना vichar karna

considerable *a* विचारणीय vicharniya

considerate *a.* ध्यान रखने वाला dhyan rakhne wala

consideration *n* विचार vichar

considering *prep.* विचार करते हुए vichar karte huye

consign *v.t.* भेजना bhejna

consign *v. t.* सुपुर्द करना supurd karna

consignment *n.* प्रेषित माल preshit maal

consist *v. i* निहित होना nihit hona

consistency *n.* सामंजस्य samanjasya

consistent *a* अविरोधी awirodhi

consolation *n* सांत्वना santwana

console *v. t* सांत्वना देना santwana dena

consolidate *v. t.* संघटित करना sangathit hona

consolidation *n* चकबंदी chakbandi

consonance *n.* अविरोध avirodh

consonant *n.* व्यंजन vyanjan

consort *n.* साथी sathi

conspectus *n.* रूपरेखा ruprekha

conspicuous *a.* विशिष्ट vishishita

conspiracy *n.* षड्यंत्र shadyantra

conspirator *n.* षड्यंत्रकर्त्ता shadyantra

conspire *v. i.* मिल जाना mil jana

constable *n* सिपाही sipahi

constant *a* स्थिर sthir

constellation *n.* नक्षत्रों का समूह nakshatron ka samuh

constipation *n.* कब्ज़ kabz

constituency *n* मतदाता क्षेत्र matdata kshetra

constituent *n.* मतदाता matdata

constituent *adj.* संविधान निर्माणकारी sanvidhan nirmankari

constitute *v. t* नियुक्त करना niyukt karna

constitution *n* विधान vidhan

constrict *v.t.* दबाना dabaana

construct *v. t.* निर्माण करना nirman karna

construction *n* निर्माण nirman

consult *v. t* परामर्श लेना paramarsh lena

consultation *n* परामर्श paramarsh

consumption *n* उपयोग upyog

consumption *n* क्षयरोग kshay rog

contact *n.* संपर्क sampark

contact *v. t* संपर्क स्थापित करना sampark sthapit karna

contagious *a* संक्रामक sankramak

contain *v.t.* नियंत्रित करना niyantrit karna

contaminate *v.t.* दूषित करना dushit karna

contemplate *v. t* विचार करना vichar karna

contemplation *n* अवलोकन avlokan

contemporary *a* समकालीन samakalin

contempt *n* अपमान apmaan

contemptuous *a* तिरस्कारपूर्ण tiraskaarpurna

contend *v. i* विरोध करना virodh karna

content *a.* संतुष्ट santusht

content *v. t* संतुष्टि प्रदान करना| santushti pradan karna

content *n* संतुष्टि santushti

content *n.* विषय सूची vishay soochi

contention *n* तर्क tark

contentment *n* संतोष santosh

contest *v. t* संघर्ष करना sangharsh karna

contest *n.* प्रतियोगिता pratiyogita

context *n* प्रसंग prasang

continent *n* महाद्वीप mahadvip

continental *a* महाद्वीपीय mahadvipiya

contingency *n.* आकस्मिक घटना aakasmik ghatna

continual *adj.* निरन्तर nirantar

continuation *n.* विस्तार vistar

continue *v. i.* जारी रखना jari rakhna

continuity *n* निरंतरता nirantarta

continuous *a* निरन्तर nirantar

contour *n* रूपरेखा rup rekha

contra *pref.* विमुख vimukh

contraception *n.* गर्भ निरोध garbh nirodh

contract *n* संविदा sanvida

contract *v. t* अनुबंध anubandh

contractor *n* ठेकेदार thekedar

contradict *v. t* विरोध करना virodh karna

contradiction *n* प्रतिवाद prativad

contrary *a* विरोधात्माक virodhatmak

contrast *v. t* विषमता दिखाना vishamta dikhana

contrast *n* विरोध virodh

contribute *v. t* योग देना yog dena

contribution *n* योगदान yogdaan

control *n* नियंत्रण niyantran

control *v. t* नियंत्रण रखना niyantran rakhna

controller *n.* नियंत्रक niyantrak

controversy *n* विवाद vivad

contuse *v.t.* कुचलना kuchalna

conundrum *n.* पहेली paheli

convene *v. t* आयोजित करना aayojit karna

convener *n* संयोजक sanyojak

convenience *n.* सुविधा suvidha

convenient *a* सुविधा जनक suvidha janak

convent *n* मठ math

convention *n.* प्रथा pratha

conversant *adj.* परिचित parichit

conversant *a* प्रवीण pravin

conversation *n* संवाद sanwad

converse *v.t.* बोलना bolna

conversion *n* रूपांतरण rupantaran

convert *v. t* रूपांतरित करना rupantarit karna

convey *v. t.* सूचित करना suchit karna

conveyance *n* सवारी sawari

convict *v. t.* अपराधी घोषित करना apradhi ghoshit karna

convict *n* अपराधी apradhi

conviction *n* धारणा dharna

convince v. t विश्वास दिलाना vishvas dilana

convivial adj. प्रफुल्ल praphul

convocation n. पादरियों का संघ paadariyon ka sangh

convoke v.t. पंचरणना pahunchana

convolve v.t. लपेटना lapetna

coo n अचरज achraj

cook v. t पकाना pakana

cook n रसोइया rasoiyaa

cooker n कुकर cooker

cool a शीतल sheetal

cool v. i. ठंडा होना thanda hona

cooler n कूलर cooler

coolie n कुली kuli

co-operate v. i सहयोग करना sahyog karna

co-operation n सहकारिता sahakarita

co-operative a सहकारी sahakari

co-ordinate a. समकक्ष samkaksh

co-ordinate v. t समायोजन करना samaayojan karna

co-ordination n समायोजन samayojan

coot n. पानी का पक्षी pani ka pakshi

co-partner n सहभागी sahabhagi

copper n तांबा tamba

coppice n. जंगल jungle

coprology n. कला कौशल की अश्लीलता kala kaushal ki ashlilta

copulate v.i. मैथुन करना maithun karna

copy n प्रतिलिपि pratilipi

copy v. t अनुकरण करना anukaran karna

coral n मूंगा munga

corbel n. ताखा takha

cord n डोरी dori

cordate adj. हृदय के आकार का hridya ke akar ka

cordial a हार्दिक hardik

core n. भीतरी हिस्सा bhitri hissa

coriander n. धनियां dhaniya

cormorant n. भुक्खड़ आदमी bhukarh aadmi

corn n अनाज anaaj

cornea n आंखों की पुतली aankhon ki putli

corner n कोना kona

cornet n. पलटन का अफसर paltan ka afsar

cornicle n. छोटा सींग chota sing

coronation n राज्याभिषेक rajyabhishek

coronet n. छोटा ताज chhota taaj

corporal a दैहिक daihik

corporate adj. संयुक्त sanyukt

corporation n निगम nigam

corps n सैन्य निकाय sainya nikaya

corpse n शव shav

correct a दोष रहित dosh rahit prasadhan

correct v. t संशोधन करना sanshodhan karna

correction n संशोधन sashodhan

correlate v.t. सहसंबंधी बनाना sahsambandhi banana

correlation n. पारस्परिक संबंध parasaparik sambandh

correspond v. i पत्र व्यवहार करना patra vyavahar karna

correspondence n. समानता samanta

correspondent n. संवाददाता samvadata

corridor n. गलियारा galiyara

corroborate v.t. प्रमाणित करना pramanit karna

corrupt v. t. दूषित करना dushit karna

corrupt a. दूषित dushit

corruption n. भ्रष्टाचार bhrasthtachar

cosmetic a. सौंदर्यवर्धक saundarya vardhak

cosmetic n. अंगराग angrag

cosmic adj. जगत संबंधी jagat sambandhi

cost v.t. मूल्य mulya

cost n. लागत laagat

costal adj. पसली संबंधी pasali sambandhi

costly a. मूल्यवान mulyawan

costume n. पोशाक poshaak

cosy **सुखकर** sukh kar
cosy *a.* **आरामदायक** aaramdayak
cot *n.* **खटिया** ghatiya
cote *n.* **झोंपड़ी** jhomparhi
cottage *n* **झोंपड़ी** jhomparhi
cotton *n.* **कपास** kapas
couch *n.* **सोफ़ा** sofa
cough *n.* **खांसी** khansi
cough *v. i.* **खांसना** khansna
coulter *n* **फाल** faal
council *n.* **परिषद्** parishad
councillor *n.* **सभासद** sabha-sad
counsel *n.* **मंत्रणा** mantrana
counsel *v. t.* **परामर्श देना** paramarsh dena
counsellor *n.* **सलाहकार** salahakar
count *n.* **संख्या** sankhya
count *v. t.* **गिनना** ginana
countenance *n.* **समर्थन** samarthan
counter *n.* **काउंटर** counter
counter *v. t* **विरोध करना** virodh karna
counteract *v.t.* **निष्फल करना** nishphal karna
counterfeit *a.* **खोटा** khota
counterfeiter *n.* **जालसाज** jaalsaaz
countermand *v.t.* **प्रतिकूल आदेश देना** pratikul aadesh dena
counterpart *n.* **प्रतिवस्तु** prativastu
countersign *v. t.* **प्रतिहस्ताक्षरित करना** pratihastaksharit karna
countess *n.* **बेगम** begam
countless *a.* **अनगिनत** an-ginat
country *n.* **देश** desh
county *n.* **प्रदेश** pradesh
coup *n.* **ताकता पलट** takhta palat
couple *n* **जोड़ा** jorha
couple *v. t* **जोड़ना** jorhna
couplet *n.* **दोहा** doha
coupon *n.* **कूपन** coupan
courage *n.* **साहस** saahas
courageous *a.* **साहसि** saahasi

courier *n.* **संदेशवाहक** sandeshvahak
course *n.* **कार्यप्रणाली** karyapranali
court *n.* **कचहरी** kachahri
court *v. t.* **प्रेम करना** prem karna
courteous *a.* **शिष्ट** shisht
courtesan *n.* **वेश्या** vaishya
courtesy *n.* **सौजन्य** saujanya
courtier *n.* **दरबारी** darbari
courtship *n.* **प्रणय निवेदन** pranay nivedan
courtyard *n.* **चौक** chowk
cousin *n.* **ममेरा भाई** mamera bhai
covenant *n.* **प्रतिज्ञा पत्र** pratigya patra
cover *v. t.* **ढकना** dhakna
cover *n.* **आवरण** aavaran
coverlet *n.* **पलंगपोश** palangposh
covet *v.t.* **लोभ करना** lobh karna
cow *n.* **गाय** gaay
cow *v. t.* **डराना** daarana
coward *n.* **कायर** kayar
cowardice *n.* **कायरता** kayarta
cower *v.i.* **दबकना** dabkana
crab *n* **केकड़ा** kekrha
crack *n* **दरार** daraar
crack *v. i* **तोड़ना** torhna
cracker *n* **पटाखा** patakha
crackle *v.t.* **कड़ाके का शब्द करना** karhake ka shabd karna
cradle *n* **पालना** palna
craft *n* **चालाकी** chalaki
craftsman *n* **शिल्पी** shilpi
crafty *a* **चालाक** chalak
cram *v. t* **रटना** ratna
crambo *n.* **तुकबंदी का खेल** tukbandi ka khel
crane *n* **क्रेन** crane
crankle *v.t.* **घुमाना** ghumana
crash *v. i* **धमाके के साथ गिरना** dhamakay ke sath gherna
crash *n* **धमाका** dhamaka
crass *adj.* **मूर्ख** murkh

crate *n.* ढाँचा dhancha

crave *v.t.* याचना करना yachna karna

crawl *v. t* घिसटना ghisatna

crawl *n* मंदगति mandgati

craze *n* पागलपन pagalpan

crazy *a* सनकी sanki

creak *v. i* चरमराना charmarana

creak *n* चरमराहट charmarahat

cream *n* मलाई malai

crease *n* तह का निशान taha ka nisan

create *v. t* सर्जन करना sarjan karna

creation *n* रचना rachna

creative *adj.* उत्पादक utpadak

creator *n* निर्माता nirmata

creature *n* प्राणी prani

credible *a* प्रामाणिक pramanik

credit *n* प्रसिद्घि prasidhi

creditor *n* ऋणदाता rindata

credulity *adj.* सन्देह शून्य sandeh shunya

creed *n.* धर्म dharm

creed *n* पंथ panth

creek *n.* खाड़ी khaari

creep *v. i* पेट के बल खिसकना pet ke bal khisakna

creeper *n* लता lata

cremate *v. t* दाहसंस्कार करना dahasanskar karna

cremation *n* दाहसंस्कार dahasanskar

crest *n* कलग़ी kalgi

crew *n.* कर्मीदल karmidal

crib *n.* चरनी charni

cricket *n* क्रिकेट cricket

crime *n* अपराध aapradh

criminal *n* अपराधी व्यक्ति apradhi vyakti

criminal *a* अपराधी apradhi

crimp *n* भरती करने वाला bharti karne wala

crimple *v.t.* मोड़ना morhna

crimson *n* गहरा लाल gehra lal

cringe *v. i.* चापलूसी करना chaplusi karna

cripple *n* विकलांग व्यक्ति viklang vyakti

crisis *n* संकटकाल sankat kal

crisp *a* फुर्तीला खस्ता phurtila khasta

criterion *n* मापदंड maapdand

critic *n* समालोचक samalochak

critical *a* संकटपूर्ण sankatpurna

criticism *n* आलोचना aalochna

criticize *v. t* निंदा करना ninda karna

crockery *n.* मिट्टी के बरतन mitti ke bartan

crocodile *n* घड़ियाल gharhiyal

croesus *n.* धनी dhani

crook *a* कमान kaman

crop *n* फ़सल phasal

cross *v.t.* पार करना paar karna

cross *v. t* विरोध करना virodh karna

cross *n* संकर sankar

cross *a* तिरछा tircha

crossing *n.* चौराहा chauraha

crotchet *n.* झक jhak

crouch *v. i.* ज़मीन से सट जाना zameen se sat jana

crow *n* कौआ kauwa

crow *v. i* डींग मारना ding marna

crowd *n* जनसमूह jansamuh

crown *n* राजमुकुट rajmukut

crown *v. t* मुकुट पहनाना mukut pahanana

crucial *adj.* अत्यंत महत्वपूर्ण atyant mahatva purna

crude *a* अशोधित ashodhit

cruel *a* नृशंस nrishans

cruelty *n* दयाहीनता dayahinta

cruise *v.i.* समुद्र में यात्रा करना samudra mein yatra karna

cruiser *n* युद्घपोत yudhpot

crumb *n* टुकड़ा tukrha

crumble *v. t* टुकड़े टुकड़े करना tukrhe tukrhe karna

crump *adj.* ऐंठा टेढ़ा aintha tedha

crusade *n* धर्मयुद्घ dharmayudh

crush *v. t* पीसना peesna

crust *n.* छाल chhal

crutch *n* आधार aadhar

cry *n* पशु की बोली pashu ki boli

cry *v. i* रोना rona

cryptography *n.* गुप्त लिखन की विद्या gupt lekhan ki vidya

crystal *n* बढ़िया कांच badhiya kanch

cub *n* पशुशावक pashushavak

cube *n* घनक्षेत्र dhankshetra

cubical *a* घनीय dhaniy

cubiform *adj.* घनाकार dhanakar

cuckold *n.* व्यभिचारिणी स्त्री का पति vyabhicharini stri ka pati

cuckoo *n* कोयल koyal

cucumber *n* खीरा khira

cudgel *n* गदा gada

cue *n* संकेत sanket

cuff *n* तमाचा tamacha

cuff *v. t* तमाचा मारना tamacha maarna

cuisine *n.* पकाने की विधि pakane ki widhi

culminate *v.i.* परम कोटि को प्राप्त करना param koti ko prapt karna

culpable *a* आपराधिक aaparadhik

culprit *n* अपराधी aapradhi

cult *n* पंथ panth

cultivate *v. t* जोतना jotana

cultural *a* सांस्कृतिक sanskritik

culture *n* पालन paalan

cunning *a* चालाक chalak

cunning *n* चालाकी chalaki

cup *n.* प्याला pyala

cupboard *n* अलमारी almaari

Cupid *n* कामदेव kamdev

cupidity *n* अर्थलिप्सा arthalipsa

curable *a* आरोग्य साध्य aarogya sadhya

curative *a* रोगनिवारक rognivarak

curb *n* नियंत्रण niyantran

curb *v. t* नियंत्रण करना niyantran karna

curcuma *n.* हल्दी haldi

curd *n* दही dahi

cure *n* औषध aushadh

cure *v. t.* उपचार करना upchar karna

curfew *n* निषेधाज्ञा nishedhagya

curiosity *n* कुतूहल kutuhal

curious *a* अद्भुत adbhut

curl *n.* घुंघराला बाल ghunghrala baal

currant *n.* सूखा अंगूर sukha angur

currency *n* मुद्रा mudra

current *n* धारा dhara

current *a* प्रचलित prachalit

curriculum *n* पाठ्यक्रम pathykram

curse *n* अभिशाप abhishaap

curse *v. t* अभिशाप देना abhishaap dena

cursory *a* सरसरी sarsari

curt *a* अशिष्टतापूर्ण ashishtatapurna

curtail *v. t* घटाना ghatana

curtain *n* आवरण aawaran

curve *n* वक्र vakra

curve *v. t* मोड़ना morhna

cushion *n* मसनद masnad

cushion *v. t* गद्दों से सजाना gaddo se sajana

custard *n* दूध की लपसी dudh ki lapsi

custodian *n* संरक्षक sanrakshak

custody *v* हिरासत hirasat

custom *n.* प्रथा pratha

customary *a* प्रथागत prathagat

customer *n* ग्राहक grahak

cut *v. t* कम करना kam karna

cut *n* प्रहार prahar

cutis *n.* भीतरी त्वचा bhitri tvacha

cycle *n* साइकिल cycle

cyclic *a* चक्रीय chakriya

cyclist *n* साइकिल सवार cycle sawar

cyclone *n.* चक्रवात chakrawat

cyclostyle *n* चक्रलेखित्र chakralekhitra

cyclostyle *v. t* चक्रलिपित करना chakralipit karna

cylinder *n* बेलन belan

cynic *n* निंदक nindak

# D

dacoit n. डाकू daku
dacoity n. डकैती dakaiti
dad, daddy n पिता pita
daffodil n. पीला नरगिस pila nargis
daft adj. पागल pagal
dagger n. खंजर khanjar
daily a दैनिक dainik
daily n. दैनिक समाचार पत्र dainik samachar patra
daily adv. प्रतिदिन pratidin
dainty a. नाज़ुक najuk
dainty n. स्वादिष्ट खाद्य svadisht khadya
dairy n दुग्धशाला dugdhshala
dais n. मंच manch
daisy n एक पुष्प ek pushp
dale n घाटी ghaati
dam n बांध bandh
damage v. t. क्षति पहुंचाना kshti pahuchana
damage n. हानि haani
dame n. गृहिणी grehini
damn v. t. शाप देना shap dena
damnation n. नरक यातना narak yatana
damp a आर्द्र aadra
damp v. t. गीला करना geela karna
damp n कोहरा kohara
damsel n. कुमारी कन्या kumari kaniya
dance n नृत्य nritya
dance v. t. नाचना nachana
dandle v.t. लाड करना laad karna
dandruff n रूसी roosi
dandy n छैला chaila
danger n. संकट sankat
dangerous a खतरनाक khatarnak
dangle v. t झुलाना jhulana
dank adj. गीला geela
dap v.i. कूदना kudna

dare v. i. हिम्मत रखना himmat rakhna
daring n. निर्भीकता nirbhikta
daring a हिम्मत वाला himmat wala
dark a अंधकारमय andhkarmaya
dark n अंधकार andhakar
darkle v.i. छिपे रहना chipe rehna
darling n प्रियतम priyatam
darling a प्यारा pyara
dart n. बर्छी barchi
dash v. i. पटक देना patak dena
dash n छोटी दौड़ choti daurh
date n समय samay
date v. t तिथ्यंकित करना tithyankit karna
daub n. पुताई putayee
daub v. t. पोतना potana
daughter n पुत्री putri
daunt v. t भयभीत करना bhayabhit karna
dauntless a निर्भीक nirbhik
dawdle v.i. विलम्ब करना vilamb karna
dawn n प्रभात prabhat
dawn v. i. प्रकट होना prakat hona
day n दिन का समय din ka samay
daze n स्तब्धता stabdhata
daze v. t स्तब्ध करना stabdha karna
dazzle n चकाचौंध chakachaundh
dazzle v. t. चकाचौंध करना chakachaundh karna
deacon n. छोटा पादरी chota padari
dead a गतिहीन gati hin
deadlock n गतिरोध gatirodh
deadly a भयंकर bhayankar
deaf a बधिर badhir
deal n लेन-देन len-den
deal v. i कार्य करना karya karna
dealer n व्यापारी vyapari
dealing n. व्यापार संबंध vyapar sambandh
dean n. कालेज का अध्यक्ष college ka adhyaksh
dear a. प्रिय, प्यारा priya, pyara
dear a महंगा mahanga

dearth *n* दुर्लभता dhurlabhta

death *n* मृत्यु mrityu

debar *v. t.* वर्जित करना varjit karna

debase *v. t.* पतित करना patit karna

debate *v. t.* बहस करना bahas karna

debate *n.* विवाद vivad

debauch *v. t.* भ्रष्ट करना bhrasht karna

debauch *n* लंपटता lampatata

debauchee *n* विषयी vishayi

debauchery *n* व्यभिचारिता vyabhicharita

debility *n* दुर्बलता durbalta

debit *n* नामखाता naam khata

debit *v. t* ऋणांकन करना rinankan karna

debris *n* मलबा malba

debt *n* उधार udhar

debtor *n* कर्जदार karjadar

decade *n* दशाब्दी dashabadi

decadent *a* पतनोन्मुख patonmukh

decamp *v. i* चुप चुप भाग जाना chup chup bhag jana

decay *v. i* हास होना haas hona

decay *vt* सड़न saarhna

decease *n* मृत्यु mrityu

decease *v. i* मर जाना mar jana

deceit *n* धोखा dhokha

deceive *v. t* धोखा देना dhokha dena

decency *n* शालीनता shalinta

decennary *n.* दस वर्ष का काल dus varsh ka kaal

decent *a.* शोभनीय shobh-niya

deception *n* धोखा dhokha

decide *v. t* निर्णय करना nirnaya karna

decimal *a* दशमलव dashamlav

decimate *v.t.* नष्ट करना nasht karna

decision *n* निर्णय nirnaya

decisive *a* निर्णयात्मक nirnayatmak

deck *n* जहाज़ का फ़र्श jahaz ka farsh

deck *v. t* सजाना sajaana

declaration *n* घोषणा ghosana

declare *v. t.* प्रकट करना prakat karna

decline *n* घटाव ghatav

decline *v. t.* कमज़ोर होना kamzor hona

declivitous *adj.* नीचे को झुका हुआ neeche ko jhuka hua

decompose *v. t.* सड़ना sarhna

decomposition *n.* सड़न sarhan

decontrol *v.t.* नियन्त्रण हटाना niyantran hatana

decorate *v. t* सजाना sajaana

decoration *n* सजावट sajaavat

decorum *n* शिष्टाचार shishtachar

decrease *v. t* कम करना kam karna

decrease *n* ह्वास hras

decree *n* न्यायिक निर्णय nyayik nirnaya

decree *v. i* निर्णय करना nirnaya karna

decrement *n.* कमी kami

dedicate *v. t.* समर्पण करना samarpan karna

dedication *n* समर्पण samarpan

deduct *v.t.* कम करना kam karna

deed *n* दस्तावेज़ dastavez

deem *v.i.* विचारना vicharna

deep *a.* भारी bhari

deer *n* हरिण harin

defamation *n* मान हानि maan hani

defame *v. t.* बदनाम करना badnam karna

default *n.* अपराध aapradh

defeat *n* पराजय parajaya

defeat *v. t.* परास्त करना parast karna

defect *n* दोष dosh

defence *n* बचाव bachaav

defend *v. t* रक्षा करना raksha karna

defendant *n* प्रतिवादी prativadi

defensive *adv.* सुरक्षात्मक surakshatmak

deference *n* सम्मान samman

defiance *n* चुनौती chunauti

deficient *adj.* हीन heen

deficit *n* घाटा ghaata

defile *n.* संकुचित मार्ग sankuchit marg

define *v. t* परिभाषा देना paribhasha dena

definite *a* निश्चित nishchit

definition *n* परिभाषा paribhasha

deflation *n.* अवमूल्यन avamulyan

deflect *v.t. & i.* रास्ता बदलना raasta badalna

deft *adj.* कुशल kushal

degrade *v. t* दरजा घटाना darja ghatana

degree *n* मात्रा matra

deist *n.* आस्तिक aastik

deity *n.* देवता devta

deject *v. t* हतोत्साह करना hatotsaha karna

dejection *n* निराशा nirasha

delay *v.t. & i.* समय बिताना samai bitan

delegate *n* प्रतिनिधि pratinidhi

delegation *n* प्रतिनिधान pratinidhan

delete *v. t* काट देना kaat dena

deliberate *a* जानबूझ कर किया हुआ jaanbhuj kar kiya hua

deliberate *v. i* विचारना vicharna

deliberation *n* विचार विमर्श vichar vimarsh

delicate *a* नाजुक nazuk

delicious *a* स्वादिष्ट svadisht

delight *n* आनंद anand

delight *v. t.* आनंद देना anand dena

deliver *v. t* देना dena

delivery *n* भाषण शैली bhashan shailee

delta *n* नदी मुख भूमि nadi mukh bhumi

delude *n.t.* मोहित करना mohit karna

delusion *n.* माया maya

demand *n* मांग maang

demand *v. t* मांग करना mang karna

demarcation *n.* सीमा निर्धारण sima nirdharan

dement *v.t* पागल करना pagal karna

demerit *n* दोष dosh

democracy *n* प्रजातंत्र prajatantra

democratic *a* प्रजातंत्रात्मक prajatantratmak

demolish *v. t.* समाप्त करना samapt karna

demon *n.* प्रेत prait

demonstrate *v. t* प्रदर्शन करना pradarshan karna

demonstration *n.* प्रदर्शन pradarshan

demoralize *v. t.* नैतिक पतन करना naitik patan karna

demur *n* आपत्ति aapatti

demur *v. t* आपत्ति करना apatti karna

den *n* गुहा guha

denial *n* नकार nakaar

denote *v. i* अर्थ रखना arth rakhna

denounce *v. t* निंदा करना ninda karna

dense *a* सघन saghna

density *n* सघनता saghnata

dentist *n.* दंत चिकित्सक dant chikitsak

denude *v.t.* नंगा करना nanga karna

denunciation *n.* भर्त्सना bhartasana

deny *v. t.* खंडन करना khandan karna

depart *v. i.* प्रयाण करना prayaan karna

department *n* विभाग vibhaag

departure *n* विचलन vichalan

depend *v. i.* भरोसा करना bharosa karna

dependant *n* पराधीन paradheen

dependence *n* पराधीनता pradhinta

dependent *a* निर्भर nirbhar

depict *v. t.* वर्णन करना varnan karna

deplorable *a* खेदजनक khedjanak

deploy *v.t.* पंक्ति में रखना pankti mai rakhna

deponent *n.* गवाह gavaha

deport *v.t.* देश बाहर निकालना desh bahar nikalna

depose *v. t* गवाही देना gavahi dena

deposit *n.* जमा jama

depot *n* संग्रहागार sagrahagaar

depreciate *v.t.i.* दाम कम होना daam kam hona

depredate *v.t.* शिकार करना shikar karna

depress *v. t* उदास करना udas karna

depression *n* उदासी udasi

deprive v. t वंचित करना vanchit karna

depth n गहराई gehaarai

deputation n शिष्टमंडल shisht mandal

depute v. t नियुक्त करना niyukt karna

deputy n प्रतिनिधि pratinidhi

derail v. t. पटरी से उतर जाना patri se uttar jana

derive v. t. प्राप्त करना prapt karna

descend v. i. नीचे आना neeche aana

descendant n वंशज vanshaj

descent n. उतार utaar

describe v. t वर्णन करना varnan karna

description n परिभाषा paribhasha

descriptive a वर्णनात्मक varnatmak

desert v. t. हट जाना hat jana

desert n रेगिस्तान registan

deserve v. t. योग्य होना yogya hona

design v. t. योजना बनाना yojana banana

design n. रूपरेखा ruprekha

desirable a वांछनीय vanchaniya

desire n अभिलाषा abhilasha

desire v.t कामना करना kamna karna

desirous a इच्छुक icchuk

desk n मेज़ mez

despair n निराशा nirasha

despair v. i निराश होना nirash hona

desperate a निराशाजनक nirashajanak

despicable a घृणित ghrenit

despise v. t घृणा करना ghrina karna

despot n निरंकुश शासक nirankush shasak

destination n गंतव्य gantavya

destiny n नियति niyati

destroy v. t मारना marna

destruction n विनाश vinash

detach v. t अलग करना alag karna

detachment n अलग करने की क्रिया alag karnai ki kriya

detail n गौण बात gaun baat

detail v. t विवरण vivaran

detain v. t रोके रखना roke rakhna

detect v. t खोजना khojana

detective n. जासूस jasus

determination n. दृढ़ संकल्प dridh sankalp

determine v. t तय करना tay karna

dethrone v. t गद्दी से उतारना gaddi se utarna

develop v. t. विकसित करना viksit karna

development n. विकास vikas

deviate v. i भटकना bhatkana

deviation n विचलन vichalan

device n योजना yojana

devil n शैतान shaitan

devise v. t सोच लेना soch lena

devoid a रहित rahit

devote v. t अर्पित करना arpit karna

devotee n समर्पित व्यक्ति samarpit vyakti

devotion n समर्पण samarpan

devour v. t निगल जाना nigal jana

dew n. ओस os

diabetes n मधुमेह madhumeh

diagnose v. t निदान करना nidaan karna

diagnosis n निदान nidan

diagram n आरेख aarekh

dialect n उपभाषा upbhasha

dialogue n संवाद sanvad

diameter n व्यास vyas

diamond n हीरा hira

diarrhoea n अतिसार atisaar

diary n दैनिक विवरण Dainik vivrun

dice n. पानसा paansa

dice v. i. पासे का खेल खेलना pase ka khel khelna

dictate v. t आदेश देना aadesh dena

dictation n आदेश aadesh

dictator n तानाशाह tanashaha

diction n शब्द चयन shabd chayan

dictionary n शब्दकोश shabdakosh

dictum n आदेश वाक्य aadesh vakya

didactic a उपदेशात्मक updeshatmak

die v. i मरना marna

diet *n* भोजन bhojan

differ *v. i* मत-भेद होना mat-bhed hona

difference *n* असमानता asamanta

different *a* भिन्न bhinn

difficult *a* जटिल jatil

difficulty *n* बाधा baadha

dig *v.t.* खोदना khodna

dig *n* खुदाई khudayee

digest *v. t.* पचाना pachana

digest *n.* संग्रह sangrah

digestion *n* पाचन pachan

digit *n.* अंक ank

digit *n* उंगली ungli

dignify *v.t* शोभायुक्त करना shobhayukt karna

dignity *n* गौरवपूर्ण gauravpurna

dilemma *n* दुविधा duvidha

diligence *n* परिश्रम parishram

diligent *a* परिश्रमी parishrami

dilute *v. t* पतला करना patla karna

dilute *a* पतला patla

dim *a* धुंधला dhundhala

dim *v. t* धुंधला करना dhundhala karna

dimension *n* आयाम aayam

diminish *v. t* कम करना kam karna

din *n* कोलाहल kolahal

dine *v. t.* भोजन करना bhojan karna

dinner *n* भोजन bhojan

dip *n.* गोता gota

dip *v. t* गोता लगाना gota lagana

diploma *n* प्रमाण पत्र praman patra

diplomacy *n* कूटनीति kutniti

diplomat *n* राजनयिक rajnayik

diplomatic *a* कूट नीतिक kut-nitik

dire *a* भयानक bhayanak

direct *a* सीधा sidha

direct *v. t* संचालन करना sanchalan karna

direction *n* निर्देश nirdesh

director *n.* निर्देशक nirdeshak

directory *n* निर्देशिका nirdeshika

dirt *n* धूल dhul

dirty *a* मलिन malin

disability *n* विकलांगता viklangata

disable *v. t* विकलांग बनाना viklang banana

disabled *a* विकलांग viklang

disadvantage *n* नुकसान nuksaan

disagree *v. i* असहमत होना asahamat hona

disagreeable *a.* अरुचिकर aruchikar

disagreement *n.* असहमति asahamati

disappear *v. i* अदृश्य होना adrishya hona

disappearance *n* अदृश्यता adrishyata

disappoint *v. t.* हताश करना hatash karna

disapproval *n* अस्वकृति asvikriti

disapprove *v. t* अस्वीकार करना asvikar karana

disarm *v. t* नि:शस्त्र करना ni-shastra karna

disarmament *n.* नि:शस्त्रीकरण ni:shastrikaran

disaster *n* आपदा aapada

disastrous *a* संकटपूर्ण sankatpurna

disc *n.* चकती chakati

discard *v. t* रद्द करना radd karna

discharge *v. t* मुक्त करना mukt karna

discharge *n.* मुक्ति mukti

disciple *n* अनुयायी anuyayee

discipline *n* अनुशासन anushasan

disclose *v. t* प्रकट करना prakat karna

discomfort *n* असुविधा asuvidha

disconnect *v. t* वियोजित करना viyojit karna

discontent *n* असंतोष asantosh

discontinue *v. t* बंद करना band karna

discord *n* अनबन an-ban

discount *n* छूट chhoot

discourage *v. t.* हतोत्साह करना hatotsah karna

discourse *n* प्रवचन pravachan

discourteous *a* अविनीत avinit

discover *v. t* पता लगाना pata lagana

discovery *n.* खोज khoj

discretion *n* समझदारी samajhdari

discriminate *v. t.* भेद करना bhed karna

discrimination *n* विभेदन क्षमता vibhedan kshamata

discuss *v. t.* विचार विनिमय करना vichar vinimaya karna

disdain *n* घृणा ghrina

disdain *v. t.* घृणा करना ghrina karna

disease *n* बीमारी bimari

disguise *n* छद्रमवेश chadramavesh

disguise *v. t* वेश बदलना vesh badalana

dish *n* तश्तरी tashtari

dishearten *v. t* हतोत्साह करना hatotsah karna

dishonest *a* बेईमान baiman

dishonesty *n.* बेईमानी baimani

dishonour *v. t* अनादर करना anadar karna

dishonour *n* अनादर anadar

dislike *v. t* नापसंद करना napasand karna

dislike *n* अरुचि aruchi

disloyal *a* विश्वासघाती vishvasghati

dismiss *v. t.* खारिज करना kharij karna

dismissal *n* बरखास्तगी barkhastgi

disobey *v. t* अवज्ञा करना avagya karna

disorder *n* अव्यवस्था avyavastha

disparity *n* असमानता asamanta

dispensary *n* दवाखाना davakhana

disperse *v. t* छितराना chhitarana

displace *v. t* विस्थापित करना visthapit karna

display *n* प्रदर्शन pradarshan

display *v. t* प्रदर्शित करना pradarshit karna

displease *v. t* नाराज़ करना naraaz karna

displeasure *n* क्रोध krodh

disposal *n* प्ररित्याग parityag

dispose *v. t* मामला निपटाना mamla niptana

disprove *v. t* असत्य सिद्ध करना asatya sidh karna

dispute *n* विवाद vivad

dispute *v. i* विवाद करना vivad karna

disqualification *n* अयोग्यता ayogyata

disqualify *v. t.* अयोग्य ठहराना ayogya thaharana

disquiet *n* अशांत ashaant

disregard *n* अपमान apmaan

disregard *v. t* उपेक्षा करना upeksha karna

disrepute *n* बदनामी badnami

disrespect *n* अनादर anadar

disrupt *v. t* भंग करना bhang karna

dissatisfaction *n* असंतोष asantosh

dissatisfy *v. t.* नाराज़ करना naraz karna

dissect *v. t* विभाजित करना vibhajit karana

dissection *n* विश्लेषण vishleshan

dissimilar *a* असमान asamaan

dissolve *v.t* लुप्त होना lupt hona

distance *n* दूरी duri

distant *a* दूर का dur ka

distil *v. t* शुद्घ करना shudh karna

distillery *n* भट्टी bhatti

distinct *a* अलग alag

distinction *n* अंतर antar

distinguish *v. i* अंतर समझना antar samjhana

distort *v. t* तोड़ मरोड़ देना torh marorh

distress *n* परेशानी paresani

distress *v. t* परेशान करना pareshaan karna

distribute *v. t* बांटना baantana

distribution *n* वितरण vitaran

district *n* जनपद janpad

distrust *n* अविश्वास avishvas

distrust *v. t.* विश्वास न रखना vishvas na rakhna

disturb *v. t* बाधा डालना badha dalna

ditch *v* धोखा देना dhokha dena

ditto *n.* यथोपरि yathopari

dive *v. i* पानी के नीचे जाना pani ke neechay jaana

dive *n* गोता gota

diverse *a* विविध vividh

divert *v. t* **मोड़ना** morhna

divide *v. t* **बांटना** bantna

divine *a* **दैवी** daivee

divinity *n* **देवता** devta

division *n* **विभाजन** vibhajan

divorce *n* **तलाक** talaak

divorce *v. t* **तलाक देना** talaak dena

divulge *v. t* **प्रकट करना** prakat karna

do *v. t* **करना** karna

docile *a* **विनम्र** vinamra

dock *n.* **गोदी** godi

doctor *n* **चिकित्सक** chikitsak

doctorate *n* **डॉक्टर की उपाधि** doctor ki upadhi

doctrine *n* **सिद्घांत** sidhant

document *n* **दस्तावेज़** dastavej

dodge *n* **चकमा** chakma

dodge *v. t* **चकमा देना** chakma dena

doe *n* **मृग** mrig

dog *n* **कुत्ता** kutta

dog *v. t* **पीछा करना** peecha karna

dogma *n* **धर्ममत** dharmmat

dogmatic *a* **धर्ममत संबंधी** dharmmat sambandhi

doll *n* **गुड़िया** gudiya

dollar *n* **डॉलर** dollar

domain *n* **शासन क्षेत्र** shasan kshetra

dome *n* **गुंबद** gumbad

domestic *a* **घरेलू** gharelu

domicile *n* **आवास** aawaas

dominant *a* **प्रमुख** pramukh

dominate *v. t* **शासन करना** shasan karna

domination *n* **शासन** shasan

dominion *n* **उपनिवेश** upnivesh

donate *v. t* **दान देना** daan dena

donation *n.* **दान** daan

donkey *n* **गधा** gadha

donor *n* **दाता** daata

doom *n* **विनाश** vinash

door *n* **प्रवेश मार्ग** pravesh marg

dose *n* **खुराक** khurak

dot *n* **बिंदु** bindu

dot *v. t* **बिंदु लगाना** bindu lagana

double *a* **दोगुना** doguna

double *n* **प्रतिरूप** pratirup

double *v. t.* **दोहरा करना** dohara karna

doubt *n* **शंका** shanka

doubt *v. i* **शंका करना** shanka karna

dough *n* **गुँथा हुआ आटा** guntha hua aata

dove *n* kabutar

down *prep* **नीचे की ओर** neeche ki aur

down *v. t* **गिरा देना** gira dena

downfall *n* **बर्बादी** barbadi

downpour *n* **भारी वर्षा** bhari varsha

downright *adv* **पूरी तरह से** puri tarah se

downright *a* **स्पष्टवादी** spash+D3379twadi

downward *adv* **नीचे की ओर** nechai ki aur

dowry *n* **दहेज** dahej

doze *n.* **झपकी** jhapki

doze *v. i* **ऊँघना** unghana

dozen *n* **दर्जन** darjan

draft *v. t* **प्रारूप तैयार करना** prarup taiyar karna

draftsman *a* **दस्तावेज़ लेखक** dastavez lekhak

drag *n* **बाधा** badha

drag *v. t* **घसीटना** ghaseetna

dragon *n* **अजगर** ajgar

drain *n* **गंदी नाली** gandi naali

drain *v. t* **धीरे धीरे निकालना** dheere dheere nikalana

drainage *n* **जलनिकास** jalnikas

drama *n* **नाटक** natak

dramatic *a* **नाटक संबंधी** natak sambandhi

dramatist *n* **नाटककार** natakkar

draper *n* **वस्त्र विक्रेता** vastr vikreta

drastic *a* **कठोर** kathor

draught *n* **प्रारूप तैयार करना** prarup taiyar karna

draw *v.t* अंकित करना ankit karna
drawback *n* कमी kami
drawer *n* दराज daraj
drawing *n* चित्रांकन chitrankan
drawing-room *n* बैठक baithak
dread *n* बहावाय bhayavah
dread *v.t* भयभीत होना bhyabhit hona
dread *a* आतंकमय aatankmaya
dream *n* स्वप्न svapan
dream *v. i.* स्वप्न देखना svapan dekhna
drench *v. t* सराबोर कर देना sarabor kar dena
dress *n* पोशाक poshak
dress *v. t* पहनाना pahnana
dressing *n* वस्त्र vastr
drill *n* बरमा barma
drill *v. t.* छेद करना ched karna
drink *v.t.* पीना peena
drink *n* शराब sharab
drip *n* टपकन tapkan
drip *v. i* टपकना tapkana
drive *n* संचालन sanchalan
drive *v. t* गाड़ी चलाना gaari chalana
driver *n* चालक chaalak
drizzle *n* फुहार phuhar parhna
drizzle *v. i* फुहार पड़ना phuhar parhna
drop *v. i* टपकना tapkana
drop *n* बूंद boond
drought *n* सूखा sookha
drown *v.i* डुबा देना duba dena
drug *n* औषधि aushadhi
druggist *n* औषध विक्रेता aushadh vikreta
drum *n* कान का परदा kaan ka parda
drum *v.i.* ढोल बजाना dhol bajana
drunkard *n* शराबी sharabi
dry *a* सूखा sukha
dry *v. i.* सूखना sukhna
dual *a* दोहरा dohara
duck *n.* बतख batakh
duck *v.i.* डुबकी लगाना dubki lagana
due *a* उचित uchit

due *n* उधार udhar
duke *n* राजा raja
dull *a* उदास udas
dull *v. t.* मंद बनाना mand banana
duly *adv* विधिवत् vidhivat
dumb *a* गूंगा gunga
dunce *n* मूर्ख आदमी murkh aadmi
dung *n* गोबर gobar
duplicate *a* मिलता जुलता milta julta
duplicate *n* प्रतिलिपि pratilipi
duplicate *v. t* प्रतिलिपि बनाना pratilipi banana
duplicity *n* कपट kapat
durable *a* टिकाऊ tikau
duration *n* कालावधि kalavadhi
during *prep* पर्यंत paryant
dusk *n* संध्या sandhya
dust *n* धूल dhool
dust *v.t.* धूल झाड़ना dhul jharhna
duster *n* झाड़न jharhan
dutiful *a* कर्त्तव्यनिष्ठ kartavyanishta
duty *n* कर्तव्य kartavya
dwarf *n* बौना bauna
dwell *v. i* रहना rehna
dwelling *n* घर ghar
dwindle *v. t* क्षीण होना kshin hona
dye *v. t* रंगना rangna
dye *n* रंग rang
dynamic *a* गति-शील gati-shil
dynamics *n.* गतिविज्ञान gativigyan
dynamite *n* बारूद barud
dynamo *n* विद्युत् शक्ति यंत्र vidyut shakti yantra
dynasty *n* राजवंश rajvansh
dysentery *n* पेचिश paichish

**E**

each *pron.* प्रत्येक pratyek
eager *a* व्यग्र vyagra

eagle *n* गरुड़ garud
ear *n* कान kaan
early *adv* समय से पूर्व samay se purva
earn *v. t* अपर्जन करना uparjan karna
earnest *a* जोशीला joshila
earth *n* पृथ्वी prithvi
earthen *a* मरीआमया mrinamaya
earthly *a* सांसारिक saansarik
earthquake *n* भूकंप bhukamp
ease *n* आराम aaram
ease *v. t* सुविधा देना suvidha dena
east *n* पूर्व दिशा purva disha
eastern *a* पूर्वीय puviya
easy *a* सरल saral
eat *v. t* खाना khana
eatable *n.* खाद्य पदार्थ khadya padarth
eatable *a* खाने योग्य khane yoygya
ebb *n.* अवनति avnati
ebb *n* भाटा bhata
ebb *v. i* उतर जाना utar jana
ebony *n* आबनूस aabnus
echo *n* प्रतिध्वनि pratidhvani
echo *v. t* गूंजना gunjana
eclipse *n* ग्रहण grehen
economic *a* आर्थिक aarthik
economical *a* मितव्ययी mitvyayi
economics *n.* अर्थशास्त्र arthashastra
economy *n* अर्थव्यवस्था arthvyavastha
edge *n* धार dhar
edible *a* भोज्य bhojya
edifice *n* भवन bhavan
edit *v. t* संपादन करना sampadan karna
edition *n* संस्करण sanskaran
editor *n* संपादक sampadak
editorial *a* संपादकीय sampadkiya
educate *v. t* शिक्षा देना shiksha dena
education *n* शिक्षा shiksha
efface *v. t* मिटा देना mita dena
effect *n* प्रभाव prabhav
effect *v. t* अमल में लाना amal mein laana

effective *a* प्रभावशाली prabhavshali
effeminate *a* कायर kayar
efficacy *n* प्रभावोत्पादकता prabhavotpadakta
efficiency *n* निपुणता nipunta
efficient *a* कुशल kushal
effigy *n* पुतला putla
effort *n* प्रयास prayas
egg *n* अंडा anda
ego *n* अहंकार aahankar
egotism *n* अहंभाव ahambhag
eight *n* आठ aath
eighteen *a* अठारह atharah
eighty *n* अस्सी assi
either *a.,* दो में से कोई do mein se koi
eject *v. t.* बाहर फेंकना baahar phenkna
elaborate *v. t* विस्तार से कहना vistar se kahana
elaborate *a* विस्तृत vistrit
elapse *v. t* गुज़रना guzarna
elastic *a* लचीला lachila
elbow *n* कोहनी kohani
elder *a* ज्येष्ठ jyeshth
elder *n* आयु में बड़ा व्यक्ति aayu mein barha vyakti
elderly *a* वयो-वृद्ध vayo-vridh
elect *v. t* चुनना chunana
election *n* निर्वाचन nirvachan
electorate *n* निर्वाचक मंडल nirvachak mandal
electric *a* विद्युतीय vidyutiya
electricity *n* विद्युत् vidyut
electrify *v. t* विद्युतीकरण करना vidyutikaran karna
elegance *n* सुन्दरता sunderta
elegant *adj* रमणीय ramaniya
elegy *n* शोकगीत shokgeet
element *n* मूलवस्तु mulvastu
elementary *a* सामान्य samanya
elephant *n* हाथी hathi

elevate v. t उन्नत करना uunat karna

elevation n ऊंचाई unchayee

eleven n ग्यारह gyarah

elf n परी pari

eligible a उपयुक्त upyukt

eliminate v. t हटाना hatana

elimination n हटाव hatav

elope v. i सहपलायन करना sahpalan karna

eloquence n वाक्पटुता vakpatuta

eloquent a भाषणपटु bhashanpatu

else a अतिरिक्त atirikt

else adv अन्यथा anyatha

elucidate v. t स्पष्ट करना spashta karna

elude v. t टालना taalna

elusion n छल chhal

elusive a चालाक chalaak

emancipation n. मुक्ति mukti

embalm v. t शवलेप करना shavlep karna

embankment n तटबंधन tatbandhan

embark v. t पोतारोहण करना potarohan karna

embarrass v. t मुश्किल में डालना mushkil mein dalna

embassy n दूतावास dutawas

embitter v. t कड़वा बनाना karhva banana

emblem n प्रतीक pratik

embodiment n मूर्तरूप murtrup

embody v. t. मूर्तरूप देना murtrup dena

embolden v. t. प्रोत्साहित करना protsahit karna

embrace v. t. आलिंगन करना aalingan karna

embrace n आलिंगन aalingan

embroidery n कसीदाकारी kasidakari

embryo n भ्रूण bhroon

emerald n पन्ना panna

emerge v. i प्रकट होना prakat hona

emergency n आपातकाल apaatkal

eminence n उच्चता ucchata

eminent a प्रतिष्ठित pratishtith

emissary n दूत doot

emit v. t बाहर भेजना bahar bhejna

emolument n परिलाभ parilabh

emotion n भावावेश bhavavesh

emotional a भावुक bhavuk

emperor n सम्राट samraat

emphasis n प्रमुखता pramukhta

emphasize v. t महत्व देना mahatva dena

emphatic a प्रभावी prabhavi

empire n साम्राज्य samrajya

employ v. t नौकरी देना naukri dena

employee n कर्मचारी karamchari

employer n नियोजक niyojak

employment n नौकरी naukari

empower v. t अधिकार देना adhikaar dena

empress n महारानी maharani

empty v खाली करना khali karna

empty a खाली khali

emulate v. t अनुकरण करना anukaran karna

enable v. t योग्य बनाना yogya banana

enact v. t कानून का रूप देना kanun ka rup dena

enamel n तामचीनी tamchini

enamour v. t अनुरक्त करना anurakt karna

encase v. t डिब्बे में बंद करना dibbe mein band karna

enchant v. t प्रसन्न करना prasann karna

encircle v. t. घेरना gherna

enclose v. t संगलन करना sangalan karna

enclosure n. घेरा ghera

encompass v. t घेरना gherna

encounter n. भिड़ंत bhirhant

encourage v. t प्रोत्साहित करना protsahit karna

encroach v. i अतिक्रमण करना atikraman karna

encumber v. t. बाधा डालना badha dalna

encyclopaedia n. विश्वकोश vishvakosh

end v. t समाप्त करना samapt karna

**end** *n.* अंजाम samapan

**endanger** *v. t.* विपत्ति में डालना vipatti mai dalna

**endear** *v.t* प्यारा बनाना pyara banana

**endearment** *n.* प्रीति priti

**endeavour** *n* प्रयास prayas

**endeavour** *v.i* प्रयत्न करना praytan karna

**endorse** *v. t.* समर्थन करना samarthan karna

**endow** *v. t* प्रदान करना pradan karna

**endurable** *a* सहनीय sahaniya

**endurance** *n.* सहनशीलता sahanshilta

**endure** *v.t.* सहन करना sahan karna

**enemy** *n* शत्रु shatru

**energetic** *a* शक्तिशाली shaktishali

**energy** *n.* ऊर्जा urja

**enfeeble** *v. t.* दुर्बल करना durbal karna

**enforce** *v. t.* बाध्य करना badhya karna

**enfranchise** *v.t.* मताधिकार देना matadhikaar dena

**engage** *v. t* काम पर लगाना kaam par lagana

**engagement** व्यवस्था vyastata

**engine** *n* यंत्र yantra

**engineer** *n* अभियंता abhiyanta

**english** *n* अंग्रेज़ लोग angrez log

**engrave** *v. t* उत्कीर्ण करना utkeerna karna

**engross** *v.t* व्यस्त रखना vyast rakhna

**engulf** *v.t* निगलना nigalna

**enigma** *n* पहेली paheli

**enjoy** *v. t* आनंद लेना anand lena

**enjoyment** *n* आनंद anand

**enlarge** *v. t* विस्तार करना vistar karna

**enlighten** *v. t.* समझाना samjhana

**enlist** *v. t* नाम लिखना naam likhna

**enliven** *v. t.* सजीव करना sajiv karna

**enmity** *n* शत्रुता shatruta

**ennoble** *v. t.* उदात्त बनाना udaat banana

**enormous** *a* विशाल vishal

**enough** *a* यथेष्ट yathesht

**enough** *adv* पर्याप्त paraypt

**enrage** *v. t* क्रुद्ध करना krodh karna

**enrapture** *v. t* प्रफुल्ल करना prafull karna

**enrich** *v. t* संपन्न बनाना sampaan banana

**enrol** *v. t* भरती करना bharti karna

**enshrine** *v. t* संजोना sanyojana

**enslave** *v.t.* दास बनाना das banana

**ensue** *v.i* पीछे घटित होना peche ghatit hona

**ensure** सुनिश्चित करना sunishchit karna

**entangle** *v. t* फंदे में फंसाना fande mai fasana

**enter** *v. t* प्रवेश करना pravesh karna

**enterprise** *n* उपक्रम upkram

**entertain** *v. t* मनोरंजन करना manoranjan karna

**entertainment** *n.* मनोरंजन manoranjan

**enthrone** *v. t* सिंहासनारूढ़ करना sinhasanarurh karna

**enthusiasm** *n* उत्साह utsah

**enthusiastic** *a* उत्साही utsahi

**entice** *v. t.* लुभाना lubhana

**entire** *a* संपूर्ण sampurna

**entirely** *adv* संपूर्णत: sampurnata

**entitle** *v. t.* दावेदार बनाना davedar banana

**entity** *n* सत्ता satta

**entomology** *n.* कीटविज्ञान keet vigyan

**entrails** *n.* अंतड़ियां antarhiyan

**entrance** *n* प्रवेश pravesh

**entrap** *v. t.* बहकाना behakna

**entreat** *v. t.* अनुनय करना anunay karna

**entreaty** *n.* विनती vinti

**entrust** *v. t* सौंपना saunpana

**entry** *n* प्रवेश pravesh

**enumerate** *v. t.* एक एक करके बताना ek ek karke batana

**envelop** *v. t* ढकना dhakna

**envelope** *n* लिफ़ाफ़ा lifafaa

**enviable** *a* ईर्ष्या योग्य irshya yogya

**envious** *a* ईर्ष्यालु irshyalu

environment *n.* परिवेश parivesh
envy *v. t* ईर्ष्या रखना irshya rakhna
epic *n* महाकाव्य mahakavya
epidemic *n* महामारी mahamari
epigram *n* विदग्धोक्ति vidagdhokti
epilepsy *n* मिरगी mirgi
epilogue *n* उपसंहार upsanhaar
episode *n* घटना ghatna
epitaph *n* समाधिलेख samadhilekh
epoch *n* युग yug
equal *a* समान saman
equal *v. t* कसमान होना samaan hona
equality *n* समानता samanata
equalize *v. t.* बराबर करना barabar karna
equate *v. t* समान मानना samaan manana
equation *n* संतुलन santulan
equation *n.* समीकरण samikaran
equator *n* विषुवत् रेखा vishuvat rekha
equilateral *a* समबाह sambaah
equip *v. t* सज्जित sajjit
equipment *n* साज़ सामान saaj saaman
equitable *a* न्यायोचित nyayochit
equivalent *a* समानार्थी samanarthi
equivocal *a* भ्रमात्मक bhramaatmak
era *n* काल kaal
eradicate *v. t* उन्मूलन करना unmulan karna
erase *v. t* मिटाना mitana
erect *v. t* निर्माण करना nirman karna
erection *n* निर्माण nirman
erode *v. t* खा जाना kha jana
erosion *n* कटाव katav
erotic *a* खामूक kaamuk
err *v. i* भूल करना bhul karna
errand *n* संदेश sandesh
erroneous *a* गलत galat
error *n* भूल bhul
erupt *v. i* प्रस्फुटित होना prasphutit hona
eruption *n* विस्फोट visphot
escape *n* निकास nikas

escape *v.i* मुक्त होना mukt hona
escort *n* अनुरक्षी anurakshi
escort *v. t* रक्षार्थ साथ जाना raksharth sath jana
especial *a* विशिष्ट wishisht
essay *n.* निबंध nibandh
essayist *n* निबंधकार nibhandkaar
essence *n* सार saar
essential *a* आवश्यक avashyak
establish *v. t.* स्थापित करना sthapit karna
establishment *n* स्थापना sthapana
estate *n* भूसंपत्ति bhu sampati
esteem *n* आदर aadar
esteem *v. t* आदर करना aadar karna
estimate *n.* अनुमान anuman
estimate *v. t* अनुमान लगाना anuman lagana
estimation *n* मूल्यांकन mulyankan
eternal सनातन sanatan
eternity *n* अनंत काल anant kaal
ether *n* व्योम vyom
ethical *a* नैतिक naitik
ethics *n.* नीतिग्रंथ nitigranth
etiquette *n* शिष्टाचार shishtachar
etymology *n.* व्युत्पत्तिशास्त्र vyutpatishastra
eunuch *n* हिजड़ा hijrha
evacuate *v. t* खाली करना khali karna
evacuation *n* निकास nikaas
evade *v. t* टालना talna
evaluate *v. t* मूल्यांकन करना mulyankan karna
evaporate *v. i* भाप बनाना bhap banana
evasion *n* टाल मटोल taal matol
even *a* समतल samtal
even *v. t* सम करना sam karna
evening *n* संध्या sandhya
event *n* घटना ghatna
eventually *adv.* अंततः antatah
ever *adv* किसी भी समय kisi bhi samay

evergreen *a* सदाबहार sadabahar

everlasting *a.* चिरस्थायी chirsthayee

every *a* प्रत्येक pratyek

evict *t* बेदखल करना baidakhal karna

eviction *n* बेदखली baidakhali

evidence *n* प्रमाण praman

evident *a.* सुस्पष्ट suspasht

evil *a* दुष्ट dusht

evil *n* अशुभ ashubh

evoke *v. t* पुकारना pukarna

evolution *n* विकास vikas

evolve *v.t* विकसित करना viksit karna

ewe *n* भेड़ bherh

exact *a* ठीक theek

exaggerate *v. t.* अतिरंजना करना atiranjana karna

exaggeration *n.* अतिशयोक्ति atishyokti

exalt *v. t* सराहना करना sarahana karna

examination *n.* जांच पड़ताल jaanch parhtaal

examine *v. t* परीक्षा करना pariksha karna

examinee *n* परीक्षार्थी pariksharthi

examiner *n* परीक्षक parikshak

example *n* उदाहरण udaharan

excavate *v. t.* खोखला करना khokla karna

excavation *n.* उत्खनन utkhanan

exceed *v.t* अधिक होना adhık hona

excel *v.i* अग्रगण्य होना agraganya hona

excellence *n.* उत्कृष्टता utkrishtata

excellency *n* मान्यवर manyawar

excellent *a.* उत्कृष्ट utkrisht

except *v. t* छोड़ देना chorh dena

except *prep* अतिरिक्त atirikt

exception *n* अपवाद apvaad

excess *n* बाहुल्य bahulya

excess *a* अतिरिक्त atirikt

exchange *n* आदान-प्रदान adaan-pradaan

exchange *v. t* विनिमय करना vinimaya karna

excise *n* उत्पादन शुल्क utpadan shulk

excite *v. t* उत्तेजित करना utejit karna

exclaim *v.i* चिल्लाना chillanaa

exclamation *n* विस्मयोद्गार vismayodgaar

exclude *v. t* निकालना nikaalna

exclusive *a* एकमात्र ek-maatra

excommunicate *v. t.* बहिष्कृत करना bahishkrit karna

excursion *n.* आमोद विहार aamod vihar

excuse *v.t* दोषमुक्त करना doshmukt karna

excuse *n* बहाना bahana

execute *v. t* पालन करना palan karna

execution *n* फांसी का दंड fansi ka dand

executioner *n.* फांसी देने वाला fansi dene wala

exempt *v. t.* मुक्त करना mukt karna

exempt शुल्क से मुक्त shulk se mukt

exercise *n.* प्रयोग prayog

exercise *v. t* प्रयोग करना prayog karna

exhaust *v. t.* थका देना thaka dena

exhibit *n.* प्रदर्शनीय वस्तु pradarsiniya wastu

exhibit *v. t* दिखाना dekhana

exhibition *n.* प्रदर्शनी pradarshini

exile *n.* देश निष्कासन des nishkasan

exile *v. t* देश से निकालना des se nikalna

exist *v.i* मौजूद होना maujud hona

existence *n* अस्तित्व astitva

exit *n.* प्रस्थान prasthan

expand *v.t.* फैलाना failaana

expansion *n.* विस्तार vistaar

ex-parte *a* एकपक्षीय ekpakchiya

expect *v. t* आशा करना aasha karna

expectation *n.* आशा aasha karna

expedient *a* उपयुक्त upyukt

expedite *v. t.* जल्दी करना jaldi karna

expedition *n* खोजयात्रा khoj yatra

expel *v. t.* निकाल देना nikaal dena

expend *v. t* खर्च करना kharch karna

expenditure *n* खर्चा kharchaa

expense *n.* खर्च kharch

expensive *a* महंगा mahanga

experience *n* अनुभव anubhav

experiment *n* परीक्षण parikshan

expert *a* विशेषज्ञ visheshagya

expert *n* कुशल व्यक्ति kushal vyakti

expire *v.i.* मरना marna

expiry *n* अवसान awasaan

explain *v. t.* विवरण देना vivaran dena

explanation *n* स्पष्ट करना spashti-karan

explicit *a.* सुस्पष्ट suspasht

explode *v. t.* विस्फोट करना wisfot karna

exploit *n* पराक्रम parakarm

exploit *v. t* अनुचित लाभ उठाना anuchit labh uthana

exploration *n* जांच पड़ताल janch padtaal

explore *v.t* खोजना khojna

explosion *n.* धमाका dhmaka

explosive *n.* विस्फोटक पदार्थ wisfotak padarth

explosive *a* विस्फोटक wisfotak

exponent *n* प्रतिपादक pratipadak

export *v. t.* निर्यात करना niryaat karna

export *n* निर्यात niryaat

expose *v. t* प्रकट करना prakat karna

express *v. t.* वर्णन करना warnan karna

express *n* द्रुतगामी रेलगाड़ी drutgami railgadi

expression *n.* अभिव्यक्ति abhi-vyakti

expressive *a.* द्योतक dyotak

expulsion *n.* निष्कासन nishkasan

extend *v. t* बढ़ाना barhaana

extent *n.* आकार aakar

external *a* बाहरी baahri

extinct *a* बुझा हुआ bujha hua

extinguish *v.t* नष्ट करना nasht karna

extol *v. t.* प्रशंसा करना prashansa karna

extra *a* अतिरिक्त atirikt

extra *adv* असामान्य रूप से asamanya rup se

extract *n* सार saar

extract *v. t* अर्क निकालना ark nikalana

extraordinary *a.* असाधारण asadharan

extravagance *n* फ़िज़ूलखर्ची fijulkharchi

extravagant *a* असंयमी asanyami

extreme *a* उग्र क्रांतिकारी ugra krantikari

extreme *n* अधिकतम adhiktam

extremist *n* अतिवादी atiwadi

exult *v. i* उल्लसित होना ullasit hona

eye *n* आंख aankh

eyeball *n* नेत्र गोलक naitra golak

eyelash *n* बरौनी baroni

eyelet *n* सूराख suraakh

eyewash *n* बहाना bahana

# F

fable *n.* नीति कथा niti katha

fabric *n* कपड़ा kapada

fabricate *v.t* निर्माण करना nirman karna

fabrication *n* छल रचना chaal rachna

fabulous *a* उत्कृष्ट utkrishta

facade *n* मुखौटा mukhauta

face *n* चेहरा chaihara

face *v.t* आमने सामने होना aamne samne hona

facet *n* पहलू pahulu

facial *a* मुख संबंधी mukh sambandhi

facile *a* सुगम sugam

facilitate *v.t* आसान कर देना aasan kar dena

facility *n* सुविधा suvidha

facsimile *n* फैक्स fax

fact *n* यथार्थ yatharth

faction *n* दलबंदी dalbandi

factious *a* झगड़ालू jhagralu

factor *n* अभिकर्त्ता abhikarta

factory *n* कारखाना karkhana

faculty *n* संकाय sankaya

fad *n* सनक sanak

fade *v.i* रंग उड़ना rang urhna

failure *n* असफलता asafalta

faint *a* कमज़ोर kamjor

faint *v.i* मूर्च्छित होना murchit hona

fair *a* सुंदर sundar

fair *n.* मेला mela

fairly *adv.* पर्याप्त मात्रा में paryapt matra mein

fairy *n* परी pari

faith *n* निष्ठा nishta

faithful *a* वफ़ादार wafaadar

falcon *n* बाज़ baaj

fall *vt* गिरना girna

fall *n* विनाश vinash

fallacy *n* भ्रांति bhranti

fallow *n* बञ्जर banjar

false *a* ग़लत galat

falter *v.i* हकलाना haklaana

fame *n* कीर्ति kirti

familiar *a* जानकार jaankar

family *n* परिवार pariwar

famine *n* अकाल akaal

famous *a* प्रसिद्घ prasidh

fan *n* पंखा pankha

fanatic *a* मतांध mataandh

fanatic *n* धर्मांध व्यक्ति dharmandh vyakti

fancy *n* कल्पना kalpana

fancy *v.t* पसंद करना pasand karna

fantastic *a* विलक्षण vilakshan

far *adv.* दूर door

far *a* दूरस्थ durasth

far *n* दूरी doori

farce *n* तमाशा tamasha

fare *n* भाड़ा bharha

farewell *n* विदा vida

farewell *interj.* अलविदा alvida

farm *n* कृषि भूमि krishi bhumi

farmer *n* किसान kisan

fascinate *v.t* मोहित करना mohit karna

fascination *n.* आकर्षण aakarshan

fashion *n* फ़ैशन fashion

fashionable *a* फ़ैशनपरस्त fashionparast

fast *a* पक्का pakka

fast *adv* तेज़ी से teji se

fast *n* उपवास upwas

fast *v.i* उपवास करना upwas karna

fasten *v.t* बांधना bandhana

fat *a* मोटा mota

fat *n* चर्बी charbi

fatal *a* घातक ghatak

fate *n* भाग्य bhagya

father *n* पिता pita

fathom *n* हराई का माप harayee ka maap

fathom *v.t* थाह लेना thah lena

fatigue *n* थकान thakan

fatigue *v.t* थकाना thakana

fault *n* दोषपूर्ण doshpurna

faulty *a* दोषपूर्ण doshpurna

fauna *n* जीव जंतु jeev jantu

favour *n* अनुमोदन anumodan

favour *v.t* समर्थन करना samarthan karna

favourable *a* अनुकूल anukul

favourite *n* प्रेमपात्र prempatra

fax *n* प्रतिकृति pratikirti

fear *n* भय bhaye

fear *v.i* डरना darna

fearful *a.* भयानक bhayanak

feasible *a* संभव sambhav

feast *n* प्रीतिभोज pritibhoj

feast *v.i* दावत देना davat dena

feat *n* साहसिक कार्य sahasik karya

feather *n* पंख pankh

feature *n* लक्षण lakshan

February *n* फ़रवरी farwari

federal *a* संघीय sanghiya

federation *n* संघ sangh

fee *n* शुल्क shulk

feeble *a* कमज़ोर kamjor

feed *v.t* भोजन देना bhojan dena

feed *n* भोजन bhojan

feel *v.t* महसूस करना mahsus karna

feeling *n* धारणा dhaarna
feign *v.t* बहाना करना bahana karna
felicitate *v.t* बधाई देना badhai karna
felicity *n* सौभाग्य saubhagya
fell *v.t* गिराना girna
fellow *n* साथी sathi
female *a* स्त्री जाति stri jati
female *n* मादा maada
feminine *a* स्त्री-जाति stri-jatiya
fence *n* घेरा ghera
fence *v.t* घेरना gherna
fend *v.t* रक्षा करना raksha karna
ferment *n* हंगामा hangama
ferment *v.t* खमीर उठाना khamir uthana
fermentation *n* उत्तेजना uttejana
ferocious *a* खूंखार khunkhar
ferry *n* नाव nav
ferry *v.t* नाव से पार उतारना nav se upar utarna
fertile *a* फलदायक faldayak
fertility *n* उर्वरता urwarta
fertilize *v.t* उर्वर बनाना uwar banana
fertilizer *n* खाद khaad
fervent *a* उत्साही uthsahi
fervour *n* जोश josh
festival *n* पर्व parv
festive *a* उल्लासमय ullasamai
festivity *n* आनंदमंगल anandmangal
festoon *n* बंदनवार, तोरण bandanwar, toran
fetch *v.t* लाना lana
fetter *n* ज़ंजीर janjir
fetter *v.t* बंधन लगाना bandhan lagana
feud *n.* सामंत saamant
feudal *a* सामंती saamanti
fever *n.* ज्वर jwar
few *a* थोड़े से thorhe se
fiasco *n* पूर्ण असफलता puran asafalta.
fibre *n.* धागा dhaaga
fickle *a* चंचल chanchal
fiction *n* कथा साहित्य katha sahitya

fictitious *a* काल्पनिक kaalpanik
fiddle *v.i* सारंगी बजाना saarangi bajana
fiddle *n* सारंगी saarang
fidelity *n* निष्ठा nishtha
fie *interj* धिक्कार dhikkar
field *n* कृषि भूमि krishi bhumi
field *n* कार्य क्षेत्र karya kshetra
field *n* खेल का मैदान khel ka maidaan
fiend *n* प्रेत prait
fierce *a* प्रचंड prachand
fiery *a* जोशीला joshila
fifteen *n* पंद्रह pandra
fifty *n.* पचास pachaas
fig *n* अंजीर anjeer
fight *n* झगड़ा jhagda
fight *v.t* किसी के विरुद्ध लड़ना kisi ke virudh larhna
figment *n* काल्पनिक वस्तु kalpanik wastu
figurative *a* आलंकारिक aalankarik
figure *n* आकार aakar
file *n* संचिका sanchika
file *v.t* फ़ाइल में रखना file mai rakhna
file *n* रेती reti
file *v.t* रेती लगाना reti lagana
fill *v.t* पूरा भरना pura bharna
film *n* चलचित्र chalchitra
filter *n* छन्ना chana
filter *v.t* छनना channa
filth *n* कचरा kachara
filthy *a* गंदा ganda
fin *n* मीनपक्ष meen-paksh
final *a* अंतिम antim
finance *n* अर्थ arth
finance *v.t* अर्थ व्यवस्था करना arth wayawasta karna
financial *a* आर्थिक arthik
financier *n* वित्त प्रबंधक bitth prabandhak
find *v.t* प्राप्त करना prapt karna
fine *n* जुर्माना jurmana
fine *v.t* जुर्माना करना jurmana karna

fine *a* महीन mahin
finger *n* उंगली ungli
finger *v.t* उंगलियों से छूना ungliyo se chuna
finish *n* अंत aant
finish *v.t* पूरा करना pura karna
finite *a* समापक samapak
fir *n* देवदारू devdaru
fire *n* आग aag
fire *v.t* जलाना jalana
firm *n.* व्यवसाय-संघ vyavasaya sangh
firm *a* कठोर kathore
first *a* प्रमुख pramukh
first *n* प्रथम स्थान pratham sthan
fiscal year वित्त वर्ष vitt varsh
fiscal *a* आर्थिक arthik
fish *n* मछली machli
fish *v.i* तलाश करना talash karna
fisherman *n* मछुआरा machuaara
fissure *n* दरार daraar
fist *n* घूंसा ghunsa
fistula *n* नासूर naasur
fit उपयुक्त upyukt
fit *n* दौरा daura
fit *v.t* स्वस्थ swasth
fitful *a* अस्थिर asthir
fitter *n* मिस्तरी mistari
five *n* पांच panch
fix *vt* स्थिर करना sthir karna
fix *n* परेशानी paraishani
flabby *a* दुर्बल durbal
flag *n* झंडा jhanda
flame *n* आग की लपट aag ki lapat
flame *v.i* दहकना dahakana
flannel *n* ऊनी कपड़ा uni kaprha
flare *v.i* दमकाना damaktna
flare *n* भड़क bharhak
flash *n* दमक damak
flash *v.t* चमकाना bharhak
flask *n* सुराही surahi

flat *a* एक समान ek saman
flat *n* भवन खंड bhavan khand
flatter *v.t* चापलूसी करना chaaplusi karna
flattery *n* चापलूसी chaplusi
flavour *n* सुगंध sugandh
flaw *n* दोष dosh
flea *n.* पिस्सू pissu
flee *v.i* रफूचक्कर होना rafuchakar
fleece *n* ऊन uun
fleece *v.t* लूटना lutna
fleet *n* जहाज़ी बेड़ा jahazi berha
flesh *n* मांस maans
flexible *a* लचीला lachila
flicker *n* टिमटिमाहट timtimahat
flicker *v.t* टिमटिमाना timtimana
flight *n* पलायन palayan
flimsy *a* पतला patla
fling *v.t* फेंकना phenkana
flippancy *n* छिछोरापन chichorapan
flirt *n* चोचलेबाज़ व्यक्ति chochlebaz vyakti
flirt *v.i* दिखावटी प्रेम करना dekhawati prem karna
float *v.i* मंडराना mandarna
flock *n* झुंड jhund
flock *v.i* एकत्र होना ektra hona
flog *v.t* पीटना pitna
flood *n* बाढ़ baarch
flood *v.t* जलमग्न करना jalmagan karna
floor *n* मंज़िल manzil
floor *v.t* फ़र्श बनाना farsh banana
flora *n* वनस्पति vanaspati
florist *n* फूल विक्रेता phool bikrita
flour *n* आटा aata
flourish *v.i* फलना फूलना phalna phulna
flow *n* प्रवाह prawah
flow *v.i* उमड़ना umarna
flower *n* पुष्प pushp
flowery *a* अलंकृत alangkrit
fluent *a* प्रवाह युक्त pravah yukt
fluid *a* तरल taral

fluid *n* द्रव्य dravya

flush *v.i* लज्जा से लाल हो जाना lajja se lal ho jana

flush *n* प्रवाह pravah

flute *n* बांसुरी baansuri

flute *v.i* बांसुरी बजाना baansuri bajana

flutter *n* फड़फड़ाहट pharhpharhahat

flutter *v.t* फड़फड़ाना pharhpharhana

fly *n* मक्खी makhi

fly *v.i* उड़ना udna

foam *n* झाग jhaag

foam *v.t* झाग पैदा करना jhag paida karna

focal *a* नाभीय naabhiya

focus *n* किरण केंद्र kiran kendra

focus *v.t* केंद्रित करना kendrit karna

fodder *n* चारा chara

foe *n* शत्रु shatru

fog *n* कोहरा kohara

foil *v.t* निष्फल करना nishphal karna

fold *n* बाड़ा baarha

fold *v.t* मोड़ना morna

foliage *n* पत्तियाँ patiyaan

follow *v.t* अनुसरण करना anusaaran karna

follower *n* अनुचर anuchar

folly *n* मूर्खता murkahta

foment *v.t* सेंकना senkna

fond *a* चाहनेवाला chahnewala

fondle *v.t* पुचकारना puchkarna

food *n* भोजन bhojan

fool *n* मूर्ख व्यक्ति murkh vyakti

foolish *a* मूर्ख murkh

foot path पटरी patri

foot *n* पैर pair

for *prep* के हेतु ke hetu

for *conj.* क्योंकि kyonki

forbid *v.t* निषिद्ध करना nishidh karna

force *n* शक्ति shakti

force *v.t* बाध्य करना badhya karna

forceful *a* बलशाली balshali

forcible *a* शक्ति-पूरण shakti puran

forearm *n* अग्र बाहू agra-baahu

forecast *n* पूर्वानुमान purwanuman

forecast *v.t* पूर्वानुमान करना purwanuman karna

forefather *n* पूर्वज purwaj

forefinger *n* तर्जनी tarjani

forehead *n* माथा maatha

foreign *a* विदेश videsh

foreigner *n* विदेशी व्यक्ति videshi vyakti

foreknowledge *n.* पूर्वज्ञान purvagyan

foreleg *n* अगली टांग agle tang

forelock *n* माथे पर की अलक maathe par ki alak

foreman *n* अगुआ agua

foremost *a* सर्वोत्तम sarwatam

forenoon *n* पूर्वाह्न purwahan

forerunner *n* अग्रदूत agradut

foresight *n* दूरदर्शिता durdarshita

forest *n* जंगल jungle

forestall *v.t* रोकथाम करना roktham karna

forester *n* वनरक्षक vanrakshak

forestry *n* वानिकी vaniki

foretell *v.t* भविष्यवाणी करना bhavishyavani karna

forethought *n* पूर्व विचार purwa wichar

forever *adv* सदैव के लिए sadaiv ke leya

forewarn *v.t* पूर्व चेतावनी देना purva chetawani dena

foreword *n* भूमिका bhumika

forfeit *v.t* ज़ब्त हो जाना zabt ho jana

forfeit *n* ज़ब्त zabt

forfeiture *n* ज़ब्ती jabti

forge *n* लोहार की दुकान lohar ki dokaan

forge *v.t* जाली नकल करना jali nakal karna

forgery *n* जालसाज़ी jaalsajhe

forget *v.t* भूल जाना bhul jana

forgetful *a* भुलक्कड़ bhulakaarh

forgive *v.t* क्षमा करना kshama karna

forgo *v.t* त्याग देना tyag dena

forlorn *a* अभागा abhaga

form *n* प्रकार prakar
formal *a* आकारिक aakarik
format *n* ग्रंथ का आकार granth ka aakar
formation *n* निर्माण nirman
former *a* पहला pahala
former *pron* पूर्वोक्त purvokt
formerly *adv* गतकाल में gatkaal mein
formidable *a* कठिन kathin
formula *n* नियम niyam
formulate *v.t* सूत्रबद्घ करना sutrabadh karna
forsake *v.t.* त्याग देना tyag dena
fort *n.* किला qilla
forte *n.* विशिष्टता wishishta
forth *adv.* बाहर bahar
forthcoming *a.* आगामी aagami
forthwith *adv.* तुरंत turant
fortify *v.t.* मज़बूत करना majbuth karna
fortitude *n.* धैर्य dhairya
fort-night *n.* पखवारा pakhwara
fortress *n.* किला qilla
fortunate *a.* भाग्यशाली bhagyasali
fortune *n.* अच्छा नसीब achha naseeb
forty *n.* चालीस chalis
forum *n* मंच manch
forward *a.* अग्रिम agrim
forward *adv* आगे की ओर aage ki aur
fossick *vt* तलाश करना talash karna
fossil *n.* खनिज khanij
foster *v.t.* पोषण करना poshan karna
foul *a.* बेईमान baimaan
found *v.t.* बुनियाद रखना buniyaad rakhna
foundation *n.* आधार aadhar
founder *n.* संस्थापक sansthapak
foundry *n.* ढलाई की कला dhalye ki kala
fountain *n.* फव्वारा favara
four *n.* चार chaar
fourteen *n.* चौदह chaudah
fowl *n.* चिड़िया chiriya
fowler *n.* चिड़ीमार chirimaar

fox *n.* लोमड़ी lomdi
fraction *n.* अंश ansh
fracture *n.* अस्थिभंग asthibhang
fracture *v.t* तोड़ना torhna
fragile *a.* भंगुर bhangur
fragment *n.* खंडित अंश khandit ansh
fragrance *n.* सुवास suvas
fragrant *a.* सुगंधित sugandhit
frail *a.* कमज़ोर kamzor
frame *v.t.* बनाना banana
frame *n* ढांचा dhancha
franchise *n.* मताधिकार matadhikaar
frank *a.* निष्कपट nishkapat
frantic *a.* उत्तेजित uttejit
fraternal *a.* भाई का bhai ka
fraternity *n.* भ्रातृसंघ bhratrisangh
fratricide *n.* भाई/बहिन की हत्या bhai/bahin ki hatya
fraud *n.* धोखा dhokha
fraudulent *a.* कपटी kapti
fraught *a.* भरा हुआ bhara hua
fray *n* लड़ाई larhayee
free *a.* निशुल्क nishulk
free *v.t* मुक्त करना mukt karna
freedom *n.* स्वतंत्रता swatantrata
freeze *v.i.* जम जाना jam jana
freight *n* भाड़ा bhada
French *a.* फ्रांसीसी भाषा francici bhasha
frenzy *n.* उन्माद unmaad
frequency *n.* निरन्तर nirantar
frequent *n.* बार बार baar baar
fresh *a.* अप्रयुक्त uprayukt
fret *n.* चिड़चिड़ापन chidchidapan
fret *v.t.* चिंतित करना chintitkarna
friction *n.* मनमुटाव manmutav
Friday *n.* शुक्रवार shukrawar
fridge *n.* प्रशीतियंत्र prashiti yantra
friend *n.* मित्र mitr
fright *n.* भय bhai
frighten *v.t.* भयभीत करना bhayabhit karna

frigid *a.* ठंडा thanda
frill *n.* झालर jhalar
fringe *n.* झब्बेदार किनारा jhabbedar kinara
fringe *v.t* झब्बा लगाना jhabba lagana
frivolous *a.* छिछोरा chhichhora
frock *n.* चोली choli
frog *n.* मेंढक mendhak
frolic *n.* प्रसन्नता prasanta
frolic *v.i.* उछलकूद करना ucchalkud karna
from *prep.* से se
front *n.* मोरचा morcha
front *a* सामने samaney
front *v.t* सामने होना samaney hona
frontier *n.* सीमांत simant
frost *n.* तुषार tushar
frown *n.* तेवर tevar
frown *v.i* भौहें चढ़ाना bhauhain charhana
frugal *a.* सस्ता sasta
fruit *n.* फल phal
fruitful *a.* लाभकारी labhkari
frustrate *v.t.* बौखलाना baukhalana
frustration *n.* निराशा, बौखलाहट nirasha, baukhalahat
fry *v.t.* छुंकना chhunkana
fry *n* तला हुआ tala hua
fuel *n.* इंधन indhan
fugitive *n.* भगोड़ा bhagorha
fulfil *v.t.* पूर्ण करना purna karna
fulfilment *n.* पूर्ति purti
full *a.* भरपूर bharpur
fullness *n.* प्रचुरता prachurta
fully *adv.* पूर्ण रूप से purna rup se
fumble *v.i.* गड़बड़ कर देना garhbarh kar dena
fun *n.* आमोद प्रमोद aamod pramod
function *n.* उत्सव utsav
function *v.i* काम करना kaam karna
functionary *n.* कर्म करने वाला kaam karne wala
fund *n.* खज़ाना khajana

fundamental *a.* आधारभूत adharbhut
funeral *n.* शव यात्रा shav yatra
fungus *n.* फफूंद fafundh
funny *n.* मज़ाकिया majakiya
fur *n.* पशुलोम pashulom
furious *a.* उग्र ugra
furl *v.t.* मोड़ना morna
furlong *n.* फर्लांग farlang
furnace *n.* अग्निकुंड agnikund
furnish *v.t.* सजाना sajaana
furniture *n.* साज सामान saaj samaan
furrow *n.* कूंड़ kund
further *adv.* इस के आगे iss ke aage
further *a* अतिरिक्त atirikth
further *v.t* आगे बढ़ाना aage badhana
fury *n.* गुस्सा gussa
fuse *v.t.* पिघल जाना pighal jana
fuse *n* फ्यूज़ तार fuje taar
fusion *n.* विलयन vilayan
fuss *n.* गड़बड़ी garhbarhi
fuss *v.i* गड़बड़ी करना gadwadi karna
futile *a.* व्यर्थ wayrth
futility *n.* निरर्थकता nirthakta
future *a.* भावी bhavi
future *n* भविष्य bhavishya

# G

gabble *v.i.* ऊलजलूल बातें करना uljalul bate karna
gadfly *adj* उत्तेजना utejna
gaiety *n.* प्रफुल्लता prafulta
gain *n* लाभ labhkari
gain *v.t.* प्राप्त करना prapt karna
gainsay *v.t.* प्रतिवाद करना pratiwaad karna
gait *n.* चाल chaal-dhaal
galaxy *n.* आकाश गंगा akash ganga
gale *n.* तेज़ हवा tez hawa
gallant *a.* सुंदर sundar

| | |
|---|---|
| **gallant** *n* आकर्षित akrisht | **gauntlet** *n.* हस्तत्राण hasttran |
| **gallantry** *n.* बहादुरी bahaduri | **gay** *a.* जिंदादिल zinda-dil |
| **gallery** *n.* चित्रशाला chitrasala | **gaze** *v.t.* एकटक देखना ektak dekhna |
| **gallon** *n.* गैलन galen | **gaze** *n* टकटकी taktaki |
| **gallop** *n.* चौकड़ी chokrhi | **gazette** *n.* राजपत्र rajpatra |
| **gallop** *v.t.* सरपट दौड़ाना sarpat daurna | **gear** *n.* गरारी garari |
| **gallows** *n.* . फांसी phaansi | **geld** *v.t.* बधिया करना badhiya karna |
| **galore** *adv.* प्रचुर मात्रा prachur matra | **gem** *n* रत्न ratan |
| **galvanize** *v.t.* उत्साह देना utsah dena | **gender** *n.* लिंग ling |
| **gamble** *v.i.* जुआ खेलना jua khelna | **general** *a.* साधारण saadharan |
| **gamble** *n* जुआ jua | **generally** *adv.* सामान्यत: samaniyat |
| **gambler** *n.* जुआरी juari | **generate** *v.t.* पैदा करना paida karna |
| **game** *n.* खेल khel | **generation** *n.* उत्पादन utpadan |
| **gander** *n.* हंस hans | **generator** *n.* उत्पादक utpadak |
| **gang** *n.* गिरोह giroh | **generosity** *n.* उदारता udarta |
| **gap** *n* अंतराल aantral | **generous** *a.* प्रचुर prachur |
| **gape** *v.i.* देखते रह जाना dekhte rah jana | **genius** *n.* प्रतिभा pratibha |
| **garage** *n.* यानशाला yaanshala | **gentle** *a.* भद्र bhadra |
| **garb** *n.* परिधान paridhan | **gentleman** *n.* भद्रपुरुष bhadrapurush |
| **garb** *v.t* परिधान पहनाना paridhan pahanana | **gentry** *n.* कुलीनलोग kulinlog |
| **garbage** *n.* कूड़ा कचरा kuda kachra | **genuine** *a.* असली asli |
| **garden** *n.* उद्यान udyaan | **geographer** *n.* भूगोलवेत्ता bhugolveta |
| **gardener** *n.* माली maali | **geographical** *a.* भौगोलिक bhaugolik |
| **gargle** *v.i.* ग़रारे करना garare karna | **geography** *n.* भूगोल bhugol |
| **garland** *n.* माला mala | **geological** *a.* भूविज्ञानीय bhuvigyaniya |
| **garland** *v.t.* माला पहनाना mala pahnana | **geologist** *n.* भूविज्ञान वेत्ता bhuvigyan vetta |
| **garlic** *n.* लहसुन lahasun | **geology** *n.* भूविज्ञान bhuvigyan |
| **garment** *n.* परिधान paridhan | **geometrical** *a.* रेखा गणितीय rekha ganitiya |
| **garter** *n.* मोज़ाबंध mauzabandh | **geometry** *n.* रेखागणित rekhaganit |
| **gas** *n.* गैस gas | **germ** *n.* जीवाणु jiwanu |
| **gasket** *n.* अवरोधक डोरी awarodhak dori | **germinate** *v.i.* अंकुरित होना ankurit hona |
| **gasp** *n.* हाँफा haanfa | **germination** *n.* अंकुरण ankuran |
| **gasp** *v.i* हांफना haanfna | **gerund** *n.* क्रियावाचक संज्ञा kriyawachak sangya |
| **gassy** *a.* गैस युक्त gas yukt | **gesture** *n.* संकेत sanket |
| **gastric** *a.* अंतरिक ज्वर antrik jwar | **get** *v.t.* प्राप्त करना prapt karna |
| **gate** *n.* फाटक faatak | **ghastly** *a.* भयानक bhayanak |
| **gather** *v.t.* एकत्र करना ekatra karna | **ghost** *n.* भूत bhoot |
| **gaudy** *a.* दिखाऊ dikhau | |
| **gauge** *n.* पैमाना paimana | |

giant *n.* दैत्य daitya
gibbon *n.* लंगूर langur
gibe *v.i.* ताना मारना tana marna
gibe *n* ताना tana
giddy *a.* चकराने वाला chakrane wala
gift *n.* उपहार uphar
gigantic *a.* भीमकाय bhimkaya
giggle *v.i.* फूहड़ढंग से हंसना fuharh dhang se hasna
gild *v.t.* चमकाना chamkana
gilt *a.* सुनहरा sunhara
ginger *n.* अदरक aadrak
giraffe *n.* जिराफ़ girrafe
gird *v.t.* हंसी उड़ाना hansi urana
girder *n.* शहतीर shahteer
girdle *n.* पेटी peti
girdle *v.t* पेटी से बांधना peti se bandhna
girl *n.* लड़की ladki
girlish *a.* लड़कियों की तरह larkion ki tarah
gist *n.* सार saar
give *v.t.* देना dena
glacier *n.* हिमनद himnaad
glad *a.* आनंदकारी anandkari
gladden *v.t.* प्रसन्न करना prasaan karna
glamour *n.* मोहकता mohakata
glance *n.* झांकी jhanki
glance *v.i.* झांकना jhanakna
gland *n.* ग्रंथि granthi
glare *n.* चमक chamak
glare *v.i* चमकना chamkana
glass *n.* कांच kaanch
glaucoma *n.* मोतिया बिंद motia band
glaze *v.t.* शीशा लगाना shisha lagana
glaze *n* चमक chamak
glazier *n.* कांच का काम करने वाला kanch ka kam karne wala
glee *n.* गीत geet
glide *v.t.* सरकना sarkana
glider *n.* छोटा विमान chhota viman
glimpse *n.* झलक jhalak

glitter *v.i.* चमचमाना chamchamana
glitter *n* चमक chamak
global *a.* विश्व-व्यापी vishva-vyapi
globe *n.* पृथ्वी prithvi
gloom *n.* उदासी udasi
gloomy *a.* उदास udas
glorification *n.* प्रशस्ति prashasti
glorify *v.t.* गुणगान करना gungaan karna
glorious *a.* शोभायुक्त shobha yukt
glory *n.* प्रतिष्ठता pratishtha
gloss *n.* व्याकरण vyakhya
glossary *n.* शब्दावली shabdawali
glossy *a.* चमकदार chamakdar
glove *n.* दस्ताना dastana
glow *v.i.* चमकना chamkana
glow *n* दीप्ति dipti
glucose *n.* ग्लूकोज़ glucose
glue *n.* सरेस sares
glut *v.t.* भरमार होना bharmar hona
glut *n* प्रचुरता,बहुतायत prachurta, bahutayat
glutton *n.* खाऊ ahik khaney wala
gluttony *n.* पेटूपन petupan
glycerine *n.* ग्लिसरीन glycerin
go *v.i.* जाना jana
goad *n.* अंकुश ankush
goad *v.t* प्रेरित करना prairit karna
goal *n.* लक्ष्य lakshya
goat *n.* बकरी bakri
gobble *n.* भकोसना bhakosana
goblet *n.* पहला pyala
god *n.* भगवान bhagwan
goddess *n.* देवी devi
godship *n.* देवत्व devatav
godly *a.* धार्मिक dharmik
godown *n.* गोदाम godam
godsend *n.* वरदान vardaan
goggles *n.* धूप का चश्मा dhup ka chasma
gold *n.* सोना sona
golden *a.* सुनहरा sunhara
goldsmith *n.* स्वर्णकार swarnakar

golf *n.* गॉल्फ़ golf

gong *n.* पदक padak

good *a.* उचित ucchit

goods *n* सामान saamaan

good-bye *interj.* अलविदा alvida

goodness *n.* उदारता uddarta

goodwill *n.* साख saakh

goose *n.* बत्तख batakh

gooseberry *n.* करौंदा karonda

gorgeous *a.* भव्य bhvya

gorilla *n.* वनमानुष vanmanush

gospel *n.* ईसा का उपदेश esa ka updesh

gossip *n.* गपशप gupshup

gourd *n.* लौकी lauki

gout *n.* गठिया gathiya

govern *v.t.* शासित करना shasit karna

governance *n.* शासन shasan

governess *n.* अध्यापिका adhiyapika

government *n.* शासन shasan

governor *n.* राज्यपाल rajyapaal

gown *n.* लबादा labada

grab *v.t.* छीनना chinna

grace *n.* शोभा shobha

grace *v.t.* शोभा बढ़ाना shobha badhana

gracious *a.* दयालु dayalu

gradation *n.* श्रेणी shreni

grade *n.* पदक्रम padkram

grade *v.t* वर्गीकरण करना vargikaran karna

gradual *a.* क्रमिक kramik

graduate *v.i.* स्नातक होना sanatak hona

graduate *n* स्नातक sanatak

graft *n.* पैबन्द paiband

grain *n.* अनाज anaaj

grammar *n.* व्याकरण vyakaran

grammarian *n.* व्याकरणवेत्ता vyakaranweta

gramophone *n.* ग्रामोफ़ोन gramophone

granary *n.* अन्नभंडार annabhandar

grand *a.* महान mahan

grandeur *n.* शान shaan

grant *v.t.* प्रदान करना pradan karna

grant *n* अनुदान anudaan

grape *n.* अंगूर angur

graph *n.* रेखाचित्र rekhachitra

graphic *a.* आलेखी aalekhi

grapple *n.* पकड़ pakad

grapple *v.i.* भिड़ना bhidhna

grasp *v.t.* कसकर पकड़ना kaskar pakarna

grasp *n* पकड़ pakad

grass *n* घास ghas

grate *n.* जाली jaali

grate *v.t* घिसना ghisna

grateful *a.* आभारी aabhari

gratification *n.* संतोष santosh

gratis *adv.* नि:शुल्क nishulk

gratitude *n.* कृतज्ञता kritagayta

gratuity *n.* उपदान updaan

grave *n.* कब्र kabr

grave *a.* गंभीर gambhir

gravitate *v.i.* आकर्षित होना aakarshit hona

gravitation *n.* गुरुत्वाकर्षण gurutvakarshan

gravity *n.* गंभीरता gambhirta

graze *v.i.* चरना charna

graze *n* खरोंच kharonch

grease *n* चिकनायी chiknai

grease *v.t* चिकना करना chikna karna

greasy *a.* चिकना chikna

great *a* विशाल vishal

greed *n.* लोलुपता lolupata

greedy *a.* लालची lalchi

greek *n.* यूनानी भाषा yunani bhasha

green *a.* हरित harit

green *n* हरा रंग hara rang

greenery *n.* हरियाली hariyali

greet *v.t.* अभिवादन करना abhivadan karna

grenade *n.* हथगोला hathgola

grey *a.* भूरा bhura

greyhound *n.* शिकारी कुत्ता shikari kutta

grief *n.* शोक shok

grievance *n.* शिकायत shikayat

grieve v.t. शोक मनाना shok manana
grievous a. शोक जनक shok janak
grim n. कटोरी kathore
grind v.i. पिसना pisna
grinder n. पीसने का उपकरण pisne ka upkaran
grip v.t. पकड़ना pakadna
grip n जकड़न jakdan
groan v.i. कराहना karahana
groan n कराहना karahna
grocer n. पंसारी pansaari
grocery n. किराना kirana
groom n. दूल्हा dulha
groove n. नाली naali
groove v.t नालीदार बनाना nalidaar banana
grope v.t. तलाशना talashna
gross n. बारह दर्जन barah darjan
gross a प्रचुर prachur
grotesque a. भोंडा bhonda
ground n. पृथ्वी prithvi
group n. समूह samuh
group v.t. वर्गीकृत करना vargikrit karna
grow v.t. उगाना ugaana
grower n. उत्पादक utpaadak
growl v.i. गुर्राना gurraana
growl n गुर्राहट gurahat
growth n. विकास vikas
grudge n द्रोह droh
grumble v.i. असंतोष प्रकट करना asantosh prakat karna
grunt n. असंतोष asantosh
grunt v.i. घुरघुराना ghurghurna
guarantee n. जमानत zamanat
guarantee v.t दायित्व लेना dayitva lena
guard v.i. बचाना bachana
guard रखवाली rakhwali
guardian n. अभिभावक abhibhavak
guava n. अमरूद amrud
guerrilla n. छापामार सैनिक chhapa-maar sainik
guess n. अनुमान anumaan

guess v.i अनुमान लगाना anumaan lagana
guest n. अतिथि atithi
guidance n. पथ-प्रदर्शन path-pradarshan
guide v.t. पथप्रदर्शन करना pathpradashan karna
guide n. पथप्रदर्शक path pradarshak
guild n. संघ sangh
guile n. छल कपट chhal kapat
guilt n. अपराध apradh
guilty a. अपराधी apradhi
guise n. बनावटी रूप banawati roop
guitar n. गिटार guitar
gulf n. खाड़ी khadi
gull n. जलमुर्गी jalmurgi
gull n मूर्ख murkh
gulp vt निगलना nigalna
gum n. मसूढ़ा masurha
gun n. बंदूक banduk
gust n. झोंका jhonka
gutter n. नाली nali
guttural a. कंठ संबंधी kanth sambandhi
gymnast n. व्यायामी vyayami
gymnastic a. व्यायाम संबंधी vyayam sambandhi
gymnastics n. व्यायाम विद्या vyayam vidha

habeas corpus n. बंदी प्रत्यक्षीकरण bandi pratyakshikaran
habit n. आदत aadat
habitable a. रहने योग्य rahne yogya
habitat n. प्राकृतिक वास prakartik was
habitation n. निवास niwas
habituate v.t. आदी बनाना aadi banana
hack v.t. काटना kaatna
hag n. डायन dayan
haggard a. थका मांदा thaka manda
haggle v.i. सौदेबाज़ी करना saudebaji karna

hail *n.* ओला aula
hail *v.i* ओला गिरना aula girna
hail *v.t* अभिवादन करना abhiwadan karna
hair *n* बाल baal
hale *a.* भला चंगा bhala changa
half *n.* आधा भाग aadha bhag
half *a* आधा aadha
hall *n.* बड़ा कमरा bada kamara
hallmark *n.* विशिष्टता चिन्ह wishishtata chinha
hallow *v.t.* पवित्र करना pavitra karna
halt *v. t.* रोकना rokna
halt *n* रुकाव rukaav
halve *v.t.* आधा-आधा बांटना adha -adha bantna
hamlet *n.* खेड़ा khrda
hammer *n.* हथौड़ा hathaura
hammer *v.t* पीटना peetna
hand *n* हाथ haath
handbill *n.* इश्तहार ishtehaar
handbook *n.* पुस्तिका pustika
handcuff *n.* हथकड़ी hathkadi
handcuff *v.t* हथकड़ी लगाना hathkari lagana
handful *n.* मुट्ठीभर muthibhar
handicap *n* बाधा badha
handicap *v.t.* बाधा डालना badha dalana
handicraft *n.* हस्तशिल्प hastsilp
handiwork *n.* दस्तकारी dastkari
handkerchief *n.* रूमाल rumaal
handle *n.* हत्था hattha
handle *v.t* नियंत्रण करना niyantran karna
handsome *a.* सुंदर sundar
handy *a.* सुविधाजनक suvidhajanak
hang *v.t.* फांसी देना fansi dena
hanker *v.i.* लालायित होना lalayit hona
haphazard *a.* अव्यवस्थित avayvastith
happen *v.t.* घटित होना ghatit hona
happening *n.* घटना gathna
happiness *n.* आनंद anand

happy *a.* प्रसन्न prasann
harass *v.t.* तंग करना tang karna
harassment *n.* परेशानी pareshani
harbour *n.* बंदरगाह bandargaha
harbour *v.t* शरण देना sharan dena
hard *a.* कड़ा karha
harden *v.t.* कठोर बनाना kathore banana
hardihood *n.* साहसिकता sahasikta
hardly *adv.* मुश्किल से mushkil se
hardship *n.* मुसीबत musibat
hardy *adj.* साहसी sahasi
hare *n.* खरगोश khargosh
harm *n.* चोट chot
harm *v.t* चोट पहुंचाना chot pahunchana
harmonious *a.* सामंजस्यपूर्ण saamanjasyapurna
harmonium *n.* हारमोनियम harmoniyam
harmony *n.* सुव्यवस्था suvyavastha
harness *n.* साज सज्जा saaj sajja
harness *v.t* प्रयोग करना prayog karna
harp *n.* वीणा veena
harsh *a.* कठोर kathor
harvest *n.* फ़सल की कटाई fasal ki katai
harvester *n.* फ़सल काटने वाला fasal katne wala
haste *n.* शीघ्रता shighrata
hasten *v.i.* जल्दी कराना jaldi karna
hasty *a.* हड़बड़ाहट के साथ harhbarhahat ke sath
hat *n.* टोप tope
hatchet *n.* कुल्हाड़ी kulharhi
hate *n.* घृणा ghrina
hate *v.t.* घृणा करना ghrina karna
haughty *a.* दंभी dambhi
haunt *v.t.* परेशान करना pareshan karna
haunt *n* अड्डा adda
have *v.t.* प्राप्त करना prapt karna
haven *n.* बंदरगाह bandargaha
havoc *n.* विध्वंस vidhvans
hawk *n* बाज़ baaj

hawker *n* फेरीवाला pheri wala

hawthorn *n.* वन संजली van sanjali

hay *n.* सूखी घास sookhi ghaas

hazard *n.* संयोग sanyog

hazard *v.t* संकट में डालना sankat mai dalna

haze *n.* कुहरा kohra

hazy *a.* धुंधला dhundhala

he *pron.* वह voh

head *n.* सिर sar

head *v.t* आगे बढ़ना aage badhna

headache *n.* सिरदर्द sirdard

heading *n.* शीर्षक sirsak

headlong *adv.* सिर के बल sar kai bal

headstrong *a.* स्वेच्छाचारी svechachari

heal *v.i.* ठीक होना theek hona

health *n.* आरोग्य aarogya

healthy *a.* स्वस्थ swastha

heap *n.* संग्रह sangrah

heap *v.t* संचय करना sanchay karna

hear *v.t.* बताया जाना bataya jana

hearsay *n.* अफ़वाह afwah

heart *n.* दिल dil

hearth *n.* चूल्हा chulha

heartily *adv.* हृदय से hridya se

heat *n.* गर्मी garmi

heat *v.t* गर्म करना garm karna

heave *v.i.* उठाना uthana

heaven *n.* स्वर्ग swarg

heavenly *a.* दिव्य divya

hedge *n.* झाड़ी की बाड़ jharhi ki baarh

hedge *v.t* बाड़ लगाना baarh lagana

heed *v.t.* ध्यान में रखना dhyan mein rakhna

heed *n* देखभाल dekhbhal

heel *n.* जूते का पिछला भाग jutay ka pichla bhag

hefty *a.* भारी bhari

height *n.* ऊंचाई unchai

heighten *v.t.* ऊंचा करना uncha karna

heinous *a.* घृणित ghrenit

heir *n.* उत्तराधिकारी utradhikari

hell *a.* नरक narak

helm *n.* पतवार patwar

helmet *n.* शिरस्त्राण shirstraan

help *v.t.* सहायता करना sahayta karna

help *n* सहायता sahayata

helpful *a.* सहायक sahayak

helpless *a.* असहाय asahaya

helpmate *n.* सहायक sahayak

hemisphere *n.* गोलार्ध golardh

hemp *n.* भांग bhangh

hen *n.* मुर्गी murgi

hence *adv.* यहां से yahan se

henceforth *adv.* अब से आगे ab se aage

henceforward *adv.* अब से आगे ab se aage

henchman *n.* विश्वसनीय अनुचर vishwasniya anuchar

henpecked *a.* जोरू का गुलाम joru ka gulam

her *a* उस (स्री)का us (istri)ka

herald *n.* उद्घोषक udhghoshak

herald *v.t* घोषित करना ghosit karna

herb *n.* जड़ी बूटी jadi buti

herculean *a.* अत्यंत कठिन aatyant kathin

herd *n.* पशु समूह pasu samuh

herdsman *n.* चरवाहा charwaha

here यहां yahan

hereabouts *adv.* आसपास aaspass

hereafter *adv.* इसके बाद iss ke baad

hereditary *n.* वंशानुगत vanshanugat

heredity *n.* आनुवंशिकता aanu-vanshikta

heritable *a.* वंशागत vanshagat

heritage *n.* विरासत viraasat

hermit *n.* संन्यासी sanyasi

hermitage *n.* कुटी kuttiya

hernia *n.* हर्निया harniya

hero *n.* नायक nayak

heroic *a.* नायक संबंधी nayak sambandhi

heroine *n.* नायिका nayika

heroism n. **वीरता** veerta
herring n. **हिलसा** hilsa machhli
hesitant a. **संशयशील** sanshay-sheel
hesitate v.i. **संकोच करना** sankoch karna
hesitation n. **संकोच** sankoch
hew v.t. **कुल्हाड़ी से काटना** khulhadi se katna
heyday n. **सर्वोत्तम समय** sarbotam samay
hibernation n. **शीतनिद्रा** seetnindra
hiccup n. **हिचकी** hichki
hide n. **चमड़ा** chamda
hide v.t **छिपाना** chhipana
hideous a. **भयंकर** bhayankar
hierarchy n. **पदक्रम** pad-kram
high a. **ऊँचा** uncha
Highness n. **महाराज** maharaj
highway n. **राजपथ** rajpath
hilarious a. **उल्लसित** ullasit
hilarity n. **प्रफुल्लता** prafullta
hill n. **टीला** teela
hillock n. **टीला** teela
him pron. **उसको** usko
hinder v.t. **बाधा पहुंचाना** badha pahuchana
hindrance n. **अवरोध** awrodh
hint n. **संकेत** sanket
hint v.i **इशारा करना** eshara karna
hip n **कूल्हा** kuulha
hire n. **भाड़ा** bhada
hire v.t **किराए पर देना** kiraay par dena
his pron. **उसका** uska
hiss n **सिसकारी** siskari
hiss v.i **फुफकारना** fufkarna
historian n. **इतिहासकार** itihaskaar
historic a . **इतिहास प्रसिद्ध** itihas prasidh
historical a. **ऐतिहासिक** itihasik
history n. **इतिहास** itihaas
hit n **प्रहार** prahar
hit v.t. **प्रहार करना** prahaar karna
hitch n. **अड़चन** adchan
hither adv. **इस स्थान पर** es isthan par

hitherto adv. **अब तक** ab tak
hive n. **मधुमक्खी का छत्ता** madhumakhi ka chhata
hoarse a. **बेसुरा** baisura
hoax n. **चकमा** chakma
hoax v.t **चकमा देना** chakma dena
hobby n. **शौक** shauk
hobby-horse n. **कठघोड़ा** kath-ghora
hockey n. **हॉकी का खेल** hockey ka khel
hoist v.t. **ऊपर उठाना** upar uthana
hold n. **पकड़** pakad
hold v.t **पकड़ना** pakadna
hole n **छेद** ched
hole v.t **छेद में डालना** ched mein dalna
holiday n. **अवकाश का दिन** awkash ka din
hollow a. **खोखला** khokhla
hollow n. **छेद** ched
hollow v.t **खोखला करना** khokhla karna
holocaust n. **सर्वनाश** sarvanash
holy a. **पावन** pawan
homage n. **श्रद्धा** shraddha
home n. **निवास** nivas
homicide n. **मानव हत्या** manav hatya
homoeopath n. **चिकित्सक** chiktsak
homogeneous a. **सजातीय** sajaatiya
honest a. **ईमानदार** imaandaar
honesty n. **ईमानदारी** imaandaari
honey n. **शहद** sahad
honeycomb n. **मधुकोश** madhukosh
honeymoon n. **प्रमोदकाल** pramodkaal
honorarium n. **मानदेय** maandaiya
honorary a. **सम्मानार्थ** sammanarth
honour n. **आदर** aadar
honour v. t **सम्मानित करना** sammanit karna
honourable a. **माननीय** maanniya
hood n. **टोप** top
hoodwink v.t. **आंख में धूल झोंकना** aankh mein dhool jhonkana
hoof n. **खुर** khur

hook *n.* अंकुश ankush

hooligan *n.* आवारा aawara

hoot *n.* उल्लू की बोली ullu ki boli

hoot *v.i* घृणा सूचक शोर करना grehna suchak shor karna

hop *v. i* फुदकना fudakana

hop *n* कूद kuud

hope *v.t.* आशा रखना asha rakhna

hope *n* आशा asha

hopeful *a.* आशावान ashavan

hopeless *a.* निराश nirash

horde *n.* भीड़ bhirh

horizon *n.* दिग मंडल dig mandal

horn *n.* सींग seengh

hornet *n.* भिड़ bhirh

horrible *a.* भीषण bheeshan

horrify *v.t.* भयभीत करना bhayabhit karna

horror *n.* भय bhay

horse *n.* घोड़ा ghodha

horticulture *n.* बाग़बानी bagbaani

hose *n.* रबर का पाइप rabar ka pipe

hospitable *a.* सत्कार करने वाला satkaar karne wala

hospital *n.* चिकित्सालय chikitsalaya

hospitality *n.* आतिथ्य aathitya

host *n.* मेज़बान meijbaan

hostage *n.* बंधक bandhak

hostel *n.* छात्रावास chatrawas

hostile *a.* विरोधी virodhi

hostility *n.* विरोध virodh

hot *a.* गर्म garm

hotchpotch *n.* घालमेल ghal-mel

hotel *n.* होटल hotel

hound *n.* शिकारी कुत्ता shikari kutta

hour *n.* घंटा ghanta

house *n* मकान makaan

how *adv.* कैसे kaise

however *adv.* चाहे जैसे chahe jaise

however *conj* तथापि tathapi

howl *v.t.* चिल्लाकर कहना chilla kar kahana

howl *n* चीख cheekh

hub *n.* नाभि naabhi

hubbub *n.* कोलाहल kolahaal

huge *a.* विशाल vishal

hum *v. i* गुंजन करना gunjan karna

hum *n* गुंजन gunjan

human *a.* मानवीय maanviya

humane *a.* दयालु dayaalu

humanitarian *a* मानवीय manavi

humanity *n.* मानवीयता manaviyata

humanize *v.t.* मानवीय बनाना manaviya banana

humble *a.* विनम्र vinamra

humdrum *a.* नीरस niras

humid *a.* गीला geela

humidity *n.* नमी nami

humiliate *v.t.* अपमानित करना apmanit karna

humiliation *n.* अपमान apman

humility *n.* विनमता vinamrata

humorist *n.* विनोदी vinodi

humorous *a.* विनोदपूर्ण vinod puran

humour *n.* परिहास parihaas

hunch *n.* कूबड़ kubad

hundred *n.* सौ sau

hunger *n* भूख bhukh

hungry *a.* भूखा bhukha

hunt *v.t.* शिकार करना shikaar karna

hunt *n* आखेट aakhet

hunter *n.* शिकारी shikari

huntsman *n.* आखेटक aakhetak

hurdle *n.* बाधा baadha

hurdle *v.t* बाधा खड़ी करना baadha khari karna

hurl *v.t.* उछालना ucchalana

hurrah *interj.* आनंद anand

hurricane *n.* झंझावात jhanjhawat

hurry *v.t.* जल्दी करना jaldi karna

hurry *n* शीघ्रता shigrata
hurt *v.t.* चोट पहुंचाना chot pahuchana
hurt *n* चोट chot
husband *n* पति pati
husbandry *n.* काश्तकारी kastkari
hush *n* निस्तब्धता nisthabadtha
hush *v.i* शांत होना shant hona
husk *n.* भूसी bhusi
husky *a.* छिलकेदार chhilke daar
hut *n.* कुटीर kutir
hybrid *a.* संकर जाति का sankar jati ka
hybrid *n* संकर sankar
hydrogen *n.* उदजन udjan
hyena, hyena *n.* लकड़बग्घा lakarbaggha
hygiene *n.* स्वास्थ्य विज्ञान svasthya vigyaan
hygienic *a.* स्वास्थ्य संबंधी svasthya sambandhi
hymn *n.* स्तुति stuti
hyperbole *n.* अतिशयोक्ति atishyokti
hypnotism *n.* सम्मोहन sammohan
hypnotize *v.t.* सम्मोहित करना sammohit karna
hypocrisy *n.* आडंबर aadambar
hypocrite *n* पाखंडी paakhandi
hypocritical *a.* पाखंडी paakhandi
hypothesis *n.* कल्पना kalpana
hypothetical *a.* काल्पनिक kaalpanik
hysteria *n.* उन्माद unmaad
hysterical *a.* उन्मत्त unmat

I *pron.* मैं main
ice *n.* बर्फ़ barf
iceberg *n.* हिमशैल himshail
icy *a.* बर्फ़ीला barfila
idea *n.* विचार vichar
ideal *a.* आदर्श aadarsh

idealism *n.* आदर्शवाद aadarsh waad
idealist *n.* आदर्शवादी aadarshwadi
idealistic *a.* आदर्शात्मक aadarshatmak
idealize *v.t.* आदर्श बनाना adarsh banana
identical *a.* मिलता जुलता milta julta
identification *n.* पहचान pehchan
identify *v.t.* पहचानना pehchanana
identity *n.* पहचान pahchan
idiocy *n.* मूर्खता murkhta
idiom *n.* मुहावरा muhawara
idiomatic *a.* मुहावरेदार muhavare-daar
idiot *n.* मूर्ख व्यक्ति murkha vyakti
idiotic *a.* मूर्खतापूर्ण murkhtapurna
idle *a.* बेकार bekar
idleness *n.* आलस्य aalasya
idler *n.* आलसी व्यक्ति aalasi vyakti
idol *n.* मूर्ति murti
idolater *n.* मूर्तिपूजक murtipujak
if *conj.* यदि yadi
ignoble *a.* शर्मनाक sharm-naak
ignorance *n.* अज्ञान agyan
ignorant *a.* अनजान anjaan
ignore *v.t.* उपेक्षा करना upeksha karna
ill *a.* बीमार bimar
ill *adv.* गलत ढंग से galat dhang se
tempered *n* क्रोधी krodhi
illegal *a.* अवैध avaidh
ilegality *n.* अवैधता avaidhita
illegible *a.* अपठनीय apathaniya
illegitimate *a.* अवैध avaidh
illicit *a.* निषिद्ध nishidh
illiteracy *n.* निरक्षरता niraksharta
illiterate *a.* निरक्षर nirshar
illness *n.* रोग rog
illogical *a.* तर्कविरुद्ध tarkwirodh
illuminate *v.t.* जगमगा देना jagmaga dena
illumination *n.* प्रकाश prakash
illusion *n.* मरीचिका marichika
illustrate *v.t.* सचित्र बनाना sachitra banana
illustration *n.* उदाहरण udhahran

image *n.* मूर्ति murti
imagery *n.* बिंब विधान bimb vidhan
imaginary *a.* काल्पनिक kalpanik
imagination *n.* कल्पनाशक्ति
   kalpanashakti
imaginative *a.* कल्पनाशील kalpanashil
imagine *v.t.* कल्पना करना kalpana karna
imitate *v.t.* अनुकरण करना anukaran karna
imitation *n.* नकल nakal
imitator *n.* अनुकरण करनेवाला anukaran
   karne wala
immaterial *a.* महत्वहीन mahatva-heen
immature *a.* अविकसित avikasit
immaturity *n.* अपरिपक्वता aparipakwata
immeasurable *a.* अमित amit
immediate *a* तुरंत turant
immemorial *a.* अति प्राचीन ati prachin
immense *a.* विशाल vishaal
immensity *n.* विशालता vishalta
immerse *v.t.* डुबाना dubana
immersion *n.* निमज्जन nimajjan
immigrant *n.* आप्रवासी aprawaasi
immigrate *v.i.* आप्रवासन करना aprawasan
   karna
immigration *n.* आप्रवासन aprawasan
imminent *a.* निकटस्थ nikatasth
immodest *a.* अविनीत avineet
immoral *a.* अनैतिक anaitik
immorality *n.* अनैतिकता anaitikta
immortal *a.* अमर amar
immortality *n.* अविनिष्टता avinashita
immortalize *v.t.* अमर बनाना amar banana
immovable *a.* अचल achal
immune *a.* प्रतिरक्षित pratirakshit
immunity *n.* बचाव bachao
immunize *v.t.* प्रतिरक्षित करना pratirakshit
   karna
impact *n.* प्रभाव prabhav
impart *v.t.* दीन den
impartial *a.* निष्पक्ष nishpaksh

impartiality *n.* निष्पक्षता nishpakshta
impassable *a.* अलंघ्य alanghya
impasse *n.* गतिरोध gatirodh
impatience *n.* अधीरता adhirta
impatient *a.* अधीर adhir
impeach *v.t.* अभियोग लगाना abhiyog
   lagana
impeachment *n.* अभियोग abhiyog
impede *v.t.* बाधा डालना badha dalna
impediment *n.* बाध baadha
impenetrable *a.* अभेद्य abhedya
imperative *a.* अत्यावश्यक atyavashyak
imperfect *a.* अपूर्ण apurna
imperfection *n.* अपूर्णता apurnata
imperial *a.* शाही shahi
imperialism *n.* साम्राज्यवाद samrajyawad
imperil *v.t.* संकट में डालना sankat mein
   dalna
imperishable *a.* अक्षय akshya
impersonal *a.* अवैयक्तिक awaiyaktik
impersonate *v.t.* अभिनय करना abhinaya
   karna
impersonation *n.* पररूप धारण par-roop
   dharna
impertinence *n.* गुस्ताखी gustakhi
impertinent *a.* गुस्ताख gustakh
impetuosity *n.* प्रचंड prachand
impetuous *a.* जल्दबाज़ jaldbaaz
implement *n.* उपकरण upkaran
implement *v.t.* कार्यान्वित करना
   karyaniwit karna
implicate *v.t.* फंसाना fansana
implication *n.* उलझाव uljhav
implicit *a.* निर्विवाद nirviwad
implore *v.t.* प्रार्थना करना prarthana karna
imply *v.t.* अंतर्निहित होना antarnihit hona
impolite *a.* अभद्र abhadra
import *v.t.* आयात करना aayat karna
import *n.* आयात aayat
importance *n.* महत्व mahatva

important *a.* **महत्वपूर्ण** mahatvapurna
impose *v.t.* **लगाना** lagana
imposing *a.* **प्रभावशाली** prabhavshali
imposition *n.* **आरोपण** aaropan
impossibility *n.* **असंभवता** asambhavta
impossible *a.* **असंभव** asambhav
impostor *n.* **पाखंडी** pakhandi
imposture *n.* **पाखंड** pakhand
impotence *n.* **नपुंसकता** napunsakta
impotent *a.* **नपुंसक** napunsak
impoverish *adv.* **निर्धनता** nirdhanta
impracticability *n.* **अव्यावहारिकता** avyavaharikta
impracticable *a.* **अव्यवहार्य** avyavaharya
impress *v.t.* **प्रभावित करना** prabhavit karna
impression *n.* **विचार** vichar
impressive *a.* **प्रभावशाली** prabhavshali
imprint *v.t.* **छापना** chhaapna
imprint *n.* **प्रभाव** prabhav
imprison *v.t.* **बंदी बनाना** bandi banana
improper *a.* **असंगत** asangat
impropriety *n.* **ग़लती** galti
improve *v.t.* **सुधारना** sudharna
improvement *n.* **सुधार** sudhar
imprudence *n.* **अविवेक** avivek
imprudent *a.* **अविवेकी** aviveki
Impulse *n.* **आवेग** aaveg
impulsive *a.* **आवेगशील** aavegshil
impunity *n.* **दंड मुक्ति** dand mukti
impure *a.* **मिलावटी** milavati
impurity *n.* **मिलावट** milavat
impute *v.t.* **लांछन लगाना** laanchan lagana
in *prep.* **में** mein
inability *n.* **असमर्थता** asamarthta
inaccurate *a.* **अशुद्ध** ashudh
inaction *n.* **आलस्य** aalasya
inactive *a.* **आलसी** aalasi
inadmissible *a.* **अमान्य** amanya
inanimate *a.* **अचेतन** achetan
inapplicable *a.* **अप्रयोज्य** aprayojya

inattentive *a.* **असावधान** asavdhan
inaudible *a.* **अश्राव्य** ashravya
inaugural *a.* **प्रारंभिक** prarambhik
inauguration *n.* **उद् घाटन** udghatan
inauspicious *a.* **अशुभ** ashubh
inborn *a.* **सहज** sahaj
incapable *a.* **असमर्थ** asamarth
incapacity *n.* **शक्तिहीनता** asmarthata
incarnate *a.* **मूर्तिमान** murtimaan
incarnate *v.t.* **साकार रखना** saakar rakhna
incarnation *n.* **अवतार** avataar
incense *v.t.* **सुगंधित करना** sugandhit karna
incense *n.* **सुगंध** sugandh
incentive *n.* **प्रोत्साहन** protsaahan
inception *n.* **आरंभ** aarambh
inch *n.* **इंच** inch
incident *n.* **घटना** ghatna
incidental *a.* **आकस्मिक** aakasmik
incite *v.t.* **उत्तेजित करना** uttejit karna
inclination *n.* **झुकाव** jhukaav
incline *v.i.* **झुकना** jhukna
include *v.t.* **सम्मिलित करना** sammilit karna
inclusion *n.* **समावेश** samawesh
inclusive *a.* **सम्मिलित** sammalit
incoherent *a.* **असंगत** asangat
income *n.* **आमदनी** aamdani
incomparable *a.* **अनुपम** anupam
incompetent *a.* **अयोग्य** ayogya
incomplete *a* . **अधूरा** adhura
inconsiderate *a.* **अविवेकी** awiwaiki
inconvenient *a.* **असुविधाजनक** asuwidhajanak
incorporate *v.t.* **निगमित करना** nigmit karna
incorporate *vt.* **सम्मिलित करना** sammilit karna
incorporation *n.* **संयोजन** sanyojan
incorrect *a.* **अशुद्ध** asudh
incorrigible *a.* **असंशोधनीय** asansodhaniy

incorruptible *a.* **ईमानदार** imendar

increase *n* **विस्तार** vistar

increase *v.t.* **बढ़ाना** badhna

incredible *a.* **अविश्वसनीय** awiswasniya

increment *n.* **वृद्धि** vriddhi

incriminate *v.t.* **अभियोग लगाना** aviyog lagana

incubation *v.i.* **अंडे सेना** ande sena

inculcate *v.t.* **सिखा देना** shiksha dena

incumbent *n.* **अति आवश्यक** atyavashyak

incumbent *a* **आश्रित** aashrit

incur *v.t.* **झेलना** jhelna

incurable *a.* **असाध्य** asadhya

indebted *a.* **आभारी** aabhari

indecency *n.* **अशिष्टता** ashishtatha

indecent *a.* **अनुचित** anuchit

indecision *n.* **असमंजस** asamanjas

indeed *adv.* **वास्तव में** vastav mein

indefensible *a.* **असमर्थनीय** asamarthniya

indefinite *a.* **अनिश्चित** anishchit

indecisive *adj* **अनिश्चित** anishchit

independence *n.* **स्वतंत्रता** swtantrata

independent *a.* **स्वतंत्र** swatantra

indescribable *a.* **अवर्णनीय** awarnaniya

index *n.* **सूची** suchi

Indian *a.* **भारतीय** bharatiya

indicate *v.t.* **संकेत करना** sanket karna

indication *n.* **संकेत** sanket

indicative *a.* **परिचायक** parichayak

indicator *n.* **सूचक** suchak

indict *v.t.* **अभियोग लगाना** abhiyog lagana

indictment *n.* **अभियोग** abhiyog

indifference *n.* **उदासीनता** udasinta

indifferent *a.* **उदासीन** udasin

indigenous *a.* **देशज** deshaj

indigestible *a.* **अपचनीय** apachniya

indigestion *n.* **अपच** apach

indignant *a.* **क्रुद्ध** krudh

indignation *n.* **क्रोध** krodh

indigo *n.* **नील** neel

indirect *a.* **अप्रत्यक्ष** apratyaksh

indiscipline *n.* **अनुशासनहीनता** anushasanhinta

indiscreet *a.* **असावधानीपूर्ण** asavdhanipurna

indiscretion *n.* **ना-समझी** na-samjhi

indiscrimination *a.* **अन्तर** antar

indispensable *a.* **अपरिहार्य** apariharya

indisposed *a.* **अस्वस्थ** aswastha

indisputable *a.* **निर्विवाद** niwirwad

indistinct *a.* **अस्पष्ट** aspashth

individual *a.* **व्यक्तिगत** vyaktigat

individualism *n.* **व्यक्तिवाद** vyaktivad

individuality *n.* **वैयक्तिकता** vyaiktikata

indivisible *a.* **अविभाज्य** avibhajya

indolent *a.* **आलसी** aalasi

indomitable *a.* **दुर्दम** durdam

indoor *a.* **भीतरी** bhitri

indoors *adv.* **भवन के अंदर** bhawan ke andar

induce *v.t.* **प्रेरित करना** prairit karna

inducement *n.* **अभिप्रेरण** abhipreran

induct *v.t.* **अधिकारी बनाना** adhikari banana

induction *n.* **अधिष्ठापन** adhishthapan

indulge *v.t.* **मन रखना** man rakhna

indulgence *n.* **अनुग्रह** anugrah

indulgent *a.* **लिप्त** lipt

industrial *a.* **औद्योगिक** audhoyogik

industrious *a.* **मेहनती** mehaniti

industry *n.* **उद्योग** udyg

ineffective *a.* **अप्रभावी** aprabhavi

inert *a.* **निष्क्रिय** nishkriya

inertia *n.* **अचलता** achalta

inevitable *a.* **अपरिहार्य** apariharya

inexact *a.* **अशुद्ध** ashudh

inexorable *a.* **निष्ठुर** nishthur

inexpensive *a.* **मितव्ययी** mitvyayi

inexperience *n.* **अनुभवहीनता** anubhavhinta

inexplicable *a.* अव्याख्येय avyakhyaya

infallible *a.* अचूक achuk

infamous *a.* बदनाम badnam

infamy *n.* अपकीर्ति apkriti

infantilism *n.* बचपन bachpan

infant *n.* बच्चा bachha

infanticide *n.* शिशुवध shishuvadh

infantile *a.* शिशु sisu

infantry *n.* पैदल सेना paidal saina

infatuate *v.t.* मूर्ख बनाना murkh banana

infatuation *n.* मुग्धता mugdhata

infect *v.t.* भ्रष्ट करना bharasht karna

infection *n.* संक्रमण sankraman

infectious *a.* संक्रमणक sankraamak

infer *v.t.* निष्कर्ष निकालना niskars nikalana

inference *n.* अनुमान anumaan

inferior *a.* घटिया ghatiya

inferiority *n.* घटियापन ghatiyapan

infernal *a.* नारकीय naarkiya

infinite *a.* अनंत aanth

infinitive *n.* सामान्य samanya

infirm *a.* कमज़ोर kamzor

infirmity *n.* कमज़ोरी kamzori

inflame *v.t.* उत्तेजित करना uttejit karna

inflammable *a.* ज्वलनशील jwalanshil

inflammation *n.* प्रज्वलन prajwalan

inflammatory *a.* प्रज्वलनकार prajwalankar

inflation *n.* मुद्रास्फीति mudrasfriti

inflexible *a.* धीरता drirhata

inflict *v.t.* थोपना thopna

influence *n.* प्रभाव prabhav

influence *v.t.* प्रभाव डालना prabhav dalna

influential *a.* प्रभावशाली prabhavshali

influenza *n.* श्लेष्मा ज्वर sheshtama jvar

influx *n.* अंतःप्रवाह anth:pravah

inform *v.t.* सूचना देना suchna dena

informal *a.* अनौपचारिक anopacharik

information *n.* खबर khabar

informative *a.* सूचनापूर्ण suchnapurna

informer *n.* मुखबिर mukhbir

infringe *v.t.* उल्लंघन करना ulanghan karna

infringement *n.* अतिक्रमण atikraman

infuriate *v.t.* क्रुद्ध करना krudh karna

infuse *v.t.* अनुप्राणित करना anupraanit karna

infusion *n.* सम्मिश्रण sammishran

ingrained *a.* पक्का pakka

ingratitude *n.* कृतघ्नता kritdhanta

ingredient *n.* अवय awayav

inhabit *v.t.* वास करना vaas karna

inhabitable *a.* आवास योग्य aawas yogya

inhabitant *n.* निवासी niwasi

inhale *v.i.* सांस लेना saans lena

inherent *a.* जन्मजात janamjaat

inherit *v.t.* उत्तराधिकार में पाना utradhikar mai pana

inheritance *n.* उत्तराधिकार utradhikaar

inhibit *v.t.* रोकना rokna

inhibition *n.* अवरोध aworodh

inhospitable *a.* असत्कारशील asathkarsil

inhuman *a.* अमानवीय amanwiya

inimical *a.* विरोधी virodhi

inimitable *a.* अनोखा anokha

initial *a.* प्रारंभिक prarmbhik

initial *n.* आद्याक्षर adhakchar

initial *v.t* आद्याक्षरित करना adhakcharit karna

initiate *v.t.* सूत्रपात करना sutrapaat karna

initiative *n.* पहल pahal

inject *v.t.* अंतःक्षिप्त करना ant-kshipt karna

injection *n.* सूई लगाना sui lagana

injudicious *a.* अविवेकी awiwaki

injunction *n.* निषेधाज्ञा nishedhagya

injure *v.t.* क्षति करना kshati karna

injurious *a.* हानि कारक haani-kaarak

injury *n.* क्षति kshati

injustice *n.* अन्याय anyaya

ink *n.* स्याही syahi
inkling *n.* आभास abhaas
inland *adv.* अंदर-अंदर andar-andar
inland *a.* अंतर्देशीय antardeshiya
in-laws *n.* ससुराल sasural
inmate *n.* संवासी sanwasi
inmost *a.* घनिष्ट ghanishth
inn *n.* सराय sarai
innate *a.* जन्मजात janamjat
inner *a.* अंदरूनी andaruni
innermost *a.* अंतरतम antartam
innings *n.* पारी paari
innocence *n.* निरपराधता nirparadhata
innocent *a.* निर्दोष nirdosh
innovate *v.t.* नया बनाना naya banana
innovation *n.* नवोन्मेष nawonmaish
innovator *n.* प्रवर्तक prawartak
innumerable *a.* असंख्य asankhya
inoculate *v.t.* टीका लगाना tika lagana
inoculation *n.* टीकाकरण tikakaran
inoperative *a.* निष्क्रिया nishkriya
inopportune *a.* असामयिक asamayik
inquest *n.* कानूनी जांच kanuni janch
inquire *v.t.* जांच करना janch karna
inquiry *n.* जांच janch
inquisition *n.* न्यायिक जांच nayayik janch
inquisitive *a.* जिज्ञासु jigyasu
insane *a.* पागल paagal
insanity *n.* पागल-पन pagal-pan
insatiable *a.* अतोषणीय atoshniya
inscribe *v.t.* लिखना likhna
inscription *n.* अभिलेख abhilekh
insect *n.* कीट kit
insecticide *n.* कीटनाशी औषधि keet-nashi aushadhi
insecure *a.* अरक्षित archikth
insecurity *n.* असुरक्षा asuraksha
insensibility *n.* असंवेदन asamvedan
insensible *a.* बेसुध baisudh
inseparable *a.* अवियोज्य avi-yojya

insert *v.t.* सन्निविष्ट करना sannivisht karna
insertion *n.* सन्निवेश sannivesh
inside *prep.* अंदर andar
inside *a* अंदरूनी andaruni
inside *adv.* अंदर andar
inside *n.* भीतरी भाग bhitri bhag
insignificance *n.* महत्व-हीनता mahatva-hinta
insignificant *a.* महत्वहीन mahatvahin
insincere *a.* निष्ठाहीन nisthahin
insincerity *n.* निष्ठाहीनता nisthahinta
insinuate *v.t.* ईशारा करना ishara karna
insinuation *n.* कटाक्ष katash
insipid *a.* नीरस neeras
insipidity *n.* स्वादहीनता swadhhinta
insist *v.t.* आग्रह करना agrah karna
insistence *n.* अनुरोध anurodh
insistent *a.* आग्रहपूर्ण aagrahpurna
insolence *n.* गुस्ताखी gustakhi
insolent *a.* गुस्ताख gustakh
insoluble *n.* असाध्य asaadhya
insolvency *n.* दिवालियापन diwaliyapan
insolvent *a.* दिवालिया diwaliya
inspect *v.t.* परीक्षण करना parikshan karna
inspection *n.* निरीक्षण nirikshan
inspector *n.* निरीक्षक nirikshak
inspiration *n.* प्रेरणा prerna
inspire *v.t.* प्रेरित करना prerit karna
instability *n.* अस्थिरता asthirta
install *v.t.* नियुक्त करना niyukt karna
installation *n.* अधिष्ठापन adishthapan
instalment *n.* किस्त kist
instance *n.* दृष्टांत drishtant
instant *a.* आवश्यक aavashayk
instantaneous *a.* तात्कालिक tatkalik
instantly *adv.* तुरंत turant
instigate *v.t.* उकसाना uksana
instigation *n.* भड़कावा bharhkava
instill *v.t.* टपकाना tapkana

instinct *n.* प्रवृत्ति pravriti
instinctive *a.* प्रवृत्तिमूलक pravritimulak
institute/institution *n.* संस्था sanstha
instruct *v.t.* हिदायत करना hidayat karna
instruction *n.* अनुदेश anudesh
instructor *n.* शिक्षक shikshak
instrument *n.* औज़ार aujaar
instrumental *a.* सहायक sahayak
instrumentalist *n.* वादक wadak
insubordinate *a.* अवज्ञाकारी awagyakari
insubordination *n.* अवज्ञा awagya
insufficient *a.* अपर्याप्त aprayapt
insular *a.* द्वीप dwip
insularity *n.* द्वीपीयता dwipiyata
insulate *v.t.* पृथक् करना prethak karna
insulation *n.* पृथक्करण prethakaran
insulator *n.* पृथक्कारी prithakari
insult *n.* अपमान apman
insult *v.t.* अनादर करना anadar karna
insupportable *a.* असहनीय asahaniya
insurance *n.* बीमा bima
insure *v.t.* सुनिश्चित करना sunishchit
karna
insurgent *n.* विद्रोही व्यक्ति vidrohi vyakti
insurgent *a.* विद्रोही vidrohi
insurmountable *a.* कठिन kathin
insurrection *n.* विद्रोह vidroh
intact *a.* अक्षुण्ण ashuun
intangible *a.* अमूर्त amurt
integrity *n.* समग्रता samgrata
intellect *n.* प्रज्ञा pragya
intellectual *a.* बौद्धिक baudhik
intellectual *n.* बुद्धिजीवी buddhijivi
intelligence *n.* प्रज्ञा pragya
intelligent *a.* बुद्धिमान budhimaan
intelligentsia *n.* बुद्धिजीवी वर्ग budhijiwi
varg
intelligible *a.* सुबोध subodh
intend *v.t.* इरादा करना irada karna
intense *a.* अत्यधिक atyadhik

intensify *v.t.* घनीभूत करना ghanivhut
karna
intensity *n.* उत्कटता utkatata
intensive *a.* सघन saghan
intent *n.* अभिप्राय abhipray
interest *adj* ब्याज byaj
intention *n.* आशय aashay
intentional *a.* सोद्देश्य swadeshya
intercept *v.t.* मार्ग में रोकना marg me
rokna
interception *n.* अवरोधन awrodhan
interchange *v.* परस्पर विनिमय paraspar
vinimay
intercourse *n.* संभोग sambhog
interdependence *n.* परस्पर निर्भरता
paraspar nirbharta
interdependent *a.* परस्पर निर्भर paraspar
nirbhar
interest *n.* अधिकार adhikar
interested *a.* रुचि लेने वाला ruchi lene wala
interesting *a.* रुचिकर ruchikar
interfere *v.i.* हस्तक्षेप करना hastakshep
karna
interference *n.* हस्तक्षेप hastakshep
interim *n.* अंतरिम antarim
interior *a.* आंतरिक antarik
interior *n.* आंतरिक भाग antarik bhag
interjection *n.* विस्मयादिबोधक
vismyadibodhak
interlock *v.t.* गूंथना ghuthana
interlude *n.* अंतराल antaral
intermediary *n.* मध्यस्थ madhyasth
intermediate *a.* मध्यवर्ती madhyawarti
interminable *a.* अनंत anant
intermingle *v.t.* परस्पर मिश्रित करना
paraspar misrith karna
intern *v.t.* नज़रबंद कर देना najarband kar
dena
internal *a.* भीतरी bhitari
international *a.* अंतर्राष्ट्रीय antarastriya

**interplay** *n.* अन्योन्य क्रिया anyonya kriya
**interpret** *v.t.* व्याख्या करन vyakhya karna
**interpreter** *n.* दुभाषिया dubhashiya
**interrogate** *v.t.* प्रश्न करना prashan karna
**interrogation** *n.* पूछताछ puchtach
**interrogative** *a.* प्रश्तमक prashanatmak
**interrogative** *n* प्रश्नवाचक शब्द prashanvachak shabd
**interrupt** *v.t.* क्रमभंग करना krambhang karna
**interruption** *n.* बाधा baadha
**intersect** *v.t.* काटना kaatna
**intersection** *n.* प्रतिच्छेद pratichhed
**interval** *n.* मध्यांतर madhyantar
**intervene** *v.i.* हस्तक्षेप करना hastkshep karna
**intervention** *n.* हस्तक्षेप hastkshep
**interview** *n.* साक्षात्कार saakshatkar
**interview** *v.t.* साक्षात्कार करना saakshatakaar karna
**intestinal** *a.* आंत्र संबंधी aantra sambandhi
**intestine** *n.* आंत aant
**intimacy** *n.* घनिष्ठता ghanishtata
**intimate** *a.* घनिष्ठ ghanist
**intimate** *v.t.* सूचना देना suchana dena
**intimation** *n.* सूचना suchana
**intimidate** *v.t.* भयभीत करना bhaybhit karna
**intimidation** *n.* संत्रास santras
**into** *prep.* के अंदर ke andar
**intolerable** *a.* असह्य asahayam
**intolerance** *n.* असहिष्णुता asahishunta
**intolerant** *a.* असहिष्णु asahishnu
**intoxicant** *n.* मादक maadak
**intoxicate** *v.t.* मदोन्मत्त करना madonmat karna
**intoxication** *n.* मादकता maadakta
**intransitive** *a.* *(verb)* अकर्मक akarmak
**intrepid** *a.* बहादुर bahadur
**intrepidity** *n.* निर्भीकता nirbhakata

**intricate** *a.* पेचीदा pechida
**intrigue** *v.t.* षड्यंत्र करना shadyantra karna
**intrigue** *n* षड्यंत्र shadyantra
**intrinsic** *a.* भीतरी bhitri
**introduce** *v.t.* परिचित करना parichit karna
**introduction** *n.* परिचय parichay
**introductory** *a.* परिचयात्मक parichaytamak
**introspect** *v.i.* आत्मनिरीक्षण करना atmanirikshana karna
**introspection** *n.* अंतर्दर्शन antardarshan
**intrude** *v.t.* अनुचित रूप से घुस पड़ना anuchit rup se ghus padna
**intrusion** *n.* अतिक्रमण aatikraman
**intuition** *n.* अंतर्बोध antarbodh
**invade** *v.t.* आक्रमण करना aakraman karna
**invalid** *a.* अमान्य aamaniya
**invalid** *n* अपंग व्यक्ति apang vyakti
**invalidate** *v.t.* अमान्य करना amaniya karna
**invaluable** *a.* अमूल्य amulya
**invasion** *n.* हमला hamla
**invective** *n.* गाली गलौज gali galoj
**invent** *v.t.* आविष्कार करना aviskaar karna
**invention** *n.* आविष्कार aviskaar
**inventive** *a.* आविष्कारशील aviskaarshil
**inventor** *n.* आविष्कारक avishkaarak
**invert** *v.t.* औंधा करना aundha karna
**invest** *v.t.* पूंजी लगाना punji lagana
**investigate** *v.t.* अनुसंधान करना anusandhan karna
**investigation** *n.* अनुसंधान anusandhan
**investment** *n.* पूंजी निवेश punji nivesh
**invigilate** *v.t.* निरीक्षण करना nirikshan karna
**invigilation** *n.* निरीक्षण nirikshan
**invigilator** *n.* निरीक्षक nirekshak
**invincible** *a.* अपराजेय aparajeya
**inviolable** *a.* अनुल्लंघनीय anulanghaniya
**invisible** *a.* अंतर्धान antardhan

invitation *v.* आमंत्रण aamantran
invite *v.t.* आमंत्रित करना aamantrit karna
invocation *n.* वंदना vandana
invoice *n.* बीजक bijak
involve *v.t.* फंसाना fansana
inward *a.* आंतरिक aantrik
inwards *adv.* अंदर को andar ko
ire *a.* नाराज़ naraaz
ire *n.* क्रोध krodh
Irish *a.* आयरलैंड का aayerland ka
Irish *n.* आयरलैंड की भाषा aayerland ki
bhasha
irksome *a.* बोझिल bhojhil
iron *n.* लोहा loha
iron *v.t.* इस्तरी करना istari karna
ironical *a.* वक्रोक्तिपूर्ण vakrotipurna
irony *n.* विडंबना vidambana
irradiate *v.i.* प्रकाशित करना prakasit karna
irrational *a.* तर्कशून्य tarkshunya
irreconcilable *a.* असंगत asangat
irrecoverable *a.* अपूरणीय apurniya
irrefutable *a.* अकाट्य akaatiya
irregular *a.* अनियमित aniyamit
irregularity *n.* अनियमितता aniyamitta
irrelevant *a.* विसंगत visangat
irrespective *a.* निरपेक्ष nirpeksh
irresponsible *a.* लापरवाह laparwah
irrigate *v.t.* सींचना sinchna
irrigation *n.* सिंचाई sinchai
irritable *a.* चिड़चिड़ा chhidchhida
irritant *a.* प्रकोपक prakopak
irritant *n.* उत्तेजक पदार्थ uttejak padarth
irritate *v.t.* उकसाना uksaana
irritation *n.* जलन jalan
irruption *n.* आक्रमण akraman
island *n.* टापू tapu
isle *n.* टापू tapu
isobar *n.* समदाब रेखा samdaab rekha
isolate *v.t.* पृथक् करना prithak karna
isolation *n.* अलगाव algaaw

issue *v.i.* परिणाम होना parinam hona
issue *n.* निकास nikas
it *pron.* यह yeh
Italian *a.* इटली का itali ka
Italian *n.* इटली की भाषा itali ki bhasha
italic *a.* तिरछा tircha
italics *n.* तिरछा मुद्रण tircha mudran
itch *n.* खुजली khujli
itch *v.i.* खुजली होना khujli hona
item *n.* विषय vishyai
ivory *n.* हाथी दांत haathi dant
ivy *n* सदाबहार लता sadabahar lata

jab *v.t.* चुभाना chubhana
jabber *v.t.* बड़बड़ करना badbad karna
jack *n.* मज़दूर mazdur
jack *v.t.* जैक द्वारा उठाना jaik duwara
uthana
jackal *n.* सियार seyaar
jacket *n.* कोट coat
jade *n.* जीमती पथरी घोडा qimti patharl
ghoda
jail *n.* बंदीगृह bandigreh
jailer *n.* कारापाल karapaal
jam *n.* अवरोध avrodh
jam *n.* मुरब्बा murabba
jar *n.* मर्तबान martbaan
jargon *n.* अनर्थक बोली anarthak boli
jasmine *n.* चमेली chameli
jaundice *n.* पीलिया piliya
javelin *n.* भाला bhaala
jaw *n.* जबड़ा jabrha
jay *n.* नीलकंठ nilkanth
jealous *a.* द्वेषी dveshi
jealousy *n.* ईर्ष्या irshya
jean *n.* मज़बूत सूती कपड़ा mazbut suti
kapda

jeer *v.i.* मज़ाक उड़ाना mazak udana

jelly *n.* लाबाबदार मिष्ठान lababdar mishtann

jeopardize *v.t.* खतरे में डालना khatrey mein dalna

jeopardy *n.* खतरा khatra

jerk *n.* झटका jhataka

jerkin *n.* मिरज़ई mirzai

jerky *a.* झटकेदार jhatkedar

jersey *n.* जर्सी jarsi

jest *n.* हंसी hansi

jest *v.i.* व्यंग्य करना vayngya karna

jet *n.* धार dhaar

Jew *n.* यहूदी yahudi

jewel *n.* मणि mani

jewel *v.t.* रत्नमंडित करना ratranmandith karna

jeweller *n.* जौहरी jauhari

jewellery *n.* रत्नाभूषण ratnabhushan

jingle *n.* झनकार jhankar

jingle *v.i.* झनझनाना jhanjhanna

job *n.* काम kaam

jobber *n.* दलाल dalal

jobbery *n.* भ्रष्टाचार bhrashtachaar

jog *v.t.* हिलाना hilaana

join *v.t.* जोड़ना jorhna

joiner *n.* योजक yojak

joint *n.* जोड़ jorna

jointly *adv.* मिलजुलकर mil-jul kar

joke *n.* परिहास parihaas

joke *v.i.* हंसी मज़ाक करना hansi majak karna

joker *n.* मसखरा maskhara

jollity *n.* आमोद प्रमोद aamodh pramodh

jolly *a.* प्रफुल्ल prafull

jolt *n.* झटका jhatka

jolt *v.t.* हिचकोले देना hichkole dena

jostle *n.* धक्कमधक्का dhakamdhakka

jostle *v.t.* धक्का देना dhakka dena

jot *n.* कण kann

journal *n.* पत्रिका patrika

journalism *n.* पत्रकारिता patrakarita

journalist *n.* पत्रकार patrakar

journey *n.* यात्रा yatra

journey *v.i.* यात्रा करना yatra karna

jovial *a.* उल्लासपूर्ण ullaspurna

joviality *n.* जिंदादिली zindadili

joy *n.* आनंद anand

joyful, joyous *n.* हर्षित harshit

jubilant *a.* उल्लसित ullasit

jubilation *n.* आनंदोत्सव anandotsav

jubilee *n.* वर्षगांठ varsh ganth

judge *n.* निर्णायक nirnayak

judge *v.i.* निर्णय करना nirnaya karna

judgement *n.* निर्णय nirnaya

judicature *n.* न्यायालय nyayalaya

judicial *a.* न्याय संबंधी nyay-sambandhi

judiciary *n.* न्यायतंत्र nyay-tantra

judicious *a.* विवेकशील vivekshil

jug *n.* लोटा lota

juggle *v.t.* जादूगरी करना jadugari karna

juggler *n.* बाज़ीगर bazigar

juice *n* रस rass

juicy *a.* रसदार rasdaar

jumble *n.* घालमेल ghalmail

jumble *v.t.* गड्मड्ड करना gadmadd karna

jump *n.* छलांग chalang

jump *v.i* कूदना kudna

junction *n.* संधि sandhi

juncture *n.* संगम sangam

jungle *n.* जंगल jungle

junior *a.* कनिष्ठ kanist

junior *n.* अवर व्यक्ति avar vyakti

junk *n.* कचरा kachra

Jupiter *n.* बृहस्पति ग्रह brehaspati grah

jurisdiction *n.* अधिकार क्षेत्र adhikar kshetra

jurisprudence *n.* न्यायशास्त्र nayayshastra

jurist *n.* कानूनविद kanunvidh

juror *n.* जूरी का सदस्य juri ka sadasya

jury *n.* न्यायपीठ naiypith

juryman *n.* जूरी का सदस्य juri ka sadasyai

just *a.* उचित ucchit

just *adv.* केवल kewal

justice *n.* अदालती निर्णय adalati nirnaya

justifiable *a.* तर्कसंगत tarksangat

justification *n.* औचित्य auchitiya

justify *v.t.* उचित प्रमाणित करना ucchit pramanit karna

justly *adv.* उचित रूप में ucchit rup mein

jute *n.* पटसन patsan

juvenile *a.* किशोर संबंधी kishore sambandhi

# K

keen *a.* इक्चुख ichhuk

keen *a.* तेज़ tez

keenness *n.* उत्सुकता utsukta

keep *v.t.* पास रखना paas rakhna

keeper *n.* देखभाल करनेवाला dekhbhal karnewala

keepsake *n.* स्मृतिचिन्ह smriti chinha

kennel *n.* कुत्ताघर kuttaghar

kerchief *n.* रूमाल rumal

kernel *n.* सार saar

kerosene *n.* मिट्टी का तेल mitti ka tel

ketchup *n.* चटनी chatni

kettle *n.* पतीली patili

key *n.* कुंजी kunji

key *v.t* चाबी से बंद करना chabi se band karna

kick *n.* ठोकर thokar

kick *v.t.* ठोकर मारना thokare marna

kid *n.* छोटा बच्चा chhota baccha

kidnap *v.t.* अपहरण करना apharan karna

kidney *n.* गुर्दा gurda

kill *v.t.* मारना marna

killer *n.* मारने वाला maarne wala

kiln *n.* भट्टा bhatta

kin *n.* परिजन parijan

kind *n.* प्रकार prakar

kind *a* कृपालु kripalu

kindergarten ; *n.* बाल विहार baal vihar

kindle *v.t.* चमकाना chamkana

kindly *adv.* कृपया kripiya

king *n.* राजा raja

kingdom *n.* सामाज्य samrajya

kino *n.* संतरा santra

kiss *n.* चुंबन chumban

kit *n.* साज़ सामान saaj saman

kitchen *n.* रसोईघर rasoi ghar

kite *n.* पतंग patang

kith *n.* रिश्तेदार rishtedar

kitten *n.* बिल्ली का बच्चा billi ka baccha

knave *n.* दुष्ट dusht

knavery *n.* दुष्टता dushtata

knee *n.* घुटना ghutna

kneel *v.i.* घुटने टेकना ghutne tekna

knife *n.* चाकू chaku

knight *n.* योद्धा yodha

knit *v.t.* बुनना bunna

knock *v.t.* खटखटाना khat-khatana

knot *n.* गांठ gaanth

knot *v.t.* बांधना bandhna

know *v.t.* जानना jaanana

knowledge *n.* जानकारी jaankari

# L

label *n.* नाम पत्र naam patra

label *v.t.* लेबिल लगाना lebal lagana

labial *a.* ओष्ठ संबंधी oshth sambandhi

laboratory *n.* प्रयोगशाला prayogsala

laborious *a.* कठिन kathin

labour *n.* प्रसव पीड़ा prasv peerha

laboured *a.* प्रभाव-हीन pravah-hin

labourer *n.* श्रमिक shramik

labyrinth n. उलझन uljhan

lac / lakh n एक लाख ek lakh

lace v.t. फ़ीतों से बांधना phiton se bandhana

lace n. किनारी kinari

lacerate v.t. यंत्रणादेना yantrana dena

lachrymose a. रुदनकारी rudankari

lack n. कमी kami

lack v.t. अभाव होना avhav hona

lackey n. नौकर naukar

lacklustre a. निस्तेज nistej

laconic a. संक्षिप्त sankshipt

lactate v.i. दुग्ध स्रावित करना dughad srawit karna

lactometer n. दुग्धमापी dughadmapi

lactose n. दुग्धशर्करा dughasharkara

lacuna n. कमी kami

lacy a. लेसदार lesdaar

lad n. लड़का ladka

ladder n. सीढ़ी sidhe

lade v.t. लादना ladana

ladle n. करछुल karchhul

ladle v.t. करछुल से देना karchhul se dena

lady n. महिला mahila

lag v.i. धीरे धीरे चलना dhere dhere chalna

laggard n. शक्तिहीन व्यक्ति saktihin baykti

lair n. मांद maand

lake n. झील jheel

lama n. बौध- भिक्षु bouddh bhikshu

lamb n. मेमना memna

lambaste v.t. मारना maarna

lambkin n. छोटा मेमना chota memna

lame a. असंतोषजनक asantoshjanak

lame v.t. पंगु बनाना pangu banana

lament n विलाप wilaap

lament v.i. शोक प्रकट करना soak prakat karna

lamentable a. खेद योग्य khed yogya

lamentation n. विलाप vilap

lamp n. दीपक deepak

lampoon v.t. व्यंग्य करना vyangya karna

lance n. भाला bhala

lance v.t. चुभाना chubhana

lancer n. बल्लमधारी योद्धा ballamdhari yodha

lancet a. छुरिका chhurika

land n. भूमि bhumi

large बड़ा bara

landing vy जहाज़ का उतरना jahaz ka utarna

landscape n. प्राकृतिक दर्शय स्थल prakirtik drishya sthal

lane n. गली gali

language n. भाषा bhasha

languish v.i. मुरझाना murjhana

lank a. लंबा और पतला lamba aur patla

lantern n. लालटेन lal tain

lap n. गोदी godi

lapse v.i. भूल चूक buool chook

lapse n भूल bhool

lard n. सुअर की चरबी suar ki charbi

large a. उदार udaar

largess n. उपहार upahar

lark n. दिल-लगी dil-lagi

lascivious a. कामुक kaamuk

lash a. कोड़ा मारना korha marna

lash n कोड़ा korha

lass n. किशोरी kishori

last v.i. टिकना tikna

last n अंतिम वस्तु antim vastu

last a. अंतिम antim

lasting a. टिकाऊ tikau

lastly adv. अंतिम तौर से antim taur se

latch n. कुंडी kundi

late a. देर der

late fee adv. विलम्ब शुल्क vilamb shulk

lately हाल ही में haal he mein

latent a. गुप्त gupt

lath n. पत्ता phatta

lathe n. खराद kharaad

lathe *n.* खराद मशीन kharaad machine

lather *n.* झाग jhaag

latitude *n.* छूट chhoot

latrine *n.* शौचालय shauchalaya

latter *a.* पिछला pichhla

lattice *n.* जाली jaali

laud *v.t.* प्रशंसा करना prashansa karna

laud *n* प्रशंसा prashansa

laudable *a.* प्रशंसनीय prashansniya

laugh *n.* हंसी hansi

laugh *v.i* हंसना hansna

laughable *a.* मनोरंजक manoranjak

laughter *n.* हंसी hansi

launch *n.* जलावतरण jalavatran

laundress *n.* धोबिन dhobin

laundry *n.* धुलाईघर dhulai ghar

laureate *a.* अलंकृत alankrit

laurel *n.* कीर्ति kirti

lava *n.* लावा lava

lavatory *n.* शौचालय shauchalya

lavish *a.* प्रचुर prachur

lavish *v.t.* दिल खोलकर खर्च करना dil kholkar kharch karna

law *n.* कानून qanoon

lawfulness *a.* कानून के अनुसार qanoon ke anusar

lawless *a.* अवैध avaidh

lawn *n.* घास का मैदान ghaas ka maidan

lawyer *n.* वकील vakil

lax *a.* ढीला dhila

laxative *n.* रेचक औषधि rechak aushadhi

leader नेता neta

laxity *n.* रेचन rechan

lay *n* लिटा देना litta dena

lay *v.t.* रखना rakhna

lay clerk *a.* गिरजा का गायक girja ka gayak

layer *n.* परत parat

layman *n.* साधारण व्यक्ति sadharan vykati

laze *v.i.* सुस्त रहना sust rehna

laziness *n.* आलस्य aalasya

lazy *n.* आलसी aalasi

lea *n.* खुला मैदान khula maidan

leach *v.t.* घोलकर बहाना gholkar bahana

lead *n.* सीसा sisa

lead *v.t.* मार्गदर्शन करना margdarsan karna

lead *n.* मार्गदर्शन margdarsan

leaden *a.* बोझिल bhojhil

leader *n.* अगुआ aguwa

leadership *n.* नेतृत्व naitritva

leaf *n.* पत्ता patta

leaflet *n.* पुस्तिका pustika

leafy *a.* पत्तियों से भरा pattiyon se bhara

league *n.* संघ sangh

leak *n.* दरार darar

leak *v.i.* रिसना risnaa

leakage *n.* रिसन risan

lean *n.* पतला patla

lean *v.i.* झुकना jhukna

leap *v.i.* कूदना kudna

leap *n* कूद kud

learn *v.i.* सीखना seekhna

learned *a.* विद्वान vidvaan

learner *n.* शिष्य shishya

learning *n* शिक्षा shiksha

lease *n.* पट्टा patta

lease *v.t.* पट्टे पर देना patte par dena

least *a.* अल्पतम alpatam

least *adv.* कम से कम मात्रा में kam se kam matra mein

leather *n.* चमड़ा chamrha

leave behind *n.* पीछे छोड़ना peechhe chhorna

leave *v.t.* छोड़ना chorhna

lecture *n.* व्याकरण vyakhayan

lecture *v* भाषण देना bhashan dena

lecturer *n.* प्रवक्ता pravakta

ledger *n.* खाता बही khata bahi

lee *n.* आश्रय ashray

leech *n.* जोंक jonk

leek n. प्याज़ जैसी सब्ज़ी pyaaz jaisi sabzi

left a. बायां bayan

left adj छोड़ा हुआ chhora hua

leftist n प्रगतिवादी व्यक्ति pragatiwadi vyakti

leg n. तंग taang

legacy n. वसीयत vasiyat

legal a. कानूनी kaanuni

legality n. वैधता vaidhata

legalize v.t. कानूनी बनाना kaanuni banana

legend n. किंवदंती kinv-vadanti

legendary a. प्रसिद्घ prasiddh

legible a. सुपाठ्य supathya

legibly adv. सुपाठ्य रूप में supathya rup mein

legion n. विशाल संख्या vishal sankhya

legionary n. सेना का सदस्य saina ka sadasya

legislate v.i. कानून बनाना kanun banana

legislation n. विधान vidhan

legislative a. विधायी vidhayi

legislator n. कानून निर्माता kanun nirmata

legislature n. विधानमंडल vidhanmandal

legitimacy n. वैधता vaidhata

legitimate a. वैध vaidh

leisure n. अवकाश avkash

leisure a फुर्सत phursat

leisurely a. इत्मिनान से itminan se

leisurely adv. धीरे धीरे dheere dheere

lemon n. नींबू nimbu

lemonade n. शिकंजी shikanji

lend v.t. उधार देना udhar dena

length n. लम्बाई lambai

lengthen v.t. लंबा करना lamba karna

lengthy a. लंबा lamba

lenience, leniency n. उदारता udaarta

lenient a. कोमल komal

lens n. दूरबीन का शीशा durbin ka shisha

lentil n. डाल daal

Leo n. सिंह राशि sinha rashi

leonine a सिंह जैसा sinha jaisa

leopard n. तेंदुआ tendua

leper n. कुष्ठरोगी kushtrogi

leprosy n. कुष्ठ kusht

less a. कम kam

less adv. इतना नहीं itna nahi

less prep. अल्प मात्रा alp matra

lessee n. पट्टेदार pattedar

lessen v.t कम होना kam hona

lesser a. लघुतर laghu-tar

lesson n. सबक sabaq

lest conj. अन्यथा anyatha

let v.t. अनुमति देना anumati dena

lethal a. प्राणघातक pranghatak

lethargic a. शक्तिहीन shaktihin

lethargy n. सुस्ती sust

letter n चिट्ठी chithhi

level n. दरजा darja

level a समतल samtal

level v.t. समतल करना samtal karna

lever n. उत्तोलक uttolak

lever n ढेकली dhekli

leverage n. उत्तोलक की शक्ति uttolok ki sakti

levity n. छिछोरापन chichorapan

levy v.t. वसूल करना vasul karna

levy n. आरोपित राशि aaropit rashi

lewd a. कामुक kamuk

lexicography n. कोश रचना kosh rachna

lexicon n. शब्दकोश shabadkosh

liability n. दायित्व dayitva

liable a. ज़िम्मेदार zimmedaar

liaison n. सम्पर्क sampark

liar n. झूठा jhutha

libel n. अभियोग पत्र abhiyog patra

liberal a. उधार udaar

liberalism n. उदारवाद udarvad

liberality n. उदारता udarta

liberate v.t. मुक्त करना mukt karna

liberation n. मुक्ति mukti

liberator *n.* मुक्तिदाता muktidata

libertine *n.* व्यभिचारी vyabhichari

liberty *n.* स्वतंत्रता swatantrata

librarian *n.* पुस्तकालयाध्यक्ष pustakalayadhayaksh

library *n.* पुस्तकालय pustakalaya.

licence *n.* अनुज्ञा पत्र anugya patra

license *v.t.* अनुज्ञा देना anugya dena

licensee *n.* अनुज्ञापत्रधारी anugyapatradhari

licentious *a.* पतित patit

lick *v.t.* जीभ से चाटना jibh se chatna

lick *n* चाटने की क्रिया chatne ki kriya

lid *n.* पलक palak

lie *n* असत्य asatya

lie *v.i.* पड़ा रहना parha rahana

lie *v.i* झूठ बोलना jhut bolna

lien *n.* वैध अधिकार vaidh adhikaar

lieu *n.* बदले में badle mein

lieutenant *n.* सेना का अफ़सर saina ka afsar

life *n* जीवनकाल jivankaal

lifeless *a.* जीवन रहित jivanrahit

lifelong *a.* आजीवन aajiwan

lift *n.* विद्युत सीढ़ी vidyut seerhi

lift *v.t.* चुराना churna

light *n.* प्रकाश prakash

light *a* सरल saral

light *v.t.* प्रकाशित होना prakashit hona

lighten *v.i.* हलका होना halka hona

lightening *n.* आकाशीय विद्युत् aakashiya vidyut

light house *n.* प्रकाश स्तम्भ prakash stambh

lightly *adv.* हलके से halke se

lignite *n.* भूरा कोयला bhura koyala

like *v.t.* पसंद करना pasand karna

like *a.* अनुरूप anurup

like *n.* पसंद pasand

ligneous *prep* खस्त-वात kashth-vat

likelihood *n.* संभव्यता sambhavyata

likely *a.* उपयुक्त upyukt

liken *v.t.* तुलना करना tulna karna

likeness *n.* अनुरूपता anurupta

likewise *adv.* उसी तरह usi tarah

liking *n.* पसंद pasand

lilac *n.* कसनी रंग का फूल kasni rang ka phool

lily *n.* कुमुदिनी kumudini

limb *n.* शाखा shakha

limber *v.t.* लचीला होना lachila hona

limber *n* गाड़ी का जुआ garhi ka juwa

lime *n.* चकोतरा chakotara

lime *n.* लासा lasa

lime *v.t* चूना लगाना chuna lagana

limelight *n.* तीव्र प्रकाश tivra prakash

limit *n.* सीमा seema

limit *v.t.* सीमित करना simit karna

limitation *n.* बाधा badha

limited *a.* संकुचित sankuchit

limitless *a.* असीम asim

line *n.* रेखा rekha

line *v.t.* अस्तर लगाना astar lagana

lineage *n.* वंशावली wanshavali

linen *n.* क्षोमवस्त्र kshomvastr

linger *v.i.* विलंब करना vilamb karna

lingo *n.* विदेशी भाषा videshi bhasha

lingua franca *n.* सामान्य भाषा samaniya bhasha

linguist *n.* भाषाविद् bhashavid

linguistic *a.* भाषा संबंधी bhasha sambandhi

linguistics *n.* भाषा विज्ञान bhasa vigyan

lining *n* अस्तर astar

link *n.* ज़ंजीर की कड़ी zanzir ki kadi

link *v.t* जोड़ना jodna

linseed *n.* अलसी alsi

lintel *n.* सरदल sardal

lion *n* शेर sher

lioness *n.* शेरनी sherni

lip *n.* अधर adhar

liquefy *v.t.* द्रव बनना drav banana

liquid *a.* तरल taral

liquid *n* पदार्थ padarth
liquidate *v.t.* मिटा देना mita dena
liquidation *n.* परिशोधन parishodhan
liquor *n.* मदिरा madira
lisp *v.t.* तुतलाना tutlana
lisp *n* तुतलाहट tutlahat
list *n.* सूचीपत्र suchipatra
list *v.t.* सूचीबद्घ करना suchibadh karna
listen *v.i.* ध्यान देना dhyan dena
listener *n.* श्रोता shrota
listless *a.* उदासीन udashin
lists *n.* अखाड़ा akharha
literacy *n.* साक्षरता saksharta
literal *a.* शाब्दिक shabdik
literary *a.* साहित्यिक sahitiyik
literate *a.* साक्षर sakshar
literature *n.* साहित्य sahitiya
litigant *n.* मुकदमेबाज़ muqadamebaaz
litigate *v.t.* मुकदमेबाज़ी करना muqadme-
baazi karna
litigation *n.* मुकदमा muqadma
litre *n.* लीटर litre
litter *v.t.* जन्म देना janam dena
litter *n.* पालकी paalki
litterateur *n.* साहित्यिक व्यक्ति sahitiyik
vyakti
little *n.* अल्प मात्रा alp matra
little *a.* छोटा chhota
little *adv.* थोड़ा सा thora se
littoral *a.* तटवर्ती tatwarti
live *v.i.* निवास करना niwas karna
live *a.* जीवंत jiwant
livelihood *n.* आजीविका aajiwika
lively *a.* सक्रिय sakriya
liver *n.* जिगर jigar
livery *n.* नौकरों की वर्दी naukaro kai vardi
living *a.* जीवंत jivant
living *n* जीविका jivika
lizard *n.* छिपकली chhipkali
load *n.* शोक भार shoak bhar

load *v.t.* लादना ladna
loadstar *n.* ध्रुवतारा dhruvatara
loadstone *n.* चुंबक पत्थर chumbak pathar
loaf *n.* पावरोटी pawroti
loaf *v.i.* आवारागर्दी करना awaragardi karna
loafer *n.* आवारा आदमी awara aadmi
loan *n.* उधार uddhar
loan *v.t.* उधार देना uddhar dena
loath *a.* अनिच्छुक anichhuk
loathe *v.t.* घृणा रखना grhena rakna
loathsome *a.* घिनौना ghinauna
lobby *n.* उपांतिका upantika
lobe *n.* पिंडक pindak
lobster *n.* महाचिंगट mahachingat
local *a.* स्थानीय sthaniya
locale *n.* घटना स्थल ghatna sthal
locality *n.* स्थान sthan
localize *v.t.* स्थानीय बनाना sthaniya
banana
locate *v.t.* स्थान से जोड़ना sthan se jodna
location *n.* स्थान sthan
lock *v.t* ताला लगाना tala lagana
lock *n* बंदूक का घोड़ा banduk ka ghoda
locker *n.* तालेदार अलमारी taledaar almarhi
locus *n.* रेखापथ rekhapath
locust *n.* टिड्डी tiddi
lodge *n.* तंबू tambu
lodge *v.t.* रखना rakhna
lodging *n.* अस्थायी आवास asthai aawas
loft *n.* अटारी atari
lofty *a.* अभिमानी avimani
log *n.* कुंदा kunda
logarithm *n.* प्रमापक pramapak
loggerhead *n.* मूढ़ mudh
logic *n.* तर्कशास्त्र tarkshastra
logical *a.* तर्कसम्मत tarksammat
logician *n.* तर्कशास्त्री tarksastri
loin *n.* नितंब nitamb
loiter *v.i.* आवारागर्दी करना aawargardi
karna

**lollipop** *n.* चूसने की मिठाई chusne ki mithai
**lone** *a.* अकेला akela
**loneliness** *n.* निर्जनता nirjanta
**lonely** *a.* निर्जन nirjan
**lonesome** *a.* निर्जन nirjan
**long** *adv* लंबे समय तक lambe samay tak
**long** *v.i* लालायित होना lalayit hona
**long** *a.* लंबा lamba
**longevity** *n.* दीर्घायुता dhirghayuta
**longing** *n.* तीव्र इच्छा tibra iccha
**longitude** *n.* देशांतर daishantar
**look** *v.i* अभिमुख होना abhimukh hona
**look** *a* रूप rup
**loom** *n* करघा kargha
**loom** *v.i.* धुंधला दिखाई देना dhundala dekhai dena
**loop** *n.* रेलवे शाखा railway shakha
**loop-hole** *n.* बचाव का रास्ता bachao ka rasta
**loose** *a.* बंधनमुक्त bandhanmukt
**loose** *v.t.* मुक्त करना mukt karna
**loosen** *v.t.* रिहा करना riha karna
**loot** *n.* लूटमार lutmar
**loot** *v.i.* लूटपाट करना lutpaat karna
**lop** *v.t.* छांटना chatna
**lop** *n.* काट छांट kaat chhant
**lord** *n.* प्रभु pravhu
**lordly** *a.* घमंडी ghamandi
**lordship** *n.* आधिपत्य adhipatya
**lore** *n.* विद्या vidha
**lorry** *n.* ठेला thela
**lose** *v.t.* खो देना kho dena
**loss** *n.* हानि haani
**lot** *n.* भाग्य bhagya
**lot** *n* बड़ी मात्रा badi matra
**lotion** *n.* लोशन loshan
**lottery** *n.* लॉटरी lotary
**lotus** *n.* कमल kamal
**loud** *a.* कोलाहलपूर्ण kolahalpurna

**lounge** *v.i.* मौज करना mauj karna
**lounge** *n.* बरामदा baramada
**louse** *n.* जूं joon
**lovable** *a.* प्रीतिकर pritikar
**love** *n* प्रणय pranaya
**love** *v.t.* प्रेम करना prem karna
**lovely** *a.* सुंदर sundar
**lover** *n.* प्रेमी premi
**loving** *a.* अनुरागशील anuragshil
**low** *adv.* निम्न स्थिति में nimn sthiti mein
**low** *a.* निचला nichla
**low** *v.i.* रंभाना rambhana
**low** *n.* रंभाहट rambhahat
**lower** *v.t.* झुकाना jhukana
**lowliness** *n.* दीनता dinta
**lowly** *a.* विनयशील vinayshil
**loyal** *a.* निष्ठावान nisthavan
**loyalist** *n.* राजभक्त rajbhakt
**loyalty** *n.* निष्ठा nistha
**lubricant** *n.* चिकनाई chiknai
**lubricate** *v.t.* चिकनाना chiknana
**lubrication** *n.* स्नेहन snehan
**lucent** *a.* चमकदार chamakdar
**lucerne** *n.* रिजका rijka
**lucid** *a.* चमकदार chamakdar
**lucidity** *n.* चमक chamak
**luck** *n.* भाग्य bhagya
**luckily** *adv.* सौभाग्य से saubhagya se
**luckless** *a.* अभागा abhaga
**lucky** *a.* भाग्यशाली vhagyasali
**lucrative** *a.* लाभप्रद labhprad
**lucre** *n.* धन dhan
**luggage** *n.* सामान saman
**lukewarm** *a.* गुनगुना gunguna
**lull** *n.* शांति काल shanti kaal
**lullaby** *n.* लोरी lori
**luminary** *n.* महान विद्वान् mahan vidwan
**luminous** *a.* प्रकाशमान prakashman
**lump** *n.* पिंड pind
**lump** *v.t.* ढेर लगाना dher lagana

lunacy *n.* पागलपन pagalpan
lunatic *n.* पागल व्यक्ति pagal vykti
lunatic *a.* पागल pagal
lunch *v.i.* भोजन करना bhojan karna
lunch *n.* दोपहर का भोजन dophar ka bhojan
lung *n* फेफड़ा fefra
lunge *n.* तलवार का वार talwar ka war
lunge *v.i* तलवार घोंपना talwar ghopna
lurch *v.i.* लड़खड़ाना ladkhadana
lure *n.* प्रलोभन pralobhan
lure *v.t.* प्रलोभित करना pralobhit karna
lurk *v.i.* दुबकना dubkana
luscious *a.* सुस्वाद suswad
lush *a.* रसीला rasila
lust *n.* काम वासना kaam vasna
lustful *a.* कामुक kamuk
lustre *n.* चमक chamak
lustrous *a.* चमकदार chamakdar
lusty *a.* हृष्ट पुष्ट harsht pusht
lute *n.* वीणा vina
luxuriance *n.* प्रचुरता prachurta
luxuriant *a.* प्रचुर prachur
luxurious *a.* विलासमय vilasmaya
luxury *n.* विलासिता vilasita
lyric *n.* गीतिकाव्य gitikawya
lyric *a.* गेय gay
lyricist *n.* प्रगीतकार pragatikaar

# M

magical *a.* जादू संबंधी jadu sambandhi
magician *n.* जादूगर jadugar
magistracy *n.* दंडाधिकरण dandadhikaran
magistrate *n.* दंडाधिकारी dandadhikari
magnanimity *n.* उदारहृदयता udarhridayata
magnanimous *a.* विशाल हृदय vishal hridya

magnate *n.* महापुरुष mahapursh
magnet *n.* चुंबक chumbak
magnetism *n.* चुंबकत्व chumbaktwa
magnificent *a.* शानदार saandar
magnify *v.t.* प्रशंसा करना prasansa karna
magnitude *n.* महानता mahaanta
magpie *n.* मुटरी mutari
mahout *n.* महावत mahawat
maid *n.* कुमारी kumari
maiden *n.* कन्या kanya
maiden *a* प्रथम pratham
mail *n.* डाक daak
mail *v.t.* डाक में डालना daak mai dalna
mail *n* कवच kavach
main *a* प्रधान pradhan
main *n* मुख्य भाग mukhya bhag
mainly *adv.* मुख्य रूप से mukhya ruup se
mainstay *n.* मुख्य सहारा mukhya sahara
maintain *v.t.* बनाए रखना banaye rakhna
maize *n.* मक्का makka
majestic *a.* राजसी raajhse
majesty *n.* प्रभुसत्ता prabhusatta
major *a.* गंभीर gambhir
major *n* मेजर major
majority *n.* बहुमत bahumat
make *v.t.* निर्माण करना nirmaan karna
make *n* प्रकार prakaar
maker *n.* निर्माता nirmaata
mal adjustment *n.* कुसमायोजन kusmayojan
mal administration *n.* कुशासन kushasan
maladroit *a.* अनाड़ी anaadi
malady *n.* बीमारी bemari
malafide *a.* जाली jaali
malafide *adv* बेईमानी से baimaani se
malaise *n.* अनमनापन anmanaapan
malaria *n.* मलेरिया malaria
malcontent *a.* असंतुष्ट asantust
malcontent *n* असंतुष्ट व्यक्ति asantust baykti

male *a.* पुलिंग puling
male *n* नर nar
malediction *n.* अभिशाप avisaap
malefactor *n.* अपराधी apraadhi
maleficent *a.* अपकारी apkaari
malice *n.* द्वेष भावना dyesh bhawana
malicious *a.* विद्वेषी vidyashi
malign *v.t.* निंदा करना ninda karna
malign *a* हानिकर haanikaar
malignancy *n.* विद्वेष vidyesh
malignant *a.* अहितकर ahitkaar
malignity *n.* गहन gahan
malmsey *n.* मधुर मदिरा madhur madira
malnutrition *n.* कुपोषण kuposhan
malpractice *n.* दुराचार durachar
malt *n.* शराब बनाना saraab banana
mal-treatment *n.* दुर्व्यवहार duwrybhar
mamma *n.* माता mata
mammal *n.* स्तनपायी sthanpaye
mam/mary *a.* स्तन संबंधी sthansambandhi
mammon *n.* संपत्ति sampatti
mammoth *n.* विशालकाय हाथी
vishaalkaaya haathi
mammoth *a* विशालकाय vishaalkaaya
man *n.* मानव manav
manage *v.t.* प्रबंध करना prabandh karna
manageable *a.* नियंत्रण योग्य niyantran
yogya
management *n.* प्रबंधन prabandhan
manager *n.* प्रबंधक prabandhak
managerial *a.* प्रबंध से संबंधित prabandh
se sambandhit
mandate *n.* आदेश aadesh
mandatory *a.* अनिवार्य aniwarya
mane *n.* अयाल ayaal
manes *n.* पितर pitar
manful *a.* पराक्रमी parakrami
manganese *n.* मैंगनीज़ manganese
manger *n.* नांद naand
mangle *v.t.* विकृत करना vikrit karna

mango *n* आम aam
manhandle *v.t.* मार पीट करना maar peet
karna
manhole *n.* प्रवेश pravesh
manhood *n.* पुरुषत्व purustwa
maniac *n.* पागल व्यक्ति paagal vaykti
manicure *n.* नख प्रसाधन nakh prasadhan
manifest *a.* व्यक्त vaykt
manifest *v.t.* प्रकट करना prakat karna
manifesto *n.* घोषणापत्र ghoshanapatra
manifold *a.* विविध vividh
manipulation *n.* छल साधन chhal sadhan
mankind *n.* मानव जाति manav jaati
manlike *a.* पुरुषोचित purushochit
manliness *n* पौरुष paurush
manly *a.* पुरुषोचित purushochit
manna *n.* दिव्यान्न divyaan
mannequin *n.* पुतला putlaa
manner *n.* रीति रिवाज riti riwaaj
mannerism *n.* कृत्रिमता kritrimata
mannerly *a.* शिष्ट sista
manoeuvre *n.* चालाकी chalaki
manoeuvre *v.i.* चालाकी कराना chalaki
karana
manor *n.* जागीर jaagir
manorial *a.* जागीर संबंधी jaagir
sambandhi
mansion *n.* विशाल भवन vishal vhawan
mantel *n.* कार्निस kaarnas
mantle *n* गैस लालटेन की बत्ती gas lalten ki
batti
mantle *v.t* ढक लेना, छिपाना dhak lena,
chhipana
manual *a.* हाथ का haath ka
manufacture *v.t.* निर्माण करना nirman
karna
manufacturer *n* उत्पादक utpaadak
manumission *n.* छुटकारा chhutkara
manumit *v.t.* मुक्त करना mukt karna
manure *n.* खाद khaad

manure *v.t.* खाद देना khaad dena

manuscript *n.* पांडुलिपि pandulipi

many *a.* अनेक aanek

map *v.t.* मानचित्र बनाना manchitra banana

map *n* मानचित्र manchitra

mar *v.t.* क्षति पहुंचाना chhati pahuchna

marathon *n.* लंबी दौड़ lambi daud

maraud *v.i.* लूटमार करते फिरना lutmaar karte firna

marauder *n.* लुटेरा lutera

marble *n.* संगमरमर sangmarmar

march *n* सीमांत simaant

march *n.* मार्च का महीना march ka mahina

mare *n.* घोड़ी ghodi

margarine *n.* कृत्रिम मक्खन kritrim makkhan

margin *n.* किनारा kinaara

marginal *a.* मामूली सा mamuli sa

marigold *n.* गेंदा genda

marine *a.* जलसेना संबंधी jalsena sambandhi

mariner *n.* पोतवाहक potwahak

marionette *n.* कठपुतली katputli

marital *a.* पति विषयक pati vishyak

maritime *a.* समुद्री तटीय samudri tatiya

mark *n.* निशाना nisaana

mark *v.t* अंकित करन ankit karan

marker *n.* अंकगणक ankganak

market *n* बाज़ार bazar

market *v.t* क्रय विक्रय करना kraya vikraya karna

marketable *a.* विक्रेय vikreya

marksman *n.* निशानेबाज़ nishanebaaj

marl *n.* चिकनी मिट्टी chikni mitti

marmalade *n.* फलपाग phallpaag

maroon *n.* भूरा लाल रंग bhura lal rang

maroon *a* भूरे लाल रंग का bhure lal rang ka

maroon *v.t* अलग थलग कर देना alag thalag kar dena

marriage *n.* शादी shadi

marriageable *a.* विवाह योग्य vivah yogya

marry *v.t.* शादी करना shadi karna

Mars *n* मंगल ग्रह mangal greh

marsh *n.* दलदल daldal

marshal *n* सेनापति sainapati

marshal *v.t* क्रमबद्घ करना krambadh karna

marshy *a.* दलदली daldali

marsupial *n.* शिशुधानी जीव shishudhani jeev

mart *n.* बाज़ार bazar

martial *a.* बहादुर bahadur

martinet *n.* कठोर अनुशासक kathor anushasak

martyr *n.* शहीद shahid

martyrdom *n.* आत्मबलिदान aatmabalidaan

marvel *n.* अद्भुत उदाहरण adhbhut udaharan

marvel *v.i* विस्मित हो जाना vismit ho jana

marvellous *a.* अद्भुत adbhut

mascot *n.* शुभंकर ताबीज़ subhankar tabiz

masculine *a.* पुंलिंग puling

mash *v.t* मसलना masalna

mash *n.* दलिया daliya

mask *n.* मुखौटा mukhauSta

mason *n.* राजगीर rajgeer

masonry *n.* राजगीरी rajgire

masquerade *n.* धोखा dhokha

mass *n.* पिंड pind

mass *v.i* जमा करना jama karna

massacre *n.* जनसंहार jansanhar

massacre *v.t.* जनसंहार करना jansanhar karna

massage *n.* मालिश maalish

massage *v.t.* मालिश करना maalish karna

masseur *n.* अंगमर्दक angmardak

massive *a.* विशाल vishal

massy *a.* भारी bhari

mast *n.* मस्तूल mastol

master *n.* स्वामी swami

master *v.t.* वशीभूत करना vashibhut karna

masterly *a.* स्वामिजनोचित swamijnochit

masterpiece *n.* सर्वोत्कृष्ट कृति sarvotkrist kriti

mastery *n.* प्रभुत्व prabhutwa

masticate *v.t.* चबाना chabana

masturbate *v.i.* हस्तमैथुन करना hastmaithun karna

mat *n.* चटाई chattai

matador *n .* वृषहंता vrish hanta

match *v.i.* समान होना samaan hona

match *n* दियासलाई diyasalai

match *n.* जोड़ jood

matchless *a.* बेजोड़ baijorh

mate *n.* साथी sathi

mate *v.t.* जोड़ा खाना joda khana

mate *n* शहमात sahamaat

mate *v.t.* शहमात देना shahmaat dena

material *a.* भौतिक bhautik

material *n* पदार्थ padarth

materialism *n.* मायाजाल mayajaal

materialize *v.t.* मूर्तरूप देना murtroop dena

maternal *a.* मातृक matrak

maternity *n.* मातृत्व matritwa

mathematical *a.* गणितशास्त्रीय ganitshastriya

mathematician *n.* गणितशास्त्री ganitshastri

mathematics *n* गणित ganit

matriarch *n.* कुलमाता kulmaata

matricidal *a.* मातृघातक matrighatak

matricide *n.* मातृवध matrivadh

matrimonial *a.* वैवाहिक vaivahik

matrimony *n.* परिणय parinaya

matrix *n* गर्भाशय सांचा garbhashay sancha

matron *n.* कार्याधीक्षिका karyadhikshaka

matter *n.* पदार्थ padarath

matter *v.i.* महत्वपूर्ण होना mathatwapurna hona

mattock *n.* गैंती gainte

mattress *n.* गद्दा gaddha

mature *a.* परिपक्व paripakwa

mature *v.i* विकसित होना viksit hona

maturity *n.* परिपक्वता paripakwata

maudlin *a* मूर्खतापूर्ण murkhtapurna

maul *n.* मूसल musal

maul *v.t* चोट पहुंचाना chot pahuchana

maulstick *n.* हाथ टेकने की छड़ी haath tekne ke chhadi

mausoleum *n.* मकबरा makbara

mawkish *a.* रूखा rukha

maxilla *n.* जंभिका jamvika

maxim *n.* उक्ति uktti

maximum *n* अधिकतम मात्रा adhiktam matra

maximum *a.* अधिकतम adhiktam

May *n.* मई मास may maas

may *v* संभावना sambhavana

mayor *n.* नगरप्रमुख nagarpramukh

maze *n.* भूलभुलैया bholbhulaya

me *pron.* मुझको mujhako

mead *n.* शहद की मदिरा shahad ki madira

meadow *n.* चारागाह charagaha

meagre *a.* थोड़ा thoda

meal *n.* भोजन का समय bhojan ka samay

mealy *a.* कोमल komal

mean *n.* साधन saadhan

mean *v.t* अभिप्राय रखना abhipray rakhna

mean *a.* मझला majhla

meander *v.i.* चक्कर लगाना chakkar lagana

meaning *n.* अभिप्राय abhipraya

meaningful *a.* सार्थक sarthak

meaningless *a.* निरर्थक nirarthak

meanness *n.* नीचता neechta

means *n* साधन sadhan

**meanwhile** *adv.* इसी बीच में ese beech mein

**measles** *n* खसरा khasra

**measurable** *a.* परिमेय parimay

**measure** *v.t* नापना naapna

**measure** *n.* योजना yojna

**measureless** *a.* असीमित aseemit

**measurement** *n.* नाप naap

**meat** *n.* मांस maans

**mechanic** *n.* मिस्त्री mistri

**mechanic** *a* यांत्रिक yaantrik

**mechanical** *a.* यांत्रिक yaantrik

**mechanics** *n.* यांत्रिकी yaantrika

**mechanism** *n.* तंत्र tantra

**medal** *n.* पदक padak

**medallist** *n.* पदक प्राप्त व्यक्ति padak prapt vaykti

**meddle** *v.i.* बाधा डालना baadha daalna

**median** *a.* मध्यगामी madhyagami

**mediate** *v.i.* मध्यस्थता करना madhyasthata karna

**mediation** *n.* मध्यस्थता madhyasthata

**mediation** *n.* ध्यान dhyaan

**mediator** *n.* मध्यस्थ madhyayasth

**medical** *a.* आयुर्वैज्ञानिक aayurvaigyanik

**medicament** *n.* औषध तत्व aushadh tatya

**medicinal** *a.* औषधीय aushadhiya

**medicine** *n.* औषधि aushadhi

**medico** *n.* चिकित्सक chikitsak

**medieval** *a.* मध्ययुग का madhyug ka

**mediocre** *a.* सामान्य saamanya

**mediocrity** *n.* सामान्य अवस्था saamanya avastha

**meditate** *v.t.* विचार करना vichar karna

**meditative** *a.* मननशील manansheel

**medium** *n* संचार-साधन sanchar-saadhan

**medium** *a* मंझला manjhala

**meek** *a.* विनम्र vinamra

**meet** *n.* बैठक baithak

**meet** *v.t.* पूरा करना puraa karna

**meeting** *n.* सभा sabha

**megalith** *n.* महा पाषाण maha paashan

**megalithic** *a.* महापाषाणीय mahapaashniya

**megaphone** *n.* ध्वनिप्रवर्धी dyanipravardhi

**melancholia** *n.* विषाद रोग vishaad rog

**melancholic** *a.* विषादग्रस्त vishaadgrast

**melancholy** *n.* खिन्नता khinnta

**melancholy** *adj* निराश nirash

**melee** *n.* हंगामा hungama

**meliorate** *v.t.* सुधारना sudharna

**mellow** *a.* समझदार samajhdaar

**melodious** *a.* सुरीला sureela

**melodrama** *n.* अतिनाटकीय व्यवहार ati-natakiya vyavhar

**melodramatic** *a.* सनसनीखेज़ sansani khez

**melody** *n.* राग raag

**melon** *n.* तरबूज़ tarbooj

**melt** *v.i.* गलाना galaana

**member** *n.* अंग angh

**membership** *n.* सदस्य sadasyata

**membrane** *n.* झिल्ली jhilli

**memento** *n.* स्मृतिचिह्न smritichinh

**memoir** *n.* आत्मचरित aatmacharit

**memorable** *a.* स्मरणीय smarniya

**memorandum** *n* स्मरण पत्र smaran patra

**memorial** *n.* स्मारक smarak

**memorial** *a* स्मरण विषयक smaran vishayak

**memory** *n.* यादगार yaadgaar

**menace** *n* धमकी dhamki

**menace** *v.t* धमकी देना dhamki dena

**mend** *v.t.* ठीक करना theek karna

**mendacious** *a.* मिथ्यावादी mithyawadi

**menial** *a.* दासोचित dasochhit

**menial** *n* सेवक sewak

**meningitis** *n.* गर्दन तोड़ बुखार gardan torh bukhar

**menopause** *n.* रजोनिवृत्ति rajoniwirti

**menses** *n.* ऋतुस्राव ritustrav

menstrual *a.* ऋतुस्राव विषयक ritu-strav vishayak

menstruation *n.* ऋतुस्राव ritu-strav

mental *a.* मानसिक maansik

mentality *n.* मनोवृत्ति manovriti

mention *n.* उल्लेख ullekh

mention *v.t.* चर्चा करना charcha karna

mentor *n.* सलाहकार salaahkaar

menu *n.* भोज्य सूची bhojaya suchi

mercantile *a.* वाणिज्य- संबंधी wanijya-sambandhi

mercenary *a.* लालची laalchi

merchandise *n.* सौदा sauda

merchant *n.* व्यापारी vyapaari

merciful *a.* दयालु dayalu

merciless *adj.* निष्ठुर nisthur

mercurial *a.* चंचल chanchal

mercury *n.* पारद paarad

mercy *n.* दया daya

mere *a.* केवल keval

merge *v.t.* मिला लेना mila lena

merger *n.* विलयन williyan

meridian *a.* दोपहरी का dophari ka

merit *n.* सद् गुण sadgun

merit *v.t* योग्य होना yogya hona

meritorious *a.* योग्य yogya

mermald *n.* जलपरी jalpari

merman *n.* जलपुरुष jalpurush

merriment *n.* आनंद anand

merry *a* सानंद sanand

mesh *n.* जाली jaali

mesmerism *n.* सम्मोहन sammohan

mesmerize *v.t.* मंत्रमुग्ध करना mantramugadh karna

mess *n.* भोजनालय bhojnaalya

mess *v.i* भोजन करना bhojan karna

message *n.* समाचार samachar

messenger *n.* संदेशवाहक sandeswahak

messiah *n.* ईसा मसीह isa masih

Messrs *n.* सर्वश्री sarawsri

metal *n.* रोड़ी rodi

metallic *a.* धातुवत्र dhatuwatra

metallurgy *n.* धातुकर्म विज्ञान dhatukarma vigyan

metamorphosis *n.* रूपांतरण rupantran

metaphor *n.* रूपक rupak

metaphysical *a.* गूढ़ gurh

metaphysics *n.* तत्वमीमांसा tatwamimansa

mete *v.t* बांटना baantana

meteor *n.* उल्का ulka

meteoric *a.* चमकीला chamkeela

meteorologist *n.* ऋतुविज्ञानी rituwigyani

meteorology *n.* मौसम विज्ञान mausam vigyan

meter *n.* मापक maapak

method *n.* विधि vidhi

methodical *a.* सुव्यवस्थित suwaywasthit

metre *n.* मीटर meter

metric *a.* मीटर संबंधी metersambandhi

metrical *a.* छंद संबंधी chhand sambandhi

metropolis *n.* महानगर mahanagar

metropolitan *n.* महानगर का mahanagar ka

mettle *n.* उत्साह utsah

mettlesome *a.* साहसी sahasi

mew *n.* म्याऊँ mewaun

mica *n.* अभ्रक abrak

microfilm *n.* अणुचित्र anuchitra

micrometer *n.* सूक्ष्ममापी suuksmmaape

microphone *n.* ध्वनिविस्तारक dyanivistarak

microscope *n.* सूक्ष्मदर्शी यंत्र sukshamdarshi yantra

microscopic *a.* अति सूक्ष्म ati suksham

microwave *n.* सूक्ष्म तरंग suksham tarang

mid *a.* मध्यवर्ती madhyavarti

midday *n.* मध्याह्न madhyaharn

middle *n* मध्य बिंदु madhya bindu

middle *a.* मध्यवर्ती madhyawarti

middleman *n.* बिचौलिया bechaouliya

middling *a.* साधारण saadharan

midget *n.* बौना bona

midland *n.* मध्यदेश madhyadesh

midnight *n.* अद्धरात्रि ardharatri

midriff *n.* मध्य-जिली madhya-jhilli

midst मध्य madhy

midsummer *n.* मध्यग्रीष्म ऋतु madhygrisham ritu

midwife *n.* दाई daayi

might *n.* पराक्रम parakram

mighty *adj.* बहादुर bahadur

midwifery *n.* प्रसूती विद्या prasuti vidya

migrant *n.* प्रवासी pravaasi

migrate *v.i.* प्रव्रजन करना pravarjan karna

migration *n.* प्रव्रजन pravarjan

migrator *a.* व्यवहार yayawar

mild *a.* नम namra

mildew *n.* फफूंदी fafundi

mile *n.* मील meel

mill *n.* कारखाना karkhaana

milestone *n.* मील का पत्थर meel ka patthar

mildness *n.* कोमलता komalta

militant *a.* योद्धा yodha

militarization *n* युद्धकर्त्ता sainyikaran

militarily *a.* सैनिक ढंग से sainik dhang se

military *n* सेना sena

militate *v.i.* युद्ध करना yudh karna

militia *n.* नागरिक सेना naagrik saina

milk *v.t.* दूध देना dudh dena

milk *n.* दूध dudh

milky *a.* दूधिया dudhiya

mill *v.t.* पीसना peesna

milkiness *n* दुधियापन dudhiapan

millennium *n.* सहस्राब्दी sahsrabdi

miller *n.* आटा पीसने वाला aata pisne wala

millet *n.* बाजरा baajra

million *n.* दस लाख das lakh

millionaire *n.* करोड़पति karorpati

mime *n.* प्रहसन prahasan

mime *v.i* स्वांग भरना svang bharna

mimesis *n.* अनुकरण anukaran

mimic *a.* अनुकरणात्मक anukarnatmak

mimic *n* नकलची nakalchi

mimic *v.t* नकल उतारना nakal utarna

mimicry *n* नकल nakal

minaret *n.* मीनार minaar

mince *v.t.* पिसी हुई चीज़ pisi hui cheez

mind *n.* बुद्धि, मन budhi, man

mind *v.t.* बुरा मानना bura manana

mindful *a.* सावधान savdhan

mindless *a.* मूर्ख murkh

mine *pron.* मेरा mera

mine *n* खान khan

miner *n.* खनिक khanik

mineral *a* खनिज संबंधी khanij sambandhi

mineral *n.* खनिज khanij

mineralogist *n.* खनिज विज्ञानी khanij vigyaani

mineralogy *n.* खनिज शास्त्र khanij shastra

mingle *v.t.* मिलाना milaana

miniature *a.* छोटा chota

miniature *n.* लघु प्रतिरूप laghhu pratirup

minify *vt* छोटा करना chhota karna

minimal *a.* अल्पतम alpatam

minimize *v.t.* कम करना kam karna

minimum *a* अल्पतम alpatam

minimum *n.* न्यूनतम मात्रा nyunatam matra

minion *n.* चापलूस chaploos

minister *v.i.* सेवा करना sewa karna

minister *n.* मंत्री mantri

ministrant *a.* सेवक sewak

ministry *n.* मंत्रिमंडल mantrimandal

minor *n* अवयस्क व्यक्ति awayasak vyakti

minor *a.* छोटा chhota

minority *n.* अल्प संख्या alp sankhya

mint *n.* पुदीना pudina

mint *n* टकसाल taksaal

mint *v.t.* ढालना dhaalna

minus *a* नकारात्मक nakaratmak

minus *n* ऋण का चिह्न rean ka chihan

minus *prep.* के बिना ke bena

minuet *a.* नृत्य-संगीत nritya sangit

minute *n.* मिनट minute

minutely *adv.* बारीकी से bariki se

minx *n.* ढीठ लड़की dhit ladki

miracle *n.* चमत्कार chamatkaar

miraculous *a.* चमत्कारिक chamatkarik

mirage *n.* मरीचिका marichika

mire *v.t.* दलदल में फंसाना daldal mai fansana

mire *n.* कीचड़ kichhad

mirror *v.t.* प्रतिबिंबित करना pratibembit karna

mirror *n* दर्पण darpan

mirth *n.* आनंद anand

mirthful *a.* आनंदपूर्ण anandpurna

misadventure *n.* दुर्घटना durghatna

misalliance *n.* बेमेल संबंध be-mail sambandh

misanthrope *n.* मानवद्वेषी manavdyashi

misapplication *n.* अनुचित प्रयोग anuchhit prayog

misapprehend *v.t.* ग़लत समझना galat samjhana

misapprehension *n* मिथ्या बोध mithya bodh

misappropriate *v.t.* ग़बन करना gaban karna

misappropriation *n.* ग़बन gaban

misbehave *v.i.* बुरा व्यवहार करना bura vaywahar karna

misbehaviour *n.* बुरा व्यवहार bura vaywahar

misbelief *n.* भ्रांत धारणा bhrant dharna

miscalculate *v.t.* ग़लत गणना करना galat ganna karna

miscalculation *n.* अशुद्घ गणना asudh ganna

miscarriage *n.* गर्भ-पात garabh-paat

miscarry *v.i.* विफल होना vifal hona

miscellaneous *a.* विभिन्न vibhinn

miscellany *n.* विविधतापूर्ण संग्रह vividhtapurna sangrah

mischance *n.* दुर्भाग्य durbhagya

mischief *n* शरारत shararat

mischievous *a.* हानिप्रद hanipradh

misconceive *v.t.* ग़लत समझना galat samjhana

misconception *n.* ग़लत धारणा galat dharna

misconduct *n.* दुराचरण duracharan

misconstrue *v.t.* ग़लत समझना galat samjhana

miscreant *n.* बदमाश badmash

misdeed *n.* दुष्कर्म duskarm

misdemeanour *n.* दुराचरण duracharan

misdirect *v.t.* गुमराह करना gumraha karna

misdirection *n.* अपनिदेशन apnidesan

miser *n.* कंजूस kanjous

miserable *a.* निकम्मा nikamma

miserably *vt* दुख से dukh se

misery *n.* कंगाली kangaali

misfire *v.i.* चालू न होना chalu na hona

misfortune *n.* दुर्भाग्य durbhagya

misgiving *n.* संदेह sandheh

misguide *v.t.* गुमराह करना gumraha karna

mishap *n.* दुर्घटना durghatna

misjudge *v.t.* ग़लत निर्णय करना galat nirnaya karna

mislead *v.t.* बहकाना bahakana

mismanagement *n.* कुप्रबंध kuprabandh

misnomer *n.* मिथ्या नाम mithya naam

misprint *n.* अशुद्घ मुद्रण ashudh mudran

misprint *v.t.* ग़लत छापना galat chhpana

misrule *n.* कुशासन kushasan

miss *v.t.* खोना khona

miss *n.* कुमारी kumari

missile *n.* प्रक्षेपास्त्र prachepaastra

mission *n.* शिष्ट मंडल shisht mandal

missionary *n.* धर्म प्रचारक dharma pracharak

missive *n.* लिखित संदेश sandesh patra

missus *n..* सुश्री sushri

mist *n.* कुहरा kuhara

mistake *n.* भूल bhoul

mister *n.* श्रीमान srimaan

mistletoe *n.* आकाश बेल aakash bail

mistreat *d* दुर्व्यवहार करना durvyawahar karna

mistress *n.* रखैल rakhel

mistrust *v.t.* अविश्वास करना aviswas karna

mistrust *n.* अविश्वास aviswas

mistrial *a.* ग़लत जांच galat jaanch

misunderstand *v.t.* ग़लत समझना galat samjhana

misunderstanding *n.* ग़लतफ़हमी galatfahami

misuse *n.* दुरुपयोग durpayog

misuse *v.t.* दुरुपयोग करना durpayog karna

mite *n.* छोटी वस्तु chhoti vastu

mite *n* मकड़ी makri

mithridate *n.* ज़हर की दवा jahar ki dawa

mitigate *v.t.* कम करना kam karna

mitigation *n.* अल्पीकरण alpikaran

mitre *n.* लम्बी टोपी lambi topi

mix *v.i* मिलना milana

mixture *n.* मिश्रण misran

moan *v.i.* विलाप करना vilaap karna

moan *n.* विलाप vilaap

moat *n.* खंदक khandak

mob *n.* जनसाधारण jansaadharan

mobile *a.* गतिशील gatiseel

mobility *n.* गतिशीलता gatisheelta

mobilize *v.t.* संचालित करना sanchalit karna

mock *v.i.* हंसी उड़ाना hansi udaana

mock *adj* दिखावटी dekhavati

mockery *n.* मज़ाक majjak

modality *n.* रीति riti

mode *n.* विधि vidhi

model *v.t.* रूप देना rup dena

model *n.* नमूना adarsh

moderate *a.* मध्यम madhyam

moderate *v.t.* धीमा करना dhima karna

moderation *n.* संतुलन santulan

modern *a.* आधुनिक adhunik

modernity *n.* आधुनिकता aadhunikta

modernize *v.t.* आधुनिकीकरण करना aadhunikikaran karna

modest *a.* विनम्र vinamra

modesty *n* संकोच sankoch

modicum *n.* अल्प परिमाण alp pariman

modification *n.* परिवर्तन parivartan

modify *v.t.* बदलना badalna

modulate *v.t.* ठीक करना theek karna

moil *v.i.* कठोर परिश्रम करना kathor parisram karna

moist *a.* गीला geela

moisten *v.t.* नम करना nam karna

moisture *n.* नमी nami

molar *a* सामूहिक samuhik

molar *n.* दाढ़ daarh

molasses *n* शीरा sheera

mole *n.* छछूंदर chhachhuchhandar

molecularity *a.* अनविक्ता aanvikta

molecule *n.* अणु anu

molest *v.t.* तंग करना tang karna

molestation *n.* छेड़खानी chher-khani

moly *n* जंगली लहसुन jangli lahsun

moment *n.* क्षण chhan

momentary *a.* क्षणिक chhanik

momentous *a.* महत्वपूर्ण mahatvapurna

momentum *n.* गति मात्रा gati matara

monarch *n.* राजा raja

monarchy *n.* राज-तंत्र raj-tantra

monastery *n.* मठ math

monasticism *n* संन्यासभाव sanyaasbhav

Monday *n.* सोमवार somvaar

monetary a. आर्थिक aarthik

money n. मुद्रा mudra

monger n. व्यवसायी vyavasayi

mongoose n. नेवला naiwala

mongrel a संकर जाति sankar jatiya

monitor n. कक्षा नायक kaksha nayak

monitory a. प्रबोधक prabodhak

monk n. मठवासी mathvashi

monkey n. बंदर bandar

monocle n चश्मा, ऐनक chashma, ainak

monody n. शोकगीत shokgeet

monogamy n. एकविवाह प्रथा ekwiwah pratha

monogram n. नाम चिह्न naam chinha

monograph n. प्रबंध prabandh

monolith n. एकाश्म akasham

monologue n. एकालाप akalap

monopolist n. एकाधिकारी akadhikari

monopolize v.t. एकाधिकार करना ekadhikaar karna

monopoly n. एकाधिकार akadhikar

monosyllabic a. एकाक्षरीय akakakshariya

monosyllable n. एकाक्षर akakshar

monotheism n. एकेश्वरवाद ekaksharvad

monotheist n. एकेश्वरवाद ekaksharvad

monotonous a. नीरस niras

monotony n नीरसता nirasta

monsoon n. मौसमी हवा mausami hava

monster n. राक्षस rakshas

monstrous a. असंगत asangat

monstrous n. विशालकाय vishal-kaaya

month n. महीना mahina

monthly adv प्रतिमाह pratimaah

monthly n मासिक maasik

montane n पहाड़ी pahari

monument n. स्मारक smaarak

monumental a. स्मारकीय smarkiya

moo v.i रंभाना rambhana

mood n. मनोदशा manodasha

moody a. उदास udaas

moon n. चंद्रमा chandrama

moor n. बंजर प्रदेश banjar pradesh

moor v.t बांधना bandhana

moor cock n. जंगली मुर्गा jangli murgha

moot n. बहस bahas

mop v.t. झाड़पोंछ करना jhar-ponchh karna

mop n. झाड़ू jharhu

mope v.i. उदास होना udaas hona

moral n. सीख seekh

moral a. सदाचार पूर्ण sadachaar purna

morale n. मनोबल manobal

moralist n. नैतिकतावादी naitekthawadi

morality n. सदाचार sadachhar

moralize v.t. नीतिगत बात करना nitigat baat karna

morbid a. बीमार bimar

morbidity n रूग्णता ruganta

more adv अधिक adhik

morel n गुछी guchhi

moreover adv. इसके अतिरिक्त iske atirikt

morganatic marriage a. अनुलोम विवाह anulom vivah

morning prayer n. प्रातःकालीन प्रार्थना prataha kalin prarthana

moribund a. मरणासन्न marnasan

morning n. सुबह subah

moron n. मंदबुद्धि व्यक्ति mandabudhi vyakti

morose a. उदास udaas

morphology n. आकृति विज्ञान akriti vigyan

morrow n. आगामी दिन agami din

morsel n. निवाला niwaala

mortal n नश्वर nashwar

mortal a. नाशवान naashwan

mortality n. मरण स्थल maran-shilta

mortar v.t. गोलाबारी करना golabari karna

mortgage v.t. बंधक रखना bandhak rakhna

mortgage n. बंधक bandhak

mortgagee n. गिरवीदार girvidaar

mortgagor n. गिरवी रखने वाला girwi rakhne wala

mortify v.t. अपमानित करना apmanit karna

mortuary n. मुर्दाघर murda ghar

mosaic n. पच्चीकारी vibhin rang

mosque n. मस्जिद masjid

mosquito n. मच्छर machhar

moss n. दलदल daldal

most a. सबसे अधिक sabse adhik

most adv. सर्वाधिक मात्रा में sarvadhik matra mai

mote n. धूलिकण dhulikan

moth n. पतंगा patanga

mother v.t. मां होना maa hona

mother n माता maata

mother like a. मातृसुलभ matrisulabh

motherhood n. मातृत्व matritva

motherly a. मां जैसा maa jaisa

motif n. मूल भाव mul bhav

motion v.i. इशारा करना ishara karna

motion n. प्रस्ताव prastav

motionless a. स्थिर esthir

motivate v प्रेरित करना prerit karna

motivation n. प्रेरणा prerna

motive n. इरादा irada

motley a. बहुरंगी bahurangi

motor n कार car

motor vt गाड़ी gaari

motorist n. मोटर चालक motar chalak

mottle vt चित्रित करना chitrit karna

motto n. आदर्श वाक्य adarsh vakya

mould v.t. आकार देना akaar dena

mould n फफूंदी phaphundi

moulder vt गल जाना gal jaana

mould n. सांचा sancha

mouldy a. फफूंदीदार fafundidaar

mound n. टीला teela

mount v.t. सवार होना sawaar hona

mount n धारक dharak

mount n. पहाड़ी paharhi

mountain n. पहाड़ pahar

mountaineer n. पहाड़ पर चढ़ने वाला pahar par chadhne wala

mountainous a. पहाड़ी pahari

mourn v.i. विलाप करना vilap karna

mourner n. विलाप करनेवाला vilap karnewala

mournful n. शोकाकुल shokakul

mourning n. मातम maatam

mouse n. चूहा chuha

moustache n. मूंछ moonch

mouth n. मुंह munh

mouthful n. निवाला niwaala

movable a. चलने योग्य chalaane yogya

movables n. चल संपत्ति chhal sampati

move n. चाल chhal

move v.t. हटाना hatana

movement n. आंदोलन aandolan

mover n. प्रस्तावक prastavak

movies n. चलचित्र chalchitra

mow v.t. काटना kaatna

much adv अधिक मात्रा में adhik matra mein

much a अधिक adhik

mucilage n. चिपचिपा पदार्थ chipchipa padarth

muck n. गोबर koora

mucus a. कफ़ जैसा kaf jaisa

mucro n. नुकीला nukila

mud n. कीचड़ kichhad

muddle v.t. भ्रम में डालना bhram mein dalna

muddle n. गड़बड़ी garhbarhi

muffle v.t. ढकना dhakna

muffler n. गुलूबंद guluband

mug n. जलपात्र jalpatra

muggy a. धुंधभरा dhundbhara

mulatto n. सांवला saanwala

mulberry n. शहतूत shahatut

mule *n.* खच्चर khachhar

mulish *a.* खच्चर जैसा khachhar jaisa

mull *n.* घालमेल ghalmail

mull *v.t.* गड़बड़ करना garhbarh karna

mullah *n.* मुल्ला mulla

mullion *n* खिड़की khirki

multifarious *a.* विभिन्न प्रकार के vibhin prakar ka

multifarious *a.* बहुप्रसवा vividh

multiform *n.* बहुरूपी bahurupi

multilateral *a.* बहुदेशीय bahudaishiya

multiple *adj* बहु-भागीय bahu-bhagiya

multiple *a.* बहुखंडीय bahukhandiya

multiplex *a.* बहुविध bahuvidh

multiplicand *n.* गुण्य राशि gunya rashi

multiplication *n.* गुणन gunan

multiplicity *n.* बहुलता bahulata

multiply *v.t.* गुणा करना guna karna

multitude *n.* समूह samuh

mum *a.* चुप chhup

mum *n* चुप्पी chhupi

mumble *v.i.* बुदबुदाना budbudana

mummer *n.* मूक अभिनेता muk abhineta

mummy *n* रक्षित मृत शरीर rakshit mrit sharir

mummy *adj* माता maata

mumps *n.* कनपेड़ा kanpeda

munch *v.t.* चबाना chabana

mundane *a.* सांसारिक sansaarik

municipal *a.* नगरपालिका संबंधी nagarpalika sambandhi

municipality *n.* नगरपालिका nagarpalika

munificent *a.* दानशील daansheel

muniments *n.* अधिकार पत्र adhikar patra

munition *n.* युद्घ सामग्री yudh saamagri

mural *n.* भित्तिचित्र bhittichitra

mural *a.* भित्तीय bhittiya

murder *n.* हत्या hatya

murder *v.t.* हत्या करना hatya karna

murderer *n.* हत्यारा hatyara

murderous *a.* प्राणघातक pran ghatak

murmur *v.t.* बड़बड़ाना barhbarhana

murmur *n.* गुनगुनाहट gungunahat

muscle *n.* मांसपेशी manspeshi

muscovite *n.* श्वेत shwet

muscular *a.* शक्तिशाली shaktishali

muse *v.i.* ध्यान लगाना dhyan lagana

muse *n* सरस्वती saraswati(Hindu goddess)

museum *n.* अजायबघर ajayabghar

mush *n.* दलिया daliya

mushroom *n.* कुकुरमुत्ता kukurmutta

music *n.* संगीत sangit

musical *a.* सांगीतिक saangitik

musician *n.* संगीतकार sangitkaar

musk *n.* कस्तूरी kasturi

musket *n.* बंदूक banduk

musketeer *n.* बंदूकधारी सिपाही bandukdhari sipahi

muslin *n.* मलमल malmal

must *v.* अनिवार्य होना aniwarya hona

must *n.* अनिवार्यता aniwaryata

must *n* भुक्रि bhukri

mustang *n.* जंगली घोड़ा jangli ghoda

mustard *n.* सरसों sarson

muster *n* सैनिक नामावली sainik namavali

muster *v.t.* एकत्र होना ekatra hona

musty *a.* फफूंददार fafundar

mutation *n.* परिवर्तन parivartan

mutative *a.* परिवर्तनशील pariwartansil

mute *a.* गूंगा gunga

mute *vt* आवाज धीमी करना awaz dhimi karna

mutilate *v.t.* अंगभंग करना angbhang karna

mutilation *n.* अंगच्छेद angchhed

mutinous *a.* बागी baghi

mutiny *v. i* बग़ावत करना bagavat karna

mutiny *n.* ग़दर gadar

mutter *v.i.* बड़बड़ाना badbadana

mutton *n.* मांस maans

mutual *a.* आपसी aapsi
muzzle *v.t* छींका लगाना chinka lagana
muzzle *n.* मुहरा muhara
my *a.* मेरा mera
myalgia *n.* पुट्ठो में दर्द puttho mai dard
myopia *n.* अल्पदृष्टि alpdristi
myopic *a.* निकटदृष्टिक nikatdristi
myosis *vt* आंख की पूतली का सुकड़ना ankh putli ka sukarna
myriad *a* असंख्य asankhya
myriad *n.* विशाल संख्या vishal sankhya
myrrh *n.* गंधरस gandhras
myrtle *n.* हिना hina
myself *pron.* स्वयं swayam
mysterious *a.* रहस्यमय rahasmay
mystery *n.* रहस्य rahasya
mystic *n* रहस्यवादी rahasywadi
mysticism *n.* रहस्यवाद rahasywad
mystify *v.t.* भ्रमित करना bhramit karna
myth *n.* पौराणिक कथा pauranik katha
mythical *a.* पुराणकथा संबंधी purankatha sambandhi
mythological *a.* पौराणिक pauranik
mythology *n.* पुराण संग्रह purana sangrah
mythopoetry *n* पौराणिक कविता pauranik kavita

nab *v.t.* बंदी बनाना bandi banana
nabob *n.* नवाब nawab
nadir *n.* पादबिंदु padbindu
nag *v.t.* कष्ट देना kasht dena
nag *n.* टट्टू tattu
nail *v.t.* कीलों से जड़ना kilon se jadna
nail *n.* नाखून nakhun
naive *a.* भोला-भाला bhola-bhala
naivete *a.* भोला bhola
naivety *n.* भोला-पन bhola pan

naked *a.* नंगा nanga
name *n.* नाम naam
name *v.t.* नाम रखना naam rakhna
namesake *n.* नामराशि naamrashi
nap *v.i.* झपकी लेना jhapki lena
nap *n.* झपकी jhapki
nap *n* लोम-हेन्न lom-hiin
napery *n.* भोजन- मेज की चादर bhojan-mez ki chadar
napkin *n.* रूमाल rumal
narcissism *n.* आत्मरति atm-rati
narcissus *n* नरगिस nargis
narcosis *n.* उनींदापन unidrapan
narcotic *n.* नशीली औषधि nasile aushadhi
narrate *v.t.* बताना batana
narration *n.* कथन kathan
narrative *a.* कथात्मक kathatmak
narrative *n.* वर्णन varnan
narrator *n.* वाचक vachak
narrow *v.t.* संकरा करना sankara karna
narrow *a.* तंग tang
nasalize *vt* नाक से बोलना naak se bolna
nasal *n* नासिक्य naasikya
nascent *a.* नवजात nav-jaat
nasty *a.* गंदा ganda
nasal *a.* जन्म संबन्धि janam sambandhi
natant *a* तैरने वाला tairane wala
nation *n.* राष्ट्र rashtra
national *a.* राष्ट्रीय rashtriya
nationalism *n.* राष्ट्रप्रेम rashtraprem
nationalist *n.* राष्ट्रवादी rashtriyawadi
nationality *n.* राष्ट्रीयता rashtriyata
nationalization *n.* राष्ट्रीयकरण rashtriyakaran
nationalize *v.t.* राष्ट्रीय बनाना rashtriya banana
native *n* मूल निवासी mul nivasi
native *a.* जन्मजात janamjaat
nativity *n.* जन्म janam
natural *a.* प्राकृतिक prakritik

naturalist *n.* प्रकृतिविज्ञानी prakritivigyani

naturalism *a* प्रकृति-वाद prakriti-vad

naturally *adv.* प्रकृति रूप से prakritik rup se

nature *n.* प्रकृति prakriti

naughty *a.* नट-खट nat-khat

nausea *n.* मतली matali

nautical *a.* समुद्रिक samudrik

naval *a.* जहाज़ी jahazi

nave *n.* चक्रनाभि chakranabhi

navigable *a.* नौगम्य naugamya

navigate *v.i.* नौचालन करना nauchhalan karna

navigation *n.* नौचालन nauchalan

navigator *n.* नौ-चालक nau-chalak

navy *n.* नौ-सेना nau-sena

nay *adv.* नहीं nahi

neap *a.* नीचा nicha

near *prep.* के पास ke paas

near *adv.* निकट nikat

near *v.i.* पास आना paas aana

near *a.* घनिष्ट ghanishth

nearly *adv.* निकट से nikat se

neat *a.* निर्मल nirmal

nebula *n.* आंख की फूली aankah kai phuli

necessary *a* अनिवार्य anivarya

necessary *n.* आवश्यक वस्तु avyashak vastu

necessitate *v.t.* आवश्यक बनाना avyaskhak banana

necessity *n.* आवश्यकता avashyakta

neck *n.* गर्दन gardan

necklace *n.* कंठहार kanth-haar

necklet *n.* कंठाभूषण kanthabhushan

necromancer *n.* ओझा ojha

necropolis *n.* कब्रिस्तान kabristan

nectar *n.* अमृत amrit

need *v.t.* आकांक्षा करना akansha karna

need *n.* आवश्यकता avashyakta

needful *a.* आवश्यक avyashak

necromancy जादुई क्रिया jadui kriya

needless *a.* अनावश्यक anavyshak

needments *adv.* आवश्यक सामान avashyak saman

needy *a.* निर्धन nirdhan

nefarious *a.* दुष्टतापूर्ण dushtatapurna

negation *n.* विरोध virodh

negative *n.* नकारात्मक nakaratmak

negativvity *adv.* निषेदामित्का nishedhatimikta

negative *a.* प्रतिरूप pratirup

neglect *v.t.* उपेक्षा करना upekchha karna

neglect *n* उपेक्षा upeksha

negligence *n.* उपेक्षा upeksha

negligent *a.* लापरवाह la parvah

negligible *a.* महत्त्वहीन mahatvahin

negotiable *a.* वार्ता योग्य varta yogya

negotiate *v.t.* सौदा करना sauda karna

negotiation *n.* वार्ता varta

negotiator *n.* वार्ताकार vartakaar

negress *n.* निग्रो महिला negro mahila

negro *n.* हबशी habshi

neigh *n.* हिनहिनाहट hinhinahat

neigh *v.i.* हिनहिनाना hinhinana

neighbour *n.* पड़ोसी padosi

neighbourhood *n.* पड़ोस pados

neighbourly *a.* पड़ोसी के नाते parosi ke naate

neither *conj.* कोई भी नहीं koi vi nahi

nemesis *n.* प्रतिरोध देवी pratirodh devi

neolithic *a.* उत्तर पाषाणकालीन uttar pashankalin

neonsign *n.* विद्युत संकेत vidyut sanket

nephew *n.* भतीजा या भांजा bhatija ya bhanja

nepotism *n.* भाई-भतीजावाद bhai-bhatijavad

nephritis *n.* गुर्दा-शोध gurda-shoth

nerve *n* नस nass

nerveless *a.* शक्तिहीन shaktihin

nervous *a.* डरपोक darpok

nest *n.* निवास nivas

nestor *v.t.* अनुभवी anubhavi

nestle *v.i.* चैन से बैठना chain se baithna

nestorian *n.* सिद्धांत वादी sidhant vadi

nestling *n* पक्षी का नवजात बच्चा pakshi ka navjaat baccha

nest *n* ठिकाना thikaana

net *n.* जाल jaal

nether *a.* निचला nichla

nettle *n.* बिच्छू बूटी bichhu buti

nettle *v.t.* डंक मारना dank marna

network *n.* तंत्र tantra

neurologist *n.* तंत्रिका विज्ञानी tantrika vigyani

neurology *n.* तंत्रिका विज्ञान tantrika vigyan

neurosis *n.* स्नायु रोग snayu rog

neuter *a.* नपुंसक napunsak

neuter *n* निराला nirala

neutral *a.* निशप्रकाश nishpaksh

neutralize *v.t.* तटस्थ बनाना tathasth banana

neutron *n.* विद्युत कण vidyut kan

never *adv.* कभी नहीं kabhi nahin

nevertheless *conj.* तिस पर भी tis par bhi

new *a.* ताज़ा taza

news *n.* खबर khabar

next *adv.* इसके उपरांत iss ke uprant

next *a.* अगला agla

nib *n.* निब nib

nibble *n* कुतरने की क्रिया kutarne ki kriya

nibble *v.t.* नुकता चीनी करना nukta chini karna

nice *a.* सु-सुभाव su-svabhav

nicety *n.* शिष्टाचार shishtachar

niche *n.* झरोखा jharokha

nick *vt* दंते-दार बनाना dante-daar banana

nickel *n.* गिलट gilat

nickname *v.t.* उपनाम देना upnam dena

nickname *n.* उपनाम upnaam

nicotine *n.* निकोटीन nikotin

niece *n.* भांजी bhanji

niggard *n.* कंजूस kanjus

niggardly *a.* कम-खर्च kam-kharch

nigger *n.* काले रंग की तितली kale rang ki titli

niggerdom *n* हबशियों का परदेश habshiyon ka prades

night long *prep.* रात भर raat bhar

night *n.* रात्रि ratri

nightingale *n.* बुलबुल bhulbhul

nightly *adv.* रात का raat ka

nihilism *n.* नाशवाद nash-vad

nil *n.* कुछ नहीं kuchh nahi

nimble *a.* चपल chapal

nimbus *n.* प्रभा मंडल prabha mandal

nine *n.* नौ nau

nineteen *n.* उन्नीस unnis

nineteenth *a.* उन्नीसवां unnisvan

ninetieth *a.* नब्बेवां nabbevan

ninety *n.* नब्बे nabbe

ninth *a.* नवां nava

nip *v.t* नोचना nochna

nipple *n.* स्तनाग्र stanagra

nitrogen *n.* गंधहीन gandh-hin

nitwit मंद बुद्धि mand budhi

no *adv.* नहीं nahin

no *n* इंकार inkar

nobility *n.* कुलीन वर्ग kulin warg

noble *a.* उत्तम uttam

noble *n.* कुलीन व्यक्ति kulin baykti

nobleman *n.* कुलीनपुरुष kulin prush

nobody *pron.* कोई नहीं koi nahi

nocturnal *a.* रात का raat ka

nod *v.i.* सिर हिलाना seer hilana

node *n.* ग्रंथि granthi

noise *n.* शोर soar

noisy *a.* कोलाहलकारी kolahalkari

nomad *n.* खानाबदोश khanabdosh

nomadic *a.* भ्रमणशील vhramansil

nomenclature *n.* नामावली namawali

nominal *a.* बहुत थोड़ा bahut thorha

nominate *v.t.* नामांकित करना naamankit karna

nomination *n.* नामांकन namankan

nominee *n* नामांकित व्यक्ति namamkit vyakti

non-alignment *n.* गुटनिरपेक्षता gutnirpekshhta

nonchalance *n.* उदासीनता udasinta

nonchalant *a.* अविचलित avichalit

nonconformist *adv.* धर्म विरोधी dharm virodhi

none *pron.* कोई नहीं koi nahi

nonentity *n.* अस्तित्वहीन वस्तु astitvahin vastu

nonetheless *adv.* फिर भी phir bhi

nonparalell *n.* अद्वितीय advitiya

nonpareil *a.* अद्वितीय advitiya

nonsense *n.* बकवास bakvas

nonsensical *a.* बेहूदा behuda

nook *n.* निर्जन स्थान nirjan sthan

noon *n.* दोपहर dopahar

noose *n.* फंदा phanda

nor *conj* और न aur na

norm *n.* मानक manak

norm *n* नियम niyam

normal *a.* नियमित niyamit

normalcy *n.* सामान्यता samanayata

north *a* उत्तरी uttari

northwards *adv.* उत्तर की ओर uttar ki or

north *n.* उत्तर uttar

northerly *adv.* उत्तर की ओर uttar ki ore ka

northerly *a.* उत्तरी uttari

northern *a.* उत्तरी uttari

nose *n.* नाक naak

nosegay *n.* गुलदस्ता guldasta

nosey *a.* कुतूहली kutuhali

nostalgia *n.* घर की याद ghar ki yaad

nostril *n.* नथुना nathuna

nostrum *n.* रामबाण ram baan

not *adv.* नहीं nahi

notability *n.* प्रसिद्धि prasiddhi

notable *a.* उल्लेखनीय ullekhniya

notary *n.* लेख्य प्रमाणक lekhya pramanak

notation *n.* अंकन ankan

notch *n.* दांता danta

notionalist *adj* कल्पना वादी kalpna vadi

note *n.* सूचना suchna

noteworthy *a.* उल्लेखनीय ullekhniya

nothing *adv.* बिल्कुल नहीं bilkul nahin

nothing *n.* कुछ नहीं kuch nahin

notice *v.t.* देख लेना dekh lena

notice *a.* सूचना suchna

notification *n.* अधि-सूचना adhi-suchana

notify *v.t.* सूचना देना suchna dena

notion *n.* विचार vichar

notional *a.* मनोगत manogat

notoriety *n.* कुख्याति kukhyati

notorious *a.* कुख्यात kukhyat

notoriety *adj* कुख्याती kukhyati

noumenon *adv.* बोधी तत्व budhi tatva

notwithstanding *conj.* यद्यपि yathapi

nought *n.* कुछ नहीं kuch nahin

noun *n.* संज्ञा sangya

nourish *v.t.* पोषण करना poshan karna

nourishment *n* पोषण poshan

novel *a.* नया naya

novel *n* उपन्यास upnayas

novelette *n.* लघु उपन्यास laghu upnayas

novelist *n.* उपन्यासकार upnayaskar

novelty *n.* नवीनता navinta

november *n.* नवंबर november

novitiate *n.* नौसिखुआ nausikhuva

now *conj.* अब ab

no near *adv.* कहीं भी नहीं kahin bhi nahin

now-a-days *adv* आजकल aajkal

nowhere *adv.* कहीं नहीं kahi nahi

noxious *a.* अहितकर ahitkar

nozzle *n.* टोंटी tonti

nubile *a.* **मोहक** mohak
nuclear *a.* **नाभिकीय** nabhikiya
nucleus *n.* **केंद्र** kendra
nude *a.* **नग्न** nagan
nudge *v.t.* **कोहनी से चूना** kohni se chhuna
nudity *n.* **नग्नता** naganta
nugget *n.* **स्वर्णपिंड** svarnapind
nuisance *n.* **उत्पाद** utpaat
null *a.* **अमान्य** amaanya
nullification *n.* **निष्प्रभावीकरण** nishprabhavikaran
nullify *v.t.* **रद्द करना** raddh karna
numb *a.* **सुन्न** sunn
number *v.t.* **अंक डालना** ank dalna
number *n.* **संख्याॅ** sankhya
numberless *a.* **अगणित** anganit
numeral *a.* **अंक बोधक** ank bodhak
numerator *n.* **अंश** ansh
numerical *a.* **संख्यात्मक** sankhyatmak
numerous *a.* **बहुत** bahut
nun *n.* **भिक्षुणी** bhikshuni
nunnery *n.* **भिक्षुणियों का मठ** bhishuni ka math
nuptial *a.* **वैवाहिक** vaivahik
nuptials *n.* **विवाह संबंधी** vivah sambandhi
nurse *n.* **परिचारिका** paricharika
nursery *n.* **शिशु-सदन** shishu-sadan
nurture *v.t.* **पालन-पोषण करना** palan-poshan karna
nurture *n.* **भोजन** bhojan
nut *n* **गिरीदार मेवा** giridaar meva
nutrition *n.* **पोषण** poshan
nutritious *a.* **पोषक** poshak
nutritive *a.* **पोषण-संबंधी** poshan sambandhi
nuzzle *v.* **सुंघाना** sunghana
nylon *n.* **नाइलॉन** nylon
nymph *n.* **अप्सरा** apsara
nympholept **संन्धि** shaidayi

oak *n.* **शाहबलूत** shah-balut
oar *n.* **पतवार** patwaar
oarsman *n.* **नाविक** naavik
oasis *n.* **नखलिस्तान** nakhlistaan
oat *n.* **जई** jae
oath *n.* **शपथ** sapath
obduracy *n.* **ज़िद** jid
obdurate *a.* **हठी** hathi
obedience *n.* **आज्ञाकारिता** aagyakarita
obedient *a.* **आज्ञाकारी** aagyakari
obeisance *n.* **श्रद्घापूर्ण नमन** shradhapurna naman
obesity *n.* **मोटापा** motapa
obey *v.t.* **आज्ञा मानना** agya manana
obey *v.t.* **आज्ञाकारी होना** aagyakari hona
obituary *a.* **निधन सूचना** nidhan suchna
object *n.* **वस्तु** vastu
object *v.t.* **विरोध करना** virodh karna
objection *n.* **आपत्ति** apatti
objectionable *a.* **आपत्तिजनक** aapattijanak
objective *n.* **वास्तविक** vastavik
objective *a.* **कर्मवाची** karmawachi
oblation *n.* **बलि** bali
obligation *n.* **बंधन** bandhan
obligatory *a.* **अनिवार्य** aniwarya
oblige *v.t.* **अनुग्रह करना** anugrah karna
oblique *a.* **तिरछा** tircha
obliterate *v.t.* **विनष्ट करना** vinast karna
obliteration *n.* **विनाश** vinash
oblivion *n.* **विस्मरण** vismaran
oblivious *a.* **स्मृतिहीन** smirtihin
oblong *a.* **आयताकार** aayatkaar
oblong *n.* **आयत** aayat
obnoxious *a.* **अप्रिय** apriya
obscene *a.* **अश्लील** asrial

obscenity _n._ अश्लीलता asrilalta

obscure _v.t._ छिपाना chhipaana

obscure _ADJ_ धुंधला dhundhala

obscurity _n._ अंधेरा andhera

observance _n._ अनुपालन anupalan

observant _a._ सावधान sawdhan

observation _n._ टिप्पणी tippni

observatory _n._ वैधशाला vaidhsalla

observe _v.t._ पालन करना palan karna

obsess _v.t._ परेशान करना paresaan karna

obsession _n._ परेशानी parisani

obsolete _a._ अप्रचलित aprachalit

obstacle _n._ बाधा badha

obstinacy _n._ ज़िद jidh

obstinate _a._ हठी hatthi

obstruct _v.t._ अवरूद्घ करना awarudh karna

obstruction _n._ बाधा badha

obstructive _a._ बाधक badhak

obtain _v.t._ प्राप्त करना prapt karna

obtainable _a._ प्राप्य prapaya

obtuse _a._ मूर्ख murkh

obvious _a._ स्पष्ट spasht

occasion _v.t_ कारण बनना karan banna

occasion _n._ अवसर awsar

occasionally _adv._ यदा कदा yada kada

occidental _a._ पाश्चात्य pashchatya

occult _a._ गुप्त gupt

occupancy _n._ आधिपात्य aadhipatya

occupant _n._ कब्जा धारी qabza dhari

occupation _n._ कब्ज़ा kabza

occupier _n._ अंधविश्वासी adhivaasi

occupy _v.t._ कब्ज़ा करना qabza karna

occur _v.i._ घटित होना ghatit hona

occurrence _n._ घटना ghatna

ocean _n._ सागर saagar

oceanic _a._ सागरीय sagariya

octagon _n._ अष्टकोण aastkon

octangular _a._ अष्टकोणी aastkoni

octave _n._ अष्टपदी aastpadi

October _n._ अक्टूबर october

oceanographic _n_ सुमद्री विज्ञान संबन्धी samudri vigyan sambandhi

octroi _n._ चुंगी chungi

oculist _n._ नेत्ररोग विशेषज्ञ netrarog visaisahgya

odd _a._ विषम visham

oddity _n._ अनोखापन anokhapan

oddish _n._ विचित्र vichitra

ode _n._ गीत geet

odious _a._ घृणास्पद grehnaspad

odium _n._ घृणाभाव grehnabhav

odorous _a._ सुगंधि sugandhi

odour _n._ गंध gandh

offence _n._ अपराध apradh

offend _v.t._ नाराज़ करना naraj karna

offender _n._ अपराधी apradhi

offensive _n_ आक्रमिक akramik

offensiveness _a._ नागवारी naagwari

offer _n_ पेश-कश pesh-kash

offer _v.t._ प्रस्तुत करना prastut karna

offering _n._ उपहार uphar

office _n_ कार्यालय karyalaya

officer _n._ अधिकारी adhikari

official _n_ राजकीय rajkiya

official _a._ आधिकारिक adhikaarik

officially _adv._ अधिकृत adhikrit

offing _n._ दृश्य क्षितिज drishya kshitij

offset _n_ ऑफ़सैट छपाई offset chhapai

offset _v.t._ हरजाना harjana

offshoot _n._ उप शाखा up-shakha

offspring _n._ संतति santati

oft _adv._ प्राय praya

often _adv._ अनेक बार anek baar

ogle _v.t._ ताकना taakna

ogle _n_ कामुक दृष्टि kamuk drishti

oil _n._ तेल tel

oil _v.t_ तेल लगाना tel lagana

oily _a._ चिकना chikna

ointment _n._ मरहम marham

old _a._ पुराना purana

oligarchy *n.* अल्पतंत्र alp-tantra

olive *n.* जैतून zaitoon

omega *n.* चरमोत्कर्ष charmotkarsh

omelette *n.* आमलेट omlet

omen *n.* अप-शगुन ap-shakun

ominous *a.* अमंगलकार amangalkaar

omission *n.* भूल bhool

omit *v.t.* छोड़ देना chhod dena

omnipotence *n.* सर्वशक्तिमत्ता sarvashaktimata

omnipotent *a.* सर्वशक्तिमान sarvashaktiman

omnipresence *n.* सर्वव्यापकता sarva-vyapakta

omnipresent *a.* सर्वव्यापी sarvaypi

omniscience *n.* सर्वज्ञता sarvagyata

omniscient *a.* सर्वज्ञ sarvagy

on *prep.* पर par

omanism *n* हस्त-मैथून hast-maithun

once *adv.* एक बार ek baar

one *pron.* अकेला akela

one *a.* एक ek

oneness *n.* एकता ekta

onerous *a.* भारी bhari

onion *n.* प्याज़ payaj

on-looker *n.* दर्शक darshak

only *adv.* मात्र matra

only *conj.* परंतु parantu

only *a.* एक-मात्र ek-matra

onomatopoeia *n.* ध्वनि dhwani

onrush *n.* प्रवाह prawah

onset *n.* हमला hamla

onslaught *n.* भीषण आक्रमण vhisan aakraman

onus *n.* दायित्व dayitva

onward *a.* आगे aage

onwards *adv.* आगे की ओर aage ki aur

ooze *v.i.* बाहर फेंकना bhahar fekhna

ooze *n.* कीचड़ kichhad

opacity *n.* अपारदर्शिता apaardarsita

opal *n.* पोलकी polki

opaque *a.* अपारदर्शी apardarsi

open *v.t.* खोलना kholna

open *a.* खुला khula

opening *n.* आरंभ aarambh

openly *adv.* खुले रूप में khulai roop mein

opera *n.* संगीत नाटक sangit natak

operate *v.t.* चालू करना chalu karna

operation *n.* शल्य चिकित्सा shalya chikitsa

operative *a.* प्रभाव पूर्ण prabhav puran

operator *n.* प्रचालक prachalak

opine *v.t.* मत-रखना mat-rakhna

opinion *n.* मत mat

opium *n.* अफ़ीम afeem

opponent *n.* विरोधी virodhi

opportune *a.* उचित uchit

opportunism *n.* अवसरवादिता awsar-vadita

opportunity *n.* सुअवसर suawsar

oppose *v.t.* विरोध करना virodh karna

opposite *a.* विरोधी virodhi

opposition *n.* विरोधी दल virodhi dal

oppress *v.t.* तंग करना tang karna

oppression *n.* दमन daman

oppressive *a.* दमनकारी damankari

oppressor *n.* दमनकर्त्ता damankarta

opt *v.i.* चयन करना chayan karna

optic *a.* दृष्टि संबंधी dristi sambandhi

optician *n.* चश्मे का निर्माता chashme ke nirmatta

optimism *n.* आशावाद ashawad

optimist *n.* आशावादी ashawadi

optimistic *a.* आशावादी ashawadi

optimum *a* अनुकूलतम anukooltam

optimum *n.* अनुकूलतम परिस्थिति anukooltam paristhiti

option *n.* चयनाधिकार chyandhikar

optional *a.* वैकल्पिक vaikalpik

opulence *n.* प्रचुरता prachurta

opulent *a.* भरपूर bharpoor
oracle *n.* तीर्थ मंदिर tirth mandir
oracular *a.* देव वाक्य dev vakya
oral *a.* मौखिक maukhik
orally *adv.* मौखिक रूप से maukhik rup se
orange *a* नारंगी narangi
orange *n.* संतरा santara
oration *n.* भाषण bhashan
orator *n.* कुशल वक्ता khusal vakta
oratorical *a.* भाषण संबंधी bhashan sambandhi
oratory *n.* भाषणकला bhasan kala
orb *n.* पृथ्वी मंडल prithivi mandal
orbit *n.* परिक्रमापथ parikramapath
orchard *n.* फलोद्यान phalodhyan
orchestra *n.* वादकवृंद vadakvrind
orchestral *a.* वाद्यवृंदीय vadyavrindiya
ordeal *n.* अग्नि परीक्षा agni pariksha
order *v.t* आदेश देना aadesh dena
order *n.* आदेश aadesh
orderly *n.* सर्वश्रेष्ठा suvyavstha
orderly *a.* नियमित niyamit
ordinance *n.* अध्यादेश adyadesh
ordinarily *adv.* साधारणत sadharanta
ordnance *n.* तोपखाना top khana
ore *n.* कच्ची धातु khanij dhatu
organ *n.* स्वर swar
organdie *n* अर्गगांधी argandi
organic *a.* संगठित sangathit
organizable *n* प्रबन्धियां prabandhniya
organism *n.* शरीर रचना sharir rachna
organization *n.* संघटन sanghatan
organize *v.t.* संघटित करना sanghatit karna
orient *n.* पूर्व purva
oriental *n* पूर्ववासी purvawasi
oriental *a.* प्राच्य prachya
origin *n.* मूल mool
original *n* मूल रूप mool roop
original *a.* मौलिक maulik
originality *n.* मौलिकता maulikta

originate *v.t.* निर्मित करना nirmit karna
originator *n.* जन्मदाता janamdata
ornament *n.* अलंकरण alangkaran
ornament *v.t.* अलंकृत करना alankrit karna
ornamental *a.* शोभाकारी sobhakaari
ornamentation *n.* सजावट sajawat
orphan *v.t* अनाथ बनाना anath banana
orphan *n.* अनाथ बालक anath balak
orphanage *n.* अनाथालय anathlaya
orthodox *a.* रूढ़िवादी rudhivadi
orthodoxy *n.* रूढ़िवादिता rudhivaditha
oscillate *v.i.* डोलना dolna
oscillation *n.* दोलन dolan
ossify *v.t.* कठोर बनाना kathore banana
ostracize *v.t.* निर्वासित करना nirvasit karna
ostrich *n.* शुतुरमुर्ग shuturmurg
other *a.* दूसरा dusra
other *pron.* अन्य व्यक्ति या वस्तु anya vyakti ya vastu
otherwise *conj.* नहींतो anyatha
otherwise *adv.* भिन्न प्रकार से bhinn prakar se
otter *n.* ऊदबिलाव udhbilaav
ottoman *n.* गद्देदार चौकी gaddedar chauki
ounce *n.* औस ounce
our *pron.* हमारा hamara
oust *v.t.* निकाल देना nikaal dena
out *adv.* बाहर baahar
outbreak *n.* प्रकोप prakop
outburst *n.* प्रस्फोटन prasphotan
outcast *a* बहिष्कृत bahishkrit
outcast *n.* जातिच्युत jatichyut
outcome *n.* परिणाम parinaam
outcry *a.* चीख chikh
outdated *a.* पुराना purana
outdo *v.t.* पछाड़ना pachadana
outdoor *a.* बाहरी bahari
outer *a.* बाहरी bahari
outfit *n.* सजा sajja

outfit *v.t* सज्जित करना sajjit karna

outgrow *v.t.* अधिक बढ़ जाना adhik barh jana

outhouse *n.* उपभवन upbhawan

outing *n.* सैर सपाटा sair sapaata

outlandish *a.* परदेशी pardesi

outlaw *v.t* प्रतिबंध लगाना pratibandh lagana

outlaw *n.* अपराधी apradhi

outline *v.t.* चित्रित करना chitrit karna

outline *n.* रूपरेखा rooprekha

outlook *n.* भावी संभावना bhavi sambhavana

outmoded *a.* पुराना purana

outpatient *n.* बहिरोगी bahirogi

outpost *n.* दूरवर्ती चौकी durvarti chowki

output *n.* उत्पादन utpadan

outrage *n.* नृशंसता nrishansata

outrage *v.t.* भंग करना bhang karna

outright *a* पूर्ण रूप से puran rup se

outright *adv.* स्पष्ट रूप से spast roop se

outrun *v.t.* तेज़ दौड़ना tej daurhna

outset *n.* प्रांरभ prarambh

outshine *v.t.* मात कर देना maat kar dena

outside *n* बाहरी सतह bahari satah

outside *adv* बाहर की ओर bahar kai aur

outside *prep* बाहर bahar

outside *a.* बाह्य bahya

outsider *n.* बाहरी व्यक्ति bahari baykti

outsize *a.* सामान्य से बड़ा samaniya se bada

outspeed *adh* तेज़ रफ्तार tez raftar

outspoken *a.* स्पष्टवादी spastwadi

outstanding *a.* बकाया bakaaya

outward *adv* बाहर की ओर bahar kai aur

outward *a.* ऊपरी uppari

outwardly *adv.* बाहर से bahar se

outwards *adv* बाहर की ओर bahar ke aur

oval *n* अंडाकार वस्तु andakaar vastu

oval *a.* अंडाकार andakaar

ovary *n.* अंडाशय andashay

ovation *n.* जय-जयकार jay-jaykaar

oven *n.* चूल्हा chulha

over *adv* ऊपर की ओर uppar ke aur

overdose *vt* अधिक दवा देना adhik dawa dena

over *prep.* ऊपर upar

overact *v.t.* अत्याभिनय करना atyabhinay karna

overall *a* कुल kul

overall *n.* लबादा labada

overarch *v.t.* मेहराब बनाना mehrab banana

overburden *v.t.* अधिक बोझ डालना adhik bhoj dalna

overcare *a.* आहक देखभाल करना ahik dekhbhaal dena

overcharge *v.t.* अधिक मूल्य वसूलना adhik mulya vasulna

overcharge *n* अधिमूल्य adhik mulya

overcoat *n.* लंबा कोट lamba kot

overcome *v.t.* अभिभूत कर देना abhibhut kar dena

overdo *v.t.* अति करना ati karna

overdose *n.* ओषधि की अतिमात्रा aushadhi ki atimatra

overdraw *v.t.* अतिशयोक्ति करना atishyokti karna

overdue *a.* विलंबित vilambit

overhaul *n.* पूरी मरम्मत pure marammat

overhaul *v.t.* पुरानी मरम्मत करना puri murammat karna

overhear *v.t.* चुपके से सुनना chupke se sunna

overjoyed *a* अति प्रसन्न aati prasann

overlap *n* ढकने वाला भाग dhakne wala bhag

overlap *v.t.* ढक लेना dhak lena

overleaf *adv.* पन्ने की दूसरी ओर panne ki dusre aur

overload *n* क अधिक भार adhik bhaar

overload *v.t.* अधिक भार लादना adhik bhaar laadna

overlook *v.t.* ऊपर से देखना uppar se dekhna

overnight *a* रात्रि भर ratri bhar

overnight *adv.* रात के समय raat kai samai

overpower *v.t.* पराजित करना parajit karna

overrule *v.t.* रद्द करना radd karna

overrun *v.t* रौंद डालना raund dalna

oversee *v.t.* पर्यवेक्षक payavekshak

overseer *n.* पर्यवेक्षक paryavekshak

overshadow *v.t.* छाया डाना dhup se bachaana

oversight *n.* चूक chook

overstrain *a.* अधिक थकान adhik thakaan

overtake *v.t.* आगे निकल जाना aage nikal jana

overthrow *n* विनाश vinash

overthrow *v.t.* तख़्ता उलट देना takhta ulat jana

overtime *n* अधिसमय adhisamay

overture *n.* संधि प्रस्ताव sandhi prastav

overture *vt* गिरा देना gira dena

overwhelm *v.t.* पराजित करना parajit karna

overwork *v.i.* अतिश्रम करना aatisram karna

overwork *n.* अतिश्रम atishram

owe *v.t* कर्ज़दार होना karzdaar hona

owl *n.* उल्लू ullu

own *v.t.* अपनाना apnaana

own *a.* अपना apna

owner *n.* स्वामी swami

ownership *n.* स्वामित्व swamitwa

ox *n.* बैल bail

oxygen *n.* ऑक्सीजन oxygen

oyster *n.* घोंघा ghongha

oxymel *n* शहद और सिकरा का शरबत shahd aur sirka ka sharbat

# P

pace *v.i.* चलना chalna

pace *n* चाल chaal

pacific *a.* शांत shant

pacify *v.t.* शांत करना shant karna

pack *n.* गठरी gathri

pack *v.t.* बाँधना baandhana

package *n.* पुलिंदा pulinda

packet *n.* छोटा पार्सल chhota parcel

packing maaterial *n.* बांधने की सामग्री bandhne ki saamagri

pact *n.* संधि sandhi

pad *n* नरम गढ़ढा naram gadda

pad *n.* दस्ता dasta

padding *n.* गद्दी gaddi

paddle *n* छोटा चापू chhota chappu

paddle *v.i.* पानी में पैर pani mein pair

paddy *n.* धान dhan

page *n.* प्रसिद्ध prishth

pageant *n.* शानदार झांकियां shaandar jhankian

pageantry *n.* आडंबर andbar

pagoda *n.* मेरु मंदिर meru mandir

pail *n.* बाल्टी baalti

pain *v.t.* पीड़ा होना pira hona

pain *n.* पीड़ा pida

painful *a.* दुःखदायी dukhyi

painstaking *a.* उद्यमी uddhami

painless पीड़ा रहित pira rahit

paint *n.* रंग rang

painter *n.* चित्रकार chitrakaar

painting *n.* चित्रकला chitrakala

pair *n.* जोड़ा jorha

pyjama *n* पेजामा pajaama

pal *n.* मित्र mitr

palace *n.* महल mahal

palanquin *n.* पालकी paalki

palatable *a.* स्वादिष्ट swadisht

palatal *a.* तालु संबंधी taalu sambandhi

palate *n.* तालु taalu

palatial *a.* भवन जैसा bhawan jaisa

pale *a* पीला peela

pale *v.i.* पीला होना peela hona

palaver *n.* मनाना manana

palm *n.* हथेली hatheli

palm *v.t.* हथेली में छिपाना hatheli mein chhipana

palm *vt* घूस देना ghoos dena

palmistry *adj* हस्त रेखा विज्ञान hast rekha vigyan

palpable *a.* स्पर्शनीय sparshaniya

palpitate *v.i.* धड़कना dharkana

palpitation *n.* धड़कन dharhkan

palsy *n.* पक्षाघात pakshaghat

paltry *a.* नीच neech

pamper *v.t.* संतुष्ट करना santusht karna

pamphlet *n.* विज्ञापन पत्र vigyapna patra

pamphleteer *n.* पर्चा लिखने वाला parcha likhne wala

panacea *n.* आचूक दवा achuk dawa

pandemonium *n.* पिशाच निवास pishach nivas

pane *n.* कांच kanch

pang *n.* पीरा peera

panel *n.* दीवर का ताकत diwar ka takhta

pang *n.* वेदना vedna

panic *n.* आतंक atank

panorama *n.* चित्रमाला chitramala

panopticon *n* गोल क़ैद खाना gol qaid khana

pant *v.i.* हांफना haafna

pantaloon *n.* पतलून patlun

panther *n.* चीता chita

pantomime *n.* मूक अभिनेता muk abhineta

pantry *n.* भंडारघर bhandarghar

popal *a.* पोप संबंधी pop sambandhi

paper *n.* सचारपत्र kaaghaz

par *n.* बराबरी barabari

parable *n.* नीतिकथा nitikatha

parachute *n.* हवाई छतरी havai chhatri

parade *v.t.* परेड करना pared karna

parade *n.* झालोन jaloos

paradox *n.* असत्याभास asatyabhas

paradoxical *a.* विरोधाभासात्मक virodhabhasaatmak

paragon *n.* अत्युत्तम पदार्थ atyuttam padarth

paragraph *n.* प्रकरण prakaran

parallel *v.t.* समानांतर करना samaanatar karna

parallel *a.* समानांतर samaantar

parallelism *n.* समानता samanta

parallelogram *n.* समानांतर चतुर्भुज samaantar chaturvurj

paralyse *v.t.* लकवा मारना lakva marna

paralysis *n.* लकवा रोग lakva rog

paralytic *a.* लकवा मारा हुआ lakva mara hua

paramount *n.* सर्वोत्तम sarvottam

paramour *n.* प्रेमिका premika

paraphernalia *n. pl* साज़ सामान saaz saaman

paraphrase *n.* भावानुवाद bhaavaanuvaad

parcel *v.t.* बांटना bantana

parcel *n.* बंडल bandal

parch *v.t.* झुलसाना jhulsana

pardon *n.* क्षमा kshama

pardon *v.t.* क्षमा करना kshama karna

pardonable *a.* क्षमा के योग्य kshama ke yogay

parent *n.* माता या पिता mata ya pita

parentage *n.* पितृत्व pitritva

parental *a.* पैतृक paitrik

parenthesis *n.* वाक्यांश vakyaansh

parish *n.* पादरी का प्रदेश padari ka pradesh

parity *n.* समानता samanta

parietal *n* भीतिया bhitiya

park *n* उद्यान udyaan
parlance *n.* बोल-चाल bol-chaal
parley *v.i* सभा करना sabha karna
parley *n.* विवादग्रस्त सम्मेलन vivaadgrast sammelan
parliament *n.* संसद sansad
parliamentarian *n.* संसद सदस्य sansad sadasya
parliamentary *a.* संसदीय sansadiya
parlour *n.* बैठक baithak
parody *v.t.* वियोग-कविता लिखना vyang-kavita likhna
parody *n.* हास्यानुकृति hasyanukriti
parole *n* प्रतीती सामोचान pratiti samochan
parrot *n.* तोता tota
parry *n.* छेकान taal-matol
parry *v.t.* तल देना taal dena
parson *n.* पादरी padari
part *v.t.* अलग होना alag hona
part *n.* अंश aansh
partake *v.i.* भाग लेना bhag lena
partial *a.* आंशिक aanshik
partiality *n.* प्रकाश-पथ paksh-paat
participant *n.* भाग लेने वाला bhag lene wala
participate *v.i.* हिस्सा लेना hissa lena
participation *n.* हिस्सेदारी hissedari
particle *a.* कण kan
particular *n.* विस्तृत वर्णन vistrit varnan
particular *a.* सावधान savdhan
partisan *a.* पक्षपातपूर्ण pakchhpathpurna
partisan *n.* पक्षधर pakshaghar
partition *v.t.* बांटना bantana
partition *n.* बंटवारा bantwara
partner *n.* साथी sathi
partnership *n.* साझा sajha
party *n.* दल dal
pass *n* रास्ता rasta
pass *v.i.* पार करना paar karna
passage *n.* अवतरण avaataran

passenger *n.* यात्री yatri
passion *n.* आवेश aavesh
passionate *a.* क्रोधी krodhi
passive *a.* निष्क्रिय nishkriya
passport *n.* पार-पत्र paar-patra
past *n.* भूतपूर्व काल bhutpurva kaal
past *prep.* गुज़रा हुआ guzra hua
past *a.* पहले का pahle ka
paste *v.t.* लेई से चिपकाना lei se chipkana
paste *n.* साना हुआ आटा saana huwa aata
pastel *n.* रंगीन खड़िया rangin khadiya
pastime *n.* क्रीड़ा krida
pasture *v.t.* चरना charna
pasture *n.* चारा chara
pat *n* थपकी thapki
pat *adv* उचित uchit
pat *v.t.* थपथपाना thapthapna
patch *n* पैबंद paiband
patch *v.t.* मरम्मत करना marammat karna
patent *n* एकस्व ekasva
paternity *adg* पितृत्व pitratava
patent *a.* स्पष्ट spasht
paternal *a.* पैतृक paitrik
path *n.* मार्ग marg
pathetic *a.* कारुणिक karunik
pathos *n.* करुणा karuna
patience *n.* सहनशीलता sahanshilta
patient *n* रोगी rogi
patio *n* आंगन aangan
patricide *n.* पितृहत्या pritrihatya
patrimony *n.* विरासत virasat
patriot *n.* देशभक्त deshbhakt
patriotic *a.* देशभक्तिपूर्ण deshbhaktipurna
patriotism *n.* देशभक्ति deshbhakti
pathological *n* रोगात्मक rogatmak
patrol *v.i.* पहरा देना pahara dena
patron *n.* पोषक poshak
patronage *n.* संस्करण sanrakshan
patronize *v.t.* सहायता देना sahayata dena
pattern *n.* प्रतिरूप pratiroop

paucity *n.* कमी kami

pauper *n.* दरिद्र daridra

pause *v.i.* ठहरना thaharna

pause *n.* विराम viram

pave *v.t.* मार्ग बनाना marg banana

pavement *n.* सड़क की पटरी sarhak ki patri

pavilion *n.* मंडप mandap

paw *v.t.* पंजे से खुरचना panje se khurachna

paw *n.* पंजा panja

pay *n* वेतन vaitan

pay *v.t.* भुगतान देना bhugtan dena

payable *a.* भुगतान योग bhugtan yogya

payee *n.* राशि पानेवाला rashi panewala

payment *n.* भुगतान bhugtan

pea *n.* मटर matar

peace *n.* शांति shanti

peaceable *a.* शांतिप्रिय shantpriya

peaceful *a.* शांत shant

peach *n.* आड़ू aarhu

peacock *n.* मोर mor

peahen *n.* मयूरी mayuri

peak *n.* शिखर sikhar

pear *n.* नाशपाती naaspati

pearl *n.* मोती moti

peasant *n.* किसान kisan

peasantry *n.* किसान वर्ग kisan varg

pebble *n.* कंकड़ kankar

peck *v.i.* चोंच मारना chonch marna

pectoral *n* कवच kavach

peculiar *a.* असाधारण asadharan

peculiarity *n.* विशेषता visheshta

pecuniary *a.* धन संबंधी dhan sambandhi

pedagogue *n.* अध्यापक adhyapak

pedagogy *n.* शिक्षणशास्त्र shikshan shastra

pedal *n.* फेरी का pair ka

peddle *v* फेरी लगना pheri lagana

pedant *n.* विद्याडंबरी vidyadambari

pedantry *n.* विद्याडंबर vidyadambar

pedestal *n.* पीठिका pithika

pedigree *n.* वंशावली vansavali

peel *n.* छिलका chhilka

peep *n* झांकी jhanki

peep *v.i.* चोरी से देखना chori se dekhna

peer *n.* अभिजात abhijaat

peerless *a.* अनुपम anupam

peg *v.t.* स्थिर करना sthir karna

peg *n.* खोंटी khunti

pelf *n.* धन दौलत dhan daulat

pell-mell *adv.* गॉड-मड्ड gadd-madd

pen *v.t.* लिखना lekhna

pen *n.* लेखनी lekhni

penal *a.* दंडविषयक dandvishayak

penalize *v.t.* दंड देना dand dena

penalty *n.* दंड dand

pencil *n.* पेंसिल pencil

pendragon *adj* अधिराज adhiraaj

pending *a* विचाराधीन vicharadhin

pendulate *vt* झूलना jhulna

penetrate *v.t.* चुभाना chubhana

penetration *n.* बेधन baidhan

penis *n.* लिंग ling

penniless *a.* निर्धन nirdhan

pension *v.t.* पेंशन देना pension dena

pension *n.* निवृत्ति वेतन nivriti-vetan

pensive *a.* चिंताग्रस्त chintagrast

pentagon *n.* पंचकोण panchkon

peon *n.* चपरासी chaprasi

people *v.t.* बसाना basana

people *n.* जनता janta

pepper *n.* मिर्च mirch

pepper *v.t.* मिर्च मिलाना mirch milana

per *prep.* प्रति prati

per cent *adv.* प्रति सैकड़ा prati sainkrha

perambulator *n.* बच्चागाड़ी bachhagarhi

perceive *v.t.* समझना samajhna

percentage *n.* प्रतिशत pratishat

perception *n.* बोध bodh

perceptive *a.* प्रत्यक्ष ज्ञानशील pratyaksh gyanshil

perch *n* धंधा dhandha

perch *n.* मीठे जल की मछली mitthe jal ki machhli

perennis *n.* बारहमासी baarah-maasi

perennial *a.* वर्ष-भर रहने वाली varsh-bhar rahne wali

perfect *a.* श्रेष्ठ shreshtha

perfect *v.t.* निर्दोष बनाना nirdosh banana

perfection *n.* निर्दोषता nirdoshta

perfidy *n.* विश्वासघात vishvasghat

perforate *v.t.* छेद करना chhed karna

perforce *adv.* हठ से hatth se

perform *v.t.* करना karna

performance *n.* प्रदर्शन pradarshan

performer *n.* प्रदर्शन करने वाला pradarshan karne wala

perfume *n.* सुगंध sugandh

perfume *v.t.* सुगंधित करना sugandith karna

perhaps *adv.* कदाचित्र kadachitra

peril *v.t.* विपत्ति में डालना vipatti mein daalna

peril *n.* संकट पूरण sankat puran

perilous *a.* संकटमय sankatmai

period *n.* समय samay

periodical *a.* नियतकालिक niyatkalik

periodical *n.* पत्रिका patrika

periphery *n.* परिधि paridhi

perish *v.i.* सड़ना sadna

perishable *a.* नाश होने योग्य nash hone yogya

perjure *v.i.* झूठी गवाही देना jhuti gavahi dena

perjury *n.* झूठी शपथ jhuti shapath

permanence *n.* स्थिरता sthirta

permanent *a.* टिकाऊ tikau

permissible *a.* आज्ञा पाने योग्य agya pane yogya

permission *n.* अनुमति anumati

permit *v.t.* आज्ञा देना aagya dena

permit *n.* अनुमति पत्र anumati patra

permutation *n.* क्रमवय kramavaya

pernicious *a.* नाशक naashak

perpetration *n* अप्रदान-कर्म apradh-karm

perpendicular *n.* समकोणिक रेखा samkonik rekha

perpetual *a.* लगातार lagatar

perpetuate *v.t.* जारी रखना jari rakhna

perplex *v.t.* व्याकुल करना vyakul karna

perplexity *n.* झंझट jhanjhat

persecute *v.t.* कष्ट देना kasht dena

persecution *n.* उत्पीड़न utpeeran

perseverance *n.* दृढ़ता drirhta

persist *v.i.* दृढ़ रहना drirh rahna

persian *n.* फारसी भाषा Farsi bhasha

persistent *a.* आग्रही aagrahi

person *n.* व्यक्ति vyakti

personage *n.* संभ्रांत जन sambhrant jan

personal *a.* निजी niji

personality *n.* व्यक्तित्व vyakatitva

personification *n.* मूर्तीकरण murtikaran

personify *v.t.* मानवीकरण करना manavikaran karna

personnel *n.* कर्मचारी दल karmachari dal

perspective *n.* दृष्टिकोण drishtikona

perspiration *n.* पसीना pasina

perspire *v.i.* पसीना निकलना pasina nikalna

persuade *v.t.* उकसाना uksana

persuasion *n.* प्रयत्न-करना prataya-karan

pertain *v.i.* से सम्बधित se sambandhit

pertinence *a.* उचित uchit

perturb *v.t.* व्याकुल करना vyakul karna

perusal *n.* वाचन vachan

peruse *v.t.* अनुशीलन anushilan

pervade *v.t.* व्याप्त होना vyapt hona

perverse *a.* विकृत vikrit

perversion *n.* विकृति vikriti

perversity *n.* दुःशीलता dushilta

pervert *v.t.* दूषित करना dusit karna

pessimism *n.* निराशावाद nirashavad

pessimist *n.* निराशावादी nirasavadi
pessimistic *a.* निराश niraash
pest *n.* नाशक जीव naashak jeev
pesticide *n.* कीटनाशक kitnashak
pestilence *n.* महामारी mahamari
pet *v.t.* प्यार करना pyar karna
pet *n.* पालतू जानवर paaltu janawar
petal *n.* फूल की पंखुरी phool ki pankhuri
petition *n.* याचिका yachika
petitioner *n.* निवेदक nivedak
petrol *n.* पेट्रोल petrol
petroleum *n.* खनिज तैल khanij tel
petticoat *n.* पेटीकोट paitikot
petty *a.* छोटा chhota
petulance *n.* दुःशीलता duhshilta
petulant *a.* चिड़चिड़ा chirhchira
phantom *n.* प्रेत pret
pharmacy *n.* दवाखाना davakhana
phase *n.* चरण charan
phenomenal *a.* अद्भुत adbhut
philatelist *adj* टिकट संग्रहरी ticket sangrahi
phial *n.* छोटी बोतल chhoti bottle
philanthropic *a.* उदार udaar
philanthropist *n.* समाजसेवी samajsevi
philanthropy *n.* लोकोपकार lokopakaar
philological *a.* भाषाशास्त्रीय bhashashastriya
philologist *n.* भाषाविद् bhashavid
philology *n.* भाषाविज्ञान bhashavigyan
philosopher *n.* दार्शनिक darshanik
philosophical *a.* दार्शनिक darshanik
philosophy *n.* दर्शनशास्त्र darshanshastra
phone *n.* टेलिफ़ोन telephone
phonetic *a.* ध्वनि संबंधी dhavni sambandhi
phonetics *n.* स्वर शास्त्र swar shastra
phosphate *n.* भास्वीय लवण bhasviya lavan
photochemistry *n.* प्रकाश-रसायन prakash-rasayan

photo *n* फ़ोटो photo
photograph *n* छाया चित्र chhaya chitra
photograph *v.t.* फ़ोटो उतारना photo utarna
photographer *n.* फ़ोटो उतारने वाला photo utarnay wala
photographic *a.* फ़ोटो संबंधी photo sambandhi
photography *n.* फ़ोटो खींचने की कला photo khinchne ki kala
phrase *n.* मुहावरा muhawara
phraseology *n.* वाक्य-शैली vakya-shaili
physic *v.t.* इलाज करना ilaj karna
phrenology *n.* कपाल विज्ञान kapaal vigyan
physical *a.* शरीरिक shaaririk
physician *n.* डॉक्टर docter
physicist *n.* भौतिकशास्त्री bhautikshastri
physics *n.* भौतिक विज्ञान bhautik vigyan
physiognomy *n.* आकृति विज्ञान akriti vigyan
physique *n.* शरीर रचना sharir rachna
pianist *n.* पियानोवादक piyanovadak
piano *n.* पियानो peyano
pick *n.* चुनाव chunav
pick *v.t.* उठाना uthaana
picket *n.* खूंटा khoonta
pickle *n.* अचार achaar
picnic *n.* वन-विहार मनोरंजन van-vihar manoranjan
pictorial *a.* सचित्र sachitra
picture *n.* चित्र chitra
piece *n.* खंड khand
pie *n* कचौरी kachauri
pierce *v.t.* छेदना chhedna
piety *n.* भक्ति bhakti
pigeon *n.* कबूतर kabutar
pigmy *n.* बौना bauna
pile *n* ढेर dher
pile *n.* चिता chita
piles *n.* बवासीर bavaseer
pilgrim *n.* तीर्थयात्री tirthyatri

pilgrimage n. तीर्थ tirth sthal
pill n. गुटिका gutika
pillar n. खम्बा khamba
pillow v.t. तकिया लगाना takiya lagana
pillow n तकिया takiya
pilot v.t. मार्ग दिखलाना marg dekhlana
pilot n. विमान चालक viman chalak
pimple n. मुंहासा muhaasa
pin v.t. नत्थी करना nathi karna
pincer n. चिमटा chimta
pinch v. चिकोट chikot
pinch v.t. चिकोटी काटना chikoti katna
pine v.i. लालायित होना lalayit hona
pine n. देवदार devdaar
pineapple n. अनन्नास ananas
pink a हल्के गुलाबी रंग का halke gulabi
rang ka
pinchpenny adj कंजूस kanjoos
pinkish a. हल्का गुलाबी halka gulabi
pinnacle n. शिखर shikhar
pioneer v.t. मार्ग दिखलाना marg dekhlana
pioneer n. मार्ग दर्शक marg darshak
pious a. पवित्र pavitra
pipe n. बांसुरी bansuri
piquant a. तीखा teekha
piracy n. समुद्री डकैती samudri daketi
pirate n. समुद्री डाकू samudri daku
pistol n. पिस्तौल pistol
piston n. मुषली mushli
pitch n. तारकोल taarkoal
pitch v.t. फेंकना phenkana
pitcher n. घड़ा gharha
piteous a. दीन deen
pitfall n. चोर गड्ढा chor gaddha
pitiable a. दया का पात्र daya ka patra
pitiful a. दयापूर्ण daya purna
pitiless a. कठोर kathor
pittance n. क्षुद्र वेतन kshudra vetan
pity v.t. तरस खाना taras khana
pity n. करुणा karuna

pivot n. केंद्र-बिंदु kendra-bindu
pivot v.t. चूल पर घुमाना chool par
ghumana
placard n. विज्ञापन पत्र vigyapan patra
place v.t. नियुक्त करना niyukt karna
place n. स्थल sthal
placid a. शांत shant
placet n स्वीकृति swikriti
plague a. महामारी mahamaari
plain a. सीधा sidha
plain n. मैदान maidan
plaintiff n. वादी vaadi
plan v.t. योजना बनाना yojana banana
plan n. योजना yojana
plane v.t. सम-तल sam-tal
plane a. चौरस chauras
plane n वायुयान vayuyan
plane vt चौरस बनाना chauras banana
planet n. ग्रह greh
planetary a. ग्रह संबंधी greh sambandhi
plank v.t. तख्ते लगाना takhte lagana
plank n. लकड़ी का तख्ता lakrhi ka takhta
plant n. पौधा paudha
plant v.t. वनस्पति जगत vanaspati jagat
plantain n. केले का वृक्ष kele ka vriksh
plantation n. खेत khet
plaster v.t. लेप लगाना lep lagana
plaster n. औषधि का लेप aushadhi ka lep
plate n. प्लेट plate
plate v.t. मुलम्मा करना mulumma karna
plateau n. पठार patthar
platform n. मंच manch
platonic a. अफलातूनी aflatooni
platoon n. पलटन paltan
play v.i. नाटक करना natak karna
play n. खेल khel
player n. खिलाड़ी khilarhi
plea n. बहाना bahana
plead v.i. वकालत करना vakalat karna
pleader n. वकील vakil

pleasant *a.* मनोहर manohar
pleasantry *n.* आनंद anand
please *v.t.* प्रसन्न करना prasann karna
pleasure *n.* आनंद anand
plebiscite *n.* जनमत संग्रह janmat sangrah
pledge *v.t.* बंधक रखना bandhak rakhna
pledge *n.* बंधक bandhak
plenty *n.* प्रचुरता prachurta
plight *n.* दुर्दशा durdasha
plenary *adj* परिपूर्ण pari-puran
pleirs *n* जंबूरा jambura
plot *n.* भू-खण्ड bhu-khand
plough *v.i* हल से जुताई करना hal se jutai karna
plough *n.* हल hal
ploughman *n.* हलवाहा halwaha
pluck *n* झटका jhatka
pluck *v.t.* तोड़ना torhna
plug *n.* गुल्ली gulli
plum *n.* आलूबुखारा aalubukhara
plumber *n.* नलकार nalkaar
plunder *n* लूट का माल lut ka maal
plunder *v.t.* लूटना lutna
plunge *n* डुबकी dubki
plunge *v.t.* ग़ोता लगाना gota lagana
plural *a.* बहुवचन bahuvachan
plurality *n.* अनेकता anekta
plus *a.* अधिक adhik
plush *n* मखमल makhmal
ply *n* परत parat
ply *v.t.* काम में लाना kaam mein lana
pneumonia न्यूमोनिया neumonia
pocket *n.* जेब jeb
pod *n.* फली phali
poem *n.* कविता kavita
poetry *n.* काव्य रचना kavya rachna
poet *n.* कवि kavi
poetaster *n.* तुक्कड़ tukkarh
poetess *n.* कवयित्री kavyitri
poetic *a.* कविता संबंधी kavita sambandhi

poetics *n.* काव्यशास्त्र kavyashastra
pock *n.* फुंसी phunsi
poignancy *n.* तीखापन tikhapan
poignant *a.* तीखा tikha
point *n.* बिंदु bindu
point *v.t.* नोकदार बनाना nokdar banana
poise *n* संतुलन santulan
poise *v.t.* सभालना sambhalna
poison *v.t.* ज़हर देना zahar dena
poison *n.* विष vish
poisonous *a.* विषैला vishaila
poke *n.* धक्का dhakka
poke *v.t.* कोचना konchna
polar *n.* ध्रुवीय dhruwiya
pole *n.* लंबा डंडा lamba danda
police *n.* पुलिस police
policeman *n.* पुलिस का सिपाही police ka sipahi
policy *n.* नीति युक्ति niti yukti
polish *n* चमक chamak
polish *v.t.* चमकाना chamkana
polite *a.* विनीत vinit
politeness *n.* विनय vinay
politic *a.* नीति चतुर niti chatur
political *a.* राजनीतिक rajnitik
politician *n.* राजनीतिज्ञ rajnitigya
politics *n.* राजनीतिशास्त्र rajnitishastra
polity *n.* राजतंत्र rajtantra
political science *n* राजनीति शास्त्र rajniti shastra
poll *n.* मस्तक mastak
poll *n* मत-दान mat-daan
pollen *n.* पराग parag
pollute *v.t.* दूषित करना dushit karna
pollution *n.* प्रदूषण pradushan
poltergeist *n.* भूत bhoot
polygamy *n.* बहुविवाह प्रथा bahuvivah pratha
polyglot *n.* बहुभाषी bahubhashi
polyglot *a.* बहुभाषाविद् bahubhashavidh

polypod *n.* बहुपाद कीड़ा bahupad kidha

polytechnic *a.* बहु-शिल्प bahu-shilp

polytechnic *n.* विविधकला विद्यालय vividhkala vidhaylaya

polytheism *n.* बहुदेववाद bahudev vad

polytheist *n.* बहुदेवपूजक bahudevpujak

polytheistic *a.* बहुदेववादी bahudev vadi

pomp *n.* आडंबर adambar

pompous *a.* आडंबरी aadambari

pond *n.* छोटा तालाब chhota talab

ponder *v.t.* विचार करना vichar karna

pony *n.* छोटा घोड़ा chhota ghoda

poor *a.* निर्धन nirdhan

pop *v.i.* पटकना patkna

popinjay *n* दंभी व्यक्ति dambhi vyakti

pope *n.* रोम का बड़ा पादरी rome ka bada paadari

poplar *n.* चिनार वृक्ष chinar vriksh

poplin *n.* पॉपलीन कपड़ा paplin kapda

populace *n.* साधारण लोग sadharan log

popular *a.* लोकप्रिय lokpriya

popularity *n.* प्रसिद्धि prasiddhi

popularize *v.t.* प्रसिद्ध बनाना prasiddh banana

populate *v.t.* बसाना basana

population *n.* आबादी abadi

populous *a.* बहुसंख्यक bahusankhyak

porcelain *n.* चीनी के मिट्टी बर्तन chini mitti ke bartan

porch *n.* द्वार-मंडप dwar-mandap

pore *n.* रोमकूप romkup

pork *n.* सुअर का मांस suar ka mans

porridge *n.* दलिया dalia

port *n.* बंदरगाह bandargaha

portable *a.* ले जाने योग्य le jane yogya

portage *n.* परिवहन parivahan

portal *n.* सदर दरवाज़ा sadar darwaza

portend *v.t.* पूर्वसूचना देना purv-suchna dena

porter *n.* कुली kuli

portico *n.* बरामदा baramada

portion *n* भाग bhaag

portion *v.t.* बांटना bantana

portrait *n.* छविचित्र chhavichitra

portraiture *n.* चित्रकला chitra-kala

portray *v.t.* वर्णन करना varnan karna

portrayal *n.* चित्रण chitran

pose *v.i.* प्रस्तुतिकरण prastutikaran

pose *n.* मुद्रा mudra

position *n.* स्थान sthan

position *n* अवस्थिति avasthiti

positive *a.* साकारत्माक sakaratmak

possess *v.t.* अधिकार में रखना adhikar mein rakhna

possession *n.* अधिकार adhikar

possibility *n.* संभावना sambhavana

possible *a.* संभव sambhava

post *n.* खंभा khambha

post *v.t.* खंभे पर लगाना khamve par lagana

post *n* अधिकार adhikaar

post *v.t.* नियुक्त करना niyukt karna

postage *n.* डाक महसूल daak mahusul

postal *a.* डाक संबंधी daak sambandhi

post-date *v.t.* उत्तरदिनांकित करना utterdinankit karna

poster *n.* इश्तिहार ishtihaar

posterity *n.* वंश vansh

posthumous *a.* मरणोत्तर maronotar

postman *n.* डाकिया dakiya

postmaster *n.* पत्रपाल patrapaal

posticoos *a.* बहिर्मुख bahirmukh

post-mortem *n.* शव परीक्षा shav pariksha

post-office *n.* डाकघर daakghar

postpone *v.t.* टालना talna

postponener *n.* स्थगन sthagan

postscript *n.* अनुलेख anulekh

posture *n.* मुद्रा mudra

pot *n.* बरतन bartan

potash *n.* पोटाश potash

potassium *n.* पोटैशियम युक्त potassium yukt

potato *n.* आलू aalu

potency *n.* शक्ति shakti

potent *a.* प्रबल prabal

potential *a.* शक्य shakya

potentiality *n.* संभावना sambhawana

potter *n.* कुम्हार kumhar

pottery *n.* मिट्टी के पात्र mitte ki patra

pouch *n.* थैली thaile

poultry *n.* घरेलू मुर्गी gharelu murgi

pounce *n* झपट्टा jhapatta

pounce *v.i.* झपटना jhapatna

pound *v.t.* कूटना kutna

pour *v.i.* बहना bahana

poverty *n.* कमी kami

powder *v.t.* बुकनी करना bookni karna

powder *n.* पाउडर powder

power *n.* शक्ति shakti

powerful *a.* शक्तिशाली shaktishali

practicability *n.* साध्यता sadhyata

practicable *a.* करने योग्य karne yogya

practical *a.* उपयोगी upyogi

practice *n.* क्रिया kriya

practise *v.t.* अभ्यास करना abhyas karna

practitioner *n.* व्यवसायी vyavasayee

pragmatic *a.* व्यवहारमूलक vyavaharmulak

praise *n.* प्रशंसा prashansa

praise *v.t.* प्रशंसा करना prashansa karna

praiseworthy *a.* सराहने योग्य sarhane yogya

prank *n.* क्रीड़ा krirha

prattle *n.* बचकानी बात bachkani baat

pray *v.i.* प्रार्थना करना prathana karna

prayer *n.* प्रार्थना prathana

preacher *n.* धर्मोपदेशक dharmopadeshak

preamble *n.* भूमिका bhumika

precaution *n.* चौकसी chaukasi

precede *v.* आगे होना aage hona

precedence *n.* पूर्व आगमन purva agman

precedent *n.* नज़ीर najir

precept *n.* उपदेश updesh

preceptor *n.* गुरु guru

precious *a.* महंगा mahanga

precis *n.* संक्षेप sankshep

precise *n.* यथार्थ yatharth

precision *n.* यथार्थता yatharthta

precursor *n.* अग्रदूत agradut

predecessor *n.* पूर्वाधिकारी purvadhikari

predestination *n.* पूर्वनियति purvaniyati

predicament *n.* कठिन परिस्थिति kathin paristhiti

predicate *n.* विधेय vidhaya

predict *v.t.* भविष्यवाणी करना bhavishvani karna

prediction *n.* भविष्यवाणी bhavishvani

predominance *n.* प्रबलता prabalta

predominant *a.* प्रबल prabal

predominate *v.i.* प्रमुख होना pramukh hona

pre-eminence *n.* उत्कृष्टता uthkrishta

pre-eminent *a.* उत्कृष्ट uthkrisht

preface *n.* प्रस्तावना prastavana

preface *v.t.* भूमिका लिखना bhumika lekhna

preference *n.* पसंद pasand

preferential *a.* तरजीही jarjihi

prefix *n.* उपसर्ग upsarga

prefix *v.t.* उपसर्ग लगाना upsarga lagana

pregnancy *n.* गर्भावस्था garbhavastha

pregnant *a.* गर्भवती garbhavarti

prehistoric *a.* प्रागैतिहासिक pragetihasik

prejudice *n.* पूर्वधारणा purvadharna

prelate *n.* धर्माधिकारी dharmadhikari

preliminary *a.* प्राथमिक prathamik

preliminary *n* प्रारंभिक कार्यवाही prarrmbhik karyavahi

prelude *n.* मंगलाचरण manglacharan

prelude *v.t.* परिचित कराना parichit karna

premarital *a.* विवाह से पूर्व का vivah se purva ka

premature *a.* कालपूर्व kaal purva

premeditate *v.t.* पूर्वयोजन करना purvayojan karna

premeditation *n.* पूर्वचिंतन purvachintan

premier *a.* प्रमुख pramukh

premier *n* प्रधानमंत्री pradhanmantri

premiere *n.* प्रथम प्रदर्शन pratham pradarshan

premium *n.* बीमा शुल्क bima shulk

premonition *n.* पूर्वबोध purvavbodh

preoccupation *n.* मानसिक व्यस्तता mansik vyastata

preoccupy *v.t.* तल्लीन करना tallin karna

preparatory *a.* प्रारंभिक prarambhik

prepare *v.t.* तैयार करना taiyyar karna

preponderance *n.* प्रमुखता pramukhta

preponderate *v.i.* प्रबल prabal

preposition *n.* पूर्वसर्ग purvasarg

prerequisite *a.* पूर्वापेक्षित purvapekshit

prerequisite *n* पूर्वापेक्षा purvapeksha

prerogative *n.* परमाधिकार parmadhikaar

prescience *n.* पूर्वबोध purvabodh

prescribe *v.t.* निर्धारित करना nirdharit karna

prescription *n.* निर्धारण nirdharan

presence *n.* उपस्थिति upasthiti

present *a.* विद्यमान vidyaman

present *n.* वर्तमान vartaman

present *v.t.* प्रस्तुत करना prastut karna

presentation *n.* उपहार प्रदान करना uphar pradan karna

presently *adv.* शीघ्र shighrah

preservation *n.* परिरक्षण parirakshan

preservative *n.* परिरक्षक parirakshak

preservative *a.* परिरक्षी parirakshi

preserve *v.t.* बनाए रखना banay rakhna

preserve *n.* परिरक्षित वस्तु parirakshit vastu

preside *v.i.* सभापति होना sabhapati hona

press *v.t.* जल्दी करना jaldi karna

press *n* छपाई की मशीन chhapai ki machine

pressure *n.* कष्ट kashth

pressurize *v.t.* दबाव डालना dabav dalna

prestige *n.* प्रतिष्ठा pratishtha

prestigious *a.* प्रतिष्ठा संबंधी pratishtha sambandhi

presume *v.t.* साहस करना sahas karna

presumption *n.* अनुमान anuman

presuppose *v.t.* मान लेना maan lena

presupposition *n.* पूर्वधारणा purvadharna

pretence *n.* बहाना bahana

pretend *v.t.* बहाना करना bahana karna

pretension *n.* दावा dava

pretentious *a.* मिथ्या दावेदार mithya daavaidaar

pretext *n* बहाना bahana

prettiness *n.* सुंदरता sundarta

pretty *a* सुंदर sundar

pretty *adv.* बहुत कुछ bahut kuch

prevail *v.i.* सफल होना safal hona

prevalence *n.* प्रचलन prachalan

prevalent *a.* प्रबल prabal

prevent *v.t.* बाधा डालना badha dalna

prevention *n.* निवारण nivaran

preventive *a.* निवारक nivarak

previous *a.* पहला pahla

prey *n.* शिकार shikaar

prey *v.i.* शिकार करना shikaar karna

price *n.* महत्व mahatva

prick *v.t.* प्रेरित करना prairet karna

prick *n.* कांटा kanta

pride *n.* अभिमान abhiman

pride *v.t.* अभिमान करना abhiman karna

priest *n.* पुरोहित purohit

priestess *n.* पुजारिन pujarin

priesthood *n.* पुरोहित वर्ग purohit varg

prima facie *adv.* प्रथम द्रष्टया pratham dristiya

primarily *adv.* मूलत: mulat:

primary *a.* प्रधान pradhan

prime *a.* आधारभूत adharbhut

prime *n.* यौवन yuvan

primer *n.* प्रवेशिका pravishika

primeval *a.* आदि युगीन adi yugin

primitive *a.* पुरातन puratan

prince *n.* राजकुमार rajkumar

princely *a.* शानदार shandar

princess *n.* राजकुमारी rajkumari

principal *n.* प्रधान व्यक्ति pradhan vyakti

principal *a* प्रथम pratham

principle *n.* ईमानदारी imandari

print *n* निशान nishan

printer *n.* मुद्रक mudrak

prior *a.* पूर्ववर्ती purvavarti

prior *n* मठाध्यक्ष mathadhyaksh

prioress *n.* मठाध्यक्षा mathadhyaksha

priority *n.* प्रथमता prathamta

prison *n.* कारागार karagaar

prisoner *n.* बंदी bandi

privacy *n.* एकांत ekant

private *a.* गैर सरकारी ghair sarkari

privation *n.* असुविधा asuvidha

privilege *n.* विशेषाधिकार vishaishadhikar

prize *n.* पुरस्कार puraskar

prize *v.t.* कद्र करना kadra karna

probability *n.* संभावना sambhavana

probable *a.* संभावित sambhavit

probably *adv.* संभवतया sambhavayata

probation *n.* परिवीक्षा काल pariviksha kaal

probationer *n.* परिवीक्षार्थी parivishharthi

probe *n* जांच पड़ताल janch padtal

problem *n.* समस्या samasya

problematic *a.* समस्यात्मक samasyatmak

procedure *n.* कार्यपद्धति karyapaddhati

proceed *v.i.* कार्य जारी रखना karya jari rakhna

proceeding *n.* कानूनी कार्यवाही kanuni karyavahi

process *n.* प्रगति pragati

procession *n.* जुलूस julus

proclaim *v.t.* घोषणा करना ghoshna karna

proclamation *n.* घोषणा ghoshna

proclivity *n.* झुकाव jhukao

procrastinate *v.i.* टालमटोल करना taalmatol karna

procrastination *n.* टालमटोल taalmatol

proctor *n.* अनुशासन अधिकार anushasan adhikaari

procure *v.t.* प्राप्त करना prapt karna

procurement *n.* प्राप्ति prapti

prodigal *a.* अपव्यय apvyaya

prodigality *n.* उदारता udarta

produce *v.t.* पूर्ति करना purti karna

produce *n.* कृषि उत्पादन krishi utpaadan

product *n.* परिणाम parinaam

production *n.* उत्पादन utpadan

productive *a.* उत्पादक uthpadak

productivity *n.* उत्पादकता uthpadakta

profane *v.t.* अपवित्र करना apvitra karna

profane *a.* अश्लील ashlil

profession *n.* घोषणा ghoshna

professional *a.* व्यवसाय संबंधी vyavasay sambandhi

professor *n.* प्राध्यापक pradhyapak

proficiency *n.* निपुणता nipunnta

proficient *a.* प्रवीण pravin

profile *n.* रेखाचित्र rekhachitra

profit *n.* लाभ labh

profit *v.t.* लाभ पहुंचाना labh pahuchana

profitable *a.* लाभकारी labhkari

profiteer *n.* मुनाफ़ाखोर munafakhor

profiteer *v.i.* मुनाफ़ाखोरी करन munafakhori karna

profligacy *n.* अनैतिकता anaitekta

profligate *a.* लापरवाह laparvah

profound *a.* गहन gahan

profundity *n.* गहराई geharai

profuse *a.* प्रचुर prachur

profusion *n.* प्रचुरता prachurta

progeny *n.* संतान santan

programme *n.* योजना yojana

programme *v.t.* कार्यक्रम बनाना karyakarm banana

progress *n.* प्रगति pragati

progress *v.i.* प्रगति करना pragati karna

progressive *a.* प्रगतिशील pragatishil

prohibit *v.t.* मना करना mana karna

prohibition *n.* निषेध nishedh

prohibitory *a.* निषेधात्मक nishedhatmak

project *n.* योजना yojana

projectile *n.* प्रक्षेपणास्त्र prakshepanastra

projectile *a* प्रक्षेप्य prakshepya

projector *n.* प्रक्षेपित्र prakshepitr

proliferation *n.* तीव्र बृद्धि tivra vridhi

prolific *a.* फलदायक faldayak

prologue *n.* भूमिका bhumika

prolong *v.t.* लंबा करना lamba karna

prolongation *n.* दीर्घीकरण dirghikaran

prominence *n.* विशिष्टता vishishitata

prominent *a.* विशिष्ट vishishit

promise *v.t* वचन देना vachan dena

promise *n* वादा vada

promising *a.* होनहार honehaaı

promissory *a.* प्रतिज्ञात्मक pratigyatmak

promote *v.t.* बढ़ावा देना badhava dena

promotion *n.* विकास vikas

prompt *a.* तत्पर tatpar

prompt *v.t.* प्रेरित करना prairet karna

prompter *n.* अनुबोधक anubodhak

prone *a.* इच्छुक icchuk

pronoun *n.* सर्वनाम sarvanaam

pronunciation *n.* उच्चारण uccharan

proof *n.* प्रमाण pramaan

prop *n.* थूनी thuni

prop *v.t.* सहारा देना sahara dena

propaganda *n.* प्रचार prachar

propagandist *n.* प्रचारक pracharak

propagate *v.t.* फैलाना failana

propagation *n.* प्रसारण prasaran

propel *v.t.* ठेलना thelna

proper *a.* उचित ucchit

property *n.* गुणधर्म gundharm

prophecy *n.* भविष्यकथन bhavishyakathan

prophesy *v.t.* पहले से बता देना pahle se bata dena

prophet *n.* पैग़ंबर paighambar

prophetic *a.* पैग़ंबरी paighambari

proportion *n.* अनुपात anupat

proportion *v.t.* समानुपातन करना samanupatan karna

proportional *a.* समानुपातिक samanupatik

proportionate *a.* समानुपाती samanupati

proposal *n.* सुझाव sujhao

propose *v.t.* प्रस्तावित करना prastavit karna

proposition *n.* कथन kathan

propound *v.t.* प्रस्तावित करना prastavit karna

proprietary *a.* मालिकाना malikana

proprietor *n.* स्वामी swami

propriety *n.* उपयुक्तता upyuktata

prorogue *v.t.* अवसान करना avasan karna

prosaic *a.* नीरस niras

prose *n.* गद्य gadhya

prosecute *v.t.* मुक़दमा चलाना muqaddma chalana

prosecution *n.* अभियोजन abhiyojan

prosecutor *n.* अभियोक्ता abhiyokta

prosody *n.* छंदशास्त्र chhandshastra

prospect *n.* आशा asha

prospective *a.* भावी bhavi

prospectus *n.* विवरण पुस्तिका vivran pustika

prosper *v.i.* सफल होन safal hona

prosperity *n.* सफलता safalta

prosperous *a.* सफल safal

**prostitute** *n.* वेश्या veshya
**prostitute** *v.t.* दुरूपयोग करना durupyog karna
**prostitution** *n.* दुरूपयोग durpayog
**prostrate** *a.* पराजित parajit
**prostrate** *v.t.* गिरा देना gira dena
**prostration** *n.* दंडवत् अवस्था dandvat karna
**protagonist** *n.* नायक nayak
**protection** *n.* बचाव bachav
**protective** *a.* संरक्षी sanrakshi
**protector** *n.* रक्षक rakshak
**protein** *n.* प्रोटीन protein
**protest** *n.* विरोध virodh
**protest** *v.i.* प्रतिवाद करना prativad
**protestation** *n.* विरोध virodh
**prototype** *n.* आदिरूप adirup
**proud** *a.* घमंडी ghamandi
**prove** *v.t.* प्रमाणित करना pramanit karna
**proverb** *n.* कहावत kahavat
**proverbial** *a.* सर्वविदित sarvavadit
**provide** *v.i.* तैयारी करना taiyari karna
**providence** *n.* दूरदृष्टि durdrishti
**provident** *a.* दूरदर्शी durdarshi
**providential** *a.* शुभ shubh
**province** *n.* प्रांत prant
**provincial** *a.* प्रान्तीय prantiya
**provincialism** *n.* संकीर्णता sankirnata
**provision** *n.* भंडार bhandar
**provisional** *a.* अस्थायी asthayi
**proviso** *n.* शर्त shart
**provocation** *n.* चिढ़ने का कारण chirdhne ka karan
**provocative** *a.* उत्तेजक uttejak
**provoke** *v.t.* चिढ़ाना chhedna
**prowess** *n.* वीरता virta
**proximate** *a.* निकट संबंधी nikat sambandhi
**proximity** *n.* निकटता nikatta

**proxy** *n.* अधिकृत कार्यकर्ता adhikrit karyakarta
**prudence** *n.* सावधानी savdhani
**prudent** *a.* विवेक vivek
**prudential** *a.* विवेकपूर्ण vivekpurna
**prune** *v.t.* छंटाई करना chhantai karna
**pry** *v.i.* ताक झांक करना taak jhaank karna
**psalm** *n.* धार्मिक भजन dharmik bhajan
**pseudonym** *n.* छद्‌नाम chhadram
**psyche** *n.* मानसिकता mansikta
**psychiatrist** *n.* मनश्चिकित्सक manashchikitsak
**psychiatry** *n.* मनश्चिकित्सा manashchikitsa
**psychic** *a.* मनोवैज्ञानिक manovaigyanik
**psychological** *a.* मनोवैज्ञानिक manovaigyanik
**psychologist** *n.* मनोविज्ञानी manovigyani
**psychology** *n.* मनोविज्ञान manovigyan
**psychopath** *n.* मनोरोगी manorogi
**psychosis** *n.* मनोविकृति manovikriti
**psychotherapy** *n.* मनश्चिकित्सा manashchikitsa
**puberty** *n.* तारुण्य tarunya
**public** *a.* सार्वजनिक sarvajanik
**public** *n.* जनता janta
**publication** *n.* प्रकाशन prakashan
**publicity** *n.* प्रचार prachar
**publicize** *v.t.* प्रचारित करना pracharit karna
**publish** *v.t.* प्रकाशित करना prakashit karna
**publisher** *n.* प्रकाशक rakashak
**pudding** *n.* पुडिंग pudding
**puddle** *n.* पोखर pokhar
**puddle** *v.t.* गंदला करना gandala karna
**puerile** *a.* बचकाना bachkana
**puff** *n.* झोंका jhonka
**pull** *v.t.* उखाड़ना ukhadana
**pull** *n.* प्रभाव prabhav
**pulley** *n.* घिरनी ghirni

pullover *n.* जरसी jarsi
pulp *n.* गूदा gooda
pulp *v.t.* लुग्दी बनाना lugdi banana
pulpit *a.* प्रवचन मंच pravachan manch
pulpy *a.* गूदेदार goodedar
pulsate *v.i.* धड़कना dhadkana
pulsation *n.* धड़कन dhadkan
pulse *n.* नब्ज़ nabz
pulse *v.i.* स्पंदित होना sampadit hona
pulse *n* दाल dal
pump *n.* पंप pump
pump *v.t.* पंप से उठाना pump se uthana
pumpkin *n.* कद्दू kaddu
pun *n.* यमक yamak
punch *n.* मुक्का mukka
punch *v.t.* मुक्का मारना mukka marna
punctual *a.* समय का पाबंद samay ka
    paband
punctuality *n.* समय की पाबंदी samay ki
    pabandi
punctuation *n.* विराम चिह्न विधान viram
    chihn vidhan
puncture *n.* छेदन chhedan
puncture *v.t.* नोक से छेद करना nok se
    chhed karna
pungency *n.* तीखापन tikhapan
pungent *a.* तीव्र tivra
punish *v.t.* दंड देना dand dena
punishment *n.* दंड dand
punitive *a.* दंडात्मक dandatmak
puny *a.* छोटा व दुर्बल chhota va durlabh
pupil *n.* पुतली putli
puppet *n.* अधीन व्यक्ति adhin vyakti
puppy *n.* पिल्ला pilla
purblind *n.* चुंधा chhundha
purchase *v.t.* खरीदना kharidana
purchase *n.* खरीद kharid
pure *a* पवित्र pavitra
purgation *n.* विरेचन virechen

purgative *n.* विरेचक पदार्थ virechek
    padarth
purgative *a* शोधक shodhak
purgatory *n.* शुद्धि का स्थान shudhi ka
    sthan
purge *v.t.* पवित्र करना pavitra karna
purification *n.* शुद्धिकरण shudhikaran
purify *v.t.* पवित्र करना pavitra karna
purist *n.* शुद्धिवादी shudhivadi
puritan *n.* नियमनिष्ठ व्यक्ति niyamnishth
    vyakti
puritanical *a.* नैतिकतावादी naitikatavadi
purity *n.* शुचिता shuchita
purple *adj./n.* बैंगनी baingani
purport *v.t.* दावा करना dawa karna
purpose *n.* प्रयोजन paryojan
purpose *v.t.* उद्देश्य रखना uddeshya rakhna
purposely *adv.* जानबूझकर jaanbhujkar
purr *v.i.* म्याऊँ करना miaun karna
purse *n.* बटुआ batua
pursuance *n.* पालन palan
pursue *v.t.* पीछा करना peecha karna
pursuit *n.* धंधा dhanda
purview *n.* परिधि paridhi
pus *n.* मवाद mavad
push *v.t.* ज़ोर देना zor dena
push *n.* धक्का dhakka
put *v.t.* रखना rakhna
puzzle *n.* उलझन uljhan
pygmy *n.* बौना bauna
pyorrhoea *n.* पायरिया payaria
pyramid *n.* पिरामिड piramid
pyre *n.* चिता chita
python *n.* अजगर ajgar

quack *n* बतख का शब्द batakh ka shabd
quackery *n.* नीमहकीमी neemhakimi

quadrangle *n.* चौकोर आंगन chaukor angan

quadrangular *a.* चतुष्कोणीय chatushkoniya

quadrilateral *a. & n.* चार भुजा की chaar bhuja ki

quadruped *n.* चौपाया chaupaya

quadruple *a.* चौगुना chauguna

quadruple *v.t.* चौगुना करना chauguna karna

quail *n.* बटेर batair

quaint *a.* विचित्र vichitra

quake *n* कंपकंपी kapkampi

quake *v.i.* कांपना kampna

qualification *n.* मर्यादा maryada

qualify *v.i.* सीमित करना seemit karna

qualitative *a.* जाति jaati

quality *n.* पद pad

quandary *n.* दुविधा duvidha

quantitative *a.* परिणाम संबंधी parinam sambandhi

quantity *n.* विस्तार vistaar

quarrel *v.i.* झगड़ना jhagarhna

quarrel *n.* झगड़ा jhagrha

quarrelsome *a.* लड़ाका larhaka

quarry *n.* खदान khadaan

quarter *v.t.* चार भाग करना char bhag karna

quarter *n.* स्थान sthan

queen *n.* महारानी maharani

queer *a.* अनूठा anutha

quell *v.t.* वश में करना vash mein karna

quench *v.t.* शांत करना shant karna

query *n* प्रश्न prashan

query *v.t* प्रश्न करना prashan karna

query *n.* पूछताछ puchtach

quest *n.* अनुसंधान anusandhan

quest *v.t.* खोज करना khoj karna

question *v.t.* संदेह करना sandeh karna

question *n.* जांच janch

questionable *a.* संदेहयुक्त sandehyukt

questionnaire *n.* प्रश्नमाला prashanmaala

queue *n.* पंक्ति pankti

quibble *v.i.* वाक्रछल करना vakrchal karna

quibble *n.* वाक्रछल vakrchal

quick *a.* फुर्तीला furteela

quicksilver *n.* पारद paarad

quiet *a.* चुपचाप chupchaap

quiet *n.* शांति shaanti

quiet *v.t.* स्थिर करना sthir karna

quilt *n.* तोषक की खोली tooshak ki kholi

quinine *n.* कुनैन kunain

quintessence *n.* मुख्य लक्षण mukhya lakshan

quit *v.t.* छोड़ना chodna

quite *adv.* बिलकुल bilkul

quiver *v.i.* कांपना kampana

quiver *n.* तरकस tarkas

quixotic *a.* वीरतापूर्ण virtapurna

quiz *v.t.* प्रश्न पूछना prashan puchna

quorum *n.* कोरम koram

quota *n.* कोटा kota

quotation *n.* प्रचलित मूल्य prachlit mulya

quote *v.t.* मूल्य बतलाना mulya batana

quotient *n.* भागफल bhagphal

# R

rabbit *n.* खरगोश khargosh

rabies *n.* जलातंक jalatank

race *v.i* तेज़ दौड़ना tez daurhana

race *n.* वंश vansh

rack *n.* शिकंजा shikanja

rack *v.t.* मरोड़ना marorhna

racket *n.* टेनिस का बल्ला tenis ka balla

radiance *n.* चमक chamak

radiant *a.* चमकीला chamakeea

radiate *v.i.* प्रसारित करना prasarit karna

radiation *n.* प्रसारण prasaran

radical *a.* मौलिक maulik

radio *n.* बिना तार का यंत्र bina taar ka yantr

radish *n.* मूली mauli

radium *n.* रेडियम धातु radium dhatu

radius *n.* त्रिज्या trijya

rag *v.t.* कष्ट देना kasht dena

rag *n.* वस्त्रखंड vastrkhand

rage *v.i.* क्रोध करना krodh karna

rage *n.* क्रोध krodh

raid *v.t.* धावा बोलना dhava bolna

raid *n.* छापा chapa

rail *v.t.* गाली देना gaali dena

rail *n.* रेलमार्ग railmarg

railing *n.* घेरा ghera

raillery *n.* मज़ाक mazaak

railway *n.* रेलपथ railpath

rain *n* वर्षा varsha

rain *v.i.* वर्षा होना varsha hona

rainy *a.* वर्षावाला varshwala

raise *v.t.* निर्माण करना nirman karna

raisin *n.* किशमिश kishmish

rally *n* लंबी भिड़ंत lambi bhindant

rally *v.t.* शक्ति जुटाना shakti jutaana

ram *v.t.* टक्कर मारना takkar maarna

ram *n.* भेड़ा bhera

ramble *n* पर्यटन paryatan

ramble *v.t.* घूमना ghumana

rampant *a.* अनियंत्रित aniyantrit

rampart *n.* किले की दीवार kile ki diwar

rancour *n.* गहरी शत्रुता gahari shatruta

random *a.* एकाएक किया हुआ eka- ek kiya hua

range *n.* चांदमारी chandmari

range *v.t.* क्रम से रखना kram se rakhna

ranger *n.* वनपाल vanpal

rank *v.t.* स्थान रखना sthan rakhna

rank *a* अशिष्ट ashisht

rank *n.* पंक्ति pankti

ransack *v.t.* खोजना khojna

ransom *n.* रिहाई rihayee

rape *v.t.* बलात्कार करना balatkar karna

rape *n.* बलात्कार balaatkar

rapid *a.* तीव्र tivra

rapidity *n.* तीव्रता tivrata

rapier *n.* हल्की तलवार halki

rapport *n.* मेल mail

rapt *a.* तन्मय tanmaya

rapture *n.* हर्षातिरेक harshatirek

rare *a.* विरल viral

rarefaction *n* सुखाने का कार्य sukhane ka karya

rascal *n.* धूर्त व्यक्ति dhurt vyakti

rash *a.* जल्दबाज़ jaldbaaz

rat *n.* चूहा chuha

rate *n.* अनुपात anupaat

rate *v.t.* मूल्यांकन करना mulyankan karna

rather *adv.* कुछ-कुछ kuch kuch

ratify *v.t.* पुष्टि करना pushti karna

ratio *n.* अनुपात anupaat

ration *n.* रसद rasad

rational *a.* विवेकशील viveksheel

rationality *n.* तर्कशक्ति tarkshakti

rattle *v. t* खड़खड़ाना kharhkharhana

rattle *n* खड़खड़ kharhkharh

ravage *v.t.* तहस नहस करना tahas nahas karna

ravage *n.* विध्वंस vidhwans

rave *v.i.* बड़बड़ाना badbadana

raven *n.* काला कौआ kala kawa

ravine *n.* कंदरा kandra

raw *a.* अनिर्मित anirmit

ray *n.* किरण kiran

raze *v.t.* भूमिसात करना bhumisat karna

razor *n.* उस्तरा ustara

reach *v.t.* प्राप्त करना prapt karna

react *v.i.* प्रतिकार करना pratikar karna

reaction *n.* विरुद्ध क्रिया virudh kriya

read *v.t.* बोलना bolna

reader *n.* रीडर reader

readily *adv.* सुख से sukh se

readiness *n.* इच्छा ichcha

ready *a.* तैयार taiyar

real *a.* असली asali

realism *n.* यथार्थ yatharth

realist *n.* यथार्थवादी yatharthavadi

realistic *a.* यथार्थवादी yatharthavadi

reality *n.* वास्तविकता vastvikta

realization *n.* वसूली vasuli

realize *v.t.* वसूल करना vasool karna

really *adv.* वास्तव में vastav mein

realm *a.* राज्य rajya

reaper *n.* फ़सल-कट मशीन fasal kat machine

rear *v.t.* पालन पोषण करना palan poshan karna

rear *n.* पिछला भाग pichla bhag

reason *v.i.* तर्क करना tark karna

reason *n.* कारण karan

reasonable *a.* तर्कशील tarksheel

reassure *v.t.* पुन: विश्वास दिलाना puna vishwas dilana

rebate *n.* छूट chut

rebel *v.i.* विद्रोह करना vidroh karna

rebel *n.* विद्रोही vidroohi

rebellion *n.* बग़ावत bagawat

rebellious *a.* बाग़ी baagi

rebirth *n.* पुनर्जन्म punarjanm

rebound *v.i.* प्रतिक्षिप्त होना pratikshipt hona

rebound *n.* उच्छलन uchalana

rebuff *v.t.* रोकना rokana

rebuff *n.* पराजय parajay

rebuke *n.* फटकार phatkaar

rebuke *v.t.* फटकारना phatkarna

recall *n.* वापस बुलाना vapas bulaana

recede *v.i.* पीछे या दूर जाना piche ya dur jana

receipt *n.* पावती pavati

receive *v.t.* स्वीकार करना swikaar karna

receiver *n.* पानेवाला panewaala

recent *a.* ताज़ा taaza

recently *adv.* हाल ही में haal hi mein

reception *n.* स्वागत swagat

receptive *a.* शीघ्र ग्रहणकारी shighra grahankari

recess *n.* गुप्त स्थान gupt sthan

recession *n.* वापसी vapasi

recipe *n.* पाक विधि paak vidhi

recipient *n.* प्रापक prapak

reciprocal *a.* पारस्परिक parasparik

reciprocate *v.t.* अदल बदल करना adal badal karna

recital *n.* गायन प्रस्तुति gayan prastuti

recitation *n.* पाठ path

recite *v.t.* सुनाना sunana

reckless *a.* जल्दबाज़ jaldbaazi

reckon *v.t.* अनुमान लगाना anuman lagana

reclaim *v.t.* सुधारना sudharana

reclamation *n* सुधार sudhar

recluse *n.* एकांतवासी ekantvasi

recognition *n.* पहचान pehchan

recognize *v.t.* पहचान लेना pehchan lena

recoil *v.i.* वापस निकल जाना vapas nikal jana

recoil *adv.* वापसी vapasi

recollect *v.t.* स्मरण करना smaran karna

recollection *n.* स्मरण smaran

recommend *v.t.* प्रशंसा करना prashansa

recommendation *n.* संस्तुति sanstuti

recompense *n.* पुरस्कार puruskar

recompense *v.t.* प्रतिफल देना pratifal dena

reconcile *v.t.* मेलमिलाप कराना mailmilap karna

reconciliation *n.* मित्रता का नवीनीकरण mitrata ka navinikaran

record *v.t.* अंकित करना ankit karna

record *n.* कीर्तिमान kirtiman

recorder *n.* लेखक lekhak

recount *v.t.* ब्यौरा देना byora dena

recoup *v.t.* क्षतिपूर्ति करना kshatipurti karna

recourse *n.* आश्रय ashrya

recover *v.t.* वापिस पाना vapis pana

recovery *n.* वसूली vasuli

recreation *n.* मनोरंजन manoranjan

recruit *v.t.* भर्ती करना barti karna

recruit *n.* रंगरूट rangroot

rectangle *n.* आयत aayat

rectangular *a.* आयताकार aytaakaar

rectification *n.* समाधान samaadhaan

rectify *v.i.* सही करना sahi karna

rectum *n.* गुदा, मलद्वार gudda, maldwar

recur *v.i.* पुनरावृत्ति होना punravrati hona

recurrence *n.* पुनरागमन punragaman

recurrent *a.* आवर्तक avartak

red *n.* लाल रंग laal rang

red *a.* लाल रंग का laal rang ka

redden *v.t.* लाल होना laal hona

reddish *a.* ललछौंहां lalchauhan

redeem *v.t.* मुक्त करना mukt karna

redemption *n.* छुटकारा chutkara

redouble *v.t.* बढ़ाना badhana

redress *n* सुधार sudhaar

redress *v.t.* उपाय करना upaya karna

reduce *v.t.* कम करना kam karna

reduction *n.* कमी kami

redundancy *n.* फ़ालतूपन phaltupan

redundant *a.* अनावश्यक anavashyak

reel *n.* रील reel

reel *v.i.* लड़खड़ाना ladkhadana

refer *v.t.* भेजना bhejana

referee *n.* निर्णयकर्त्ता nirnayakarta

reference *n.* निर्देशन nirdeshan

referendum *n.* जनमत संग्रह janmat sangreh

refine *v.t.* शुद्घ करना shudh karna

refinement *n.* शुद्घता shudhata

refinery *n.* परिशोधनशाला parishodhan shala

reflect *v.t.* परावर्तित करना paravartit karna

reflection *n.* परावर्तन paravartan

reflective *a.* परावर्तक paravartak

reflector *n.* प्रतिक्षेपक pratikshepak

reflex *a* परावर्तित paravartit

reflex *n.* अनैच्छिक क्रिया anaichik kriya

reflexive *a* कर्त्ता संबंधी karta sambandhi

reform *n.* सुधार sudhaar

reform *v.t.* सुधारना sudharna

reformation *n.* सुधार sudhaar

reformatory *n.* सुधार गृह sudhar greha

reformatory *a* सुधारात्मक sudharatmak

reformer *n.* सुधारक sudharak

refrain *v.i.* अलग रहना alag rehna

refresh *v.t.* नया करना naya karna

refreshment *n.* जलपान jalpaan

refrigerate *v.t.* शीतल करना sheetal karna

refrigeration *n.* प्रशीतन prashitan

refrigerator *n.* प्रशीतित्र prashititr

refuge *n.* शरण sharan

refugee *n.* शरणार्थी sharanarthi

refulgence *n.* चमक chamak

refulgent *a.* देदीप्यमान dedipyaman

refund *v.t.* लौटाना lautana

refund *n.* धन की वापसी dhan ki wapasi

refusal *n.* प्रतिषेध pratishedh

refuse *v.t.* मना करना mana karna

refuse *n.* मल mal

refutation *n.* खंडन khandan

refute *v.t.* खंडन करना khandan karna

regal *a.* राजकीय rajkiya

regard *n.* ध्यान dhyan

regard *v.t.* आदर करना aadar karna

regenerate *v.t.* सुधारना sudharna

regeneration *n.* सुधार sudhar

regicide *n.* राजहंता rajhanta

regime *n.* प्रशासन prashasan

regiment *n.* सैन्यदल sainyadal

regiment *v.t.* संगठित करना sangathit karna

region *n.* भूभाग bhubhaag
regional *a.* क्षेत्रीय kshetriya
register *n.* लेखा lekha
register *v.t.* दर्ज करना darj karna
registrar *n.* पंजीयक panjiyak
registration *n.* पंजीयन panjiyan
registry *n.* पंजीयन panjiyan
regret *n* खेद khed
regret *v.i.* दु:खी होना dukhi hona
regular *a.* औपचारिक aupacharik
regularity *n.* नियमितता niyamitata
regulate *v.t.* नियमित करना niyamit karna
regulation *n.* व्यवस्थापन vyvasthapan
regulator *n.* प्रबंधकर्त्ता prabandhakarta
rehabilitate *v.t.* पूर्व अवस्था में लाना purva awastha
rehabilitation *n.* पुनर्निवेशन punarnirveshan
rehearsal *n.* पूर्व प्रयोग purv prayog
rehearse *v.t.* दुहराना duharana
reign *v.i.* राज्य करना rajya karna
reign *n* राज्यकाल rajyakal
reimburse *v.t.* लौटाना lautana
rein *v.t.* रोकना rokana
rein *n.* लगाम lagam
reinforce *v.t.* सुदृढ़ बनाना sudridh banana
reinforcement *n.* सुदृढ़ीकरण sudhridhikaran
reinstate *v.t.* बहाल करना behal karna
reinstatement *n.* बहाली bahaali
reiterate *v.t.* बार बार दुहराना baar baar duhrana
reiteration *n.* पुनरावृत्ति punravrati
reject *v.t.* अस्वीकार करना aswikar karana
rejection *n.* अस्वीकार aswikar
rejoice *v.i.* प्रसन्न होना prasanna hona
rejoin *v.t.* प्रत्युत्तर देना pratyuttar dena
rejoinder *n.* प्रत्युत्तर pratyuttar
rejuvenation *n.* नई जवानी nayee jawani
relapse *n.* पतन patan

relate *v.t.* बताना bataana
relation *n.* संबंध sambandh
relative *n.* रिश्तेदार rishtedar
relative *a.* सापेक्ष sapeksh
relax *v.t.* शिथिल करना shithil karna
relaxation *n.* शिथिलता shithilta
relay *n.* नई टोली nayee toli
relay *v.t.* प्रसारित करना prasarit karana
release *n* प्रकाशन prakashan
release *v.t.* मुक्त करना mukt karana
relent *v.i.* नरम पड़ना naram padana
relentless *a.* दयाहीन dayaheen
relevance *n.* प्रासंगिकता prasangikta
relevant *a.* प्रासंगिक prasangik
reliable *a.* विश्वसनीय vishvasaniya
reliance *n.* भरोसा bharosa
relic *n.* निशानी nishani
relief *n.* आराम aaram
relieve *v.t.* कम करना kam karana
religion *n.* धर्म dharm
religious *a.* धार्मिक dharmik
relinquish *v.t.* त्याग देना tyag dena
relish *n* स्वाद swad
relish *v.t.* स्वाद लेना swad lena
reluctance *n.* अनिच्छा anichcha
reluctant *a.* अनिच्छुक anichchuk
rely *v.i.* निर्भर होना nirbhar hona
remain *v.i.* रहना rehna
remainder *n.* शेष shesh
remains *n.* अवशेष avshesh
remand *n* जेल वापसी jail wapasi
remand *v.t.* पुन: जेल भेजना punh jail bhejna
remark *n.* टिप्पणी tippani
remarkable *a.* असाधारण asadharan
remedial *a.* उपचारी upchaari
remedy *n.* उपाय upaya
remedy *v.t* ठीक करना thik karana
remember *v.t.* स्मरण रखना smaran karna
remembrance *n.* स्मारक smarak

remind *v.t.* याद दिलाना yaad dilaana

reminder *n.* स्मरणपत्र smaran patar

reminiscence *n.* स्मरण smaran

remission *n.* कमी kami

remit *v.t.* शिथिल करना shithil karna

remittance *n.* प्रेषण preshan

remorse *n.* पश्चाताप pashchatap

remote *a.* दूरस्थ durasth

removable *a.* हटाने योग्य hatane yogya

removal *n.* हटाने का कार्य hatane ka karya

remove *v.t.* हटाना hatana

remunerate *v.t.* मज़दूरी देना mazdoori dena

remuneration *n.* पुरस्कार puraskar

remunerative *a.* लाभकारी labhkari

renaissance *n.* पुनर्जन्म punarjanam

render *v.t.* लौटाना lautana

rendezvous *n.* मिलन स्थल milan sthal

renew *v.t.* नया करना naya karna

renewal *n.* नवीकरण navikaran

renounce *v.t.* छोड़ना chodna

renovate *v.t.* नया करना naya karna

renovation *n.* नवीकरण navikaran

renown *n.* यश yash

renowned *a.* प्रसिद्ध prasidh

rent *v.t.* किराये पर लेना kiraye par lena

rent *n.* मालगुजारी malgujari

renunciation *n.* आत्मत्याग atmatyag

repair *n.* मरम्मत marramat

repair *v.t.* मरम्मत करना marammat karana

reparable *a.* क्षतिपूर्ति योग्य kshatipurti yogya

repartee *n.* व्यंग्य उक्ति vyangya ukti

repatriate *v.t.* स्वदेश भेजना swadesh bhejna

repatriate *n* प्रत्यावर्तित व्यक्ति pratyavartit vykati

repatriation *n.* देश प्रत्यावर्तन desh pratyavartan

repay *v.t.* वापस करना vapas karna

repayment *n.* वापसी vapasi

repeal *n* निरसन nirsan

repeal *v.t.* निरस्त करना nirast karna

repel *v.t.* पीछे को हटाना peeche ko hatana

repellent *n* विकर्षक वस्तु vikarshak vastu

repellent *a.* विकर्षक vikarshak

repent *v.i.* पश्चात्ताप करना pashchatap karna

repentance *n.* पश्चात्ताप pashchatap

repentant *a.* पछतावा करनेवाला pachtava karnewala

repercussion *n.* प्रतिध्वनि pratidhvani

repetition *n.* आवृत्ति aavrati

replace *v.t.* पुन: स्थापित करना puna sthapit karna

replacement *n.* प्रतिस्थापन pratisthapan

replenish *v.t.* फिर से भरना phir se bharna

replete *a.* भरपूर bharpur

replica *n.* प्रतिकृति pratikrati

reply *v.i.* उत्तर देना uttar dena

reply *n* उत्तर uttar

report *n.* विवरण vivran

report *v.t.* बयान करना bayan karna

reporter *n.* संवाददाता samvaddata

repose *v.i.* आराम करना aaram karna

repose *n.* शांति shanti

repository *n.* भंडार गृह bhandar greh

represent *v.t.* वर्णन करना varnan karna

representation *n.* विरोध पत्र virodh patr

representative *a.* प्रदर्शक pradarshak

representative *n.* प्रतिनिधि pratinidhi

repress *v.t.* रोकना rokna

repression *n.* निदबाव nidbav

reprimand *v.t.* निंदा करना ninda karna

reprimand *n.* घुड़की ghudki

reprint *v.t.* पुन: मुद्रित करना puna mudrit karna

reprint *n.* पुनर्मुद्रण punar mudran

reproach *n.* धिक्कार dhikkar

reproach *v.t.* धिक्कारना dhikkarana
reproduction *n* प्रजनन prajnan
reproductive *a.* पुनरुत्पादक punrutpadan
reproof *n.* निंदा ninda
reptile *n.* रेंगनेवाला जंतु rengne wala jantu
republic *n.* प्रजातंत्र राज्य prajatantra rajya
republican *n* लोकतंत्रवादी loktantravaadi
republican *a.* लोकतंत्र संबंधी loktantra sambandhi
repudiate *v.t.* अस्वीकार करना aswikar karna
repudiation *n.* तिरस्कार tiraskaar
repugnance *n.* घृणा ghrina
repugnant *a.* अरुचिकर aruchikar
repulse *n.* खदेड़ने की क्रिया khaderne ki kriya
repulse *v.t.* खदेड़ना khaderna
repulsion *n.* घृणा ghrina
repulsive *a.* प्रतिकारक pratikarak
reputation *n.* यश yash
repute *n.* कीर्ति kirti
repute *v.t.* गणना करना ganana karna
request *n* प्रार्थना pratharna
request *v.t.* प्रार्थना करना pratharna karna
require *v.t.* मांगना maangna
requirement *n.* मांग maang
requisite *n* आवश्यक वस्तु awashyak vastu
requisite *a.* आवश्यक awashyak
requisition *n.* मांग mang
requisition *v.t.* मांगना mangna
requite *v.t.* लौटाना lautana
rescue *v.t.* मुक्त करना mukt karna
rescue *n* निस्तार nistaar
research *v.i.* अनुसंधान करना anusandhan karna
research *n* अनुसंधान anusabdhan
resemblance *n.* सादृश्य होना sadrishya hona
resemble *v.t.* के सदृश होना ke sadrashya hona

resent *v.t.* बुरा मानना bura manana
resentment *n.* अपमान apmaan
reservation *n.* छिपाव chhipaav
reserve *v.t.* बचा रखना bacha rakhna
reservoir *n.* कोश kosh
reside *v.i.* निवास करना nivas karna
residence *n.* निवासस्थान nivas sthan
resident *a.* निवासी nivasi
resident *n* रहने वाला rehne wala
residual *a.* शेष (भाग) shesh bhag
residue *n.* अवशेष avshesh
resign *v.t.* छोड़ना chodna
resignation *n.* परित्याग parityag
resist *v.t.* रोकना rokna
resistance *n.* विरोध virodh
resistant *a.* बाधक badhak
resolute *a.* कृतसंकल्प kritsankalp
resolution *n.* समाधान samadhan
resolve *v.t.* विश्लेषण करना vishleshan karna
resonance *n.* गूंज goonj
resonant *a.* गुंजायमान gunjayamaan
resort *v.i.* सहारा लेना sahara lena
resort *n* गमन gaman
resound *v.i.* गूंजना goonjana
resource *n.* साधन sadhan
resourceful *a.* उपाय कुशल upaya kushal
respect *v.t.* आदर करना aadar karna
respect *n.* आदर aadar
respectful *a.* श्रद्धालु shradhalu
respective *a.* निजी neji
respiration *n.* श्वसन shwasan
respire *v.i.* सांस लेना saans lena
resplendent *a.* देदीप्यमान dedipyman
respond *v.i.* उत्तर देना uttar dena
respondent *n.* प्रतिवादी prativadi
response *n.* उत्तर uttar
responsibility *n.* उत्तरदायित्व uttardayitva
responsible *a.* उत्तरदायी uttardayi
rest *v.i.* स्थिर होना sthir hona

rest *n* अवशेष awshesh
restaurant *n.* भोजनालय bhojanalaya
restive *a.* अड़ियल adiyal
restoration *n.* वापसी yaapasi
restore *v.t.* मरम्मत करना marammat
karna
restrain *v.t.* नियंत्रित करना niyantrit karna
restrict *v.t.* दबाना dabana
restriction *n.* सीमा seema
restrictive *a.* प्रतिबंधक pratibandhak
result *n.* परिणाम parinam
resume *n.* सार, संक्षेप saar, sanksep
resumption *n.* पुनर्ग्रहण punargrahan
resurgence *n.* पुरुत्थान purruthan
resurgent *a.* पुनरुत्थानशील punruthanshil
retail *v.t.* फुटकर बिक्री phutkar bikri
retail *adv.* खुदरा द्वारा khudra dwara
retail *a* खुदरा khudra
retailer *n.* फुटकर विक्रेता phutkar vikreta
retain *v.t.* रोक रखना rok rakhna
retaliate *v.i.* प्रतिकार करना pratikar karna
retaliation *n.* प्रतिकार pratikar
retard *v.t.* धीमा करना dheema karna
retardation *n.* गतिरोध gatirodh
retention *n.* अवधारणा avdharna
retentive *a.* धारणा शक्ति dharana shakti
reticence *n.* अल्पभाषिता alpbhashita
reticent *a.* अल्पभाषी alpbhashi
retinue *n.* नौकर चाकर naukar chakar
retirement *n.* कार्यमुक्ति karyamukti
retort *v.t.* जैसे को तैसा लौटाना jaisai ko
taisa lautana
retort *n.* मुंह तोड़ जवाब munh tor jawab
retouch *v.t.* परिष्कृत करना parishkrit
karna
retrace *v.t.* पर वापस जाना par vapas jana
retread *n.* रबर चढ़ा टायर rubber chadha
tyre
retreat *v.i.* पीछे हटना peeche hatna
retrench *v.t.* व्यय vyaya

retrenchment *n.* व्यय में कमी vyaya mein
kami
retrieve *v.t.* पुन: प्राप्त करना punh prapt
karna
retrospect *n.* पश्चात् दृष्टि pashchat
drishiti
retrospection *n.* सिंहावलोकन
sinhavalokan
retrospective *a.* पूर्वप्रभावी purvprabhavi
return *v.i.* लौटना lautana
return *n.* वापसी vapasi
revel *v.i.* आनंद लेना anand lena
revel *n.* आमोद प्रमोद aamod pramod
revelation *n.* प्रकटन prakatan
reveller *n.* मौज उड़ाने वाला mauj udane
wala
revelry *n.* रंगरलियां rangraliayan
revenge *v.t.* बदला लेना badla lena
revenge *n.* प्रतिकार pratikar
revengeful *a.* प्रतिशोधी pratishodhi
revenue *n.* आय aay
revere *v.t.* सम्मान करना sammaan karna
reverence *n.* आदर aadar
reverend *a.* माननीय mananiya
reverent *a.* श्रद्धालु shradhalu
reverential *a.* श्रद्धापूर्ण shraddhapurna
reverie *n.* दिवास्वप्न divaswapan
reversal *n.* उल्टाव ultaav
reverse *a.* विपरीत viprit
reverse *n* विपर्यय viparyaya
reverse *v.t.* अधोमुख करना adhomukh
karna
reversible *a.* पलटने योग्य palatane yogya
revert *v.i.* लौट आना lautana
review *n* पुनर्परीक्षण punarparikshan
review *v.t.* पुनर्विचार करना punarvichar
karna
revise *v.t.* दुबारा विचार करना dubara vichar
karna
revision *n.* संशोधन sashodhan

revival *n.* पुररुत्थान purruthan
revive *v.i.* पुनर्जीवित होना punarjivit hona
revocation *n.* निरसन nirasan
revoke *v.t.* रद्द करना radd karana
revolt *v.i.* राजद्रोह करना rajdroh karna
revolt *n.* बलवा balwa
revolution *n.* चक्कर chakkar
revolutionary *a.* क्रांतिकारी krantikari
revolve *v.i.* चक्कर खाना chakkar khana
revolver *n.* रिवाल्वर revolver
reward *n.* पारितोषिक paritoshik
reward *v.t.* इनाम देना inaam dena
rhetoric *n.* वाक्पटुता vaakpatuta
rhetorical *a.* शब्दाडंबरपूर्ण shabdandpurna
rheumatic *a.* गठिया संबंधी gathiya
  sambandhi
rheumatism *n.* गठिया gathiya
rhinoceros *n.* गैंडा gainda
rhyme *n.* तुक tuk
rhyme *v.i.* पद्य लिखना padya likhna
rhymester *n.* पद्यकार padyakar
rhythm *b.* ताल taal
rhythmic *a.* तालबद्ध taalbadh
rib *n.* पसली pasli
ribbon *n.* रेशम का पतला फ़ीता resham ka
  patla feeta
rice *n.* धान dhan
rich *a.* धनी dhani
riches *n.* धन dhan
richness *a.* धनाढ्यता dhanadhayata
rickets *n.* सूखा रोग sukha rog
rickety *a.* सूखा रोगी sukha rogi
rickshaw *n.* रिक्शा riksha
rid *v.t.* मुक्त करना mukt karna
riddle *n.* पहेली paheli
riddle *v.i.* पहेली कहना paheli karna
ride *n* गाड़ी से यात्रा gadi se yatra
ride *v.t.* सवारी करना sawari karna
rider *n.* सवार sawaar
ridge *n.* चोटी choti

ridicule *v.t.* उपहास करना uphas karna
ridicule *n.* उपहास uphaas
ridiculous *a.* बेहूदा behudaa
rifle *v.t.* खोजकर लूटना khojkar lutana
rifle *n* राइफ़ल rifal
rift *n.* फटन phatan
right *a.* सही sahi
right *adv* दाहिनी ओर का dahini aur ka
right *n* न्याय nyaya
righteous *a.* न्याय परायण nyaya parayan
rigid *a.* कड़ा karha
rigorous *a.* दृढ़ dridh
rigour *n.* कठिनता kathinata
rim *n.* किनारा kinara
ring *n.* अंगूठी anguthi
ring *v.t.* घंटी ghanti
ringlet *n.* बालों का लच्छा balon ka lachcha
ringworm *n.* दाद daad
rinse *v.t.* धो डालना dho dalna
riot *n.* दंगा danga
riot *v.t.* बलवा करना balwa karna
rip *v.t.* फाड़ना pharhana
ripe *a* पका हुआ paka hua
ripen *v.i.* पकना, पकाना pakana
ripple *n.* लहर lehar
ripple *v.t.* लहराना lehrana
rise *v.* उठना uthana
rise *n.* उदय uday
risk *v.t.* खतरे में डालना khatre mein dalna
risk *n.* खतरा khatra
risky *a.* खतरनाक khatarnak
rite *n.* धार्मिक उत्सक dharmik utsav
ritual *n.* धार्मिक संस्कार dharmik sanskar
rival *n.* प्रतिस्पर्धी pratispardhi
rival *v.t.* प्रतिद्वंद्वी होना pratidwandi hona
rivalry *n.* प्रतिस्पर्धा pratispardha
river *n.* नदी nadi
rivet *n.* कीलक kilak
rivet *v.t.* केंद्रित करना kendrit karna
rivulet *n.* नाला naala

road *n.* सड़क sadak
roam *v.i.* घूमना फिरना ghumna phirna
roar *n.* गर्जन garjan
roar *v.i.* गर्जन करना garjan karna
roast *v.t.* भूनना bhunana
roast *a* भुना हुआ bhuna hua
roast *n* भुना हुआ मांस bhuna hua maans
rob *v.t.* लूटना lutana
robber *n.* लुटेरा lutera,
robbery *n.* लूटपाट, डकैती lutpat,dakaiti
robe *n.* लबादा labada
robe *v.t.* कपड़े पहनाना kapade pehanana
robot *n.* यंत्र मानव yantr manav
robust *a.* हृष्ट-पुष्ट hrisht-pusht
rock *v.t.* झुलाना jhulana
rock *n.* चट्टान chattan
rocket *n.* राकेट rocket
rod *n.* छड़ chhar
rodent *n.* कृतंक kritank
roe *n.* छोटा हिरन chota hiran
rogue *n.* दुष्ट dusht
roguery *n.* दुष्टता dushtata
roguish *a.* दुष्टतापूर्ण dushtatapurna
role *n.* भूमिका bhumika
roll *n.* बेलनाकार belnakar
roll *v.i.* चक्कर खाना chakkar khana
roll-call *n.* हाज़िरी haaziri
roller *n.* रोलर roler
romance *n.* प्रेम लीला prem leela
romantic *a.* प्रेम प्रसंगयुक्त prem prasangyukt
romp *n.* उछल कूद uchal kud
roof *n.* छत chat
roof *v.t.* छत से पाटना chat se patna
rook *n.* धोखेबाज़ dhokhebaz
rook *v.t.* ठगना thagana
room *n.* कमरा, अवसर kamara, awasar
roomy *a.* विशाल vishal
roost *n.* बसेरा basera
roost *v.i.* बैठना baithna

root *n.* जड़ jarh
root *v.i.* जड़ जमना jarh jamana
rope *n.* रस्सी rassi
rosary *n.* सुमिरनी sumirani
rosary *n.* माला maala
rose *n.* गुलाब gulab
roseate *a.* गुलाबी gulabi
rostrum *n.* मंच manch
rosy *a.* गुलाबी gulabi
rot *n.* दुर्गंध durgandh
rot *v.i.* सड़ना sarhana
rotary *a.* घूमनेवाला ghumnewala
rotate *v.i.* चक्कर खाना chakkar khana
rotation *n.* नियमित आवर्तन niyamit avartan
rote *n.* दुहराव duhrav
rouble *n.* रूस की मुद्रा, रूबल roos ki mudra
rough *a.* ऊबड़खाबड़ ubarh khabarh
rough *a.* रूखा rukha
rough *a.* कठोर kathor
round *a.* बेलनाकार belanakar
round *adv.* चारों ओर charon or
rouse *v.i.* उत्तेजित करना uttejit karna
rout *v.t.* भगदड़ करना bhagdarh karna
rout *n* हुड़दंगी भीड़ hurdangi bhirh
rout *n* घोर पराजय ghor parajaya
route *n.* मार्ग marg
routine *n.* नियमित niyamit
rove *v.i.* घूमना ghumana
rover *n.* घुमंतू ghumantu
row *n.* पंक्ति pankti
row *v.t.* नाव खेना nava khena
row *n.* झगड़ा jhagra
rowdy *a.* कोलाहलपूर्ण kolahalpurna
royal *a.* राजसी rajasi
royalist *n.* राजभक्त raj bhakt
rub *v.t.* रगड़ना ragarna, ghisna
rubber *n.* रबड़ rubber
rubbish *n.* कूड़ा करकट kuda karkat
rubble *n.* मलबा malba

ruby *n.* माणिक, गहरा लाल रंग manik

rude *a.* असभ्य asabhya

rudiment *n.* मूल तत्व mul tatva

rudimentary *a.* प्रारंभिक मूल prarambhik muul

rue *v.t.* दुःखी होना dukhi hona

rueful *a.* दुःखी dukhi

ruffian *n.* गुंडा gunda

ruffle *v.t.* चिढ़ाना chidhana

rug *n.* ग़लीचा galicha

rugged *a.* खुरदरा khurdara

ruin *n.* खंडहर khandhar

ruin *v.t.* बिगाड़ना bigarana

rule *n.* नियम niyam

rule *v.t.* शासन करना shasan karna

ruler *n.* शासक shasak

ruling *n.* व्यवस्था vyvastha

rum *n.* शराब sharab

rum *a* विलक्षण vilakshan

rumble *n.* गड़गड़ाहट garhgarhahat

ruminant *a.* जुगाली करने वाला jugali karne wala

ruminant *n.* जुगाली वाला पशु jugali wala pashu

ruminate *v.i.* जुगाली करना jugali karna

rumination *n.* चिंतन chintan

rummage *n* छान बीन chan been

rummy *n.* ताश का रमी खेल tash ka rami khel

rumour *n.* अफ़वाह aphwah

rumour *v.t.* अफ़वाह फैलाना aphwah phailana

run *v.i.* दौड़ना daudana,

run *n.* दौड़ daud

run *n.* क्रिकेट का एक 'रन' cricket ka run,

rung *n.* सीढ़ी का डंडा sidhi ka danda

runner *n.* धावक dhavak

rupee *n.* रुपया rupiya

rupture *v.t.* तोड़ना todna,

rupture *n.* संबंध विच्छेद sambandh viched

rural *a.* देहाती dehati

ruse *n.* चाल chaal

rush *n.* व्यस्तता का समय vyastata ka samay

rush *v.t.* तेज़ी से ले जाना tezi se le jana

rush *n* जलबेंत jal baint

rust *n.* जंग jang

rust *v.i* जंग लगाना jang lagana

rustic *a.* ग्राम्य gramya

rustic *n* गँवार ganwar

rusticate *v.t.* निष्कासित करना dandaswarup nishkasit karna

rustication *n.* निष्कासन nishkasan

rusticity *n.* गँवारूपन ganwarupan

rusty *a.* ज़ंग खाया हुआ jang khaya hua

rut *n.* लीक, पक्की आदत lik, pakki aadat

ruthless *a.* निर्दय nirdya

rye *n.* राई raye

# S

sabotage *n.* तोड़फोड़ tor phor

sabotage *v.t.* सतोड़ फोड़ करना tor phor karna

sabre *n.* तलवार talwar

saccharin *n.* सैकरिन sakarin

sack *n.* बोरी bori

sacrament *n.* धार्मिक उत्सव dharmik utsav

sacred *a.* पवित्र pavitra

sacrifice *n.* अर्पण arpan

sacrifice *v.t.* बलिदान करना balidan karna

sacrificial *a.* बलिदान संबंधी balidan sambandhi

sacrilege *n.* अपवित्रीकरण apivtrikaran

sacrilegious *a.* देवत्व का अपहारी devatwa ka apahari

sacrosanct *a.* पवित्र pavitra

sad *a.* दुःखी dukhi

sadden *v.t.* दुःखी करना dukhi karna

saddle *n.* काठी kaathi
sadism *n.* परपीड़न रति parpiran rati
sadist *n.* परपीड़न कामुक parpirhan kamuk
safe *a.* सुरक्षित surakshit
safe *n.* तिजोरी tijori
safeguard *vt.* रक्षा करना raksha karna
safety *n.* सुरक्षा suraksha
saffron *n.* केसर kesar
saffron *a* केसरिया kesariya
sagacious *a.* समझदार samajhdar
sagacity *n.* चतुराई chaturayee
sage *n.* ऋषि rishi
sage *a.* बुद्धिमान budhiman
sail *v.i.* जलयात्रा करना jal yatra karna
sail *n.* खेवन khevan
sailor *n.* नाविक navik
saint *n.* संत sant
saintly *a.* पुण्यात्मा punyaatma
sake *n.* कारण kaaran
salad *n.* सलाद salad
salary *n.* वेतन vetan
sale *n.* बिक्री bikri
saleable *a.* विक्रय vikray
salesman *n.* विक्रेता vikreta
salient *a.* मुख्य mukhya
saline *a.* नमकीन namkeen
salinity *n.* खारापन kharapan
saliva *n.* लार laar
sally *n.* छलांग chalang
sally *n.* विहार vihar
sally *v.i.* झपट्टा मारना jhapatta maarna
saloon *n.* स्वागत कक्ष svagat kaksh
salt *n.* नमक namak
salt *v.t* नमक छिड़कना namak chirhakana
salty *a.* नमकीन namkeen
salutary *a.* लाभकारी labhkari
salutation *n.* अभिवादन abhivadan
salute *v.t.* नमस्कार करना namaskar karna
salute *n* अभिवादन abhivadan
salvage *n.* नाशरक्षण naashrakshan

salvage *v.t.* क्षति से बचाना kshati se bachana
salvation *n.* पापों से मुक्ति paapon se mukti
same *a.* वही vahi
sample *n.* नमूना namuna
sample *v.t.* चुनना chunana
sanatorium *n.* आरोग्यआश्रम arogyashram
sanctification *n.* पवित्रीकरण pavitrikaran
sanction *n.* अनुमोदन anumodan
sanction *v.t.* आज्ञा देना agya
sanctity *n.* पवित्रता pavitrata
sanctuary *n.* मंदिर mandir
sand *n.* रेत ret
sandal *n.* चप्पल chappal
sandalwood *n.* चंदन chandan
sandwich *n.* सैंडविच sandwich
sandy *a.* रेतीला retila
sane *a.* स्वस्थ चित्त का swasth chit ka
sanguine *a.* रक्त वर्ण का rakt varna ka
sanity *n.* मानसिक स्वास्थ्य mansik swasthya
sap *n.* शक्ति shakti
sap *v.t.* शक्तिहीन करना shaktiheen karna
sapling *n.* छोटा पौधा chota paudha
sapphire *n.* गहरा नीला रंग gehra neela rang
sarcasm *n.* व्यंग्य कथन vyangya kathan
sarcastic *a.* व्यंग्यपूर्ण vyangyapurna
sardonic *a.* निंदापूर्ण nindapurna
satan *n.* शैतान shaitan
satchel *n.* झोला thaila
satellite *n.* उपग्रह upgreha
satiable *a.* तृप्त tript
satiate *v.t.* तृप्त कर देना tript kar dena
satiety *n.* तृप्ति अघाव tripti aghav
satire *n.* व्यंग्य vyangya
satirical *a.* व्यंग्यपूर्ण vyangyapurna
satirist *n.* व्यंग्य लेखक vyangya lekhak
satirize *v.t.* व्यंग्य करना vyangya karna
satisfaction *n.* संतोष santosh

satisfactory *a.* संतोषजनक santoshjanak

satisfy *v.t.* संतुष्ट करना santusht karna

saturate *v.t.* परिपूर्ण करना paripurna karna

saturation *n.* संतुष्टि santushtii

Saturday *n.* शनिवार shaniwar

sauce *n.* चटनी chatni

saucer *n.* तश्तरी tashtari

saunter *v.t.* बेकार घूमना bekar ghumna

savage *a.* जंगली jangali

savage *n* हबशी habashi

savagery *n.* क्रूरता krurta

save *v.t.* सुरक्षित रखना surakshit rakhna

save *prep* सिवाय siwaya

saviour *n.* रक्षक rakshak

savour *n.* स्वाद swad

savour *v.t.* स्वादिष्ट होना swadisht hona

saw *n.* आरा ara

saw *v.t.* आरे से काटना arey se katana

say *v.t.* बोलना bolna

say *n.* व्याख्यान vyakhyan

scabbard *n.* म्यान myan

scabies *n.* खुजली की बीमारी khujli ki bimari

scaffold *n.* फांसी का तख्ता phansi ka takhta

scale *v.t.* तराज़ू में तोलना tarazoo mein tolana

scamper *v.i* इधर उधर दौड़ना idhar udhar daurhna

scamper *n* तेज़ दौड़ tez daurh

scan *v.t.* सूक्ष्म परीक्षण करना sukshm parikshan karna

scandal *n* बदनामी badnami

scandalize *v.t.* बदनाम करना badnam karna

scant *a.* अपर्याप्त aparyapt

scanty *a.* कम kam

scapegoat *n.* बलि का बकरा bali ka bakra

scar *n* घाव का निशान ghav ka nishan

scar *v.t.* धब्बा लगाना dhabba lagna

scarce *a.* अल्प alp

scarcely *adv.* मुश्किल से ही mushkil se hi

scarcity *n.* अल्पता alpata

scare *n.* अकारण भय akaaran bhaya

scare *v.t.* डराना daraana

scarf *n.* दुपट्टा dupatta

scatter *v.t.* फैलाना phailana

scavenger *n.* सफ़ाई कर्मचारी safai karamchari

scene *n.* नाटक का दृश्य natak ka drishya

scenery *n.* दृश्यभूमि drishyabhumi

scenic *a.* चित्रात्मक chitratmak

scent *n.* सुगंध sugandh

sceptic *n.* संदेहवादी sandehwadi

sceptical *a.* संशयात्मक sanshayatmak

scepticism *n.* संशयात्मकता sanshayatmakta

sceptre *n.* राजदंड rajdand

schedule *n.* कार्यक्रम karyakram

schedule *v.t.* अनुसूची बनाना anusuchi banana

scheme *n.* पद्धति padhati

scheme *v.i.* योजना बनाना yojana banana

scholar *n.* विद्वान् vidyan

scholarly *a.* विद्वत्तापूर्ण vidvatapurna

scholarship *n.* छात्रवृत्ति chatravrati

scholastic *a.* विद्वान् संबंधी vidyan sambandhi

school *n.* विद्यालय vidyalaya

science *n.* विज्ञान vigyan

scientific *a.* वैज्ञानिक vaigyanik

scientist *n.* वैज्ञानिक vaigyanik

scintillate *v.i.* चमकना chamakna

scintillation *n.* चमक chamak

scissors *n.* कैंची kainchi

scoff *n.* ताना tana

scoff *v.i.* उपहास करना upahas karna

scold *v.t.* दोष निकालना dosh nikalana

scooter *n.* स्कूटर scooter

scope *n.* गुंजाइश kshetra

scorch *v.t.* झुलसाना jhulsana

score *n.* गणना ganana
score *v.t.* अंक बनाना ank banana
scorn *n.* तिरस्कार tiraskar
scorn *v.t.* घृणा करना ghrina karna
scorpion *n.* बिच्छू bichchu
Scot *n.* स्कॉटलैंड का निवासी scotland ka niwasi
scotch *n.* स्कॉटलैंड निवासी scotland niwasi
scotch *n.* एक प्रकार की शराब ek prakar ki sharab
scot-free *a.* सुरक्षित surakshit
scoundrel *n.* दुष्ट dusht
scourge *n.* विपत्ति vipatti
scourge *v.t.* कड़ा दंड देना karha dand dena
scout *n* गुप्तचर guptchar
scout *v.i* गुप्तचर्या करना guptcharya karna
scowl *v.i.* त्योरी चढ़ाना tyori chadhna
scowl *n.* भ्रूभंग bhrubhang
scramble *v.i.* ऊपर चढ़ना upar chadhna
scrap *n.* रद्दी raddi
scratch *n.* खरोंच kharonch
scratch *v.t.* खुरचना khurachna
scrawl *n* घसीट ghasit
scrawl *v.t.* घसीटना ghasitana
scream *n* चीख cheekh
scream *v.i.* चीखना cheekhna
screen *v.t.* बचाना bachana
screen *n.* चित्रपट chitrpat
screw *v.t.* पेच से कसना pech se kasna
screw *n.* पेच pech
scribble *n.* घसीट ghasit
script *n.* लिखावट likhawat
scripture *n.* धर्मग्रंथ dharamgranth
scroll *n.* काग़ज़ का खर्रा kagaz ka kharra
scrutiny *n.* सूक्ष्म जांच sukshm janch
scuffle *v.i.* हाथापाई करना hathapayee karna
scuffle *n.* हाथापाई hathapayee
sculpture *n.* मूर्तिकला murtikala

scythe *v.t.* दरांती से काटना daranti se katana
scythe *n.* दांती danti
sea *n.* सागर sagar
seal *n.* मुहर muhar
seam *v.t.* सिलाई से जोड़ना silayee se jodna
seam *n.* परत parat
seamy *a.* सीवनदार sivandar
search *v.t.* खोजना khojana
search *n.* खोज khoj
season *n.* ऋतु ritu
seasonal *a.* मौसमी mausami
seat *v.t.* बैठाना baithana
seat *n.* बैठने का आसन baithane ka aasan
secede *v.i.* पृथक् हो जाना prithak ho jana
secession *n.* अपगमन apgaman
secessionist *n.* अलगाववादी algavwadi
secluded *a.* एकांत ekant
seclusion *n.* एकांतता ekantata
second *a.* दूसरा dusra
second *v.t.* अनुमोदित करना anumodit karna
secondary *a.* अनुपूरक anupurak
secrecy *n.* गुप्तता guptata
secret *n.* गुप्त gupt
secret *a.* छिपा हुआ chipa huw
secretariat (e) *n.* सचिवालय sachivalaya
secretary *n.* सचिव sachiv
secrete *v.t.* छिपाना chipana
secrete *v.t.* स्रावित करना stravit karna
secretion *n.* स्राव strav
secretive *a.* गोपनशील gopansheel
sect *n.* पंथ panth
section *n.* अनुभाग anubhag
sector *n.* व्यावसायिक क्षेत्र vyavasayik kshetra
secure *a.* सुरक्षित surakshit
secure *v.t.* सुरक्षित करना surakshit karna
security *n.* सुरक्षा suraksha
sedan *n.* पालकी palaki

sedate *a.* गंभीर, शांत gambhir

sedative *n* शामक औषध shamak aushadh

sedative *a.* शामक shamak

sedentary *a.* आसीन aasin

sediment *n.* तलछट talchat

sedition *n.* विद्रोह vidroha

seditious *a.* विप्लवकारी viplavkari

seduce *n.* बहकाना behakana

seduction *n.* सतीत्व हरण satitva haran

seductive *a* लुभावना lubhawana

see *v.t.* देखना dekhana

seed *n.* बीज beej

seed *v.t.* बोना bona

seek *v.t.* मांगना mangaana

seem *v.i.* जान पड़ना jaan parhna

seemly *a.* उपयुक्त upyukt

seep *v.i.* रिसना risna

seer *n.* सिद्धपुरुष sidhpurush

seethe *v.i.* उबलना ubalna

segment *v.t.* विभाजित करना vibhajit karna

segment *n.* भाग bhag

segregate *v.t.* पृथक् करना prithak karna

segregation *n.* अलगाव algav

seismic *a.* भूकंप संबंधी bhukamp sambandhi

seize *v.t.* छीनना chheenana

seizure *n.* पकड़ pakarh

seldom *adv.* यदा कदा yada kada

select *a* चुनिंदा, उत्कृष्ट chuninda

select *v.t.* चुनना chunana

selection *n.* चयन chayan

selective *a.* चयन योग्य chayan yogya

selfish *a.* स्वार्थी swarthi

selfless *a.* स्वार्थरहित swarth-rahit

sell *v.t.* बेचना bechna

seller *n.* विक्रेता vikreta

semblance *n.* सादृश्य dikhava

semen *n.* वीर्य virya

semester *n.* अद्‌र्घवार्षिक सत्र ardhwarshik satr

seminal *a.* वीर्य संबधी virya sambandhi

seminar *n.* गोष्ठी goshthi

senate *n.* प्रबंधकारिणी समिति prabandhkarini samiti

senator *n.* समिति सदस्य samiti sadasya

send *v.t.* भेजना bhejana

senile *a.* वृद्घावस्था संबंधी vridhavastha sambandhi

senility *n.* बुढ़ापे की दुर्बलता budhape ki durbalata

senior *n.* वयोवृद्घ व्यक्ति vyovridh vyakati

senior *a.* वयोवृद्घ vayovridh

seniority *n.* वरीयता variyata

sensation *n.* अनुभूति anubhuti

sensational *a.* संवेदनात्मक samvedanatamak

sense *v.t.* अनुभव करना anubhav karana

sense *n.* इंद्रिय indriya

senseless *a.* बेहोश behosh

sensibility *n.* संवेदनशीलता samvedansheelta

sensible *a.* समझदार samajhdar

sensitive *a.* संवेदनशील samvedansheel

sensual *a.* कामुक kaamuk

sensualist *n.* भोगवादी bhogwadi

sensuality *n.* कामुकता kamukta

sentence *v.t.* दंड देना dand dena

sentence *n.* वाक्य wakya

sentience *n.* चेतना chetana

sentient *a.* संवेदनशील sanvedansheel

sentiment *n.* भावुकता bhaavukta

sentimental *a.* भावुक bhaavuk

sentinel *n.* संतरी santari

sentry *n.* संतरी santari

separable *a.* वियोज्य viyojya

separate *v.t.* अलग करना alag karna

separate *a.* विभक्त vibhakt

separation *n.* पृथक्करण prithakaran

sepsis *n.* पूर्ति, पूतिता purti,

September *n.* सितंबर setambar
septic *a.* विषाक्त vishakt
sepulchre *n.* समाधि samadhi
sepulchre *n.* दफ़न dafan
sequel *n.* परिणाम parinaam
sequence *n.* अनुक्रम anukram
sequester *v.t.* अलग करना alag karna
serene *a.* शांत shant
serenity *n.* शांति shanti
serf *n.* कृषि मज़दूर krishi mazdoor
sergeant *n.* सारजेंट sarjent
serial *n.* धारावाहिक dharawahik
serial *a.* क्रमिक kramik
series *n.* क्रम kram
serious *a* गंभीर gambhir
sermon *n.* नीतिवचन nitivachan
serpent *n.* सर्प sarp
serpentine *n.* चालाक chalaak
servant *n.* सेवक sewak
serve *n.* सर्विस service
serve *v.t.* नौकरी करना naukari karna
service *n.* नौकरी naukari
serviceable *a.* चालू हालत में chalu halat mein
servile *a.* दासतापूर्ण dastapurna
servility *n.* दासता dasta
session *n.* बैठक baithak
set *a* निर्धारित nirdharit
settle *v.i.* बसना basna
settlement *n.* समझौता samjhauta
settler *n.* उपनिवेशी upniveshi
seven *a* सात saat
seven *n.* सात की संख्या saat ki sankhya
seventeen *n., a* सत्रह satrah
seventeenth *a.* सत्रहवां satrehwan
seventh *a.* सातवां satwan
seventieth *a.* सत्तरवां sattarwan
seventy *n., a* सत्तर sattar
sever *v.t.* काट देना kaat dena
several *a* कई kayee

severance *n.* विच्छेद vichhed
severe *a.* सख्त sakht
severity *n.* कठिनता kathinta
sew *v.t.* सिलना silna
sewage *n.* मलजल maljal
sewer *n* नाला naalaa
sewerage *n.* मलव्यवस्था mal-vyawastha
sex *n.* लिंग ling
sex *n.* यौन क्रिया yaun kriya
sexual *a.* लैंगिक laingik
sexuality *n.* काम वासना kaam vasna
sexy *n.* कामुक kamuk
shabby *a.* फटेहाल phatehal
shackle *v.t.* बेड़ी डालना berhi dalna
shackle *n.* बेड़ी berhi
shade *v.t.* छायित करना chayit karana
shade *n.* छाया chaya
shadow *n.* परछाई parchayee
shadowy *a.* छायादार chayadaar
shaft *n.* दस्ता dasta
shake *n* झटका jhatka
shake *v.i.* हिलना hilna
shaky *a.* अस्थिर asthir
shallow *a.* उथला uthla
sham *n* दिखावा dikhawa
sham *a* दिखावटी dikhawati
sham *v.i.* बहाना करना bahana karna
shame *v.t.* लज्जित करना lajjit karna
shame *n.* शरम sharam
shameful *a.* लज्जाजनक lajjajanak
shameless *a.* निर्लज्ज nirlajj
shampoo *n.* केशमार्जक keshmarjak
shanty *a.* कुटी kuti
shape *v.t* आकार देना akaar dena
shape *n.* आकार akaar
shapely *a.* सुघड़ sugharh
share *v.t.* सहभागी होना sahabhagi hona
share *n.* भाग bhag
shark *n.* हांगर hangar
sharp *adv.* ठीक समय से theek samay se

sharp *a.* **नुकीला** nukila
sharpen *v.t.* **तेज़ करना** tez karana
sharper *n.* **ठग** thag
shatter *v.t.* **नष्ट करना** nasht karna
shave *n* **हजामत** hajamat
shave *v.t.* **हजामत बनाना** hajamat banana
shawl *n.* **शॉल** shaul
she *pron.* **वह (स्त्री)** veh (stri)
sheaf *n.* **पूला** pulaa
shear *v.t.* **भेड़ मूंडना** bherh mundana
shears *n. pl.* **कैंची** kaincha
shed *n* **छप्पर** chappar
shed *v.t.* **गिरा देना** gira dena
sheep *n.* **भेड़** bherh
sheepish *a.* **संकोची** sankochi
sheer *a.* **निरा** nira
sheet *v.t.* **चादर डालना** chadar dalna
sheet *n.* **चादर** vistar
shelf *n.* **टांड** taand
shell *v.t.* **गोले बरसाना** goley barsana
shell *n.* **छिलका** chhilka
shelter *v.t.* **पनाह देना** panah dena
shelter *n.* **शरणस्थल** sharansthal
shelve *v.t.* **ताक पर रखना** taak par rakhana
shepherd *n.* **गड़ेरिया** gadeheriya
shield *v.t.* **बचाना** bachana
shield *n.* **ढाल** dhaal
shift *n* **परिवर्तन** parivartan
shift *v.t.* **स्थानांतरित करना** sthanantarit karana
shifty *a.* **धोखेबाज** dhokhebaaz
shilling *n.* **ब्रिटिश मुद्रा** british mudra
shilly-shally *v.i.* **हिचकिचाना** hichkichana
shilly-shally *n.* **अनिर्णय** anirnaya
shine *n* **चमक** chamak
shine *v.i.* **चमकना** chamakna
shiny *a.* **चमकदार** chamakdar
ship *n.* **जहाज़** jahaz
shipment *n.* **जहाज़ पर लदान** jahaz par ladan

shire *n.* **प्रांत** prant
shirk *v.t.* **जी चुराना** ji churana
shirker *n.* **कामचोर** kamchor
shirt *n.* **कमीज़** kamiz
shiver *v.i.* **कांपना** kampana
shoal *n.* **मछलियों का झुंड** machliyon ka jhund
shock *n.* **झटका** jhatka
shoe *v.t.* **नाल लगाना** naal lagana
shoe *n.* **जूता** joota
shoot *n* **टहनी** tahani
shoot *n* **शिकार** shikaar
shoot *v.t.* **अंकुरना** ankurna
shop *v.i.* **खरीददारी करना** khariddari karana
shop *n.* **दुकान** dukaan
shore *n.* **समुद्रतट** samudra tat
short *adv.* **अचानक** achanak
short *a.* **छोटा** chota
shortage *n.* **अभाव** abhav
shortcoming *n.* **दोष** dosh
shorten *v.t.* **छोटा होना** chota hona
shortly *adv.* **शीघ्र ही** shighra hi
shorts *n. pl.* **निकर** nikkar
shot *n.* **निशाना** nishana
shot *n.* **फ़ोटो** photo
shoulder *v.t.* **दायित्व लेना** dayitva lena
shoulder *n.* **कंधा** kandha
shout *v.i.* **चिल्लाना** chilana
shout *n.* **चीख** cheekh
shove *n.* **ठेला, धक्का** thela
shove *v.t.* **धकेलना** dhakelana
shovel *v.t.* **बेलचे से हटाना** belche se hataana
shovel *n.* **बेलचा** belcha
show *n.* **प्रदर्शन** pradarshan
show *v.t.* **दिखाना** dikhana
shower *v.t.* **बरसाना** barasna
shower *n.* **बौछार** bauochar
shrew *n.* **कर्कशा** karkasha
shrewd *a.* **चालाक** chaalaak

| | |
|---|---|
| shriek *v.i.* चीखना cheekhna | sightly *a.* रमणीय ramaniya |
| shriek *n.* चीख cheekh | sign *v.t.* हस्ताक्षर करना hastakshar karna |
| shrill *a.* तीक्ष्ण आवाज़ tikshna awaz | sign *n.* संकेत sanket |
| shrine *n.* पवित्र स्थान pavitra sthan | signal *a.* उल्लेखनीय ulekhaniya |
| shrink *v.i* सिकुड़ना sikurhna | signal *v.t.* संकेत करना sanket karna |
| shrinkage *n.* सिकुड़न sikurhan | signal *n.* संकेत sanket |
| shroud *v.t.* ढकना, छिपाना dhakana, chipana | signatory *n.* हस्ताक्षरकर्त्ता hastakshar karna |
| shroud *n.* परदा pardaa | signature *n.* हस्ताक्षर hastakshar |
| shrub *n.* झाड़ी jhaarhi | significance *n.* महत्व mahtya |
| shrug *v.t.* कंधे उचकाना kandhe uchkana | significant *a.* अर्थपूर्ण arthapurna |
| shudder *n* कंपकंपी kampkampi | signification *n.* अर्थ arth |
| shudder *v.i.* कांप उठना kamp uthna | signify *v.t.* अर्थ रखना arth rakhna |
| shuffle *n.* घसीटन ghasitan | silence *v.t.* चुप करना chup karna |
| shuffle *v.i.* पैर घसीटना pair ghasitna | silence *n.* शांति shanti |
| shun *v.t.* दूर रहना dur rehna | silencer *n.* साइलैंसर silencer |
| shunt *v.t.* मोड़ना morhna | silent *a.* शांत shant |
| shut *v.t.* बंद होना band hona | silhouette *n.* पार्श्व छायाचित्र parshva chayachitra |
| shuttle *v.t.* आगे पीछे aage peeche | silk *n.* रेशम resham |
| shuttle *n.* ढरकी dharki | silken *a.* रेशमी reshami |
| shuttlecock *n.* चिड़िया chirhiya | silky *a.* रेशम जैसा resham jaisa |
| shy *v.i.* बिदकना bidakna | silly *a.* मूर्ख murkh |
| shy *n.* संकोची sankochi | silt *n.* गाद gaad |
| sick *a.* मिचलीग्रस्त, michligrast | silver *n.* चांदी chandi |
| sickle *n.* हंसिया hansiya | silver *v.t.* चांदी चढ़ाना chandi chadhana |
| sickly *a.* अस्वस्थ, रुग्ण asvastha | similar *a.* सदृश sadrishya |
| sickness *n.* बीमारी bimari | similarity *n.* समानता samanta |
| side *v.i.* पक्ष लेना paksh lena | simile *n.* उपमा upmaa |
| side *n.* सतह satah | similitude *n.* समानता samanta |
| siege *n.* घेराबंदी gherabandi | simmer *v.i.* उबलना ubalna |
| siesta *n.* दोपहर की झपकी dopahar ki jhapaki | simple *a.* सादा saada |
| sieve *v.t.* छानना chanana | simpleton *n.* बुद्धू budhu |
| sieve *n.* छलनी chalni | simplicity *n.* सादगी saadagi |
| sift *v.t.* बारीकी से जांच करना bariki se janch karna | simplification *n.* सरलीकरण sarlikaran |
| sigh *v.i.* आह भरना aha bharna | simplify *v.t.* सरल बनाना saral banana |
| sigh *n.* आह aha | simultaneous *a.* समकालिक samkalik |
| sight *v.t.* देखना dekhna | sin *v.i.* पाप करना paap karna |
| sight *n.* दृष्टि drishti | sin *n.* पाप कर्म paap karm |
| | since *conj.* के बाद से ke baad se |

since *adv.* तब से अब तक tab se ab tak
sincere *a.* ईमानदार imandar
sincerity *n.* सच्चाई sachayee
sinful *a.* पापी paapi
sing *v.i.* गाना gaana
singe *n* झुलसन jhulsan
singe *v.t.* झुलसाना jhulsana
singer *n.* गायक gayak
single *n.* एकतरफ़ा टिकट ektarpha ticket
single *v.t.* चुनना chunana
single *a.* केवल एक kewal ek
singular *a.* एकवचन ekvachan
singularity *n.* अनोखापन anokhapan
singularly *adv.* अनोखे ढंग से anokhe dhang se
sinister *a.* अशुभ ashubh
sink *n* चहबच्चा chahbachcha
sink *v.i.* डूबना daubna
sinner *n.* पापी paapi
sinuous *a.* टेढ़ा मेढ़ा tedha medha
sip *n.* चुस्की chuski
sip *v.t.* चुस्की लगाकर पीना chuski lagakar
sir *n.* श्रीमान shriman
siren *n.* भोंपू bhaupun
sister *n.* बहन behan
sisterhood *n.* बहनापा behenapa
sisterly *a.* भगिनीवत् bhaginivat
sit *v.i.* बैठना baithna
site *n.* स्थान sthan
situation *n.* परिस्थिति paristhiti
six *n., a* छ: cheh
sixteen *n., a.* सोलह solaha
sixteenth *a.* सोलहवां solahawan
sixth *a.* छठा chata
sixtieth *a.* साठवां saathwan
sixty *n., a.* साठ saatth
sizable *a.* विशाल vishal
size *n.* आकार aakaar
skate *n.* स्केट skait

skate *v.t.* स्केटों पर फिसलना skaiton par phisalna
skein *n.* लच्छी lachchi
skeleton *n.* कंकाल kankal
sketch *v.t.* नक्शा बनाना naksha banana
sketch *n.* संक्षिप्त वर्णन sankshipt
sketchy *a.* संक्षिप्त, अधूरा sankshipt
skid *v.i.* फिसलना phisalna
skilful *a.* निपुण nipun
skill *n.* निपुणता nipunata
skin *v.t* खाल khal
skin *n.* त्वचा tvacha
skip *n* उछाल uchaal
skip *v.i.* फुदकना phudakna
skipper *n.* कप्तान kaptan
skirmish *n.* झड़प jharhap
skirt *n.* घाघरा ghaghra
skit *n.* प्रहसन prahasan
skull *n.* खोपड़ी khoprhi
sky *n.* आकाश aakash
slab *n.* पटिया patiya
slack *a.* ढीला dheela
slacken *v.t.* ढीला करना dheela karnaa
slacks *n.* ढीला पाजामा dheela pajama
slake *v.t.* प्यास बुझाना pyas bujhana
slam *v.t.* ज़ोर से बंद करना zor se band karna
slander *n.* झूठी निंदा jhoothi ninda
slander *v.t.* झूठी निंदा करना jhoothi ninda karna
slanderous *a.* निंदात्मक nindatmak
slang *n.* बोलचाल की भाषा bolchal ki bhasha
slant *n* झुकाव jhukav
slant *v.t.* तिरछा करना tircha karna
slap *v.t.* तमाचा मारना tamacha maarana
slap *n.* चांटा chaanta
slash *n* चीरा cheera
slash *v.t.* चीर देना cheer dena
slate *n.* स्लेट slate

slattern *n.* फूहड़ स्त्री phuhar istri

slatternly *a.* फूहड phuhar

slaughter *v.t.* वध करना vadh karna

slaughter *n.* पशुवध pashu vadh

slave *v.i.* दास daas

slavery *n.* दास प्रथा daas pratha

slavish *a.* दासतापूर्ण daastapuran

slay *v.t.* वध करना vadh karna

sleek *a.* चिकना chikna

sleep *n.* नींद neend

sleep *v.i.* सोना sona

sleeper *n.* शयनिका shayanika

sleepy *a.* उनींदा uninda

sleeve *n* आस्तीन aastin

sleight *n.* कौशल kaushal

slender *n.* पतला patla

slice *n.* फांक phank

slick *a* चिकना chikna

slide *n* चिकनी chikni steh

slide *v.i.* सरकाना sarakna

slide *v.i.* खिसकाना khisakana

slight *n.* अपमान apmaan

slight *a.* थोड़ा thorha

slim *v.i.* वज़न कम करना vazan kam karna

slim *a.* पतला patla

slime *n.* कीचड़ keechar

slimy *a.* पंकयुक्त pank-yukt

sling *n.* गोफन gophan

slip *n.* परची parchi

slip *v.i.* फिसलना phisalna

slippery *a.* फिसलन वाला phislan wala

slipshod *a.* फूहड़िया phuhariya

slit *v.t.* दरार करना darar karna

slit *n.* दरार darar

slogan *n.* नारा nara

slope *v.i.* ढालू होना dhalu hona

slope *n.* ढाल dhaal

sloth *n.* आलस्य alasya

slothful *n.* आलसी alasi

slough *v.t.* केंचुली गिराना kenchuli girana

slough *n.* दलदल daldal

slough *n.* केंचुली kenchuli

slovenly *a.* मैला कुचैला maila kuchaila

slow *v.i.* धीमा होना dheema hona

slow *a* धीमा dheema

slowly *adv.* धीमी गति से dheemi gati se

slowness *n.* धीमापन dheemapan

sluggard *n.* सुस्त sust

sluice *n.* जलद्वार jaldwar

slum *n.* गंदी बस्ती gandi basti

slumber *n.* नींद neend

slumber *v.i.* सोना sona

slump *v.i.* गिर पड़ना gir padhna

slump *n.* मंदी mandi

slur *n.* कलंक kalank

slush *n.* कीचड़ kicharh

slushy *a.* कीचड़दार kicharhdaar

slut *n.* बदनाम स्त्री badnam stri

sly *a.* धोखेबाज़ dhokhebaz

smack *n* मत्स्य नौका matsya nauka

smack *v.t.* चांटा मारना chaanta marna

smack *n.* स्वाद swaad

small *n* कमर का पतला भाग kamar ka patla bhag

small *a.* छोटा chota

smallness *adv.* छोटापन chotapan

smallpox *n.* चेचक chechak

smart *v.i* टीस लगना tees lagna

smart *n* टीस tees

smart *a.* फुर्तीला phurtila

smash *n* भारी प्रहार bhari prahar

smash *v.t.* झटके से तोड़ना jhatke se torhna

smear *n.* दाग़ daag

smell *v.t.* सूंघना soonghna

smell *n.* गंध gandh

smelt *v.t.* पिघलाना pighlana

smile *v.i.* मुस्काना muskana

smile *n.* मुस्कान muskan

smith *n.* धातु कर्मी dhatu karmi

smock *n.* लबादा labada

smog *n.* धूम कोहरा dhoom kohra

smoke *v.i.* धूम्रपान करना dhumra-paan karna

smoke *n.* धुआं dhuan

smoky *a.* धुआंयुक्त dhuanyukt

smooth *v.t.* चिकना करना chikna karna

smooth *a.* चिकना chikna

smother *v.t.* दम घोंटना dam ghontana

smoulder *v.i.* सुलगना sulagna

smug *a.* आत्मसंतुष्ट atm-santusht

smuggle *v.t.* तस्करी करना taskari karna

smuggler *n.* तस्कर taskar

snack *n.* हल्का भोजन halka bhojan

snag *n.* कठिनाई kathinayee

snail *n.* घोंघा ghongha

snake *v.i.* रेंगना rengna

snake *n.* सर्प sarp

snap *n* तड़क tarhak

snap *a* आकस्मिक akasmik

snap *v.t.* फ़ोटो लेना photo lena

snare *v.t.* फंसाना fasana

snare *n.* जाल jaal

snarl *v.i.* गुर्राना gurrana

snarl *n.* गुर्राहट gurrahat

snatch *n.* बलपूर्वक ग्रहण bal-purvak grahan

snatch *v.t.* छीनना chheenana

sneak *n* उचक्का uchakka

sneer *n* तिरस्कार tiraskar

sneer *v.i* अवहेलना दिखाना avhelana dikhana

sneeze *n* छींक cheenk

sneeze *v.i.* छींकना cheenkana

sniff *n* सुड़क surhak

snob *n.* वर्गदंभी varg dambhi

snobbery *n.* वर्गदंभ varg dambh

snobbish *v* दंभपूर्ण dambh puran

snore *n* खर्राटा kharrata

snore *v.i.* खर्राटे लेना kharrate lena

snort *n.* फुफकार fufkar

snort *v.i.* फुंकारना, फुफकारना phunkarna

snout *n.* थूथन thuthan

snow *n.* बर्फ़ barph

snowy *a.* बर्फ़ सफ़ेद barph jaisa safed

snub *n.* अपमान apmaan

snub *v.t.* झिड़कना jhirakna

snuff *n.* सुंघनी sunghani

snug *n.* गर्म garam

so *adv.* इतना itna

so *conj.* अत: atah

soak *n.* शुष्कन shushkan

soak *v.t.* भिगोना bhigona

soap *v.t.* साबुन लगाना sabun lagana

soap *n.* साबुन sabun

soapy *a.* साबुन जैसा sabun jaisa

soar *v.i.* ऊंची उड़ान भरना unchi urhaan bharna

sob *n* सुबकी subki

sob *v.i.* सुबकना subakna

sober *a.* सादा sada

sobriety *n.* गांभीर्य gambhirya

sociability *n.* मिलनसारी milansari

sociable *a.* मिलनसार milansar

social *n.* सामाजिक samajik

socialism *n* समाजवाद samajvad

socialist *n,a* समाजवादी samajvadi

society *n.* समाज samaj

sociology *n.* समाजशास्त्र samaj shastra

sock *n.* मौज़ा mauza

socket *n.* गर्तिका gartika

sod *n.* तृणभूमि trin-bhumi

sodomite *n.* लौंडेबाज़ laundebaz

sodomy *n.* लौंडेबाज़ी laundebazi

sofa *n.* सोफ़ा sofa

soft *n.* कोमल komal

soften *v.t.* कोमल बनाना komal banana

soil *n.* मिट्टी mitti

sojourn *n* ठहराव thahrav

sojourn *v.i.* ठहरना thahrana

solace *v.t.* सांत्वना देना santvana dena

solace *n.* सांत्वना santvana

solar *a.* सौर saur

solder *v.t.* टांके से जोड़ना tanke se jodna

solder *n.* टांका tanka

soldier *n.* सैनिक sainik

sole *v.t* तल्ला लगाना talla lagana

sole *a* अकेला akela

sole *n.* तल्ला talla

solemn *a.* गंभीर gambhir

solemnity *n.* गंभीरता gambhirta

solemnize *v.t.* समारोह मनाना samaroh manana

solicit *v.t.* विनती करना vinti karna

solicitation *n.* विनती vinti

solicitor *n.* न्यायाभिकर्त्ता nyayabhikarta

solicitous *a.* चिंतित chintit

solicitude *n.* चिंता chinta

solid *n* ठोस पदार्थ thos padarth

solid *a.* ठोस thos

solidarity *n.* एकजुटता ek jutata

soliloquy *n.* स्वगत swagat

solitary *a.* अकेला akela

solitude *n.* अकेलापन akelapan

solo *a.* एकल ekal

solo *adv.* अकेले akele

solo *n* एकल संगीत ekal sangeet

soloist *n.* एकल गायक ekal gayak

solubility *n.* घुलनशीलता ghulan shilta

soluble *a.* समाधेय samadhey

solution *n.* समाधान samadhan

solve *v.t.* हल करना hal karna

solvency *n.* ऋणशोध क्षमता rinshodh kshamta

solvent *n* विलायक द्रव vilayak drav

solvent *a.* ऋणशोधक्षम् rinshodhksham

sombre *a.* कालिमामय kalimamaya

some *pron.* कुछ kuch

some *a.* कोई, कुछ koi kuch

somebody *n.* विशिष्ट व्यक्ति vishisht vyakti

somebody *pron.* कोई व्यक्ति koi vyakti

somehow *adv.* जैसे तैसे jaise taise

someone *pron.* कोई व्यक्ति koi vyakti

somersault *v.i.* कलाबाज़ी खाना kalabazi khana

somersault *n.* कलाबाज़ी kalabazi

something *adv.* कुछ सीमा तक kuch seema tak

something *pron.* कुछ kuch

sometime *adv.* कभी कभी kabhi kabhi

sometimes *adv.* कभी कभी kabhi kabhi

somewhat *adv.* कुछ कुछ kuch kuch

somewhere *adv.* कहीं, किसी जगह kahin

somnambulism *n.* निद्राभ्रमण nidra bhraman

somnambulist *n.* निद्राचारी nidrachari

somnolence *n.* निद्रालुता nidraluta

somnolent *n.* निद्राजनक nidra janak

son *n.* पुत्र putr

song *n.* गायन gayan

singer *n.* गायक gayak

sonic *a.* ध्वनि संबंधी dhwani sambandhi

sonnet *n.* चतुर्दश-पदी chaturdash-padi

sonority *n.* निनादिता ninadita

soon *adv.* शीघ्र jaldi

soot *v.t.* काजल लगाना kajal lagana

soot *n.* कालिख kalikh

soothe *v.t.* शांत करना shant karna

sophism *n.* कुतर्क kutark

sophist *n.* कुतर्की kutarki

sophisticate *v.t.* कृत्रिम बनाना kritrim banana

sophisticated *a.* जटिल jatil

sophistication *n.* कृत्रिमता kritrimata

sorcerer *n.* जादूगर jadugar

sorcery *n.* जादू jadu

sordid *a.* नीच eeich

sore *n* फोड़ा phora

sore *a.* पीड़ादायक pirhadayak

sorrow *v.i.* दुःखी होना dukh hona

sorrow *n.* दुःख, पीड़ा dukh, peerha

sorry *a.* दुःखी, खेदपूर्ण dukhi, khedpurna

sort *n.* प्रकार prakar

soul *n.* आत्मा aatma

sound *v.i.* ध्वनि करना dhwani karna

sound *n* ध्वनि dhwani

sound *a.* अच्छा achcha

soup *n.* शोरबा shorba

sour *v.t.* खट्टा करना khatta karna

sour *a.* खट्टा khatta

source *n.* उद्गम udgam

south *n.* दक्षिण dakshin

south *adv* दक्षिण की ओर dakshin ki aur

southerly *a.* दक्षिणी dakshini

southern *a.* दक्षिणी dakshini

souvenir *n.* यादगार yadgar

sovereign *a* सर्वश्रेष्ठ sarva-shreshth

sovereignty *n.* प्रभुसत्ता prabhusatta

sow *v.t.* बोना bauna

space *n.* अंतरिक्ष antriksh

spacious *a.* विस्तृत vistrit

spade *v.t.* फावड़े से खोदना phavrhe se khodna

spade *n.* फावड़ा phaawra

span *v.t.* ऊपर फैला होना upar faila hona

span *n.* सीमा seema

Spaniard *n.* स्पेन का निवासी spain ka nivasi

spaniel *n.* कुत्ते की एक नस्ल kutte ki ek nasal

Spanish *n.* स्पेन की भाषा spain ki bhasha

Spanish *a.* स्पेन का spain ka

spanner *n.* रिंच rinch

spare *a* अतिरिक्त atirikt

spare *n.* फ़ालतू पुर्ज़ा faltu purja

spare *v.t.* बख्श देना bakhsh dena

spark *v.i.* चमकना chamakna

spark *n.* छैला chaila

spark *n.* चिंगारी chingari

sparkle *n.* चमक chamak

sparkle *v.i.* चमकना chamakna

sparrow *n.* गौरैया gaurayiya

sparse *a.* अपर्याप्त aparyapt

spasm *n.* जकड़न jakran

spate *n.* प्रचुरता prachurta

spatial *a.* स्थान विषयक sthan vishayak

spawn *v.i.* अंडे देना ande dena

spawn *n.* जलजीवों के अंडे jaljivon ke ande

speak *v.i.* बोलना bolna

speaker *n.* वक्ता wakta

spear *v.t.* भाले से बींधना bhaale se bindhane

spear *n.* भाला bhaala

spearhead *v.t.* नेतृत्व करना netritva karna

spearhead *n.* भाले की नोक bhale ki nok

special *a.* असाधारण asadharan

specialist *n.* विशेषज्ञ visheshagya

speciality *n.* विशेषता visheshta

specialization *n.* विशिष्टीकरण vishishtikaran

specialize *v.i.* विशेषज्ञ बनना visheshagya banana

species *n.* जाति jaati

specific *a.* निश्चित nishchit

specification *n.* विशिष्ट निर्देशन vishisht nirdeshan

specimen *n.* नमूना namuna

speck *n.* धब्बा dhabba

spectacle *n.* चश्मा chashma

spectacular *a.* भव्य bhavya

spectator *n.* दर्शक darshak

spectre *n.* काली छाया kali chaya

speculate *v.i.* अटकल लगाना atkal lagana

speculation *n.* अटकलबाज़ी atkalbazi

speech *n.* वाणी vani

speed *v.i.* तेज़ी से चलना tezi se chalna

speed *n.* तेज़ी tezi

speedy *a.* तीव्र tivra

spell *v.t.* संकेत करना sanket karna

spell *n* अवधि avadhi

spend *v.t.* व्यय करना vyaya karna

spendthrift *n.* अपव्ययी व्यक्ति apvyayai vyakti

sperm *n.* शुक्राणु shukranu

sphere *n.* गोला gola

spherical *a.* गोलाकार golakar

spice *v.t.* मसालों से छोंकना masalon se chonkna

spice *n.* मसाला masala

spicy *a.* रुचिकर ruchikar

spider *n.* मकड़ी makarhi

spike *v.t.* कील से बींधना keel se bindhna

spike *n.* नोक nauk

spill *n* गिराव girav

spill *v.i.* छलकना chalakna

spin *n.* चक्रण chakran

spin *v.i.* घूमना ghumna

spinach *n.* पालक palak

spinal *a.* मेरुदंडीय merudandiya

spindle *n.* तकला takla

spine *n.* रीढ़ ridh

spinner *n.* कातनेवाला katnewala

spinster *n.* अविवाहिता स्त्री avivahita stri

spiral *a.* घुमावदार ghumavdar

spiral *n.* सर्पिल आकार sarpil aakar

spirit *n.* आत्मा atma

spirited *a.* उत्साही utsahi

spiritual *a.* आध्यात्मिक adhyatmik

spiritualism *n.* अध्यात्मवाद adhyatmavad

spiritualist *n.* अध्यात्मवादी adhytmavadi

spirituality *n.* आध्यात्मिकता adhyatmikta

spit *n* थूक thuk

spit *v.i.* थूकना thukna

spite *n.* द्वेष dvesh

spittle *n* थूक thuk

spittoon *n.* पीकदान peekdaan

splash *n* छिड़काव chirhkava

splash *v.i.* छिड़का जाना chidka jana

spleen *n.* तिल्ली tilli

splendid *a.* शानदार shandar

splendour *n.* भव्यता bhavyata

splinter *n.* किरच kirch

split *n* विभाजन vibhajan

split *v.i.* चीरना cheerna

spoil *v.t.* बिगड़ जाना bigarh jana

spoke *n.* आरा aara

spokesman *n.* प्रवक्ता pravakta

sponge *n.* स्पंज spanj

sponsor *v.t.* प्रयोजित करना prayojit karna

sponsor *n.* प्रायोजक prayojak

spontaneity *n.* स्वाभाविकता svabhavikta

spontaneous *a.* स्वैच्छिक svaichik

spoon *n.* चम्मच chammach

spoonful *n.* चम्मच भर chammach bhar

sporadic *a.* छुट पुट chut put

sport *v.i.* खिलवाड़ करना khilvarh karna

sport *n.* मनोरंजन manoranjan

sportive *a.* क्रीड़ाशील krirhasheel

sportsman *n.* खिलाड़ी khiladi

spot *v.t.* धब्बे डालना dhabbe dalna

spot *n.* निशान nishan

spotless *a.* दोषरहित doshrahit

spousal *n.* विवाह vivah

spouse *n.* पति अथवा पत्नी pati athwa patni

spout *v.i.* तेज़ी से बाहर निकलना tezi se bahar nikalna

spout *n.* पनाला panala

sprain *n.* मोच moch

sprain *v.t.* मुड़काना murhkana

spray *v.t.* छिड़कना chidakana

spray *n.* फुहार phuhar

spread *n.* विस्तार vistar

spread *v.i.* फैलना phailna

spree *n.* मौज मस्ती mauj masti

sprig *n.* टहनी tahani

sprightly *a.* उत्साहपूर्ण utsahpurna

spring *n* उछाल uchal

spring *v.i.* उछलना uchhalna

sprinkle *v.t.* छिड़कना chhirakana

sprint *v.i.* तेज़ी से दौड़ना tezi se daurana

sprout *n* अंकुर ankur

**sprout** *v.i.* अंकुरित होना ankurit hona

**spur** *v.t.* एड़ लगाना add lagana

**spur** *n.* महमेज़ mehmez

**spurious** *a.* नकली nakali

**spurn** *v.t.* ठुकरा देना thukara dena

**spurt** *n* झपट्टा jhapatta

**spurt** *v.i.* फूट निकलना, phut nikalna

**sputnik** *n.* कृत्रिम उपग्रह kritrim upgreh

**sputum** *n.* थूक thuk

**spy** *v.i.* जासूसी करना jasusi karna

**spy** *n.* गुप्तचर guptchar

**squad** *n.* दस्ता dasta,

**squadron** *n.* स्क्वाड्रन squadran

**squalid** *a.* गंदा ganda

**squalor** *n.* गंदगी gandagi

**squander** *v.t.* उड़ा देना udha dena

**square** *v.t.* वर्गाकार बनाना vargakar banana

**square** *n.* वर्ग varg

**squash** *n* फलरस पेय phalras pay

**squash** *v.t.* भुर्ता बना देना bhurta bana dena

**squat** *v.i.* पालथी मारना palthi marna

**squeak** *v.i.* चूं चूं करना choon choon karana

**squeeze** *v.t.* दबाना dabana

**squint** *n* भेंगापन bhengapan

**squint** *v.i.* भेंगा होना bhenga hona

**squire** *n.* ज़मींदार zamindar

**squirrel** *n.* गिलहरी gilahari

**stab** *n.* हथियार से प्रहार hathiyar se prahar

**stab** *v.t.* छुरा घोपना churra ghopna

**stability** *n.* स्थायित्व sthayitva

**stabilization** *n.* स्थिरीकरण sthirikaran

**stabilize** *v.t.* स्थिर बनाना sthir banana

**stable** *n* अस्तबल astabal

**stable** *a.* स्थिर sthir

**stadium** *n.* क्रीड़ा स्थल krida sthal

**staff** *n.* कर्मचारीगण karamchari-gan

**stag** *n.* हिरण hiran

**stage** *v.t.* मंचन करना manchan karna

**stage** *n.* मंच manch

**stagger** *n.* लड़खड़ाहट larhkharhahat

**stagger** *v.i.* लड़खड़ाकर चलना larhkhara kar chalna

**stagnant** *a.* स्थिर sthir

**stagnate** *v.i.* गतिहीन होना gatihin hona

**stagnation** *n.* गतिहीनता gatihinta

**staid** *a.* गंभीर gambhir

**stain** *n.* धब्बा dhabba

**stainless** *a.* बेदाग़ bedag

**stair** *n.* पैड़ी, pairhi

**stake** *v.t.* जोखिम लेना jokhim lena,

**stake** *n* खूंटा khoonta

**stale** *v.t.* बासी करना basi karna

**stale** *a.* बासी basi

**stalemate** *n.* शतरंज में ज़िच shatranj mein zich

**stalk** *v.i.* अकड़कर चलना akarkar chalna

**stalk** *n* गर्वीली चाल garvili chal

**stalk** *n.* डंठल danthal

**stall** *v.t.* थान पर रखना than par rakhna

**stall** *n.* छोटी दुकान choti dukan

**stalwart** *a.* मज़बूत mazboot

**stamina** *n.* दम-खम dam-kham

**stammer** *v.i.* हकलाना haklana

**stammer** *n* हकलाहट haklahat

**stamp** *v.i.* मुद्रांकित करना mudrankit karna

**stamp** *n.* पैर की थाप pair ki thaap

**stampede** *v.i* भगदड़ मचना bhagdarh machna

**stampede** *n.* भगदड़ bhagdarh

**stand** *n.* ठहराव thahrav

**stand** *v.i.* खड़ा होना khara hona

**standard** *a* सामान्य samanya

**standard** *n.* मानक manak

**standardization** *n.* मानकीकरण mankikaran

**standardize** *v.t.* मानकीकरण करना manakikaran karna

**standpoint** *n.* दृष्टिकोण drishtikon

**standstill** *n.* विराम viraam

stanza *n.* बंद band

staple *n.* मुख्य उपज mukhya upaj

star *n.* तारा tara

starch *v.t.* कलफ़ लगाना kalaf lagana

starch *n.* श्वेत सार shwet saar

stare *n.* टकटकी taktaki

stare *v.i.* घूरना ghoorna

stark *adv.* सरासर sarasar

stark *n.* फीका fheeka

starry *a.* तारामय taramaya

start *n* प्रारंभ prarambh

start *v.t.* प्रारंभ करना prarambh karna

startle *v.t.* चौंकाना chaunkana

starvation *n.* भूखमरी bhukhmari

starve *v.i.* भूखों मरना bhukhon marna

state *v.t* कहना kehna

state *n.* अवस्था avastha

stateliness *n.* शान shan

stately *a.* भव्य bhavya

statement *n.* कथन kathan

statesman *n.* राजनेता rajneta

static *n.* स्थिर sthir

statics *n.* स्थैतिकी sthaitiki

station *n* स्टेशन station

station *v.t.* तैनात करना tainaat karna

stationary *a.* स्थिर sthir

stationery *n.* लेखन सामग्री lekhan samagri

statistical *a.* सांख्यिकीय sankhyikiya

statistician *n.* सांख्यिकीविद् sankhyikivid

statistics *n.* सांख्यिकी sankhyiki

statue *n.* मूर्ति murti

stature *n.* महानता mahanata

status *n.* पद pad

statute *n.* कानून kanoon

statutory *a.* वैधानिक vaidhanik

staunch *a.* विश्वसनीय vishvasniya

stay *n* ठहराव thahrav

stay *v.i.* रहना rehna

steadfast *a.* दृढ़, अटल dridh, atal

steadiness *n.* दृढ़ता dridhta

steady *v.t.* दृढ़ बनना dridh banana

steady *a.* नियमित niyamit

steal *v.i.* चोरी करना chori karna

stealthily *adv.* चोरी छुपे chori chupe

steam *n* भाप bhaap

steam *v.i.* भाप छोड़ना bhaap chhorna

steed *n.* घोड़ा ghoda

steel *n.* इस्पात ispat

steep *v.t.* तर करना tar karna

steep *a.* तीव्र ढलान वाला tivra dhalan wala

steeple *n.* मीनार minar

steer *v.t.* मार्गदर्शन करना margdarshan karna

stellar *a.* नक्षत्रीय nakshatriya

stem *v.i.* पैदा होना paida hona

stem *n.* जलयान का अग्र भाग jalyan ka agra bhag

stench *n.* दुर्गंध durgandh

stenographer *n.* आशुलिपिक ashu lipik

stenography *n.* आशुलिपि aashulipi

step *v.i.* चलना chalna

step *n.* कदम kadam

steppe *n.* घास का मैदान ghas ka maidan

stereotype *v.t.* घिसा पिटा रूप देना ghisa pita rup dena

stereotyped *a.* परंपरागत paramparagat

sterile *a.* बांझ banjh

sterility *n.* बांझपन banjhpan

sterilization *n.* जीवाणु नाशन jivanu nashan

sterilize *v.t.* जीवाणुरहित बनाना jivanu-rahit banana

sterling *n.* ब्रिटिश मुद्रा british mudra

sterling *a.* खरा khara

stern *a.* कठोर kathor

stethoscope *n.* स्टैथोस्कोप stethoscope

stew *n.* उत्तेजना uttejana

steward *n.* प्रबंधक prabandhak

stick *v.t.* चुभोना chobhona

stick *n.* लाठी lathi

sticker *n.* चिप्पी chippi
stickler *n.* आग्रही agrahi
sticky *n.* चिपचिपा chipchipa
stiff *n.* जटिल jatil
stiffen *v.t.* कठोर बनाना kathor banana
stifle *v.t.* दबाना dabana
stigma *n.* लांछन anchan
still *adv.* अब तक ab tak
still *n* शांत shaant
still *n.* अचल चित्र achal chitr
still *a.* स्थिर sthir
stillness *n.* स्थिरता sthirta
stilt *n.* पैरबांसा pairbansa
stimulant *n.* प्रेरक पदार्थ prerak padarth
stimulate *v.t.* उभारना ubharana
stimulus *n.* प्रेरणा prerna
sting *v.t.* डंक मारना dank maarana
stingy *a.* कंजूस kanjus
stink *n* दुर्गंध durgandh
stink *v.i.* बदबूदार होना badbudar hona
stipend *n.* वज़ीफ़ा vazifa
stipulate *v.t.* शर्त लगाना shart lagana
stipulation *n.* व्यवस्था vyvasthata
stir *v.i.* हिलना hilna
stirrup *n.* रकाब rakab
stitch *v.t.* सिलना silna
stitch *n.* सीवन siwan
stock *v.t.* भंडारण bhandaran
stock *n.* माल maal
stocking *n.* मौज़ा mauza
stoic *n.* वैरागी vairagi
stoke *v.t.* ईंधन झोंकना indhan jhonkana
stoker *n.* ईंधन झोंकने वाला indhan jhonkane wala
stomach *n.* पेट pet
stone *v.t.* पत्थर फेंकना pathar phenkna
stone *n.* पत्थर pathar
stony *a.* पथरीला patharila
stool *n.* स्टूल stool
stoop *n* झुकाव jhukav

stoop *v.i.* झुकना jhukna
stop *n* विराम viram
stop *v.t.* रोकना rokna
stoppage *n* रूकावट rukawat
storage *n.* भंडारण bhandaran
store *v.t.* बचा रखना bacha rakhna
store *n.* गोदाम godam
storey *n.* मंज़िल manzil
stork *n.* सारस saras
storm *n.* तूफ़ान toofan
stormy *a.* तूफ़ानी toofani
story *n.* कहानी kahani
stout *a.* स्थूलकाय sthulkaya
stove *n.* स्टोव stove
stow *v.t.* बांधकर रख देना bandhakar rakh dena
straggle *v.i.* भटक जाना bhatak jana
straggler *n.* भटकैया bhatkaiya
straight *a.* सीधा, sidha
straighten *v.t.* सीधा करना seedha karna
straightforward *a.* सीधा सादा sidha sada
straightway *adv.* तुरंत turant
straiten *v.t.* संकीर्ण बनाना sakirna banana
strand *n* समुद्र तट samudra tat
strand *v.i.* परेशानी में छोड़ना pareshani mein chorna
strange *a.* अनोखा anokha
stranger *n.* अजनबी ajnabi
strangulation *n.* श्वास अवरोधन shvas avrodhan
strap *n.* पट्टा patta
stratagem *n.* चाल chaal
strategic *a.* युद्धनीति विषयक yudhniti vishayak
strategist *n.* युद्धनीतिज्ञ yudhnitigya
strategy *n.* समूची योजना samuchi yojana
stratum *n.* स्तर estar
straw *n.* भूसा bhusa
strawberry *n.* झरबेर jharber
stray *a* कोई-कोई koi-koi

stray *v.i.* घूमना ghumna

stream *v.i.* बहना behna

stream *n.* नदी nadi

streamer *n.* पताका pataka

streamlet *n.* नदिया nadiya

street *n.* गली gali, sadak

strength *n.* शक्ति shakti

strengthen *v.t.* मज़बूत बनाना mazbut banana

strenuous *a.* ज़ोरदार zordaar

stress *v.t* बल देना bal dena

stress *n.* बल bal

stretch *n* खिंचाव kinchav

stretch *v.t.* फैलाना phailana

strew *v.t.* बिखेरना bikherna

strict *a.* कठोर kathor

strict *a.* अपवादरहित apvadrahit

stricture *n.* कटु आलोचना katu alochana

stride *n* लंबा डग lamba dag

strident *a.* कर्णभेदी karnabhedi

strife *n.* झगड़ा jhagarha

strike *v.t.* आक्रमण करना akraman karna

strike *n* हड़ताल harhtaal

striker *n.* हड़तालकर्त्ता harhtalkaita

string *n.* रस्सी rassi

stringency *n.* सख्ती sakhti

stringent *a.* कठोर kathor

strip *v.t.* नंगा करना nanga karna

strip *n.* पट्टी patti

stripe *n.* धारी dhaari

strive *v.i.* संघर्ष करना sangharsh karna

stroke *n.* प्रहार prahar

stroll *v.i.* टहलना tahalna

strong *a.* शक्तिशाली shaktishali

stronghold *n.* केंद्र kendra

structural *a.* संरचनात्मक saranchanatamak

structure *n.* संरचना saranchana

struggle *n* संघर्ष sangharsh

strumpet *n.* वेश्या veshya

strut *n* गर्वीली चाल garvili chaal

strut *v.i.* इठलाना ithlana

stub *n.* पेंसिल का टुकड़ा pencil ka tukrha

stubble *n.* खूंटी khunti

stubble *n.* दाढ़ी के छोटे बाल daarhi ke chhote baal

stubborn *a.* जिद्दी jiddi

stud *v.t.* जड़ना jarhna

stud *n.* दुहरा बटन duhra batan

student *n.* विद्यार्थी vidyarthi

studio *n.* प्रसारण कक्ष prasaran kaksh

studious *a.* अध्ययनशील adhyayansheel

study *n.* अध्ययनकक्ष adhyayankaksh

study *v.i.* अध्ययन करना adhyayan karna

stuff 2 *v.t.* ठूंसकर भरना thunskar bharna

stuff *n.* कोई पदार्थ koi padarth

stuffy *a.* घुटन भरा ghutan bhara

stumble *n.* ठोकर thokar

stumble *v.i.* ठोकर खाना thokar khana

stump *v.t* आउट करना out karna

stump *n.* टुकड़ा tukrha

stun *v.t.* आश्चर्यचकित करना ashcharyachakit karna

stunt *n* करतब kartab

stunt *v.t.* विकास रोकना vikas rokna

stupefy *v.t.* मूर्ख बनाना murkh banana

stupendous *a.* विशाल vishal

stupid *a* मंदबुद्धि mandbudhi

stupidity *n.* मूर्खता murkhta

sturdy *a.* मज़बूत mazboot

style *n.* ढंग dhang

subdue *v.t.* वश में करना vash mein karna

subject *a* संभाव्य sambhavya

subject *n.* विषयवस्तु vishayvastu

subject *n.* प्रजा praja

subjection *n.* आधिपत्य adhipatya

subjective *a.* आत्मपरक atmaparak

sub-judice *a.* विधि विचाराधीन vidhi vicharadhin

subjugate *v.t.* अधीन करना adhin karna

**subjugation** *n.* आधिपत्य adhipatya

**sublimate** *v.t.* उदात्तीकरण करना udattikaran karna

**sublime** *a.* उदात्त udaatt

**sublimity** *n.* उदात्तता udattata

**submarine** *a* अंतःसागरी antah sagari

**submarine** *n.* पनडुब्बी pandubbi

**submerge** *v.i.* डूबना dubna

**submerge** *v.i.* गोता लगाना gota lagana

**submission** *n.* समर्पण samarpan

**submissive** *a.* आज्ञाकारी agyakaari

**submit** *v.t.* प्रस्तुत करना prastut karna

**subordinate** *a.* कम महत्व का kam mahtva ka

**subordinate** *n* अधीनस्थ कर्मचारी adhinasth karamchari

**subordination** *n.* अधीनीकरण adhinikaran

**subscription** *n.* चंदा chanda

**subsequent** *a.* आगामी aagami

**subservience** *n.* उपयोगिता upyogita

**subservient** *a.* सहायक sahayak

**subside** *v.i.* कम होना kam hona

**subsidiary** *a.* सहायक sahayak

**subsidize** *v.t.* आर्थिक सहायता देना arthik sahayata dena

**subsidy** *n.* आर्थिक सहायता arthik sahayata

**subsist** *v.i.* जीवित रहना jeevit rehna

**subsistence** *n.* जीविका jeevika

**substance** *n.* पदार्थ padarth

**substantial** *a.* ठोस thos

**substantially** *adv.* पर्याप्त मात्रा में paryapt matra mein

**substantiate** *v.t.* प्रमाणित करना pramanit karna

**substantiation** *n.* प्रमाणीकरण pramanikaran

**substitute** *n.* स्थानापन्न sthanapann

**substitution** *n.* प्रतिस्थापन pratisthapan

**subterranean** *a.* भूमिगत bhumigat

**subtle** *n.* बारीक baarik

**subtlety** *n.* बारीकी baariiki

**subtract** *v.t.* घटाना ghatnaa

**subtraction** *n.* घटाव ghatav

**suburb** *n.* उपनगरीय क्षेत्र upnagariya kshetra

**suburban** *a.* उपनगरीय upnagariya

**suburban** *a.* संकीर्णतापूर्ण sankirnatapurna

**subversion** *n.* समाप्ति samaapati

**subversive** *a.* विनाशकारी vinashkaari

**subvert** *v.t.* उलट देना ulat dena

**succeed** *v.i.* सफल होना saphal hona

**success** *n.* सफलता saphalta

**successful** *a* सफल saphal

**succession** *n.* अनुक्रमण anukraman

**successive** *a.* क्रमिक kramik

**successor** *n.* उत्तराधिकारी uttradhikari

**succumb** *v.i.* हार मानना haar manana

**succumb** *v.i.* मर जाना mar jana

**such** *pron.* ऐसे व्यक्ति aise vyakti

**such** *a.* ऐसा aisa

**suck** *n.* चूषण chushan

**suck** *v.t.* चूसना chusana

**suckle** *v.t.* स्तनपान कराना stanpan karana

**sudden** *n.* आकस्मिक akasmik

**suddenly** *adv.* अचानक achanak

**sue** *v.t.* मुकदमा चलाना mukadama chalana

**suffer** *v.t.* भुगतना bhugatna

**suffice** *v.i.* पर्याप्त होना paryapt hona

**sufficiency** *n.* पर्याप्त मात्रा paryapt matra

**sufficient** *a.* पर्याप्त paryapt

**suffix** *v.t.* जोड़ना jorhna

**suffix** *n.* प्रत्यय pratyaya

**suffocate** *v.t* दम घुटकर मरना dam ghutkar marna

**suffocation** *n.* घुटन ghutan

**suffrage** *n.* मताधिकार matadhikaar

**sugar** *v.t.* मीठा करना meetha karna

**sugar** *n.* चीनी, शक्कर cheeni

**suggest** *v.t.* प्रस्तावित करना prastavit karna

**suggestion** *n.* प्रस्ताव prastav

**suggestive** *a.* विचारोत्तेजक vicharotejak

suicidal *a.* आत्मघाती atmaghati

suicide *n.* आत्महत्या atmahatya

suit *v.t.* उपयुक्त बनाना upyukt banana

suit *n.* मुकदमा mukadama

suitability *n.* उपयुक्तता upyuktata

suitable *a.* उचित uchit

suitor *n.* प्रार्थी prarthi

sullen *a.* रूठा हुआ rootha hua

sulphur *n.* गंधक gandhak

sulphuric *a.* गंधक युक्त gandhak yukt

sultry *a.* उमसदार umasdar

sum *v.t.* जोड़ना jorhna

sum *n.* धनराशि dhanrashi

summarily *adv.* तुरंत turant

summarize *v.t.* संक्षिप्त करना sankshipt karna

summary *a* संक्षिप्त sankshipt

summary *n.* संक्षिप्त विवरण sankshipt vivran

summer *n.* ग्रीष्म ऋतु grishma ritu

summit *n.* चोटी choti

summon *v.t.* बुला भेजना bula bhejna

summon *n.* अदालत का बुलावा adalat ka bulava

sumptuous *a.* शानदार shandaar

sun *v.t.* धूप dhoop

sun *n.* सूर्य surya

sunday *n.* रविवार raviwar

sunder *v.t.* अलग करना alag karna

sundry *a.* विभिन्न vibhinn

sunny *a.* गर्म garam

super tax *n.* अधिकर adhikar

superabundance *n.* आधिक्य aadhikya

superabundant *a.* भरपूर bharpoor

superb *a.* उत्तम uttam

superficial *a.* अगंभीर agambhir

superficiality *n.* छिछलापन chichalapan

superfine *a.* अति उत्तम ati uttam

superfluity *n.* आधिक्य aadhikya

superfluous *a.* फ़ालतू, अति अधिक faltu, ati adhik

superhuman *a.* अतिमानवीय atimanviya

superintend *v.t.* संचालन करना sanchalan karna

superintendence *n.* संचालन sanchalan

superintendent *n.* प्रबंधक prabandhak

superior *a.* उच्च uccha

superiority *n.* श्रेष्ठता shreshthata

superlative *n.* मावस्था mavastha

superlative *a.* श्रेष्ठतासूचक shreshthatasuchak

superman *n.* अतिमानव atimanav

supernatural *a.* अलौकिक alaukik

supersede *v.t.* स्थान लेना sthan lena

supersonic *a.* पराध्वनिक paradhvanik

superstition *n.* अंधविश्वास andhvishvas

superstitious *a.* अंधविश्वासी andhvishvasi

supervise *v.t.* निर्देशित करना nirdeshit karna

supervision *n.* देख रेख dekh rekh

supervisor *n.* निरीक्षक nirikshak

supper *n.* रात्रि का भोजन ratri ka bhojan

supple *a* सुनम्य sunamya

supplement *n.* परिशिष्ट parishisht

supplement *v.t.* पूरा करना pura karna

supplementary *a.* पूरक purak

supplier *n.* प्रदायक pradayak

supply *n* भंडार bhandaar

supply *v.t.* प्रदान करना pradaan karna

support *n.* सहारा sahara

support *v.t.* सहारा sahara

suppose *v.t.* कल्पना करना kalpana karna

supposition *n.* कल्पना kalpana

suppress *v.t.* कुचलना kuchalna

suppression *n.* दमन daman

supremacy *n.* उच्चता uchchata

supreme *a.* सर्वोच्च sarvoch

surcharge *v.t.* अधिभार लगाना adhibhar lagana

surcharge n. अधिशुल्क adhishulk

sure a. निश्चित nishchit

surely adv. निश्चित रूप से nishchit rup se

surety n. ज़मानत jamanat

surf n. तटीय लहरें tatitya leharain

surface n. सतह satah

surface v.i ऊपर आना uppar aana

surfeit n. आधिक्य aadhikya

surge v.i. हिलोर मारना hilor maarna

surge n. आवेश avesh

surgeon n. शल्य चिकित्सक shalya chikitsak

surgery n. शल्य चिकित्सा shalya chikitsa

surmise v.t. अंदाज़ा लगाना andaza labgana

surmise n. अनुमान anumaan

surmount v.t. विजय पाना vijay pana

surname n. कुलनाम kulnaam

surpass v.t. अधिक होना adhik hona

surplus n. अधिशेष adhishesh

surprise v.t. आश्चर्यचकित करना ashcharyachakit karna

surrender n आत्मसमर्पण atmasamarpan

surrender v.t. हार मानना haar manana

surround v.t. घेरना gherna

surroundings n. प्रतिवेश prativesh

surtax n. अधिकर adhikar

surveillance n. निगरानी nigrani

survey n. सर्वेक्षण sarvekshan

survey v.t. निरीक्षण करना nirikshan karna

survival n. उत्तरजीविता uttarjeevita

survive v.i. जीवित बचना jeevit bachna

suspect n संदिग्ध व्यक्ति sandigdh vyakti

suspect v.t. संदेह करना sandeh karna

suspect a. संदिग्ध sandighdh

suspend v.t. निलंबित करना nilambit karna

suspense n. अनिश्चय की स्थिति anishchya ka sthiti

suspension n. निलंबन nilamban

suspicion n. संदेह sandeh

suspicious a. शक्की shakki

sustain v.t. जीवित रखना jeevit rakhna

sustenance n. जीवनाधार jeevanadhar

swagger n इठलाती चाल ithlaati chaal

swagger v.i. इठलाना ithlana

swallow n. निगरण nigaran

swallow n. अबाबील ababeel

swallow v.t. निगलना nigalna

swamp n. दलदल daldal

swan n. हंस hans

swarm v.i. भीड़ लगाना bheerh lagana

swarm n. दल dal

swarthy a. सांवला sanvala

sway n प्रभाव prabhav

sway v.i. हिलना डुलना hilna dulna

swear v.t. कसम खिलाना kasam khilana

sweat v.i. पसीना आना paseena aana

sweat n. पसीना paseena

sweater n. स्वेटर sweater

sweep n. साफ़ सफ़ाई saaf safai

sweep v.i. झाड़ू लगाना jhaadu lagana

sweeper n. झाड़ू लगानेवाला jharhu laganewala

sweet a. मीठा meetha

sweeten v.t. मीठा करना meetha karna

sweetmeat n. मिष्ठान, मिठाई mithai, methae

sweetness n. मिठास mithas

swell n फुलाव fulav

swell v.i. बढ़ना badna

swift a. तीव्र, तत्पर tivra, tatper

swim n तैराकी tairaki

swim v.i. तैरना tairana

swimmer n. तैराक tairak

swindle n. ठगी, झांसा thagi

swindle v.t. ठगना thagna

swindler n. झांसिया, ठग thag

swine n. सूअर suar

swine n. घृणित व्यक्ति ghrinit vyakti

swing n झूला jhula

swing v.i. झूलना jhulna

**Swiss** *n.* स्विटज़रलैंड का निवासी
switzerland ka nivasi

**switch** *v.t.* बदलना badalna

**switch** *n.* स्विच switch

**swoon** *v.i* मूर्च्छित होना murchit hona

**swoon** *n.* मूर्च्छा murcha

**swoop** *v.i.* झपट्टा मारना jhapatta marna

**swoop** *n* झपट्टा jhapatta

**sword** *n.* तलवार talwar

**sycamore** *n.* गूलर gular

**sycophancy** *n.* चाटुकारिता, चापलूसी
chaplusi

**sycophant** *n.* चापलूस chaplus

**syllable** *n.* उच्चारण इकाई ucharan ikayee

**syllabus** *n.* पाठ्यक्रम pathyakram

**sylph** *n.* परी pari

**sylvan** *a.* वृक्षीय vrikshiya

**symbol** *n.* चिह्न, प्रतीक chinh, prateek

**symbolic** *a.* प्रतीकात्मक pratikatmak

**symbolism** *n.* प्रतीकवाद pratikvad

**symbolize** *v.t.* प्रतीक होना pratik hona

**symmetrical** *a.* सममित sammit

**symmetry** *n.* संतुलन santulan

**sympathetic** *a.* सहानुभूतिपूर्ण sahanubhuti-
purna

**sympathize** *v.i.* सहानुभूति रखना
sahanubhuti rakhna

**sympathy** *n.* सहानुभूति sahanubhuti

**symphony** *n.* वाद्यवृंद रचना vadyavrind
rachna

**symphony** *n.* सुरीलापन surilapan

**symposium** *n.* विचार गोष्ठी vichar goshthi

**symptom** *n.* लक्षण lakshan

**symptomatic** *a.* लक्षणसूचक
lakshansuchak

**synonym** *n.* पर्याय paryaya

**synonymous** *a.* पर्यायवाची, paryayavachi

**synopsis** *n.* रूपरेखा ruperekha

**syntax** *n.* वाक्य रचना vakya rachna

**synthesis** *n.* संश्लेषण sankshaleshan

**synthetic** *n* कृत्रिम उत्पादन kritrim utpadan

**synthetic** *a.* संश्लेषणात्मक
sankshaleshanatmak

**syringe** *n.* पिचकारी pichkari

**syrup** *n.* शरबत sharbat

**system** *n.* योजना yojna

**systematic** *a.* पद्धतिबद्ध padhatibadh

**systematize** *v.t.* सुव्यवस्थित करना
suvyavasthit karna

# T

**table** *n.* मॅज mez

**table** *v.t.* प्रस्तुत करना prastut karna

**tablet** *n.* गोली goli

**taboo** *a* निषिद्ध nishidh

**taboo** *v.t.* निषिद्ध करना nishidh karna

**taboo** *n.* निषेध nishedh

**tabular** *a.* तालिकाबद्ध talika badh

**tabulate** *v.t.* तालिकाबद्ध करना talikabadh
karna

**tabulation** *n.* सारणीयन sarniyan

**tabulator** *n.* सारणीयक sarniyak

**tacit** *a.* अनकहा ankaha

**tacit** *a.* मौन maun,ankaha

**taciturn** *a.* अल्पभाषी alpbhashi

**tackle** *v.t.* भिड़ना bhirhna

**tackle** *n.* विरोधी पर काबू virodhi par kabu

**tact** *n.* व्यवहार कौशल vyvahar kaushal

**tactician** *n.* रणनीतिज्ञ rannitigya

**tactics** *n.* रणनीति ranniti

**tactile** *a.* स्पर्श योग्य sparsh yogya

**tag** *n.* घिसा पिटा कथन ghisa pita kathan

**tag** *v.t.* संलग्न करना sanlagna karna

**tail** *n.* पूंछ poonch

**tailor** *n.* दर्ज़ी darzi

**taint** *v.t.* दूषित करना dushit karna

**taint** *n.* दोष dosh

**take** *v.t.* लेना lena

take *v.t* पकड़ना pakarhna

tale *n.* कहानी kahani

talent *n.* प्रतिभा pratibha

talisman *n.* तावीज़ taveez

talk *v.i.* बोलना bolna

talkative *a.* बातूनी batuni

tall *a.* लंबा lamba

tallow *n.* चरबी charbi

tally *v.t.* अनुरूप होना anurup hona

tally *n.* हिसाब hisab

tamarind *n.* इमली का वृक्ष imli ka vriksh

tame *v.t.* पालना palna

tame *a.* पालतू paltu

tamper *v.i.* हस्तक्षेप hastakshep

tan *v.i.* भूरा होना bhoora hona

tangent *n.* स्पर्शज्या sparshjya

tangible *a.* स्पर्शनीय sparshniya

tangle *v.t.* उलझाना uljhana

tangle *n.* उलझन uljhan

tank *n.* टंकी tanki

tanker *n.* तेल पोत tel pot

tanner *n.* चर्म शोधक sharm shodhak

tannery *n.* चर्म शोधनशाला sharm shodhanshala

tantalize *v.t.* तरसाना tarsana

tantamount *a.* समान saman

tap *n.* टोंटी tonti

tap *v.t.* द्रव निकालना dravya nikalna

tape *v.t* अभिलेखन करना abhilekhan karna

tape *n.* पट्टी patti

taper *n* पतलापन patlapan

tapestry *n.* दीवार दरी deewar dari

tar *v.t.* तारकोल पोतना tarkol potna

tar *n.* तारकोल tarkol

target *n.* निशाना nishana

tariff *n.* सीमा शुल्क seema shulk

tarnish *v.t.* बदरंग करना badrang karna

task *n.* कार्य karya

task *v.t.* कार्य सौंपना karya saunpana

taste *n.* स्वाद svad

tasteful *a.* रुचिकर ruchikar

tasty *a.* स्वादिष्ट svadisht

tatter *v.t* चिथड़े करना chithrhe karna

tatter *n.* चिथड़ा chithrha

tattoo *v.i.* लीला गोदना leela godna

tattoo *n.* गोदने का चिह्न godne ka chinh

tattoo *n.* बिगुल का नाद bigul ka nad

tattoo *n.* सेना का प्रदर्शन sena ka pradarshan

taunt *n* ताना tana

taunt *v.t.* ताना मारना tana maarna

tavern *n.* मधुशाला madhushala

tax *v.t.* कर लगाना kar lagana

tax *n.* कर kar

taxable *a.* कर योग्य kar yogya

taxation *n.* करारोपण kararopan

taxi *v.i.* टैक्सी में जाना taxi mein jaana

taxi *n.* टैक्सी taxi

tea *n* चाय chai

teach *v.t.* शिक्षा देना shiksha dena

teacher *n.* शिक्षक shikshak

team *n.* टोली toli

tear *n.* चीरा cheera

tear *v.t.* फाड़ना pharhna

tear *n.* आंसू aansu

tearful *a.* अश्रुपूर्ण ashrupurna

tease *v.t.* चिढ़ाना chidhana

teat *n.* स्तनाग्र stanagra

technical *n.* तकनीकी takniki

technicality *n.* प्राविधिकता pravidhikta

technician *n.* तकनीक जाननेवाला takneek jananevala

technique *n.* प्रविधि pravidhi

technological *a.* प्रौद्योगिकीय praudyogikiya

technologist *n.* प्रौद्योगिकीविद् praudyogikivad

technology *n.* प्रौद्योगिकी praudyogiki

tedious *a.* उबाऊ या उकताने वाला ubane ya thakane wala

tedious *a.* नीरस neeras

tedium *n.* नीरसता neerasta

teem *v.i.* प्रचुरता में होना prachurata mein hona

teem *v.i.* उमड़ना umarhna

teenager *n.* किशोर, किशोरी kishor, kishori

teens *n. pl.* किशोरावस्था kishoravastha

teethe *v.i.* दूध के दांत निकलना dudh ke dant nikalna

teetotal *a.* मद्यत्यागी madyatyagi

teetotaller *n.* मद्यत्यागी madyatyagi

telecommunications *n.* दूरसंचार doosanchar

telegram *n.* तार संदेश taar sandesh

telegraph *v.t.* तार द्वारा भेजना taar dwara bhejana

telegraph *n.* तार यंत्र taar yantra

telegraphic *a.* तार द्वारा प्रेषित taar dwara preshit

telegraphist *n.* तार यांत्रिक taar yantrik

telegraphy *n.* तारसंचार taarsanchar

telepathic *a.* दूर संवेदी door sanvadi

telepathist *n.* दूरसंवेदनविद् doorsanvedanvid

telepathy *n.* दूरसंवेदन dursanvedan

telephone *n.* दूरभाष doorbhash

telescope *n.* दूरबीन doorbin

telescopic *a.* दूरबीनी doorbini

television *n.* दूरदर्शन doordashan

tell *v.t.* बताना batana

teller *n.* कथक kathak

temper *v.t.* मंद करना mand karna

temper *n.* मानसिकता maansikta

temperament *n.* प्रकृति prakriti

temperamental *a.* स्वाभाविक svabhavik

temperance *n.* मद्यत्याग madyatyag

temperate *a.* शीतोष्ण sheetoshna

temperature *n.* तापमान taapman

tempest *n.* तूफ़ान toofan

tempestuous *a.* तूफ़ानी toofani

temple *n* कनपटी kanpati

temple *n.* मंदिर mandir

temporal *a.* कालिक kalik

temporary *a.* अस्थायी asthai

tempt *v.t.* लुभाना lubhana

temptation *n.* प्रलोभन pralobhan

tempter *n.* लुभानेवाला lubhanewala

ten *n., a* दस dus

tenable *a.* समर्थनीय samarthniya

tenacity *n.* तीव्रता tivrata

tenancy *n.* किरायेदारी kirayadari

tenant *n.* किरायेदार kirayadar

tend *v.i.* प्रवृत्त होना pravrat hona

tendency *n.* झुकाव jhukao

tender *v.t.* प्रस्तुत करना prastut karna

tender *n* सेवक sevak

tender *a* मुलायम mulayam

tender *n* निविदा nivida

tenet *n.* सिद्घांत siddhant

tennis *n.* टैनिस tennis

tense *a.* कसा हुआ kasa hua

tense *n.* काल kaal

tension *n.* कसाव kasav

tent *n.* तंबू tambu

tentative *a.* आज़माइशी azmaishi

tenure *n.* धारण dharan

term *n.* अवधि avadhi

term *n.* शब्द shabdh

term *v.t.* पुकारना pukarna

term *n.pl.* सम्बन्ध sambandh

terminable *a.* समाप्य samapya

terminal *n* सिरा sira

terminal *a.* अंतिम antim

terminate *v.t.* समाप्त होना samapt hona

termination *n.* समाप्ति samapati

terminology *n.* पारिभाषिक शब्दावली paribhashik shabdawali

terminus *n.* अंतिम स्टेशन antim station

terrace *n.* चबूतरा chabutara

terrible *a.* गंभीर gambhir

terrier *n.* कुत्ते की एक नस्ल kutte ki ek nasal

terrific *a.* अति अधिक ati adhik

terrify *v.t.* आतंकित करना atankit karna

territorial *a.* प्रादेशिक kshetriya

territory *n.* क्षेत्र kshetra

terror *n.* आतंक aatank

terrorism *n.* आतंकवाद aatankvad

terrorist *n.* आतंकवादी aatankvadi

terrorize *v.t.* आतंकित करना aatankit karna

terse *a.* संक्षिप्त sankshipt

test *n* परीक्षण parikshan

test *v.t.* जांचना janchna

testament *n.* वसीयत vasiyat

testicle *n.* अंडग्रंथि andgranthi

testify *v.i.* प्रमाण देना praman dena

testimonial *n.* प्रमाणपत्र pramanpatra

testimony *n.* साक्ष्य sakshya

tete-a-tete *n.* व्यक्तिगत वार्तालाप vyaktigat vartalap

tether *v.t.* पगहे से बांधना pageh se bandhna

tether *n.* रस्सी rassi

text *n.* मूल पाठ mool path

textile *n* वस्त्र vastra

texture *n.* गठन gathan

thank *v.t.* धन्यवाद देना dhanyavad dena

thankful *a.* कृतज्ञ, kritagya

thankless *a.* कृतघ्न kritagna

thanks *n.* आभार aabhaar

that *dem. pron.* उसने usne

that *rel. pron.* जो jo

that *adv.* ताकि taki

that *conj.* कि ki

that *a.* वह vah

thatch *v.t.* छप्पर डालना chappar dalna

thatch *n.* छप्पर chappar

thaw *v.i* पिघलना pighalna

thaw *n* पिघलन pighalna

theatre *n.* नाट्यशाला natyashala

theatrical *a.* नाट्यशाला विषयक natyashala vishayak

theft *n.* चोरी chori

their *a.* उनका unka

theirs *pron.* उनका unka

theism *n.* आस्तिकता aastikta

theist *n.* आस्तिक aastik

them *pron.* उनको unko

thematic *a.* विषयगत vishaygat

theme *n.* विषय vishay

then *a* तत्कालीन tatkaleen

then *adv.* उस समय us samay

thence *adv.* वहां से vahan se

theocracy *n.* धर्मतंत्र, dharamtantra

theologian *n.* धर्मविज्ञानी dharam vigyani

theological *a.* धर्मविज्ञान विषयक dharmavigyan vishayak

theology *n.* ईश्वरमीमांसा ishwarmimansa

theorem *n.* प्रमेय pramay

theoretical *a.* सैद्धांतिक saidhantik

theorist *n.* सिद्धांतशास्त्री siddhantshastri

theorize *v.i.* सिद्धांत स्थापित करना siddhant sthapit karna

theory *n.* सैद्धांतिक ज्ञान saidhantik gyan

therapy *n.* चिकित्सा chikitsa

there *adv.* वहां vahan

thereabouts *adv.* लगभग उतना lagbhag utarna

thereafter *adv.* तदनंतर tadantar

thereby *adv.* उसके द्वारा uske dwara

therefore *adv.* अतः atah

thermal *a.* ऊष्मीय ushmiya

thermometer *n.* तापमापी taapmapi

thermos (flask) *n.* थर्मस tharmas

thesis *n.* शोध ग्रंथ shodh granth

thick *a.* घना ghana

thick *adv.* प्रचुर मात्रा में prachur matra mein

thicken *v.i.* मोटा होना mota hona

thicket *n.* झुरमुट jhurmut

thief *n.* चोर chori

thigh *n.* जंघा jangha

thimble *n.* अंगुश्ताना angushtana

thin *v.t.* पतला करना patla karna

thin *a.* पतला patla

thing *n.* वस्तु vastu

think *v.t.* मानना manana

thinker *n.* विचारक vicharak

third *n.* तिहाई भाग tihayee bhag

third *a.* तीसरा teesra

thirdly *adv.* तीसरे स्थान पर teesre sthan par

thirst *v.i.* प्यासा होना pyasa hona

thirst *n.* प्यास pyas

thirsty *a.* प्यासा pyasa

thirteen *n.* तेरह की संख्या terah ki sankhya

thirteen *a* तेरह terah

thirteenth *a.* तेरहवां terahawan

thirtieth *n* तीसवां भाग teesvan bhag

thirtieth *a.* तीसवां teesvan

thirty *a* तीस tees

thirty *n.* तीस की संख्या tees ki sankhya

thistle *n.* ऊंटकटारा untkataara

thither *adv.* उस ओर, वहां को us aur, vahan ko

thorn *n.* कांटा kanta

thorny *a.* कंटकमय, कष्टप्रद kantakmay

thorough *a* पूर्ण purna

thoroughfare *n.* आम रास्ता aam rasta

though *adv.* तथापि tathapi

though *conj.* यद्यपि yadyapi

thought *n* सोच विचार soch-vichar

thoughtful *a.* लिहाज़ करनेवाला lihaz karnewala

thousand *a* हज़ार hazar

thousand *n.* हज़ार की संख्या hazar ki sankhya

thraldom *n.* दासता dasta

thrall *n.* दास daas

thrash *v.t.* पीटना pitna

thread *v.t* धागा डालना dhaa dalna

thread *n.* धागा dhaga

threadbare *a.* जीर्ण jirna

threat *n.* धमकी dhamki

threaten *v.t.* धमकी देना dhamki dena

three *a* तीन teen

three *n.* तीन की संख्या teen ki sankhya

thresher *n.* मड़ाई की मशीन madhai ki machine

threshold *n.* दहलीज़ dahleez

thrice *adv.* तीन बार teen baar

thrift *n.* मितव्ययिता mitvyayata

thrifty *a.* मितव्ययी mitvyayi

thrill *v.t.* पुलकित करना pulkit karna

thrill *n.* पुलक pulak

thrive *v.i.* फलना फूलना phalna phulna

throat *n.* गला gala

throaty *a.* बैठी हुई आवाज़ baithee hui awaz

throb *n.* स्पंदन sampadan

throb *v.i.* धड़कना dharhakna

throe *n.* तीव्र पीड़ा tivra peerha

throne *v.t.* राजगद्दी पर बिठाना rajgaddi par bithana

throne *n* राजगद्दी rajgaddi

throng *n.* भीड़ bheerh

throng *v.t.* ठसाठस भर देना thasathas bhar dena

throttle *v.t.* गला घोंटना gala ghontana

throttle *n.* उपरोधक uprodhak

through *adv.* आद्योपांत adyopant

through *a* बिना रुके जानेवाला bina ruke janewala

through *prep.* के आर पार ke aar paar

throughout *prep.* के प्रत्येक भाग में ke pratyek bhag mein

throughout *adv.* सर्वत्र sarvatra

throw *n.* फेंक phenk

throw *v.t.* फेंकना phenkna

thrust *n* ज़ोरदार धक्का zordaar dhakka

thrust *v.t.* धक्का देना dhakka dena

thud *v.i.* धम की आवाज़ करना dham ki awaz

thud *n.* धम dham

thug *n.* गुंडा gunda

thumb *n.* अंगूठा angutha

thump *v.t.* मुक्का मारना mukka maarna

thump *n.* मुक्का mukka

thunder *v.i.* गरजना garjana

thunder *n.* गरज़ garaz

thunderous *a.* गर्जनशील garjanshil

Thursday *n.* गुरूवार guruvar

thus *adv.* इस प्रकार is prakar

thwart *v.t.* रोकना rokna

tiara *n.* मुकुट mukut

tick *v.i.* टिक टिक करना tik tik karna

tick *n.* टिक टिक की ध्वनि tik tik ki dhwani

ticket *n.* टिकट ticket

tickle *v.t.* हंसाना hansana

ticklish *a.* गुदगुदी gudgudi

tidal *a.* ज्वारीय jvariya

tide *n.* ज्वार jvaar

tidiness *n.* स्वच्छता, सुव्यवस्था svachata

tidings *n. pl.* समाचार samachar

tidy *v.t.* सुव्यवस्थित करना suvyavasthit karna

tidy *a.* सुव्यवस्थित suvyavasthit

tie *v.t.* बांधना bandhana

tie *n* गांठ ganth

tie *n* टाई tie

tiger *n.* बाघ bagh

tight *a.* कसा हुआ kasa hua

tighten *v.t.* कसना, kasna

tigress *n.* बाघिन baghin

tile *v.t.* खपरों से पाटना khapron se patna

tile *n.* खपरा khapra

till *n. conj.* जब तक कि jab tak ki

till *v.t.* जोतना jotna, jutai karna

till *prep.* के समय तक ke samay tak

tilt *v.i.* झुकना jhukna

tilt *n.* झुकाव jhukao

timber *n.* इमारती लकड़ी imarati lakri

time *v.t.* का समय नापना ka samay naapna

time *n.* समय samay

timely *a.* समयोचित samyochit

timid *a.* डरपोक darphok

timidity *n.* भीरुता bheeruta

timorous *a.* भीरु bheeru

tin *v.t.* डिब्बों में रखना dibbon mein rakhna

tin *n.* टिन tin

tin *n.* टिन का डिब्बा tin ka dabba

tincture *v.t.* हल्का रंग चढ़ाना halka rang chadhana

tincture *n.* झलक jhalak

tinge *v.t.* की पुट देना ki put dena

tinge *n.* आभा aabha

tinker *n.* ठठेरारा thathera

tinsel *n.* पन्नी panni

tint *v.t.* रंगना rangna

tint *n.* रंग rang

tiny *a.* बहुत छोटा bahut chhota

tip *v.t.* नोकदार बनाना nokdaar banana

tip *n.* संकेत sanket

tip *v.t.* बख़िशश देना bakhshish dena

tip *v.t.* हल्का सा छूना halka sa choona

tip *n.* नोक nok

tipsy *a.* हल्के नशे में halke nashe mein

tirade *n.* फटकार भरा भाषण phatkar bhara bhashan

tire *v.t.* थक जाना thaka jana

tiresome *a.* थकाऊ thakau

tissue *n.* मुलायम काग़ज़ mulayam kagaz

titanic *a.* विशाल vishal

tithe *n.* दशमांश कर dashmansh kar

title *n.* पुस्तक का नाम pustak ka naam

titular *a.* औपाधिक upadhik

toad *n.* भेक bhek

tobacco *n.* तंबाकू tambaku

today *n.* यह दिन yeh din

today *adv.* आज, आजकल aaj

toe *v.t.* पैर से छूना pair se choona

toe *n.* पैर की उंगली pair ki ungli

toffee *n.* टॉफी toffee

toga *n.* चोग़ा choga

together *adv.* साथ साथ saath saath

toil *v.i.* कठिन परिश्रम करना kathin parishram karna

toil *n.* कठिन परिश्रम kathin parishram

toilet *n.* शौचघर shauchghar

toils *n. pl.* जाल jaal

token *n.* प्रतीक pratik

tolerable *a.* सहनीय sahaniya

tolerance *n.* सहनशीलता sahanshilta

tolerant *a.* सहिष्णु sahishnu

tolerate *v.t.* होने देना hone dena

toleration *n.* धार्मिक सहिष्णुता dharmik sahishunta

toll *n* घंटा नाद ghanta naad

toll *v.t.* घंटा बजाना ghanta bajana

toll *n.* पथकर pathkar

tomato *n.* टमाटर tamatar

tomb *n.* कब्र kabra

tomboy *n.* मरदानी लड़की mardani larhki

tomcat *n.* बिलाव bilav

tome *n.* विशाल ग्रंथ vishal granth

tomorrow *adv.* कल को kal ko

tomorrow *n.* आने वाला कल aane wala kal

ton *n.* टन tan

tone *n.* स्वर svar

tone *v.t.* तानबद्ध करना taanbadh karna

tongs *n. pl.* चिमटा chimta

tongue *n.* जीभ jeebh

tonic *n.* स्वास्थ्यवर्धक औषधि svasthavardhak aushadhi

tonic *n.* मूलस्वर moolsvar

tonic *a.* तान विषयक taan vishayak

tonight *adv.* आज रात को aaj rat ko

to-night *n.* आज की रात aaj ki raat

tonne *n.* मीटरी टन meetri tan

tonsil *n.* टॉन्सिल tonsil

tonsure *n.* मुंडन mundan

too *adv.* बहुत अधिक bahut adhik

tool *n.* औज़ार auzaar

tooth *n.* दांत dant

toothache *n.* दांत दर्द dant dard

toothsome *a.* स्वादिष्ट svadisht

top *v.t.* चोटी पर पहुंचना choti par pahunchna

top *n.* लट्टू lattu

top *n.* चोटी choti

topaz *n.* पुखराज pukhraj

topic *n.* विषय vishay

topical *a.* सामयिक samayik

topographer *n.* स्थलाकृति विशेषज्ञ sthalakriti visheshagya

topographical *a.* स्थलाकृतिक sthalakritik

topography *n.* स्थलाकृति sthalakriti

topple *v.i.* उलट जाना ulat jaana

topsy turvy *a.* औंधा aundha

topsy turvy *adv* उलट पुलट स्थिति में ulat pulat sthiti mein

torch *n.* मशाल mashal

torment *n.* यातना yatna

torment *v.t.* यातना देना yatna dena

tornado *n.* तूफ़ान toofan

torpedo *n.* पनडुब्बी pandubbi

torrent *n.* प्रचंड धारा prachand dhara

torrential *a.* प्रचंड धारा जैसा prachand dhara jaisa

torrid *a.* अति उष्ण ati ushna

tortoise *n.* कछुआ kachhua

tortuous *a.* टेढ़ा मेढ़ा tedha medha

torture *v.t.* यातना देना yatna dena

torture *n.* यातना yatna

toss *n* उछाल uchchal

toss *v.t.* झटका देना jhatka dena

total *n.* पूर्ण मात्रा purna matra

total *v.t.* जोड़ना jorhna

total *a.* संपूर्ण, समूचा sampurna

totality *n.* संपूर्णता sampurnata

touch *n* स्पर्श sparsh

touch *v.t.* स्पर्श करना sparsh karna

touch *v.t.* संपर्क में आना sampark mein ana

touchy *a.* नाराज़ naraz

tough *a.* मज़बूत mazboot

toughen *v.t.* कड़ा बनाना karha banana

tour *v.i.* भ्रमण करना bhraman karna

tour *n.* भ्रमण, यात्रा bhraman, yatra

tourism *n.* पर्यटन paryatan

tourist *n.* पर्यटक paryatak

tournament *n.* खेलकूद प्रतियोगिता khelkud pratiyogita

towards *prep.* की ओर ki aur

towel *v.t.* तौलिये से पोंछना tauliye se paunchna

towel *n.* तौलिया tauliya

tower *v.i.* ऊंचा उठना uncha uthna

tower *n.* मीनार minar

town *n.* कसबा kasba

township *a.* कसबा kasba

toy *v.i.* खिलवाड़ करना khilvarh karna

toy *n.* खिलौना khilauna

trace *v.t.* सुराग़ पा लेना surag pa lena

trace *n.* निशान nishan

traceable *a.* खोजने योग्य khojne yogya

track *v.t.* ढूंढ लेना dhoondh lena

track *n.* मार्ग marg

tract *n* पुस्तिका pustika

tract *n.* विस्तृत भूभाग vistrit bhubhag

traction *n.* खिंचाव khinchav

tractor *n.* ट्रैक्टर tractor

trade *v.i* व्यापार करना vyapar karna

trade *n.* व्यापार vyapar

trader *n.* व्यापारी vyapari

tradesman *n.* दुकानदार dukandar

tradition *n.* परंपरा parampara

traditional *a.* परंपरागत paramparagat

traffic *n.* यातायात yatayaat

tragedian *n.* त्रासदीकार trasadikar

tragedy *n.* दु:खद घटना dukhad ghatna

tragic *a.* दु:खांत dukhant

trail *v.t.* घसीटना ghasitna

trail *n.* मार्ग marg

trailer *n* फिल्म की झलकियां film ki jhalkiyan

train *v.t.* प्रशिक्षण देना prashikshan dena

train *n.* रेलगाड़ी railgarhi

trainee *n.* प्रशिक्षणार्थी prashikshanarthi

training *n.* प्रशिक्षण prashikshan

trait *n.* विशेषता visheshta

traitor *n.* विश्वासघाती vishvasghati

tram *n.* ट्रामगाड़ी tramgarhi

trample *v.t.* कुचलना, रौंदना kuchalna

trance *n.* बेहोशी behoshi

tranquil *a.* शांत shant

tranquillity *n.* शांति shanti

tranquillize *v.t.* शांत करना shant karna

transact *v.t.* संपादित करना sampadit karna

transaction *n.* संपादन sampadan

transcend *v.t.* मानव के अनुभव manav ke anubhav

transcendent *a.* अनुभवातीत anubhavatit

transcription *n.* प्रतिलिपि लेखन pratilipi lekhan

transfer *v.t.* स्थानांतरित करना sthanantarit karna

transfer *n.* स्थानातंरण sthananataran

transferable *a.* स्थानांतरणीय sthanantaraniya

transfiguration *n.* रूपांतरण rupantaran

transfigure *v.t.* रूपांतरित करना rupantarit karna

transform *v.* रूप बदल देना rup badal dena

transformation *n.* रूपांतरण rupantaran

transgress *v.t.* अतिक्रमण करना atikraman karna

transgression *n.* अतिक्रमण atikraman

transit *n.* परिवहन parivahan

transition *n.* परिवर्तन parivartan

transitive *n.* सकर्मक क्रिया sakarmak

transitory *n.* अस्थायी asthayee

translate *v.t.* अनुवाद करना anuvad karna

translation *n.* अनुवाद anuvad

transmigration *n.* देहांतरण dehantaran

transmission *n.* संचारण sancharan karna

transmit *v.t.* प्रेषित करना preshit karna

transmitter *n.* प्रेषक preshak

transparent *a.* पारदर्शी pardarshi

transplant *v.t.* प्रतिरोपित करना pratiropit karna

transport *n.* परिवहन साधन parivahan sadhan

transport *v.t.* ले जाना le jana

transportation *n.* परिवहन parivahan

trap *v.t.* धोखा देकर पकड़ना dhokha dekar pakarhna

trap *n.* ढका हुआ गड्ढा dhaka hua gaddha

trash *n.* कूड़ा करकट koorha karkat

travel *v.i.* यात्रा करना yatra karna

travel *n* यात्रा yatra

traveller *n.* यात्री yatri

tray *n.* ट्रे tray

treacherous *a.* विश्वासघाती dhokhebaz,vishvaghati

treachery *n.* धोखा dhokha

tread *n* पदचाप padchap

tread *v.t.* कुचलना kuchalna

treason *n.* विश्वासघात vishvasghat

treasure *v.t.* संचित करना sanchit karna

treasure *n.* भंडार bhandar

treasurer *n.* कोषाध्यक्ष koshadhyaksha

treasury *n.* ख़ज़ाना khazana

treat *n* दावत dawat

treat *v.t.* बरताव करना bartav karna

treat *v.t.* इलाज करना ilaj karna

treatise *n.* प्रबंध prabandh

treatment *n.* व्यवहार vyavahar

treaty *n.* संधि sandhi

tree *n.* पेड़ ped

trek *n.* लंबी, कठोर पैदल यात्रा lambi, kathor paidal yatra

trek *v.i.* पैदल चलना paidal chalna

tremble *v.i.* कांपना kampana

tremendous *a.* विशाल vishal

tremor *n.* कंपन kampan

trench *v.t.* (में) खांचा बनाना (mein) khancha banana

trench *n.* खाई, खंदक khandak

trend *n.* प्रवृत्ति pravrati

trespass *n.* अतिक्रमण atikraman

trespass *v.i.* अतिक्रमण करना atikraman karna

trial *n.* जांच janch

triangle *n.* त्रिभुज tribhuj

triangular *a.* त्रिभुजाकार tribhujakar

tribal *a.* जनजातीय janjatiya

tribe *n.* जन जाति jan jati

tribulation *n.* मुसीबत musibat

tribunal *n.* न्यायालय, न्यायाधिकरण nyayalaya

tributary *n.* सहायक नदी saayak nadi

tributary *a.* सहायक sahayak

trick *v.t.* धोखा देना dhokha dena

trick *n* धोखा dhokha

trickery *n.* धोखा dhokha

trickle *v.i.* टपकना, tapakna

trickster *n.* कपटी kapati

tricky *a.* चालाक chalak

tricolour *a.* तिरंगा tiranga

tricycle *n.* तिपहिया साइकिल tipahiya cycle

trifle *v.i* खिलवाड़ करना khilvarh karna

trifle *n.* नगण्य वस्तु, अल्पमात्रा naganya vastu

trigger *n.* लिबलिबी liblibi

trim *n* सज्जा sajja

trim *v.t.* छांटना chantana

trim *a.* साफ़ सुथरा saf suthra

trinity *n.* त्रिक trik

**trio** *n.* त्रिक trik

**trip** *n.* सैर sair

**trip** *v.t.* गिरा देना gira dena

**tripartite** *a.* त्रिपक्षीय tripakshiya

**triple** *a.* तिगुना tiguna

**triple** *adj* तिगुना करना tiguna karna

**triplicate** *v.t.* तिगुना करना tiguna karna

**triplicate** *a.* तिगुना tiguna

**triplication** *n.* त्रिगुणन trigunan

**tripod** *n.* तिपाई tipayee

**triumph** *v.i.* विजय प्राप्त करना vijay prapt karna

**triumph** *n.* विजय vijay

**triumphal** *a.* विजय संबंधी vijay sambandhi

**triumphant** *a.* विजयी vijayayi

**trivial** *a.* हल्का halka

**troop** *v.i* टोली में चलना toli mein chalna

**troop** *n.* टोली toli

**trooper** *n.* घुड़सवार सैनिक ghurhsawar sainik

**trophy** *n.* पुरस्कार puraskar

**tropic** *n.* कर्क अथवा मकर रेखा kark athva makar rekha

**tropical** *a.* अति उष्ण ati ushna

**trot** *n* दुलकी dulki

**trot** *v.i.* दुलकी चलना dulki chalna

**trouble** *v.t.* चिंतित करना chintit karna

**trouble** *n.* व्यवधान vyavdhan

**troublesome** *a.* कष्टप्रद kashtprad

**troupe** *n.* मंडली mandali

**trousers** *n. pl* पतलून patlun

**trowel** *n.* करनी karni

**truce** *n.* युद्धविराम yudhviram

**truck** *n.* ट्रक truck

**true** *a.* तथ्यात्मक tathyatmak

**trump** *v.t.* (पर) तुरुप मारना (par) turup marna

**trump** *n.* तुरुप turup

**trumpet** *v.i.* तुरही बजाना turahi banana

**trumpet** *n.* तुरही turahi

**trunk** *n.* पेड़ का तना perh ka tana

**trust** *v.t* (पर) भरोसा करना (par) bharosa karna

**trust** *n.* विश्वास vishvas

**trustee** *n.* न्यासी nyasi

**trustful** *a.* विश्वासी vishvasi

**trustworthy** *a.* भरोसे का bharose ka

**trusty** *n.* निष्ठावान nishthavan

**truth** *n.* वास्तविकता vastvikta

**truthful** *a.* सत्यवादी satyavadi

**try** *n* प्रयत्न prayatna

**try** *v.i.* प्रयत्न करना pryatna karna

**tryst** *n.* पूर्व निश्चित भेंट purva nishchit bhent

**tub** *n.* टब tub

**tube** *n.* नली nali

**tuberculosis** *n.* क्षेय रोग ksheya rog

**tubular** *a.* नलिकाकार nalikakar

**tug** *v.t.* ज़ोर से खींचना zor se khinchna

**tuition** *n.* अनुशिक्षण anushikshan

**tumble** *n.* गिराव girav

**tumble** *v.i.* गिर जाना gir jana

**tumbler** *n.* गिलास gilas

**tumour** *n.* अर्बुद aburdh

**tumult** *n.* तीव्र कोलाहल tivra kolahal

**tumultuous** *a.* कोलाहलपूर्ण kolahalpurna

**tune** *v.t.* समस्वरित करना samsvarit karna

**tune** *n.* धुन dhun

**tunnel** *v.i.* सुरंग बनाना surang banana

**tunnel** *n.* सुरंग surang

**turban** *n.* पगड़ी pagrhi

**turbine** *n.* टरबाइन turbine

**turbulence** *n.* उग्रता ugrata

**turbulent** *a.* अशांत ashant

**turf** *n.* तृणभूमि trinbhumi

**turkey** *n.* पीरू peeru

**turmeric** *n.* हल्दी haldi

**turmoil** *n.* घबराहट ghabrahat

**turn** *n* घुमाव ghumav

urge *v.t* समझाना samjhana
urge *n* तीव्र इच्छा tivra ichcha
urgency *n.* अत्यावश्यकता atyavashyakta
urgent *a.* अति आवश्यक ati avashyak
urinal *n.* मूत्रालय mutralaya
urinary *a.* मूत्रीय mutriya
urinate *v.i.* लघुशंका करना laghushanka karna
urination *n.* मूत्र त्याग mutra tyag
urine *n.* मूत्र mutra
urn *n* कलश kalash
usage *n.* प्रयोग prayog
use *n.* लाभ labh
use *v.t.* काम में लाना kaam mein laana
useful *a.* उपयोगी upyogi
usher *n.* प्रवेशक praveshak
usher *v.t.* अंदर ले जाना andar le jana
usual *a.* सामान्य samanya
usually *adv.* नियमत niyamit
usurer *n.* सूदखोर soodkhor
usurp *v.t.* हथियाना hathiyana
usurpation *n.* अनाधिकार ग्रहण anadhikar grahan
usury *n.* सूदखोरी soodkhori
utensil *n.* बरतन bartan
uterus *n.* गर्भाशय garbhashay
utilitarian *a.* उपयोगी upyogi
utility *n.* लाभ labh
utilization *n.* उपयोग upyog
utilize *v.t.* प्रयोग करना prayog karna
utmost *a.* अधिकतम adhiktam
utmost *n* अधिकतम मात्रा adhiktam matra
utopia *n* . आदर्श राज्य adarsh rajya
utopian *a.* आदर्श adarsh
utter *v.t.* कहना kehna
utter *a* पूर्ण purna
utterance *n.* बोली boli
utterly *adv.* पूर्णतया purnataya

vacancy
vacancy
vacant
vacate
vacation
vaccina
vaccina
vaccina
    lagan
vaccine
vacillate
vacuum
vagabo
vagabo
vagary
vagina
vague
vaguen
vain *a.*
vainglo
vainglo
vainly
vale *n.*
valiant
valid *a.*
validat
validity
valley
valour
valuab
valuati
value
valve
van *n.*
vanish
vanity

turn *v.i.* घूमना ghumna
turner *n.* खरादी kharadi
turnip *n.* शलजम shaljam
turpentine *n.* तारपीन taarpin
turtle *n.* समुद्री कच्छप samudari kachchap
tusk *n.* गजदंत gajdant
tussle *v.i.* संघर्ष करना sangharsh karna
tussle *n.* संघर्ष sangharsh
tutor *n.* निजी शिक्षक niji shikshak
tutorial *n.* निजी शिक्षक के शिक्षण का समय niji shikshak ke shikshan ka samay
tutorial *a.* शिक्षकीय shikshakiya
twelfth *n.* बारहवां भाग barhavan bhag
twelfth *a.* बारहवां barhavan
twelve *n* बारह barah
twelve *n.* बारह की संख्या barah ki sankhya
twentieth *n* बीसवां भाग beesvan bhag
twentieth *a.* बीसवां beesvan
twenty *n* बीस की संख्या bees ki sankhya
twenty *a.* बीस bees
twice *adv.* दो बार do baar
twig *n.* टहनी tahani
twilight *n* धुंधला प्रकाश dhundhala prakash
twin *a* जुड़वा jurhva
twin *n.* जुड़वां जोड़े में से एक jurhva jorhe mein se ek
twinkle *n.* झिलमिलाहट jhilmilahat
twinkle *v.i.* झिलमिलाना, चमकना chamakna
twist *n.* ऐंठन ainthan
twist *v.t.* गूथना guthna
twitter *v.i.* चहकना chahakna
twitter *n.* चहक chahak
two *a.* दो do
two *n.* दो की संख्या do ki sankhya
twofold *a.* दोगुना doguna
type *v.t.* टंकित करना tankit karna
type *n.* श्रेणी shreni
typhoid *n.* आंत्रज्वर antrajvar
typhoon *n.* प्रचंड तूफ़ान prachand tufan

typhus *n.* तंद्रिक ज्वर tandrik jvar
typical *a.* प्रारूपिक विशिष्ट prarupik vishisht
typify *v.t.* प्रारूप होना prarup hona
typist *n.* टंकक tankak
tyranny *n.* तानाशाही tanashahi
tyrant *n.* तानाशाह tanashah
tyre *n.* टायर tyre

udder *n.* अयन ayan
uglify *v.t.* कुरूप बनाना, बिगाड़ना kurup banana, bigaadna
ugliness *n.* कुरूपता kurupta
ugly *a.* कुरूप kurup
ulcer *n.* फोड़ा, व्रण fhora, vran
ulcerous *a.* व्रणीय, व्रणयुक्त vraniya, vranyukt
ulterior *a.* गुप्त gupt
ultimate *a.* अंतिम, सर्वोच्च महत्व का antim, sarvoch mahatwa ka
ultimately *adv.* अंतत: antatah
ultimatum *n.* अंतिम शर्त antim shart
umbrella *n.* छाता chata
umpire *n.* निर्णायक nirnayak
umpire *adj* निर्णायक होना nirnayak hona
unable *a.* असमर्थ asamarth
unanimity *n.* सर्वसम्मति sarvasammati
unanimous *a.* सर्वसम्मत sarvasammat
unaware *a.* अनजान anjaan
unawares *adv.* अनजाने में anjane mein
unburden *v.t.* बोझ उतारना bojh utarna
uncanny *a.* रहस्यमय rahasyamaya
uncertain *a.* अपरिवर्तनशील aparivartan sheel
uncle *n.* चाचा chacha
uncouth *a.* भद्दा bhadda
under *prep.* नीचे neeche

under adv नीचे neeche
undercurrent n. अंतर्धारा antardhara
underdog n दलित व्यक्ति dalit vyakti
undergo v.t. गुज़रना guzarna
undergraduate n. पूर्वस्नातक purvasnatak
underhand a. गुप्त gupt
underline v.t. रेखांकित करना rekhankit karna
undermine v.t. सुरंग बनाना surang banana
underneath adv. नीचे neeche
understand v.t. समझना samajhana
undertake v.t. वचन देना vachan dena
undertone n. मंद स्वर mand swar
underwear n. अंतरीय antariya
underworld n. अधोलोक adholok
undo v.t. नष्ट करना nasht karna
undue a. अनुचित anuchit
undulate v.i. लहराना lehrana
unearth v.t. खोजना khojana
uneasy a. चिंतित chintit
unfair a. अनुचित anuchit
unfold v.t. खोलना kholna
unfortunate a. खेदजनक khedjanak
ungainly a. भद्दा bhadda
unhappy a. दुःखपूर्ण dukhapurna
unification n. एकीकरण ekikaran
union n. एकता ekta
unionist n. संघवादी sanghwadi
unique a. अद्वितीय advitiya
unison n. सामंजस्य samanjasya
unit n. मात्रक matrak
unite v.t. एक करना ek karna
unity n. एकता ekta
universal a. विश्वव्यापी viswavyapi
universality n. विश्वव्यापकता vishwayopakata
universe n. विश्व vishwa
university n. विश्वविद्यालय vishv vidyalaya
unjust a. अन्यायी anyayi

unless
unlike
unlike
unlikel
unman
unprin
unrelia
unrest
unruly
unsettl
unshea
se ni
until p
until c
untowa
unwell
unwitti
up adv.
upbrai
upheav
uphold
upkeep
uplift v
uplift n
upon p
upper
upright
uprisin
uproar
uproar
uproot
upset v
upshot
up-to-d
upward
upward
urban
urbane
urbanit
urchin

vanity n. सारहीनता saarhinta
vanquish v.t. पराजित करना parajit karna
vaporize v.t. वाष्प में बदल जाना vashp mein badal jaana
vaporous a. वाष्प जैसा vashp jaisa
vapour n. वाष्प vashp
variable a. परिवर्तनीय parivartaniya
variance n. अनबन anban
variation n. परिवर्तन parivartan
varied a. विभिन्न vibhinn
variety n. विविधता vividhata
various a. विविध, विभिन्न vividh,vibhinn
various a. vibhinn
varnish v.t. रोग़न करना rogan karna
varnish n. रोग़न rogan
vary v.t. बदल जाना badal jaana
vasectomy n. नसबंदी nasbandi
vaseline n. वैसलीन vaseline
vast a. विशाल vishal
vault n. मेहराबी छत mehrabi chhat
vault v.i. कूदना koodna
vault n. तहखाना tahakhana
vegetable n. साग sabzi
vegetarian n. शाकाहारी shakahari
vegetarian a निरामिष niramish
vegetation n. पेड़ पौधे perh paudhe
vehemence n. तीव्रता tivrata
vehement a. प्रचंड prachand
vehicle n. वाहन vahan
vehicular a. यानयुक्त yanyukt
veil v.t. ढकना dhakna
veil n. ओढ़नी odhni
vein n. शिरा shira
velocity n. गति gati
velvet n. मखमल makhmal
velvety a. मखमली makhmali
venal a. भ्रष्ट bhrasht
venality n. भ्रष्टता bhrashtata
vendor n. विक्रेता vikreta
venerable a. आदरणीय adarniya

venerate v.t. आदर करना adar karna
veneration n. श्रद्धा shraddha
vengeance n. प्रतिशोध pratishodh
venial क्शमया kshamya
venial a. लघु laghu
venom n. विष vish
venomous a. विषैला vishaila
vent n. छेद ched
ventilate v.t. हवादार बनाना havadar banana
ventilation n. वातापूर्ति हवादारी vatapurti
ventilator n. हवाकश havakash
venture v.t. साहस करना sahas karna
venture n. जोखिम jokhim
venturesome a. जोखिम भरा jokhim bhara
venturous a. साहसी sahasi
venue n. सभा स्थल sabha sthal
veracity n. सच्चाई sachchayee
veranda n. बरामदा baramada
verb क्रिया kriya
verbal a. मौखिक maukhik
verbally adv. मौखिक रूप में maukhik rup mein
verbatim adv. शब्दशः shabdashah
verbatim a. शाब्दिक shaabdik
verbose a. शब्दबहुल shabdabahul
verbosity n. शब्दबहुलता shabdabahulata
verdant a. हरा भरा hara bhara
verdict n. अभिनिर्णय abhinirnaya
verge n. किनारा kinara
verification n. प्रमाणन satyapan
verify v.t. जांच करना janch karna
verisimilitude n. सत्याभास satyabhas
veritable a. वास्तविक सच्चा vastvik sach
vermillion a. गहरा लाल gehra lal
vermillion n. गहरा लाल रंग gehra lal rang
vernacular a. देशी deshi
vernacular n. सामान्य भाषा samanya bhasha
vernal a. वासंतिक vasantik

versatile *a.* बहुमुखी bahumukhi

versatility *n.* संपन्नता pratibha sampannata

verse *n.* काव्य kavya

versed *a.* प्रवीण pravin

versification *n.* पद्यरचना padyarachna

versify *v.t.* पद्यबद्ध करना padya-baddh karna

version *n.* कथन kathan

versus *prep.* बनाम banaam

vertical *a.* ऊपर kharha

verve *n.* उत्साह utsah

very *a.* यही yahi

very *a.* वही vahi

very *a.* बिल्कुल bilkul

vessel *n.* बरतन bartan

vest *n.* फातूही fatuhi

vest *v.t.* (से) समपन्न करना (se) sampann karna

vest *v.t.* कपड़ा पहनाना kapda pehanana

vestige *n.* निशानी nishani

vestment *n.* परिधान paridhan

veteran *a.* अनुभवी anubhavi

veteran *n.* अनुभवी व्यक्ति anubhavi vyakti

veterinary *a.* पशुचिकित्सा संबंधी pashuchikitsa

veto *v.t.* निषिद्ध करना nishidh karna

veto *n.* निषेधाधिकार nishedhadhikar

vex *v.t.* तंग करना tang karna

vexation *n* परेशानी pareshani

via *prep.* के मार्ग से ke marg se

viable *a.* व्यवहार्य vyavaharya

vial *n.* शीशी sheeshi

vibrate *v.i.* आवाज़ का कांपना awaaz ka kampana

vibration *n.* कंपन kampan

vicar *n.* पुरोहित purohit

vicarious *a.* स्थानापन्न sthanapann

vice *n.* व्यसन vyasan

vice-versa *adv.* विलोमत: vilomatah

vicinity *n.* पड़ोस pados

vicious *a.* खतरनाक khatarnak

vicissitude *n.* भाग्य का फेर bhagya ka pher

victim *n.* शिकार shikar

victimize *v.t.* को शिकार बनाना ko shikar banana

victor *n.* विजेता vijeta

victorious *a.* विजयी vijayi

victory *n.* विजय vijay

victuals *n. pl* खाद्य khadya

vie *v.i.* मुकाबला करना mukabala karna

view *n.* दृश्य drishya

view *v.t.* देखना dekhna

vigil *n.* रखवाली rakhwali

vigilance *n.* निगरानी nigrani

vigilant *a.* सतर्क satark

vigorous *a.* शक्तिशाली shaktishali

vile *a.* घृणित ghrinit

vilify *v.t.* निंदा करना ninda karna

villa *n.* देहाती बंगला dehati bangla

village *n.* देहात dehat

villager *n.* देहाती dehati

villain *n.* दुष्ट dusht

vindicate *v.t.* सच सिद्ध करना sach sidh karna

vindication *n.* दोष मुक्ति dosh mukti

vine *n.* अंगूर की बेल angur ki bel

vinegar *n.* सिरका sirka

vintage *n.* अंगूरी शराब anguri sharab

violate *v.t.* भंग करना bhang karna

violation *n.* उल्लंघन ulanghan

violence *n.* हिंसा hinsa

violent *a.* हिंसात्मक hinsatmak

violent *a.* तीव्र tivra

violet *n.* बैंगनी रंग baingani rang

violin *n.* वायलिन violin

violinist *n.* वायलिन वादक violin vadak

virgin *n* पवित्र pavitra

virgin *n.* कुंआरी kunwari

virginity *n.* शुचिता shuchita

virile *a.* शक्तिशाली shaktishali

virility *n.* पौरुष paurush

virtual *a* वास्तविक vastvik

virtue *n.* नैतिकता naitikta

virtuous *a.* पावन pavan

virulence *n.* द्वेषभाव dveshbhav

virulent *a.* विषाक्त vishakt

virus *n.* विषाक्त तत्व vishakt tatva

visage *n.* चेहरा chehra

visibility *n.* दृष्टिसीमा drishyasima

visible *a.* दृश्यमान drishyaman

vision *n.* दृष्टि drishti

visionary *n.* स्वप्न दृष्टा svapan drishta

visionary *a.* काल्पनिक kalpanik

visit *v.* घूमने आना ghoomne ana

visit *n.* ठहराव thaharav

visit *v.t.* (से) मिलने जाना (se) milne jana

visitor *n.* मेहमान mehman

vista *n.* दृश्य drishya

visual *a.* दृष्टि विषयक drishti vishayak

visualize *v.t.* कल्पना करना kalpana karna

vital *a.* प्राणाधार pranadhar

vitality *n.* जीवन शक्ति jeevan shakti

vitalize *v.t.* जीवन प्रदान करना jeevan pradan karna

vitamin *n.* विटामिन vitamin

vitiate *v.t.* बिगाड़ना bigarhna

vivacious *a.* फुर्तीला furtila

vivacity *n.* आनंदमयता anandmayata

viva-voce *a* मौखिक maukhik

viva-voce *n* मौखिक परीक्षा maukhik pariksha

viva-voce *adv.* मौखिक रूप में maukhik rup mein

vivid *a.* सजीव sajiv

vivid *a.* चमकदार chamakdar

vixen *n.* कर्कशा karkasha

vocabulary *n.* शब्द सूची shabd soochi

vocal *a.* कथित kathit

vocalist *n.* गायक gayak

vocation *n.* व्यवसाय vyvasaya

vogue *n.* प्रचलन prachlan

voice *n.* आवाज़ awaaz

voice *v.t.* अभिव्यक्त करना abhivyakt karna

void *v.t.* रद्द करना radd karna

void *n.* शून्य shunya

void *a.* रिक्त rikt

volcanic *a.* ज्वालामुखीय jwalamukhiya

volcano *n.* ज्वालामुखी jwalamukhi

volition *n.* संकल्प शक्ति sankalp shakti

volley *v.t.* उड़ती गेंद पर मार urhati gend par maar

volt *n.* वोल्ट volt

voltage *n.* वोल्टता voltata

volume *n.* परिमाण pariman

volume *n.* ढेर dher

voluminous *a.* विशाल vishal

voluntarily *adv.* स्वेच्छा से svaicha se

voluntary *a.* स्वैच्छिक svaichik

volunteer *v.t.* स्वेच्छा से देना svecha se dena

volunteer *n.* स्वयंसेवक svayamsevak

voluptuary *n.* विषयासक्त vishyasakt

voluptuous *a.* भोगपूर्ण bhogpurna

vomit *n* वमन क्रिया vaman kriya

vomit *v.t.* मुंह से उलट देना muhn se ulat dena

voracious *a.* अति भूखा ati bhukha

votary *n.* अनुयायी anuyayi

vote *v.i.* मत देना mat dena

vote *n.* मतदान matdan

voter *n.* मतदाता matdata

vouch *v.i.* आश्वासन देना ashvasan dena

voucher *n.* व्यय की रसीद vyaya ki rasid

vow *v.t.* व्रत लेना vrat lena

vow *n.* व्रत vrat

vowel *n.* स्वर svar

voyage *n.* समुद्र यात्रा samudra yatra

voyage *v.i.* समुद्र यात्रा करना samudra yatra karna

voyager *n.* समुद्र यात्री samudra yatri

vulgar *a.* अश्लील ashalil

vulgar *a.* भद्दा bhadda

vulgarity *n.* अश्लीलता ashalilta

vulnerable *a.* जिस पर वार किया जा सके jis par var kiya ja sake

vulture *n.* गिद्ध giddh

# W

waddle *v.i.* डगमगाकर चलना dagmagakar chalna

waft *n* महक mehak

wag *n* हिलने की क्रिया hilane ki kriya

wag *v.i.* हिलना hilna

wage *n.* मज़दूरी mazdoori

wager *v.i.* बाज़ी लगाना bazi lagana

wager *n.* शर्त shart

wagon *n.* मालडिब्बा maldibba

wail *n* विलाप vilap

wail *v.i.* विलाप करना vilap karna

wain *n.* बैलगाड़ी bailgarhi

waist *n.* कमर kamar

waistband *n.* कमरबंद kamarband

waistcoat *n.* वास्कट vaskat

wait *n.* प्रतीक्षा pratiksha

wait *v.i.* प्रतीक्षा करना pratiksha karna

waiter *n.* बैरा baira

waitress *n.* परिचारिका paricharika

waive *v.t.* छोड़ देना chhod dena

wake *n* जागरण jagran

wake *n* अनुजल anujal

wake *v.t.* जगाना jagana

wakeful *a.* निद्रा रहित nidra rahit

walk *n* भ्रमण bhraman

walk *v.i.* चलना chalna

wall *n.* दीवार diwar

wall *v.t.* दीवार से घेरना diwar se gherna

wallet *n.* थैली thaili

wallop *v.t.* आघात करना aghaat karna

wallow *v.i.* लोट पोट करना lot pot karna

walnut *n.* अखरोट akhrot

walrus *n.* समुद्री घोड़ा samudari ghoda

wan *a.* पीला peela

wand *n.* छड़ी charhi

wander *v.i.* घूमना ghumana

wane *n* ह्रास hwas

wane *v.i.* घटना ghatana

want *n* आवश्यकता avashyakata

want *v.t.* इच्छा रखना ichha rakhna

wanton *a.* उदेश्यहीन udeshyahin

war *v.i.* लड़ना larhna

war *n.* युद्ध yuddh

warble *n* कूजन kujan

warble *v.i.* कूजना kujana

warbler *n.* गायक पक्षी gayak pakshi

ward *v.t.* रक्षा करना raksha karna

ward *n.* आश्रित ashrit

warden *n.* वार्डन warden

warder *n.* जेलर jailer

wardrobe *n.* वस्त्र vastra

wardship *n.* अभिरक्षा abhiraksha

ware *n.* वस्तुएं vastuen

warehouse *v.t* गोदाम godaam

warfare *n.* संग्राम sangraam

warlike *a.* युद्धप्रिय yudhpriya

warm *a.* गुनगुना gunguna

warm *v.t.* गरम करना garam karna

warmth *n.* गरमी garami

warn *v.t.* सचेत करना sachet karna

warning *n.* पूर्वसूचना purvasuchna

warrant *v.t.* ज़िम्मा लेना zimma lena

warrant *n.* आज्ञापत्र agyapatr

warrantor *n.* आश्वासनदाता ashwasandaata

warranty *n.* अधिकार, adhikar

warren *n.* खरगोशों का बाड़ा khargoshon ka barha

warrior *n.* योद्धा yodha

wart *n.* मस्सा massa

wary *a.* सतर्क satark

wash *n* धुलाई dhulayee

wash *v.t.* धोना dhona

washable *a.* धुलाई योग्य dhulayee yogya

washer *n.* वाशर washer

wasp *n.* ततैया tatiya

waspish *a.* चिड़चिड़ा chirhchirha

wassail *n.* उत्सवगान utsav gaan

wastage *n.* छीजन, हानि hani

waste *n.* निर्थक nirarthak

waste *v.t.* नष्ट करना nasht karna

waste *a.* व्यर्थ vyartha

wasteful *a.* विनाशकारी vinashkari

watch *n.* चौकसी chaukasi

watch *v.t.* अवलोकन करना avlokan karna

watchful *a.* सतर्क satark

watchword *n.* नारा naara

water *n.* पानी pani

waterfall *n.* जल प्रपात jal prapat

water-melon *n.* तरबूज़ tarbooz

waterproof *n* जलसह वस्त्र jalsah vastra

waterproof *v.t.* जलसह बनाना jalsah banana

waterproof *a.* जलसह jalsah

watertight *a.* जलरोधी jalrodhi

watery *a.* अश्रुमय ashrumya

watt *n.* वाट watt

wave *v.t.* हिलाना hilana

wave *n.* लहर lehar

waver *v.i.* अस्थिर होना asthir hona

wax *v.t.* मोम लगाना mom lagana

wax *n.* मोम mom

way *n.* मार्ग marg

way *n.* ढंग dhang

wayfarer *n.* राही rahi

waylay *v.t.* घात में बैठना ghat mein baithna

wayward *a.* हठी hathi

weak *a.* कमज़ोर kamzor

weaken *v.t. & i* कमज़ोर बनाना kamzor banana

weakling *n.* कमज़ोर प्राणी kamzor prani

weakness *n.* कमज़ोरी kamzori

weal *n.* कल्याण kalyan

wealth *n.* धन दौलत dhan daulat

wealthy *a.* धनी dhani

weapon *n.* हथियार hathiyar

wear *v.t.* प्रदर्शित करना pradarshit karna

weary *v.t. & i* थकना thakana

weary *a.* नीरस niras

weary *v.t.* थकाना thakaana

weary *a.* थका मांदा thaka manda

weather *n* मौसम mausam

weather *v.t.* झेलना jhelna

weave *v.t.* बुनना bunana

weaver *n.* बुनकर bunkar

web *n.* मकड़ी का जाला makrhi ka jaala

webby *a.* झिल्लीदार jhillidar

wed *v.t.* विवाह करना vivah karna

wedding *n.* विवाहोत्सव vivahutsav

wedge *n.* पच्चर pachchar

wedlock *n.* विवाह vivah

Wednesday *n.* बुधवार budhvar

weed *v.t.* निराना nirana

weed *n.* अपतृण apitrin

week *n.* सप्ताह saptah

weekly *adv.* प्रत्येक सप्ताह pratyek saptah

weekly *n.* साप्ताहिक saptahik

weekly *a.* साप्ताहिक saptahik

weep *v.i.* रोना rona

weevil *n.* घुन ghun

weigh *v.t.* तोलन tolan

weight *n.* वज़न vazan

weightage *n.* बढ़त badhat

weighty *a.* भारी bhari

weir *n.* सेतु setu

weird *a.* अनोखा anokha

welcome *n* अभिनंदन abhinandan

welcome *v.t* स्वागत करना svagat karna

welcome *a.* सुखद sukhad

weld *n* जोड़ jorh

weld *v.t.* मिलाना milana

welfare *n.* कल्याण kalyan

well *adv.* भली भांति bhali bhanti

well *n.* कुआं kuan

well *v.i.* बहना behna

well *a.* स्वस्थ swastha

wellington boot *n.* लंबा जूता lamba juta

well-known *a.* सुपरिचित suparichit

well-read *a.* विद्वान vidvan

well-timed *a.* समयानुकूल samayanukul

well-to-do *a.* संपन्न sampann

welt *n.* चाबुक chabuk

welter *n.* आंदोलन andolan

wen *n.* गिल्टी gilti

wench *n.* लड़की larki

west *a.* पश्चिमी, पछुवां pashchimi

west *adv.* पश्चिम की ओर pashchim ki or

west *n.* पश्चिम pashchim

westerly *a.* पश्चिमी pashchimi

western *a.* पश्चिमी pashchimi

wet *v.t.* गीला करना geela karna

wet *a.* गीला geela

wetness *n.* गीलापन geelapan

whack *v.t.* प्रहार करना prahar karna

whale *n.* वेल whale

wharfage *n.* घाट शुल्क ghat shulk

what *a.* कौनसा kaun sa

what *pron.* जो वस्तु jo vastu

what *interj.* क्या ! kya!

whatever *pron.* जो कुछ भी, कुछ भी kuch bhi

wheat *n.* गेहूं का पौधा gehun ka paudha

wheedle *v.t.* फुसलाना phuslana

wheel *v.t.* घुमाना ghumana

wheel *a.* पहिया pahiya

whelm *v.t.* अभिभूत करना abhibhut karna

whelp *n.* पिल्ला pilla

when *conj.* जिस समय jis samay

when *adv.* कब kab

whence *adv.* जहां से jahan se

whenever *adv. conj* जब कभी jab kabhi

where *conj.* जहां jahan

where *adv.* कहां kahan

whereabouts *adv.* कहां kahan

whereas *conj.* जबकि jabki

whereat *conj.* जिस पर, जहां jis par, jahan

wherein *adv.* किस दृष्टि से kis drishti se

whereupon *conj.* जिसके बाद jis ke baad

wherever *adv.* जहां कहीं jahan kahin

whet *v.t.* तेज़ करना tez karana

whether *conj.* यदि yadi

which *pron.* जो jo

which *a* कौनसा kaun sa

whichever *pron* जो कोई jo koi

whiff *n.* झोंका jhonka

while *conj.* जब तक jab tak

while *v.t.* समय गंवाना samay gawana

while *n.* समय samay

whim *n.* सनक sanak

whimper *v.i.* रिरियाना ririyana

whimsical *a.* अनोखा anokha

whine *n* चिल्लाहट chilhat

whine *v.i.* रोना चिल्लाना rona chilana

whip *n.* कोड़ा korha

whip *v.t.* फेंटना phentana

whipcord *n.* चाबुक की डोरी chabuk ki dori

whir *n.* भिनभिनाहट bhinbhinahat

whirl *n* घुमाव ghumao

whirl *n.i.* घूमना ghumna

whirligig *n.* लट्टू, चक्रदोला lattu

whirlpool *n.* भंवर bhanwar

whirlwind *n.* चक्रवात, बगूला chakravat, bagula

whisk *n* फेंटनी phentani

whisker *n.* पशु की मूंछ pashu ki moonch

whisky *n.* शराब sharab

whisper *n* फुसफुस phus-phus

whisper *v.t.* फुसफुसा कर कहना phuphusa kar kehna

whistle *n* सीटी की आवाज़ seeti ki awaaz

whistle *v.i.* सीटी बजाना seeti bajana

white *n* सफ़ेद रंग saphed rang

white *a.* सफ़ेद saphed

whiten *v.t.* सफ़ेद करना saphed karna

whitewash *v.t.* सफ़ेदी करना saphedi karna

whitewash *n.* सफ़ेदी saphedi

whither *adv.* कहां kahan

whitish *a.* सफ़ेद सा saphed sa

whittle *v.t.* छीलना chheenanaa

whiz *v.i.* सनसनाना sansanana

who *pron.* कौन kaun

whole *n* संपूर्ण sampurna

whole *a.* संपूर्ण sampurna

whole-hearted *a.* हार्दिक hardik

wholesale *a* थोक संबंधी thok sambandhi

wholesale *adv.* थोक में thok mein

wholesale *n.* थोक बिक्री thok bikri

wholesaler *n.* थोक व्यापारी thok vyapari

wholesome *a.* हितकारी hitkari

wholly *adv.* पूर्णतया purntaya

whom *pron.* किसे kise

whore *n.* वेश्या vaishya

whose *pron.* किसका kiska

why *adv.* क्यों kyon

wick *n.* दीपक की बत्ती deepak ki batti

wicked *a.* पापी paapi

wicker *n.* खपची khapchi

wicket *n.* छोटा फाटक chhota phatak

wide *adv.* पूर्णरूप से purna rup se

wide *a.* चौड़ा chaurha

widen *v.t.* चौड़ा करना chaura karna

widespread *a.* व्यापक vyapak

widow *v.t.* विधवा बनाना vidhva banana

widow *n.* विधवा vidhva

widower *n.* विधुर vidhur

width *n.* चौड़ाई chaurhayi

wield *v.t.* प्रयोग में लाना prayog mein laana

wife *n.* पत्नी patni

wig *n.* विग vig

wight *n.* प्राणी prani

wigwam *n.* कुटिया kutiya

wild *a.* जंगली jangli

wilderness *n.* बीहड़, biharh

wile *n.* चाल chaal

will *v.t.* इच्छा रखना ichcha rakhna

will *n.* संकल्पशक्ति sankalpshakti

willing *a.* तत्पर tatpar

willingness *n.* तत्परता tatparta

willow *n.* भिंसा, bhinsa,

wily *a.* धूर्त, चालाक chalak

wimble *n.* बरमा, बरमी burma, burmi

wimple *n.* शिरोवस्त्र shirovastra

win *n* विजय vijay

win *v.t.* प्राप्त करना prapt karna

wince *v.i.* सिकुड़ जाना sikurh jana

wind *n.* अफारा aphaara

wind *v.t.* लपेटना lapetna

windbag *n.* गप्पी व्यक्ति gappi vyakti

winder *n.* चाबी भरने का यंत्र chabi bharne ka yantr

windlass *v.t.* बेलन चरखा belan charkha

windmill *n.* पवनचक्की pawanchakki

window *n.* खिड़की khirhki

windy *a.* तूफ़ानी tufani

wine *n.* अंगूरी शराब anguri sharab

wing *n.* पंख pankh

wink *v.i.* पलक झपकना palak jhapakna

wink *n* झपक jhapak

winner *n.* विजेता vijeta

winnow *v.t.* ओसाना, बरसाना osana, barsana

winsome *a.* आकर्षक akarshak

winter *v.i* जाड़ा बिताना jarha bitana

winter *n.* शीत ऋतु sheet ritu

wintry *a.* ठंडा thanda

wipe *n.* पोंछन ponchan

wipe *v.t.* पोंछना ponchna
wire *n.* तार taar
wireless *n* रेडियो radio
wireless *a.* बेतार का betaar ka
wiring *n.* बिजली के तार bijli ka taar
wisdom *n.* समझदारी samajhdari
wisdom-tooth *n.* अक्ल दाढ़ akal dadh
wise *a.* समझदार budhiman
wish *v.t.* चाहना chahana
wish *n.* इच्छा ichcha
wishful *a.* आकांक्षी akanshi
wisp *n.* घास का गट्ठर ghas ka gaththar
wistful *a.* उत्कंठित utkanthit
wit *n.* बुद्धि की प्रखरता buddhi ki prakharta
witch *n.* जादूगरनी jadugarni
witchcraft *n.* जादू टोना jadu tona
witchery *n.* जादू टोना jadu tona
with *prep.* साथ saath
withdraw *v.t.* पीछे हटाना peeche hatana
withdrawal *n.* वापसी vapasi
withe *n.* लचीली टहनी lachili tahani
wither *v.i.* मुरझाना murjhana
withhold *v.t.* रोक रखना rok rakhna
within *adv.* घर में, अंदर ghar mein,andar
within *n.* भीतरी भाग bhitri bhag
within *prep.* अंदर andar
without *prep.* रहित rahit
withstand *v.t.* (सामना करना samana karna
witless *a.* बुद्धिहीन buddhihin
witness *v.i.* गवाही देना gavahi dena
witness *n.* प्रत्यक्ष दर्शक pratyaksh darshak
witticism *n.* चुटीला कथन chutila katan
witty *a.* वाग्विदग्ध vagvidagdh
wizard *n.* जादूगर jadugar
wobble *v.i* हिलना hilna
woe *n.* विषाद shok
woebegone *a.* उदास udas
woeful *n.* शोकपूर्ण shokpurna
wolf *n.* भेड़िया bherhiya
woman *n.* नारी nari

womanhood *n.* नारीत्व naritva
womanise *v.t.* वेश्यागमन करना veshyagaman karna,
womanish *n.* ज़नाना janana
womb *n.* गर्भाशय barbhashya
wonder *v.i.* आश्चर्य करना ashcarya karna
wonder *n* आश्चर्य ashcarya
wonderful *a.* आश्चर्यजनक ashcaryajanak
wondrous *a.* आश्चर्यजनक, अद्भुत, अत्युत्कृष्ट ashcaryajanak
wont *n* रिवाज, आदत riwaaz,adat
wont *a.* आदी aadi
wonted *a.* अभ्यस्त, सामान्य abhyast,samanya
woo *v.t.* प्रणय करना pranaya karna
wood *n.* लकड़ी lakri
wooden *a.* लकड़ी का lakri ka
woodland *n.* वनस्थली vansthali
woods *n.* जंगल jangal
woof *n.* बाना bana
wool *n.* ऊन oon
woollen *n* ऊनी कपड़ा ooni kaparha
woollen *a.* ऊनी ooni
word *n.* शब्द shabd
wordy *a.* शब्दाडंबरपूर्ण shabdadambarpurna
work *v.t.* काम करना kaam karna
work *n.* व्यवसाय vyvasaya
workable *a.* व्यवहार्य vyavaharya
workaday *a.* सादा sada
worker *n.* मज़दूर mazdoor
workman *n.* मज़दूर mazdoor
workmanship *n.* शिल्प shilp
workshop *n.* कारखाना karkhana
world *n.* विश्व vishv
worldling *n.* सांसारिक आनंद sansarik anand
worldly *a.* पार्थिव parthiv
worm *n.* कीड़ा kirha
wormwood *n.* नागदौन naagdaun

worn *a.* घिसा हुआ ghisa hua

worry *v.i.* चिंतित होना chintit hona

worry *n.* चिंता chinta

worsen *v.t.* बिगाड़ना bigarhana

worship *v.t.* पूजा करना, puja karna

worship *n.* पूजा puja

worshipper *n.* पुजारी, उपासक pujari,upasak

worst *n.* सबसे बुरी बात sabse buri baat

worst *a* सब से बुरा sab se bura

worst *v.t.* पराजित करना parajit karna

worsted *n.* ऊनी धागा ooni dhaga

worth *a* निश्चित मूल्य का nishchit mulya ka

worth *n.* उपयोगिता upyogita

worthless *a.* व्यर्थ vyarth

worthy *a.* योग्य, सम्मान्य yogya

would-be *a.* होने वाला hone wala

wound *v.t.* घायल करना ghayal karna

wound *n.* घाव ghav

wrack *n.* समुद्री शैवाल samudri shaiwal

wraith *n.* प्रेत pret

wrangle *v. t* कलह करना kalah karna

wrangle *n.* लड़ाई ladai

wrangle *v.i.* लड़ना ladna

wrap *n* आवरण avaran

wrap *v.t.* लपेटना lapetana

wrapper *n.* कागज़ की लपेटन kagaz ka lapetan

wrath *n.* क्रोध krodh

wreath *n.* माला mala

wreathe *v.t.* गूथना guthna

wreck *v.t.* नष्ट करना nasht karna

wreck *n.* पोतभंग potbhang

wreckage *n.* पोतावशेष potavashesh

wrecker *n.* ध्वंसकर्त्ता dhvanskarta

wren *n.* पिटपिटी pitpiti

wrench *v.t.* मरोड़ना marorhana

wrench *n.* मरोड़ marorh

wrest *v.t.* छीनना, मरोड़ना marorhana

wrestle *v.i.* कुश्ती लड़ना, संघर्ष करना kushti larhna

wrestler *n.* कुश्ती लड़ने वाला kushti larhne wala

wretch *n.* अभागा व्यक्ति abhaga vyakti

wretched *a.* दु:खी dukhi

wrick *n* मोच moch

wriggle *n* रेंगने की क्रिया rengne ki kriya

wriggle *v.i.* रेंगना rengna

wring *v.t* ऐंठना ainthana

wrinkle *v.t.* सिलवट डालना silwat dalna

wrinkle *n.* झुर्री jhurri

wrist *n.* कलाई kalai

writ *n.* हुक्मनामा hukmnama

write *v.t.* लिखना, likhna

writer *n.* लिखनेवाला likhnewala

writhe *v.i.* छटपटाना chatpatana

wrong *adv.* ग़लत ढंग से galat dhang se

wrong *a.* ग़लत galat

wrongful *a.* अन्यायपूर्ण anyayapurna

wry *a.* टेढ़ा tedha

xerox *n.* छायाप्रति chayaprati

Xmas *n.* बड़ा दिन bada din

x-ray *n.* एक्स किरण aiks kiran

x-ray *v.t.* एक्सकिरण फोटो लेना aikskikaran photo lena

xylophilous *a.* काष्ठ प्रेमी kashth premi

xylophone *n.* काष्ठ तरंग kashth tarang

yacht *n.* हलकी नौका halki nauka

yacht *v.i* नौका विहार करना nauka vihar karna

yak *n.* सुरागाय, चमर suragaya, chamar

yap *n* भौं भौं bhaun bhaun
yap *v.i.* भौं भौं करना bhaun bhaun karna
yard *n.* गज़ gaz
yarn *n.* सूत sut
yawn *v.i.* जम्हाई लेना jamahi lena
yawn *n.* जम्हाई jamahi
year *n.* वर्ष varsh
yearly *a.* वार्षिक varshik
yearly *adv.* प्रतिवर्ष prativarsh
yearn *v.i.* लालायित होना lalayit hona
yearning *n.* लालसा lalasa
yeast *n.* खमीर khamir
yell *v.i.* चिल्लाना chilana
yell *n* पुकार pukar
yellow *a.* पीला peela
yellow *n* पीला रंग peela rang
yellow *v.t.* पीला करना peela karna
yellowish *a.* पीला-सा peela sa
Yen *n.* जापानी मुद्रा japani mudra
yeoman *n.* छोटा ज़मींदार chota zamindar
yes *adv.* सचमुच sachmuch
yesterday *n.* बीता हुआ दिन beeta hua din
yesterday *adv.* कल kal
yet *adv.* अब तक ab tak
yet *conj.* तथापि tathapi
yield *v.t.* पैदा करना paida karna
yield *n* उपज upaj
yoke *n.* बंधन bandhan
yoke *v.t.* युग्मित करना yugmit karna
yolk *n.* अंडे की ज़रदी ande ki zardi
yonder *a.* वहाँ का vahan ka
yonder *adv.* वहाँ wahan
young *a.* छोटा chota
young *n* बच्चे bachche
youngster *n.* लौंडा launda
youth *n.* यौवन yauvan
youthful *a.* युवा yuva

# Z

zany *a.* हास्यपूर्ण hasyapurna
zeal *n.* उत्साह utsa
zealot *n.* कट्टर समर्थक kattar samarthak
zealous *a.* उत्साही utsahi
zebra *n.* ज़ेबरा zebra
zenith *n.* चरम बिंदु charam bindu
zephyr *n.* मंद समीर mand samir
zero *n.* शून्य shunya
zest *n.* उत्साह utsah
zigzag *a.* टेढ़ा मेढ़ा tedha medha
zinc *n.* जस्ता jasta
zip *n.* ज़िप zip
zodiac *n* राशिचक्र rashichakra
zonal *a.* मंडलीय mandaliya
zone *n.* क्षेत्र kshetra
zoo *n.* जंतुशाला jantushala
zoological *a.* प्राणि विज्ञान विषयक prani vigyan vishayak
zoologist *n.* प्राणि विज्ञानी prani vigyani
zoology *n.* प्राणि विज्ञान prani vigyan
zoom *n.* तेज़ ऊर्ध्व उड़ान tez udharv udan

# Hindi-English

## A

aab tak *adv.* अब तक already
aabha *n.* आभा tinge
aabhaar *n.* आभार thanks
aabhari *a.* आभारी grateful
aabhari *a.* आभारी indebted
aabnus *n* आबनूस ebony
aachaar *v.t.* अचार condite
aachar vyavahar *n* आचार व्यवहार conduct
aacharan *n* आचरण bearing
aacharan *n* आचरण behaviour
aacharan karna *v. i.* आचरण करना behave
aadambar *n.* आडंबर hypocrisy
aadambari *a.* आडंबरी pompous
aadar *n* आदर esteem
aadar *n.* आदर honour
aadar *n.* आदर respect
aadar *n.* आदर reverence
aadar karna *v. t* आदर करना esteem
aadar karna *v.t.* आदर करना regard
aadar karna *v.t.* आदर करना respect
aadarsh *a.* आदर्श ideal
aadarsh waad *n.* आदर्शवाद idealism
aadarshatmak *a.* आदर्शात्मक idealistic
aadarshwadi *n.* आदर्शवादी idealist
aadat *n.* आदत habit
aadesh *n* आदेश command
aadesh *n* आदेश dictation
aadesh *n.* आदेश mandate
aadesh *n.* आदेश order
aadesh dena *v. t* आदेश देना command
aadesh dena *v. t* आदेश देना dictate
aadesh dena *v.t* आदेश देना order
aadesh vakya *n* आदेश वाक्य dictum
aadha *a* आधा half
aadha bhag *n.* आधा भाग half
aadhar *n.* आधार backbone

aadhar *n.* आधार base
aadhar *n* आधार crutch
aadhar *n.* आधार foundation
aadharit karna *v.t.* आधारित करना base
aadhikya *n.* आधिक्य superabundance
aadhikya *n.* आधिक्य superfluity
aadhikya *n.* आधिक्य surfeit
aadhipatya *n.* आधिपातय occupancy
aadhunikikaran karna *v.t.* आधुनिकीकरण करना modernize
aadhunikta *n.* आधुनिकता modernity
aadi *a.* आदी accustomed
aadi *a.* आदी wont
aadi banana *v.t.* आदी बनाना accustom
aadi banana *v. t.* आदी बनाना habituate
aadi hona *v.t.* आदी होना addict
aadra *a* आर्द्र damp
aadrak *n.* अदरक ginger
aag *n* आग fire
aag ki lapat *n* आग की लपट flame
aag par *adv.* आग पर aflame
aagami *a* आगामी after
aagami *a.* आगामी forthcoming
aagami *a.* आगामी subsequent
aage *prep. & adv.* आगे afore
aage *a.* आगे onward
aage *adv.* आगे ahead
aage badhana *v.t* आगे बढ़ाना further
aage badhna *v.t* आगे बढ़ना head
aage hona *v.* आगे होना precede
aage ki aur *adv* आगे की ओर forward
aage ki aur *adv.* आगे की ओर onwards
aage nikal jana *v.t.* आगे निकल जाना overtake
aage peeche *v.t.* आगे पीछे shuttle
aage-peeche karna *v.t.* आगे-पीछे करना alternate
aagman *n.* आगमन advent
aagman *n.* आगमन approach
aagman *n.* आगमन arrival
aagrahi *a.* आग्रही persistent

aagrahpurna *a.* आग्रहपूर्ण insistent
aagya dena *v.t.* आज्ञा देना permit
aagyakari *a.* आज्ञाकारी obedient
aagyakari hona *v.t.* आज्ञाकारी होना obey
aagyakarita *n.* आज्ञाकारिता compliance
aagyakarita *n.* आज्ञाकारिता obedience
aagzani *n* आगज़नी arson
aahankar *n* अहंकार ego
aaj *adv.* आज, आजकल today
aaj ki raat *n.* आज की रात to-night
aaj rat ko *adv.* आज रात को tonight
aajiwan *a.* आजीवन lifelong
aajiwika *n.* आजीविका livelihood
aajkal *adv* आजकल now-a-days
aakaar *n.* आकार size
aakar *n* आकार bulk
aakar *n.* आकार extent
aakar *n* आकार figure
aakarashit karna *v. t.* आकर्षित करना captivate
aakarik *a* आकारिक formal
aakarshan *n.* आकर्षक वस्तु attraction
aakarshan *n.* आकर्षण charm
aakarshan *n.* आकर्षण fascination
aakarshit hona *v.i.* आकर्षित होना gravitate
aakarshit karna *v.t.* आकर्षित करना allure
aakarshit karna *v.t.* आकर्षित करना attract
aakash *n.* आकाश sky
aakash bail *n.* आकाश बेल mistletoe
aakash mein *adv.* आकाश में aloft
aakashiya vidyut *n.* आकाशीय विद्युत् lightening
aakasmik *a* आकस्मिक abrupt
aakasmik *a* आकस्मिक accidental
aakasmik *a.* आकस्मिक casual
aakasmik *a.* आकस्मिक incidental
aakasmik ghatna *n.* आकस्मिक घटना contingency
aakhet *n* आखेट hunt
aakhetak *n.* आखेटक huntsman

aakraman karna *v.t.* आक्रमण करना assault
aakraman karna *v.t.* आक्रमण करना invade
aakrashak *a.* आकर्षक attractive
aakriti *n.* आकृति aspect
aalankarik *a* आलंकारिक figurative
aalasi *a.* आलसी inactive
aalasi *a.* आलसी indolent
aalasi *n.* आलसी lazy
aalasi vyakti *n.* आलसी व्यक्ति idler
aalasya *n.* आलस्य idleness
aalasya *n.* आलस्य inaction
aalasya *n.* आलस्य laziness
aalekhi *a.* आलेखी graphic
aalingan *n* आलिंगन embrace
aalingan karna *v. t.* आलिंगन करना embrace
aalochna *n* आलोचना criticism
aalu *n.* आलू potato
aalubukhara *n.* आलूबुखारा plum
aam *n* आम mango
aam rasta *n.* आम रास्ता thoroughfare
aamaniya *a.* अमान्य invalid
aamantran *v.* आमंत्रण invitation
aamantrit karna *v.t.* आमंत्रित करना invite
aamdani *n.* आमदनी income
aamne samne hona *v.t* आमने सामने होना face
aamod pramod *n.* आमोद प्रमोद fun
aamod pramod *n.* आमोद प्रमोद revel
aamod vihar *n.* आमोद विहार excursion
aamodh pramodh *n.* आमोद प्रमोद jollity
aana *v. i.* आना come
aandolan *n* आंदोलन agitation
aandolan *n.* आंदोलन movement
aane wala kal *n.* आने वाला कल tomorrow
aanek *a.* अनेक many
aangan *n* आंगन patio
aankah kai phuli *n.* आंख की फूली nebula
aankh *n* आंख eye

aankh ki jhilli *n* आँख की झिल्ली choroid
aankh ki jhilli *n.* आंख की झिल्ली conjunctive
aankh mein dhool jhonkana *v.t.* आंख में धूल झोंकना hoodwink
aankhon ki putli *n* आंखों की पुतली cornea
aansh *n.* अंश part
aanshik *a.* आंशिक partial
aansu *n.* आंसू tear
aant *n.* अंत close
aant *n* अंत finish
aant *n.* आंत intestine
aante *n.* आंतें bowel
aanth *a.* अनंत infinite
aantra sambandhi *a.* आंत्र संबंधी intestinal
aantral *n* अंतराल gap
aantrik *a.* आंतरिक inward
aantrik gun *n.* आंतरिक गुण attribute
aanu-vanshikta *n.* आनुवंशिकता heredity
aanvikta *a.* अनविक्ता molecularity
aapada *n* आपदा disaster
aaparadhik *a* आपराधिक culpable
aapatti *n* आपत्ति demur
aapattijanak *a.* आपत्तिजनक objectionable
aapradh *n* अपराध crime
aapradh *n.* अपराध default
aapradhi *n* अपराधी culprit
aapsi *a.* आपसी mutual
aar paar *prep.* आर पार athwart
aara *n.* आरा spoke
aaram *n.* आराम comfort
aaram *n* आराम ease
aaram *n.* आराम relief
aaram karna *v.i.* आराम करना repose
aarambh *n* आरम्भ alpha
aarambh *n.* आरंभ inception
aarambh *n.* आरंभ opening
aaramdayak *a* आरामदायक comfortable
aaramdayak *a.* आरामदायक cosy
aararot *n.* अरारोट arrowroot

aarekh *n* आरेख diagram
aarhu *n.* आड़ू peach
aarogya *n.* आरोग्य health
aarogya sadhya *a* आरोग्य साध्य curable
aarop *n* आरोप accusation
aaropan *n.* आरोपण allegation
aaropan *n.* आरोपण imposition
aaropit karna *v.t.* आरोपित करना allege
aaropit karna *v.t.* आरोपित करना attribute
aaropit rashi *n.* आरोपित राशि levy
aar-paar *adv.* आर-पार across
aarthik *a* आर्थिक economic
aarthik *a.* आर्थिक monetary
aasan kar dena *v.t* आसान कर देना facilitate
aasha karna *v. t* आशा करना expect
aasha karna *n.* आशा expectation
aashay *n.* आशय intention
aashcharyachakit *a.* आश्चर्यचकित aghast
aashrit *a* आश्रित incumbent
aashulipi *n.* आशुलिपि stenography
aasin *a.* आसीन sedentary
aaspass *adv* आसपास around
aaspass *adv.* आसपास hereabouts
aastik *n.* आस्तिक deist
aastik *n.* आस्तिक theist
aastikta *n.* आस्तिकता theism
aastin *n* आस्तीन sleeve
aastkon *n.* अष्टकोण octagon
aastkoni *a.* अष्टकोणी octangular
aastpadi *n.* अष्टपदी octave
aata *n* आटा flour
aata pisne wala *n.* आटा पीसने वाला miller
aatank *n.* आतंक terror
aatankit karna *v.t.* आतंकित करना terrorize
aatankmaya *a* आतंकमय dread
aatankvad *n.* आतंकवाद terrorism
aatankvadi *n.* आतंकवादी terrorist
aath *n* आठ eight
aathitya *n.* आतिथ्य hospitality

aati prasann *a* अति प्रसन्न overjoyed
aatikraman *n.* अतिक्रमण intrusion
aatisram karna *v.i.* अतिश्रम करना
overwork
aatma *n.* आत्मा soul
aatmabalidaan *n.* आत्मबलिदान
martyrdom
aatmacharit *n.* आत्मचरित memoir
aatmakatha *n.* आत्मकथा autobiography
aatyant kathin *a.* अत्यंत कठिन herculean
aavantan *n.* आवंटन allocation
aavaran *n.* आवरण cover
aavashayk *a.* आवश्यक instant
aaveg *n.* आवेग impulse
aavegshil *a.* आवेगशील impulsive
aavesh *n.* आवेश passion
aavrati *n.* आवृत्ति repetition
aawaas *n* आवास domicile
aawara *n.* आवारा hooligan
aawaran *n* आवरण curtain
aawargardi karna *v.i.* आवारागर्दी करना
loiter
aawas yogya *a.* आवास योग्य inhabitable
aay *n.* आय revenue
aayam *n* आयाम dimension
aayat *n.* आयात import
aayat *n.* आयत oblong
aayat *n.* आयत rectangle
aayat karna *v.t.* आयात करना import
aayatkaar *a.* आयताकार oblong
aayerland ka *a.* आयरलैंड का Irish
aayerland ki bhasha *n.* आयरलैंड की भाषा
Irish
aayog *n.* आयोग commission
aayojit karna *v. t* आयोजित करना
convene
aayu mein barha vyakti *n* आयु में बड़ा
व्यक्ति elder
aayudhagar *n.* आयुधागार arsenal
aayukt *n.* आयुक्त commissioner
aayurvaigyanik *a.* आयुर्वैज्ञानिक medical

ab *conj.* अब now
ab se aage *adv.* अब से आगे henceforth
ab se aage *adv.* अब से आगे henceforward
ab tak *adv.* अब तक hitherto
ab tak *adv.* अब तक still
ab tak *adv.* अब तक yet
ababeel *n.* अबाबील swallow
abadi *n.* आबादी population
abhaas *n.* आभास inkling
abhadra *a.* अभद्र impolite
abhaga *a.* अभागा accursed
abhaga *a* अभागा forlorn
abhaga *a.* अभागा luckless
abhaga vyakti *n.* अभागा व्यक्ति wretch
abhav *n.* अभाव shortage
abhedya *a.* अभेद्य impenetrable
abhibhavak *n.* अभिभावक guardian
abhibhut kar dena *v.t.* अभिभूत कर देना
overcome
abhibhut karna *v.t.* अभिभूत करना whelm
abhigrahan *n.* अभिग्रहण acquisition
abhijaat *n.* अभिजात peer
abhikarta *n* अभिकर्त्ता factor
abhilasha *n.* अभिलाषा appetence
abhilasha *n.* अभिलाषा aspiration
abhilasha *n* अभिलाषा desire
abhilekh *n.* अभिलेख inscription
abhilekhagar *n.pl.* अभिलेखागार archives
abhilekhan karna *v.t* अभिलेखन करना
tape
abhiman *n.* अभिमान pride
abhiman karna *v.t.* अभिमान करना pride
abhimantrit karna *v.t.* अभिमंत्रित करना
auspicate
abhimukh hona *v.i* अभिमुख होना look
abhinandan *n* अभिनंदन welcome
abhinay *n.* अभिनय acting
abhinay karna *v.i.* अभिनय करना act
abhinaya karna *v.t.* अभिनय करना
impersonate
abhineta *n.* अभिनेता actor

185

abhinetri *n.* अभिनेत्री actress
abhinirnaya *n.* अभिनिर्णय verdict
abhipray *n.* अभिप्राय intent
abhipray rakhna *v.t* अभिप्राय रखना mean
abhipraya *n.* अभिप्राय meaning
abhipreran *n.* अभिप्रेरण inducement
abhiraksha *n.* अभिरक्षा wardship
abhishaap *n* अभिशाप curse
abhishaap dena *v. t* अभिशाप देना curse
abhivadan *n* अभिवादन salute
abhivadan *n.* अभिवादन salutation
abhivadan karna *v.t.* अभिवादन करना greet
abhivyakt karna *v.t.* अभिव्यक्त करना voice
abhi-vyakti *n.* अभिव्यक्ति expression
abhiwadan karna *v.t* अभिवादन करना hail
abhiyanta *n* अभियंता engineer
abhiyog *n.* अभियोग indictment
abhiyog *n.* अभियोग impeachment
abhiyog lagana *v.t.* अभियोग लगाना impeach
abhiyog lagana *v.t.* अभियोग लगाना indict
abhiyog patra *n.* अभियोग पत्र libel
abhiyojan *n.* अभियोजन prosecution
abhiyokta *n.* अभियोक्ता prosecutor
abhyas karna *v.t.* अभ्यास करना practise
abhyast,samanya *a.* अभ्यस्त, सामान्य wonted
abrak *n.* अभ्रक mica
aburdh *n.* अर्बुद tumour
achaar *n.* अचार pickle
achal *a.* अचल immovable
achal chitr *n.* अचल चित्र still
achalta *n.* अचलता inertia
achanak *adv.* अचानक short
achanak *adv.* अचानक suddenly
achanak avrodh *n* अचानक अवरोध breakdown
achcha *a.* अच्छा sound
achetan *a.* अचेतन inanimate

achetan avastha *n.* अचेतन अवस्था coma
achha naseeb *n.* अच्छा नसीब fortune
achraj *n* अचरज coo
achuk *a.* अचूक infallible
achuk dawa *n.* आचूक दवा panacea
acre *n.* एकड़ acre
adaan-pradaan *n* आदान-प्रदान exchange
adal badal karna *v. t* अदल बदल करना commute
adal badal karna *v.t.* अदल बदल करना reciprocate
adalat *n* अदालत bench
adalat ka bulava *n.* अदालत का बुलावा summon
adalat mein talab karna *v. t* अदालत में तलब करना cite
adalati nirnaya *n.* अदालती निर्णय justice
adambar *n.* आडंबर pomp
adar karna *v.t.* आदर करना venerate
adarniya *a.* आदरणीय venerable
adarsh *n.* नमूना model
adarsh *a.* आदर्श utopian
adarsh banana *v.t.* आदर्श बनाना idealize
adarsh rajya *n .* आदर्श राज्य utopia
adarsh vakya *n.* आदर्श वाक्य motto
adbhut *a* अद्भुत curious
adbhut *a.* अद् भुत marvellous
adbhut *a.* अद् भुत phenomenal
adchan *n.* अड़चन hitch
add lagana *v.t.* एड़ लगाना spur
adda *n* अड्डा haunt
adesh dena *v.t* आदेश देना bid
adha -adha bantna *v.t.* आधा-आधा बांटना halve
adhakchar *n.* आद्याक्षर initial
adhakcharit karna *v.t* आद्याक्षरित करना initial
adhakhula *adv.* अधखुला ajar
adham *a.* अधम abject
adhar *n.* अधर lip

adhar sambandhi *adj.* आधार सम्बन्धी basal

adharbhut *a.* आधारभूत fundamental

adharbhut *a.* आधारभूत prime

adhbhut udaharan *n.* अद्भुत उदाहरण marvel

adhibhar lagana *v.t.* अधिभार लगाना surcharge

adhik *adv* अधिक more

adhik *a* अधिक much

adhik *a.* अधिक plus

adhik barh jana *v.t.* अधिक बढ़ जाना outgrow

adhik bhaar *n* क अधिक भार overload

adhik bhaar laadna *v.t.* अधिक भार लादना overload

adhik bhoj dalna *v.t.* अधिक बोझ डालना overburden

adhik dawa dena *vt* अधिक दवा देना overdose

adhik hona *v.t* अधिक होना exceed

adhik hona *v.t.* अधिक होना surpass

adhik madira peena *v. i* अधिक मदिरा पीना booze

adhik matra mein *adv* अधिक मात्रा में much

adhik mulya *n* अधिमूल्य overcharge

adhik mulya vasulna *v.t.* अधिक मूल्य वसूलना overcharge

adhik thakaan *a.* अधिक थकान overstrain

adhikaar *n* अधिकार post

adhikaar dena *v. t* अधिकार देना empower

adhikaarik *a.* आधिकारिक official

adhikar *n.* अधिकार interest

adhikar *n.* अधिकार possession

adhikar *n.* अधिकर super tax

adhikar *n.* अधिकर surtax

adhikar *n.* अधिकार, warranty

adhikar karna *v.t.* अधिकार करना annex

adhikar kshetra *n.* अधिकार क्षेत्र jurisdiction

adhikar mein rakhna *v.t.* अधिकार में रखना possess

adhikar patra *n.* अधिकार पत्र muniments

adhikar virodh *n.* अधिकार विरोध antinomy

adhikari *n.* अधिकारी officer

adhikari banana *v.t.* अधिकारी बनाना induct

adhikarik *a.* आधिकारिक authoritative

adhikrit *adv.* अधिकृत officially

adhikrit karyakarta *n.* अधिकृत कार्यकर्ता proxy

adhiktam *n* अधिकतम extreme

adhiktam *a.* अधिकतम maximum

adhiktam *a.* अधिकतम utmost

adhiktam matra *n* अधिकतम मात्रा maximum

adhiktam matra *n* अधिकतम मात्रा utmost

adhin karna *v.t.* अधीन करना subjugate

adhin vyakti *n.* अधीन व्यक्ति puppet

adhinasth karamchari *n* अधीनस्थ कर्मचारी subordinate

adhinikaran *n.* अधीनीकरण subordination

adhipatya *n.* आधिपत्य lordship

adhipatya *n.* आधिपत्य subjection

adhipatya *n.* आधिपत्य subjugation

adhir *a.* अधीर impatient

adhiraaj *adj* अधिराज pendragon

adhirta *n.* अधीरता impatience

adhisamay *n* अधिसमय overtime

adhishesh *n.* अधिशेष surplus

adhishthapan *n.* अधिष्ठापन induction

adhishulk *n.* अधिशुल्क surcharge

adhi-suchana *n.* अधि-सूचना notification

adhivaasi *n.* अंधविश्वासी occupier

adhiyapika *n.* अध्यापिका governess

adholok *n.* अधोलोक underworld

adhomukh karna *v.t.* अधोमुख करना reverse

adhunik *a.* आधुनिक modern

adhuniktam *a.* आधुनिकतम up-to-date

adhura *a* . अधूरा incomplete
adhyapak *n.* अध्यापक pedagogue
adhyatmavad *n.* अध्यात्मवाद spiritualism
adhyatmik *a.* आध्यात्मिक spiritual
adhyatmikta *n.* आध्यात्मिकता spirituality
adhyaya *n.* अध्याय chapter
adhyayan karna *v.i.* अध्ययन करना study
adhyayankaksh *n.* अध्ययनकक्ष study
adhyayansheel *a.* अध्ययनशील studious
adhytmavadi *n.* अध्यात्मवादी spiritualist
adi yugin *a.* आदि युगीन primeval
adirup *n.* आदिरूप prototype
adishthapan *n.* अधिष्ठापन installation
adiyal *a.* अडियल restive
adla-badli karna *v.t.* अदला-बदली करना barter
adlatiya *ns.* अदलतिया barrator
adrishya hona *v. i* अदृश्य होना disappear
adrishyata *n* अदृश्यता disappearance
advitiya *a.* अद्वितीय nonpareil
adwjtiya *a.* अद्वितीय unique
advitiya *n.* अद्वितीय nonparalell
adyadesh *n.* अध्यादेश ordinance
adyopant *adv.* आद्योपांत through
afeem *n.* अफीम opium
aflatooni *a.* अफलातूनी platonic
afwaha *n.* अफ़वाह hearsay
agambhir *a.* अगंभीर superficial
agami din *n.* आगामी दिन morrow
agay badhana *v.t.* आगे बढ़ाना advance
aghaat karna *v.t.* आघात करना wallop
agla *a.* अगला next
agla hona *v.t.* अगला होना adjoin
agle tang *n* अगली टांग foreleg
agni pariksha *n.* अग्नि परीक्षा ordeal
agnikund *n.* अग्निकुंड furnace
agra-baahu *n* अग्र बाहू forearm
agradut *n* अग्रदूत forerunner
agradut *n.* अग्रदूत precursor
agraganya hona *v.i* अग्रगण्य होना excel
agrah karna *v.t.* आग्रह करना insist

agrahi *n.* आग्रही stickler
agrim *a.* अग्रिम forward
agua *n* अगुआ foreman
aguwa *n.* अगुआ leader
agya *v.t.* आज्ञा देना sanction
agya manana *v.t.* आज्ञा मानना obey
agya pane yogya *a.* आज्ञा पाने योग्य permissible
agyakaari *a.* आज्ञाकारी submissive
agyan *n.* अज्ञान ignorance
agyapatr *n.* आज्ञापत्र warrant
agyat hone ki awastha *n.* अज्ञात होने की अवस्था anonymity
aha *n.* आह sigh
aha bharna *v.i* आह भरना sigh
ahaata *n* अहाता compound
ahambhag *n* अहंभाव egotism
ahik dekhbhaal dena *a.* आहक देखभाल करना overcare
ahik khaney wala *n.* खाऊ glutton
ahitkaar *a.* अहितकर malignant
ahitkar *a.* अहितकर noxious
aiks kiran *n.* एक्स किरण x-ray
aikskikaran photo lena *v.t.* एक्सकिरण फोटो लेना x-ray
aintha tedha *adj.* ऐंठा टेढ़ा crump
ainthan *n.* ऐंठन twist
ainthana *v.t* ऐंठना wring
aisa *a.* ऐसा such
aise vyakti *pron.* ऐसे व्यक्ति such
ajayabghar *n.* अजायबघर museum
ajgar *n* अजगर dragon
ajgar *n.* अजगर python
ajib karya athawa bahawayar *n* अजीब कार्य अथवा व्यवहार antic
ajnabi *a.* अजनबी alien
ajnabi *n.* अजनबी stranger
akaal *n* अकाल famine
akaar *n.* आकार shape
akaar dena *v.t.* आकार देना mould
akaar dena *v.t* आकार देना shape

akaaran bhaya *n.* अकारण भय scare

akaatiya *a.* अकाट्य irrefutable

akadami *n* अकादमी academy

akadhikar *n.* एकाधिकार monopoly

akadhikari *n.* एकाधिकारी monopolist

akakakshariya *a.* एकाक्षरीय monosyllabic

akakshar *n.* एकाक्षर monosyllable

akal dadh *n.* अक्ल दाढ़ wisdom-tooth

akalap *n.* एकालाप monologue

akansha karna *v.t.* आकांक्षा करना need

akanshi *a.* आकांक्षी wishful

akarkar chalna *v.i.* अकड़कर चलना stalk

akarmak *a.* *(verb)* अकर्मक intransitive

akarshak *a.* आकर्षक winsome

akash ganga *n.* आकाश गंगा galaxy

akasham *n.* एकाश्म monolith

akash-neel *a* आकाश-नील blue

akasmik *a* आकस्मिक snap

akasmik *n.* आकस्मिक sudden

akela *a.* अकेला alone

akela *a.* अकेला lone

akela *pron.* अकेला one

akela *a* अकेला sole

akela *a.* अकेला solitary

akelapan *n.* अकेलापन solitude

akele *adv.* अकेले solo

akharh *a.* अक्खड़ arrogant

akharha *n* अखाड़ा arena

akharha *n.* अखाड़ा lists

akhrot *n.* अखरोट walnut

akramak *n.* आक्रामक aggressor

akraman *n* आक्रमण aggression

akraman *n.* आक्रमण irruption

akraman karna *v.* आक्रमण करना assail

akraman karna *v. t* आक्रमण करना besiege

akraman karna *v.t.* आक्रमण करना strike

akramik *n* आक्रमिक offensive

akrisht *n* आकर्षित gallant

akriti vigyan *n.* आकृति विज्ञान morphology

akriti vigyan *n.* आकृति विज्ञान physiognomy

akshar yojak *n.* अक्षर योजक compositor

aksharekha *n.* अक्षरेखा axis

akshya *a.* अक्षय imperishable

alag *adv.* अलग aloof

alag *adv.* अलग aside

alag *adv.* अलग away

alag *a* अलग distinct

alag hona *v.t.* अलग होना part

alag karna *v.t* अलग करना abstract

alag karna *v. t* अलग करना detach

alag karna *v.t.* अलग करना separate

alag karna *v.t.* अलग करना sequester

alag karna *v.t.* अलग करना sunder

alag karnai ki kriya *n* अलग करने की क्रिया detachment

alag rehna *v.i.* अलग रहना refrain

alag se *adv.* अलग से apart

alag thalag kar dena *v.t* अलग थलग कर देना maroon

alag-alag *adv.* अलग-अलग asunder

alanghya *a.* अलंघ्य impassable

alangkaran *n.* अलंकरण ornament

alangkrit *a* अलंकृत flowery

alankrit *a.* अलंकृत laureate

alankrit karna *v.t.* अलंकृत करना ornament

alasi *n.* आलसी slothful

alasya *n.* आलस्य sloth

alaukik *a.* अलौकिक supernatural

algaaw *n.* अलगाव isolation

algav *n.* अलगाव avulsion

algav *n.* अलगाव segregation

algavwadi *n.* अलगाववादी secessionist

alingan *n* आलिंगन clasp

almaari *n* अलमारी cupboard

alochana karna *v.t.* आलोचना करना attack

alp *a.* अल्प scarce

alp matra *prep.* अल्प मात्रा less

alp matra *n.* अल्प मात्रा little

**alp pariman** *n.* अल्प परिमाण modicum
**alp sankhya** *n.* अल्प संख्या minority
**alpata** *n.* अल्पता scarcity
**alpatam** *a.* अल्पतम least
**alpatam** *a.* अल्पतम minimal
**alpatam** *a* अल्पतम minimum
**alpawiram chinah** *n* अल्पविराम चिह्न comma
**alpbhashi** *a.* अल्पभाषी reticent
**alpbhashi** *a.* अल्पभाषी taciturn
**alpbhashita** *n.* अल्पभाषिता reticence
**alpdristi** *n.* अल्पदृष्टि myopia
**alpikaran** *n.* अल्पीकरण mitigation
**alp-tantra** *n.* अल्पतंत्र oligarchy
**alsi** *n.* अलसी linseed
**aluminium** *n.* अल्युमीनियम aluminium
**aluminium** *n* एल्यूमिनियम argil
**alvida** *interj.* अलविदा adieu
**alvida** *interj.* अलविदा bye-bye
**alvida** *interj.* अलविदा farewell
**alvida** *interj.* अलविदा good-bye
**amaanya** *a.* अमान्य null
**amal** *a* अम्ल acid
**amal mein laana** *v. t* अमल में लाना effect
**amangalkaar** *a.* अमंगलकार ominous
**amaniya karna** *v.t.* अमान्य करना invalidate
**amanwiya** *a.* अमानवीय inhuman
**amanya** *a.* अमान्य inadmissible
**amar** *a.* अमर immortal
**amar banana** *v.t.* अमर बनाना immortalize
**amit** *a.* अमित immeasurable
**amlata** *n.* अम्लता acidity
**amlatv** *adj.* अम्लत्व antacid
**amrit** *n.* अमृत nectar
**amrud** *n.* अमरूद guava
**amulya** *a.* अमूल्य invaluable
**amurt** *a* अमूर्त abstract
**amurt** *a.* अमूर्त intangible
**anaadi** *a.* अनाड़ी maladroit

**anaaj** *n* अनाज corn
**anaaj** *n.* अनाज grain
**anaam** *a.* अनाम anonymous
**anadar** *n* अनादर dishonour
**anadar** *n* अनादर disrespect
**anadar karna** *v. t* अनादर करना dishonour
**anadar karna** *v.t.* अनादर करना insult
**anadhikar grahan** *n.* अनाधिकार ग्रहण usurpation
**anaichik kriya** *n.* अनैच्छिक क्रिया reflex
**anaitekta** *n.* अनैतिकता profligacy
**anaitik** *a.* अनैतिक immoral
**anaitikta** *n.* अनैतिकता immorality
**anakani** *n.* आनाकानी connivance
**anamata** *n.* अनामता anonymity
**ananas** *n.* अनन्नास pineapple
**anand** *n* आनंद delight
**anand** *n* आनंद enjoyment
**anand** *n.* आनंद happiness
**anand** *interj.* आनंद hurrah
**anand** *n.* आनंद joy
**anand** *n.* आनंद merriment
**anand** *n.* आनंद mirth
**anand** *n.* आनंद pleasantry
**anand** *n.* आनंद pleasure
**anand dena** *v. t.* आनंद देना charm
**anand dena** *v. t.* आनंद देना delight
**anand ka geet** *n* आनन्द का गीत carol
**anand ki savari** *n* आनन्द की सवारी chaise
**anand lena** *v.i.* आनंद लेना bask
**anand lena** *v. t* आनंद लेना enjoy
**anand lena** *v.i.* आनंद लेना revel
**anand utsav** *n* आनन्द उत्सव carnival
**anandkari** *a.* आनंदकारी glad
**anandmangal** *n* आनंदमंगल festivity
**anandmayata** *n.* आनंदमयता vivacity
**anandotsav** *n.* आनंदोत्सव jubilation
**anandprad** *a* आनंदप्रद comic
**anandpurna** *a.* आनंदपूर्ण mirthful
**anant** *a.* अनंत interminable
**anant kaal** *n* अनंत काल eternity

anari *a* अनाड़ी clumsy

anarthak boli *n.* अनर्थक बोली jargon

anath balak *n.* अनाथ बालक orphan

anath banana *v.t* अनाथ बनाना orphan

anathlaya *n.* अनाथालय orphanage

anavashyak *a.* अनावश्यक redundant

anavyshak *a.* अनावश्यक needless

anayatha *adv.* अन्यथा alias

anban *n.* अनबन variance

an-ban *n* अनबन discord

anchan *n.* लांछन stigma

anda *n* अंडा egg

andakaar *a.* अंडाकार oval

andakaar vastu *n* अंडाकार वस्तु oval

andar *prep.* अंदर inside

andar *prep.* अंदर within

andar *adv.* अंदर inside

andar ko *adv.* अंदर को inwards

andar le jana *v.t.* अंदर ले जाना usher

andar-andar *adv.* अंदर-अंदर inland

andaruni *a.* अंदरूनी inner

andaruni *a* अंदरूनी inside

andashay *n.* अंडाशय ovary

andaza labgana *v.t.* अंदाज़ा लगाना
surmise

andbar *n.* आडंबर pageantry

ande dena *v.i.* अंडे देना spawn

ande ki saphedi *n* अंडे की सफेदी albumen

ande ki zardi *n.* अंडे की ज़रदी yolk

ande sena *v.i.* अंडे सेना incubation

andgranthi *n.* अंडग्रंथि testicle

andha *a* अंधा blind

andhakar *n* अंधकार dark

andhapan *n* अंधापन blindness

andha-pan *n* अन्धापन ablepsy

andhera *n.* अंधेरा obscurity

andhkarmaya *a* अंधकारमय dark

andhvishvas *n.* अंधविश्वास superstition

andhvishvasi *a.* अंधविश्वासी superstitious

andolan *n.* आंदोलन campaign

andolan *n.* आंदोलन welter

anek baar *adv.* अनेक बार often

anekarthi *a.* अनेकार्थी ambiguous

anekta *n.* अनेकता plurality

anganit *a.* अगणित numberless

angbhang karna *v.t.* अंगभंग करना
mutilate

angchhed *n.* अंगच्छेद mutilation

angh *n.* अंग member

angikar karna *v.t.* अंगीकार करना concede

angikaran *n* अंगीकरण adoption

an-ginat *a.* अनगिनत countless

angmardak *n.* अंगमर्दक masseur

angrag *n.* अंगराग cosmetic

angrakshak *n.* अंगरक्षक bodyguard

angrez *adj* अंग्रेज़ British

angrez log *n* अंग्रेज़ लोग english

angur *n.* अंगूर grape

angur ki bel *n.* अंगूर की बेल vine

anguri sharab *n.* अंगूरी शराब vintage

anguri sharab *n.* अंगूरी शराब wine

angushtana *n.* अंगुश्ताना thimble

angutha *n.* अंगूठा thumb

anguthi *n.* अंगूठी ring

anichcha *n.* अनिच्छा reluctance

anichchuk *a.* अनिच्छुक reluctant

anichhuk *a.* अनिच्छुक loath

anirmit *a.* अनिर्मित raw

anirnaya *n.* अनिर्णय shilly-shally

anishchit *a.* अनिश्चित indefinite

anishchit *adj* अनिश्चित indecisive

anishchya ka sthiti *n.* अनिश्चय की स्थिति
suspense

anivarya *a* अनिवार्य binding

anivarya *a* अनिवार्य compulsory

anivarya *a* अनिवार्य necessary

aniwarya *a.* अनिवार्य mandatory

aniwarya *a.* अनिवार्य obligatory

aniwarya hona *v.* अनिवार्य होना must

aniwaryata *n.* अनिवार्यता must

aniyamit *a* अनियमित anomalous

aniyamit *a.* अनियमित irregular

**aniyamitta** *n.* अनियमितता irregularity
**aniyantrit** *a.* अनियंत्रित rampant
**anjaan** *a.* अनजान ignorant
**anjaan** *a.* अनजान unaware
**anjane mein** *adv.* अनजाने में unawares
**anjane mein** *adv.* अनजाने में unwittingly
**anjeer** *n* अंजीर fig
**ank** *n.* अंक digit
**ank banana** *v.t.* अंक बनाना score
**ank bodhak** *a.* अंक बोधक numeral
**ank dalna** *v.t.* अंक डालना number
**ankaha** *a.* अनकहा tacit
**ankan** *n.* अंकन notation
**ankekshak** *n.* अंकेक्षक auditor
**ankekshan** *n.* अंकेक्षण audit
**ankekshan karna** *v.t.* अंकेक्षण करना audit
**ankganak** *n.* अंकगणक marker
**ankganit** *n.* अंकगणित arithmetic
**ankganit-sambandhi** *a.* अंकगणित-संबंधी
  arithmetical
**ankh putli ka sukarna** *vt* आंख की पूतली
  का सुकड़ना myosis
**ankit karan** *v.t* अंकित करन mark
**ankit karna** *v.t* अंकित करना draw
**ankit karna** *v.t.* अंकित करना record
**ankur** *n* अंकुर sprout
**ankuran** *n.* अंकुरण germination
**ankurit hona** *v.i.* अंकुरित होना germinate
**ankurit hona** *v.i.* अंकुरित होना sprout
**ankurna** *v.t.* अंकुरना shoot
**ankush** *n.* अंकुश goad
**ankush** *n.* अंकुश hook
**anmanaapan** *n.* अनमनापन malaise
**ann** *n.* अन्न cereal
**annabhandar** *n.* अन्नभंडार granary
**annmaya** *a* अन्नमय cereal
**anokha** *a.* अनोखा inimitable
**anokha** *a.* अनोखा strange
**anokha** *a.* अनोखा weird
**anokha** *a.* अनोखा whimsical
**anokhapan** *n.* अनोखापन oddity

**anokhapan** *n.* अनोखापन singularity
**anokhe dhang se** *adv.* अनोखे ढंग से
  singularly
**anopacharik** *a.* अनौपचारिक informal
**ansh** *n.* अंश fraction
**ansh** *n.* अंश numerator
**antah sagari** *a* अंत:सागरी submarine
**antar** *n* अंतर distinction
**antar** *a.* अन्तर indiscrimination
**antar samjhana** *v. i* अंतर समझना
  distinguish
**antaral** *n.* अंतराल interlude
**antarastriya** *a.* अंतर्राष्ट्रीय international
**antarbodh** *n.* अंतर्बोध intuition
**antardarshan** *n.* अंतर्दर्शन introspection
**antardeshiya** *a.* अंतर्देशीय inland
**antardhan** *a.* अंतर्धान invisible
**antardhara** *n.* अंतर्धारा undercurrent
**antarhiyan** *n.* अंतड़ियां entrails
**antarik** *a.* आंतरिक interior
**antarik bhag** *n.* आंतरिक भाग interior
**antarim** *n.* अंतरिम interim
**antariya** *n.* अंतरीय underwear
**antarnihit hona** *v.t.* अंतर्निहित होना imply
**antartam** *a.* अंतरतम innermost
**antatah** *adv.* अंतत: eventually
**antatah** *adv.* अंतत: ultimately
**antenna** *n.* एंटिना aerial
**antenna** *n.* एंटिना antennae
**anth:pravah** *n.* अंत:प्रवाह influx
**antim** *a* अंतिम final
**antim** *a.* अंतिम last
**antim** *a.* अंतिम terminal
**antim shart** *n.* अंतिम शर्त ultimatum
**antim station** *n.* अंतिम स्टेशन terminus
**antim taur se** *adv.* अंतिम तौर से lastly
**antim vastu** *n* अंतिम वस्तु last
**antim, sarvoch mahatwa ka** *a.* अंतिम,
  सर्वोच्च महत्व का ultimate
**ant-kshipt karna** *v.t.* अंत:क्षिप्त करना
  inject

**antrajvar** *n.* आंत्रज्वर typhoid
**antreep** *n.* अंतरीप cape
**antrik jwar** *a.* अंतरिक ज्वर gastric
**antriksh** *n.* अंतरिक्ष space
**antriksh-yatri** *n.* अंतरिक्ष- यात्री astronaut
**anu** *n.* अणु molecule
**anubandh** *n* अनुबंध bond
**anubandh** *v. t* अनुबंध contract
**anubhag** *n.* अनुभाग section
**anubhav** *n* अनुभव experience
**anubhav karana** *v.t.* अनुभव करना sense
**anubhavatit** *a.* अनुभवातीत transcendent
**anubhavhin** *adj* अनुभवहीन callow
**anubhavhinta** *n.* अनुभवहीनता
  inexperience
**anubhavi** *v.t.* अनुभवी nestor
**anubhavi** *ı.* अनुभवी veteran
**anubhavi vyakti** *n.* अनुभवी व्यक्ति
  veteran
**anubhuti** *n.* अनुभूति sensation
**anubodhak** *n.* अनुबोधक prompter
**anuchar** *n* अनुचर follower
**anuchhit prayog** *n.* अनुचित प्रयोग
  misapplication
**anuchit** *a.* अनुचित indecent
**anuchit** *a.* अनुचित unduc
**anuchit** *a* अनुचित unfair
**anuchit labh uthana** *v. t* अनुचित लाभ
  उठाना exploit
**anuchit rup se** *adv.* अनुचित रूप में amiss
**anuchit rup se ghus padna** *v.t.* अनुचित
  रूप से घुस पड़ना intrude
**anuchitra** *n.* अणुचित्र microfilm
**anudaan** *n* अनुदान grant
**anudesh** *n.* अनुदेश instruction
**anugami** *a* अनुगामी consequent
**anugrah** *n.* अनुग्रह indulgence
**anugrah karna** *v.t.* अनुग्रह करना oblige
**anugya dena** *v.t.* अनुज्ञा देना license
**anugya patra** *n.* अनुज्ञा पत्र licence

**anugyapatradhari** *n.* अनुज्ञापत्रधारी
  licensee
**anujal** *n* अनुजल wake
**anukaran** *n.* अनुकरण mimesis
**anukaran karna** *v.t.* अनुकरण करना ape
**anukaran karna** *v. t* अनुकरण करना copy
**anukaran karna** *v. t* अनुकरण करना
  emulate
**anukaran karna** *v.t.* अनुकरण करना
  imitate
**anukaran karne wala** *n.* अनुकरण
  करनेवाला imitator
**anukarnatmak** *a.* अनुकरणात्मक mimic
**anukooltam** *a* अनुकूलतम optimum
**anukooltam paristhiti** *n.* अनुकूलतम
  परिस्थिति optimum
**anukram** *n.* अनुक्रम sequence
**anukraman** *n.* अनुक्रमण succession
**anukul** *a* अनुकूल congenial
**anukul** *a* अनुकूल favourable
**anukul banana** *v.t* अनुकूल बनाना
  accommodate
**anukul banana** *v.t.* अनुकूल बनाना adapt
**anukulan** *n.* अनुकूलन adaptation
**anukulan** *n.* अनुकूलन adjustment
**anukulit karna** *v.t.* अनुकूलित करना adjust
**anukulta** *n.* अनुकूलता conformity
**anukulta** *n.* अनुकूलता consensus
**anulanghaniya** *a.* अनुल्लंघनीय inviolable
**anulekh** *n.* अनुलेख postscript
**anulom vivah** *a.* अनुलोम विवाह
  morganatic marriage
**anumaan** *n* अनुमान conjecture
**anumaan** *n.* अनुमान guess
**anumaan** *n.* अनुमान inference
**anumaan** *n.* अनुमान surmise
**anumaan lagana** *v.i* अनुमान लगाना guess
**anuman** *n.* अनुमान estimate
**anuman** *n.* अनुमान presumption
**anuman lagana** *v.t.* अनुमान लगाना assess

**anuman lagana** *v. t* अनुमान लगाना estimate

**anuman lagana** *v.t.* अनुमान लगाना reckon

**anumati** *n.* अनुमति allowance

**anumati** *n.* अनुमति assent

**anumati** *n.* अनुमति permission

**anumati dena** *v.t.* अनुमति देना allow

**anumati dena** *v.t.* अनुमति देना let

**anumati patra** *n.* अनुमति पत्र permit

**anumodan** *n.* अनुमोदन approbation

**anumodan** *n.* अनुमोदन approval

**anumodan** *n* अनुमोदन favour

**anumodan** *n.* अनुमोदन sanction

**anumodan karna** *v.t* अनुमोदन करना approbate

**anumodan karna** *v.t.* अनुमोदन करना approve

**anumodit karna** *v.t.* अनुमोदित करना second

**anunay karna** *v. t.* अनुनय करना entreat

**anupaat** *n.* अनुपात rate

**anupaat** *n.* अनुपात ratio

**anupajau** *a.* अनउपजाऊ barren

**anupalan** *n.* अनुपालन observance

**anupam** *a.* अनुपम incomparable

**anupam** *a.* अनुपम peerless

**anupasthit** *a* अनुपस्थित absent

**anupasthit rakhna** *v.t* अनुपस्थित रखना absent

**anupasthiti** *n* अनुपस्थिति absence

**anupat** *n.* अनुपात proportion

**anupraanit karna** *v.t.* अनुप्राणित करना infuse

**anupras** *n.* अनुप्रास alliteration

**anuprayog** *n.* अनुप्रयोग application

**anupurak** *a* अनुपूरक complementary

**anupurak** *a.* अनुपूरक secondary

**anuragshil** *a.* अनुरागशील loving

**anurakshi** *n* अनुरक्षी escort

**anurakt karna** *v. t* अनुरक्त करना enamour

**anurodh** *n.* अनुरोध insistence

**anurodh karna** *v.t.* अनुरोध करना conjure

**anurup** *a.* अनुरूप analogous

**anurup** *a.* अनुरूप like

**anurup hona** *v.t.* अनुरूप होना tally

**anurupta** *n.* अनुरूपता analogy

**anurupta** *n.* अनुरूपता likeness

**anusaaran karna** *v.t* अनुसरण करना follow

**anusabdhan** *n* अनुसंधान research

**anu-sambandhi** *a.* अणु-संबंधी atomic

**anusandhan** *n.* अनुसंधान investigation

**anusandhan** *n.* अनुसंधान quest

**anusandhan karna** *v.t.* अनुसंधान करना investigate

**anusandhan karna** *v.i.* अनुसंधान करना research

**anushasan** *n* अनुशासन discipline

**anushasan adhikaari** *n.* अनुशासन अधिकार proctor

**anushasanhinta** *n.* अनुशासनहीनता indiscipline

**anushikshan** *n.* अनुशिक्षण tuition

**anushilan** *v.t.* अनुशीलन peruse

**anusuchi banana** *v.t.* अनुसूची बनाना schedule

**anutha** *a.* अनूठा queer

**anuvad** *n.* अनुवाद translation

**anuvad karna** *v.t.* अनुवाद करना translate

**anuyayee** *n* अनुयायी disciple

**anuyayi** *n.* अनुयायी votary

**anya** *a* अन्य another

**anya vyakti ya vastu** *pron.* अन्य व्यक्ति या वस्तु other

**anyatha** *adv* अन्यथा else

**anyatha** *conj.* अन्यथा lest

**anyatha** *conj.* नहींतो otherwise

**anyatra upasthit** *n.* अन्यत्र उपस्थिति alibi

**anyaya** *n.* अन्याय injustice

anyayapurna *a.* अन्यायपूर्ण wrongful

anyayi *a.* अन्यायी unjust

anyokti *n.* अन्योक्ति allegory

anyokti-sambandhi *a.* अन्योक्ति-संबंधी allegorical

anyonya kriya *n.* अन्योन्य क्रिया interplay

apaardarsita *n.* अपारदर्शिता opacity

apaatkal *n* आपातकाल emergency

apach *n.* अपच indigestion

apachniya *a.* अपचनीय indigestible

apaharan *n* अपहरण abduction

apaharan karna *v.t.* अपहरण करना abduct

apang vyakti *n* अपंग व्यक्ति invalid

aparajeya *a.* अपराजेय invincible

apardarsi *a.* अपारदर्शी opaque

apariharya *a.* अपरिहार्य indispensable

apariharya *a.* अपरिहार्य inevitable

aparipakwata *n.* अपरिपक्वता immaturity

aparivartan sheel *a.* अपरिवर्तनशील uncertain

aparyapt *a.* अपर्याप्त scant

aparyapt *a.* अपर्याप्त sparse

apathaniya *a.* अपठनीय illegible

apatti *n.* आपत्ति objection

apatti karna *v. t* आपत्ति करना demur

apeel *n.* अपील appeal

apeelkarta *n.* अपीलकर्त्ता appellant

apgaman *n.* अपगमन secession

aphaara *n.* अफारा wind

apharan karna *v.t.* अपहरण करना kidnap

aphwah *n.* अफ़वाह rumour

aphwah phailana *v.t.* अफ़वाह फैलाना rumour

apitrin *n.* अपतृण weed

apivtrikaran *n.* अपवित्रीकरण sacrilege

apkaari *a.* अपकारी maleficent

apkriti *n.* अपकीर्ति infamy

apmaan *n* अपमान contempt

apmaan *n* अपमान disregard

apmaan *n.* अपमान resentment

apmaan *n.* अपमान slight

apmaan *n.* अपमान snub

apmaanit karna *v.t.* अपमानित करना attaint

apman *n* अपमान abasement

apman *n* अपमान affront

apman *n.* अपमान humiliation

apman *n.* अपमान insult

apmanit karna *v.t.* अपमानित करना abase

apmanit karna *v.t.* अपमानित करना affront

apmanit karna *v.t.* अपमानित करना humiliate

apmanit karna *v.t.* अपमानित करना mortify

apmanjanak *a* अपमानजनक abusive

apna *a.* अपना own

apnaana *v.t.* अपनाना own

apnana *v.t.* अपनाना adopt

apnidesan *n.* अपनिदेशन misdirection

apraadhi *n.* अपराधी malefactor

aprabhavi *a.* अप्रभावी ineffective

aprachalit *a.* अप्रचलित antique

aprachalit *a.* अप्रचलित archaic

aprachalit *a.* अप्रचलित obsolete

apradh *n.* अपराध guilt

apradh *n.* अपराध offence

apradh ka saathi *n* अपराध का साथी accomplice

apradhi *n.* अपराधी accused

apradhi *n* अपराधी convict

apradhi *a* अपराधी criminal

apradhi *a.* अपराधी guilty

apradhi *n.* अपराधी offender

apradhi *n.* अपराधी outlaw

apradhi ghoshit karna *v. t.* अपराधी घोषित करना convict

apradhi thaharana *v.t.* अपराधी ठहराना accuse

apradhi vyakti *n* अपराधी व्यक्ति criminal

apradh-karm *n* अप्रदान-कर्म perpetration

apratyaksh *a.* अप्रत्यक्ष indirect

**aprawaasi** *n.* आप्रवासी immigrant

**aprawasan** *n.* आप्रवासन immigration

**aprawasan karna** *v.i.* आप्रवासन करना immigrate

**aprayapt** *a.* अपर्याप्त insufficient

**aprayojya** *a.* अप्रयोज्य inapplicable

**apriya** *a.* अप्रिय obnoxious

**apsara** *n.* अप्सरा nymph

**apshabd** *n* अपशब्द abuse

**ap-shakun** *n.* अप-शगुन omen

**apurna** *a.* अपूर्ण imperfect

**apurna viram** *n* अपूर्ण विराम colon

**apurnata** *n.* अपूर्णता imperfection

**apurniya** *a.* अपूरणीय irrecoverable

**apvaad** *n* अपवाद exception

**apvadrahit** *a.* अपवादरहित strict

**apvitra karna** *v.t.* अपवित्र करना profane

**apvyaya** *a.* अपव्यय prodigal

**apvyayai vyakti** *n.* अपव्ययी व्यक्ति spendthrift

**ara** *n.* आरा saw

**aradhana** *n.* आराधना adoration

**aradhya** *a.* आराध्य adorable

**arajakata** *n* अराजकता anarchy

**arajkatavaad** *n.* अराजकतावाद anarchism

**arajkatavaadi** *n* अराजकतावादी anarchist

**archikth** *a.* अरक्षित insecure

**ardh saptahik** *adj* अर्ध साप्ताहिक bi-weekly

**ardharatri** *n.* अर्धरात्रि midnight

**ardhwarshik satr** *n.* अर्धवार्षिक सत्र semester

**arey se katana** *v.t.* आरे से काटना saw

**argandi** *n* अर्गांधी organdie

**ark nikalana** *v. t* अर्क निकालना extract

**arogyashram** *n.* आरोग्याश्रम sanatorium

**aropit karna** *v.t.* आरोपित करना ascribe

**arpan** *n.* अर्पण sacrifice

**arpit karna** *v. t* अर्पित करना devote

**arth** *n* अर्थ finance

**arth** *n.* अर्थ signification

**arth rakhna** *v. i* अर्थ रखना denote

**arth rakhna** *v.t.* अर्थ रखना signify

**arth wayawasta karna** *v.t* अर्थ व्यवस्था करना finance

**arthalipsa** *n* अर्थलिप्सा cupidity

**arthapurna** *a.* अर्थपूर्ण significant

**arthashastra** *n.* अर्थशास्त्र economics

**arthi** *n* अरथी bier

**arthik** *a* आर्थिक financial

**arthik** *a* आर्थिक fiscal

**arthik sahayata** *n.* आर्थिक सहायता subsidy

**arthik sahayata dena** *v.t.* आर्थिक सहायता देना subsidize

**arthvyavastha** *n* अर्थव्यवस्था economy

**aruchi** *n* अरुचि dislike

**aruchikar** *a.* अरुचिकर disagreeable

**aruchikar** *a.* अरुचिकर repugnant

**arunodaya** *n* अरुणोदय aurora

**asaadhya** *n.* असाध्य insoluble

**asabhya** *a.* असभ्य barbarous

**asabhya** *a.* असभ्य rude

**asabhya vyakti** *n.* असभ्य व्यक्ति barbarian

**asabhyata** *n.* असभ्यता barbarism

**asadharan** *a.* असाधारण extraordinary

**asadharan** *a.* असाधारण peculiar

**asadharan** *a.* असाधारण remarkable

**asadharan** *a.* असाधारण special

**asadhya** *a.* असाध्य incurable

**asafalta** *n* असफलता failure

**asahamat hona** *v. i* असहमत होना disagree

**asahamati** *n.* असहमति disagreement

**asahaniya** *a.* असहनीय insupportable

**asahaya** *a.* असहाय helpless

**asahayam** *a.* असह्य intolerable

**asahishnu** *a.* असहिष्णु intolerant

**asahishunta** *n.* असहिष्णुता intolerance

**asainik** *a* असैनिक civil

**asainik vyakti** *n* असैनिक व्यक्ति civilian

asali *a.* असली real
asamaan *a* असमान dissimilar
asamaan *a* असमान unlike
asamanjas *n.* असमंजस indecision
asamanta *n* असमानता difference
asamanta *n* असमानता disparity
asamanya *a* असामान्य abnormal
asamanya rup se *adv* असामान्य रूप से extra
asamarth *a.* असमर्थ incapable
asamarth *a.* असमर्थ unable
asamarthniya *a.* असमर्थनीय indefensible
asamarthta *n.* असमर्थता inability
asamayik *a.* असामयिक inopportune
asambhav *a.* असंभव impossible
asambhavta *n.* असंभवता impossibility
asambhavya *a.* असंभाव्य unlikely
asamvedan *n.* असंवेदन insensibility
asangat *a.* असंगत improper
asangat *a.* असंगत incoherent
asangat *a.* असंगत irreconcilable
asangat *a.* असंगत monstrous
asankhya *a.* असंख्य innumerable
asankhya *a* असंख्य myriad
asansodhaniy *a.* असंशोधनीय incorrigible
asantosh *n* असंतोष discontent
asantosh *n* असंतोष dissatisfaction
asantosh *n.* असंतोष grunt
asantosh prakat karna *v.i.* असंतोष प्रकट करना grumble
asantoshjanak *a.* असंतोषजनक lame
asantust *a.* असंतुष्ट malcontent
asantust baykti *n* असंतुष्ट व्यक्ति malcontent
asanyami *a* असंयमी extravagant
asathkarsil *a.* असत्कारशील inhospitable
asatya *n* असत्य lie
asatya sidh karna *v. t* असत्य सिद्घ करना disprove
asatyabhas *n.* असत्याभास paradox
asavdhan *a.* असावधान careless

asavdhan *a.* असावधान inattentive
asavdhanipurna *a.* असावधानीपूर्ण indiscreet
aseemit *a.* असीमित measureless
asha *n* आशा hope
asha *n.* आशा prospect
asha karna *v.t.* आशा करना await
asha karna *v.t.* आशा करना bank
asha rakhna *v.t.* आशा रखना hope
ashaant *n* अशांत disquiet
ashalil *a.* अश्लील vulgar
ashalilta *n.* अश्लीलता vulgarity
ashanka *n.* आशंका apprehension
ashankit *a.* आशंकित apprehensive
ashant *a.* अशांत turbulent
ashant karna *v.t.* अशांत करना unsettle
ashanti *n* अशांति unrest
ashavan *a.* आशावान hopeful
ashawad *n.* आशावाद optimism
ashawadi *n.* आशावादी optimist
ashawadi *a.* आशावादी optimistic
ashcarya karna *v.i.* आश्चर्य करना wonder
ashcharya *n* आश्चर्य wonder
ashcharyachakit karna *v.t.* आश्चर्यचकित करना stun
ashcharyachakit karna *v.t.* आश्चर्यचकित करना surprise
ashcharyajanak *a.* आश्चर्यजनक wonderful
ashcharyajanak *a.* आश्चर्यजनक, अद् भुत, अत्युत्कृष्ट wondrous
ashisht *a* अशिष्ट rank
ashisht *a* अशिष्ट unmannerly
ashishtatapurna *a* अशिष्टतापूर्ण curt
ashishtatha *n.* अशिष्टता indecency
ashlil *a.* अश्लील profane
ashodhit *a* अशोधित crude
ashravya *a.* अश्राव्य inaudible
ashray *n.* आश्रय lee
ashrit *n.* आश्रित ward
ashrumya *a.* अश्रुमय watery

**ashrupurna** *a.* अश्रुपूर्ण tearful
**ashrya** *n.* आश्रय recourse
**ashu lipik** *n.* आशुलिपिक stenographer
**ashubh** *n* अशुभ evil
**ashubh** *a.* अशुभ inauspicious
**ashubh** *a.* अशुभ sinister
**ashudh** *a.* अशुद्घ inaccurate
**ashudh** *a.* अशुद्घ inexact
**ashudh mudran** *n.* अशुद्घ मुद्रण misprint
**ashuun** *a.* अक्षुण्ण intact
**ashvasan dena** *v.i.* आश्वासन देना vouch
**ashvast** *a.* आश्वस्त confident
**ashwasan-daata** *n.* आश्वासनदाता warrantor
**asim** *a.* असीम limitless
**asli** *a.* असली genuine
**asmarthata** *n.* शक्तिहीनता incapacity
**aspasht** *a.* अस्पष्ट vague
**aspashtata** *n.* अस्पष्टता vagueness
**aspashth** *a.* अस्पष्ट indistinct
**asrilal** *a.* अश्लील obscene
**asrilalta** *n.* अश्लीलता obscenity
**assi** *n* अस्सी eighty
**astabal** *n* अस्तबल stable
**astar** *n* अस्तर lining
**astar lagana** *v.t.* अस्तर लगाना line
**astha** *n.* आस्था belief
**asthai** *a.* अस्थायी temporary
**asthai aawas** *n.* अस्थायी आवास lodging
**asthayee** *n.* अस्थायी transitory
**asthayi** *a.* अस्थायी provisional
**asthibhang** *n.* अस्थिभंग fracture
**asthir** *adj.* अस्थिर astatic
**asthir** *a* अस्थिर fitful
**asthir** *a.* अस्थिर shaky
**asthir hona** *v.i.* अस्थिर होना waver
**asthirta** *n.* अस्थिरता instability
**astitva** *n* अस्तित्व existence
**astitvahin vastu** *n.* अस्तित्वहीन वस्तु nonentity
**astra-shastra** *n.* अस्त्र-शस्त्र ammunition

**asudh** *a.* अशुद्घ incorrect
**asudh ganna** *n.* अशुद्घ गणना miscalculation
**asuraksha** *n.* असुरक्षा insecurity
**asuvidha** *n* असुविधा discomfort
**asuvidha** *n.* असुविधा privation
**asuvidhajanak** *a.* असुविधाजनक untoward
**asuwidhajanak** *a.* असुविधाजनक inconvenient
**asvastha** *a.* अस्वस्थ, रुग्ण sickly
**asvastha** *a.* अस्वस्थ unwell
**asvikar karana** *v. t* अस्वीकार करना disapprove
**asvikriti** *n* अस्वकृति disapproval
**aswastha** *a.* अस्वस्थ indisposed
**aswikar** *n.* अस्वीकार rejection
**aswikar karana** *v.t.* अस्वीकार करना reject
**aswikar karna** *v.t.* अस्वीकार करना repudiate
**atah** *conj.* अत: so
**atah** *adv.* अत: therefore
**atank** *n.* आतंक panic
**atankit karna** *v.t.* आतंकित करना terrify
**atari** *n.* अटारी loft
**atharah** *a* अठारह eighteen
**ati adhik** *a.* अति अधिक terrific
**ati avashyak** *a.* अति आवश्यक urgent
**ati bhukha** *a.* अति भूखा voracious
**ati karna** *v.t.* अति करना overdo
**ati mahan** *a.* अति महान awful
**ati prachin** *a.* अति प्राचीन immemorial
**ati suksham** *a.* अति सूक्ष्म microscopic
**ati ushna** *a.* अति उष्ण torrid
**ati ushna** *a.* अति उष्ण tropical
**ati utsuk** *adj.* अति उत्सुक appetent
**ati uttam** *a.* अति उत्तम superfine
**atikraman** *n.* अतिक्रमण infringement
**atikraman** *n.* अतिक्रमण transgression
**atikraman** *n.* अतिक्रमण trespass
**atikraman karna** *v. i* अतिक्रमण करना encroach

atikraman karna *v.t.* अतिक्रमण करना
transgress

atikraman karna *v.i.* अतिक्रमण करना
trespass

atimanav *n.* अतिमानव superman

atimanviya *a.* अतिमानवीय superhuman

ati-natakiya vyavhar *n.* अतिनाटकीय
व्यवहार melodrama

atiranjana karna *v. t.* अतिरंजना करना
exaggerate

atirikt *a.* अतिरिक्त additional

atirikt *a* अतिरिक्त else

atirikt *prep* अतिरिक्त except

atirikt *a* अतिरिक्त excess

atirikt *a* अतिरिक्त extra

atirikt *a* अतिरिक्त spare

atirikth *a* अतिरिक्त further

atisaar *n* अतिसार diarrhoea

atishram *n.* अतिश्रम overwork

atishyokti *n.* अतिशयोक्ति exaggeration

atishyokti *n.* अतिशयोक्ति hyperbole

ati-shyokti karna *v.t.* अतिशयोक्ति करना
overdraw

atithi *n.* अतिथि guest

atiwadi *n* अतिवादी extremist

atkal lagana *v.i.* अटकल लगाना speculate

atkalbazi *n.* अटकलबाज़ी speculation

atma *n.* आत्मा spirit

atmaghati *a.* आत्मघाती suicidal

atmahatya *n.* आत्महत्या suicide

atmanirikshana karna *v.i.* आत्मनिरीक्षण
करना introspect

atmaparak *a.* आत्मपरक subjective

atmasamarpan *n* आत्मसमर्पण surrender

atmatyag *n.* आत्मत्याग renunciation

atm-rati *n.* आत्मरति narcissism

atm-santusht *a.* आत्मसंतुष्ट smug

atoshniya *a.* अतोषणीय insatiable

atyabhinay karna *v.t.* अत्याभिनय करना
overact

atyadhik *a.* अत्यधिक intense

atyant mahatva purna *adj.* अत्यंत
महत्वपूर्ण crucial

atyavashyak *a.* अत्यावश्यक imperative

atyavashyak *n.* अति आवश्यक incumbent

atyavashyakta *n.* अत्यावश्यकता urgency

atyuttam padarth *n.* अत्युत्तम पदार्थ
paragon

auchitiya *n.* औचित्य justification

auchitya *n.* औचित्य aptitude

audhoyogik *a.* औद्योगिक industrial

August *n.* अगस्त August

aujaar *n.* औज़ार instrument

aula *n.* ओला hail

aula girna *v.i* ओला गिरना hail

aundha *a.* औंधा topsy turvy

aundha karna *v.t.* औंधा करना invert

aupacharik *a.* औपचारिक regular

aupcharik *a.* औपचारिक ceremonious

aur *conj.* और and

aur aache dhang se *adv.* और अच्छे ढंग से
better

aur na *conj* और न nor

ausat *n.* औसत average

ausat darjay ka *a.* औसत दर्जे का average

aushadh *n* औषध cure

aushadh tatya *n.* औषध तत्व medicament

aushadh vikreta *n.* औषध-विक्रेता chemist

aushadh vikreta *n* औषध विक्रेता druggist

aushadhi *n* औषधि drug

aushadhi *n.* औषधि medicine

aushadhi banane wala *n.* औषधि बनाने
वाला compounder

aushadhi ka lep *n.* औषधि का लेप plaster

aushadhi ki atimatra *n.* औषधि की
अतिमात्रा overdose

aushadhiya *a.* औषधीय medicinal

auzaar *n.* औजार tool

avaataran *n.* अवतरण passage

avadhi *n* अवधि spell

avadhi *n.* अवधि term

avagya karna *v. t* अवज्ञा करना disobey

avaidh *a.* अवैध illegal
avaidh *a.* अवैध illegitimate
avaidh *a.* अवैध lawless
avaidhita *n.* अवैधता ilegality
avamulyan *n.* अवमूल्यन deflation
avar vyakti *n.* अवर व्यक्ति junior
avaran *n* आवरण wrap
avarodh *n* अवरोध check
avartak *a.* आवर्तक recurrent
avasan karna *v.t.* अवसान करना prorogue
avashyak *a* आवश्यक essential
avashyak saman *adv.* आवश्यक सामान needments
avashyakata *n* आवश्यकता want
avashyakta *n.* आवश्यकता necessity
avashyakta *n.* आवश्यकता need
avastha *n.* अवस्था state
avasthiti *n* अवस्थिति position
avataar *n.* अवतार incarnation
avayvasthit *adv.* अव्यवस्थित chaotic
avayvastith *a.* अव्यवस्थित haphazard
avdharan *n* अवधारण conception
avdharna *n.* अवधारणा retention
avesh *n.* आवेश surge
avgat *a.* अवगत aware
avhav hona *v.t.* अभाव होना lack
avhelana dikhana *v.i* अवहेलना दिखाना sneer
avibhajya *a.* अविभाज्य indivisible
avichalit *a.* अविचलित nonchalant
avikasit *a.* अविकसित immature
avimani *a.* अभिमानी lofty
avinashita *n.* अविनिष्टता immortality
avineet *a.* अविनीत immodest
avinit *a* अविनीत discourteous
avirodh *n.* अविरोध consonance
avisaap *n.* अभिशाप malediction
avishkaarak *n.* आविष्कारक inventor
avishvas *n* अविश्वास distrust
avishvasniya *a.* अविश्वसनीय unreliable
aviskaar *n.* आविष्कार invention

aviskaar karna *v.t.* आविष्कार करना invent
aviskaarshil *a.* आविष्कारशील inventive
aviswas *n.* अविश्वास mistrust
aviswas karna *v.t.* अविश्वास करना mistrust
avivahit jeevan *n.* अविवाहित जीवन celibacy
avivahit vyakti *n.* अविवाहित व्यक्ति bachelor
avivahita stri *n.* अविवाहिता स्त्री spinster
avivechit *a.* अविवेचित automatic
avivek *n.* अविवेक imprudence
aviveki *a.* अविवेकी imprudent
aviyog lagana *v.t.* अभियोग लगाना incriminate
avi-yojya *a.* अवियोज्य inseparable
avkaash *n.* अवकाश vacation
avkash *n.* अवकाश leisure
avlokan *n* अवलोकन contemplation
avlokan karna *v.t.* अवलोकन करना watch
avnati *n.* अवनति ebb
avrodh *n.* अवरोध barrier
avrodh *n.* अवरोध jam
avrudh karna *v.t* अवरुद्ध करना block
avshesh *n.* अवशेष ash
avshesh *n.* अवशेष remains
avshesh *n.* अवशेष residue
avyakhyaya *a.* अव्याख्येय inexplicable
avyashak *a.* आवश्यक needful
avyashak vastu *n.* आवश्यक वस्तु necessary
avyaskhak banana *v.t.* आवश्यक बनाना necessitate
avyavaharikta *n.* अव्यावहारिकता impracticability
avyavaharya *a.* अव्यवहार्य impracticable
avyavastha *n.* अव्यवस्था chaos
avyavastha *n* अव्यवस्था confusion
avyavastha *n* अव्यवस्था disorder

**avyavasthit karna** *v. t* अव्यवस्थित करना
confuse
**avyavyasayee** *n.* अव्यवसायी amateur
**awaara** *n.* आवारा vagabond
**awaaz** *n.* आवाज़ voice
**awaaz ka kampana** *v.i.* आवाज़ का कांपना
vibrate
**awagya** *n.* अवज्ञा insubordination
**awagyakari** *a.* अवज्ञाकारी insubordinate
**awaidh** *a* अवैध bastard
**awaidh santan** *n.* अवैध संतान bastard
**awaiyaktik** *a.* अवैयक्तिक impersonal
**awara aadmi** *n.* आवारा आदमी loafer
**awaragardi karna** *v.i.* आवारागर्दी करना
loaf
**awarnaniya** *a.* अवर्णनीय indescribable
**awarodhak dori** *n.* अवरोधक डोरी gasket
**awarudh karna** *v.t.* अवरूद्घ करना
obstruct
**awasaan** *n* अवसान expiry
**awashyak** *a.* आवश्यक requisite
**awashyak vastu** *n* आवश्यक वस्तु requisite
**awayasak vyakti** *n* अवयस्क व्यक्ति minor
**awayav** *n.* अवय ingredient
**awaz dhimi karna** *vt* आवाज धीमी करना
mute
**awirodhi** *a* अविरोधी consistent
**awiswasniya** *a.* अविश्वसनीय incredible
**awiwaiki** *a.* अविवेकी inconsiderate
**awiwaki** *a.* अविवेकी injudicious
**awkash ka din** *n.* अवकाश का दिन holiday
**aworodh** *n.* अवरोध inhibition
**awrodh** *n.* अवरोध hindrance
**awrodhan** *n.* अवरोधन interception
**awsar** *n.* अवसर occasion
**awsar-vadita** *n.* अवसरवादिता
opportunism
**awshesh** *n* अवशेष rest
**ayaal** *n.* अयाल mane
**ayan** *n.* अयन udder
**ayogya** *a.* अयोग्य incompetent

**ayogya thaharana** *v. t.* अयोग्य ठहराना
disqualify
**ayogyata** *n* अयोग्यता disqualification
**aytaakaar** *a.* आयताकार rectangular
**ayu** *n.* आयु age
**azmaishi** *a.* आज़माइशी tentative

# B

**baad mein** *adv.* बाद में afterwards
**baadal** *n.* बादल cloud
**baadha** *n.* बाधा bar
**baadha** *n* बाधा difficulty
**baadha** *n.* बाधा hurdle
**baadha** *n.* बाध impediment
**baadha** *n.* बाधा interruption
**baadha daalna** *v.i.* बाधा डालना meddle
**baadha khari karna** *v.t* बाधा खड़ी करना
hurdle
**baagi** *a.* बाग़ी rebellious
**baahar** *adv.* बाहर out
**baahar phenkna** *v. t.* बाहर फेंकना eject
**baahri** *a* बाहरी external
**baaj** *n* बाज़ falcon
**baaj** *n* बाज़ hawk
**baajra** *n.* बाजरा millet
**baal** *n* बाल bristle
**baal** *n* बाल hair
**baal vihar** *n.* बाल विहार kindergarten ;
**baalti** *n.* बाल्टी pail
**baandh** *n* बाँध causeway
**baandhana** *v.t* बांधना bind
**baandhana** *v.t.* बाँधना pack
**baansuri** *n* बांसुरी flute
**baansuri bajana** *v.i* बांसुरी बजाना flute
**baantana** *v. t* बांटना distribute
**baantana** *v.t* बांटना mete
**baar baar** *n.* बार बार frequent
**baar baar duhrana** *v.t.* बार बार दुहराना
reiterate

baarah-maasi *n.* बारहमासी perennis

baarch *n* बार्च flood

baarh lagana *v.t* बाड़ लगाना hedge

baarha *n* बाड़ा fold

baariiki *n.* बारीकी subtlety

baarik *n.* बारीक subtle

baat-chit karna *v. t* बातचीत करना commune

bacha rakhna *v.t.* बचा रखना reserve

bacha rakhna *v.t.* बचा रखना store

bachaav *n* बचाव defence

bachana *v.i.* बचाना guard

bachana *v.t.* बचाना screen

bachana *v.t.* बचाना shield

bachao *n.* बचाव immunity

bachao ka rasta *n.* बचाव का रास्ता loophole

bachav *n.* बचाव avoidance

bachav *n.* बचाव protection

bachcha *n* बच्चा child

bachche *n* बच्चे young

bachha *n.* बच्चा babe

bachha *n.* बच्चा bantling

bachha *n.* बच्चा infant

bachhagarhi *n.* बच्चागाड़ी perambulator

bachhra *n.* बछड़ा calf

bachkana *a.* बचकाना childish

bachkana *a.* बचकाना puerile

bachkani baat *n.* बचकानी बात prattle

bachna *v.i.* बचना abstain

bachpan *n.* बचपन infantilism

bada din *n.* बड़ा दिन Xmas

bada kamara *n.* बड़ा कमरा hall

badal dena *v. t.* बदल देना change

badal jaana *v.t.* बदल जाना vary

badalna *v.t.* बदलना modify

badalna *v.t.* बदलना switch

badbad karna *v.t.* बड़बड़ करना jabber

badbadana *v.i.* बड़बड़ाना mutter

badbadana *v.i.* बड़बड़ाना rave

badbudar hona *v.i.* बदबूदार होना stink

badha *n.* बाधा barricade

badha *n* बाधा drag

badha *n* बाधा handicap

badha *n.* बाधा limitation

badha *n.* बाधा obstacle

badha *n.* बाधा obstruction

badha dalana *v.t.* बाधा डालना handicap

badha dalna *v. t* बाधा डालना disturb

badha dalna *v. t.* बाधा डालना encumber

badha dalna *v.t.* बाधा डालना impede

badha dalna *v.t.* बाधा डालना prevent

badha pahuchana *v.t.* बाधा पहुंचाना hinder

badhai *n* बधाई congratulation

badhai dena *v. t* बधाई देना congratulate

badhai ka auzaar *n* बढ़ाई का औज़ार brace

badhai karna *v.t* बधाई देना felicitate

badhak *a.* बाधक obstructive

badhak *a.* बाधक resistant

badhana *v.t.* बढ़ाना amplify

badhana *v.t.* बढ़ना augment

badhana *v.t.* बढ़ना redouble

badhat *n.* बढ़त weightage

badhava dena *v. t* बढ़ावा देना boost

badhava dena *v.t.* बढ़ावा देना promote

badhir *a* बधिर deaf

badhiya kanch *n* बढ़िया कांच crystal

badhiya karna *v.t.* बधिया करना geld

badhna *v.t.* बढ़ना accumulate

badhna *v.t.* बढ़ाना increase

badhya karna *v. t.* बाध्य करना enforce

badhya karna *v.t* बाध्य करना force

badhyakaran *n* बाध्यकरण compulsion

badi matra *n* बड़ी मात्रा lot

badla lena *v.t.* बदला लेना revenge

badle mein *n.* बदले में lieu

badmash *n.* बदमाश miscreant

badminton *n.* बैडमिंटन badminton

badna *v.i.* बढ़ना swell

badnam *a.* बदनाम infamous

badnam karna *v. t.* बदनाम करना defame

**badnam karna** *v.t.* बदनाम करना
scandalize
**badnam stri** *n.* बदनाम स्त्री slut
**badnami** *n* बदनामी disrepute
**badnami** *n* बदनामी scandal
**badrang karna** *v.t.* बदरंग करना tarnish
**bagavat karna** *v. i* बग़ावत करना mutiny
**bagawat** *n.* बग़ावत rebellion
**bagbaani** *n.* बाग़बानी horticulture
**bagh** *n.* बाघ tiger
**baghi** *a.* बाग़ी mutinous
**baghin** *n.* बाघिन tigress
**bahaali** *n.* बहाली reinstatement
**bahadur** *a* बहादुर brave
**bahadur** *a.* बहादुर intrepid
**bahadur** *a.* बहादुर martial
**bahadur** *adj.* बहादुर mighty
**bahaduri** *n* बहादुरी bravery
**bahaduri** *n.* बहादुरी gallantry
**bahakana** *v.t.* बहकाना mislead
**bahana** *n* बहाना excuse
**bahana** *n* बहाना eyewash
**bahana** *n.* बहाना plea
**bahana** *v.i.* बहना pour
**bahana** *n.* बहाना pretence
**bahana** *n* बहाना pretext
**bahana karna** *v.t.* बहाना करना pretend
**bahana karna** *v.t* बहाना करना feign
**bahana karna** *v.i.* बहाना करना sham
**bahar** *adv.* बाहर forth
**bahar** *prep* बाहर outside
**bahar bhejna** *v. t* बाहर भेजना emit
**bahar kai aur** *adv* बाहर की ओर outside
**bahar kai aur** *adv* बाहर की ओर outward
**bahar ke aur** *adv* बाहर की ओर outwards
**bahar se** *adv.* बाहर से outwardly
**bahari** *a.* बाहरी outdoor
**bahari** *a.* बाहरी outer
**bahari baykti** *n.* बाहरी व्यक्ति outsider
**bahari satah** *n* बाहरी सतह outside
**bahas** *n.* बहस moot

**bahas karna** *v. t.* बहस करना debate
**bahata hua** *adv.* बहता हुआ afloat
**bahirmukh** *a.* बहिरमुख posticoos
**bahirogi** *n.* बहिरोगी outpatient
**bahishkar** *n* बहिष्कार boycott
**bahishkrit** *a* बहिष्कृत outcast
**bahishkrit karna** *v. t.* बहिष्कृत करना
excommunicate
**bahiskar karna** *v. t.* बहिष्कार करना
boycott
**bahta hua** *adj.* बहता हुआ confluent
**bahu-bhagiya** *adj* बहू-भागीय multiple
**bahubhashavidh** *a.* बहुभाषाविद् polyglot
**bahubhashi** *n.* बहुभाषी polyglot
**bahudaishiya** *a.* बहुदेशीय multilateral
**bahudev vad** *n.* बहुदेववाद polytheism
**bahudev vadi** *a.* बहुदेववादी polytheistic
**bahudevpujak** *n.* बहुदेवपूजक polytheist
**bahukhandiya** *a.* बहुखंडीय multiple
**bahulata** *n.* बहुलता multiplicity
**bahulya** *n* बाहुल्य excess
**bahumat** *n.* बहुमत majority
**bahumukhi** *a.* बहुमुखी versatile
**bahupad kidha** *n.* बहुपाद कीड़ा polypod
**bahurangi** *a.* बहुरंगी motley
**bahurupi** *n.* बहुरूपी multiform
**bahusankhyak** *a.* बहुसंख्यक populous
**bahu-shilp** *a.* बहु-शिल्प polytechnic
**bahut** *a.* बहुत numerous
**bahut adhik** *adv.* बहुत अधिक too
**bahut chhota** *a.* बहुत छोटा tiny
**bahut kuch** *adv.* बहुत कुछ pretty
**bahut samay pahley** *adv.* बहुत समय पहले
ago
**bahut tez** *n* बहुत तेज़ breakneck
**bahut thorha** *a.* बहुत थोड़ा nominal
**bahuvachan** *a.* बहुवचन plural
**bahuvidh** *a.* बहुविध multiplex
**bahuvivah pratha** *n.* बहुविवाह प्रथा
polygamy
**bahya** *a.* बाह्य outside

baidakhal karna v. t बेदख़ल करना evict
baidakhali n बेदख़ली eviction
baidhan n. बेधन penetration
baijorh a. बेजोड़ matchless
bail n. बैल ox
bailgarhi n. बैलगाड़ी wain
baimaan a. बेईमान foul
baimaani se adv बेईमानी से malafide
baiman a बेईमान dishonest
baimani n. बेईमानी dishonesty
baingan n बैंगन brinjal
baingani adj./n. बैंगनी purple
baingani rang n. बैंगनी रंग violet
bair n बैर antagonism
baira n. बैरा waiter
baisudh a. बेसुध insensible
baisura a. बेसुरा hoarse
baithak n. बैठक session
baithak n बैठक drawing-room
baithak n. बैठक meet
baithak n. बैठक parlour
baithana v.t. बैठाना seat
baithane ka aasan n. बैठने का आसन seat
baithee hui awaz a. बैठी हुई आवाज़ throaty
baithna v.i. बैठना roost
baithna v.i. बैठना sit
bajana v.i. बजाना blow
bakaaya a. बकाया outstanding
bakaya n.pl. बकाया arrears
bakery n बेकरी bakery
bakhsh dena v.t. बख़्श देना spare
bakhshish dena v.t. बख़्शिश देना tip
bakri n. बकरी goat
baksua n बकसुआ buckle
bakvas n. बकवास nonsense
bakvas karna v. t बकवास करना chatter
bakwas n. बकवास babble
bakwas karna v.i. बकवास करना babble
bal n. बल stress
bal dena v.t बल देना stress

balaatkar n. बलात्कार rape
balak n बालक boy
balatkar karna v.t. बलात्कार करना rape
bali n. बलि oblation
bali ka bakra n. बलि का बकरा scapegoat
balidan karna v.t. बलिदान करना sacrifice
balidan sambandhi a. बलिदान संबंधी sacrificial
balivedi n. बलिवेदी altar
balla n बल्ला bat
ballamdhari yodha n. बल्लमधारी योद्धा lancer
ballebaj n. बल्लेबाज batsman
balon ka lachcha n. बालों का लच्छा ringlet
bal-purvak grahan n. बलपूर्वक ग्रहण snatch
balshali a बलशाली forceful
balti n बाल्टी bucket
balut ka phal n. बलूत का फल acorn
balwa n. बलवा revolt
balwa karna v.t. बलवा करना riot
balwan a. बलवान athletic
bam n बम bomb
bam girana v. t बम गिराना bomb
bambari karna v. t बमबारी करना bombard
bambbari n बमबारी bombardment
bambvarshak n बमवर्षक bomber
bana n. बाना woof
banaam prep. बनाम versus
banana v.t. बनाना frame
banaspati wigyan n वनस्पति विज्ञान botany
banawati roop n. बनावटी रूप guise
banay rakhna v.t. बनाए रखना preserve
banaye rakhna v.t. बनाए रखना maintain
band n. बंद stanza
band gaahi n. बंद गाड़ी van
band hona v.t. बंद होना shut
band karna v. i. बंद करना cease
band karna v. t बंद करना close

band karna *v. t* बंद करना discontinue
bandal *n.* बंडल parcel
bandanwar, toran *n* बंदनवार, तोरण
festoon
bandar *n.* बंदर monkey
bandargaha *n.* बंदरगाह harbour
bandargaha *n.* बंदरगाह haven
bandargaha *n.* बंदरगाह port
bandgobhi *n.* बन्दगोभी cabbage
bandh *n* बांध dam
bandhak *n.* बंधक hostage
bandhak *n.* बंधक mortgage
bandhak *n.* बंधक pledge
bandhak rakhna *v.t.* बंधक रखना
mortgage
bandhak rakhna *v.t.* बंधक रखना pledge
bandhakar rakh dena *v.t.* बांधकर रख देना
stow
bandhan *n.* बंधन obligation
bandhan *n.* बंधन yoke
bandhan lagana *v.t* बंधन लगाना fetter
bandhana *v.t* बांधना fasten
bandhana *v.t* बांधना moor
bandhana *v.t.* बांधना tie
bandhanmukt *a.* बंधनमुक्त loose
bandhna *v.t.* बांधना knot
bandhne ki saamagri *n.* बांधने की सामग्री
packing maaterial
bandi *n.* बंदी captive
bandi *n.* बंदी prisoner
bandi bana hua *a.* बंदी बना हुआ captive
bandi banana *v. t.* बंदी बनाना capture
bandi banana *v.t.* बंदी बनाना imprison
bandi banana *v.t.* बंदी बनाना nab
bandi dasha *n.* बंदी दशा captivity
bandi pratyakshikaran *n.* बंदी
प्रत्यक्षीकरण habeas corpus
bandigreh *n.* बंदीगृह jail
bandikaran *n.* बंदीकरण capture
banduk *n.* बंदूक gun
banduk *n.* बंदूक musket

banduk ka ghoda *n* बंदूक का घोड़ा lock
banduk ke naal *n.* बंदूक की नाल barrel
bandukdhari sipahi *n.* बंदूकधारी सिपाही
musketeer
bangla *n* बंगला bungalow
banjar *n* बञ्जर fallow
banjar pradesh *n.* बंजर प्रदेश moor
banjh *n* बांझ barren
banjh *a.* बांझ sterile
banjh *adj.* बाँझ acarpous
banjhpan *n.* बांझपन sterility
bank *n.* बैंक bank
bank-karmi *n.* बैंक-कर्मी banker
bans *n.* बांस bamboo
bansuri *n.* बांसुरी pipe
bantana *v.t.* बांटना apportion
bantana *v.t.* बांटना parcel
bantana *v.t.* बांटना partition
bantana *v.t.* बांटना portion
bantna *v. t* बांटना divide
bantwara *n.* बंटवारा partition
bara बड़ा large
bara padri *n.* बड़ा पादरी cardinal
barabar hona *v.* बराबर होना amount
barabar karna *v. t.* बराबर करना equalize
barabar mein *adv* बराबर में abreast
barabari *n.* बराबरी par
barah *n* बारह twelve
barah darjan *n.* बारह दर्जन gross
barah ki sankhya *n.* बारह की संख्या
twelve
baramada *n.* बरामदा lounge
baramada *n.* बरामदा portico
baramada *n.* बरामदा veranda
barasna *v.t.* बरसाना shower
barbadi *n* बर्बादी downfall
barbarta *n* बर्बरता barbarity
barbhashya *n.* गर्भाशय womb
barchi *n.* बर्छी dart
barf *n.* बर्फ़ ice
barfila *a.* बर्फ़ीला icy

bargad *n.* बरगद banyan

barha bandar *n.* बड़ा बन्दर baboon

barhaana *v. t* बढ़ाना extend

barhavan *a.* बारहवां twelfth

barhavan bhag *n.* बारहवां भाग twelfth

barhayee *n.* बढ़ई carpenter

barhayeegiri *n.* बढ़ईगीरी carpentry

barhbarh karna *v. i* बड़बड़ करना blether

barhbarhana *v.t.* बड़बड़ाना murmur

barhi antarhi *n* बड़ी अंतड़ी colon

barhi lal mirch *n* बड़ी लाल मिर्च capsicum

bariki se *adv.* बारीकी से minutely

bariki se janch karna *v.t.* बारीकी से जांच करना sift

barkhastgi *n* बरखास्तगी dismissal

barma *n.* बरमा auger

barma *n* बरमा drill

baroni *n.* बरौनी eyelash

barph *n.* बर्फ़ snow

barph jaisa safed *a.* बर्फ़ सफ़ेद snowy

bartan *n.* बरतन pot

bartan *n.* बरतन utensil

bartan *n.* बरतन vessel

bartav karna *v.t.* बरताव करना treat

barti karna *v.t.* भर्ती करना recruit

barud *n* बारूद dynamite

basana *v.t.* बसाना people

basana *v.t.* बसाना populate

basera *n.* बसेरा roost

basi *a.* बासी stale

basi karna *v.t.* बासी करना stale

basna *v.i.* बसना settle

bataana *v.t.* बताना relate

batair *n.* बटेर quail

batakh *n.* बतख duck

batakh *n.* बत्तख goose

batakh ka shabd *n* बतख का शब्द quack

batan *n* बटन button

batan lagana *v. t.* बटन लगाना button

batana *v.t.* बताना narrate

batana *v.t.* बताना tell

bataya jana *v.t.* बताया जाना hear

batchit karna *v. i.* बातचीत करना chat

batua *n.* बटुआ purse

batuni *a.* बातूनी talkative

baudhik *a.* बौद्धिक intellectual

baukhalana *v.t.* बौखलाना frustrate

bauna *n* बौना dwarf

bauna *n.* बौना pigmy

bauna *n.* बौना pygmy

bauna *v.t.* बोना sow

bauochar *n.* बौछार shower

bavaseer *n.* बवासीर piles

bawal *n* बवाल babel

bayan *a.* बायां left

bayan karna *v.t.* बयान करना report

bayeen aur jhuka hua lekh *n.* बाई ओर झुका हुआ लेख backhand

bazar *n* बाज़ार market

bazar *n.* बाज़ार mart

bazi lagana *v.i.* बाज़ी लगाना wager

bazigar *n.* बाज़ीगर juggler

bechaouliya *n.* बिचौलिया middleman

bechna *v.t.* बेचना sell

bedag *a.* बेदाग़ stainless

bedhi *n* बेड़ी chain

beech mein *prep.* बीच में among

beech mein *prep.* बीच में amongst

beej *n.* बीज seed

beejganit *n.* बीजगणित algebra

beekar *n* बीकर beaker

beemar hona *v.i.* बीमार होना ail

beemari *n.* बीमारी ailment

bees *a.* बीस twenty

bees ki sankhya *n* बीस की संख्या twenty

beesvan *a.* बीसवां twentieth

beesvan bhag *n* बीसवां भाग twentieth

beeta hua din *n.* बीता हुआ दिन yesterday

begam *n.* बेगम countess

behakana *n.* बहकाना seduce

behakna *v. t.* बहकाना entrap

behal karna *v.t.* बहाल करना reinstate

behalana v. *t* बहलाना coax
behan n. बहन sister
behenapa n. बहनापा sisterhood
behna v.i. बहना stream
behna v.i. बहना well
behosh a. बेहोश senseless
behoshi n बेहोशी anaesthesia
behoshi n. बेहोशी trance
behuda a. बेहूदा nonsensical
behudaa a. बेहूदा ridiculous
bekar a. बेकार idle
bekar ghumna v.t. बेकार घूमना saunter
belan n बेलन cylinder
belan charkha v.t. बेलन चरखा windlass
belanakar a. बेलनाकार round
belcha n. बेलचा shovel
belche se hataana v.t. बेलचे से हटाना
   shovel
bell n बैल bullock
belle nritya sn. बैले नृत्य ballet
belnakar n. बेलनाकार roll
be-mail sambandh n. बेमेल संबंध
   misalliance
bemari n. बीमारी malady
bent n. बेंत cane
bent se marna v. t. बेंत से मारना cane
berhi n. बेड़ी shackle
berhi dalna v.t. बेड़ी डालना shackle
betaar ka a. बेतार का wireless
bhaag n भाग portion
bhaala n. भाला javelin
bhaala n. भाला spear
bhaale se bindhane v.t. भाले से बींधना
   spear
bhaap n भाप steam
bhaap chhorna v.i. भाप छोड़ना steam
bhaavaanuvaad n. भावानुवाद paraphrase
bhaavuk a. भावुक sentimental
bhaavukta n. भावुकता sentiment
bhada n. भाड़ा freight
bhada n. भाड़ा hire

bhadda a. भद्दा, uncouth
bhadda a. भद्दा ungainly
bhadda a. भद्दा vulgar
bhadra a. भद्र gentle
bhadrapurush n. भद्रपुरुष gentleman
bhag n. भाग segment
bhag n. भाग share
bhag lena v.i. भाग लेना partake
bhag lene wala n. भाग लेने वाला
   participant
bhagdarh n. भगदड़ stampede
bhagdarh karna v.t. भगदड़ करना rout
bhagdarh machna v.i भगदड़ मचना
   stampede
bhaginivat a. भगिनीवत् sisterly
bhagorha n. भगोड़ा fugitive
bhagphal n. भागफल quotient
bhagwan n. भगवान god
bhagya n भाग्य fate
bhagya n. भाग्य lot
bhagya n. भाग्य luck
bhagya ka pher n. भाग्य का फेर
   vicissitude
bhagyasali a. भाग्यशाली fortunate
bhahar fekhna v.i. बाहर फेकना ooze
bhai n भाई brother
bhai n. भय fright
bhai ka a. भाई का fraternal
bhai/bahin ki hatya n. भाई/बहिन की हत्या
   fratricide
bhai-bhatijavad n. भाई-भतीजावाद
   nepotism
bhaichara n. भाईचारा confraternity
bhainsa n. भैंसा buffalo
bhajan n भजन anthem
bhajan n भजन chant
bhakosana n. भकोसना gobble
bhakti n. भक्ति piety
bhala n. भाला lance
bhala changa a. भला चंगा hale
bhale ki nok n. भाले की नोक spearhead

bhali bhanti *adv.* भली भांति well
bhalmansi *n.* भलमन्सी complaisance
bhalu *n* भालू bear
bhandaar *n* भंडार supply
bhandar *n.* भण्डार ambry
bhandar *n.* भंडार provision
bhandar *n.* भंडार treasure
bhandar greh *n.* भंडार गृह repository
bhandaran *v.t.* भंडारण stock
bhandaran *n.* भंडारण storage
bhandarghar *n.* भंडारघर pantry
bhang karna *v. t* भंग करना disrupt
bhang karna *v.t.* भंग करना outrage
bhang karna *v.t.* भंग करना violate
bhangh *n.* भांग hemp
bhangur *a.* भंगुर fragile
bhanjan *n* भंजन break
bhanji *n.* भांजी niece
bhanwar *n.* भंवर whirlpool
bhap banana *v. i* भाप बनाना evaporate
bhara hua *a.* भरा हुआ fraught
bharasht karna *v.t.* भ्रष्ट करना infect
bharatiya *a.* भारतीय Indian
bharha *n* भाड़ा fare
bharhak *n* भड़क flare
bharhak *v.t* चमकाना flash
bharhkava *n.* भड़कावा instigation
bhari *a* भारी bulky
bhari *a.* भारी deep
bhari *a.* भारी hefty
bhari *a.* भारी massy
bhari *a.* भारी onerous
bhari *a.* भारी weighty
bhari bhul *n* भारी भूल blunder
bhari bhul karna *v.i* भारी भूल करना
   blunder
bhari golabari *n.* भारी गोलाबारी barrage
bhari prahar *n* भारी प्रहार smash
bhari varsha *n* भारी वर्षा downpour
bharmar hona *v.t.* भरमार होना glut
bharosa *n.* भरोसा reliance

bharosa karna *v. i.* भरोसा करना depend
bharosa rakhna *v. t* भरोसा रखना believe
bharose ka *a.* भरोसे का trustworthy
bharpoor *a.* भरपूर opulent
bharpoor *a.* भरपूर superabundant
bharpur *a.* भरपूर full
bharpur *a.* भरपूर replete
bhartasana *n.* भर्त्सना denunciation
bharti karna *v. t* भरती करना enrol
bharti karne wala *n* भरती करने वाला
   crimp
bhasa vigyan *n.* भाषा विज्ञान linguistics
bhasan kala *n.* भाषणकला oratory
bhasha *n.* भाषा language
bhasha sambandhi *a.* भाषा संबंधी
   linguistic
bhashan *n.* भाषण oration
bhashan dena *v* भाषण देना lecture
bhashan sambandhi *a.* भाषण संबंधी
   oratorical
bhashan shailee *n* भाषण शैली delivery
bhashanpatu *a* भाषणपटु eloquent
bhashashastriya *a.* भाषाशास्त्रीय
   philological
bhashavid *n.* भाषाविद् linguist
bhashavid *n.* भाषाविद् philologist
bhashavigyan *n.* भाषाविज्ञान philology
bhashyakar *n* भाष्यकार commentator
bhasviya lavan *n.* भास्वीय लवण
   phosphate
bhata *n* भाटा ebb
bhatak jana *v.i.* भटक जाना straggle
bhatija ya bhanja *n.* भतीजा या भांजा
   nephew
bhatkaiya *n.* भटकैया straggler
bhatkana *v. i* भटकना deviate
bhatta *n.* भट्टा kiln
bhatti *n* भट्टी distillery
bhauchakka *adv.* भौचक्का aback
bhaugolik *a.* भौगोलिक geographical
bhauhain charhana *v.i* भौहें चढ़ाना frown

bhaun bhaun *n* भौं भौं yap

bhaun bhaun karna *v.i.* भौं भौं करना yap

bhaunh *n* भौंह brow

bhaunkna *v.t.* भौंकना bark

bhaupun *n.* भोंपू siren

bhautik *a.* भौतिक material

bhautik vigyan *n.* भौतिक विज्ञान physics

bhautikshastri *n.* भौतिकशास्त्री physicist

bhavan *n* भवन edifice

bhavan khand *n* भवन खंड flat

bhavan samuh *n* भवन समूह complex

bhavavesh *n* भावावेश emotion

bhavi *a.* भावी future

bhavi *a.* भावी prospective

bhavi sambhavana *n.* भावी संभावना outlook

bhavishvani *n.* भविष्यवाणी prediction

bhavishvani karna *v.t.* भविष्यवाणी करना predict

bhavishya *n* भविष्य future

bhavishyakathan *n.* भविष्यकथन prophecy

bhavishyavani karna *v.t* भविष्यवाणी करना foretell

bhavuk *a* भावुक emotional

bhavya *n* भव्य august

bhavya *a.* भव्य spectacular

bhavya *a.* भव्य stately

bhavyata *n.* भव्यता splendour

bhawan jaisa *a.* भवन जैसा palatial

bhawan ke andar *adv.* भवन के अंदर indoors

bhay *n.* भय horror

bhay se peela parh jana *v. t. & i* भय से पीला पड़ जाना blanch

bhayabhit karna *v. t* भयभीत करना daunt

bhayabhit karna *v.t.* भयभीत करना frighten

bhayabhit karna *v.t.* भयभीत करना horrify

bhayanak *a* भयानक dire

bhayanak *a.* भयानक fearful

bhayanak *a.* भयानक ghastly

bhayankar *a.* भयंकर atrocious

bhayankar *a* भयंकर deadly

bhayankar *a.* भयंकर hideous

bhayavah *n* बहावाय dread

bhaybhit karna *v. t.* भयभीत करना bully

bhaybhit karna *v.t.* भयभीत करना intimidate

bhaybhith *a.* भयभीत afraid

bhaye *n* भय fear

bhed karna *v. t.* भेद करना discriminate

bhed khol dena *v. t. & i* भेद खोल देना blab

bheekh mangte phirna *v. i* भीख माँगते फिरना cadge

bheerh *n.* भीड़ throng

bheerh lagana *v.i.* भीड़ लगाना swarm

bheerh se dar lagna *n.* भीड़ से डर लगना agoraphobia

bheeru *a.* भीरु timorous

bheeruta *n.* भीरुता timidity

bheeshan *a.* भीषण horrible

bhejana *v.t.* भेजना refer

bhejana *v.t.* भेजना send

bhejna *v.t.* भेजना consign

bhek *n.* भेक toad

bhenga hona *v.i.* भेंगा होना squint

bhengapan *n* भेंगापन squint

bhera *n.* भेड़ा ram

bherh *n* भेड़ ewe

bherh *n.* भेड़ sheep

bherh mundana *v.t.* भेड़ मूंडना shear

bherhiya *n.* भेड़िया wolf

bhidhna *v.i.* भिड़ना grapple

bhigona *v.t.* भिगोना soak

bhikhari *n* भिखारी beggar

bhiksha *n.* भिक्षा alms

bhikshuni *n.* भिक्षुणी nun

bhimkaya *a.* भीमकाय gigantic

bhinbhinahat *n.* भिनभिनाहट buzz

bhinbhinahat *n.* भिनभिनाहट whir
bhinn *prep* भिन्न unlike
bhinn *a* भिन्न different
bhinn prakar se *adv.* भिन्न प्रकार से
    otherwise
bhinsa, *n.* भिंसा, willow
bhirh *n.* भीड़ horde
bhirh *n.* भिड़ hornet
bhirhant *n* भिंड़त collision
bhirhant *n.* भिंड़त encounter
bhirhna *v. i.* भिड़ना collide
bhirhna *v.t.* भिड़ना tackle
bhishuni ka math *n.* भिक्षुणियों का मठ
    nunnery
bhitari *a.* भीतरी internal
bhitari chat *n.* भीतरी छत ceiling
bhitiya *n* भीतिया parietal
bhitri *a.* भीतरी indoor
bhitri *a.* भीतरी intrinsic
bhitri bhag *n.* भीतरी भाग inside
bhitri bhag *n.* भीतरी भाग within
bhitri hissa *n.* भीतरी हिस्सा core
bhitri tvacha *n.* भीतरी त्वचा cutis
bhittichitra *n.* भित्तिचित्र mural
bhittiya *a.* भित्तीय mural
bhogpurna *a.* भोगपूर्ण voluptuous
bhogwadi *n.* भोगवादी sensualist
bhojan *n* भोजन boarding
bhojan *n* भोजन diet
bhojan *n* भोजन dinner
bhojan *n* भोजन feed
bhojan *n* भोजन food
bhojan *n.* भोजन nurture
bhojan dena *v.t* भोजन देना feed
bhojan ka samay *n.* भोजन का समय meal
bhojan karna *v. t.* भोजन करना dine
bhojan karna *v.i.* भोजन करना lunch
bhojan karna *v.i* भोजन करना mess
bhojanalaya *n.* भोजनालय restaurant
bhojan-mez ki chadar *n.* भोजन- मेज की
    चादर napery

bhojaya suchi *n.* भोज्य सूची menu
bhojha *n* बोझा burden
bhojhil *a.* बोझिल irksome
bhojhil *a.* बोझिल leaden
bhojnaalya *n.* भोजनालय mess
bhojpatra *n.* भोजपत्र birch
bhojya *a* भोज्य edible
bhola *n.* भोला naivete
bhola pan *n.* भोला-पन naivety
bhola-bhala *a.* भोला-भाला naive
bholbhulaya *n.* भूलभुलैया maze
bhonda *a.* भोंडा grotesque
bhool *n* भूल lapse
bhool *n.* भूल omission
bhoora *a* भूरा brown
bhoora hona *v.i.* भूरा होना tan
bhoora rang *n* भूरा रंग brown
bhoot *n.* भूत ghost
bhoot *n.* भूत poltergeist
bhootkal ki aur *adv.* भूतकाल की ओर
    backward
bhoul *n.* भूल mistake
bhram mein dalna *v.t.* भ्रम में डालना
    muddle
bhramaatmak *a* भ्रमात्मक equivocal
bhraman *n* भ्रमण walk
bhraman karna *v.i.* भ्रमण करना tour
bhraman, yatra *n.* भ्रमण, यात्रा tour
bhramit karna *v.t.* भ्रमित करना mystify
bhrant dharna *n.* भ्रांत धारणा misbelief
bhranti *n* भ्रांति fallacy
bhrasht *a.* भ्रष्ट venal
bhrasht karna *v. t.* भ्रष्ट करना debauch
bhrashtachaar *n.* भ्रष्टाचार jobbery
bhrashtata *n.* भ्रष्टता venality
bhrasthtachar *n.* भ्रष्टाचार corruption
bhratrisangh *n.* भ्रातृसंघ fraternity
bhratritva *n* भ्रातृत्व brotherhood
bhring *n* भृंग beetle
bhroon *n* भ्रूण embryo
bhrubhang *n.* भ्रूभंग scowl

bhu sampati *n* भूसंपत्ति estate
bhubhaag *n.* भूभाग region
bhu-bhag *n.* भू-भाग area
bhugatna *v.t.* भुगतना suffer
bhugol *n.* भूगोल geography
bhugolveta *n.* भूगोलवेत्ता geographer
bhugtan *n.* भुगतान payment
bhugtan dena *v.t.* भुगतान देना pay
bhugtan yogya *a.* भुगतान योग payable
bhuja *n.* भुजा arm
bhukamp *n* भूकंप earthquake
bhukamp sambandhi *a.* भूकंप संबंधी
  seismic
bhukarh aadmi *n.* भुक्खड़ आदमी
  cormorant
bhukh *n.* भूख appetite
bhukh *n* भूख hunger
bhukha *a.* भूखा hungry
bhu-khand *n.* भू-खण्ड plot
bhukhmari *n.* भूखमरी starvation
bhukhon marna *v.i.* भूखों मरना starve
bhukri *n* भुक्रि must
bhul *n* भूल error
bhul jana *v.t* भूल जाना forget
bhul karna *v. i* भूल करना err
bhulakaarh *a* भुलक्कड़ forgetful
bhulbhul *n.* बुलबुल nightingale
bhumi *n.* भूमि land
bhumigat *a.* भूमिगत subterranean
bhumika *n* भूमिका foreword
bhumika *n.* भूमिका preamble
bhumika *n.* भूमिका prologue
bhumika *n.* भूमिका role
bhumika lekhna *v.t.* भूमिका लिखना
  preface
bhumi-sambandhi *a.* भूमि-संबंधी agrarian
bhumisat karna *v.t.* भूमिसात करना raze
bhuna hua *a* भुना हुआ roast
bhuna hua maans *n* भुना हुआ मांस roast
bhunana *v.t.* भूनना roast
bhura *a.* भूरा grey

bhura koyala *n.* भूरा कोयला lignite
bhura lal rang *n.* भूरा लाल रंग maroon
bhure lal rang ka *a* भूरे लाल रंग का
  maroon
bhurta bana dena *v.t.* भुर्ता बना देना
  squash
bhusa *n.* भूसा straw
bhusi *n.* भूसी husk
bhutpurva kaal *n.* भूतपूर्व काल past
bhuvigyan *n.* भूविज्ञान geology
bhuvigyan vetta *n.* भूविज्ञान वेत्ता
  geologist
bhuvigyaniya *a.* भूविज्ञानीय geological
bhvya *a.* भव्य gorgeous
bhyabhit hona *v.t* भयभीत होना dread
bichchu *n.* बिच्छू scorpion
bichhu buti *n.* बिच्छू बूटी nettle
bicycle *n.* बाइसिकिल bicycle
bidakna *v.i.* बिदकना shy
bigarana *v.t.* बिगाड़ना ruin
bigarh jana *v.t.* बिगड़ जाना spoil
bigarhana *v.t.* बिगाड़ना aggravate
bigarhana *v. t* बिगाड़ना bungle
bigarhana *v.t.* बिगाड़ना worsen
bigarhna *v.t.* बिगाड़ना vitiate
bigul *n* बिगुल bugle
bigul ka nad *n.* बिगुल का नाद tattoo
biharh *n.* बीहड़, wilderness
bijak *n.* बीजक invoice
bijju *n.* बिज्जू badger
bijkosh sambandhi *adj* बीजकोष सम्बन्धी
  capsular
bijli ka taar *n.* बिजली के तार wiring
bikherna *v.t.* बिखेरना strew
bikri *n.* बिक्री sale
bilav *n.* बिलाव tomcat
bilkul *adv.* बिलकुल quite
bilkul *a.* बिल्कुल very
bilkul nahin *adv.* बिल्कुल नहीं nothing
bill *n* बिल burrow
bill, prapayak *n* बिल, प्रपायक bill

**billa** *n.* बिल्ला badge
**billi** *n.* बिल्ली cat
**billi ka baccha** *n.* बिल्ली का बच्चा kitten
**bilona** *v. t. & i.* बिलोना churn
**bima** *n.* बीमा insurance
**bima karna** *v.t.* बीमा करना assure
**bima shulk** *n.* बीमा शुल्क premium
**bimar** *a.* बीमार ill
**bimar** *a.* बीमार morbid
**bimari** *n* बीमारी disease
**bimari** *n.* बीमारी sickness
**bimari ka daura** *n* बीमारी का दौरा bout
**bimb vidhan** *n.* बिंब विधान imagery
**bina dhuain ka barud** *n.* बिना धुऐं का बारूद amberite
**bina rang ka** *adj* बिना रंग का achromatic
**bina ruke janewala** *a* बिना रुके जानेवाला through
**bina sir ka** *adj.* बिना सिर का acephalous
**bina taar ka yantr** *n.* बिना तार का यंत्र radio
**bindu** *n* बिंदु dot
**bindu** *n.* बिंदु point
**bindu lagana** *v. t* बिंदु लगाना dot
**biscuit** *n* बिस्कुट biscuit
**bishap** *n* बिशप bishop
**bistar par** *adv.* बिस्तर पर abed
**bitth prabandhak** *n* वित्त प्रबंधक financier
**blouse** *n* ब्लाउज़ blouse
**bodh** *n.* बोध perception
**bojh utarna** *v.t.* बोझ उतारना unburden
**bol-chaal** *n.* बोल-चाल parlance
**bolchal ki bhasha** *n.* बोलचाल की भाषा slang
**boli** *n.* बोली utterance
**bolna** *v.t.* बोलना converse
**bolna** *v.t.* बोलना read
**bolna** *v.t.* बोलना say
**bolna** *v.i.* बोलना speak
**bolna** *v.i.* बोलना talk

**bona** *n.* बौना midget
**bona** *v.t.* बोना seed
**bonnet** *n* बोनिट bonnet
**bonus** *n* बोनस bonus
**bookni karna** *v.t.* बुकनी करना powder
**boond** *n* बूंद drop
**bori** *n.* बोरी sack
**botal** *n* बोतल bottle
**bouddh bhikshu** *n.* बौध- भिक्षु lama
**brandi** *n* ब्रांडी brandy
**break** *n* ब्रेक brake
**break lagana** *v. t* ब्रेक लगाना brake
**brehaspati grah** *n.* बृहस्पति ग्रह Jupiter
**brigadier** *n* ब्रिगेडियर brigadier
**british mudra** *n.* ब्रिटिश मुद्रा shilling
**british mudra** *n.* ब्रिटिश मुद्रा sterling
**budbudana** *v.i.* बुदबुदाना mumble
**buddhi ki prakharta** *n.* बुद्धि की प्रखरता wit
**buddhihin** *a.* बुद्धिहीन witless
**buddhijivi** *n.* बुद्धिजीवी intellectual
**budhape ki durbalata** *n.* बुढ़ापे की दुर्बलता senility
**budhi tatva** *adv.* बोधी तत्व noumenon
**budhi, man** *n.* बुद्धि, मन mind
**budhihin karna** *v. t* बुद्धिहीन करना bemuse
**budhijiwi varg** *n.* बुद्धिजीवी वर्ग intelligentsia
**budhimaan** *a.* बुद्धिमान्न intelligent
**budhiman** *a.* बुद्धिमान sage
**budhiman** *a.* समझदार wise
**budhu** *n.* बुद्धू simpleton
**budhvar** *n.* बुधवार Wednesday
**bujha hua** *a* बुझा हुआ extinct
**bukhar** *n* बुखार ague
**bula bhejna** *v.t.* बुला भेजना summon
**bulana** *v.* बुलाना calling
**bulbula** *n* बुलबुला bubble
**bunana** *v.t.* बुनना weave

**buniyaad rakhna** *v.t.* बुनियाद रखना found

**buniyadi** *a.* बुनियादी basic

**bunkar** *n.* बुनकर weaver

**bunna** *v.t.* बुनना knit

**buool chook** *v.i.* भूल चूक lapse

**bura** *a.* बुरा bad

**bura manana** *v.t.* बुरा मानना mind

**bura manana** *v.t.* बुरा मानना resent

**bura vaywahar** *n.* बुरा व्यवहार misbehaviour

**bura vaywahar karna** *v.i.* बुरा व्यवहार करना misbehave

**bure prakar se** *adv.* बुरे प्रकार से badly

**burma,burmi** *n.* बरमा, बरमी wimble

**bus** *n* बस bus

**byaj** *adj* ब्याज interest

**byora dena** *v.t.* ब्योरा देना recount

# C

**cafighar** *n.* काफीघर cafe

**cake** *n.* केक cake

**camera** *n.* कैमरा camera

**cancer** *n.* कैंसर cancer

**car** *n* कार motor

**carbon** *n.* कार्बन carbon

**cartoon** *n.* कार्टून cartoon

**cartoos** *n.* कारतूस cartridge

**cassette** *n.* कैसिट cassette

**cement** *n.* सीमेंट cement

**chaal** *n* चाल pace

**chaal** *n.* चाल ruse

**chaal** *n.* चाल stratagem

**chaal** *n.* चाल wile

**chaal rachna** *n* छल रचना fabrication

**chaala** *n* छाला blain

**chaalaak** *a.* चालाक shrewd

**chaalak** *n* चालक driver

**chaal-dhaal** *n.* चाल gait

**chaanta** *n.* चांटा slap

**chaanta marna** *v.t.* चांटा मारना smack

**chaaplusi karna** *v.t* चापलूसी करना flatter

**chaar** *n.* चार four

**chaar bhuja ki** *a. & n.* चार भुजा की quadrilateral

**chaaron aur** *prep.* चारों ओर around

**chaati** *n* छाती bosom

**chabana** *v. t* चबाना chew

**chabana** *v.t.* चबाना masticate

**chabana** *v.t.* चबाना munch

**chabi bharne ka yantr** *n.* चाबी भरने का यंत्र winder

**chabi se band karna** *v.t* चाबी से बंद करना key

**chabuk** *n.* चाबुक welt

**chabuk ki dori** *n.* चाबुक की डोरी whipcord

**chabutara** *n.* चबूतरा terrace

**chacha** *n.* चाचा uncle

**chachi** *n.* चाची aunt

**chadai karna** *v.i* चड़ाई करना climb

**chadar dalna** *v.t.* चादर डालना sheet

**chadhayee** *n.* चढ़ाई ascent

**chadhayee** *n.* चढ़ाई climb

**chadi** *n* छड़ी baton

**chadramavesh** *n* छद्मवेश disguise

**chahak** *n.* चहक twitter

**chahakna** *v.i.* चहकना twitter

**chahana** *v.t.* चाहना wish

**chahbachcha** *n* चहबच्चा sink

**chahe jaise** *adv.* चाहे जैसे however

**chahnewala** *a* चाहनेवाला fond

**chai** *n* चाय tea

**chaihara** *n* चेहरा face

**chaila** *n* छैला dandy

**chaila** *n.* छैला spark

**chain se baithna** *v.i.* चैन से बैठना nestle

**chaine** *n* छेनी chisel

**chaine se katna** *v. t.* छेनी से काटना chisel

**chaitavani** *n.* चेतावनी caution

**chaitavani dena** *v. t.* चेतावनी देना caution

chajja *n.* छज्जा balcony
chakachaundh *n* चकाचौंध dazzle
chakachaundh karna *v. t.* चकाचौंध करना dazzle
chakati *n.* चकती disc
chakbandi *n* चकबंदी consolidation
chakit karna *v.t* चकित करना astound
chakkar *n.* चक्कर revolution
chakkar khana *v.i.* चक्कर खाना revolve
chakkar khana *v.i.* चक्कर खाना roll
chakkar khana *v.i.* चक्कर खाना rotate
chakkar lagana *v.i.* चक्कर लगाना meander
chakma *n* चकमा dodge
chakma *n.* चकमा hoax
chakma dena *v. t* चकमा देना dodge
chakma dena *v.t* चकमा देना hoax
chakotara *n.* चकोतरा lime
chakralekhitra *n* चक्रलेखित्र cyclostyle
chakralipit karna *v. t* चक्रलिपित करना cyclostyle
chakran *n.* चक्रण spin
chakranabhi *n.* चक्रनाभि nave
chakrane wala *a.* चकराने वाला giddy
chakravat,bagula *n.* चक्रवात, बगूला whirlwind
chakrawat *n.* चक्रवात cyclone
chakrha *n.* छकड़ा cart
chakriya *a* चक्रीय cyclic
chaku *n.* चाकू knife
chalaak *a* चालाक elusive
chalaak *n.* चालाक serpentine
chalaane yogya *a.* चलने योग्य movable
chalak *a.* चालाक artful
chalak *a* चालाक crafty
chalak *a* चालाक cunning
chalak *a.* चालाक tricky
chalak *a.* धूर्त, चालाक wily
chalaki *n* चालाकी craft
chalaki *n* चालाकी cunning
chalaki *n.* चालाकी manoeuvre

chalaki karana *v.i.* चालाकी कराना manoeuvre
chalakna *v.i.* छलकना spill
chalang *n.* छलांग jump
chalang *n.* छलांग sally
chalchitra *n* चलचित्र film
chalchitra *n.* चलचित्र movies
chalis *n.* चालीस forty
chalna *v.i.* चलना pace
chalna *v.i.* चलना step
chalna *v.i.* चलना walk
chalni *n.* छलनी sieve
chalu halat mein *a.* चालू हालत में serviceable
chalu karna *v.t.* चालू करना operate
chalu na hona *v.i.* चालू न होना misfire
chamak *n* चमक blaze
chamak *n* चमक brilliance
chamak *n.* चमक glare
chamak *n* चमक glaze
chamak *n* चमक glitter
chamak *n.* चमक lucidity
chamak *n.* चमक lustre
chamak *n* चमक polish
chamak *n.* चमक radiance
chamak *n.* चमक refulgence
chamak *n.* चमक scintillation
chamak *n* चमक shine
chamak *n.* चमक sparkle
chamakana *v. i* चमकना beam
chamakdaar *a* चमकदार bright
chamakdar *a.* चमकदार glossy
chamakdar *a.* चमकदार lucent
chamakdar *a.* चमकदार lucid
chamakdar *a.* चमकदार lustrous
chamakdar *a.* चमकदार shiny
chamakdar *a.* चमकदार vivid
chamakeea *a.* चमकीला radiant
chamakna *v.i.* चमकना scintillate
chamakna *v.i.* चमकना shine
chamakna *v.i.* चमकना spark

chamakna *v.i.* चमकना sparkle
chamakna *v.i.* झिलमिलाना, चमकना
 twinkle
chamakta hua *adv.* चमकता हुआ aglow
chamatkaar *n.* चमत्कार miracle
chamatkarik *a.* चमत्कारिक miraculous
chamchamana *v.i.* चमचमाना glitter
chamda *n.* चमड़ा hide
chameli *n.* चमेली jasmine
chamgaadharh *n* चमगादड़ bat
chamkana *v.t.* चमकाना polish
chamkana *v. t* चमकाना brighten
chamkana *v.t.* चमकाना gild
chamkana *v.i* चमकना glare
chamkana *v.i.* चमकना glow
chamkana *v.t.* चमकाना kindle
chamkeela *a.* चमकीला meteoric
chammach *n.* चम्मच spoon
chammach bhar *n.* चम्मच भर spoonful
chamrha *n.* चमड़ा leather
chan been *n* छान बीन rummage
chana *n* छन्ना filter
chanana *v.t.* छानना sieve
chanchal *a* चंचल fickle
chanchal *a.* चंचल mercurial
chanda *n.* चंदा subscription
chandan *n.* चंदन sandalwood
chandi *n.i.* चांदी silver
chandi chadhana *v.t.* चांदी चढ़ाना silver
chandmari *n.* चांदमारी range
chandrama *n.* चंद्रमा moon
changul *n* चंगुल clutch
channa *v.t* छनना filter
chantana *v.t.* छांटना trim
chap *n.* चाप arc
chapa *n.* छापा raid
chapal *a.* चपल active
chapal *adj* चपल brisk
chapal *a.* चपल nimble
chapalta *n.* चपलता activity
chapalta *n.* चपलता agility

chaploos *n.* चापलूस minion
chaplus *n.* चापलूस sycophant
chaplusi *n* चापलूसी adulation
chaplusi *n* चापलूसी flattery
chaplusi *n.* चाटुकारिता, चापलूसी
 sycophancy
chaplusi karna *v. i.* चापलूसी करना cringe
chappal *n.* चप्पल sandal
chappar *n* छप्पर shed
chappar *n.* छप्पर thatch
chappar dalna *v.t.* छप्पर डालना thatch
chaprasi *n.* चपरासी peon
char bhag karna *v.t.* चार भाग करना
 quarter
chara *n* चारा fodder
chara *n.* चारा pasture
charagaha *n.* चारागाह meadow
charam bindu *n.* चरम बिंदु zenith
charan *n.* चरण phase
charbi *n* चर्बी fat
charbi *n.* चरबी tallow
charcha karna *v.t.* चर्चा करना mention
charhi *n.* छड़ी wand
charitra *n.* चरित्र character
charmarahat *n* चरमराहट creak
charmarana *v. i* चरमराना creak
charmotkarsh *n.* चरमोत्कर्ष omega
charna *v.i.* चरना graze
charna *v.t.* चरना pasture
charni *n.* चरनी crib
charon aur rahne wala *adj.* चारों ओर रहने
 वाला ambient
charon or *adv.* चारों ओर round
charpai *n* चारपाई bed
charwaha *n.* चरवाहा herdsman
chashma *n.* चश्मा spectacle
chashma, ainak *n* चश्मा, ऐनक monocle
chashme ke nirmatta *n.* चश्मे का निर्माता
 optician
chat *n.* छत roof
chat se patna *v.t.* छत से पाटना roof

**chata** *a.* छठा sixth
**chata** *n.* छाता umbrella
**chatna** *v.t.* छांटना lop
**chatne ki kriya** *n* चाटने की क्रिया lick
**chatni** *n.* चटनी ketchup
**chatni** *n.* चटनी sauce
**chatpatana** *v.i.* छटपटाना writhe
**chatravrati** *n.* छात्रवृत्ति scholarship
**chatrawas** *n.* छात्रावास hostel
**chattai** *n.* चटाई mat
**chattan** *n.* चट्टान rock
**chatukari karna** *v. t* चाटुकारी करना beslaver
**chatur** *a.* चतुर clever
**chaturayee** *n.* चतुराई sagacity
**chaturdash-padi** *n.* चतुर्दश-पदी sonnet
**chatushkoniya** *a.* चतुष्कोणीय quadrangular
**chaudah** *n.* चौदह fourteen
**chauguna** *a.* चौगुना quadruple
**chauguna karna** *v.t.* चौगुना करना quadruple
**chaukas rehna** *v.i.* चौकस रहना beware
**chaukasi** *n.* चौकसी precaution
**chaukasi** *n.* चौकसी watch
**chaukor angan** *n.* चौकोर आंगन quadrangle
**chaunkana** *v.t.* चौंकाना startle
**chaupaya** *n.* चौपाया quadruped
**chaura karna** *v.t.* चौड़ा करना widen
**chauraha** *n.* चौराहा crossing
**chauras** *a.* चौरस plane
**chauras banana** *vt* चौरस बनाना plane
**chaurha** *a* चौड़ा broad
**chaurha** *a.* चौड़ा wide
**chaurha karna ya hona** *v. t. & i* चौड़ा करना या होना broaden
**chaurhayee** *n* चौड़ाई breadth
**chaurhayi** *n.* चौड़ाई width
**chaya** *n.* छाया shade
**chayadaar** *a.* छायादार shadowy

**chayan** *n.* चयन selection
**chayan karna** *v.i.* चयन करना opt
**chayan yogya** *a.* चयन योग्य selective
**chayanika** *n.* चयनिका anthology
**chayaprati** *n.* छायाप्रति xerox
**chayit karana** *v.t.* छायित करना shade
**chechak** *n.* चेचक smallpox
**ched** *n* छेद bore
**ched** *n* छेद hole
**ched** *n.* छेद hollow
**ched** *n.* छेद vent
**ched karna** *v. t.* छेद करना drill
**ched mein dalna** *v.t* छेद में डालना hole
**chedna** *v. t* छेदना bore
**cheekh** *n* चीख howl
**cheekh** *n* चीख scream
**cheekh** *n.* चीख shout
**cheekh** *n.* चीख shriek
**cheekhna** *v.i.* चीखना scream
**cheekhna** *v.i.* चीखना shriek
**cheeni** *n.* चीनी, शक्कर sugar
**cheenk** *n* छींक sneeze
**cheenkana** *v.i.* छींकना sneeze
**cheer dena** *v.t.* चीर देना slash
**cheera** *n* चीरा slash
**cheera** *n.* चीरा tear
**cheerna** *v.i.* चीरना split
**cheh** *n., a* छः six
**chehra** *n.* चेहरा visage
**cheque** *n.* चेक cheque
**chetana** *v.t.* चेताना admonish
**chetana** *n.* चेतना sentience
**chetavani** *n.* चेतावनी admonition
**chetavani** *n* चेतावनी alarm
**chhaal** *n.* छाल bark
**chhaapna** *v.t.* छापना imprint
**chhaati** *n* छाती breast
**chhachhuchhandar** *n.* छछूंदर mole
**chhadram** *n.* छद्मनाम pseudonym
**chhal** *n.* छाल crust
**chhal** *n* छल elusion

chhal *n.* चाल move
chhal kapat *n.* छल कपट guile
chhal sadhan *n.* छल साधन manipulation
chhal sampati *n.* चल संपत्ति movables
chhan *n.* क्षण moment
chhand sambandhi *a.* छंद संबंधी metrical
chhandshastra *n.* छंदशास्त्र prosody
chhanik *a.* क्षणिक momentary
chhantai karna *v.t.* छंटाई करना prune
chhapai ki machine *n* छपाई की मशीन press
chhapa-maar sainik *n.* छापामार सैनिक guerrilla
chhar *n.* छड़ rod
chhati *n* छाती chest
chhati pahuchna *v.t.* क्षति पहुंचाना mar
chhatri *n.* छतरी canopy
chhavani *n.* छावनी cantonment
chhavichitra *n.* छविचित्र portrait
chhaya chitra *n* छाया चित्र photograph
chhed karna *v.t.* छेद करना perforate
chhedan *n.* छेदन puncture
chhedna *v.t.* छेदना pierce
chhedna *v.t.* चिढ़ाना provoke
chheenana *v.t.* छीनना seize
chheenana *v.t.* छीनना snatch
chheenanaa *v.t.* छीलना whittle
chher-khani *n.* छेड़खानी molestation
chhichhora *a.* छिछोरा frivolous
chhidchhida *a.* चिड़चिड़ा irritable
chhidra *n.* छिद्र aperture
chhilka *n.* छिल्का peel
chhilka *n.* छिलका shell
chhilke daar *a.* छिलकेदार husky
chhinti *n* चींटी ant
chhipa hua *adj.* छिपा हुआ clandestine
chhipaana *v.t.* छिपाना obscure
chhipaav *n.* छिपाव reservation
chhipana *v.t* छिपाना hide
chhipkali *n.* छिपकली lizard
chhirakana *v. t.* छिड़कना sprinkle

chhitarana *v. t* छितराना disperse
chhod dena *v.t.* छोड़ देना omit
chhod dena *v.t.* छोड़ देना waive
chhoot *n* छूट concession
chhoot *n* छूट discount
chhoot *n.* छूट latitude
chhora hua *adj* छोड़ा हुआ left
chhota *a.* छोटा little
chhota *a.* छोटा minor
chhota *a.* छोटा petty
chhota baccha *n.* छोटा बच्चा kid
chhota chappu *n* छोटा चापू paddle
chhota ghoda *n.* छोटा घोड़ा pony
chhota karna *vt* छोटा करना minify
chhota parcel *n.* छोटा पार्सल packet
chhota phatak *n.* छोटा फाटक wicket
chhota taaj *n.* छोटा ताज coronet
chhota talab *n.* छोटा तालाब pond
chhota va durlabh *a.* छोटा व दुर्लभ puny
chhota viman *n.* छोटा विमान glider
chhoti bottle *n.* छोटी बोतल phial
chhoti pustak *n* छोटी पुस्तक brochure
chhoti vastu *n.* छोटी वस्तु mite
chhundha *n.* चुंधा purblind
chhunkana *v.t.* छुंकना fry
chhup *a.* चुप mum
chhupi *n* चुप्पी mum
chhurika *a.* छुरिका lancet
chhutkara *n.* छुटकारा manumission
chichalapan *n.* छिछलापन superficiality
chichorapan *n* छिछोरापन flippancy
chichorapan *n.* छिछोरापन levity
chidakana *v.t.* छिड़कना spray
chidchidapan *n.* चिड़चिड़ापन fret
chiddh, gussa *n.* चिढ़, गुस्सा annoyance
chiddhana *v.t.* चिढ़ाना annoy
chidh *n.* चिढ़ allergy
chidhana *v.t.* चिढ़ाना ruffle
chidhana *v.t.* चिढ़ाना tease
chidka jana *v.i.* छिड़का जाना splash
chikh *a.* चीख outcry

chikitsa *n.* चिकित्सा therapy
chikitsak *n* चिकित्सक doctor
chikitsak *n.* चिकित्सक medico
chikitsalaya *n.* चिकित्सालय clinic
chikitsalaya *n.* चिकित्सालय hospital
chikna *a.* चिकना greasy
chikna *a.* चिकना oily
chikna *a.* चिकना sleek
chikna *a* चिकना slick
chikna *a.* चिकना smooth
chikna karna *v.t* चिकना करना grease
chikna karna *v.t.* चिकना करना smooth
chiknai *n* चिकनायी grease
chiknai *n.* चिकनाई lubricant
chiknana *v.t.* चिकनाना lubricate
chikni mitti *n.* चिकनी मिट्टी marl
chikni steh *n* चिकनी slide
chikot *v.* चिकोट pinch
chikoti katna *v.t.* चिकोटी काटना pinch
chiktsak *n.* चिकित्सक homoeopath
chilahat *n* चिल्लाहट whine
chilakar bolna *n.i.* चिल्लाकर बोलना bawl
chilakar bolna *v. t* चिल्लाकर बोलना blare
chilamachi *n.* चिलमची basin
chilana *v.i.* चिल्लाना shout
chilana *v.i.* चिल्लाना yell
chilla kar kahana *v.t.* चिल्लाकर कहना howl
chillakar dhaudna *v. t* चिल्लाकर दौड़ना clutter
chillanaa *v.i* चिल्लाना exclaim
chimni *n.* चिमनी chimney
chimta *n.* चिमटा pincer
chimta *n. pl.* चिमटा tongs
chinar vriksh *n* चिनार वृक्ष poplar
chinchin *n* चींचीं chirp
chinchin karna *v.i.* चींची करना chirp
chingari *n.* चिंगारी spark
chinh, prateek *n.* चिह्न, प्रतीक symbol
chini mitti ke bartan *n.* चीनी के मिट्टी बर्तन porcelain

chinka lagana *v.t* छींका लगाना muzzle
chinna *v.t.* छीनना grab
chinta *a* चिंता anxiety
chinta *n.* चिंता care
chinta *n* चिंता concern
chinta *n.* चिंता solicitude
chinta *n.* चिंता worry
chintagrast *a.* चिंताग्रस्त pensive
chintajanak *a.* चिंताजनक anxious
chintan *n.* चिंतन rumination
chintana *v. t* छींटना bestrew
chintit *a.* चिंतित solicitous
chintit *a.* चिंतित uneasy
chintit hona *v.i.* चिंतित होना worry
chintit karna *v. t* चिंतित करना concern
chintit karna *v.t.* चिंतित करना trouble
chintitkarna *v.t.* चिंतित करना fret
chipa huw *a.* छिपा हुआ secret
chipakane wala *a.* चिपकनेवाला adhesive
chipakna *v.i.* चिपकना adhere
chipana *v. t.* छिपाना conceal
chipana *v.t.* छिपाना secrete
chipchipa *n.* चिपचिपा sticky
chipchipa padarth *n.* चिपचिपा पदार्थ mucilage
chipe rehna *v.i.* छिपे रहना darkle
chipkana *v.t.* चिपकाना affix
chipkane wala padarth *n.* चिपकाने वाला पदार्थ adhesive
chipkav *n.* चिपकाव adhesion
chippi *n.* चिप्पी sticker
chiptana *v. i.* चिपटना cling
chirdhne ka karan *n.* चिढ़ने का कारण provocation
chirhchira *a.* चिड़चिड़ा petulant
chirhchirha *a.* चिड़चिड़ा waspish
chirhiya *n.* चिड़िया shuttlecock
chirhiyakhana *n.* चिड़ियाखाना aviary
chirhkava *n* छिड़काव splash
chirimaar *n.* चिड़ीमार fowler
chiriya *n.* चिड़िया fowl

chirsthayee *a.* चिरस्थायी everlasting

chita *n.* चीता panther

chita *n.* चिता pile

chita *n.* चिता pyre

chithhi *n* चिट्ठी letter

chithrha *n.* चिथड़ा tatter

chithrhe karna *v.t* चिथड़े करना tatter

chitra *n.* चित्र picture

chitradhar *n.* चित्राधार album

chitrakaar *n.* चित्रकार painter

chitrakala *n.* चित्रकला painting

chitra-kala *n.* चित्रकला portraiture

chitrakari ke liye kapda *n.* चित्रकारी के लिए कपड़ा canvas

chitramala *n.* चित्रमाला panorama

chitran *n.* चित्ररण portrayal

chitrankan *n* चित्रांकन drawing

chitrasala *n.* चित्रशाला gallery

chitratmak *a.* चित्रात्मक scenic

chitrit karna *vt* चित्रित करना mottle

chitrit karna *v.t.* चित्रित करना outline

chitrpat *n.* चित्रपट screen

chobhona *v.t.* चुभोना stick

chochlebaz vyakti *n* चोचलेबाज़ व्यक्ति flirt

chocolate *n* चोकोलेट chocolate

chodna *v.t.* छोड़ना quit

chodna *v.t.* छोड़ना renounce

chodna *v.t.* छोड़ना resign

choga *n.* चोग़ा cloak

choga *n.* चोग़ा toga

chokrhi *n.* चौकड़ी gallop

choli *n* चोली bodice

choli *n.* चोली frock

chonch *n* चोंच beak

chonch marna *v.i.* चोंच मारना peck

chook *n.* चूक oversight

chool par ghumana *v.t.* चूल पर घुमाना pivot

choon choon karana *v.i.* चूं चूं करना squeak

chor *n* चोर burglar

chor gaddha *n.* चोर गड्ढा pitfall

chorh dena *v. t* छोड़ देना except

chorhna *v.t.* छोड़ना leave

chori *n* चोरी burglary

chori *n.* चोरी theft

chori *n.* चोर thief

chori chupe *adv.* चोरी छुपे stealthily

chori karna *v.i.* चोरी करना steal

chori se dekhna *v.i.* चोरी से देखना peep

chot *n* चोट bruise

chot *n.* चोट harm

chot *n* चोट hurt

chot pahuchana *v.t.* चोट पहुंचाना hurt

chot pahuchana *v.t* चोट पहुंचाना maul

chot pahunchana *v.t* चोट पहुंचाना harm

chota *a.* छोटा miniature

chota *a.* छोटा short

chota *a.* छोटा small

chota *a.* छोटा young

chota hiran *n.* छोटा हिरन roe

chota hona *v.t.* छोटा होना shorten

chota memna *n.* छोटा मेमना lambkin

chota padari *n.* छोटा पादरी deacon

chota paudha *n.* छोटा पौधा sapling

chota sing *n.* छोटा सींग cornicle

chota zamindar *n.* छोटा ज़मींदार yeoman

chotapan *adv.* छोटापन smallness

choti *n.* चोटी ridge

choti *n.* चोटी summit

choti *n.* चोटी top

choti anguthi *n* छोटी अँगूठी annulet

choti daurh *n* छोटी दौड़ dash

choti dukan *n.* छोटी दुकान stall

choti kharhi *n.* छोटी खाड़ी bight

choti nadi *n.* छोटी नदी brook

choti par pahunchna *v.t.* चोटी पर पहुंचना top

chowk *n.* चौक courtyard

chubhana *v.t.* चुभाना jab

chubhana *v.t.* चुभाना lance

**chubhana** *v.t.* चुभाना penetrate
**chudi** *n.* चूड़ी bangle
**chugli khana** *v.t.* चुगली खाना backbite
**chuha** *n.* चूहा mouse
**chuha** *n.* चूहा rat
**chuja** *n.* चूजा chicken
**chukandar** *n.* चुकन्दर artichoke
**chukandar** *n* चुकंदर beet
**chulha** *n.* चूल्हा hearth
**chulha** *n.* चूल्हा oven
**chumbak** *n.* चुंबक magnet
**chumbak pathar** *n.* चुंबक पत्थर loadstone
**chumbaktwa** *n.* चुंबकत्व magnetism
**chumban** *n.* चुंबन kiss
**chuna lagana** *v.t* चूना लगाना lime
**chunana** *v. t.* चुनना choose
**chunana** *v. t* चुनना elect
**chunana** *v.t.* चुनना sample
**chunana** *v.t.* चुनना select
**chunana** *v.t.* चुनना single
**chunauti** *n.* चुनौती challenge
**chunauti** *n* चुनौती defiance
**chunauti dena** *v. t.* चुनौती देना challenge
**chunav** *n.* चुनाव pick
**chune ka tatva** *n* चूने का तत्त्व calcium
**chungi** *n.* चुंगी octroi
**chuninda** *a* चुनिंदा, उत्कृष्ट select
**chup chup bhag jana** *v. i* चुप चुप भाग जाना decamp
**chup karna** *v.t.* चुप करना silence
**chupchaap** *a.* चुपचाप quiet
**chupke se sunna** *v.t.* चुपके से सुनना overhear
**churna** *v.t.* चुराना lift
**churra ghopna** *v.t.* छुरा घोपना stab
**chusana** *v.t.* चूसना suck
**chushan** *n.* चूषण suck
**chuski** *n.* चुस्की sip
**chuski lagakar** *v.t.* चुस्की लगाकर पीना sip
**chusne ki mithai** *n.* चूसने की मिठाई lollipop

**chut** *n.* छूट rebate
**chut put** *a.* छुट पुट sporadic
**chutila katan** *n.* चुटीला कथन witticism
**chutkara** *n.* छुटकारा redemption
**chyandhikar** *n.* चयनाधिकार option
**cigrate** *n.* सिगरेट cigarette
**cinemaghar** *n.* सिनेमाघर cinema
**coat** *n* कोट bulwark
**coat** *n* कोट coat
**coat** *n.* कोट jacket
**coffee ke beej** *n* कॉफ़ी के बीज़ coffee
**college ka adhyaksh** *n.* कालेज का अध्यक्ष dean
**cooker** *n* कुकर cooker
**cooler** *n* कूलर cooler
**counter** *n.* काउंटर counter
**coupan** *n.* कूपन coupon
**crane** *n* क्रेन crane
**cricket** *n* क्रिकेट cricket
**cricket ka run,** *n.* क्रिकेट का एक 'रन' run
**cycle** *n* साइकिल cycle
**cycle sawar** *n* साइकिल सवार cyclist

# D

**daad** *n.* दाद ringworm
**daag** *n.* दाग blot
**daag** *n.* दाग़ smear
**daak** *n.* डाक mail
**daak mahusul** *n.* डाक महसूल postage
**daak mai dalna** *v.t.* डाक में डालना mail
**daak sambandhi** *a.* डाक संबंधी postal
**daakghar** *n.* डाकघर post-office
**daal** *n.* डाल lentil
**daalchini** *n* दालचीनी cinnamon
**daam kam hona** *v.t.i.* दाम कम होना depreciate
**daan** *n.* दान donation
**daan dena** *v. t* दान देना donate
**daansheel** *a.* दानशील munificent

**daanshil** *a.* दानशील charitable
**daarana** *v. t.* डराना cow
**daarh** *n.* दाढ़ molar
**daarhi ke chhote baal** *n.* दाढ़ी के छोटे बाल stubble
**daas** *n.* दास adscript
**daas** *v.i.* दास slave
**daas** *n.* दास thrall
**daas pratha** *n.* दास प्रथा slavery
**daasta** *n* दासता bondage
**daastapuran** *a.* दासतापूर्ण slavish
**daata** *n* दाता donor
**daayi** *n.* दाई midwife
**dabaana** *v.t.* दबाना constrict
**dabana** *v. t.* दबाना compress
**dabana** *v.t.* दबाना restrict
**dabana** *v.t.* दबाना squeeze
**dabana** *v.t.* दबाना stifle
**dabav dalana** *v. t* दबाव डालना compel
**dabav dalna** *v.t.* दबाव डालना pressurize
**dabi hansi hansna** *v. i* दबी हँसी हँसना chuckle
**dabkana** *v.i.* दबकना cower
**dadhi** *n* दाढ़ी beard
**dafan** *n* दफ़न burial
**dafan** *n.* दफ़न sepulchre
**dafnana** *v. t.* दफनाना bury
**dagmagakar chalna** *v.i.* डगमगाकर चलना waddle
**dahakana** *v.i* दहकना blaze
**dahakana** *v.i* दहकना flame
**dahasanskar** *n* दाहसंस्कार cremation
**dahasanskar karna** *v. t* दाहसंस्कार करना cremate
**dahej** *n* दहेज dowry
**dahi** *n* दही curd
**dahini aur ka** *adv* दाहिनी ओर का right
**dahleez** *n.* दहलीज़ threshold
**daihik** *a* दैहिक corporal
**dainik** *a* दैनिक daily

**dainik samachar patra** *n.* दैनिक समाचार पत्र daily
**Dainik vivrun** *n* दैनिक विवरण diary
**daishantar** *n.* देशांतर longitude
**daitya** *n.* दैत्य giant
**daivee** *a* दैवी divine
**dakaar** *n* डकार belch
**dakaar lena** *v. t* डकार लेना belch
**dakaiti** *n.* डकैती dacoity
**dakiya** *n.* डाकिया postman
**dakshin** *n.* दक्षिण south
**dakshin dhruviya** *a.* दक्षिणध्रुवीय Antarctic
**dakshin ki aur** *adv* दक्षिण की ओर south
**dakshini** *a.* दक्षिणी southerly
**dakshini** *a.* दक्षिणी southern
**daku** *n.* डाकू bandit
**daku** *n.* डाकू dacoit
**dal** *n.* दल party
**dal** *n* दाल pulse
**dal** *n.* दल swarm
**dalal** *n* दलाल broker
**dalal** *n.* दलाल jobber
**dalbandi** *n* दलबन्दी collusion
**dalbandi** *n* दलबंदी faction
**daldal** *n* दलदल bog
**daldal** *n.* दलदल marsh
**daldal** *n.* दलदल moss
**daldal** *n.* दलदल slough
**daldal** *n.* दलदल swamp
**daldal mai fansana** *v.t.* दलदल में फंसाना mire
**daldali** *a.* दलदली marshy
**dalia** *n.* दलिया porridge
**dalit vyakti** *n* दलित व्यक्ति underdog
**daliya** *n.* दलिया mash
**daliya** *n.* दलिया mush
**dam ghontana** *v.t.* दम घोंटना smother
**dam ghutkar marna** *v.t* दम घुटकर मरना suffocate
**dama** *n.* दमा asthma

**damak** *n* दमक flash
**damaktna** *v.i* दमकाना flare
**daman** *n.* दमन oppression
**daman** *n.* दमन suppression
**damankari** *a.* दमनकारी oppressive
**damankarta** *n.* दमनकर्त्ता oppressor
**dambh** *n.* दंभ vainglory
**dambh puran** *v* दंभपूर्ण snobbish
**dambhi** *a.* दंभी haughty
**dambhi** *a.* दंभी vainglorious
**dambhi vyakti** *n* दंभी व्यक्ति popinjay
**dam-kham** *n.* दम-खम stamina
**dand** *n.* दंड penalty
**dand** *n.* दंड punishment
**dand dena** *v. t.* दंड देना castigate
**dand dena** *v.t.* दंड देना penalize
**dand dena** *v.t.* दंड देना punish
**dand dena** *v.t.* दंड देना sentence
**dand mukti** *n.* दंड मुक्ति impunity
**dandadhikaran** *n.* दंडाधिकरण magistracy
**dandadhikari** *n.* दंडाधिकारी magistrate
**dandaswarup nishkasit karna** *v.t.*
  निष्कासित करना rusticate
**dandatmak** *a.* दंडात्मक punitive
**dandvat karna** *n.* दंडवत् अवस्था
  prostration
**dandvishayak** *a.* दंडविषयक penal
**danga** *n.* दंगा riot
**dani sanstha** *n.* दानी संस्था charity
**dank maarana** *v.t.* डंक मारना sting
**dank marna** *v.t.* डंक मारना nettle
**dant** *n.* दांत tooth
**dant chikitsak** *n* दंत चिकित्सक dentist
**dant dard** *n.* दांत दर्द toothache
**danta** *n.* दांता notch
**dante-daar banana** *vt* दंते-दार बनाना nick
**danthal** *n.* डंठल stalk
**danti** *n.* दांती scythe
**dantna** *v. t.* डाँटना chide
**danvadol hona** *v.i.* डावांडोल होना vacillate

**dara kar vasul karna** *n, v.t.* डरा कर वसूल
  करना blackmail
**daraana** *v.t.* डराना scare
**daraar** *n* दरार crack
**daraar** *n* दरार fissure
**daraj** *n* दराज drawer
**daranti se katana** *v.t.* दरांती से काटना
  scythe
**darar** *n* दरार cleft
**darar** *n.* दरार leak
**darar** *n.* दरार slit
**darar karna** *v.t.* दरार करना slit
**darbari** *n.* दरबारी courtier
**daridra** *n.* दरिद्र pauper
**darj karna** *v.t.* दर्ज करना register
**darja** *n.* दरजा level
**darja ghatana** *v. t* दरजा घटाना degrade
**darjan** *n* दर्जन dozen
**darna** *v.t.* डरना apprehend
**darna** *v.i* डरना fear
**darpan** *n* दर्पण mirror
**darphok** *a.* डरपोक timid
**darpok** *a.* डरपोक nervous
**darshak** *n.* दर्शक on-looker
**darshak** *n.* दर्शक spectator
**darshanik** *n.* दार्शनिक philosopher
**darshanik** *a.* दार्शनिक philosophical
**darshanshastra** *n.* दर्शनशास्त्र philosophy
**darzi** *n.* दर्ज़ी tailor
**das banana** *v.t.* दास बनाना enslave
**das lakh** *n.* दस लाख million
**dashabadi** *n* दशाब्दी decade
**dashamlav** *a* दशमलव decimal
**dashmansh kar** *n.* दशमांश कर tithe
**dasochhit** *a.* दासोचित menial
**dasta** *n.* दस्ता pad
**dasta** *n.* दासता servility
**dasta** *n.* दस्ता shaft
**dasta** *n.* दासता thraldom
**dasta,** *n.* दस्ता squad
**dastana** *n.* दस्ताना glove

dastapurna *a.* दासतापूर्ण servile
dastavej *n* दस्तावेज़ document
dastavez *n* दस्तावेज़ deed
dastavez lekhak *a* दस्तावेज़ लेखक draftsman
dastkari *n.* दस्तकारी handiwork
daubna *v.i.* डूबना sink
daud *n.* दौड़ run
daudana, *v.i.* दौड़ना run
daura *n* दौरा fit
dauran *prep.* दौरान amid
dauran *prep* दौरान by
dav ya bazi lagane wala *n* दाँव या बाजी लगाने वाला bidder
dava *n* दावा claim
dava *n.* दावा pretension
dava karna *v.t.* दावा करना assert
dava karna *v. t* दावा करना claim
davakhana *n* दवाखाना dispensary
davakhana *n.* दवाखाना pharmacy
davat dena *v.i* दावत देना feast
davay se kahana *v.t.* दावे से कहना affirm
davedar *n* दावेदार claimant
davedar banana *v. t.* दावेदार बनाना entitle
dawa karna *v.t.* दावा करना purport
dawat *n.* दावत banquet
dawat *n* दातत treat
dawat dena *v.t.* दावत देना banquet
daya *n.* दया mercy
daya ka patra *a.* दया का पात्र pitiable
daya karna *v. t* दया करना commiserate
daya purna *a.* दयापूर्ण pitiful
dayaalu *a.* दयालु humane
dayaheen *a.* दयाहीन relentless
dayahinta *n* दयाहीनता cruelty
dayalu *adj* दयालु benign
dayalu *a.* दयालु gracious
dayalu *a.* दयालु merciful
dayaluta se *adv* दयालुता से benignly
dayan *n.* डायन hag
dayitva *n.* दायित्व liability

dayitva *n.* दायित्व onus
dayitva lena *v.t* दायित्व लेना guarantee
dayitva lena *v.t.* दायित्व लेना shoulder
dedipyaman *a.* देदीप्यमान refulgent
dedipyman *a.* देदीप्यमान resplendent
deen *a.* दीन piteous
deepak *n.* दीपक lamp
deepak ki batti *n.* दीपक की बत्ती wick
deevaliya *n.* दिवालिया bankrupt
deevaliyapan *n.* दिवालियापन bankruptcy
deewar dari *n.* दीवार दरी tapestry
deg *n* देग ****boiler
dehantaran *n.* देहांतरण transmigration
dehat *n.* देहात village
dehati *a.* देहाती rural
dehati *n.* देहाती villager
dehati bangla *n.* देहाती बंगला villa
dekh lena *v.t.* देख लेना notice
dekh rekh *n.* देख रेख supervision
dekhana *v. t* दिखाना exhibit
dekhana *v.t.* देखना see
dekhavati *adj* दिखावटी mock
dekhawati prem karna *v.i* दिखावटी प्रेम करना flirt
dekhbhal *n* देखभाल heed
dekhbhal karnewala *n.* देखभाल करनेवाला keeper
dekhna *v.t.* देखना sight
dekhna *v.t.* देखना view
dekh-rekh *n.* देख-रेख care
dekhte rah jana *v.i.* देखते रह जाना gape
demaag *n* दिमाग़ brain
den *v.t.* दीन impart
dena *v. t* देना deliver
dena *v.t.* देना give
der *a.* देर late
der se aane wala *adj.* देर से आने वाला belated
des nishkasan *n.* देश निष्कासन exile
des se nikalna *v. t* देश से निकालना exile
desh *n.* देश country

desh bahar nikalna *v.t.* देश बाहर निकालना deport

desh pratyavartan *n.* देश प्रत्यावर्तन repatriation

deshaj *a.* देशज indigenous

deshbhakt *n.* देशभक्त patriot

deshbhakti *n.* देशभक्ति patriotism

deshbhaktipurna *a.* देशभक्तिपूर्ण patriotic

deshi *a.* देशी vernacular

dev vakya *a.* देव वाक्य oracular

devatav *n.* देवत्व godship

devatwa ka apahari *a.* देवत्व का अपहारी sacrilegious

devdaar *n.* देवदार pine

devdar ka vriksh *n.* देवदार का वृक्ष cedar

devdaru *n* देवदारू fir

devdoot *n* देवदूत angel

devi *n.* देवी goddess

devta *n* देवता divinity

devta *n.* देवता deity

devta tulya nirman *n.* देवता तुल्य निर्माण apotheosis

dhaa dalna *v.t* धागा डालना thread

dhaaga *n.* धागा fibre

dhaal *n.* ढाल shield

dhaal *n.* ढाल slope

dhaalna *v.t.* ढालना mint

dhaan *n* घान batch

dhaar *n.* धार jet

dhaari *n.* धारी stripe

dhaarna *n* धारणा feeling

dhabba *n.* धब्बा speck

dhabba *n.* धब्बा stain

dhabba lagana *v. t* धब्बा लगाना blot

dhabba lagna *v.t.* धब्बा लगाना scar

dhabbe dalna *v.t.* धब्बे डालना spot

dhadkan *n.* धड़कन pulsation

dhadkana *v.i.* धड़कना pulsate

dhaga *n.* धागा thread

dhairya *n.* धैर्य fortitude

dhak lena *v.t.* ढक लेना overlap

dhak lena, chhipana *v.t* ढक लेना, छिपाना mantle

dhaka hua gaddha *n.* ढका हुआ गड्ढा trap

dhakamdhakka *n.* धक्कमधक्का jostle

dhakana, chipana *v.t.* ढकना, छिपाना shroud

dhakelana *v.t.* धकेलना shove

dhakka *n.* धक्का poke

dhakka *n.* धक्का push

dhakka dena *v.t.* धक्का देना jostle

dhakka dena *v.t.* धक्का देना thrust

dhakna *n.* ढकना casing

dhakna *v. t.* ढकना cover

dhakna *v. t* ढकना envelop

dhakna *v.t.* ढकना muffle

dhakna *v.t.* ढकना veil

dhakne wala bhag *n* ढकने वाला भाग overlap

dhalana *v. t.* ढालना cast

dhalu hona *v.i.* ढालू होना slope

dhalye ki kala *n.* ढलाई की कला foundry

dham *n.* धम thud

dham ki awaz *v.i.* धम की आवाज़ करना thud

dham se band karna *v.t.* धम से बंद करना bang

dhamaka *n* धमाका blast

dhamaka *n* धमाका crash

dhamakay ke sath gherna *v. i* धमाके के साथ गिरना crash

dhamki *n* धमकी menace

dhamki *n.* धमकी threat

dhamki dena *v.t* धमकी देना menace

dhamki dena *v.t.* धमकी देना threaten

dhamni *n.* धमनी artery

dhan *n.* धन lucre

dhan *n.* धान paddy

dhan *n.* धान rice

dhan *n.* धन riches

dhan daulat *n.* धन दौलत pelf

dhan daulat *n.* धन दौलत wealth

dhan ki wapasi *n.* धन की वापसी refund

dhan sambandhi *a.* धन संबंधी pecuniary

dhanadhayata *a.* धनाढ्यता richness

dhanakar *adj.* घनाकार cubiform

dhancha *n.* ढांचा cast

dhancha *n.* ढाँचा crate

dhancha *n* ढांचा frame

dhanda *n.* धंधा pursuit

dhandha *n* धंधा perch

dhang *n.* ढंग style

dhang *n.* ढंग way

dhani *n.* धनी croesus

dhani *a.* धनी rich

dhani *a.* धनी wealthy

dhaniy *a* घनीय cubical

dhaniya *n.* धनियां coriander

dhankshetra *n* घनक्षेत्र cube

dhanrashi *n.* धनराशि sum

dhanrudhar *n* धनुर्धर archer

dhanush *n* धनुष bow

dhanvan *a.* धनवान affluent

dhanyavad dena *v.* धन्यवाद देना acknowledge

dhanyavad dena *v.t.* धन्यवाद देना thank

dhar *n* धार edge

dhara *n* धारा clause

dhara *n* धारा current

dharak *n* धारक mount

dharam vigyani *n.* धर्मविज्ञानी theologian

dharamgranth *n.* धर्मग्रंथ scripture

dharampracharak *n.* धर्मप्रचारक apostle

dharamtantra *n.* धर्मतंत्र, theocracy

dharan *n.* धारण tenure

dharana *n* धारणा comprehension

dharana shakti *a.* धारणा शक्ति retentive

dharawahik *r* धारावाहिक serial

dharhakna *v.i.* धड़कना throb

dharhkan *n.* धड़कन palpitation

dharkan *n* धड़कन beat

dharkana *v.i.* धड़कना palpitate

dharki *n.* ढरकी shuttle

dharm *n.* धर्म creed

dharm *n.* धर्म religion

dharm virodhi *adv.* धर्म विरोधी nonconformist

dharma pracharak *n.* धर्म प्रचारक missionary

dharmadhikari *n.* धर्माधिकारी prelate

dharmakriya *n.* धर्मक्रिया ceremony

dharmandh vyakti *n* धर्मांध व्यक्ति bigot

dharmandh vyakti *n* धर्मांध व्यक्ति fanatic

dharmavigyan vishayak *a.* धर्मविज्ञान विषयक theological

dharmayudh *n* धर्मयुद्घ crusade

dharmik *a.* धार्मिक godly

dharmik *a.* धार्मिक religious

dharmik bhajan *n.* धार्मिक भजन psalm

dharmik sahishunta *n.* धार्मिक सहिष्णुता toleration

dharmik sanskar *n.* धार्मिक संस्कार ritual

dharmik utsav *n.* धार्मिक उत्सक rite

dharmik utsav *n.* धार्मिक उत्सव sacrament

dharmmat *n* धर्ममत dogma

dharmmat sambandhi *a* धर्ममत संबंधी dogmatic

dharmopadeshak *n.* धर्मोपदेशक preacher

dharna *n* धारणा belief

dharna *n* धारणा conviction

dhatu karmi *n.* धातु कर्मी smith

dhatu ko galakar dhalayee *n* धातु को गलाकर ढलाई casting

dhatukarma vigyan *n.* धातुकर्म विज्ञान metallurgy

dhatuwatra *a.* धातुवत्र metallic

dhaunkani *n.* धौंकनी bellows

dhaunsiya *n* धौंसिया bully

dhava *n.* धावा assault

dhava *n.* धावा charge

dhava bolna *v.t.* धावा बोलना raid

dhavak *n.* धावक runner

dhavni sambandhi *a.* ध्वनि संबंधी phonetic

dheela *a.* ढीला slack

dheela karnaa *v.t.* ढीला करना slacken

dheela pajama *n.* ढीला पाजामा slacks

dheema *a* धीमा slow

dheema hona *v.i.* धीमा होना slow

dheema karna *v.t.* धीमा करना retard

dheemapan *n.* धीमापन slowness

dheemi gati se *adv.* धीमी गति से slowly

dheere dheere *adv.* धीरे धीरे leisurely

dheere dheere nikalana *v. t* धीरे धीरे निकालना drain

dhekli *n* ढेकली lever

dher *n.* ढेर volume

dher *n* ढेर pile

dher lagana *v.t.* ढेर लगाना lump

dhere dhere chalna *v.i.* धीरे धीरे चलना lag

dhikkar *interj* धिक्कार fie

dhikkar *n.* धिक्कार reproach

dhikkarana *v.t.* धिक्कारना reproach

dhila *a.* ढीला lax

dhima karna *v.t.* धीमा करना moderate

dhirghayuta *n.* दीर्घायुता longevity

dhit ladki *n.* ढीठ लड़की minx

dhmaka *n.* धमाका explosion

dho dalna *v.t.* धो डालना rinse

dhobin *n.* धोबिन laundress

dhoka dena *v.t.* धोखा देना bam

dhokha *n* धोखा bluff

dhokha *n.* धोखा catch

dhokha *n* धोखा deceit

dhokha *n.* धोखा deception

dhokha *n.* धोखा fraud

dhokha *n.* धोखा masquerade

dhokha *n.* धोखा treachery

dhokha *n* धोखा trick

dhokha *n.* धोखा trickery

dhokha dekar pakarhna *v.t.* धोखा देकर पकड़ना trap

dhokha dena *v. t.* धोखा देना bilk

dhokha dena *v. t* धोखा देना bluff

dhokha dena *v. t* धोखा देना deceive

dhokha dena *v* धोखा देना ditch

dhokha dena *v.t.* धोखा देना trick

dhokhebaaz *a.* धोखेबाज shifty

dhokhebaz *n.* धोखेबाज़ rook

dhokhebaz *a.* धोखेबाज़ sly

dhokhebaz,vishvaghati *a.* विश्वासघाती treacherous

dhol bajana *v.i.* ढोल बजाना drum

dhona *v.t.* धोना wash

dhool *n* धूल dust

dhoom kohra *n.* धूम कोहरा smog

dhoondh lena *v.t.* ढूंढ लेना track

dhoop *v.t.* धूप sun

dhruvatara *n.* ध्रुवतारा loadstar

dhruwiya *n.* ध्रुवीय polar

dhuan *n.* धुआं smoke

dhuanyukt *a.* धुआंयुक्त smoky

dhul *n* धूल dirt

dhul jharhna *v.t.* धूल झाड़ना dust

dhulai ghar *n.* धुलाईघर laundry

dhulayee *n* धुलाई wash

dhulayee ka kam *n.* ढुलाई का काम cartage

dhulayee yogya *a.* धुलाई योग्य washable

dhulikan *n.* धूलिकण mote

dhumra-paan karna *v.i.* धूम्रपान करना smoke

dhun *n.* धुन tune

dhundala dekhai dena *v.i.* धुंधला दिखाई देना loom

dhundbhara *a.* धुंधभरा muggy

dhundhala *a* धुंधला cloudy

dhundhala *a* धुंधला dim

dhundhala *a.* धुंधला hazy

dhundhala *ADJ* धुंधला obscure

dhundhala karna *v. t* धुंधला करना dim

dhundhala prakash *n* धुंधला प्रकाश twilight

dhup dena *v. t* धूप देना cense

dhup ka chasma *n.* धूप का चश्मा goggles

**dhup se bachaana** *v.t.* छाया डाला
overshadow
**dhuri** *n.* धुरी axle
**dhurlabhta** *n* दुर्लभता dearth
**dhurt vyakti** *n.* धूर्त व्यक्ति rascal
**dhvani sambandhi** *a* ध्वनि-संबंधी
acoustic
**dhvani shastra** *n.* ध्वनिशास्त्र acoustics
**dhvanivistarak** *n* ध्वनिविस्तारक amplifier
**dhvansh** *n* ध्वंस annihilation
**dhvanskarta** *n.* ध्वंसकर्ता wrecker
**dhwani** *n.* ध्वनि onomatopoeia
**dhwani** *n* ध्वनि sound
**dhwani karna** *v.i.* ध्वनि करना sound
**dhwani sambandhi** *a.* ध्वनि संबंधी sonic
**dhyaan** *n.* ध्यान mediation
**dhyan** *n.* ध्यान regard
**dhyan dena** *v.i.* ध्यान देना listen
**dhyan lagana** *v.i.* ध्यान लगाना muse
**dhyan mein rakhna** *v.t.* ध्यान में रखना
heed
**dhyan rakhne wala** *a.* ध्यान रखने वाला
considerate
**dhyan se dhekna** *v. t* ध्यान से देखना
behold
**dibba** *n.* डिब्बा can
**dibbai mein band karna** *v. t.* डिब्बे में बंद
करना can
**dibbe mein band karna** *v. t* डिब्बे में बंद
करना encase
**dibbon mein rakhna** *v.t.* डिब्बों में रखना
tin
**dig mandal** *n.* दिग मंडल horizon
**dikhana** *v.t.* दिखाना show
**dikhau** *a.* दिखाऊ gaudy
**dikhava** *n.* सादृश्य semblance
**dikhava** *n* दिखावा affectation
**dikhawa** *n* दिखावा sham
**dikhawati** *a* दिखावटी sham
**diksha snan** *n.* दीक्षा-स्नान baptism

**diksha snan karna** +*v.t.* दीक्षा-स्नान
कराना baptize
**dil** *n.* दिल heart
**dil kholkar kharch karna** *v.t.* दिल
खोलकर खर्च करना lavish
**diler** *a.* दिलेर valiant
**dil-lagi** *n.* दिल-लगी lark
**din ka samay** *n* दिन का समय day
**ding** *n* डींग boast
**ding** *n* डींग brag
**ding marna** *v.i* डींग मारना boast
**ding marna** *v. i* डींग मारना brag
**ding marna** *v. i* डींग मारना crow
**dinta** *n.* दीनता lowliness
**dipti** *n* दीप्ति glow
**dirghikaran** *n.* दीर्घीकरण prolongation
**divaswapan** *n.* दिवास्वप्न reverie
**divya** *adj.* दिव्य celestial
**divya** *a.* दिव्य heavenly
**divyaan** *n.* दिव्यान्न manna
**diwaliya** *a.* दिवालिया insolvent
**diwaliyapan** *n.* दिवालियापन insolvency
**diwar** *n.* दीवार wall
**diwar ka takhta** *n.* दीवर का ताकत panel
**diwar se gherna** *v.t.* दीवार से घेरना wall
**diyasalai** *n* दियासलाई match
**do** *a.* दो two
**do baar** *adv.* दो बार twice
**do dhura wala** *adj* दो धुरा वाला biaxial
**do ki sankhya** *n.* दो की संख्या two
**do kon ka** *adj.* दो कोण का biangular
**do mein se koi** *a.,* दो में से कोई either
**do saal mein hone wala** *adj* दो साल में होने
वाला biennial
**docter** *n.* डॉक्टर physician
**doctor ki upadhi** *n* डॉक्टर की उपाधि
doctorate
**doguna** *a* दोगुना double
**doguna** *a.* दोगुना twofold
**doha** *n.* दोहा couplet
**dohara** *pref* दोहरा bi

**dohara** *a* दोहरा dual
**dohara jorha** *adj* दोहरा जोड़ा binary
**dohara karna** *v. t.* दोहरा करना double
**dolan** *n.* दोलन oscillation
**dollar** *n* डॉलर dollar
**dolna** *v.i.* डोलना oscillate
**dono** *a* दोनों both
**dono log** *pron* दोनों लोग both
**door** *adv.* दूर far
**door sanvadi** *a.* दूर संवेदी telepathic
**doorbhash** *n.* दूरभाष telephone
**doorbin** *n.* दूरबीन telescope
**doorbini** *a.* दूरबीनी telescopic
**doordashan** *n.* दूरदर्शन television
**doori** *n* दूरी far
**doorsanvedanvid** *n.* दूरसंवेदनविद्
telepathist
**doosanchar** *n.* दूरसंचार
telecommunications
**doot** *n* दूत emissary
**dopahar** *n.* दोपहर noon
**dopahar ki jhapaki** *n.* दोपहर की झपकी
siesta
**dophar ka bhojan** *n.* दोपहर का भोजन
lunch
**dophari ka** *a.* दोपहरी का meridian
**dori** *n* डोरी cord
**dosh** *n* दोष blame
**dosh** *n* दोष blemish
**dosh** *n* दोष defect
**dosh** *n* दोष demerit
**dosh** *n* दोष flaw
**dosh** *n.* दोष shortcoming
**dosh** *n.* दोष taint
**dosh dena** *v. t.* दोष देना charge
**dosh lagana** *v.* दोष लगाना arraign
**dosh lagana** *v. t* दोष लगाना blame
**dosh mukti** *n.* दोष मुक्ति vindication
**dosh nekalne wala** *adj* दोष निकालने वाला
censorious
**dosh nikalana** *v.t.* दोष निकालना scold

**dosh nikalna** *v. t* दोष निकालना cavil
**dosh rahit prasadhan** *a* दोष रहित correct
**doshmukt karna** *v.t* दोषमुक्त करना
absolve
**doshmukt karna** *v.t* दोषमुक्त करना
excuse
**doshmukti ya rihai** *n.* दोषमुक्ति या रिहाई
acquittal
**doshpurna** *n* दोषपूर्ण fault
**doshpurna** *a* दोषपूर्ण faulty
**doshrahit** *a.* दोषरहित spotless
**drav banana** *v.t.* द्रव बनना liquefy
**dravya** *n* द्रव्य fluid
**dravya nikalna** *v.t.* द्रव निकालना tap
**dridh** *a.* दृढ़ rigorous
**dridh banana** *v.t.* दृढ़ बनना steady
**dridh sankalp** *n.* दृढ़ संकल्प determination
**dridh, atal** *a.* दृढ़, अटल steadfast
**dridhta** *n.* दृढ़ता steadiness
**dirh rahna** *v.i.* दृढ़ रहना persist
**drirhata** *a.* धीरता inflexible
**drirhta** *n.* दृढ़ता perseverance
**drishtant** *n.* दृष्टांत instance
**drishti** *n.* दृष्टि sight
**drishti** *n.* दृष्टि vision
**drishti vishayak** *a.* दृष्टि विषयक visual
**drishtikon** *n.* दृष्टिकोण standpoint
**drishtikona** *n.* दृष्टिकोण perspective
**drishya** *n.* दृश्य view
**drishya** *n.* दृश्य vista
**drishya kshitij** *n.* दृश्य क्षितिज offing
**drishyabhumi** *n.* दृश्यभूमि scenery
**drishyaman** *a.* दृश्यमान visible
**drishyasima** *n.* दृष्टिसीमा visibility
**dristi sambandhi** *a.* दृष्टि संबंधी optic
**droh** *n* द्रोह grudge
**drutgami railgadi** *n* द्रुतगामी रेलगाड़ी
express
**duba dena** *v.i* डुबा देना drown
**dubana** *v.t.* डुबाना immerse

**dubara namakaran** *n* दुबारा नामकरण anabaptism

**dubara vichar karna** *v.t.* दुबारा विचार करना revise

**dubhashiya** *n.* दुभाषिया interpreter

**dubkana** *v.i.* दुबकना lurk

**dubki** *n* डुबकी plunge

**dubki lagana** *v.i.* डुबकी लगाना duck

**dubna** *v.i.* डूबना submerge

**dudh** *n.* दूध milk

**dudh dena** *v.t.* दूध देना milk

**dudh ka matka** *n.* दूध का मटका churn

**dudh ke dant nikalna** *v.i.* दूध के दांत निकलना teethe

**dudh ki lapsi** *n* दूध की लपसी custard

**dudh pilana** *v. t* दूध पिलाना ablactate

**dudhiapan** *n* दुधियापन milkiness

**dudhiya** *a.* दूधिया milky

**dugdhshala** *n* दुग्धशाला dairy

**dughad srawit karna** *v.i.* दुग्ध स्रावित करना lactate

**dughadmapi** *n.* दुग्धमापी lactometer

**dughasharkara** *n.* दुग्धशर्करा lactose

**duharana** *v.t.* दुहराना rehearse

**duhra batan** *n.* दुहरा बटन stud

**duhrav** *n.* दुहराव rote

**duhshilta** *n.* दुःशीलता petulance

**dukaan** *n.* दुकान shop

**dukandar** *n.* दुकानदार tradesman

**dukh hona** *v.i.* दुःखी होना sorrow

**dukh se** *vt* दुख से miserably

**dukh, peerha** *n.* दुःख, पीड़ा sorrow

**dukhad ghatna** *n.* दुःखद घटना tragedy

**dukhant** *a.* दुःखांत tragic

**dukhapurna** *a.* दुःखपूर्ण unhappy

**dukhi** *a.* दुःखी rueful

**dukhi** *a.* दुःखी sad

**dukhi** *a.* दुःखी wretched

**dukhi hona** *v.i.* दुःखी होना regret

**dukhi hona** *v.t.* दुःखी होना rue

**dukhi karna** *v.t.* दुःखी करना sadden

**dukhi, khedpurna** *a.* दुःखी, खेदपूर्ण sorry

**dukhyi** *a.* दुःखदायी painful

**dulaar karna** *v. t* दुलार करना cocker

**dulha** *n.* दूल्हा bridegroom

**dulha** *n.* दूल्हा groom

**dulhan** *n* दुलहन bride

**dulki** *n* दुलकी trot

**dulki chalna** *v.i.* दुलकी चलना trot

**dupatta** *n.* दुपट्टा scarf

**dur ka** *a* दूर का distant

**dur rehna** *v.t.* दूर रहना shun

**durachar** *n.* दुराचार malpractice

**duracharan** *n.* दुराचरण misconduct

**duracharan** *n.* दुराचरण misdemeanour

**durasth** *a* दूरस्थ far

**durasth** *a.* दूरस्थ remote

**durbal** *a* दुर्बल flabby

**durbal karna** *v. t.* दुर्बल करना enfeeble

**durbalta** *n* दुर्बलता debility

**durbhagya** *n.* दुर्भाग्य adversity

**durbhagya** *n.* दुर्भाग्य mischance

**durbhagya** *n.* दुर्भाग्य misfortune

**durbin** *n.* दूरबीन binocular

**durbin ka shisha** *n.* दूरबीन का शीशा lens

**durdam** *a.* दुर्दम indomitable

**durdarshi** *a.* दूरदर्शी provident

**durdarshita** *n* दूरदर्शिता foresight

**durdasha** *n.* दुर्दशा plight

**durdrishti** *n.* दूरदृष्टि providence

**durg** *n.* दुर्ग castle

**durg** *n.* दुर्ग citadel

**durgandh** *n* दुर्गंध stink

**durgandh** *n.* दुर्गंध rot

**durgandh** *n.* दुर्गंध stench

**durghatna** *n* दुर्घटना accident

**durghatna** *n.* दुर्घटना casualty

**durghatna** *n.* दुर्घटना misadventure

**durghatna** *n.* दुर्घटना mishap

**duri** *n* दूरी distance

**duri par** *adv.* दूरी पर afar

**duri par** *adv.* दूरी पर beyond

durpayog n. दुरुपयोग misuse

durpayog n. दुरूपयोग prostitution

durpayog karna v.t. दुरुपयोग करना misuse

dursanvedan n. दूरसंवेदन telepathy

durupyog karna v.t. दुरूपयोग करना prostitute

durvarti chowki n. दूरवर्ती चौकी outpost

durvyawahar karna d दुर्व्यवहार करना mistreat

dus n., a दस ten

dus varsh ka kaal n. दस वर्ष का काल decennary

dushilta n. दुःशीलता perversity

dushit a. दूषित corrupt

dushit karna v.t. दूषित करना contaminate

dushit karna v. t. दूषित करना corrupt

dushit karna v.t. दूषित करना pollute

dushit karna v.t. दूषित करना taint

dushman n. दुश्मन adversary

dusht a दुष्ट evil

dusht n. दुष्ट knave

dusht n. दुष्ट rogue

dusht n. दुष्ट scoundrel

dusht n. दुष्ट villain

dushtata n. दुष्टता knavery

dushtata n. दुष्टता roguery

dushtatapurna a. दुष्टतापूर्ण nefarious

dushtatapurna a. दुष्टतापूर्ण roguish

dusit karna v.t. दूषित करना pervert

duskarm n. दुष्कर्म misdeed

dusra a. दूसरा other

dusra a. दूसरा second

dutavas ka adhikari n. दूतावास का अधिकारी attache

dutawas n दूतावास embassy

duvidha n दुविधा dilemma

duvidha n. दुविधा quandary

duwrybhar n. दुर्व्यवहार mal-treatment

dvesh n. द्वेष spite

dveshbhav n. द्वेषभाव virulence

dveshi a. द्वेषी jealous

dvibhashi a द्विभाषी bilingual

dvilingiya adj. द्विलिंगीय bisexual

dvipad n द्विपाद biped

dvishir peshi n द्विशिर पेशी biceps

dvivavah-pratha n द्विविवाह-प्रथा bigamy

dvivibhajit karna v. t द्विविभाजित करना bisect

dwar-mandap n. द्वार-मंडप porch

dwesh n द्वेष animus

dwip a. द्वीप insular

dwipiyata n. द्वीपीयता insularity

dyanipravardhi n. ध्वनिप्रवर्धी megaphone

dyanivistarak n. ध्वनिविस्तारक microphone

dyesh bhawana n. द्वेष भावना malice

dyotak a. दयोतक expressive

# E

eeich a. नीच sordid

eent n ईंट brick

ek art एक an

ek a. एक one

ek arab n एक अरब billion

ek baar adv. एक बार once

ek chota tara adj. एक छोटा तारा asteroid

ek ek karke batana v. t. एक एक करके बताना enumerate

ek jutata n. एकजुटता solidarity

ek karna v.t. एक करना unite

ek lakh n एक लाख lac / lakh

ek prakar ka baja n. एक प्रकार का बाजा banjo

ek prakar ka kutta n एक प्रकार का कुत्ता bulldog

ek prakar ki sharab n. एक प्रकार की शराब scotch

ek pushp n एक पुष्प daisy

ek saman a एक समान flat

**eka ek girna** *v. i* एकाएक गिरना collapse

**eka- ek kiya hua** *a.* एकाएक किया हुआ random

**ekadhikaar karna** *v.t.* एकाधिकार करना monopolize

**eka-ek tutna** *n* एकाएक टूटना abruption

**ekagrata** *n.* एकाग्रता concentration

**ekaksharvad** *n.* एकेश्वरवाद monotheism

**ekaksharvad** *n.* एकेश्वरवाद monotheist

**ekal** *a.* एकल solo

**ekal gayak** *n.* एकल गायक soloist

**ekal sangeet** *n* एकल संगीत solo

**ekant** *n.* एकांत privacy

**ekant** *a.* एकांत secluded

**ekantata** *n.* एकांतता seclusion

**ekantvasi** *n.* एकांतवासी recluse

**ekarhon mein nap** *n.* एकड़ों में नाप acreage

**ekasva** *n* एकस्व patent

**ekatra hona** *v.t.* एकत्र होना muster

**ekatra karna** *v.t.* एकत्र करना amass

**ekatra karna** *v.t.* एकत्र करना assemble

**ekatra karna** *v.t.* एकत्र करना gather

**ekikaran** *n.* एकीकरण unification

**ek-maatra** *a* एकमात्र exclusive

**ek-matra** *a.* एक-मात्र only

**ekpakchiya** *a* एकपक्षीय ex parte

**ekta** *n.* एकता oneness

**ekta** *n.* एकता union

**ekta** *n.* एकता unity

**ektak dekhna** *v.t.* एकटक देखना gaze

**ektantra** *n* एकतंत्र autocracy

**ektarpha ticket** *n.* एकतरफ़ा टिकट single

**ektra hona** *v.i* एकत्र होना flock

**ekvachan** *a.* एकवचन singular

**ekviwah pratha** *n.* एकविवाह प्रथा monogamy

**es isthan par** *adv.* इस स्थान पर hither

**esa ka updesh** *n.* ईसा का उपदेश gospel

**ese beech mein** *adv.* इसी बीच में meanwhile

**eshara karna** *v.i* इशारा करना hint

**estar** *n.* स्तर stratum

**esthir** *a.* स्थिर motionless

**faal** *n* फाल coulter

**faatak** *n.* फाटक gate

**fafundar** *a.* फफूंददार musty

**fafundh** *n.* फफूंद fungus

**fafundi** *n.* फफूंदी mildew

**fafundidaar** *a.* फफूंदीदार mouldy

**failaana** *v.t.* फैलाना expand

**failana** *v.t.* फैलाना propagate

**faldayak** *a* फलदायक fertile

**faldayak** *a.* फलदायक prolific

**faltu purja** *n.* फ़ालतू पुरज़ा spare

**faltu, ati adhik** *a.* फ़ालतू, अति अधिक superfluous

**fande mai fasana** *v. t* फंदे में फंसाना entangle

**fansana** *v.t.* फंसाना implicate

**fansana** *v.t.* फंसाना involve

**fansi dena** *v.t.* फांसी देना hang

**fansi dene wala** *n.* फांसी देने वाला executioner

**fansi ka dand** *n* फांसी का दंड execution

**farar hona** *v.i* फ़रार होना abscond

**farlang** *n.* फर्लांग furlong

**farsh banana** *v.t* फर्श बनाना floor

**Farsi bhasha** *n.* फारसी भाषा persian

**farwari** *n* फ़रवरी February

**fasal kat machine** *n.* फ़सल-कट मशीन reaper

**fasal katne wala** *n.* फ़सल काटने वाला harvester

**fasal ki katai** *n.* फ़सल की कटाई harvest

**fasana** *v.t.* फंसाना snare

**fashion** *n* फैशन fashion

**fashionparast** *a* फैशनपरस्त fashionable

fatuhi *n.* फातूही vest
favara *n.* फव्वारा fountain
fax *n* फैक्स facsimile
fefra *n* फेफड़ा lung
fheeka *n.* फीका stark
fhora, vran *n.* फोड़ा, व्रण ulcer
fijulkharchi *n* फ़िजूलखर्ची extravagance
file mai rakhna *v.t* फ़ाइल में रखना file
film ki jhalkiyan *n* फिल्म की झलकियां
trailer
foda *v. t* फोड़ा botch
foolgobhi *n.* फूलगोभी cauliflower
francici bhasha *a.* फ़्रांसीसी भाषा French
fudakana *v. i* फुदकना hop
fufkar *n.* फुफकार snort
fufkarna *v.i* फुफकारना hiss
fuharh dhang se hasna *v.i.* फूहड़ढंग से
हंसना giggle
fuje taar *n* फ्यूज़ तार fuse
fulav *n* फुलाव swell
furteela *a.* फ़ुर्तीला quick
furtila *a.* फ़ुर्तीला vivacious

# G

gaad *n.* गाद silt
gaadha karna *v. t* गाढ़ा करना condense
gaal *n* गाल cheek
gaali dena *v.t.* गाली देना abuse
gaali dena *v.t.* गाली देना rail
gaana *v.i.* गाना sing
gaanth *n.* गांठ bale
gaanth *n.* गांठ knot
gaanth banana *v.t.* गांठ बनाना bale
gaari *vt* गाड़ी motor
gaari chalana *v. t* गाड़ी चलाना drive
gaarivaan *n* गाड़ीवान coachman
gaay *n.* गाय cow
gaban *n.* ग़बन misappropriation

gaban karna *v.t.* ग़बन करना
misappropriate
gada *n* गदा cudgel
gadar *n.* ग़दर mutiny
gaddedar chauki *n.* गद्देदार चौकी ottoman
gaddha *n.* गड्ढा mattress
gaddi *n.* गद्दी padding
gaddi se utarna *v. t* गद्दी से उतारना
dethrone
gadd-madd *adv.* गॅड-मड्ड pell-mell
gaddo se sajana *v. t* गद् दों से सजाना
cushion
gadeheriya *n.* गड़ेरिया shepherd
gadha *n.* गधा ass
gadha *n* गधा donkey
gadhe ki renk *n* गधे की रेंक bray
gadhya *n.* गद्य prose
gadi se yatra *n* गाड़ी से यात्रा ride
gadmadd karna *v.t.* गड्मड्ड करना jumble
gadwadi karna *v.i* गड़बड़ी करना fuss
gahan *n.* गहन malignity
gahan *a.* गहन profound
gahari shatruta *n.* गहरी शत्रुता rancour
gainda *n.* गैंडा rhinoceros
gainte *n.* गैंती mattock
gajar *n.* गाजर carrot
gajdant *n.* गजदंत tusk
gal jaana *vt* गल जाना moulder
gala *n.* गला throat
gala ghontana *v.t.* गला घोंटना throttle
gala ghontna *v. t.* गला घोंटना choke
gala hua *adj* गला हुआ carious
galaana *v.i.* गलाना melt
galat *a* गलत erroneous
galat *a* ग़लत false
galat *a.* ग़लत wrong
galat chhapana *v.t.* ग़लत छापना misprint
galat dhang se *adv.* ग़लत ढंग से ill
galat dhang se *adv.* ग़लत ढंग से wrong
galat dharna *n.* ग़लत धारणा
misconception

**galat ganna karna** *v.t.* ग़लत गणना करना miscalculate

**galat jaanch** *a.* गलत जांच mistrial

**galat nirnaya karna** *v.t.* ग़लत निर्णय करना misjudge

**galat samjhana** *v.t.* ग़लत समझना misapprehend

**galat samjhana** *v.t.* ग़लत समझना misconceive

**galat samjhana** *v.t.* ग़लत समझना misconstrue

**galat samjhana** *v.t.* ग़लत समझना misunderstand

**galatfahami** *n.* ग़लतफ़हमी misunderstanding

**galen** *n.* गैलन gallon

**gali** *n.* गली alley

**gali** *n.* गली lane

**gali galoj** *n.* गाली गलौज invective

**gali, sadak** *n.* गली street

**galicha** *n.* ग़लीचा rug

**galiyara** *n.* गलियारा corridor

**galti** *n.* ग़लती impropriety

**gaman** *n* गमन resort

**gambhir** *a.* गंभीर bad

**gambhir** *a.* गंभीर grave

**gambhir** *a.* गंभीर major

**gambhir** *a.* गंभीर, शांत sedate

**gambhir** *a* गंभीर serious

**gambhir** *a.* गंभीर solemn

**gambhir** *a.* गंभीर staid

**gambhir** *a.* गंभीर terrible

**gambhirta** *n.* गंभीरता gravity

**gambhirta** *n.* गंभीरता solemnity

**gambhirya** *n.* गांभीर्य sobriety

**ganana** *n.* गणना score

**ganana** *n.* गणना calculation

**ganana karn ka yantra** *n* गणना करने का यन्त्र calculator

**ganana karna** *v. t.* गणना करना calculate

**ganana karna** *v.t.* गणना करना repute

**ganda** *a* गंदा filthy

**ganda** *a.* गंदा nasty

**ganda** *a.* गंदा squalid

**gandagi** *n.* गंदगी squalor

**gandala karna** *v.t.* गंदला करना puddle

**gandh** *n.* गंध odour

**gandh** *n.* गंध smell

**gandhak** *n.* गंधक sulphur

**gandhak yukt** *a.* गंधक युक्त sulphuric

**gandh-hin** *n.* गंधहीन nitrogen

**gandhras** *n.* गंधरस myrrh

**gandi basti** *n.* गंदी बस्ती slum

**gandi naali** *n* गंदी नाली drain

**gandmala** *n* गण्डमाला angina

**ganit** *n* गणित mathematics

**ganitshastri** *n.* गणितशास्त्री mathematician

**ganitshastriya** *a.* गणितशास्त्रीय mathematical

**ganja** *a.* गंजा bald

**gantavya** *n* गंतव्य destination

**ganth** *n* गांठ tie

**ganvar** *n* गँवार churl

**ganwar** *n* गँवार rustic

**ganwarupan** *n.* गँवारूपन rusticity

**gappi vyakti** *n.* गप्पी व्यक्ति windbag

**gapshap** *n* गपशप chat

**garabh-paat** *n.* गर्भ-पात miscarriage

**garam** *n.* गर्म snug

**garam** *a.* गर्म sunny

**garam karna** *v.t.* गरम करना warm

**garami** *n.* गरमी warmth

**garare karna** *v.i.* ग़रारे करना gargle

**garari** *n.* गरारी gear

**garaz** *n.* गरज़ thunder

**garbh nirodh** *n.* गर्भ निरोध contraception

**garbhashay** *n.* गर्भाशय uterus

**garbhashay sancha** *n* गर्भाशय सांचा matrix

**garbhavarti** *a.* गर्भवती pregnant

**garbhavastha** *n.* गर्भावस्था pregnancy

garbhpaat *n* गर्भपात abortion

garbhpaat hona *v.i* गर्भपात होना abort

gardan *n.* गर्दन neck

gardan torh bukhar *n.* गर्दन तोड़ बुखार meningitis

garhbarh kar dena *v.i.* गड़बड़ कर देना fumble

garhbarh karna *v.t.* गड़बड़ करना mull

garhbarhi *n.* गड़बड़ी fuss

garhbarhi *n.* गड़बड़ी muddle

garhgarhahat *n.* गड़गड़ाहट rumble

garhi *n.* गाड़ी car

garhi *n.* गाड़ी carriage

garhi ka juwa *n* गाड़ी का जुआ limber

garjan *n.* गर्जन roar

garjan karna *v.i.* गर्जन करना roar

garjana *v. i* गरजना bellow

garjana *v.i.* गरजना thunder

garjanshil *a.* गर्जनशील thunderous

garm *a.* गर्म hot

garm karna *v.t* गर्म करना heat

garmi *n.* गर्मी heat

garmi se jhulsa hua *adj.* गरमी से झुलसा हुआ arid

gartika *n.* गर्तिका socket

garud *n* गरुड़ eagle

garvili chaal *n* गर्वीली चाल strut

garvili chal *n* गर्वीली चाल stalk

gas *n.* गैस gas

gas lalten ki batti *n* गैस लालटेन की बत्ती mantle

gas yukt *a.* गैस युक्त gassy

gatha-geet *n.* गाथा-गीत ballad

gathan *n.* गठन texture

gathiya *n.* गठिया gout

gathiya *n.* गठिया rheumatism

gathiya sambandhi *a.* गठिया संबंधी rheumatic

gathna *n.* घटना happening

gathri *n.* गठरी pack

gati *n.* गति velocity

gati barhana *v.t* गति बढ़ाना accelerate

gati hin *a* गतिहीन dead

gati matara *n.* गति मात्रा momentum

gatihin hona *v.i.* गतिहीन होना stagnate

gatihinta *n.* गतिहीनता stagnation

gatimaan *adj.* गतिमान agog

gatirodh *n* गतिरोध deadlock

gatirodh *n.* गतिरोध impasse

gatirodh *n.* गतिरोध retardation

gatiseel *a.* गतिशील mobile

gatisheelta *n.* गतिशीलता mobility

gatishil *adv.* गतिशील astir

gati-shil *a* गति-शील dynamic

gativigyan *n.* गतिविज्ञान dynamics

gativridhi *n* गतिवृद्धि acceleration

gatkaal mein *adv* गतकाल में formerly

gatta *n.* गत्ता cardboard

gaun baat *n* गौण बात detail

gauravpurna *n* गौरवपूर्ण dignity

gaurayiya *n.* गौरैया sparrow

gaushala *n* गोशाला byre

gavaha *n.* गवाह deponent

gavahi dena *v. t* गवाही देना depose

gavahi dena *v.i.* गवाही देना witness

gay *a.* गेय lyric

gayak *n.* गायक singer

gayak *n.* गायक singer

gayak *n.* गायक vocalist

gayak pakshi *n.* गायक पक्षी warbler

gayak-dal *n.* गायक-दल chorus

gayak-mandali *n* गायक-मंडली choir

gayan *n.* गायन song

gayan prastuti *n.* गायन प्रस्तुति recital

gaz *n.* गज़ yard

geela *adj.* गीला dank

geela *a.* गीला humid

geela *a.* गीला moist

geela *a.* गीला wet

geela karna *v. t.* गीला करना damp

geela karna *v.t.* गीला करना wet

geelapan *n.* गीलापन wetness

geet *n.* गीत glee
geet *n.* गीत ode
gehaarai *n* गहराई depth
geharai *n.* गहराई profundity
gehra lal *n* गहरा लाल crimson
gehra lal *a.* गहरा लाल vermillion
gehra lal rang *n.* गहरा लाल रंग vermillion
gehra neela rang *n.* गहरा नीला रंग sapphire
gehun ka paudha *n.* गेहूं का पौधा wheat
gend *n.* गेंद ball
gend phenkna *v.i* गेंद फेंकना bowl
genda *n.* गेंदा marigold
ghaas ka maidan *n.* घास का मैदान lawn
ghaata *n* घाटा deficit
ghaati *n* घाटी dale
ghabrahat *n.* घबराहट turmoil
ghaghra *n.* घाघरा skirt
ghair sarkari *a.* गैर सरकारी private
ghalmail *n.* घालमेल jumble
ghalmail *n.* घालमेल mull
ghal-mel *n.* घालमेल hotchpotch
ghamand *n.* घमंड arrogance
ghamand *n* घमण्ड conceit
ghamandi *adj.* घमंडी arrogant
ghamandi *a.* घमंडी lordly
ghamandi *a.* घमंडी proud
ghana *a.* घना thick
ghanisht *a.* घनिष्ट close
ghanishtata *n.* घनिष्ठता association
ghanishtata *n.* घनिष्ठता intimacy
ghanishth *a.* घनिष्ट inmost
ghanishth *a.* घनिष्ट near
ghanist *a.* घनिष्ठ intimate
ghanivhut karna *v.t.* घनीभूत करना intensify
ghanta *n* घंटा bell
ghanta *n.* घंटा hour
ghanta bajana *v.t.* घंटा बजाना toll
ghanta naad *n* घंटा नाद toll
ghanti *v.t.* घंटी ring

ghapla *n* घपला bungle
ghar *n* घर abode
ghar *n* घर dwelling
ghar ki yaad *n.* घर की याद nostalgia
ghar mein,andar *adv.* घर में, अंदर within
gharelu *a* घरेलू domestic
gharelu murgi *n.* घरेलू मुर्गी poultry
gharha *n.* घड़ा pitcher
gharhi *n.* घड़ी clock
gharhiyal *n* घड़ियाल crocodile
ghas *n* घास grass
ghas ka gaththar *n.* घास का गट्ठर wisp
ghas ka maidan *n.* घास का मैदान steppe
ghaseetna *v. t* घसीटना drag
ghasit *n* घसीट scrawl
ghasit *n.* घसीट scribble
ghasitan *n.* घसीटन shuffle
ghasitana *v.t.* घसीटना scrawl
ghasitna *v.t.* घसीटना trail
ghat *n.* घात ambush
ghat mein baithna *v.t.* घात में बैठना waylay
ghat shulk *n.* घाट शुल्क wharfage
ghatak *a* घातक fatal
ghatana *v. t* घटाना curtail
ghatana *v.i.* घटना wane
ghatav *n* घटाव decline
ghatav *n.* घटाव subtraction
ghati *n.* घाटी vale
ghati *n.* घाटी valley
ghatit hona *v. t* घटित होना befall
ghatit hona *v.t.* घटित होना happen
ghatit hona *v.i.* घटित होना occur
ghatiya *a* घटिया coarse
ghatiya *n.* खटिया cot
ghatiya *a.* घटिया inferior
ghatiyapan *n.* घटियापन inferiority
ghatna *n* घटना circumstance
ghatna *n.* घटना conjuncture
ghatna *n* घटना episode
ghatna *n* घटना event

ghatna *n.* घटना incident
ghatna *n.* घटना occurrence
ghatna sthal *n.* घटना स्थल locale
ghatnaa *v.t.* घटाना subtract
ghav *n.* घाव wound
ghav ka nishan *n* घाव का निशान scar
ghayal karna *v.t.* घायल करना wound
ghera *n.* घेरा circle
ghera *n.* घेरा enclosure
ghera *n* घेरा fence
ghera *n.* घेरा railing
gherabandi *n* घेराबंदी blockade
gherabandi *n.* घेराबंदी siege
gherna *v.t.* घेरना begird
gherna *v. t.* घेरना encircle
gherna *v. t* घेरना encompass
gherna *v.t* घेरना fence
gherna *v.t.* घेरना surround
ghinauna *a* घिनौना abominable
ghinauna *a.* घिनौना loathsome
ghirni *n.* घिरनी pulley
ghisa hua *a.* घिसा हुआ worn
ghisa pita kathan *n.* घिसा पिटा कथन tag
ghisa pita rup dena *v.t.* घिसा पिटा रूप देना stereotype
ghisatna *v. t* घिसटना crawl
ghisna *v.t* घिसना grate
ghoda *n.* घोड़ा steed
ghodha *n.* घोड़ा horse
ghodi *n.* घोड़ी mare
gholkar bahana *v.t.* घोलकर बहाना leach
ghongha *n.* घोंघा oyster
ghongha *n.* घोंघा snail
ghoomne ana *v.* घूमने आना visit
ghoonsa *n* घूँसा buff
ghoorna *v.i.* घूरना stare
ghoos *n* घूस bribe
ghoos dena *vt* घूस देना palm
ghor parajaya *n* घोर पराजय rout
ghosana *n* घोषणा declaration
ghoshana karna *v.t.* घोषणा करना avow

ghoshanapatra *n.* घोषणापत्र manifesto
ghoshit karna *v.t.* घोषित करना advertise
ghoshna *n.* घोषणा proclamation
ghoshna *n.* घोषणा profession
ghoshna *n.* घोषणा announcement
ghoshna karna *v.t.* घोषणा करना announce
ghoshna karna *v.t.* घोषणा करना proclaim
ghosit karna *v.t* घोषित करना herald
ghrenit *a* घृणित despicable
ghrenit *a.* घृणित heinous
ghrina *n.* घृणा abhorrence
ghrina *n.* घृणा aversion
ghrina *n* घृणा disdain
ghrina *n.* घृणा hate
ghrina *n.* घृणा repugnance
ghrina *n.* घृणा repulsion
ghrina karna *v.t.* घृणा करना abhor
ghrina karna *v. t* घृणा करना despise
ghrina karna *v. t.* घृणा करना disdain
ghrina karna *v.t.* घृणा करना hate
ghrina karna *v.t.* घृणा करना scorn
ghrinit *a.* घृणित vile
ghrinit vyakti *n.* घृणित व्यक्ति swine
ghudki *n.* घुड़की reprimand
ghulan shilta *n.* घुलनशीलता solubility
ghumana *v.t.* घुमाना crankle
ghumana *v.t.* घूमना ramble
ghumana *v.i.* घूमना rove
ghumana *v.i.* घूमना wander
ghumana *v.t.* घुमाना wheel
ghumantu *n.* घुमंतू rover
ghumantu *a* घुमंतू vagabond
ghumao *n* घुमाव whirl
ghumav *n* घुमाव turn
ghumavdar *a.* घुमावदार spiral
ghumna *v.i.* घूमना spin
ghumna *v.i.* घूमना stray
ghumna *v.i.* घूमना turn
ghumna *n.i.* घूमना whirl
ghumna phirna *v.i.* घूमना फिरना roam

**ghumnewala** *a.* घूमनेवाला rotary

**ghun** *n.* घुन weevil

**ghunghrala baal** *n.* घुंघराला बाल curl

**ghunsa** *n* घूंसा fist

**ghurghurna** *v.i.* घुरघुराना grunt

**ghurhsawar sainik** *n.* घुड़सवार सैनिक trooper

**ghutan** *n.* घुटन suffocation

**ghutan bhara** *a.* घुटन भरा stuffy

**ghuthana** *v.t.* गूंथना interlock

**ghutna** *n.* घुटना knee

**ghutne tekna** *v.i.* घुटने टेकना kneel

**giddh** *n.* गिद्ध vulture

**gilahari** *n.* गिलहरी squirrel

**gilas** *n.* गिलास tumbler

**gilat** *n.* गिलट nickel

**gilti** *n.* गिल्टी wen

**ginana** *v. t.* गिनना count

**ginti** *n.* गिनती computation

**gir jana** *v.i.* गिर जाना tumble

**gir padhna** *v.i.* गिर पड़ना slump

**gira dena** *v. t* गिरा देना down

**gira dena** *vt* गिरा देना overture

**gira dena** *v.t.* गिरा देना prostrate

**gira dena** *v.t.* गिरा देना shed

**gira dena** *v.t.* गिरा देना trip

**giraphtari** *n.* गिरफ़्तारी arrest

**girav** *n* गिराव spill

**girav** *n.* गिराव tumble

**giridaar meva** *n* गिरीदार मेवा nut

**girja ka gayak** *a.* गिरजा का गायक lay clerk

**girja ka padadhikari** *n.* गिरजे का पदाधिकारी beadle

**girjaghar** *n.* गिरजाघर church

**girna** *vt* गिरना fall

**girna** *v.t* गिराना fell

**giroh** *n.* गिरोह gang

**girrafe** *n.* जिराफ़ giraffe

**girvidaar** *n.* गिरवीदार mortgagee

**girwi rakhne wala** *n.* गिरवी रखने वाला mortgagor

**gitikawya** *n.* गीतिकाव्य lyric

**glucose** *n.* ग्लूकोज़ glucose

**glycerin** *n.* ग्लिसरीन glycerine

**gobar** *n* गोबर dung

**godaam** *v.t* गोदाम warehouse

**godam** *n.* गोदाम godown

**godam** *n.* गोदाम store

**godi** *n.* गोदी dock

**godi** *n.* गोदी lap

**godne ka chinh** *n.* गोदने का चिह्न tattoo

**gol** *a* गोल circular

**gol qaid khana** *n* गोल कैद खाना panopticon

**gola** *n.* गोला sphere

**golabari karna** *v.t.* गोलाबारी करना mortar

**golakar** *a.* गोलाकार spherical

**golardh** *n.* गोलार्ध hemisphere

**goley barsana** *v.t.* गोले बरसाना shell

**golf** *n.* गॉल्फ़ golf

**goli** *n* गोली bullet

**goli** *n.* गोली tablet

**gomans** *n* गोमांस beef

**gooda** *n.* गूदा pulp

**goodedar** *a.* गूदेदार pulpy

**goonj** *n.* गूंज resonance

**goonjana** *v.i.* गूंजना resound

**gopansheel** *a.* गोपनशील secretive

**gophan** *n.* गोफन sling

**goshthi** *n.* गोष्ठी seminar

**gota** *n.* गोता dip

**gota** *n* गोता dive

**gota lagana** *v. t* गोता लगाना dip

**gota lagana** *v.t.* गोता लगाना plunge

**gota lagana** *v.i.* गोता लगाना submerge

**grahak** *n..* ग्राहक client

**grahak** *n* ग्राहक customer

**gramin vyavastha** *n.* ग्रामीण व्यवस्था agronomy

**gramophone** *n.* ग्रामोफोन gramophone

gramya *a.* ग्राम्य rustic

granth ka aakar *n* ग्रंथ का आकार format

granthi *n.* ग्रंथि gland

granthi *n.* ग्रंथि node

granth-suchi +*n* ग्रंथ-सूची bibliography

greh *n.* ग्रह planet

greh sambandhi *a.* ग्रह संबंधी planetary

grehen *n* ग्रहण eclipse

grehini *n.* गृहिणी dame

grehna suchak shor karna *v.i* घृणा सूचक शोर करना hoot

grehnabhav *n.* घृणाभाव odium

grehnaspad *a.* घृणास्पद odious

grhena rakna *v.t.* घृणा रखना loathe

grishma ritu *n.* ग्रीष्म ऋतु summer

grishma ritu sambandhi *adj* ग्रीष्म ऋतु सम्बन्धी aestival

gubbara *n.* गुब्बारा balloon

guchha *n* गुच्छा bunch

guchha *n* गुच्छा cluster

guchhi *n* गुछी morel

guda *n.* गुदा anus

gudda, maldwar *n.* गुदा, मलद्वार rectum

gudgudi *a.* गुदगुदी ticklish

gudiya *n* गुड़िया doll

gufa *n.* गुफ़ा cave

gufa *n.* गुफ़ा cavern

guha *n.* गुहा cavity

guha *n* गुहा den

guitar *n.* गिटार guitar

gulab *n.* गुलाब rose

gulabi *a.* गुलाबी roseate

gulabi *a.* गुलाबी rosy

gular *n.* गूलर sycamore

guldasta *n* गुलदस्ता bouquet

guldasta *n.* गुलदस्ता nosegay

gulli *n.* गुल्ली plug

gulmehndi *n.* गुलमेंहदी balsam

guluband *n.* गुलूबंद muffler

gumbad *n* गुंबद dome

gumraha karna *v.t.* गुमराह करना misdirect

gumraha karna *v.t.* गुमराह करना misguide

guna karna *v.t.* गुणा करना multiply

gunak *n.* गुणक coefficient

gunan *n.* गुणन multiplication

gunda *n.* गुंडा ruffian

gunda *n.* गुंडा thug

gundharm *n.* गुणधर्म property

gunga *a* गूंगा dumb

gunga *a.* गूंगा mute

gungaan karna *v.t.* गुणगान करना glorify

gunguna *a.* गुनगुना lukewarm

gunguna *a.* गुनगुना warm

gungunahat *n.* गुनगुनाहट murmur

gunjan *n* गूंजन hum

gunjan karna *v. i* गूंजन करना buzz

gunjan karna *v. i* गूंजन करना hum

gunjana *v. t* गूंजना echo

gunjayamaan *a.* गुंजायमान resonant

guntha hua aata *n* गुँथा हुआ आटा dough

gunya rashi *n.* गुण्य राशि multiplicand

gupshup *n.* गपशप gossip

gupt *a.* गुप्त confidential

gupt *a.* गुप्त latent

gupt *a.* गुप्त occult

gupt *n.* गुप्त secret

gupt *a.* गुप्त, ulterior

gupt *a.* गुप्त underhand

gupt bhandar *n* गुप्त भंडार cache

gupt lekhan ki vidya *n.* गुप्त लिखन की विद्या cryptography

gupt matdaan *n* गुप्त मतदान ballot

gupt rup se batana *v. i* गुप्त रूप से बताना confide

gupt sthan *n.* गुप्त स्थान recess

guptata *n.* गुप्तता secrecy

guptchar *n* गुप्तचर scout

guptchar *n.* गुप्तचर spy

ena *v.i.* हिस्सा लेना participate
ari *n.* हिस्सेदारी participation
a. हितकारी wholesome
v. i हो जाना become
ka khel *n.* हॉकी का खेल hockey
होना be
होना belong
na *v.t.* होने देना tolerate
la a. होने वाला would-be
a. होनहार promising
टल hotel
स decrease
mbandhi *adjs* हृदय सम्बन्धी

akar ka *adj.* हृदय के आकार का

adv. हृदय से heartily
t a. हृष्ट-पुष्ट robust
n. हुक्मनामा writ

हंगामा affray
हंगामा melee
irh *n* हुड़दंगी भीड़ rout
wane

क desirous
क prone
readiness
wish
v.t. इच्छा रखना will
t. इच्छा रखना want
keen
urhna *v.i* इधर उधर दौड़ना
mna *v.t* इधर उधर घूमना
ज करना physic
ज करना treat

ilaychi *n.* इलायची cardamom
imaandaar *a.* ईमानदार honest
imaandaari *n.* ईमानदारी honesty
imandar *a.* ईमानदार sincere
imandari *n.* ईमानदारी principle
imarat *n* इमारत building
imarati lakri *n.* इमारती लकड़ी timber
imendar *a.* ईमानदार incorruptible
imli ka vriksh *n.* इमली का वृक्ष tamarind
inaam dena *v.t.* इनाम देना reward
inch *n.* इंच inch
indhan *n.* ईंधन fuel
indhan jhonkana *v.t.* ईंधन झोंकना stoke
indhan jhonkane wala *n.* ईंधन झोंकने वाला stoker
indriya *n.* इंद्रिय sense
ingit karna *v.i.* इंगित करना allude
inkar *n* इंकार no
irada *n.* इरादा motive
irada karna *v.t.* इरादा करना intend
irshya *n.* ईर्ष्या jealousy
irshya rakhna *v. t* ईर्ष्या रखना envy
irshya yogya *a* ईर्ष्या योग्य enviable
irshyalu *a* ईर्ष्यालु envious
is prakar *adv.* इस प्रकार thus
is se pehle ki *conj* इससे पहले कि before
is seema tak *adv.* इस सीमा तक as
isa masih *n.* ईसा मसीह messiah
isaai dharm ka *a.* इसाई धर्म का catholic
isai *n* ईसाई Christian
isai dharma *n.* ईसाई धर्म Christianity
isai dharma-sambandhi *a.* ईसाई धर्म-संबंधी Christian
isai jagat *n.* ईसाई जगत Christendom
isai math *n.* ईसाई मठ abbey
isaiyon ki dharm pustak *n* ईसाइयों की धर्म पुस्तक bible
isa-janmotasav *n* ईसा-जन्मोत्सव Christmas
ishara karna *v. t* इशारा करना beckon
ishara karna *v.t.* ईशारा करना insinuate

guptcharya karna *v.i* गुप्तचर्या करना scout
gurahat *n* गुर्राहट growl
gurda *n.* गुर्दा kidney
gurda-shoth *n.* गुर्दा-शोध nephritis
gurh *a.* गूढ़ metaphysical
gurraana *v.i.* गुर्राना growl
gurrahat *n.* गुर्राहट snarl
gurrana *v.i.* गुर्राना snarl
guru *n.* गुरू preceptor
gurutvakarshan *n.* गुरुत्वाकर्षण gravitation
guruvar *n.* गुरूवार Thursday
gussa *n.* गुस्सा fury
gustakh *a.* गुस्ताख impertinent
gustakh *a.* गुस्ताख insolent
gustakhi *n.* गुस्ताखी impertinence
gustakhi *n.* गुस्ताखी insolence
gut *n* गुट bloc
guthna *v.t.* गूथना twist
guthna *v.t.* गूथना wreathe
gutika *n.* गुटिका pill
gutnirpekshhta *n.* गुटनिरपेक्षता non-alignment
guzarna *v. t* गुज़रना elapse
guzarna *v.t.* गुज़रना undergo
guzra hua *prep.* गुज़रा हुआ past
gyarah *n* ग्यारह eleven

# H

haafna *v.i.* हांफना pant
haal he mein हाल ही में lately
haal hi mein *adv.* हाल ही में recently
haanfa *n.* हाँफा gasp
haanfna *v.i* हांफना gasp
haani *n.* हानि damage
haani *n.* हानि loss
haanikaar *a* हानिकर malign
haani-kaarak *a.* हानि कारक injurious

haar maanna *v. t* हार मानना bend
haar manana *v.i.* हार मानना succumb
haar manana *v.t.* हार मानना surrender
haas hona *v. i* हास होना decay
haath *n* हाथ hand
haath ka *a.* हाथ का manual
haath tekne ke chhadi *n.* हाथ टेकने की छड़ी maulstick
haathi dant *n.* हाथी दांत ivory
haaziri *n.* हाज़िरी roll-call
habashi *n* हबशी savage
habshi *n.* हबशी negro
habshiyon ka prades *n* हबशियों का परदेश niggerdom
haddi *n.* हड्डी bone
haija *n.* हैज़ा cholera
hajamat *n* हजामत shave
hajamat banana *v.t.* हजामत बनाना shave
hajjam *n.* हज्जाम barber
haklaana *v.i* हकलाना falter
haklahat *n* हकलाहट stammer
haklana *v.i.* हकलाना stammer
hal *n.* हल plough
hal karna *v.t.* हल करना solve
hal se jutai karna *v.i* हल से जुताई करना plough
halanki *conj.* हालांकि albeit
halchal *n.* हलचल ado
haldi *n.* हल्दी curcuma
haldi *n.* हल्दी turmeric
halka *a.* हल्का trivial
halka bhojan *n.* हल्का भोजन snack
halka gulabi *a.* हल्का गुलाबी pinkish
halka hona *v.i.* हलका होना lighten
halka rang chadhana *v.t.* हल्का रंग चढ़ाना tincture
halka sa choona *v.t.* हल्का सा छूना tip
halkapan *n* हल्कापन buoyancy
halke gulabi rang ka *a* हल्के गुलाबी रंग का pink
halke nashe mein *a.* हल्के नशे में tipsy

halke se *adv.* हलके से lightly

halki *n.* हल्की तलवार rapier

halki nauka *n.* हल्की नौका yacht

halwaha *n.* हलवाहा ploughman

halwai *n* हलवाई confectioner

hamara *pron.* हमारा our

hamla *n.* हमला attack

hamla *n.* हमला invasion

hamla *n.* हमला onset

hangama *n* हंगामा ferment

hangar *n.* हांगर shark

hani *n.* छीजन, हानि wastage

hanikarak *a* हानिकारक adverse

hanikarak *a.* हानिकारक baleful

hanipradh *a.* हानिप्रद mischievous

hans *n.* हंस gander

hans *n.* हंस swan

hansana *v.t.* हंसाना tickle

hansi *n.* हंसी jest

hansi *n.* हंसी laugh

hansi *n.* हंसी laughter

hansi majak karna *v.i.* हंसी मज़ाक करना joke

hansi udaana *v.i.* हंसी उड़ाना mock

hansi urana *v.t.* हंसी उड़ाना gird

hansiya *n.* हंसिया sickle

hansna *v.i* हंसना laugh

hara bhara *a.* हरा भरा verdant

hara rang *n* हरा रंग green

harayee ka maap *n* हराई का माप fathom

hardik *a* हार्दिक cordial

hardik *a.* हार्दिक whole-hearted

harhap lena *v.t.* हड़प लेना appropriate

harhbarhahat ke sath *a.* हड़बड़ाहट के साथ hasty

harhtaal *n* हड़ताल strike

harhtalkarta *n.* हड़तालकर्त्ता striker

harin *n* हरिण deer

harit *a.* हरित green

hariyali *n.* हरियाली greenery

harjana *v.t.* हरजाना offset

harmoniyam *n.* हारमोनियम harmonium

harniya *n.* हर्निया hernia

harshatirek *n.* हर्षातिरेक rapture

harshit *n.* हर्षित joyful, joyous

harsht pusht *a.* हृष्ट पुष्ट lusty

hasil karna *v.t.* हासिल करना achieve

hasil karna *v.t.* हासिल करना attain

hast rekha vigyan *adj* हस्त रेखा विज्ञान palmistry

hastakshar *n.* हस्ताक्षर autograph

hastakshar *n.* हस्ताक्षर signature

hastakshar karna *v.t.* हस्ताक्षर करना sign

hastakshar karna *n.* हस्ताक्षरकर्त्ता signatory

hastakshep *n.* हस्तक्षेप interference

hastakshep *v.i.* हस्तक्षेप tamper

hastakshep karna *v.i.* हस्तक्षेप करना interfere

hastkshep *n.* हस्तक्षेप intervention

hastkshep karna *v.i.* हस्तक्षेप करना intervene

hast-maithun *n* हस्त-मैथून omanism

hastmaithun karna *v.i.* हस्तमैथुन करना masturbate

hastsilp *n.* हस्तशिल्प handicraft

hasttran *n.* हस्तत्राण gauntlet

hasya abhineta *n.* हास्य अभिनेता comedian

hasyanukriti *n.* हास्यानुकृति parody

hasyapurna *a.* हास्यपूर्ण zany

hasyaras ki patrika *n* हास्यरस की पत्रिका comic

hat jana *v.t.* हट जाना desert

hatana *v.t* हटाना eliminate

hatana *v.t.* हटाना move

hatana *v.t.* हटाना remove

hatane ka karya *n.* हटाने का कार्य removal

hatane yogya *a.* हटाने योग्य removable

hatash karna *v.t.* हताश करना disappoint

hatav *n* हटाव elimination

hathapayee *n.* हाथापाई scuffle

hathapayee karna *v.i.* हाथापाई करना scuffle

hathaura *n.* हथौड़ा hammer

hatheli *n.* हथेली palm

hatheli mein chhipana *v.t.* हथेली में छिपाना palm

hathgola *n.* हथगोला grenade

hathi *n* हाथी elephant

hathi *a.* हठी obdurate

hathi *a.* हठी wayward

hathiyaar *n.* हथियार arm

hathiyana *v.t.* हथियाना usurp

hathiyar *n.* हथियार weapon

hathiyar se prahar *n.* हथियार से प्रहार stab

hathkadi *n.* हथकड़ी handcuff

hathkari lagana *v.t* हथकड़ी लगाना handcuff

hatotsah karna *v.t.* हतोत्साह करना discourage

hatotsah karna *v.t* हतोत्साह करना dishearten

hatotsaha karna *v.t* हतोत्साह करना deject

hatth se *adv.* हठ से perforce

hattha *n.* हत्था handle

hatthi *a.* हठी adamant

hatthi *a.* हठी obstinate

hatya *n* हत्या assassination

hatya *n.* हत्या murder

hatya karna *v.t.* हत्या करना assassinate

hatya karna *v.t* हत्या करना butcher

hatya karna *v.t.* हत्या करना murder

hatyara *n.* हत्यारा assassin

hatyara *n* हत्यारा cain

hatyara *n.* हत्यारा murderer

haudi *n.* हौदी cesspool

havadar *n.* हवादार airy

havadar banana *v.t.* हवादार बनाना ventilate

havai chhatri *n.* हवाई छतरी parachute

havakash *n.* हवाकश ventilator

havayee *a.* हवाई

havayee adda *n.*

havayee jahaz

hazar *a* हज़ार

hazar ki sankh

thousand

heen *adj.* हीन

hichki *n.* हिच

hichkichana

hichkole de

hidayat ka

hijrha *n* हि

hilaana *v.t*

hilana *v.t.*

hilana *v.t.*

hilane ki

hilna *v.t*

hilna

hilna

hilna

hilna

hilna

hilor

hilsa

him

him

him

hi

hi

hi

h

hissa

hisse

hitka

ho jan

hockey

hona *v.*

hona *v.*

hone de

hone wa

honeha

hotel *n.*

hras *n* ह

hriday sa

cardiac

hridya ke

cordate

hridya se

hrisht-pus

hukmnam

hun हूँ am

hungama *n*

hungama *n*

hurdangi b

hwas *n* हना

icchuk *a* इच्छु

icchuk *a.* इच्छु

ichcha *n.* इच्छ

ichcha *n.* इच्छ

ichcha rakhna

ichha rakhna

ichhuk *a.* इच्छु

idhar udhar d

scamper

idhar udhar gh

ambulate

ilaj karna *v.t.* इ

ilaj karna *v.t.* इ

ishara karna *v.i.* इशारा करना motion
ishtehaar *n.* इश्तहार handbill
ishtihaar *n.* इश्तिहार poster
ishwarmimansa *n.* ईश्वरमीमांसा theology
iske atirikt *adv.* इसके अतिरिक्त moreover
ispat *n.* इस्पात steel
iss ke aage *adv.* इस के आगे further
iss ke baad *adv.* इसके बाद hereafter
iss ke uprant *adv.* इसके उपरांत next
istari karna *v.t.* इस्तरी करना iron
itali ka *a.* इटली का Italian
itali ki bhasha *n.* इटली की भाषा Italian
ithlaati chaal *n* इठलाती चाल swagger
ithlana *v.i.* इठलाना strut
ithlana *v.i.* इठलाना swagger
itihaas *n.* इतिहास history
itihaascar *n.* इतिहासकार annalist
itihas *n.* इतिहास chronicle
itihas prasidh *a .* इतिहास प्रसिद्घ historic
itihasik *a.* ऐतिहासिक historical
itihaskaar *n.* इतिहासकार historian
itminan se *a.* इत्मिनान से leisurely
itna *adv.* इतना so
itna nahi *adv.* इतना नहीं less

J

jaagir *n.* जागीर manor
jaagir sambandhi *a.* जागीर संबंधी manorial
jaal *n.* जाल net
jaal *n.* जाल snare
jaal *n. pl.* जाल toils
jaali *n.* जाली grate
jaali *n.* जाली lattice
jaali *a.* जाली malafide
jaali *n.* जाली mesh
jaalsaaz *n.* जालसाज counterfeiter
jaalsajhe *n* जालसाज़ी forgery
jaan parhna *v.i.* जान पड़ना seem

jaanana *v.t.* जानना know
jaanbhuj kar kiya hua *a* जानबूझ कर किया हुआ deliberate
jaanbhujkar *adv.* जानबूझकर purposely
jaanch parhtaal *n.* जांच पड़ताल examination
jaankar *a* जानकार familiar
jaankari *n.* जानकारी knowledge
jaati *a.* जाति qualitative
jaati *n.* जाति species
jab kabhi *adv. conj* जब कभी whenever
jab tak *conj.* जब तक while
jab tak ki *n. conj.* जब तक कि till
jab tak ki *conj* जब तक कि until
jabki *conj.* जबकि whereas
jabrha *n.* जबड़ा jaw
jabt karna *v. t* ज़ब्त करना confiscate
jabti *n* ज़ब्ती forfeiture
jadi buti *n.* जड़ी बूटी herb
jadu *n.* जादू sorcery
jadu karna *v.i.* जादू करना conjure
jadu sambandhi *a.* जादू संबंधी magical
jadu tona *n.* जादू टोना witchcraft
jadu tona *n.* जादू टोना witchery
jadugar *n.* जादूगर magician
jadugar *n.* जादूगर sorcerer
jadugar *n.* जादूगर wizard
jadugari karna *v.t.* जादूगरी करना juggle
jadugarni *n.* जादूगरनी witch
jadui kriya जादुई क्रिया necromancy
jae *n.* जई oat
jagana *v.t.* जगाना wake
jagat sambandhi *adj.* जगत संबंधी cosmic
jagmaga dena *v.t.* जगमगा देना illuminate
jagran *n* जागरण wake
jahan *conj.* जहां where
jahan kahin *adv.* जहां कहीं wherever
jahan se *adv.* जहां से whence
jahar ki dawa *n.* ज़हर की दवा mithridate
jahaz *n.* जहाज़ ship
jahaz ka farsh *n* जहाज़ का फ़र्श deck

**jahaz ka utarna** *vy* जहाज़ का उतरना landing

**jahaz par ladan** *n.* जहाज़ पर लदान shipment

**jahazi** *a.* जहाज़ी naval

**jahazi berha** *n* जहाज़ी बेड़ा fleet

**jaik duwara uthana** *v.t.* जैक द्वारा उठाना jack

**jail wapasi** *n* जेल वापसी remand

**jailer** *n.* जेलर warder

**jaisai ko taisa lautana** *v.t.* जैसे को तैसा लौटाना retort

**jaise taise** *adv.* जैसे तैसे somehow

**jakdan** *n* जकड़न grip

**jakran** *n.* जकड़न spasm

**jal baint** *n* जलबेंत rush

**jal prapat** *n.* जल प्रपात waterfall

**jal yatra karna** *v.i.* जलयात्रा करना sail

**jalan** *n.* जलन irritation

**jalana** *v. t* जलाना burn

**jalana** *v.t* जलाना fire

**jalatank** *n.* जलातंक rabies

**jalavatran** *n.* जलावतरण launch

**jaldbaaz** *a.* जल्दबाज़ impetuous

**jaldbaaz** *a.* जल्दबाज़ rash

**jaldbaazi** *a.* जल्दबाज़ reckless

**jaldi** *adv.* शीघ्र soon

**jaldi karna** *v. t.* जल्दी करना expedite

**jaldi karna** *v.i.* जल्दी कराना hasten

**jaldi karna** *v.t.* जल्दी करना hurry

**jaldi karna** *v.t.* जल्दी करना press

**jaldi se kam karna** *v. t* जल्दी से काम करना bustle

**jaldwar** *n.* जलद्वार sluice

**jali nakal karna** *v.t* जाली नकल करना forge

**jalidaar** *adj* जालीदार cellular

**jaljivon ke ande** *n.* जलजीवों के अंडे spawn

**jalmagan karna** *v.t* जलमग्न करना flood

**jalmurgi** *n.* जलमुर्गी gull

**jalne ki chot** *n* जलने की चोट burn

**jalnikas** *n* जलनिकास drainage

**jaloos** *n.* झालोन parade

**jalpaan** *n.* जलपान refreshment

**jalpan-greh** *n.* जलपान- गृह canteen

**jalpari** *n.* जलपरी mermaid

**jalpatra** *n.* जलपात्र mug

**jalpratap** *n.* जलप्रताप cascade

**jalpurush** *n.* जलपुरुष merman

**jalrodhi** *a.* जलरोधी watertight

**jalsah** *a.* जलसह waterproof

**jalsah banana** *v.t.* जलसह बनाना waterproof

**jalsah vastra** *n* जलसह वस्त्र waterproof

**jalsena sambandhi** *a.* जलसेना संबंधी marine

**jalta hua** *adv.* जलता हुआ ablaze

**jalwayu** *n.* जलवायु climate

**jalyan ka agra bhag** *n.* जलयान का अग्र भाग stem

**jam jana** *v.i.* जम जाना freeze

**jama** *n.* जमा deposit

**jama karna** *v.i* जमा करना mass

**jamahi** *n.* जम्हाई yawn

**jamahi lena** *v.i.* जम्हाई लेना yawn

**jamanat** *n.* ज़मानत surety

**jambura** *n* जंबूरा pleirs

**jamvika** *n.* जंभिका maxilla

**jan jati** *n.* जन जाति tribe

**jana** *v.i.* जाना go

**janam** *n.* जन्म nativity

**janam dena** *v.t.* जन्म देना litter

**janam ka dhani** *adj.* जन्म का धनी born rich

**janam sambandhi** *a.* जन्म संबन्धि nasal

**janamdata** *n.* जन्मदाता originator

**janamjaat** *a.* जन्मजात inherent

**janamjaat** *a.* जन्मजात native

**janamjat** *a.* जन्मजात innate

**janana** *n.* ज़नाना womanish

**janch** *n.* जांच inquiry

**janch** *n.* जांच question

janch *n.* जांच trial

janch karna *v.t.* जांच करना inquire

janch karna *v.t.* जांच करना verify

janch padtaal *n* जांच पड़ताल exploration

janch padtal *n* जांच पड़ताल probe

janchana *v. t.* जांचना check

janchna *v.t.* जांचना test

jang *n.* जंग rust

jang khaya hua *a.* ज़ंग खाया हुआ rusty

jang lagana *v.i* जंग लगाना rust

jangal *n.* जंगल woods

jangali *a.* जंगली barbarian

jangali *a.* जंगली savage

jangali sand *n* जंगली साँड bison

janganana *n.* जनगणना census

jangha *n.* जंघा thigh

jangli *a.* जंगली wild

jangli ghoda *n.* जंगली घोड़ा mustang

jangli lahsun *n* जंगली लहसुन moly

jangli murgha *n.* जंगली मुर्गा moor cock

janjatiya *a.* जनजातीय tribal

janjir *n* ज़ंजीर fetter

jankaari *n* जानकारी cognizance

janm *n.* जन्म birth

janm dena *v. t* जन्म देना beget

janmat sangrah *n.* जनमत संग्रह plebiscite

janmat sangreh *n.* जनमत संग्रह referendum

janpad *n* जनपद district

jansaadharan *n.* जनसाधारण mob

jansamuh *n* जनसमूह crowd

jansanhar *n.* जनसंहार massacre

jansanhar karna *v.t.* जनसंहार करना massacre

janta *n.* जनता people

janta *n.* जनता public

jantushala *n.* जंतुशाला zoo

japani mudra *n.* जापानी मुद्रा Yen

jarh *n.* जड़ root

jarh jamana *v.i.* जड़ जमना root

jarha bitana *v.i* जाड़ा बिताना winter

jarhna *v.t.* जड़ना stud

jari rakhna *v. i.* जारी रखना continue

jari rakhna *v.t.* जारी रखना perpetuate

jarjihi *a.* तरजीही preferential

jarsi *n.* जर्सी jersey

jarsi *n.* जरसी pullover

jasta *n.* जस्ता zinc

jasus *n.* जासूस detective

jasusi karna *v.i.* जासूसी करना spy

jati *n* जाति breed

jati *n* जाति caste

jatichyut *n.* जातिच्युत outcast

jatil *a* जटिल complex

jatil *a* जटिल difficult

jatil *a.* जटिल sophisticated

jatil *n.* जटिल stiff

jau *n.* जौ barley

jauhari *n.* जौहरी jeweller

jawaharat ka baksa *n* जवाहरात का बक्सा casket

jay jaykar karna *v.t* जय जयकार करना acclaim

jayanti *n.* जयंती anniversary

jay-jaykaar *n.* जय-जयकार ovation

jayjaykaar karna *v. t.* जयजयकार करना cheer

jaykar *n* जयकार acclaim

jeb *n.* जेब pocket

jeebh *n.* जीभ tongue

jeetna *v. t* जीतना conquer

jeev jantu *n* जीव जंतु fauna

jeev vigyan *n* जीव विज्ञान biology

jeev vigyani *n* जीव विज्ञानी biologist

jeevan pradan karna *v.t.* जीवन प्रदान करना vitalize·

jeevan shakti *n.* जीवन शक्ति vitality

jeevanadhar *n.* जीवनाधार sustenance

jeevani *n* जीवनी biography

jeevani-lekhak *n* जीवनी-लेखक biographer

jeevika *n.* जीविका subsistence

jeevit *a.* जीवित animate

**jeevit rakhna** *v.t.* जीवित रखना sustain

**jeevit bachna** *v.i.* जीवित बचना survive

**jeevit rehna** *v.i.* जीवित रहना subsist

**jewaanu** *n.* जीवाणु bacteria

**jhaadu lagana** *v.i.* झाड़ू लगाना sweep

**jhaag** *n* झाग foam

**jhaag** *n.* झाग lather

**jhaarhi** *n* झाड़ी bush

**jhaarhi** *n.* झाड़ी shrub

**jhabba lagana** *v.t* झब्बा लगाना fringe

**jhabbedar kinara** *n.* झब्बेदार किनारा fringe

**jhag paida karna** *v.t.* झाग पैदा करना foam

**jhagarha** *n.* झगड़ा strife

**jhagarhna** *v.i.* झगड़ना quarrel

**jhagda** *n* झगड़ा fight

**jhagra** *n.* झगड़ा row

**jhagralu** *a* झगड़ालू factious

**jhagrha** *n.* झगड़ा altercation

**jhagrha** *n.* झगड़ा quarrel

**jhak** *n.* झक crotchet

**jhalak** *n.* झलक glimpse

**jhalak** *n.* झलक tincture

**jhalar** *n.* झालर frill

**jhanakna** *v.i.* झांकना glance

**jhanda** *n* झंडा flag

**jhangiya** *n.* जांघिया breeches

**jhanjhanna** *v.i.* झनझनाना jingle

**jhanjhat** *n* झंझट botheration

**jhanjhat** *n.* झंझट perplexity

**jhanjhawat** *n.* झंझावात hurricane

**jhankar** *n.* झनकार jingle

**jhanki** *n.* झांकी glance

**jhanki** *n* झांकी pcep

**jhapak** *n* झपक wink

**jhapatna** *v.i.* झपटना pounce

**jhapatta** *n* झपट्टा pounce

**jhapatta** *n* झपट्टा spurt

**jhapatta** *n* झपट्टा swoop

**jhapatta maarna** *v.i.* झपट्टा मारना sally

**jhapatta marna** *v.i.* झपट्टा मारना swoop

**jhapki** *n.* झपकी doze

**jhapki** *n.* झपकी nap

**jhapki lena** *v.i.* झपकी लेना nap

**jharber** *n.* झरबेर strawberry

**jharhan** *n* झाड़न duster

**jharhap** *n.* झड़प skirmish

**jharhi ki baarh** *n.* झाड़ी की बाड़ hedge

**jharhu** *n* झाड़ू broom

**jharhu** *n.* झाड़ू mop

**jharhu laganewala** *n.* झाड़ू लगानेवाला sweeper

**jharokha** *n.* झरोखा niche

**jhar-ponchh karna** *v.t.* झाड़पोंछ करना mop

**jhataka** *n.* झटका jerk

**jhatka** *n* झटका blow

**jhatka** *n.* झटका jolt

**jhatka** *n* झटका pluck

**jhatka** *n* झटका shake

**jhatka** *n.* झटका shock

**jhatka dena** *v.t.* झटका देना toss

**jhatke se torhna** *v.t.* झटके से तोड़ना smash

**jhatkedar** *a.* झटकेदार jerky

**jheel** *n.* झील lake

**jhelna** *v.t.* झेलना incur

**jhelna** *v.t.* झेलना weather

**jhenp** *n* झेंप blush

**jhenpana** *v.i* झेंपना blush

**jhilli** *n.* झिल्ली membrane

**jhillidar** *a.* झिल्लीदार webby

**jhilmilahat** *n.* झिलमिलाहट twinkle

**jhirakna** *v.t.* झिड़कना snub

**jhomparhi** *n.* झोंपड़ी cote

**jhomparhi** *n* झोंपड़ी cottage

**jhonka** *n.* झोंका whiff

**jhonka** *n.* झोंका gust

**jhonka** *n.* झोंका puff

**jhoothi ninda** *n.* झूठी निंदा slander

**jhoothi ninda karna** *v.t.* झूठी निंदा करना slander

**jhukaav** *n.* झुकाव inclination
**jhukana** *v. t* झुकना bow
**jhukana** *v.t.* झुकाना lower
**jhukao** *n.* झुकाव proclivity
**jhukao** *n.* झुकाव tendency
**jhukao** *n.* झुकाव tilt
**jhukav** *n* झुकाव slant
**jhukav** *n* झुकाव stoop
**jhukna** *v.i.* झुकना incline
**jhukna** *v.i.* झुकना lean
**jhukna** *v.i.* झुकना stoop
**jhukna** *v.i.* झुकना tilt
**jhula** *n* झूला swing
**jhulana** *v. t* झुलाना dangle
**jhulana** *v.t.* झुलाना rock
**jhulna** *vt* झूलना pendulate
**jhulna** *v.i.* झूलना swing
**jhulsan** *n* झुलसन singe
**jhulsana** *v.t.* झुलसाना parch
**jhulsana** *v.t.* झुलसाना scorch
**jhulsana** *v.t.* झुलसाना singe
**jhund** *n* झुंड flock
**jhurmut** *n.* झुरमुट thicket
**jhurri** *n.* झुर्री wrinkle
**jhut bolna** *v.i* झूठ बोलना lie
**jhuta sidh karna** *v.t.* झूठा सिद्ध करना confute
**jhutha** *n* झूठा bouncer
**jhutha** *n.* झूठा liar
**jhuti shapath** *n.* झूठी शपथ perjury
**jhuti gavahi dena** *v.i.* झूठी गवाही देना perjure
**jhuti khabhar** *n* झूठी खबर bruit
**ji churana** *v.t.* जी चुराना shirk
**jibh se chatna** *v.t.* जीभ से चाटना lick
**jid** *n.* ज़िद obduracy
**jiddi** *a.* जिद्दी stubborn
**jidh** *n.* ज़िद obstinacy
**jigar** *n.* जिगर liver
**jigyasu** *a.* जिज्ञासु inquisitive
**jirna** *a.* जीर्ण threadbare

**jis ke baad** *conj.* जिसके बाद whereupon
**jis par var kiya ja sake** *a.* जिस पर वार किया जा सके vulnerable
**jis par, jahan** *conj.* जिस पर, जहां whereat
**jis samay** *conj.* जिस समय when
**jiski zamanat ho sake** *a.* जिसकी ज़मानत हो सके bailable
**jisko** *pron.* जिसको as
**jivan yukt karna** *v.t.* जीवन युक्त करना animate
**jivankaal** *n* जीवनकाल life
**jivanrahit** *a.* जीवन रहित lifeless
**jivant** *a.* जीवंत living
**jivanu nashan** *n.* जीवाणु नाशन sterilization
**jivanu-rahit banana** *v.t.* जीवाणुरहित बनाना sterilize
**jivika** *n* जीविका living
**jiwant** *a.* जीवंत live
**jiwanu** *n.* जीवाणु germ
**jo** *rel. pron.* जो that
**jo** *pron.* जो which
**jo koi** *pron* जो कोई whichever
**jo vastu** *pron.* जो वस्तु what
**joda khana** *v.t.* जोड़ा खाना mate
**jodna** *v.t* जोड़ना link
**jodne wala** *adj.* जोड़ने वाला annectant
**jokhim** *n.* जोखिम venture
**jokhim bhara** *a.* जोखिम भरा venturesome
**jokhim lena,** *v.t.* जोखिम लेना stake
**jokhim se bhara** *a.* जोखिम से भरा adventurous
**jonk** *n.* जोंक leech
**jood** *n.* जोड़ match
**joon** *n.* जूं louse
**joota** *n.* जूता boot
**joota** *n.* जूता shoe
**jordar dastakh** *n.* ज़ोरदार दस्तक bang
**jorh** *n* जोड़ weld
**jorha** *n* जोड़ा couple
**jorha** *n.* जोड़ा pair

**jorhna** *v.t.* जोड़ना ally
**jorhna** *v. t.* जोड़ना cement
**jorhna** *v. t* जोड़ना couple
**jorhna** *v.t.* जोड़ना join
**jorhna** *v.t.* जोड़ना suffix
**jorhna** *v.t.* जोड़ना sum
**jorhna** *v.t.* जोड़ना total
**jorhne ki kriya** *n.* जोड़ने की क्रिया addition
**jorhon ki sujan** *n* जोड़ों की सूजन arthritis
**jorna** *v.t.* जोड़ना add
**jorna** *v.t.* जोड़ना attach
**jorna** *v. t.* जोड़ना connect
**jorna** *n.* जोड़ joint
**joru ka gulam** *a.* जोरू का गुलाम henpecked
**josh** *n.* जोश ardour
**josh** *n* जोश fervour
**joshila** *a* जोशीला earnest
**joshila** *a* जोशीला fiery
**jotana** *v. t* जोतना cultivate
**jotna,jutai karna** *v.t.* जोतना till
**jua** *n* जुआ gamble
**jua khelna** *v.i.* जुआ खेलना gamble
**juari** *n.* जुआरी gambler
**jugali karna** *v.i.* जुगाली करना ruminate
**jugali karne wala** *a.* जुगाली करने वाला ruminant
**jugali wala pashu** *n.* जुगाली वाला पशु ruminant
**julus** *n.* जुलूस procession
**jungle** *n.* जंगल coppice
**jungle** *n* जंगल forest
**jungle** *n.* जंगल jungle
**jurhva** *a* जुड़वां twin
**jurhva jorhe mein se ek** *n.* जुड़वां जोड़े में से एक twin
**juri ka sadasya** *n.* जूरी का सदस्य juror
**juri ka sadasyai** *n.* जूरी का सदस्य juryman
**jurmana** *n* जुर्माना fine
**jurmana karna** *v.t* जुर्माना करना fine

**jutana** *v.t.* जुटाना afford
**jutay ka pichla bhag** *n.* जूते का पिछला भाग heel
**jutayee-yogya bhumi** *adj* जुताई-योग्य भूमि arable
**jvaar** *n.* ज्वार tide
**jvariya** *a.* ज्वारीय tidal
**jwalamukhi** *n.* ज्वालामुखी volcano
**jwalamukhiya** *a.* ज्वालामुखीय volcanic
**jwalanshil** *a.* ज्वलनशील inflammable
**jwar** *n.* ज्वर fever
**jyeshth** *a* ज्येष्ठ elder
**jyotish** *n.* ज्योतिष astrology
**jyotishi** *n.* ज्योतिषी astrologer

# K

**ka samay naapna** *v.t.* का समय नापना time
**kaaghaz** *n.* सचारपत्र paper
**kaal** *n* काल era
**kaal** *n.* काल tense
**kaal purva** *a.* कालपूर्व premature
**kaalam** *n* कॉलम column
**kaalkram** *n.* कालक्रम chronology
**kaalpanik** *a* काल्पनिक fictitious
**kaalpanik** *a.* काल्पनिक hypothetical
**kaam** *n.* काम job
**kaam karna** *v.i* काम करना function
**kaam karna** *v.t.* काम करना work
**kaam karne wala** *n.* कर्म करने वाला functionary
**kaam mein laana** *v.t.* काम में लाना use
**kaam mein lana** *v.t.* काम में लाना ply
**kaam par lagana** *v. t* काम पर लगाना engage
**kaam vasna** *n.* काम वासना lust
**kaam vasna** *n.* काम वासना sexuality
**kaamuk** *a* खामूक erotic
**kaamuk** *a.* कामुक lascivious

kaamuk *a.* कामुक sensual

kaan *n* कान ear

kaan ka khunt *n* कान का खूँट cerumen

kaan ka parda *n* कान का परदा drum

kaan khodni *n.* कानखोदनी auricle

kaan ki aakriti ka *adj.* कान की आकृति का auricular

kaanch *n.* कांच glass

kaanuni *a.* कानूनी legal

kaanuni banana *v.t.* कानूनी बनाना legalize

kaaran *n.* कारण cause

kaaran *n.* कारण sake

kaaran banana *v.t* कारण बनना cause

kaaran batlanay wala *adj.* कारण बतलाने वाला causal

kaarinda *n.* कारिंदा bailiff

kaarnas *n.* कार्नस mantel

kaat chhant *n.* काट छांट lop

kaat dena *v. t* काट देना delete

kaat dena *v.t.* काट देना sever

kaathi *n.* काठी saddle

kaatna *v.t.* काटना hack

kaatna *v. t.* काटना bite

kaatna *v.t.* काटना intersect

kaatna *v.t.* काटना mow

kab *adv.* कब when

kabhi kabhi *adv.* कभी कभी sometime

kabhi kabhi *adv.* कभी कभी sometimes

kabhi nahin *adv.* कभी नहीं never

kabla *n* काबला bolt

kabr *n.* कब्र grave

kabra *n.* कब्र tomb

kabristan *n.* कब्रिस्तान cemetery

kabristan *n.* कब्रिस्तान churchyard

kabristan *n.* कब्रिस्तान necropolis

kabutar *n* dove

kabutar *n.* कबूतर pigeon

kabz *n.* कब्ज़ constipation

kabza *n.* कब्ज़ा occupation

kachahri *n.* कचहरी court

kachara *n* कचरा filth

kachauri *n* कचौरी pie

kachhua *n.* कछुआ tortoise

kachra *n.* कचरा junk

kadachitra *adv.* कदाचित्र perhaps

kadam *n.* कदम step

kadam chal *n* कदम चाल canter

kaddu *n.* कद्दू pumpkin

kadra karna *v.t.* कद्र करना prize

kaf jaisa *a.* कफ़ जैसा mucus

kagar *n.* कगार brink

kagaz ka kharra *n.* कागज का खर्रा scroll

kagaz ka lapetan *n.* कागज़ की लपेटन wrapper

kahan *adv.* कहां where

kahan *adv.* कहां whereabouts

kahan *adv.* कहां whither

kahani *n.* कहानी story

kahani *n.* कहानी tale

kahavat *n.* कहावत adage

kahavat *n.* कहावत proverb

kahi nahi *adv.* कहीं नहीं nowhere

kahin *adv.* कहीं, किसी जगह somewhere

kahin bhi nahin *adv.* कहीं भी नहीं no near

kaid karna *v. t* कैद करना confine

kaincha *n. pl.* कैंचा shears

kainchi *n.* कैंची scissors

kaise *adv.* कैसे how

kajal lagana *v.t.* काजल लगाना soot

kaksh *n.* कक्ष apartment

kaksha *n* कक्षा class

kaksha nayak *n.* कक्षा नायक monitor

kal *adv.* कल yesterday

kal ko *adv.* कल को tomorrow

kala *adj.* काला black

kala karna *v. t.* काला करना blacken

kala kaushal ki ashlilta *n.* कला कौशल की अश्लीलता coprology

kala kawa *n.* काला कौआ raven

kalabaz *n.* कलाबाज़ acrobat

kalabazi *n.* कलाबाज़ी somersault

**kalabazi khana** *v.i.* कलाबाज़ी खाना somersault

**kalaf lagana** *v.t.* कलफ़ लगाना starch

**kalah karna** *v. t* कलह करना wrangle

**kalai** *n.* कलाई wrist

**kalai sambandhi** *adj* कलाई संबंधी carpal

**kalakar** *n.* कलाकार artist

**kalank** *n* कलंक blur

**kalank** *n.* कलंक slur

**kalash** *n* कलश urn

**kalatamak** *a.* कलात्मक artistic

**kalavadhi** *n* कालावधि duration

**kale rang ki titli** *n.* काले रंग की तितली nigger

**kalgi** *n* कलग़ी crest

**kali** *n.* कली bud

**kali chaya** *n.* काली छाया spectre

**kalik** *a.* कालिक temporal

**kalikh** *n.* कालिख soot

**kalimamaya** *a.* कालिमामय sombre

**kalin** *n.* कालीन carpet

**kalpana** *n* कल्पना fancy

**kalpana** *n.* कल्पना hypothesis

**kalpana** *n.* कल्पना supposition

**kalpana karna** *v.t.* कल्पना करना visualize

**kalpana karna** *v.t.* कल्पना करना assume

**kalpana karna** *v.t.* कल्पना करना imagine

**kalpana karna** *v.t.* कल्पना करना suppose

**kalpanashakti** *n.* कल्पनाशक्ति imagination

**kalpanashil** *a.* कल्पनाशील imaginative

**kalpanik** *a.* काल्पनिक imaginary

**kalpanik** *a.* काल्पनिक visionary

**kalpanik wastu** *n* काल्पनिक वस्तु figment

**kalpit katha** *n* कल्पित कथा canard

**kalpna vadi** *adj* कल्पना वादी notionalist

**kalyan** *n.* कल्याण weal

**kalyan** *n.* कल्याण welfare

**kam** *a.* कम less

**kam** *a.* कम scanty

**kam hona** *v.t* कम होना lessen

**kam hona** *v.i.* कम होना subside

**kam karana** *v.t.* कम करना relieve

**kam karna** *v.t.* कम करना abate

**kam karna** *v.t.* कम करना alleviate

**kam karna** *v. t* कम करना cut

**kam karna** *v. t* कम करना decrease

**kam karna** *v.t.* कम करना deduct

**kam karna** *v. t* कम करना diminish

**kam karna** *v.t.* कम करना minimize

**kam karna** *v.t.* कम करना mitigate

**kam karna** *v.t.* कम करना reduce

**kam mahtva ka** *a.* कम महत्व का subordinate

**kam se kam matra mein** *adv.* कम से कम मात्रा में least

**kamal** *n.* कमल lotus

**kaman** *a* कमान crook

**kamar** *n.* कमर waist

**kamar ka patla bhag** *n* कमर का पतला भाग small

**kamara, awasar** *n.* कमरा, अवसर room

**kamarband** *n.* कमरबंद waistband

**kambal** *n* कंबल blanket

**kamchor** *n.* कामचोर shirker

**kamdev** *n* कामदेव Cupid

**kami** *n.* कमी abatement

**kami** *n.* कमी alleviation

**kami** *n.* कमी decrement

**kami** *n* कमी drawback

**kami** *n.* कमी lack

**kami** *n.* कमी lacuna

**kami** *n.* कमी paucity

**kami** *n.* कमी poverty

**kami** *n.* कमी reduction

**kami** *n.* कमी remission

**kamiz** *n.* कमीज़ shirt

**kamjor** *a* कमज़ोर faint

**kamjor** *a* कमज़ोर feeble

**kam-kharch** *a.* कम-खर्च niggardly

**kamna karna** *v.t* कामना करना desire

**kamp uthna** *v.i.* कांप उठना shudder

kampan *n.* कंपन tremor

kampan *n.* कंपन vibration

kampana *v.i.* कांपना quiver

kampana *v.i.* कांपना shiver

kampana *v.i.* कांपना tremble

kampkampi *n* कंपकंपी shudder

kampna *v.i.* कांपना quake

kamuk *a.* कामुक lewd

kamuk *a.* कामुक lustful

kamuk *n.* कामुक sexy

kamuk drishti *n* कामुक दृष्टि ogle

kamukta *n.* कामुकता sensuality

kamzor *a.* कमज़ोर frail

kamzor *a.* कमज़ोर infirm

kamzor *a.* कमज़ोर weak

kamzor banana *v.t. & i* कमज़ोर बनाना weaken

kamzor hona *v. t.* कमज़ोर होना decline

kamzor prani *n.* कमज़ोर प्राणी weakling

kamzori *n.* कमज़ोरी infirmity

kamzori *n.* कमज़ोरी weakness

kan *a.* कण particle

kanastar *n.* कनस्तर canister

kanch *n.* कांच pane

kanch ka kam karne wala *n.* कांच का काम करने वाला glazier

kandha *n.* कंधा shoulder

kandhe uchkana *v.t.* कंधे उचकाना shrug

kandra *n.* कंदरा ravine

kangaali *n.* कंगाली misery

kangan *n* कंगन bracelet

kangha *n* कंघा comb

kanist *a.* कनिष्ठ junior

kanjoos *adj* कंजूस pinchpenny

kanjous *n.* कंजूस miser

kanjus *n.* कंजूस niggard

kanjus *a.* कंजूस stingy

kankal *n.* कंकाल skeleton

kankar *n.* कंकड़ pebble

kankhajura *n.* कनखजूरा centipede

kann *n.* कण jot

kanoon *n.* कानून statute

kanpati *n* कनपटी temple

kanpeda *n.* कनपेड़ा mumps

kanta *n.* कांटा prick

kanta *n.* कांटा thorn

kantakmay *a.* कंटकमय, कष्टप्रद thorny

kantedar *a.* कांटेदार barbed

kanth sambandhi *a.* कंठ संबंधी guttural

kanthabhushan *n.* कंठाभूषण necklet

kanth-haar *n.* कंठहार necklace

kanti loha *n* कान्ती लोहा cast-iron

kanun banana *v.i.* कानून बनाना legislate

kanun ka rup dena *v. t* कानून का रूप देना enact

kanun nirmata *n.* कानून निर्माता legislator

kanuni janch *n.* कानूनी जांच inquest

kanuni karyavahi *n.* कानूनी कार्यवाही proceeding

kanunvidh *n.* कानूनविद jurist

kanw-kanw *n.* कॉंव-कॉंव caw

kanw-kanw karna *v. i.* कॉंव-कॉंव करना caw

kanya *n.* कन्या maiden

kapaal vigyan *n.* कपाल विज्ञान phrenology

kapada *n* कपड़ा fabric

kapade pehanana *v.t.* कपड़े पहनाना robe

kaparhe ki sajawat patti *n* कपड़े की सजावटी पट्टी bunting

kapas *n.* कपास cotton

kapat *n* कपट duplicity

kapati *n.* कपटी trickster

kapda pehanana *v.t.* कपड़ा पहनाना vest

kapde par likha sandesh *n.* कपड़े पर लिखा संदेश banner

kaphila *n.* काफिला caravan

kapi *n* कपि ape

kapkampi *n* कंपकंपी quake

kaprha *n* कपड़ा cloth

kaprhe pahnana *v. t* कपड़े पहनाना clothe

kaptan *n.* कप्तान captain

kaptan *n.* कप्तान skipper

kaptani *n.* कप्तानी captaincy

kapti *a.* कपटी fraudulent

kapur *n.* कपूर camphor

kar *n.* कर tax

kar lagana *v.t.* कर लगाना tax

kar yogya *a.* कर योग्य taxable

karagaar *n.* कारागार prison

karahana *v.i.* कराहना groan

karahna *n* कराहना groan

karamchari *n* कर्मचारी employee

karamchari-gan *n.* कर्मचारीगण staff

karan *n.* कारण reason

karan banna *v.t* कारण बनना occasion

karanatva *n* कारणत्व causality

karapaal *n.* कारापाल jailer

kararopan *n.* करारोपण taxation

karavas *n.* कारावास confinement

kar-chalak *n.* कार-चालक chauffeur

karchhul *n.* करछुल ladle

karchhul se dena *v.t.* करछुल से देना ladle

kargha *n* करघा loom

karha *a.* कड़ा hard

karha *a.* कड़ा rigid

karha banana *v.t.* कड़ा बनाना toughen

karha dand dena *v.t.* कड़ा दंड देना scourge

karhak *n* कड़क clap

karhake ka shabd karna *v.t.* कड़ाके का शब्द करना crackle

karhva banana *v. t* कड़वा बनाना embitter

karib-karib *adv.* करीब-करीब almost

karjadar *n* कर्जदार debtor

kark athva makar rekha *n.* कर्क अथवा मकर रेखा tropic

karkash shabd *n. & v. i* कर्कश शब्द clack

karkasha *n.* कर्कशा shrew

karkasha *n.* कर्कशा vixen

karkhaana *n.* कारखाना mill

karkhana *n* कारखाना factory

karkhana *n.* कारखाना workshop

karmachari dal *n.* कर्मचारी दल personnel

karmawachi *a.* कर्मवाची objective

karmidal *n.* कर्मीदल crew

karmsthapan *n.* क्रमस्थापन arrangement

karna *v. t* करना do

karna *v.t.* करना perform

karnabhedi *a.* कर्णभेदी strident

karnal *adj.* कर्नल colonel

karne yogya *a.* करने योग्य practicable

karni *n.* करनी trowel

kar-nirdharan *n.* कर-निर्धारण assessment

karonda *n.* करोंदा gooseberry

karorpati *n.* करोड़पति millionaire

karta sambandhi *a* कर्त्ता संबंधी reflexive

kartab *n* करतब stunt

kartavya *n* कर्तव्य duty

kartavyanishta *a* कर्त्तव्यनिष्ठ dutiful

karuna *n.* करुणा pathos

karuna *n.* करुणा pity

karunik *a.* कारुणिक pathetic

karya *n.* कार्य act

karya *n.* कार्य action

karya *n.* कार्य task

karya jari rakhna *v.i.* कार्य जारी रखना proceed

karya karna *v. i* कार्य करना deal

karya kshetra *n* कार्य क्षेत्र field

karya saunpana *v.t.* कार्य सौंपना task

karya suchi *n.* कार्यसूची agenda

karyadhikshaka *n.* कार्याधीक्षिका matron

karyakarm banana *v.t.* कार्यक्रम बनाना programme

karyakram *n.* कार्यक्रम schedule

karyalaya *n.* कार्यालय office

karyamukti *n.* कार्यमुक्ति retirement

karyaniwit karna *v.t.* कार्यान्वित करना implement

karyapaddhati *n.* कार्यपद्धति procedure

karyapranali *n.* कार्यप्रणाली course

karzdaar hona *v.t* कर्ज़दार होना owe

kasa hua *a.* कसा हुआ tense

kasa hua *a.* कसा हुआ tight

**kasam khilana** *v.t.* कसम खिलाना swear
**kasav** *n.* कसाव tension
**kasayee** *n* कसाई butcher
**kasba** *n.* कसबा town
**kasba** *a.* कसबा township
**kasha** *n. & adj* काँसा bronze
**kasht dena** *v.t.* कष्ट देना agonize
**kasht dena** *v.t.* कष्ट देना nag
**kasht dena** *v.t.* कष्ट देना persecute
**kasht dena** *v.t.* कष्ट देना rag
**kashtakari** *a* कष्टकारी burdensome
**kashth** *n.* कष्ट pressure
**kashth premi** *a.* काष्ठ प्रेमी xylophilous
**kashth tarang** *n.* काष्ठ तरंग xylophone
**kashth-vat** *prep* खस्त-वात ligneous
**kashtprad** *a.* कष्टप्रद troublesome
**kasidakari** *n* कसीदाकारी embroidery
**kaskar pakarna** *v.t.* कसकर पकड़ना grasp
**kasna** *v.t.* कसना, tighten
**kasni rang ka phool** *n.* कसनी रंग का फूल lilac
**kastkari** *n.* काश्तकारी husbandry
**kasturi** *n.* कस्तूरी musk
**katash** *n.* कटाक्ष insinuation
**katav** *n* कटाव erosion
**katha sahitya** *n* कथा साहित्य fiction
**kathak** *n.* कथक teller
**kathan** *n.* कथन narration
**kathan** *n.* कथन proposition
**kathan** *n.* कथन statement
**kathan** *n.* कथन version
**kathatmak** *a.* कथात्मक narrative
**kath-ghora** *n.* कठघोड़ा hobby-horse
**kathin** *a* कठिन arduous
**kathin** *a* कठिन formidable
**kathin** *a.* कठिन insurmountable
**kathin** *a.* कठिन laborious
**kathin parishram** *n.* कठिन परिश्रम toil
**kathin parishram karna** *v.i.* कठिन परिश्रम करना toil

**kathin paristhiti** *n.* कठिन परिस्थिति predicament
**kathinata** *n.* कठिनता rigour
**kathinayee** *n.* कठिनाई snag
**kathinta** *n.* कठिनता severity
**kathinta se chadhna** *v. i* कठिनता से चढ़ना clamber
**kathit** *a.* कथित vocal
**kathor** *a.* कठोर callous
**kathor** *a.* कठोर harsh
**kathor** *a.* कठोर pitiless
**kathor** *a.* कठोर stern
**kathor** *a.* कठोर strict
**kathor** *a.* कठोर stringent
**kathor** *a* कठोर drastic
**kathor** *a.* कठोर rough
**kathor anushasak** *n.* कठोर अनुशासक martinet
**kathor banana** *v.t.* कठोर बनाना stiffen
**kathor parisram karna** *v.i.* कठोर परिश्रम करना moil
**kathore** *a* कठोर firm
**kathore** *n.* कटोरी grim
**kathore banana** *v.t.* कठोर बनाना harden
**kathore banana** *v.t.* कठोर बनाना ossify
**katna** *v. t* काटना chop
**katne ka ghav** *n* काटने का घाव bite
**katnewala** *n.* कातनेवाला spinner
**katora** *n* कटोरा bowl
**katputli** *n.* कठपुतली marionette
**kattar samarthak** *n.* कट्टर समर्थक zealot
**kattarta** *n* कट्टरता bigotry
**katu alochana** *n.* कटु आलोचना stricture
**kaular** *n* कॉलर collar
**kaun** *pron.* कौन who
**kaun sa** *a.* कौनसा what
**kaun sa** *a* कौनसा which
**kaushal** *n.* कौशल attainment
**kaushal** *n.* कौशल sleight
**kauwa** *n* कौआ crow
**kavach** *n.* कवच armour

**kavach** *n* कवच mail
**kavach** *n* कवच pectoral
**kavi** *n.* कवि bard
**kavi** *n.* कवि poet
**kavita** *n.* कविता poem
**kavita sambandhi** *a.* कविता संबंधी poetic
**kavya** *n.* काव्य verse
**kavya rachna** *n.* काव्य रचना poetry
**kavyashastra** *n.* काव्यशास्त्र poetics
**kavyitri** *n.* कवयित्री poetess
**kaya** *n* काया body
**kayar** *n.* कायर coward
**kayar** *a* कायर effeminate
**kayarta** *n.* कायरता cowardice
**kayee** *a* कई several
**ke aar paar** *prep.* के आर पार through
**ke andar** *prep.* के अंदर into
**ke atirikt** *prep* के अतिरिक्त besides
**ke baad mein** *prep.* के बाद में after
**ke baad se** *conj.* के बाद से since
**ke bena** *prep.* के बिना minus
**ke hetu** *prep* के हेतु for
**ke marg se** *prep.* के मार्ग से via
**ke neeche** *prep* के नीचे beneath
**ke paas** *prep.* के पास at
**ke paas** *prep.* के पास near
**ke paas mein** *prep.* के पास में beside
**ke pratyek bhag mein** *prep.* के प्रत्येक भाग में throughout
**ke saamney** *prep* के सामने before
**ke sadrashya hona** *v.t.* के सदृश होना resemble
**ke samay tak** *prep.* के समय तक till
**keechar** *n.* कीचड़ slime
**keel** *n.* कील clink
**keel se bindhna** *v.t.* कील से बींधना spike
**keet vigyan** *n.* कीटविज्ञान entomology
**keet-nashi aushadhi** *n.* कीटनाशी औषधि insecticide
**kehna** *v.t* कहना state
**kehna** *v.t.* कहना utter

**kekrha** *n* केकड़ा crab
**kela** *n.* केला banana
**kele ka vriksh** *n.* केले का वृक्ष plantain
**kenchuli** *n.* केंचुली slough
**kenchuli girana** *v.t.* केंचुली गिराना slough
**kendra** *n* केंद्र centre
**kendra** *n.* केंद्र nucleus
**kendra** *n.* केंद्र stronghold
**kendra se hat janai wala** *adj.* केन्द्र से हट जाने वाली centrifugal
**kendra-bindu** *n.* केंद्र-बिंदु pivot
**kendrit karna** *v. t* केंद्रित करना concentrate
**kendrit karna** *v.t* केंद्रित करना focus
**kendrit karna** *v.t.* केंद्रित करना rivet
**kendriya** *a.* केंद्रीय central
**kesar** *n.* केसर saffron
**kesariya** *a* केसरिया saffron
**keshmarjak** *n.* केशमार्जक shampoo
**keval** *a.* केवल mere
**kewal** *adv.* केवल just
**kewal ek** *a.* केवल एक single
**kha jana** *v. t* खा जाना erode
**khaad** *n* खाद fertilizer
**khaad** *n.* खाद manure
**khaad dena** *v.t.* खाद देना manure
**khaari** *n.* खाड़ी creek
**khabar** *n.* खबर information
**khabar** *n.* खबर news
**khacchar jaisa** *a.* खच्चर जैसा mulish
**khachhar** *n.* खच्चर mule
**khadaan** *n.* खदान quarry
**khaderna** *v.t.* खदेड़ना repulse
**khaderne ki kriya** *n.* खदेड़ने की क्रिया repulse
**khadi** *n.* खाड़ी gulf
**khadya** *n. pl* खाद्य victuals
**khadya padarth** *n.* खाद्य पदार्थ eatable
**khagolshastra** *n.* खगोलशास्त्र astronomy
**khagolshastri** *n.* खगोलशास्त्री astronomer
**khajana** *n.* खज़ाना fund

khajanchi *n.* ख़ज़ांची cashier
khal *v.t* खाल skin
khali *a.* खाली bare
khali *a* खाली empty
khali *a.* खाली vacant
khali karna *v* खाली करना empty
khali karna *v. t* खाली करना evacuate
khali karna *v.t.* खाली करना vacate
khalipan *n.* खालीपन vacancy
khamba *n.* खम्बा pillar
khambha *n.* खंभा post
khamir *n.* खमीर yeast
khamir uthana *v.t* खमीर उठाना ferment
khamve par lagana *v.t.* खंभे पर लगाना
  post
khan *n* खान mine
khana *v. t* खाना eat
khanabdosh *n.* खानाबदोश nomad
khand *n.* खंड piece
khandak *n.* खंदक moat
khandak *n.* खाई, खंदक trench
khandan *n.* खंडन refutation
khandan karna *v. t.* खंडन करना deny
khandan karna *v.t.* खंडन करना refute
khandhar *n.* खंडहर ruin
khandit ansh *n.* खंडित अंश fragment
khane yoygya *a* खाने योग्य eatable
khanij *n.* खनिज fossil
khanij *n.* खनिज mineral
khanij dhatu *n.* कच्ची धातु ore
khanij sambandhi *a* खनिज संबंधी
  mineral
khanij shastra *n.* खनिज शास्त्र mineralogy
khanij tel *n.* खनिज तैल petroleum
khanij vigyaani *n.* खनिज विज्ञानी
  mineralogist
khanik *n.* खनिक miner
khanjar *n.* खंजर dagger
khansi *n.* खांसी cough
khansna *v. i.* खांसना cough
khapchi *n.* खपची wicker

khapra *n.* खपरा tile
khapron se patna *v.t.* खपरों से पाटना tile
khara *a.* खरा sterling
khara hona *v.i.* खड़ा होना stand
khara pani *n* खारा पानी brine
kharaad *n.* खराद lathe
kharaad machine *n.* खराद मशीन lathe
kharadi *n.* खरादी turner
kharapan *n.* खारापन salinity
kharch *n.* खर्च expense
kharch karna *v. t* खर्च करना expend
kharchaa *n* खर्चा expenditure
khargosh *n.* खरगोश hare
khargosh *n.* खरगोश rabbit
khargoshon ka barha *n.* खरगोशों का बाड़ा
  warren
kharha *a.* ऊपर vertical
kharhi *n* खाड़ी bay
kharhi chattan *n.* खाड़ी चट्टान cliff
kharhkharh *n* खड़खड़ rattle
kharhkharhana *v. t* खड़खड़ाना rattle
kharid *n.* खरीद purchase
kharidana *v. t.* खरीदना buy
kharidana *v.t.* खरीदना purchase
khariddari karna *v.i.* खरीददारी करना
  shop
kharij karna *v. t.* खारिज करना dismiss
kharonch *n* खरोंच graze
kharonch *n.* खरोंच scratch
kharrata *n* खर्राटा snore
kharrate lena *v.i.* खर्राटे लेना snore
khasra *n* खसरा measles
khata *n.* खाता account
khata bahi *n.* खाता बही ledger
khatarnak *a* खतरनाक dangerous
khatarnak *a.* खतरनाक risky
khatarnak *a.* खतरनाक vicious
khat-khat ki awaz *n.* खटखट की आवाज़
  click
khat-khatana *v.t.* खटखटाना knock
khatmal *n.* खटमल bug

khatra *n.* खतरा jeopardy

khatra *n.* खतरा risk

khatre ki suchana *v.t* खतरे की सूचना alarm

khatre mein dalna *v.t.* खतरे में डालना risk

khatrey mein dalna *v.t.* खतरे में डालना jeopardize

khatta *adj.* खटा citric

khatta *a.* खट्टा sour

khatta karna *v.t.* खट्टा करना sour

khazana *n.* ख़ज़ाना treasury

khed *n* खेद regret

khed prakat karna *v.i.* खेद प्रकट करना apologize

khed yogya *a.* खेद योग्य lamentable

khedjanak *a* खेदजनक deplorable

khedjanak *a.* खेदजनक unfortunate

khel *n.* खेल game

khel *n.* खेल play

khel ka maidaan *n* खेल का मैदान field

khelkud *n.* खेलकूद athletics

khelkud pratiyogita *n.* खेलकूद प्रतियोगिता tournament

khet *n.* खेत plantation

khet mein *adv.* खेत में afield

khevan *n.* खेवन sail

khiladi *n.* खिलाड़ी sportsman

khilarhi *n.* खिलाड़ी player

khilauna *n.* खिलौना toy

khilna *v.i* खिलना blossom

khilvarh karna *v.i.* खिलवाड़ करना sport

khilvarh karna *v.i.* खिलवाड़ करना toy

khilvarh karna *v.i* खिलवाड़ करना trifle

khinchav *n.* खिंचाव traction

khinnta *n.* खिन्नता melancholy

khira *n* खीरा cucumber

khirhki *n.* खिड़की window

khirki *n* खिड़की mullion

khisakana *v.i.* खिसकाना slide

kho dena *v.t.* खो देना lose

khodna *v.t.* खोदना dig

khoj *n.* खोज discovery

khoj *n.* खोज search

khoj karna *v.t.* खोज करना quest

khoj yatra *n* खोजयात्रा expedition

khojana *v. t* खोजना detect

khojana *v.t.* खोजना search

khojana *v.t.* खोजना unearth

khojkar lutana *v.t.* खोजकर लूटना rifle

khojna *v.t* खोजना explore

khojna *v.t.* खोजना ransack

khojne yogya *a.* खोजने योग्य traceable

khokhla *a.* खोखला hollow

khokhla karna *v.t* खोखला करना hollow

khokla karna *v. t.* खोखला करना excavate

kholna *v.t.* खोलना open

kholna *v.t.* खोलना unfold

khona *v.t.* खोना miss

khoon behna *v. i* खून बहना bleed

khoon ki kami *n* खून की कमी anaemia

khoonta *n.* खूंटा picket

khoonta *n* खूंटा stake

khoprhi *n.* खोपड़ी skull

khot *n.* खोट alloy

khota *a* खोटा bogus

khota *a.* खोटा counterfeit

khrda *n.* खेड़ा hamlet

khubani *n.* खूबानी apricot

khudayee *n* खुदाई dig

khudra *a* खुदरा retail

khudra dwara *adv.* खुदरा द्वारा retail

khujli *n.* खुजली itch

khujli hona *v.i.* खुजली होना itch

khujli ki bimari *n.* खुजली की बीमारी scabies

khula *a.* खुला open

khula maidan *n.* खुला मैदान lea

khulai roop mein *adv.* खुले रूप में openly

khulhadi se katna *v.t.* कुल्हाड़ी से काटना hew

khun *n* खून blood

khunkhar *a* खूंखार ferocious

**khunti** *n.* खोंटी peg
**khunti** *n.* खूंटी stubble
**khur** *n.* खुर hoof
**khurachna** *v.t.* खुरचना scratch
**khurak** *n* खुराक dose
**khurdara** *a.* खुरदरा rugged
**khusal vakta** *n.* कुशल वक्ता orator
**ki** *conj.* कि that
**ki aur** *prep.* की ओर towards
**ki put dena** *v.t.* की पुट देना tinge
**kicharh** *n.* कीचड़ slush
**kicharh se ganda karna** *v. t* कीचड़ से गन्दा करना bemire
**kicharhdaar** *a.* कीचड़दार slushy
**kichhad** *n.* कीचड़ mire
**kichhad** *n.* कीचड़ mud
**kichhad** *n.* कीचड़ ooze
**kilak** *n.* कीलक rivet
**kile ki diwar** *n.* किले की दीवार rampart
**kilon se jadna** *v.t.* कीलों से जड़ना nail
**kimiyagiri** *n.* कीमियागीरी alchemy
**kinaara** *n.* किनारा margin
**kinara** *n.* किनारा rim
**kinara** *n.* किनारा verge
**kinare par** *adv.* किनारे पर ashore
**kinari** *n.* किनारी lace
**kinari lagana** *v.t* किनारी लगाना border
**kinchav** *n* खिंचाव stretch
**kintu** *conj.* किंतु but
**kinv-vadanti** *n.* किंवदंती legend
**kiraay par dena** *v.t* किराए पर देना hire
**kiran** *n* किरण beam
**kiran** *n.* किरण ray
**kiran kendra** *n* किरण केंद्र focus
**kirana** *n.* किराना grocery
**kirayadar** *n.* किरायेदार tenant
**kirayadari** *n.* किरायेदारी tenancy
**kiraye par lena** *v.t.* किराये पर लेना rent
**kirch** *n.* किरच splinter
**kirha** *n.* कीड़ा caterpillar
**kirha** *n.* कीड़ा worm

**kirti** *n* कीर्ति fame
**kirti** *n.* क्रीति laurel
**kirti** *n.* कीर्ति repute
**kirtimaan hona** *v. t.* कीर्तिमान होना commemorate
**kirtiman** *n.* कीर्तिमान record
**kis drishti se** *adv.* किस दृष्टि से wherein
**kisaan** *n.* किसान agriculturist
**kisan** *n* किसान boor
**kisan** *n* किसान farmer
**kisan** *n.* किसान peasant
**kisan varg** *n.* किसान वर्ग peasantry
**kise** *pron.* किसे whom
**kishmish** *n.* किशमिश raisin
**kishor** *a.* किशोर adolescent
**kishor, kishori** *n.* किशोर, किशोरी teenager
**kishoravastha** *n.* किशोरावस्था adolescence
**kishoravastha** *n. pl.* किशोरावस्था teens
**kishore sambandhi** *a.* किशोर संबंधी juvenile
**kishori** *n.* किशोरी lass
**kisi bhi samay** *adv* किसी भी समय ever
**kisi ke virudh larhna** *v.t* किसी के विरुद्ध लड़ना fight
**kisi na kisi tarike se** *adv.* किसी न किसी तरीके से anyhow
**kisi seema tak** *adv.* किसी सीमा तक any
**kiska** *pron.* किसका whose
**kist** *n.* किस्त instalment
**kit** *n.* कीट insect
**kitnashak** *n.* कीटनाशक pesticide
**ko shikar banana** *v.t.* को शिकार बनाना victimize
**kohani** *n* कोहनी elbow
**kohara** *n* कोहरा damp
**kohara** *n* कोहरा fog
**kohni** *n* कोहनी ancon
**kohni se chhuna** *v.t.* कोहनी से चूना nudge
**kohra** *n.* कुहरा haze
**koi** *a.* कोई any

koi kuch *a.* कोई, कुछ some
koi nahi *pron.* कोई नहीं nobody
koi nahi *pron.* कोई नहीं none
koi padarth *n.* कोई पदार्थ stuff
koi vi nahi *conj.* कोई भी नहीं neither
koi vyakti *pron.* कोई व्यक्ति somebody
koi vyakti *pron.* कोई व्यक्ति someone
koi wastu *n.* कोई वस्तु aught
koi-koi *a* कोई-कोई stray
kokeen *n* कोकीन cocaine
kolahaal *n.* कोलाहल hubbub
kolahal *n* कोलाहल clamour
kolahal *n* कोलाहल din
kolahal *n.* कोलाहल uproar
kolahal karna *v. i.* कोलाहल करना
    clamour
kolahalkari *a.* कोलाहलकारी noisy
kolahalpurna *a.* कोलाहलपूर्ण loud
kolahalpurna *a.* कोलाहलपूर्ण tumultuous
kolahalpurna *a.* कोलाहलपूर्ण uproarious
kolahalpurna *a.* कोलाहलपूर्ण rowdy
komal *a.* कोमल lenient
komal *a.* कोमल mealy
komal *n.* कोमल soft
komal banana *v.t.* कोमल बनाना soften
komalta *n.* कोमलता mildness
kona *n* कोन angle
kona *n* कोना corner
konchna *v.t.* कोंचना poke
kon-sambandhi *a.* कोण-संबंधी angular
koodna *v.i.* कूदना vault
koora *n.* गोबर muck
koorha karkat *n.* कूड़ा करकट trash
kora *a* कोरा blank
koram *n.* कोरम quorum
korha *n* कोड़ा lash
korha *n.* कोड़ा whip
korha marna *a.* कोड़ा मारना lash
kosh *n* कोष budget
kosh *n.* कोश reservoir
kosh rachna *n.* कोश रचना lexicography

koshadhyaksha *n.* कोषाध्यक्ष treasurer
kota *n.* कोटा quota
kothar *n.* कोठार barn
kothari *n.* कोठरी cell
kothari *n.* कोठरी closet
kothri *n.* कोठरी cabin
koyal *n* कोयल cuckoo
koyla *n* कोयला coal
kram *n.* क्रम array
kram *n.* क्रम series
kram mein rakhna *v.t.* क्रम में रखना
    arrange
kram se *adv* क्रम से consecutively
kram se rakhna *v.t.* क्रम से रखना range
krama se hone wala *a.* क्रम से होने वाला
    alternate
kramavaya *n.* क्रमवय permutation
krambadh karna *v.t* क्रमबद्ध करना
    marshal
krambhang karna *v.t.* क्रमभंग करना
    interrupt
kramik *a.* क्रमिक gradual
kramik *a.* क्रमिक serial
kramik *a.* क्रमिक successive
kramik vridhi *n* क्रमिक वृद्धि accretion
krantikari *a.* क्रांतिकारी revolutionary
kraya vikraya karna *v.t* क्रय विक्रय करना
    market
kreta *n.* क्रेता buyer
krida *n.* क्रीड़ा pastime
krida sthal *n.* क्रीड़ा स्थल stadium
kripa *n* कृपा benevolence
kripalu *a* कृपालु benevolent
kripalu *a* कृपालु kind
kripiya *adv.* कृपया kindly
krirha *n.* क्रीड़ा prank
krirha pratiyogi *n.* क्रीड़ा-प्रतियागी athlete
krirhasheel *a.* क्रीड़ाशील sportive
krishi *n* कृषि agriculture
krishi bhumi *n* कृषि भूमि farm
krishi bhumi *n* कृषि भूमि field

**krishi mazdoor** *n.* कृषि मज़दूर serf

**krishi utpaadan** *n.* कृषि उत्पादन produce

**krishi-sambandhi** *a* कृषि-संबंधी agricultural

**kritagayta** *n.* कृतज्ञता gratitude

**kritagna** *a.* कृतघ्न thankless

**kritagya** *a.* कृतज्ञ, thankful

**kritank** *n.* कृतंक rodent

**kritdhanta** *n.* कृतघ्नता ingratitude

**kritrim banana** *v.t.* कृत्रिम बनाना sophisticate

**kritrim makkhan** *n.* कृत्रिम मक्खन margarine

**kritrim upgreh** *n.* कृत्रिम उपग्रह sputnik

**kritrim utpadan** *n* कृत्रिम उत्पादन synthetic

**kritrimata** *n.* कृत्रिमता mannerism

**kritrimata** *n.* कृत्रिमता sophistication

**kritsankalp** *a.* कृतसंकल्प resolute

**kriya** *n.* क्रिया practice

**kriya** क्रिया verb

**kriyashil banana** *v.t.* क्रियाशील बनाना arouse

**kriya-visheshan** *n.* क्रिया-विशेषण adverb

**kriyawachak sangya** *n.* क्रियावाचक संज्ञा gerund

**krodh** *n.* क्रोध anger

**krodh** *n* क्रोध displeasure

**krodh** *n.* क्रोध indignation

**krodh** *n.* क्रोध ire

**krodh** *n.* क्रोध rage

**krodh** *n.* क्रोध wrath

**krodh karna** *v. t* क्रुद्ध करना enrage

**krodh karna** *v.i.* क्रोध करना rage

**krodhi** *a.* क्रोधी aggressive

**krodhi** *n* क्रोधी tempered

**krodhi** *a.* क्रोधी passionate

**krodhit** *a.* क्रोधित angry

**krudh** *a.* क्रुद्ध indignant

**krudh karna** *v.t.* क्रुद्ध करना infuriate

**krurta** *n.* क्रूरता savagery

**krurtapurna** *a* क्रूरतापूर्ण beastly

**kshama** *n.* क्षमा pardon

**kshama karna** *v.t* क्षमा करना forgive

**kshama karna** *v.t.* क्षमा करना pardon

**kshama ke yogay** *a.* क्षमा के योग्य pardonable

**kshama pradan** *n.* क्षमा प्रदान condone

**kshamta** *n.* क्षमता capacity

**kshamya** क्रशमया venial

**kshati** *n.* क्षति injury

**kshati karna** *v.t.* क्षति करना injure

**kshati se bachana** *v.t.* क्षति से बचाना salvage

**kshatipurti** *n.pl.* क्षतिपूर्ति amends

**kshatipurti** *n* क्षतिपूर्ति compensation

**kshatipurti karna** *v.t* क्षतिपूर्ति करना compensate

**kshatipurti karna** *v.t.* क्षतिपूर्ति करना recoup

**kshatipurti yogya** *a.* क्षतिपूर्ति योग्य reparable

**kshay rog** *n* क्षयरोग consumption

**kshetra** *n.* गुंजाइश scope

**kshetra** *n.* क्षेत्र territory

**kshetra** *n.* क्षेत्र zone

**kshetraphal** *n* क्षेत्रफल area

**kshetriya** *a.* क्षेत्रीय regional

**kshetriya** *a.* प्रादेशिक territorial

**ksheya rog** *n.* क्षेय रोग tuberculosis

**kshin hona** *v. t* क्षीण होना dwindle

**kshomvastr** *n.* क्षोमवस्त्र linen

**kshti pahuchana** *v. t* क्षति पहुंचाना damage

**kshudhavardhak vastu** *n* क्षुधावर्धक वस्तु appetizer

**kshudra vetan** *n.* क्षुद्र वेतन pittance

**kuan** *n.* कुआं well

**kubad** *n.* कूबड़ hunch

**kuch** *pron.* कुछ some

**kuch** *pron.* कुछ something

**kuch bhi** *pron.* जो कुछ भी, कुछ भी whatever

**kuch kuch** *adv.* कुछ-कुछ rather

**kuch kuch** *adv.* कुछ कुछ somewhat

**kuch nahin** *n.* कुछ नहीं nothing

**kuch nahin** *n.* कुछ नहीं nought

**kuch seema tak** *adv.* कुछ सीमा तक something

**kuchalna** *v.t.* कुचलना contuse

**kuchalna** *v.t.* कुचलना suppress

**kuchalna** *v.t.* कुचलना, रौंदना trample

**kuchalna** *v.t.* कुचलना tread

**kuchh der ke liye** *adv.* कुछ देर के लिए awhile

**kuchh nahi** *n.* कुछ नहीं nil

**kud** *n* कूद leap

**kuda kachra** *n.* कूड़ा कचरा garbage

**kuda karkat** *n.* कूड़ा करकट rubbish

**kudna** *v.i.* कूदना dap

**kudna** *v.i* कूदना jump

**kudna** *v.i.* कूदना leap

**kuhara** *n.* कुहरा mist

**kujan** *n* कूजन warble

**kujana** *v.i.* कूजना warble

**kukhyat** *n.* कुख्यात arrant

**kukhyat** *a.* कुख्यात notorious

**kukhyati** *n.* कुख्याति notoriety

**kukhyati** *adj* कुख्याती notoriety

**kukna** *v. i* कूकना cackle

**kukurmutta** *n.* कुकुरमुत्ता mushroom

**kul** *a* कुल overall

**kuladhipati** *n.* कुलाधिपति chancellor

**kulharhi** *n.* कुल्हाड़ी axe

**kulharhi** *n.* कुल्हाड़ी hatchet

**kuli** *n* कुली coolie

**kuli** *n.* कुली porter

**kulin baykti** *n.* कुलीन व्यक्ति noble

**kulin prush** *n.* कुलीनपुरुष nobleman

**kulin vyakti** *n.* कुलीन व्यक्ति aristocrat

**kulin warg** *n.* कुलीन वर्ग nobility

**kulinlog** *n.* कुलीनलोग gentry

**kulintantra** *n.* कुलीनतंत्र aristocracy

**kulmaata** *n.* कुलमाता matriarch

**kulnaam** *n.* कुलनाम surname

**kumari** *n.* कुमारी maid

**kumari** *n.* कुमारी miss

**kumari kaniya** *n.* कुमारी कन्या damsel

**kumbh rashi** *n.* कुम्भ राशि Aquarius

**kumhar** *n.* कुम्हार potter

**kumudini** *n.* कुमुदिनी lily

**kunain** *n.* कुनैन quinine

**kund** *a* कुंद blunt

**kund** *n.* कुंड furrow

**kunda** *n* कुंदा block

**kunda** *n.* कुंदा log

**kundi** *n.* कुंडी latch

**kunj** *n* कुंज bower

**kunji** *n.* कुंजी key

**kunwari** *n.* कुंआरी virgin

**kuposhan** *n.* कुपोषण malnutrition

**kuprabandh** *n.* कुप्रबंध mismanagement

**kursi** *n.* कुर्सी chair

**kurup** *a.* कुरूप ugly

**kurup banana, bigaadna** *v.t.* कुरूप बनाना, बिगाड़ना uglify

**kurupta** *n.* कुरूपता ugliness

**kushagrata** *n.* कुशाग्रता acumen

**kushal** *adj.* कुशल deft

**kushal** *a* कुशल efficient

**kushal vyakti** *n* कुशल व्यक्ति expert

**kushalta** *n.* कुशलता art

**kushasan** *n.* कुशासन mal administration

**kushasan** *n.* कुशासन misrule

**kusht** *n.* कुष्ठ leprosy

**kushti larhna** *v.i.* कुश्ती लड़ना, संघर्ष करना wrestle

**kushti larhne wala** *n.* कुश्ती लड़ने वाला wrestler

**kushtrogi** *n.* कुष्ठरोगी leper

**kusmayojan** *n.* कुसमायोजन mal adjustment

**kutark** *n.* कुतर्क sophism

**kutarki** *n.* कुतर्की sophist
**kutarne ki kriya** *n* कुतरने की क्रिया nibble
**kuti** *a.* कुटी shanty
**kutir** *n.* कुटीर hut
**kutiya** *n* कुतिया bitch
**kutiya** *n.* कुटिया wigwam
**kutna** *v.t.* कूटना pound
**kutniti** *n* कूटनीति diplomacy
**kut-nitik** *a* कूट नीतिक diplomatic
**kutta** *n* कुत्ता dog
**kuttaghar** *n.* कुत्ताघर kennel
**kutte ki ek nasal** *n.* कुत्ते की एक नस्ल spaniel
**kutte ki ek nasal** *n.* कुत्ते की एक नस्ल terrier
**kuttiya** *n.* कुटी hermitage
**kutuhal** *n* कुतूहल curiosity
**kutuhali** *a.* कुतूहली nosey
**kuud** *n* कूद hop
**kuulha** *n* कूल्हा hip
**kya!** *interj.* क्या ! what
**kyon** *adv.* क्यों why
**kyonki** *conj.* क्योंकि because
**kyonki** *conj.* क्योंकि for

# L

**la parvah** *a.* लापरवाह negligent
**laad karna** *v.t.* लाड करना dandle
**laadna** *v. t* लादना burden
**laagat** *n.* लागत cost
**laal hona** *v.t.* लाल होना redden
**laal rang** *n.* लाल रंग red
**laal rang ka** *a.* लाल रंग का red
**laalchi** *a.* लालची mercenary
**laanchan lagana** *v.t.* लांछन लगाना impute
**laar** *n.* लार saliva
**lababdar mishtann** *n.* लाबाबदार मिष्ठान jelly
**labada** *n.* लबादा gown

**labada** *n.* लबादा overall
**labada** *n.* लबादा robe
**labada** *n.* लबादा smock
**labh** *n.* लाभ advantage
**labh** *n* लाभ benefit
**labh** *n.* लाभ profit
**labh** *n.* लाभ use
**labh** *n.* लाभ utility
**labh pahuchana** *v. t.* लाभ पहुँचाना benefit
**labh pahuchana** *v.t.* लाभ पहुँचाना profit
**labh pahunchana** *v.t.* लाभ पहुंचाना advantage
**labhdayak** *a.* लाभदायक advantageous
**labhkari** *a* लाभकारी beneficial
**labhkari** *a.* लाभकारी fruitful
**labhkari** *n* लाभ gain
**labhkari** *a.* लाभकारी profitable
**labhkari** *a.* लाभकारी remunerative
**labhkari** *a.* लाभकारी salutary
**labhprad** *a.* लाभप्रद lucrative
**lachchi** *n.* लच्छी skein
**lachila** *a* लचीला elastic
**lachila** *a* लचीला flexible
**lachila hona** *v.t.* लचीला होना limber
**lachili tahani** *n.* लचीली टहनी withe
**ladai** *n.* लड़ाई wrangle
**ladana** *v.t.* लादना lade
**ladka** *n.* लड़का lad
**ladkhadana** *v.i.* लड़खड़ाना lurch
**ladkhadana** *v.i.* लड़खड़ाना reel
**ladki** *n.* लड़की girl
**ladna** *v.t.* लादना load
**ladna** *v.i.* लड़ना wrangle
**lagam** *n* लगाम bridle
**lagam** *n.* लगाम rein
**lagana** *v.t.* लगाना impose
**laga-taar** *adj.* लगातार consecutive
**lagatar** *a.* लगातार perpetual
**lagav** *n* लगाव appurtenance
**lagav** *n.* लगाव attachment
**lagbhag** *adv* लगभग about

**lagbhag utarna** *adv.* लगभग उतना thereabouts

**laghhu pratirup** *n.* लघु प्रतिरूप miniature

**laghu** *a.* लघु venial

**laghu upnyas** *n.* लघु उपन्यास novelette

**laghushanka karna** *v.i.* लघुशंका करना urinate

**laghu-tar** *a.* लघुतर lesser

**lagu karna** *v.t.* लागू करना apply

**lahasun** *n.* लहसुन garlic

**laingik** *a.* लैंगिक sexual

**lajja se lal ho jana** *v.i* लज्जा से लाल हो जाना flush

**lajjajanak** *a.* लज्जाजनक shameful

**lajjit** *a.* लज्जित ashamed

**lajjit karna** *v.t.* लज्जित करना abash

**lajjit karna** *adv* लज्जित ablush

**lajjit karna** *v.t.* लज्जित करना shame

**lakarbaggha** *n.* लकड़बग्घा hyena, hyena

**lakrhi ka takhta** *n.* लकड़ी का तख्ता plank

**lakri** *n.* लकड़ी wood

**lakri ka** *a.* लकड़ी का wooden

**lakshan** *n* लक्षण feature

**lakshan** *n.* लक्षण symptom

**lakshansuchak** *a.* लक्षणसूचक symptomatic

**lakshya** *n.* लक्ष्य aim

**lakshya** *n.* लक्ष्य goal

**lakshya sadhna** *v.i.* लक्ष्य साधना aim

**lakva mara hua** *a.* लकवा मारा हुआ paralytic

**lakva marna** *v.t.* लकवा मारना paralyse

**lakva rog** *n.* लकवा रोग paralysis

**lal mirch** *n.* लाल मिर्च chilli

**lal tain** *n.* लालटेन lantern

**lalasa** *n.* लालसा yearning

**lalayit hona** *v.i.* लालायित होना hanker

**lalayit hona** *v.i* लालायित होना long

**lalayit hona** *v.i.* लालायित होना pine

**lalayit hona** *v.i.* लालायित होना yearn

**lalchauhan** *a.* ललछौंहां reddish

**lalchi** *a.* लालची greedy

**lalsa** *n.* लालसा avarice

**lamba** *a.* लंबा lengthy

**lamba** *a.* लंबा long

**lamba** *a.* लंबा tall

**lamba aur patla** *a.* लंबा और पतला lank

**lamba dag** *n* लंबा डग stride

**lamba danda** *n.* लंबा डंडा pole

**lamba juta** *n.* लंबा जूता wellington boot

**lamba karna** *v.t.* लंबा करना lengthen

**lamba karna** *v.t.* लंबा करना prolong

**lamba kot** *n.* लंबा कोट overcoat

**lambai** *n.* लम्बाई length

**lambe samay tak** *adv* लंबे समय तक long

**lambi bhindant** *n* लंबी भिड़ंत rally

**lambi daud** *n.* लंबी दौड़ marathon

**lambi topi** *n.* लम्बी टोपी mitre

**lambi, kathor paidal yatra** *n.* लंबी, कठोर पैदल यात्रा trek

**lampatata** *n* लंपटता debauch

**lana** *v.t* लाना bring

**lana** *v.t* लाना fetch

**langar** *n.* लंगर anchor

**langar shulk** *n* लंगरशुल्क anchorage

**langur** *n.* लंगूर gibbon

**laparvah** *a.* लापरवाह profligate

**laparwah** *a.* लापरवाह irresponsible

**lapetana** *v.t.* लपेटना wrap

**lapetna** *v.t.* लपेटना convolve

**lapetna** *v.t.* लपेटना wind

**larhaka** *a.* लड़ाका quarrelsome

**larhakpan** *n* लड़कपन boyhood

**larhaku** *a* लड़ाकू bellicose

**larhayee** *n* लड़ाई fray

**larhkhara kar chalna** *v.i.* लड़खड़ाकर चलना stagger

**larhkharhahat** *n.* लड़खड़ाहट stagger

**larhna** *v.i.* लड़ना war

**larki** *n.* लड़की wench

**larkion ki tarah** *a.* लड़कियों की तरह girlish

lasa *n.* लासा lime
lata *n* लता creeper
lathi *n.* लाठी stick
lattu *n.* लट्टू top
lattu *n.* लट्टू, चक्रदोला whirligig
lauki *n.* लौकी gourd
launda *n.* लौंडा youngster
laundebaz *n.* लौंडेबाज़ sodomite
laundebazi *n.* लौंडेबाज़ी sodomy
lautana *v.t.* लौटाना refund
lautana *v.t.* लौटाना reimburse
lautana *v.t.* लौटाना render
lautana *v.t.* लौटाना requite
lautana *v.i.* लौटना return
lautana *v.i.* लौट आना revert
lava *n.* लावा lava
lavang *n* लवंग clove
laya hua *adj.* लाया हुआ borne
le jana *v.t* ले जाना bear
le jana *v.t.* ले जाना transport
le jane yogya *a.* ले जाने योग्य portable
lebal lagana *v.t.* लेबिल लगाना label
leela godna *v.i.* लीला गोदना tattoo
lehar *n* लहर billow
lehar *n.* लहर ripple
lehar *n.* लहर wave
lehrana *v.i* लहराना billow
lehrana *v.t.* लहराना ripple
lehrana *v.i.* लहराना undulate
lei se chipkana *v.t.* लेई से चिपकाना paste
lekh *n* लेख article
lekha *n.* लेखा register
lekha karna *v.t.* लेखा करना compute
lekhak *n.* लेखक author
lekhak *n.* लेखक recorder
lekhan samagri *n.* लेखन सामग्री stationery
lekhna *v.t.* लिखना pen
lekhni *n.* लेखनी pen
lekhya pramanak *n.* लेख्य प्रमाणक notary
lena *v.t.* लेना take
len-den *n* लेन-देन deal

lep lagana *v.t.* लेप लगाना plaster
lesdaar *a.* लेसदार lacy
liblibi *n.* लिबलिबी trigger
lifafaa *n* लिफ़ाफ़ा envelope
lihaz karnewala *a.* लिहाज़ करनेवाला thoughtful
lik, pakki aadat *n.* लीक, पक्की आदत rut
likhavat *n* लिखावट calligraphy
likhawat *n.* लिखावट script
likhna *v.t.* लिखना inscribe
likhna *v.t.* लिखना, write
likhnewala *n.* लिखनेवाला writer
ling *n.* लिंग gender
ling *n.* लिंग penis
ling *n.* लिंग sex
lipik *n* लिपिक clerk
lipt *a.* लिप्त indulgent
litre *n.* लीटर litre
litta dena *n* लिटा देना lay
lobh karna *v.t.* लोभ करना covet
loha *n.* लोहा iron
lohar *n* लोहार blacksmith
lohar ki dokaan *n* लोहार की दुकान forge
lokokti *n* लोकोक्ति byword
lokopakaar *n.* लोकोपकार philanthropy
lokpriya *a.* लोकप्रिय popular
loktantra sambandhi *a.* लोकतंत्र संबंधी republican
loktantravaadi *n* लोकतंत्रवादी republican
lolupata *n.* लोलुपता greed
lomcharm *n* लोमचर्म beaver
lomdi *n.* लोमड़ी fox
lom-hiin *n* लोम-हेन्न nap
lori *n.* लोरी lullaby
loshan *n.* लोशन lotion
lot pot karna *v.i.* लोट पोट करना wallow
lota *n.* लोटा jug
lotary *n.* लॉटरी lottery
lubhana *v. t.* लुभाना entice
lubhana *v.t.* लुभाना tempt
lubhanewala *n.* लुभानेवाला tempter

lubhawana *a* लुभावना seductive
lugdi banana *v.t.* लुग्दी बनाना pulp
lupt ho jaana *v.i.* लुप्त हो जाना vanish
lupt hona *v.t* लुप्त होना dissolve
lut ka maal *n* लूट का माल booty
lut ka maal *n* लूट का माल plunder
lutana *v.t.* लूटना rob
lutera *n.* लुटेरा marauder
lutera, *n.* लुटेरा robber
lutmaar karte firna *v.i.* लूटमार करते फिरना maraud
lutmar *n.* लूटमार loot
lutna *v.t* लूटना fleece
lutna *v.t.* लूटना plunder
lutpaat karna *v.i.* लूटपाट करना loot
lutpat,dakaiti *n.* लूटपाट, डकैती robbery

# M

maa hona *v.t.* मां होना mother
maa jaisa *a.* मां जैसा motherly
maada *n* मादा female
maadak *n.* मादक intoxicant
maadakta *n.* मादकता intoxication
maal *n.* माल commodity
maal *n.* माल stock
maala *n.* माला rosary
maali *n.* माली gardener
maalish *n.* मालिश massage
maalish karna *v.t.* मालिश करना massage
maan hani *n* मान हानि defamation
maan lena *v.t.* मान लेना accede
maan lena *v.t.* मान लेना presuppose
maand *n.* मांद lair
maandaiya *n.* मानदेय honorarium
maang *n* मांग demand
maang *n.* मांग requirement
maangna *v.t.* मांगना require
maanniya *a.* माननीय honourable
maans *n* मांस flesh

maans *n.* मांस meat
maans *n.* मांस mutton
maansik *a.* मानसिक mental
maansikta *n.* मानसिकता temper
maanviya *a.* मानवीय human
maapak *n.* मापक meter
maapdand *n* मापदंड criterion
maar peet karna *v.t.* मार पीट करना manhandle
maarna *v.t.* मारना lambaste
maarne wala *n.* मारने वाला killer
maasik *n* मासिक monthly
maasum *a.* मासूम candid
maat kar dena *v.t.* मात कर देना outshine
maata *n* माता mother
maata *adj* माता mummy
maatam *n.* मातम mourning
maatha *n* माथा forehead
maathe par ki alak *n* माथे पर की अलक forelock
machhar *n.* मच्छर mosquito
machli *n* मछली fish
machliyon ka jhund *n.* मछलियों का झुंड shoal
machuaara *n* मछुआरा fisherman
madhai ki machine *n.* मड़ाई की मशीन thresher
madhukosh *n.* मधुकोश honeycomb
madhumakhi *n.* मधुमक्खी bee
madhumakhi ka ghar *n.* मधुमक्खी का घर beehive
madhumakhi ka chhata *n.* मधुमक्खी का छत्ता hive
madhumakhi-paalan *n.* मधुमक्खी-पालन apiculture
madhumakhipaalan-sthan *n.* मधुमक्खीपालन-स्थान apiary
madhumeh *n* मधुमेह diabetes
madhur madira *n.* मधुर मदिरा malmsey
madhushala *n.* मधुशाला tavern
madhy मध्य midst

madhya *prep* मध्य between
madhya bindu *n* मध्य बिंदु middle
madhya nikalna *v.t.* माध्य निकालना
  average
madhyadesh *n.* मध्यदेश midland
madhyagami *a.* मध्यगामी median
madhyaharn *n.* मध्याह्न midday
madhya-jhilli *n.* मध्य-जिली midriff
madhyam *a.* मध्यम moderate
madhyantar *n.* मध्यांतर interval
madhyasth *n.* मध्यस्थ arbitrator
madhyasth *n.* मध्यस्थ intermediary
madhyastha *n.* मध्यस्थ arbiter
madhyasthata *n.* मध्यस्थता mediation
madhyasthata karna *v.t.* मध्यस्थता करना
  arbitrate
madhyasthata karna *v.i.* मध्यस्थता करना
  mediate
madhyavarti *a.* मध्यवर्ती mid
madhyawarti *a.* मध्यवर्ती intermediate
madhyawarti *a.* मध्यवर्ती middle
madhyayasth *n.* मध्यस्थ mediator
madhygrisham ritu *n.* मध्यग्रीष्म ऋतु
  midsummer
madhyug ka *a.* मध्ययुग का medieval
madira *n.* मदिरा liquor
madonmat karna *v.t.* मदोन्मत्त करना
  intoxicate
madyasar *n* मद्यसार alcohol
madyatyag *n.* मद्यत्याग temperance
madyatyagi *a.* मद्यत्यागी teetotal
madyatyagi *n.* मद्यत्यागी teetotaller
maha paashan *n.* महा पाषाण megalith
maha vidyalaya *n* महाविद्यालय college
mahaanta *n.* महानता magnitude
mahachingat *n.* महाचिंगट lobster
mahadvip *n* महाद्वीप continent
mahadvipiya *a* महाद्वीपीय continental
mahakavya *n* महाकाव्य epic
mahakna *v.i.* महकना bloom
mahal *n.* महल palace

mahamaari *a.* महामारी plague
mahamari *n* महामारी epidemic
mahamari *n.* महामारी pestilence
mahan *a* महान big
mahan *a.* महान grand
mahan vidwan *n.* महान विद्वान् luminary
mahanagar *n.* महानगर metropolis
mahanagar ka *n.* महानगर का
  metropolitan
mahanata *n.* महानता stature
mahanga *a* महंगा dear
mahanga *a* महंगा expensive
mahanga *a.* महंगा precious
mahapaashniya *a.* महापाषाणीय
  megalithic
mahapursh *n.* महापुरुष magnate
maharaj *n.* महाराज Highness
maharani *n* महारानी empress
maharani *n.* महारानी queen
mahatva *n.* महत्व importance
mahatva *n.* महत्व price
mahatva dena *v. t* महत्व देना emphasize
mahatva-heen *a.* महत्वहीन immaterial
mahatvahin *a.* महत्वहीन insignificant
mahatvahin *a.* महत्त्वहीन negligible
mahatva-hinta *a.* महत्व-हीनता
  insignificance
mahatvakanksha *v.t.* महत्वाकांक्षा aspire
mahatvapurna *a.* महत्वपूर्ण important
mahatvapurna *a.* महत्वपूर्ण momentous
mahavir *n* महावीर chevalier
mahawat *n.* महावत mahout
maheene mein do bar *adj.* महीने में दो बार
  bimonthly
mahila *n.* महिला lady
mahin *a* महीन fine
mahina *n.* महीना month
mahsus karna *v.t* महसूस करना feel
mahtvakansha *n.* महत्वाकांक्षा ambition
mahtvakanshi *a.* महत्वाकांक्षी ambitious
mahtya *n.* महत्व significance

maidan *n.* मैदान plain

mail *n* मेल coalition

mail *n.* मेल rapport

maila kuchaila *a.* मैला कुचैला slovenly

mailmilap karna *v.t.* मेलमिलाप कराना reconcile

main *pron.* मैं I

maithun karna *v.i.* मैथुन करना copulate

majakiya *a* मज़ाकिया comical

majakiya *n.* मज़ाकिया funny

majbuth karna *v.t.* मज़बूत करना fortify

majhla *a.* मझला mean

majjak *n.* मज़ाक mockery

major *n* मेजर major

makaan *n* मकान house

makar rashi *n* मकर राशि Capricorn

makarhi *n.* मकड़ी spider

makbara *n.* मकबरा mausoleum

makhan *n* मक्खन butter

makhan lagana *v. t* मक्खन लगाना butter

makhi *n* मक्खी fly

makhmal *n* मखमल plush

makhmal *n.* मखमल velvet

makhmali *a.* मखमली velvety

makka *n.* मक्का maize

makrhi ka jaala *n.* मकड़ी का जाला web

makrhi ka jala *n* मकड़ी का जाला cobweb

makri *n* मकड़ी mite

mal *n.* मल refuse

mala *n* माला anadem

mala *n.* माला garland

mala *n.* माला wreath

mala pahnana *v.t.* माला पहनाना garland

malai *n* मलाई cream

malaria *n.* मलेरिया malaria

malba *n* मलबा debris

malba *n.* मलबा rubble

maldibba *n.* मालडिब्बा wagon

malgujari *n.* मालगुजारी rent

malik *n* मालिक boss

malikana *a.* मालिकाना proprietary

malin *a* मलिन dirty

maljal *n.* मलजल sewage

malmal *n.* मलमल muslin

mal-vyawastha *n.* मलव्यवस्था sewerage

mamera bhai *n.* ममेरा भाई cousin

mamla *n.* मामला affair

mamla niptana *v. t* मामला निपटाना dispose

mamuli sa *a.* मामूली सा marginal

man rakhna *v.t.* मन रखना indulge

mana karna *v.t.* मना करना prohibit

mana karna *v.t.* मना करना refuse

manak *n.* मानक norm

manak *n.* मानक standard

manakikaran karna *v.t.* मानकीकरण करना standardize

manana *n.* मनाना palaver

manana *v.t.* मानना think

mananiya *a.* माननीय reverend

manansheel *a.* मननशील meditative

manashchikitsa *n.* मनश्चिकित्सा psychiatry

manashchikitsa *n.* मनश्चिकित्सा psychotherapy

manashchikitsak *n.* मनश्चिकित्सक psychiatrist

manav *n.* मानव man

manav hatya *n.* मानव हत्या homicide

manav jaati *n.* मानव जाति mankind

manav ke anubhav *v.t.* मानव के अनुभव transcend

manavdyashi *n.* मानवद्वेषी misanthrope

manavi *a* मानवीय humanitarian

manavikaran karna *v.t.* मानवीकरण करना personify

manaviya banana *v.t.* मानवीय बनाना humanize

manaviyata *n.* मानवीयता humanity

manch *n.* मंच dais

manch *n.* मंच forum

manch *n.* मंच platform

manch *n.* मंच rostrum

manch *n.* मंच stage

manchan karna *v.t.* मंचन करना stage

manchitra *n* मानचित्र map

manchitra banana *v.t.* मानचित्र बनाना map

manchitrawali *n.* मानचित्रावली atlas

mand banana *v. t.* मंद बनाना dull

mand budhi मंद बुद्धि nitwit

mand karna *v. t* मन्द करना blear

mand karna *v.t.* मंद करना temper

mand samir *n.* मंद समीर zephyr

mand swar *n.* मंद स्वर undertone

mandabudhi vyakti *n.* मंदबुद्धि व्यक्ति moron

mandali *n.* मंडली assembly

mandali *n* मंडली club

mandali *n.* मंडली troupe

mandaliya *a.* मंडलीय zonal

mandap *n* मंडप booth

mandap *n.* मंडप pavilion

mandarna *v.i* मंडराना float

mandbudhi *a* मंदबुद्धि stupid

mandgati *n* मंदगति crawl

mandi *n.* मंदी slump

mandir *n.* मंदिर sanctuary

mandir *n.* मंदिर temple

mang *n.* मांग requisition

mang karna *v. t* मांग करना demand

mangaana *v.t.* मांगना seek

mangal greh *n* मंगल ग्रह Mars

mangana *v.t.* माँगना ask

manganese *n.* मैंगनीज़ manganese

mangharant kahani *n.* मनगढ़ंत कहानी concoction

manglacharan *n.* मंगलाचरण prelude

mangna *v.t.* मांगना requisition

mani *n.* मणि jewel

manik *n.* माणिक, गहरा लाल रंग ruby

manjari *n* मंजरी blossom

manjhala *n* मंझला medium

manka *n* मनका bead

mankikaran *n.* मानकीकरण standardization

manmauji *a.* मनमौजी capricious

manmutav *n.* मनमुटाव friction

manobal *n.* मनोबल morale

manodasha *n.* मनोदशा mood

manogat *a.* मनोगत notional

manohar *a.* मनोहर pleasant

manoranjak *a.* मनोरंजक laughable

manoranjan *n* मनोरंजन amusement

manoranjan *n.* मनोरंजन entertainment

manoranjan *n.* मनोरंजन recreation

manoranjan *n.* मनोरंजन sport

manoranjan karna *v.t.* मनोरंजन करना amuse

manoranjan karna *v. t* मनोरंजन करना entertain

manorogi *n.* मनोरोगी psychopath

manovaigyanik *a.* मनोवैज्ञानिक psychic

manovaigyanik *a.* मनोवैज्ञानिक psychological

manovigyan *n.* मनोविज्ञान psychology

manovigyani *n.* मनोविज्ञानी psychologist

manovikriti *n.* मनोविकृति psychosis

manovriti *n.* मनोवृत्ति mentality

manovyath *n.* मनोव्यथ compunction

mansik swasthya *n.* मानसिक स्वास्थ्य sanity

mansik vyastata *n.* मानसिक व्यस्तता preoccupation

mansikta *n.* मानसिकता psyche

manspeshi *n.* मांसपेशी muscle

mantramugadh karna *v.t.* मंत्रमुग्ध करना mesmerize

mantrana *n.* मंत्रणा counsel

mantri *n.* मंत्री minister

mantrimandal *n.* मंत्रिमंडल ministry

mantri-mandal *n.* मंत्रि-मंडल cabinet

manya banana *v.t.* मान्य बनाना validate

manyata *n.* मान्यता assumption

manyawar *n* मान्यवर excellency

manzil *n* मंज़िल floor

manzil *n.* मंज़िल storey

mar jana *v. i* मर जाना decease

mar jana *v.i.* मर जाना succumb

maraham lagana *v.t.* मरहम लगाना anoint

marammat *n* मरम्मत upkeep

marammat karana *v.t.* मरम्मत करना repair

marammat karna *v.t.* मरम्मत करना patch

marammat karna *v.t.* मरम्मत करना restore

maran-shilta *n.* मरण स्थल mortality

march ka mahina *n.* मार्च का महीना march

mardani larhki *n.* मरदानी लड़की tomboy

marg *n.* मार्ग avenue

marg *n.* मार्ग path

marg *n.* मार्ग route

marg *n.* मार्ग track

marg *n.* मार्ग trail

marg *n.* मार्ग way

marg banana *v.t.* मार्ग बनाना pave

marg darshak *n.* मार्ग दर्शक pioneer

marg dekhlana *v.t.* मार्ग दिखलाना pilot

marg dekhlana *v.t.* मार्ग दिखलाना pioneer

marg me rokna *v.t.* मार्ग में रोकना intercept

margdarsan *n.* मार्गदर्शन lead

margdarsan karna *v.t.* मार्गदर्शन करना lead

margdarshan karna *v.t.* मार्गदर्शन करना steer

marham *n.* मरहम balm

marham *n.* मरहम ointment

marichika *n.* मरीचिका illusion

marichika *n.* मरीचिका mirage

marna *v. t* मारना destroy

marna *v. i* मरना die

marna *v.i.* मरना expire

marna *v.t.* मारना kill

marnasan *a.* मरणासन्न moribund

maronotar *a.* मरणोत्तर posthumous

marorh *n.* मरोड़ wrench

marorhana *v.t.* मरोड़ना wrench

marorhana *v.t.* छीनना, मरोड़ना wrest

marorhna *v.t.* मरोड़ना rack

marramat *n.* मरम्मत repair

martbaan *n.* मर्तबान jar

maryada *n.* मर्यादा qualification

masak baja *n.* मसक बाजा bagpipe

masala *n.* मसाला spice

masalna *v.t* मसलना mash

masalon se chonkna *v.t.* मसालों से छौंकना spice

mashal *n.* मशाल torch

masiha *n.* मसीहा Christ

masjid *n.* मस्जिद mosque

maskhara *n* मसखरा buffoon

maskhara *n.* मसखरा joker

masnad *n* मसनद cushion

massa *n.* मस्सा wart

mastak *n.* मस्तक poll

mastol *n.* मस्तूल mast

masurha *n.* मसूढ़ा gum

mat *n.* मत opinion

mat dena *v.i.* मत देना vote

mat patra *n.* मत पत्र ballot

mata *n.* माता mamma

mata ya pita *n.* माता या पिता parent

mataandh *a* मतांध fanatic

matadhikaar *n.* मताधिकार franchise

matadhikaar *n.* मताधिकार suffrage

matadhikaar dena *v.t.* मताधिकार देना enfranchise

matali *n.* मतली nausea

matar *n.* मटर pea

mat-bhed hona *v. i* मत-भेद होना differ

mat-daan *n* मत-दान poll

matdan *n.* मतदान vote

matdata *n.* मतदाता constituent

matdata *n.* मतदाता voter

matdata kshetra *n* मतदाता क्षेत्र constituency

math *n.* मठ cloister

math *n* मठ convent

math *n.* मठ monastery

matha *n* मट्ठा buttermilk

mathadhyaksh *n* मठाध्यक्ष prior

mathadhyaksha *n.* मठाध्यक्षा prioress

mathatwapurna hona *v.i.* महत्वपूर्ण होना matter

mathvashi *n.* मठवासी monk

matihinta *n.* मतिहीनता abstraction

matra *n* मात्रा degree

matra *adv.* मात्र only

matrak *a.* मातृक maternal

matrak *n.* मात्रक unit

mat-rakhna *v.t.* मत-रखना opine

matrighatak *a.* मातृघातक matricidal

matrisulabh *a.* मातृसुलभ mother like

matritva *n.* मातृत्व motherhood

matritwa *n.* मातृत्व maternity

matrivadh *n.* मातृवध matricide

matsya nauka *n* मत्स्य नौका smack

mauj karna *v.i.* मौज करना lounge

mauj masti *n.* मौज मस्ती spree

mauj udane wala *n.* मौज उड़ाने वाला reveller

maujud hona *v.i* मौजूद होना exist

maukhik *a.* मौखिक oral

maukhik *a.* मौखिक verbal

maukhik *a* मौखिक viva-voce

maukhik pariksha *n* मौखिक परीक्षा viva-voce

maukhik rup mein *adv.* मौखिक रूप में verbally

maukhik rup mein *adv.* मौखिक रूप में viva-voce

maukhik rup se *adv.* मौखिक रूप से orally

mauli *n.* मूली radish

maulik *a.* मौलिक original

maulik *a.* मौलिक radical

maulikta *n.* मौलिकता originality

maun,ankaha *a.* मौन tacit

mausam *n* मौसम weather

mausam vigyan *n.* मौसम विज्ञान meteorology

mausami *a.* मौसमी seasonal

mausami hava *n.* मौसमी हवा monsoon

mauza *n.* मौज़ा sock

mauza *n.* मौज़ा stocking

mauzabandh *n.* मोज़ाबंध garter

mavad *n.* मवाद pus

mavastha *n.* मावस्था superlative

maveshi *n.* मवेशी cattle

may maas *n.* मई मास May

maya *n.* माया delusion

mayajaal *n.* मायाजाल materialism

mayuri *n.* मयूरी peahen

mazaak *n.* मज़ाक raillery

mazak *n.* मज़ाक banter

mazak udana *v.i.* मज़ाक उड़ाना jeer

mazak urhana *v.t.* मज़ाक उड़ाना banter

mazboot *a.* मज़बूत stalwart

mazboot *a.* मज़बूत sturdy

mazboot *a.* मज़बूत tough

mazbut banana *v.t.* मज़बूत बनाना strengthen

mazbut suti kapda *n.* मज़बूत सूती कपड़ा jean

mazdoor *n.* मज़दूर worker

mazdoor *n.* मज़दूर workman

mazdoori *n.* मज़दूरी wage

mazdoori dena *v.t.* मज़दूरी देना remunerate

mazdur *n.* मज़दूर jack

meel *n.* मील mile

meel ka patthar *n.* मील का पत्थर milestone

meen-paksh *n* मीनपक्ष fin

meetha *a.* मीठा sweet

meetha karna *v.t.* मीठा करना sugar

meetha karna *v.t.* मीठा करना sweeten

meetri tan *n.* मीटरी टन tonne

mehak *n* महक waft

mehaniti *a.* मेहनती industrious

mehman *n.* मेहमान visitor

mehmez *n.* महमेज़ spur

mehrab banana *v.t.* मेहराब बनाना overarch

mehrabadaar banana *v.t.* मेहराबदार बनाना arch

mehrabi chhat *n.* मेहराबी छत vault

meijbaan *n.* मेज़बान host

mein *prep.* में in

mela *n.* मेला fair

memna *n* मेमना agnus

memna *n.* मेमना lamb

mendhak *n.* मेंढक frog

mera *pron.* मेरा mine

mera *a.* मेरा my

meru mandir *n.* मेरु मंदिर pagoda

merudandiya *a.* मेरुदंडीय spinal

mesh rashi *n* मेष राशि Aries

meter *n.* मीटर metre

metersambandhi *a.* मीटर संबंधी metric

mewaun *n.* म्याऊँ mew

mez *n* मेज़ desk

mez *n.* मॅज table

miaun karna *v.i.* म्याऊँ करना purr

michligrast *a.* मिचलीग्रस्त, sick

mil jana *v.t.* मिल जाना amalgamate

mil jana *v. t* मिल जाना combine

mil jana *v. i.* मिल जाना conspire

mila lena *v.t.* मिला लेना merge

milaana *v. i* मिलाना compound

milaana *v.t.* मिलाना mingle

milan *n* मिलान comparison

milan sthal *n* मिलन स्थल abuttal

milan sthal *n.* मिलन स्थल rendezvous

milana *v.i* मिलना mix

milana *v.t.* मिलाना weld

milansaar *a.* मिलनसार affable

milansar *a.* मिलनसार sociable

milansari *n.* मिलनसारी sociability

milavat *n.* मिलावट adulteration

milavat *n.* मिलावट impurity

milavat karna *v.t.* मिलावट करना adulterate

milavati *a.* मिलावटी impure

mil-jul kar *adv.* मिलजुलकर jointly

milna *v* मिलना abut

milna *v. t* मिलना blend

milta julta *a* मिलता जुलता duplicate

milta julta *a.* मिलता जुलता identical

mimiyahat *n* मिमियाहट bleat

mimiyana *v. i* मिमियाना bleat

minaar *n.* मीनार minaret

minar *n.* मीनार steeple

minar *n.* मीनार tower

minute *n.* मिनट minute

mirch *n.* मिर्च pepper

mirch milana *v.t.* मिर्च मिलाना pepper

mirgi *n* मिरगी epilepsy

mirzai *n.* मिरज़ई jerkin

mishran *n* मिश्रण amalgam

mishran *n* मिश्रण amalgamation

mishran *n* मिश्रण blend

mishrit khad *n* मिश्रित खाद compost

mishthan greha *n* मिष्ठान गृह confectionery

misran *n.* मिश्रण mixture

misri *n.* मिसरी candy

mistari *n* मिस्तरी fitter

mistri *n.* मिस्त्री mechanic

mita dena *v. t* मिटा देना efface

mita dena *v.t.* मिटा देना liquidate

mitana *v. t* मिटाना erase

mithai, methae *n.* मिष्ठान, मिठाई sweetmeat

mithas *n.* मिठास sweetness

mithya bodh *n* मिथ्या बोध misapprehension

**mithya daavaidaar** *a.* मिथ्या दावेदार pretentious

**mithya naam** *n.* मिथ्या नाम misnomer

**mithyabhiman** *n.* मिथ्याभीमान vanity

**mithyawadi** *a.* मिथ्यावादी mendacious

**mitr** *n.* मित्र ally

**mitr** *n.* मित्र friend

**mitr** *n.* मित्र pal

**mitr banana** *v. t.* मित्र बनाना befriend

**mitrabhav ka** *adj.* मित्रभाव का amicable

**mitrata** *n.* मित्रता amity

**mitrata ka navinikaran** *n.* मित्रता का नवीनीकरण reconciliation

**mitte ki patra** *n.* मिट्टी के पात्र pottery

**mitthai** *n.* मिठाई comfit

**mitthe jal ki machhli** *n.* मीठे जल की मछली perch

**mitti** *n* मिट्टी clay

**mitti** *n.* मिट्टी soil

**mitti ka tel** *n.* मिट्टी का तेल kerosene

**mitti ke bartan** *n.* मिट्टी के बरतन crockery

**mitti ke patra** *n* मिट्टी के पात्र ceramics

**mitvyayata** *n.* मितव्ययिता thrift

**mitvyayi** *a* मितव्ययी economical

**mitvyayi** *a.* मितव्ययी inexpensive

**mitvyayi** *a.* मितव्ययी thrifty

**miyaan se nikalna** *v.t.* म्यान से निकालना unsheathe

**moch** *n* मोच wrick

**moch** *n.* मोच sprain

**mochi** *n* मोची cobbler

**mohak** *a.* मोहक nubile

**mohakata** *n.* मोहकता glamour

**mohar** *n* मोहर cachet

**mohit karna** *v. t* मोहित करना beguile

**mohit karna** *v.t* मोहित करना bewitch

**mohit karna** *n.t.* मोहित करना delude

**mohit karna** *v.t* मोहित करना fascinate

**mom** *n.* मोम wax

**mom lagana** *v.t.* मोम लगाना wax

**mom se dhaka huya** *adj.* मोम से ढँका हुआ cerated

**mombatti** *n.* मोमबत्ती candle

**mool** *n.* मूल origin

**mool path** *n.* मूल पाठ text

**mool roop** *n* मूल रूप original

**moolsvar** *n.* मूलस्वर tonic

**moonch** *n.* मूंछ moustache

**mor** *n.* मोर peacock

**morcha** *n.* मोरचा front

**morh** *n* मोड़ bend

**morhna** *v.t.* मोड़ना crimple

**morhna** *v. t* मोड़ना curve

**morhna** *v. t* मोड़ना divert

**morhna** *v.t.* मोड़ना shunt

**morna** *v.t* मोड़ना fold

**morna** *v.t.* मोड़ना furl

**mota** *a* मोटा fat

**mota hona** *v.i.* मोटा होना thicken

**motapa** *n.* मोटापा obesity

**motar chalak** *n.* मोटर चालक motorist

**moti** *n.* मोती pearl

**motia band** *n.* मोतिया बिंद glaucoma

**motiyabind** *n.* मोतियाबिंद cataract

**motorcar** *n.* मोटरकार automobile

**mridu karna** *v.t.* मृदु करना assuage

**mrlg** *n* मृग doe

**mrinamaya** *a* मरीआमया earthen

**mrityu** *n* मृत्यु death

**mrityu** *n* मृत्यु decease

**mudh** *n.* मूढ़ loggerhead

**mudra** *n.* मुद्रा attitude

**mudra** *n* मुद्रा currency

**mudra** *n.* मुर्दा money

**mudra** *n.* मुद्रा pose

**mudra** *n.* मुद्रा posture

**mudrak** *n.* मुद्रक printer

**mudrankit karna** *v.i.* मुद्रांकित करना stamp

**mudrasfriti** *n.* मुद्रास्फीति inflation

**mugdhata** *n.* मुग्धता infatuation

**muhaasa** *n.* मुंहासा pimple
**muhakama** *n.* मुहकमा bureau
**muhansa** *n* मुँहासा acne
**muhar** *n.* मुहर seal
**muhara** *n.* मुहरा muzzle
**muhavare-daar** *a.* मुहावरेदार idiomatic
**muhawara** *n.* मुहावरा idiom
**muhawara** *n.* मुहावरा phrase
**muhn se ulat dena** *v.t.* मुंह से उलट देना vomit
**mujhako** *pron.* मुझको me
**muk abhineta** *n.* मूक अभिनेता mummer
**muk abhineta** *n.* मूक अभिनेता pantomime
**mukabala karna** *v.i.* मुकाबला करना vie
**mukadama** *n.* मुकदमा suit
**mukadama chalana** *v.t.* मुकदमा चलाना sue
**mukh** *n* मुख brim
**mukh sambandhi** *a* मुख संबंधी facial
**mukhauSta** *n.* मुखौटा mask
**mukhauta** *n* मुखौटा facade
**mukhbir** *n.* मुखबिर informer
**mukhiya** *n.* मुखिया chieftain
**mukhya** *a.* मुख्य chief
**mukhya** *a.* मुख्य salient
**mukhya bhag** *n* मुख्य भाग main
**mukhya lakshan** *n.* मुख्य लक्षण quintessence
**mukhya ruup se** *adv.* मुख्य रूप से mainly
**mukhya sahara** *n.* मुख्य सहारा mainstay
**mukhya upaj** *n.* मुख्य उपज staple
**mukka** *n.* मुक्का punch
**mukka** *n.* मुक्का thump
**mukka maarna** *v.t.* मुक्का मारना thump
**mukka marna** *v.t.* मुक्का मारना punch
**mukkebazee** *n* मुक्केबाज़ी boxing
**mukt hona** *v.i* मुक्त होना escape
**mukt karana** *v.t.* मुक्त करना release
**mukt karna** *v. t* मुक्त करना discharge
**mukt karna** *v. t.* मुक्त करना exempt
**mukt karna** *v.t* मुक्त करना free

**mukt karna** *v.t.* मुक्त करना liberate
**mukt karna** *v.t.* मुक्त करना loose
**mukt karna** *v.t.* मुक्त करना manumit
**mukt karna** *v.t.* मुक्त करना redeem
**mukt karna** *v.t.* मुक्त करना rescue
**mukt karna** *v.t.* मुक्त करना rid
**mukti** *n.* मुक्ति discharge
**mukti** *n.* मुक्ति emancipation
**mukti** *n.* मुक्ति liberation
**muktidata** *n.* मुक्तिदाता liberator
**mukut** *n.* मुकुट tiara
**mukut pahanana** *v. t* मुकुट पहनाना crown
**mul** *a* मूल aboriginal
**mul bhav** *n.* मूल भाव motif
**mul nivasi** *n. pl* मूल निवासी aborigines
**mul nivasi** *n* मूल निवासी native
**mul tatva** *n.* मूल तत्व rudiment
**muladhar** *n.* मूलाधार basis
**mulat:** *adv.* मूलत: primarily
**mulayam** *a* मुलायम tender
**mulayam kagaz** *n.* मुलायम काग़ज़ tissue
**mulla** *n.* मुल्ला mullah
**mulumma karna** *v.t.* मुलम्मा करना plate
**mulvastu** *n* मूलवस्तु element
**mulya** *v.t.* मूल्य cost
**mulya batana** *v.t.* मूल्य बतलाना quote
**mulyankan** *n* मूल्यांकन estimation
**mulyankan** *n.* मूल्यांकन valuation
**mulyankan karna** *v.t.* मूल्यांकन करना appraise
**mulyankan karna** *v.t.* मूल्यांकन करना appreciate
**mulyankan karna** *v. t* मूल्यांकन करना evaluate
**mulyankan karna** *v.t.* मूल्यांकन करना rate
**mulyawan** *a.* मूल्यवान costly
**munafakhor** *n.* मुनाफ़ाखोर profiteer
**munafakhori karna** *v.i.* मुनाफ़ाखोरी करन profiteer
**mundan** *n.* मुंडन tonsure

munga *n* मूंगा coral
munh *n.* मुंह mouth
munh kholay hue *adv.*, मुंह खोले हुए agape
munh tor jawab *n.* मुंह तोड़ जवाब retort
munim *n.* मुनीम accountant
munimi *n.* मुनीमी accountancy
muqadamebaaz *n.* मुकदमेबाज़ litigant
muqaddma chalana *v.t.* मुकदमा चलाना prosecute
muqdma *n.* मुकदमा litigation
muqadme-baazi karna *v.t.* मुकदमेबाज़ी करना litigate
murabba *n.* मुरब्बा jam
murcha *n.* मूर्च्छा swoon
murchit hona *v.i* मूर्च्छित होना faint
murchit hona *v.i* मूर्च्छित होना swoon
murda ghar *n.* मुर्दाघर mortuary
murga *n* मुर्गा cock
murgi *n.* मुर्गी hen
murhkana *v.t.* मुड़काना sprain
murjhana *v.i.* मुरझाना languish
murjhana *v.i.* मुरझाना wither
murkahta *n* मूर्खता folly
murkh *adj.* मूर्ख asinine
murkh *n.* मूर्ख clod
murkh *adj.* मूर्ख crass
murkh *a* मूर्ख foolish
murkh *n* मूर्ख gull
murkh *a.* मूर्ख mindless
murkh *a.* मूर्ख obtuse
murkh *a.* मूर्ख silly
murkh aadmi *n* मूर्ख आदमी dunce
murkh banana *v.t.* मूर्ख बनाना infatuate
murkh banana *v.t.* मूर्ख बनाना stupefy
murkh vyakti *n.* मूर्ख व्यक्ति ass
murkh vyakti *n* मूर्ख व्यक्ति blockhead
murkh vyakti *n* मूर्ख व्यक्ति fool
murkha vyakti *n.* मूर्ख व्यक्ति idiot
murkhata *n* मूर्खता absurdity
murkhatapurn *a* मूर्खतापूर्ण absurd

murkhta *n.* मूर्खता idiocy
murkhta *n.* मूर्खता stupidity
murkhtapurna *a.* मूर्खतापूर्ण idiotic
murkhtapurna *a* मूर्खतापूर्ण maudlin
murti *n.* मूर्ति idol
murti *n.* मूर्ति image
murti *n.* मूर्ति statue
murti ka rup dena *v. t.* मूर्ति का रूप देना carve
murtikala *n.* मूर्तिकला sculpture
murtikaran *n.* मूर्तीकरण personification
murtimaan *a.* मूर्तिमान incarnate
murtipujak *n.* मूर्तिपूजक idolater
murtroop dena *v.t.* मूर्तरूप देना materialize
murtrup *n* मूर्तरूप embodiment
murtrup dena *v. t.* मूर्तरूप देना embody
musal *n.* मूसल maul
mushkil mein dalna *v. t* मुश्किल में डालना embarrass
mushkil se *adv.* मुश्किल से barely
mushkil se *adv.* मुश्किल से hardly
mushkil se hi *adv.* मुश्किल से ही scarcely
mushli *n.* मुषली piston
musibat *n.* मुसीबत hardship
musibat *n.* मुसीबत tribulation
muskan *n.* मुस्कान smile
muskana *v.i* मुस्काना smile
mutari *n.* मुटरी magpie
muthibhar *n.* मुड़ीभर handful
mutra *n.* मूत्र urine
mutra tyag *n.* मूत्र त्याग urination
mutralaya *n.* मूत्रालय urinal
mutrashaya *n* मूत्राशय bladder
mutriya *a.* मूत्रीय urinary
myan *n.* म्यान scabbard

# N

naabhi *n.* नाभि hub
naabhiya *a* नाभीय focal

naach *n.* नाच cabaret

naagdaun *n.* नागदौन wormwood

naagrik saina *n.* नागरिक सेना militia

naagrikshastra *n* नागरिकशास्त्र civics

naagrikta *n* नागरिकता citizenship

naagwari *a.* नागवारी offensiveness

naajuk *a.* नाजुक awkward

naak *n.* नाक nose

naak se bolna *vt* नाक से बोलना nasalize

naal lagana *v.t.* नाल लगाना shoe

naala *n.* नाला rivulet

naalaa *n* नाला sewer

naali *n.* नाली groove

naam *n.* नाम name

naam chinha *n.* नाम चिह्न monogram

naam khata *n* नामखाता debit

naam likhna *v. t* नाम लिखना enlist

naam patra *n.* नाम पत्र label

naam rakhna *v.t.* नाम रखना name

naamankit karna *v.t.* नामांकित करना nominate

naamrashi *n.* नामराशि namesake

naanbaai *n.* नानबाई baker

naand *n.* नांद manger

naap *n.* नाप measurement

naapna *v.t* नापना measure

naara *n.* नारा watchword

naarkiya *a.* नारकीय infernal

naashak *a.* नाशक pernicious

naashak jeev *n.* नाशक जीव pest

naashrakshan *n.* नाशरक्षण salvage

naashwan *a.* नाशवान mortal

naasikya *n* नासिक्य nasal

naaspati *n.* नाशपाती pear

naasur *n* नासूर fistula

naavik *n.* नाविक oarsman

nabbe *n.* नब्बे ninety

nabbevan *a.* नब्बेवां ninetieth

nabhikiya *a.* नाभिकीय nuclear

nabz *n.* नब्ज़ pulse

nachana *v. t.* नाचना dance

nadi *n.* नदी river

nadi *n.* नदी stream

nadi mukh bhumi *n* नदी मुख भूमि delta

nadiya *n.* नदिया streamlet

nagad dhan *n.* नकद धन cash

nagadi mein badalna *v. t.* नगदी में बदलना cash

nagan *a.* नग्न nude

naganta *n.* नग्नता nudity

naganya vastu *n.* नगण्य वस्तु, अल्पमात्रा trifle

nagar *n* नगर city

nagar ka *a* नगर का civic

nagar-nivasi *n* नगर-निवासी citizen

nagarpalika *n.* नगरपालिका municipality

nagarpalika sambandhi *a.* नगरपालिका संबंधी municipal

nagarpramukh *n.* नगरप्रमुख mayor

nagphani *n.* नागफनी cactus

nagriya *a.* नगरीय urban

nahar *n* नहर aqueduct

nahar *n.* नहर canal

nahi *adv.* नहीं nay

nahi *adv.* नहीं not

nahin *adv.* नहीं no

naitekthawadi *n.* नैतिकतावादी moralist

naitik *a* नैतिक ethical

naitik patan karna *v. t.* नैतिक पतन करना demoralize

naitikatavadi *a.* नैतिकतावादी puritanical

naitikta *n.* नैतिकता virtue

naitikta-nirpeksha *a.* नैतिकता-निरपेक्ष amoral

naitra golak *n* नेत्र गोलक eyeball

naitritva *n.* नेतृत्व leadership

naiwala *n.* नेवला mongoose

naiypith *n.* न्यायपीठ jury

najarband kar dena *v.t.* नज़रबंद कर देना intern

najir *n.* नज़ीर precedent

najuk *a.* नाजुक dainty

**nakaar** *n* नकार denial
**nakal** *n.* नकल imitation
**nakal** *n* नकल mimicry
**nakal utarna** *v.t* नकल उतारना mimic
**nakalchi** *n* नकलची mimic
**nakali** *a.* नकली artificial
**nakali** *a.* नकली spurious
**nakaratmak** *a* नकारात्मक minus
**nakaratmak** *n.* नकारात्मक negative
**nakh prasadhan** *n.* नख प्रसाधन manicure
**nakhlistaan** *n.* नखलिस्तान oasis
**nakhun** *n.* नाखून nail
**naksha** *n.* नक्शा chart
**naksha banana** *v.t.* नक्शा बनाना sketch
**nakshatriya** *a.* नक्षत्रीय stellar
**nakshatron ka samuh** *n.* नक्षत्रों का समूह constellation
**nala** *n* नाला channel
**nali** *n.* नाली gutter
**nali** *n.* नली tube
**nalidaar banana** *v.t* नालीदार बनाना groove
**nalikakar** *a.* नलिकाकार tubular
**nalkaar** *n.* नलकार plumber
**nam karna** *v.t.* नम करना moisten
**namak** *n.* नमक salt
**namak chirhakana** *v.t* नमक छिड़कना salt
**namamkit vyakti** *n* नामांकित व्यक्ति nominee
**naman** *n* नमन bow
**namankan** *n.* नामांकन nomination
**namaskar karna** *v.t.* नमस्कार करना salute
**namawali** *n.* नामावली nomenclature
**nami** *n.* नमी humidity
**nami** *n.* नमी moisture
**namkeen** *a.* नमकीन saline
**namkeen** *a.* नमकीन salty
**namra** *a.* नम्र mild
**namuna** *n.* नमूना sample
**namuna** *n.* नमूना specimen

**nanga** *a.* नंगा naked
**nanga karna** *v.t.* नंगा करना bare
**nanga karna** *v.t.* नंगा करना denude
**nanga karna** *v.t.* नंगा करना strip
**napasand karna** *v. t* नापसंद करना dislike
**napunsak** *a.* नपुंसक impotent
**napunsak** *a.* नपुंसक neuter
**napunsakta** *n.* नपुंसकता impotence
**nar** *n* नर male
**nara** *n.* नारा slogan
**naraaz** *a.* नाराज़ ire
**naraaz karna** *v. t* नाराज़ करना displease
**naraj karna** *v.t.* नाराज़ करना offend
**narak** *a.* नरक hell
**narak yatana** *n.* नरक यातना damnation
**naram gadda** *n* नरम गद्ढा pad
**naram padana** *v.i.* नरम पड़ना relent
**narangi** *a* नारंगी orange
**naraz** *a.* नाराज़ touchy
**naraz karna** *v. t.* नाराज़ करना dissatisfy
**nargis** *n* नरगिस narcissus
**nari** *n.* नारी woman
**naritva** *n.* नारीत्व womanhood
**nariyal** *n* नारियल coconut
**nariyal ki jata** *n* नारियल की जटा coir
**na-samjhi** *n.* ना-सामझी indiscretion
**nasbandi** *n.* नसबंदी vasectomy
**nash hone yogya** *a.* नाश होने योग्य perishable
**nasht karna** *v.t.* नष्ट करना decimate
**nasht karna** *v.t.* नष्ट करना annihilate
**nasht karna** *v.i* नष्ट करना blast
**nasht karna** *v. t* नष्ट करना break
**nasht karna** *v.t* नष्ट करना extinguish
**nasht karna** *v.t.* नष्ट करना shatter
**nasht karna** *v.t.* नष्ट करना undo
**nasht karna** *v.t.* नष्ट करना waste
**nasht karna** *v.t.* नष्ट करना wreck
**nashta** *n* नाश्ता breakfast
**nash-vad** *n.* नाशवाद nihilism
**nashwar** *n* नश्वर mortal

**nasile aushadhi** *n.* नशीली औषधि narcotic
**nass** *n* नस nerve
**nastik** *n* नास्तिक antitheist
**nastik** *n* नास्तिक atheist
**nastikta** *n* नास्तिकता atheism
**nata purush** *n.* नाटा पुरुष bantam
**natak** *n* नाटक drama
**natak ka drishya** *n.* नाटक का दृश्य scene
**natak karna** *v.i.* नाटक करना play
**natak sambandhi** *a* नाटक संबंधी dramatic
**natakkar** *n* नाटककार dramatist
**nathi karna** *v.t.* नत्थी करना pin
**nathuna** *n.* नथुना nostril
**nat-khat** *a.* नट-खट naughty
**natkhat larhka** *n.* नटखट लड़का urchin
**natodar** *adj.* नतोदर concave
**natyashala** *n.* नाट्यशाला theatre
**natyashala vishayak** *a.* नाट्यशाला विषयक theatrical
**nau** *n.* नौ nine
**nau-chalak** *n.* नौ-चालक navigator
**nauchalan** *n.* नौचालन navigation
**nauchhalan karna** *v.i.* नौचालन करना navigate
**naugamya** *a.* नौगम्य navigable
**nauk** *n.* नोक spike .
**nauka par** *adv* नौका पर aboard
**nauka vihar karna** *v.i* नौका विहार करना yacht
**naukar** *n.* नौकर lackey
**naukar chakar** *n.* नौकर चाकर retinue
**naukari** *n.* नौकरी appointment
**naukari** *n* नौकरी employment
**naukari** *n.* नौकरी service
**naukari karna** *v.t.* नौकरी करना serve
**naukaro kai vardi** *n.* नौकरों की वर्दी livery
**naukarshahi** *n.* नौकरशाही bureaucracy
**naukri dena** *v. t* नौकरी देना employ
**nau-sena** *n.* नौ-सेना navy
**nausena adhyaksha** *n.* नौसेनाध्यक्ष admiral

**nausikhuva** *n.* नौसिखुआ novitiate
**nav** *n.* नाव barge
**nav** *n* नाव boat
**nav** *n* नाव ferry
**nav khena** *v.i* नाव खेना boat
**nav se upar utarna** *v.t* नाव से पार उतारना ferry
**nava** *a.* नवां ninth
**nava khena** *v.t.* नाव खेना row
**navik** *n.* नाविक sailor
**navikaran** *n.* नवीकरण renewal
**navikaran** *n.* नवीकरण renovation
**navinta** *n.* नवीनता novelty
**nav-jaat** *a.* नवजात nascent
**nawab** *n.* नवाब nabob
**nawonmaish** *n.* नवोन्मेष innovation
**naya** *a.* नया novel
**naya banana** *v.t.* नया बनाना innovate
**naya karna** *v.t.* नया करना refresh
**naya karna** *v.t.* नया करना renew
**naya karna** *v.t.* नया करना renovate
**nayain sire se** *adv.* नए सिरे से afresh
**nayak** *n* नायक commander
**nayak** *n.* नायक hero
**nayak** *n.* नायक protagonist
**nayak sambandhi** *a.* नायक संबंधी heroic
**nayayik janch** *n.* न्यायिक जांच inquisition
**nayayshastra** *n.* न्यायशास्त्र jurisprudence
**nayee jawani** *n.* नई जवानी rejuvenation
**nayee pattiyan** *n* नई पत्तियाँ browse
**nayee toli** *n.* नई टोली relay
**nayika** *n.* नायिका heroine
**nazuk** *a* नाजुक delicate
**nechai ki aur** *adv* नीचे की ओर downward
**neech** *a.* नीच paltry
**neechay** *adv* नीचे below
**neechay aana** *v.i.* नीचे आना alight
**neeche** *prep.* नीचे under
**neeche** *adv* नीचे beneath
**neeche** *adv* नीचे under
**neeche** *adv.* नीचे underneath

**neeche aana** *v. i.* नीचे आना descend
**neeche ki aur** *prep* नीचे की ओर down
**neeche ko jhuka hua** *adj.* नीचे को झुका हुआ declivitous
**neechta** *n.* नीचता meanness
**neel** *n.* नील indigo
**neelaam karna** *v.t.* नीलाम करना auction
**neelaami** *n* नीलामी auction
**neelvarna** *n* नीलवर्ण blue
**neemhakimi** *n.* नीमहकीमी quackery
**neend** *n.* नींद sleep
**neend** *n.* नींद slumber
**neeras** *a.* नीरस insipid
**neeras** *a.* नीरस tedious
**neerasta** *n.* नीरसता tedium
**negro mahila** *n.* निग्रो महिला negress
**neji** *a.* निजी respective
**nerankush** *a* निरंकुश autocratic
**nerankush shasak** *n* निरंकुश शासक autocrat
**neta** नेता leader
**netrarog visaisahgya** *n.* नेत्ररोग विशेषज्ञ oculist
**netritva karna** *v. t* नेतृत्व करना conduct
**netritva karna** *v.t.* नेतृत्व करना spearhead
**neumonia** न्यूमोनिया pneumonia
**ni:shastrikaran** *n.* निः शस्त्रीकरण disarmament
**nib** *n.* निब nib
**nibandh** *n.* निबंध essay
**nibhandkaar** *n* निबंधकार essayist
**nicha** *a.* नीचा neap
**nichla** *a.* निचला low
**nichla** *a.* निचला nether
**nidaan karna** *v. t* निदान करना diagnose
**nidan** *n* निदान diagnosis
**nidar** *a.* निडर bold
**nidbav** *n.* निदबाव repression
**nidhan suchna** *a.* निधन सूचना obituary
**nidra bhraman** *n.* निद्राभ्रमण somnambulism

**nidra janak** *n.* निद्राजनक somnolent
**nidra rahit** *a.* निद्रा रहित wakeful
**nidrachari** *n.* निद्राचारी somnambulist
**nidraluta** *n.* निद्रालुता somnolence
**nigal jana** *v. t* निगल जाना devour
**nigalna** *v.t* निगलना engulf
**nigalna** *vt* निगलना gulp
**nigalna** *v.t.* निगलना swallow
**nigam** *n* निगम corporation
**nigaran** *n.* निगरण swallow
**nigmit karna** *v.t.* निगमित करना incorporate
**nigrani** *n.* निगरानी surveillance
**nigrani** *n.* निगरानी vigilance
**nihaye** *n.* निहाई anvil
**nihit hona** *v. i* निहित होना consist
**niji** *a.* निजी personal
**niji shikshak** *n.* निजी शिक्षक tutor
**niji shikshak ke shikshan ka samay** *n.* निजी शिक्षक के शिक्षण का समय tutorial
**nikaal dena** *v. t.* निकाल देना expel
**nikaal dena** *v.t.* निकाल देना oust
**nikaalna** *v. t* निकालना exclude
**nikaas** *n* निकास evacuation
**nikaasi** *n* निकासी clearance
**nikamma** *a.* निकम्मा miserable
**nikas** *n* निकास escape
**nikas** *n.* निकास issue
**nikat** *adv.* निकट near
**nikat sambandhi** *a.* निकट संबंधी proximate
**nikat se** *adv.* निकट से nearly
**nikatasth** *a.* निकटस्थ imminent
**nikatdristi** *a.* निकटदृष्टिक myopic
**nikatta** *n.* निकटता proximity
**nikkar** *n. pl.* निकर shorts
**nikotin** *n.* निकोटीन nicotine
**nilamban** *n.* निलंबन suspension
**nilambit karna** *v.t.* निलंबित करना suspend
**nilkanth** *n.* नीलकंठ jay

nimajjan *n.* निमज्जन immersion

nimbu *n.* नींबू lemon

nimn sthiti mein *adv.* निम्न स्थिति में low

nimnastariya *a.* निम्नस्तरीय banal

ninadita *n.* निनादिता sonority

ninda *n.* निंदा censure

ninda *n* निंदा condemnation

ninda *n.* निंदा reproof

ninda karna *v.t.* निंदा करना vilify

ninda karna *v.* निन्दा करना asperse

ninda karna *v. t.* निन्दा करना calumniate

ninda karna *v. t.* निंदा करना censure

ninda karna *v. t.* निंदा करना condemn

ninda karna *v. t* निंदा करना criticize

ninda karna *v. t* निंदा करना denounce

ninda karna *v.t.* निंदा करना malign

ninda karna *v.t.* निंदा करना reprimand

nindak *n* निंदक cynic

nindapurna *a.* निंदापूर्ण sardonic

nindatmak *a.* निंदात्मक slanderous

nindra ka samay *n.* निद्रा का समय bedtime

nipun *a.* निपुण skilful

nipun *adj.* निपुण adept

nipun vyakti *n.* निपुण व्यक्ति adept

nipunata *n.* निपुणता skill

nipunnta *n.* निपुणता proficiency

nipunta *n.* निपुणता accomplishment

nipunta *n* निपुणता efficiency

nira *a.* निरा sheer

niraash *a.* निराश pessimistic

niraksharta *n.* निरक्षरता illiteracy

nirala *n* निराला neuter

niramish *a.* निरामिष vegetarian

nirana *v.t.* निराना weed

nirankush *a.* निरंकुश arbitrary

nirankush shasak *n* निरंकुश शासक despot

nirantar ~*a.* निरंतर ceaseless

nirantar *adj.* निरन्तर continual

nirantar *a* निरन्तर continuous

nirantar *n.* निरन्तर frequency

nirantarta *n* निरंतरता continuity

nirarthak *a.* निरर्थक meaningless

nirarthak *n.* निर्थक waste

niras *a.* नीरस humdrum

niras *a.* नीरस monotonous

niras *a.* नीरस prosaic

niras *a.* नीरस weary

nirasan *n.* निरसन revocation

nirasavadi *n.* निराशावादी pessimist

nirash *a.* निराश hopeless

nirash *adj* निराश melancholy

nirash hona *v. i* निराश होना despair

nirasha *n* निराशा dejection

nirasha *n* निराशा despair

nirasha, baukhalahat *n.* निराशा, बौखलाहट frustration

nirashajanak *a* निराशाजनक desperate

nirashavad *n.* निराशावाद pessimism

nirast karna *v.t.* निरस्त करना repeal

nirasta *n* नीरसता monotony

nirbhakata *n.* निर्भीकता intrepidity

nirbhar *a* निर्भर dependent

nirbhar hona *v.i.* निर्भर होना rely

nirbhik *a* निर्भीक dauntless

nirbhikta *n* निर्भीकता boldness

nirbhikta *n.* निर्भीकता daring

nirdaya *a* निर्दय bloody

nirdaya *a* निर्दय brutal

nirdesh *n* निर्देश direction

nirdeshak *n* निर्देशक conductor

nirdeshak *n.* निर्देशक director

nirdeshan *n.* निर्देशन reference

nirdeshika *n* निर्देशिका directory

nirdeshit karna *v.t.* निर्देशित करना supervise

nirdhan *a.* निर्धन needy

nirdhan *a.* निर्धन penniless

nirdhan *a.* निर्धन poor

nirdhanta *adv.* निर्धनता impoverish

nirdharan *n.* निर्धारण prescription

nirdharit *a* निर्धारित set

**nirdharit karna** *v.t.* निर्धारित करना allocate

**nirdharit karna** *v.t.* निर्धारित करना prescribe

**nirdosh** *a.* निर्दोष innocent

**nirdosh banana** *v.t.* निर्दोष बनाना perfect

**nirdosh ghoshit karna** *v.t.* निर्दोष घोषित करना acquit

**nirdoshta** *n.* निर्दोषता perfection

**nirdya** *a.* निर्दय ruthless

**nirekshak** *n.* निरीक्षक invigilator

**nirikshak** *n.* निरीक्षक inspector

**nirikshak** *n.* निरीक्षक supervisor

**nirikshan** *n.* निरीक्षण inspection

**nirikshan** *n.* निरीक्षण invigilation

**nirikshan karna** *v. t.* निरीक्षण करना censor

**nirikshan karna** *v.t.* निरीक्षण करना invigilate

**nirikshan karna** *v.t.* निरीक्षण करना survey

**nirjan** *a.* निर्जन lonely

**nirjan** *a.* निर्जन lonesome

**nirjan sthan** *n.* निर्जन स्थान nook

**nirjanta** *n.* निर्जनता loneliness

**nirlajj** *a.* निर्लज्ज shameless

**nirmaan karna** *v.t.* निर्माण करना make

**nirmaata** *n.* निर्माता maker

**nirmal** *a.* निर्मल neat

**nirman** *n* निर्माण construction

**nirman** *n* निर्माण erection

**nirman** *n* निर्माण formation

**nirman karna** *v. t* निर्माण करना build

**nirman karna** *v. t.* निर्माण करना construct

**nirman karna** *v. t* निर्माण करना erect

**nirman karna** *v.t* निर्माण करना fabricate

**nirman karna** *v.t.* निर्माण करना manufacture

**nirman karna** *v.t.* निर्माण करना raise

**nirman shaili** *n.* निर्माण शैली architecture

**nirmata** *n* निर्माता creator

**nirmit karna** *v. t* शांत होना compose

**nirmit karna** *v.t.* निर्मित करना originate

**nirmul** *a.* निर्मूल baseless

**nirnay karna** *v.t.* निर्णय करना adjudge

**nirnaya** *n.* निर्णय conclusion

**nirnaya** *n* निर्णय decision

**nirnaya** *n.* निर्णय judgement

**nirnaya karna** *v. t* निर्णय करना decide

**nirnaya karna** *v. i* निर्णय करना decree

**nirnaya karna** *v.i.* निर्णय करना judge

**nirnayak** *a* निर्णायक conclusive

**nirnayak** *n.* निर्णायक judge

**nirnayak** *n.* निर्णायक umpire

**nirnayak hona** *adj* निर्णायक होना umpire

**nirnayakarta** *n.* निर्णयकर्ता referee

**nirnayatmak** *a* निर्णयात्मक decisive

**nirparadhata** *n.* निरपराधता innocence

**nirpeksh** *a.* निरपेक्ष irrespective

**nirsan** *n* निरसन repeal

**nirshar** *a.* निरक्षर illiterate

**nirthakta** *n.* निरर्थकता futility

**nirvachak mandal** *n* निर्वाचक मंडल electorate

**nirvachan** *n* निर्वाचन election

**nirvasan** *n.* निर्वासन banishment

**nirvasit karna** *v.t.* निर्वासित करना banish

**nirvasit karna** *v.t.* निर्वासित करना ostracize

**nirvivad** *a* निर्विवाद certain

**nirviwad** *a.* निर्विवाद implicit

**niryaat** *n* निर्यात export

**niryaat karna** *v. t.* निर्यात करना export

**nisaana** *n.* निशाना mark

**nisandeh** *adv.* निःसंदेह certainly

**nishan** *n* निशान print

**nishan** *n.* निशान spot

**nishan** *n.* निशान trace

**nishana** *n.* निशाना shot

**nishana** *n.* निशाना target

**nishanebaaj** *n.* निशानेबाज़ marksman

**nishani** *n.* निशानी relic

nishani *n.* निशानी vestige

ni-shastra karna *v. t* निःशस्त्र करना disarm

nishchit *a* निश्चित definite

nishchit *a.* निश्चित specific

nishchit *a.* निश्चित sure

nishchit karna *v.t.* निश्चित करना ascertain

nishchit mulya ka *a* निश्चित मूल्य का worth

nishchit rup se *adv.* निश्चित रूप से surely

nishedh *n.* निषेध prohibition

nishedh *n.* निषेध taboo

nishedhadhikar *n.* निषेधाधिकार veto

nishedhagya *n* निषेधाज्ञा curfew

nishedhagya *n.* निषेधाज्ञा injunction

nishedhatimikta *adv.* निषेदामिक्ता negativvity

nishedhatmak *a.* निषेधात्मक prohibitory

nishidh *a.* निषिद्घ illicit

nishidh *a* निषिद्घ taboo

nishidh karna *v.t* निषिद्घ करना forbid

nishidh karna *v.t.* निषिद्घ करना taboo

nishidh karna *v.t.* निषिद्घ करना veto

nishkapat *a.* निष्कपट frank

nishkapatata *n.* निष्कपटता candour

nishkasan *n.* निष्कासन expulsion

nishkasan *n.* निष्कासन rustication

nishkriya *a.* निष्क्रिय inert

nishkriya *a.* निष्क्रिया inoperative

nishkriya *a.* निष्क्रिय passive

nishpaksh *a.* निष्पक्ष impartial

nishpaksh *a.* निशप्रकाश neutral

nishpakshta *n.* निष्पक्षता impartiality

nishphal *adv* निष्फल abortive

nishphal karna *v.t.* निष्फल करना counteract

nishphal karna *v.t* निष्फल करना foil

nishprabhavikaran *n.* निष्प्रभावीकरण nullification

nishta *n* निष्ठा faith

nishtha *n* निष्ठा fidelity

nishthavan *n.* निष्ठावान trusty

nishthur *a.* निष्ठुर inexorable

nishulk *a.* निशुल्क free

nishulk *adv.* निःशुल्क gratis

niskars nikalana *v.t.* निष्कर्ष निकालना infer

nistaar *n* निस्तार rescue

nistej *a.* निस्तेज lacklustre

nistha *n.* निष्ठा allegiance

nistha *n.* निष्ठा loyalty

nisthabadtha *n* निस्तब्धता hush

nisthahin *a.* निष्ठाहीन insincere

nisthahinta *n.* निष्ठाहीनता insincerity

nisthavan *a.* निष्ठावान loyal

nisthur *adj.* निष्ठुर merciless

nitamb *n.* नितंब loin

niti chatur *a.* नीति चतुर politic

niti katha *n.* नीति कथा fable

niti yukti *n.* नीति युक्ति policy

nitigat baat karna *v.t.* नीतिगत बात करना moralize

nitigranth *n.* नीतिग्रंथ ethics

nitikatha *n.* नीतिकथा parable

nitivachan *n.* नीतिवचन sermon

nivarak *a.* निवारक preventive

nivaran *n.* निवारण prevention

nivas *n.* निवास accommodation

nivas *n.* निवास home

nivas *n.* निवास nest

nivas karna *v.i.* निवास करना reside

nivas sthan *n.* निवासस्थान residence

nivasi *a.* निवासी resident

nivden karna *v.t.* निवेदन करना ask

nivedak *n.* निवेदक petitioner

nivedan karna *v. t.* निवेदन करना beg

nivida *n* निविदा tender

nivriti-vetan *n.* निवृत्ति वेतन pension

niwaala *n.* निवाला morsel

niwaala *n.* निवाला mouthful

niwas *n.* निवास habitation

**niwas karna** *v.i.* निवास करना live

**niwasi** *n.* निवासी inhabitant

**niwirwad** *a.* निर्विवाद indisputable

**niyam** *n* नियम formula

**niyam** *n.* नियम norm

**niyam** *n.* नियम rule

**niyam virodh** *n* नियम-विरोध anomaly

**niyamit** *a.* नियमित normal

**niyamit** *a.* नियमित orderly

**niyamit** *n.* नियमित routine

**niyamit** *a.* नियमित steady

**niyamit** *adv.* नियमत usually

**niyamit avartan** *n.* नियमित आवर्तन rotation

**niyamit karna** *v.t.* नियमित करना regulate

**niyamitata** *n.* नियमितता regularity

**niyamnishth vyakti** *n.* नियमनिष्ठ व्यक्ति puritan

**niyantrak** *n.* नियंत्रक censor

**niyantrak** *n.* नियंत्रक controller

**niyantran** *n* नियंत्रण control

**niyantran** *n* नियंत्रण curb

**niyantran hatana** *v.t.* नियंत्रण हटाना decontrol

**niyantran karna** *v. t* नियंत्रण करना curb

**niyantran karna** *v.t* नियंत्रण करना handle

**nIyantran rakhna** *v. t* नियन्त्रण रखना control

**niyantran yogya** *a.* नियंत्रण योग्य manageable

**niyantrit karna** *v.t.* नियंत्रित करना contain

**niyantrit karna** *v.t.* नियंत्रित करना restrain

**niyat karna** *v.t.* नियत करना allot

**niyati** *n* नियति destiny

**niyatkalik** *a.* नियतकालिक periodical

**niyojak** *n* नियोजक employer

**niyukt karna** *v. t* नियुक्त करना depute

**niyukt karna** *v.t.* नियुक्त करना appoint

**niyukt karna** *v.t.* नियुक्त करना assign

**niyukt karna** *v. t* नियुक्त करना constitute

**niyukt karna** *v.t.* नियुक्त करना install

**niyukt karna** *v.t.* नियुक्त करना place

**niyukt karna** *v.t.* नियुक्त करना post

**nochna** *v.t* नोचना nip

**nok** *n.* नोक tip

**nok se chhed karna** *v.t.* नोक से छेद करना puncture

**nokdaar banana** *v.t.* नोकदार बनाना tip

**nokdar banana** *v.t.* नोकदार बनाना point

**november** *n.* नवंबर november

**nrishans** *a* नृशंस cruel

**nrishansata** *n* नृशंसता atrocity

**nrishansata** *n.* नृशंसता outrage

**nritya** *n* नृत्य dance

**nritya sangit** *a.* नृत्य-संगीत minuet

**nukila** *n.* नुकीला mucro

**nukila** *a.* नुकीला sharp

**nuksaan** *n* नुकसान disadvantage

**nukta chini karna** *v.t.* नुकता चीनी करना nibble

**nupur** *n* नुपूर anklet

**nyasi** *n.* न्यासी trustee

**nyaya** *n* न्याय right

**nyaya parayan** *a.* न्याय परायण righteous

**nyaya virudh** *adj* न्याय विरुद्ध absonant

**nyayabhikarta** *n.* न्यायाभिकर्ता solicitor

**nyayalaya** *n.* न्यायालय judicature

**nyayalaya** *n.* न्यायालय, न्यायाधिकरण tribunal

**nyayaochit** *a* न्यायोचित equitable

**nyayik nirnaya** *n* न्यायिक निर्णय decree

**nyay-sambandhi** *a.* न्याय संबंधी judicial

**nyay-tantra** *n.* न्यायतंत्र judiciary

**nylon** *n.* नाइलॉन nylon

**nyunatam matra** *n.* न्यूनतम मात्रा minimum

**O**

**october** *n.* अक्टूबर October

**odhni** *n.* ओढ़नी veil

**offset chhapai** *n.* ऑफ़सैट छपाई offset
**ojha** *n.* ओझा necromancer
**omlet** *n.* आमलेट omelette
**oon** *n.* ऊन wool
**ooni** *a.* ऊनी woollen
**ooni dhaga** *n.* ऊनी धागा worsted
**ooni kaparha** *n* ऊनी कपड़ा woollen
**os** *n.* ओस dew
**osana, barsana** *v.t.* ओसाना, बरसाना winnow
**oshth sambandhi** *a.* ओष्ठ संबंधी labial
**ounce** *n.* औंस ounce
**out karna** *v.t* आउट करना stump
**oxygen** *n.* ऑक्सीजन oxygen

# P

**paadariyon ka sangh** *n.* पादरियों का संघ convocation
**paadri** *n* पाद्री clergy
**paagal** *a.* पागल insane
**paagal vaykti** *n.* पागल व्यक्ति maniac
**paagana** *v. t.* पागना candy
**paak vidhi** *n.* पाक विधि recipe
**paakhandi** *n.* पाखंडी hypocrite
**paakhandi** *a.* पाखंडी hypocritical
**paalan** *n* पालन culture
**paalki** *n.* पालकी litter
**paalki** *n.* पालकी palanquin
**paaltu janawar** *n.* पालतू जानवर pet
**paan** *n* पान betel
**paangar** *n* पांगर chestnut
**paansa** *n.* पानसा dice
**paap karm** *n.* पाप कर्म sin
**paap karna** *v.i.* पाप करना sin
**paap se mukt karna** *v.t.* पाप से मुक्त करना assoil
**paap svikaran** *n* पाप स्वीकरण confession
**paapi** *a.* पापी sinful
**paapi** *n.* पापी sinner

**paapi** *a.* पापी wicked
**paapon se mukti** *n.* पापों से मुक्ति salvation
**paar karna** *v.t.* पार करना cross
**paar karna** *v.i.* पार करना pass
**paarad** *n.* पारद mercury
**paarad** *n.* पारद quicksilver
**paari** *n.* पारी innings
**paar-patra** *n.* पार-पत्र passport
**paas aana** *v.i.* पास आना near
**paas mein** *adv* पास में by
**paas pahunchana** *v.t.* पास पहुंचना approach
**paas rakhna** *v.t.* पास रखना keep
**paathak** *n* पाठक book-worm
**pachaas** *n.* पचास fifty
**pachadana** *v.t.* पछाड़ना outdo
**pachan** *n* पाचन digestion
**pachana** *v.i.* पचाना assimilate
**pachana** *v. t.* पचाना digest
**pachchar** *n.* पच्चर wedge
**pachtava karnewala** *a.* पछतावा करनेवाला repentant
**pad** *n.* पद chair
**pad** *n.* पद quality
**pad** *n.* पद status
**pad tyag** *n* पद-त्याग abdication
**padak** *n.* पदक gong
**padak** *n.* पदक medal
**padak prapt vaykti** *n.* पदक प्राप्त व्यक्ति medallist
**padarath** *n.* पदार्थ matter
**padari** *n.* पादरी parson
**padari ka pradesh** *n.* पादरी का प्रदेश parish
**padarth** *n* पदार्थ liquid
**padarth** *n* पदार्थ material
**padarth** *n.* पदार्थ substance
**padbindu** *n.* पादबिंदु nadir
**padchap** *n* पदचाप tread
**padhaku** *n.* पढ़ाक्कू bookish

padhati *n.* पद्धति scheme

padhatibadh *a.* पद्धतिबद्ध systematic

padkram *n.* पदक्रम grade

pad-kram *n.* पदक्रम hierarchy

pados *n.* पड़ोस neighbourhood

pados *n.* पड़ोस vicinity

padosi *n.* पड़ोसी neighbour

padri ki vriti *n* पादरी की वृत्ति benefice

padya likhna *v.i.* पद्य लिखना rhyme

padya-baddh karna *v.t.* पद्यबद्ध करना versify

padyakar *n.* पद्यकार rhymester

padyarachna *n.* पद्यरचना versification

pagal *adj* पागल bizarre

pagal *adj.* पागल daft

pagal *a.* पागल lunatic

pagal karna *v.t* पागल करना dement

pagal vykti *n.* पागल व्यक्ति lunatic

pagalpan *n* पागलपन craze

pagalpan *n.* पागलपन lunacy

pagal-pan *n.* पागल-पन insanity

pageh se bandhna *v.t.* पगहे से बांधना tether

paglakar *adv.* पगलाकर amuck

pagrhi *n.* पगड़ी turban

pahal *n.* पहल initiative

pahala *a* पहला former

pahar *n.* पहाड़ mountain

pahar par chadhne wala *n.* पहाड़ पर चढ़ने वाला mountaineer

pahara dena *v.i.* पहरा देना patrol

paharhi *n.* पहाड़ी mount

paharhi nala ya nadi *n.* पहाड़ी नाला या नदी beck

pahari *n* पहाड़ी montane

pahari *a.* पहाड़ी mountainous

pahchan *n.* पहचान identity

paheli *n.* पहेली conundrum

paheli *n* पहेली enigma

paheli *n.* पहेली riddle

paheli karna *v.i.* पहेली कहना riddle

pahiya *a.* पहिया wheel

pahiye ka danta *n* पहिये का दाँता cog

pahla *a.* पहला previous

pahle ka *a.* पहले का past

pahle se bata dena *v.t.* पहले से बता देना prophesy

pahnana *v. t* पहनाना dress

pahulu *n* पहलू facet

pahunch पहुँच access

pahunch ke andar *a* पहुंच के अंदर available

pahunchana *v.i.* पहुंचना arrive

pahunchana *v.t.* पंचरणना convoke

paiband *n.* पैबन्द graft

paiband *n* पैबंद patch

paichish *n* पेचिश dysentery

paida hona *v.i.* पैदा होना stem

paida hua *v.* पैदा हुआ born

paida karna *v.t.* पैदा करना generate

paida karna *v.t.* पैदा करना yield

paidal chalna *v.i.* पैदल चलना trek

paidal saina *n.* पैदल सेना infantry

paighambar *n.* पैग़ंबर prophet

paighambari *a.* पैग़ंबरी prophetic

paimana *n.* पैमाना gauge

paina *a.* पैना acute

pair *n* पैर foot

pair ghasitna *v.i.* पैर घसीटना shuffle

pair ka *n.* फेरी का pedal

pair ki thaap *n.* पैर की थाप stamp

pair ki ungli *n.* पैर की उंगली toe

pair se choona *v.t.* पैर से छूना toe

pairbansa *n.* पैरबांसा stilt

pairhi *n.* पैड़ी, stair

paitikot *n.* पेटीकोट petticoat

paitrik *a.* पैतृक parental

paitrik *a.* पैतृक paternal

pajaama *n* पेजामा pyjama

paka hua *a* पका हुआ ripe

pakad *n.* पकड़ grapple

pakad *n* पकड़ grasp

pakad *n.* पकड़ hold

pakadna *v.t.* पकड़ना grip

pakadna *v.t* पकड़ना hold

pakana *v. t* पकाना concoct

pakana *v. t* पकाना cook

pakana *v.i.* पकना, पकाना ripen

pakane ki widhi *n.* पकाने की विधि cuisine

pakarh *n.* पकड़ seizure

pakarhna *v. i.* पकड़ना bag

pakarhna *v.t* पकड़ना take

pakarna *v. t.* पकड़ना catch

pakchhpathpurna *a.* पक्षपातपूर्ण partisan

pakhand *n.* पाखंड imposture

pakhandi *n.* पाखंडी impostor

pakhwara *n.* पखवारा fort-night

pakka *a* पक्का fast

pakka *a.* पक्का ingrained

paksh lena *v.i.* पक्ष लेना side

pakshaghar *n.* पक्षधर partisan

pakshaghat *n.* पक्षाघात palsy

pakshapat *n* पक्षपात bias

pakshapatpurna banana *v. t* पक्षपातपूर्ण बनाना bias

pakshi ka navjaat baccha *n* पक्षी का नवजात बच्चा nestling

paksh-paat *n.* प्रकाश-पथ partiality

pakshposhan *n.* पक्षपोषण advocacy

pakshposhit karna *v.t.* पक्षपोषित करना advocate

pala *n* पाला blight

palak *n.* पलक lid

palak *n.* पालक spinach

palak jhapakna *v.i.* पलक झपकना wink

palaki *n.* पालकी sedan

palan *n.* पालन pursuance

palan karna *v.i* पालन करना abide

palan karna *v. i* पालन करना comply

palan karna *v. t* पालन करना execute

palan karna *v.t.* पालन करना observe

palan karte hue *a* पालन करते हुए abiding

palan poshan karna *v.t.* पालन पोषण करना rear

palangposh *n.* पलंगपोश coverlet

palan-poshan karna *v.t* पालन- पोषण करना breed

palan-poshan karna *v.t.* पालन-पोषण करना nurture

palatane yogya *a.* पलटने योग्य reversible

palayan *n* पलायन flight

palna *n* पालना cradle

palna *v.t.* पालना tame

paltan *n.* पलटन platoon

paltan ka afsar *n.* पलटन का अफसर cornet

palthi marna *v.i.* पालथी मारना squat

paltu *a.* पालतू tame

panah dena *v.t.* पनाह देना shelter

panala *n.* पनाला spout

panch *n* पांच five

panch faisla *n.* पंचफैसला arbitration

panchang *n.* पंचांग almanac

panchang *n.* पंचांग calendar

panchi *n* पक्षी bird

panchkon *n.* पंचकोण pentagon

pandra *n* पंद्रह fifteen

pandubbi *n.* पनडुब्बी submarine

pandubbi *n.* पनडुब्बी torpedo

pandulipi *n.* पांडुलिपि manuscript

panewaala *n.* पानेवाला receiver

pangu banana *v.t.* पंगु बनाना lame

pani *n.* पानी water

pani ka pakshi *n.* पानी का पक्षी coot

pani ke neechay jaana *v. i* पानी के नीचे जाना dive

pani mein pair *v.i.* पानी में पैर paddle

panir *n.* पनीर cheese

panja *n* पंजा claw

panja *n.* पंजा paw

panje se khurachna *v.t.* पंजे से खुरचना paw

panjiyak *n.* पंजीयक registrar

panjiyan *n.* पंजीयन registration

panjiyan *n.* पंजीयन registry

pankh *n* पंख feather

pankh *n.* पंख wing

pankha *n* पंखा fan

pankti *n.* पंक्ति queue

pankti *n.* पंक्ति rank

pankti *n.* पंक्ति row

pankti mai rakhna *v.t.* पंक्ति में रखना deploy

pank-yukt *a.* पंकयुक्त slimy

panna *n* पन्ना emerald

panne ki dusre aur *adv.* पन्ने की दूसरी ओर overleaf

panni *n.* पन्नी tinsel

pansaari *n.* पंसारी grocer

panth *n* पंथ creed

panth *n* पंथ cult

panth *n.* पंथ sect

paplin kapda *n.* पॉपलीन कपड़ा poplin

par *prep.* पर on

par *prep* पर upon

par vapas jana *v.t.* पर वापस जाना retrace

paradheen *n* पराधीन dependant

paradhvanik *a.* पराध्वनिक supersonic

parag *n.* पराग pollen

paraishani *n* परेशानी fix

parajay *n.* पराजय rebuff

parajaya *n* पराजय defeat

parajit *a.* पराजित prostrate

parajit karna *v. t.* पराजित करना beat

parajit karna *v.t.* पराजित करना overpower

parajit karna *v.t.* पराजित करना overwhelm

parajit karna *v.t.* पराजित करना vanquish

parajit karna *v.t.* पराजित करना worst

parakarm *n* पराक्रम exploit

parakram *n.* पराक्रम might

parakrami *a.* पराक्रमी manful

param koti ko prapt karna *v.i.* परम कोटि को प्राप्त करना culminate

paramarsh *n* परामर्श advice

paramarsh *n* परामर्श consultation

paramarsh dena *v.t.* परामर्श देना advise

paramarsh dena *v. t.* परामर्श देना counsel

paramarsh lena *v. t* परामर्श लेना consult

parampara *n.* परंपरा tradition

paramparagat *a.* परंपरागत stereotyped

paramparagat *a.* परंपरागत traditional

parampriya *a* परमप्रिय beloved

parangat *a* पारंगत accomplished

parantu *conj.* परंतु only

parasaparik sambandh *n.* पारस्परिक संबंध correlation

paraspar misrith karna *v.t.* परस्पर मिश्रित करना intermingle

paraspar nirbhar *a.* परस्पर निर्भर interdependent

paraspar nirbharta *n.* परस्पर निर्भरता interdependence

paraspar vinimay *v.* परस्पर विनिमय interchange

parasparik *a.* पारस्परिक reciprocal

parast karna *v. t.* परास्त करना defeat

parat *n.* परत layer

parat *n* परत ply

parat *n.* परत seam

paravartak *a.* परावर्तक reflective

paravartan *n.* परावर्तन reflection

paravartit *a* परावर्तित reflex

paravartit karna *v.t.* परावर्तित करना reflect

paraya karna *v.t.* पराया करना alienate

paraypt *adv* पर्याप्त enough

parcha likhne wala *n.* पर्चा लिखने वाला pamphleteer

parchayee *n.* परछाई shadow

parchi *n.* पर्ची chit

parchi *n.* पर्ची slip

pardaa *n.* परदा shroud

**pardar** *adj.* परदार aliform
**pardarshi** *a.* पारदर्शी transparent
**pardesi** *a.* परदेशी outlandish
**pared karna** *v.t.* परेड करना parade
**paresaan karna** *v.t.* परेशान करना obsess
**paresani** *n* परेशानी distress
**pareshaan karna** *v. t* परेशान करना distress
**pareshan hona** *v. t* परेशान होना bother
**pareshan karna** *v.t.* परेशान करना haunt
**pareshani** *n.* परेशानी harassment
**pareshani** *n* परेशानी vexation
**pareshani mein chorna** *v.i.* परेशानी में छोड़ना strand
**parha rahana** *v.i.* पड़ा रहना lie
**parhav dalna** *v. i.* पड़ाव डालना camp
**pari** *n* परी elf
**pari** *n* परी fairy
**pari** *n.* परी sylph
**paribhasha** *n* परिभाषा definition
**paribhasha** *n* परिभाषा description
**paribhasha dena** *v. t* परिभाषा देना define
**paribhashik shabdawali** *n.* पारिभाषिक शब्दावली terminology
**paricharika** *n.* परिचारिका nurse
**paricharika** *n.* परिचारिका waitress
**parichay** *n.* परिचय introduction
**parichay karna** *v.t.* परिचय कराना acquaint
**parichayak** *a.* परिचायक indicative
**parichaytamak** *a.* परिचयात्मक introductory
**parichit** *adj.* परिचित conversant
**parichit karna** *v.t.* परिचित करना introduce
**parichit karna** *v.t.* परिचित कराना prelude
**parichit vyakti** *n.* परिचित व्यक्ति acquaintance
**paridhan** *n.* परिधान attire
**paridhan** *n.* परिधान clothes
**paridhan** *n* परिधान clothing

**paridhan** *n.* परिधान garb
**paridhan** *n.* परिधान garment
**paridhan** *n.* परिधान vestment
**paridhan pahanana** *v.t* परिधान पहनाना garb
**paridhi** *n.* परिधि circuit
**paridhi** *n.* परिधि circumference
**paridhi** *n.* परिधि periphery
**paridhi** *n.* परिधि purview
**parihaas** *n.* परिहास humour
**parihaas** *n.* परिहास joke
**parijan** *n.* परिजन kin
**parikramapath** *n.* परिक्रमापथ orbit
**pariksha karna** *v. t* परीक्षा करना examine
**parikshak** *n* परीक्षक examiner
**parikshan** *n* परीक्षण experiment
**parikshan** *n* परीक्षण test
**parikshan karna** *v.t.* परीक्षण करना inspect
**pariksharthi** *n.* परीक्षार्थी candidate
**pariksharthi** *n* परीक्षार्थी examinee
**parilabh** *n* परिलाभ emolument
**pariman** *n.* परिमाण volume
**parimarjan karna** *v. t* परिमार्जन करना cleanse
**parimay** *a.* परिमेय measurable
**parinaam** *n.* परिणाम outcome
**parinaam** *n.* परिणाम product
**parinaam** *n.* परिणाम sequel
**parinaam** *n.* परिणाम upshot
**parinam** *n* परिणाम consequence
**parinam** *n.* परिणाम result
**parinam hona** *v.i* परिणाम होना amount
**parinam hona** *v.i.* परिणाम होना issue
**parinam sambandhi** *a.* परिणाम संबंधी quantitative
**parinaya** *n.* परिणय matrimony
**paripak karna** *v.* परिपाक करना assimilate
**paripakwa** *a.* परिपक्व mature
**paripakwata** *n.* परिपक्वता maturity
**paripatra** *n.* परिपत्र circular

**pari-puran** *adj* परिपूर्ण plenary
**paripurna karna** *v.t.* परिपूर्ण करना
saturate
**parirakshak** *n.* परिरक्षक preservative
**parirakshan** *n.* परिरक्षण preservation
**parirakshi** *a.* परिरक्षी preservative
**parirakshit vastu** *n.* परिरक्षित वस्तु
preserve
**parisani** *n.* परेशानी obsession
**parishad** *n.* परिषद् council
**parishisht** *n.* परिशिष्ट appendix
**parishisht** *n.* परिशिष्ट supplement
**parishkrit karna** *v.t.* परिष्कृत करना
retouch
**parishodhan** *n.* परिशोधन liquidation
**parishodhan shala** *n.* परिशोधनशाला
refinery
**parishram** *n* परिश्रम diligence
**parishrami** *a* परिश्रमी diligent
**paristhiti** *n.* परिस्थिति situation
**paristithi** *n.pl.* परिस्थिति circumstance
**paritaap** *n.* परिताप anguish
**paritoshik** *n.* पारितोषिक reward
**parityag** *n* प्ररित्याग disposal
**parityag** *n.* परित्याग resignation
**parivahan** *n.* परिवहन portage
**parivahan** *n.* परिवहन transit
**parivahan** *n.* परिवहन transportation
**parivahan sadhan** *n.* परिवहन साधन
transport
**parivartan** *n.* परिवर्तन change
**parivartan** *n.* परिवर्तन modification
**parivartan** *n.* परिवर्तन mutation
**parivartan** *n* परिवर्तन shift
**parivartan** *n.* परिवर्तन transition
**parivartan** *n.* परिवर्तन variation
**parivartaniya** *a.* परिवर्तनीय variable
**parivartit karna** *v.t.* परिवर्तित करना alter
**parivesh** *n.* परिवेश environment
**pariviksha kaal** *n.* परीविक्षा काल
probation

**parivishharthi** *n.* परिवीक्षार्थी probationer
**pariwar** *n* परिवार family
**pariwartansil** *a.* परिवर्तनशील mutative
**parkar** *n* परकार compass
**parmadhikaar** *n.* परमाधिकार prerogative
**parmanand** *n* परमानंद bliss
**parmanu** *n.* परमाणु atom
**parosi ke naate** *a.* पड़ोसी के नाते
neighbourly
**parpiran rati** *n.* परपीड़न रति sadism
**parpirhan kamuk** *n.* परपीड़न कामुक
sadist
**par-roop dharna** *n.* परस्वरूप धारण
impersonation
**parshva chayachitra** *n.* पार्श्व छायाचित्र
silhouette
**parthiv** *a.* पार्थिव worldly
**parv** *n* पर्व festival
**parvat ki choti** *n.* पर्वत की चोटी alp
**paryant** *prep* पर्यंत during
**paryapt** *a.* पर्याप्त adequate
**paryapt** *a.* पर्याप्त sufficient
**paryapt hona** *v.i.* पर्याप्त होना suffice
**paryapt matra** *n.* पर्याप्त मात्रा sufficiency
**paryapt matra mein** *adv.* पर्याप्त मात्रा में
fairly
**paryapt matra mein** *adv.* पर्याप्त मात्रा में
substantially
**paryatak** *n.* पर्यटक tourist
**paryatan** *n* पर्यटन ramble
**paryatan** *n.* पर्यटन tourism
**paryavekshak** *n.* पर्यवेक्षक overseer
**paryaya** *n.* पर्याय synonym
**paryayavachi** *a.* पर्यायवाची, synonymous
**paryojan** *n.* प्रयोजन purpose
**pasali sambandhi** *adj.* पसली संबंधी costal
**pasand** *n.* पसंद choice
**pasand** *n.* पसंद like
**pasand** *n.* पसंद liking
**pasand** *n.* पसंद preference
**pasand karna** *v.t* पसंद करना‌ fancy

pasand karna *v.t.* पसंद करना like

pase ka khel khelna *v. i.* पासे का खेल खेलना dice

paseena *n.* पसीना sweat

paseena aana *v.i.* पसीना आना sweat

pashchat drishiti *n.* पश्चात् दृष्टि retrospect

pashchatap *n.* पश्चाताप remorse

pashchatap *n.* पश्चात्ताप repentance

pashchatap karna *v.i.* पश्चात्ताप करना repent

pashchatya *a.* पाश्चात्य occidental

pashchim *n.* पश्चिम west

pashchim ki or *adv.* पश्चिम की ओर west

pashchimi *a.* पश्चिमी, पछुवां west

pashchimi *a.* पश्चिमी westerly

pashchimi *a.* पश्चिमी western

pashu *n* पशु beast

pashu *n* पशु brute

pashu ki boli *n* पशु की बोली cry

pashu ki moonch *n.* पशु की मूंछ whisker

pashu vadh *n.* पशुवध slaughter

pashuchikitsa *a.* पशुचिकित्सा संबंधी veterinary

pashulom *n.* पशुलोम fur

pashupala *n.* पशुपाला barn

pashushavak *n* पुशुशावक cub

pasina *n.* पसीना perspiration

pasina nikalna *v.i.* पसीना निकलना perspire

pasli *n.* पसली rib

pasu samuh *n.* पशु समूह herd

pata *n.* पता address

pata lagana *v. t* पता लगाना discover

patak dena *v. i.* पटक देना dash

pataka *n.* पताका streamer

patakha *n* पटाखा cracker

patan *n.* पतन relapse

patang *n.* पतंग kite

patanga *n.* पतंगा moth

path *n.* पाठ recitation

path pradarshak *n.* पथप्रदर्शक guide

pathar *n.* पत्थर stone

pathar ka sanduk *n* पत्थर का सन्दूक cist

pathar phenkna *v.t.* पत्थर फेंकना stone

patharila *a.* पथरीला stony

pathbhrasht *adv.,* पथभ्रष्ट astray

pathkar *n.* पथकर toll

path-pradarshan *n.* पथ-प्रदर्शन guidance

pathpradashan karna *v.t.* पथप्रदर्शन करना guide

pathyakram *n.* पाठ्यक्रम syllabus

pathykram *n* पाठ्यक्रम curriculum

pati *n* पति husband

pati athwa patni *n.* पति अथवा पत्नी spouse

pati vishyak *a.* पति विषयक marital

patili *n.* पतीली kettle

patit *a.* पतित licentious

patit hona *v.i.* पतित होना backslide

patit karna *v. t.* पतित करना debase

patiya *n.* पटिया slab

patiyaan *n* पत्तियाँ foliage

patjharh *n.* पतझड़ autumn

patkna *v.i.* पटकना pop

patla *a* पतला dilute

patla *a* पतला flimsy

patla *n.* पतला lean

patla *n.* पतला slender

patla *a.* पतला slim

patla *a.* पतला thin

patla karna *v. t* पतला करना dilute

patla karna *v.t.* पतला करना thin

patlapan *n* पतलापन taper

patlun *n.* पतलून pantaloon

patlun *n. pl* पतलून trousers

patni *n.* पत्नी wife

patnonmukh *a* पतनोन्मुख decadent

patra pane wala *n.* पत्र पाने वाला addressee

patra vyavahar karna *v. i* पत्र व्यवहार करना correspond

**patrakar** *n.* पत्रकार journalist
**patrakarita** *n.* पत्रकारिता journalism
**patrapaal** *n.* पत्रपाल postmaster
**patri** पटरी foot path
**patri se uttar jana** *v. t.* पटरी से उतर जाना derail
**patrika** *n.* पत्रिका journal
**patrika** *n.* पत्रिका periodical
**patsan** *n.* पटसन jute
**patta** *n* पट्टा belt
**patta** *n.* पत्ता leaf
**patta** *n.* पट्टा lease
**patta** *n.* पट्टा strap
**patte par dena** *v.t.* पट्टे पर देना lease
**pattedar** *n.* पट्टेदार lessee
**patthar** *n.* पठार plateau
**patti** *n.* पट्टी band
**patti** *n.* पत्ती blade
**patti** *n.* पट्टी strip
**patti** *n.* पट्टी tape
**patti bandhana** *v.t* पट्टी बांधना bandage
**pattiyon se bhara** *a.* पत्तियों से भरा leafy
**patwaar** *n.* पतवार oar
**patwar** *n.* पतवार helm
**paudha** *n.* पौधा plant
**pauranik** *a.* पौराणिक mythological
**pauranik katha** *n.* पौराणिक कथा myth
**pauranik kavita** *n* पौराणिक कविता mythopoetry
**paurush** *n* पौरुष manliness
**paurush** *n.* पौरुष virility
**pavan** *a.* पावन virtuous
**pavati** *n.* पावती receipt
**pavitra** *a.* पवित्र chaste
**pavitra** *a.* पवित्र pious
**pavitra** *a.* पवित्र sacred
**pavitra** *a.* पवित्र sacrosanct
**pavitra** *n* पवित्र virgin
**pavitra** *a* पवित्र pure
**pavitra karna** *v.t.* पवित्र करना hallow
**pavitra karna** *v.t.* पवित्र करना purge

**pavitra karna** *v.t.* पवित्र करना purify
**pavitra sthan** *n.* पवित्र स्थान shrine
**pavitrata** *n.* पवित्रता sanctity
**pavitrikaran** *n.* पवित्रीकरण sanctification
**pawan** *a.* पावन holy
**pawanchakki** *n.* पवनचक्की windmill
**pawroti** *n.* पावरोटी loaf
**payaj** *n.* प्याज़ onion
**payaria** *n.* पायरिया pyorrhoea
**payavekshak** *v.t.* पर्यवेक्षक oversee
**paye** *n* पेय beverage
**pech** *n.* पेच screw
**pech se kasna** *v.t.* पेच से कसना screw
**peche ghatit hona** *v.i* पीछे घटित होना ensue
**pechida** *a.* पेचीदा intricate
**pechila** *adj* पेचीला anfractuous
**ped** *n.* पेड़ tree
**peecha karna** *v. t* पीछा करना dog
**peecha karna** *v.t.* पीछा करना pursue
**peeche hatana** *v.t.* पीछे हटाना withdraw
**peeche hatna** *v.i.* पीछे हटना retreat
**peeche ki aur** *adv* पीछे की ओर behind
**peeche ko hatana** *v.t.* पीछे को हटाना repel
**peechhe chhorna** *n.* पीछे छोड़ना leave behind
**peekdaan** *n.* पीकदान spittoon
**peela** *a* पीला pale
**peela** *a.* पीला yellow
**peela** *a.* पीला wan
**peela hona** *v.i.* पीला होना pale
**peela karna** *v.t.* पीला करना yellow
**peela rang** *n* पीला रंग chrome
**peela rang** *n* पीला रंग yellow
**peela sa** *a.* पीला-सा yellowish
**peena** *v.t.* पीना drink
**peera** *n.* पीरा pang
**peerha** *n.* पीड़ा ache
**peerha hona** *v.i.* पीड़ा होना ache
**peerhit karna** *v.t.* पीड़ित करना aggrieve
**peeru** *n.* पीरू turkey

peesna *v. t* पीसना crush
peesna *v.t.* पीसना mill
peetal *n.* पीतल brass
peetna *v.t.* पीटना beat
peetna *v. t* पीटना belabour
peetna *v.t* पीटना hammer
pehchan *n.* पहचान identification
pehchan *n.* पहचान recognition
pehchan lena *v.t.* पहचान लेना recognize
pehchanana *v.t.* पहचानना identify
pehle hi *adv.* पहले ही beforehand
pehle se *adv.* पहले से already
pehle se acchha *a* पहले से अच्छा better
pehlu *n.* पहलू aspect
pencil *n.* पेंसिल pencil
pencil ka tukrha *n.* पेंसिल का टुकड़ा stub
pension dena *v.t.* पेंशन देना pension
perh ka tana *n.* पेड़ का तना trunk
perh paudhe *n.* पेड़ पौधे vegetation
pesh-kash *n* पेश-कश offer
pet *n* पेट abdomen
pet *n* पेट belly
pet *n.* पेट stomach
pet band *n.* पेटबंद apron
pet ke bal khisakna *v. i* पेट के बल
  खिसकना creep
peti *n.* पेटी girdle
peti se bandhna *v.t* पेटी से बांधना girdle
petrak *a.* पैतृक ancestral
petrol *n.* पेट्रोल petrol
pet-sambandhi *a.* पेट-संबंधी abdominal
petupan *n.* पेटूपन gluttony
peyano *n.* पियानो piano
phaansi *n. .* फांसी gallows
phaawra *n.* फावड़ा spade
phailana *v.t.* फैलाना scatter
phailana *v.t.* फैलाना stretch
phailna *v.i.* फैलना spread
phal *n.* फल fruit
phali *n.* फली pod
phallpaag *n.* फलपाग marmalade

phalna phulna *v.i* फलना फूलना flourish
phalna phulna *v.i.* फलना फूलना thrive
phalodhyan *n.* फलोद्यान orchard
phalras pay *n* फलरस पेय squash
phaltupan *n.* फालतूपन redundancy
phanda *n.* फंदा noose
phank *n.* फांक slice
phans jana *v.i* फंस जाना bog
phansi ka takhta *n.* फांसी का तख्ता
  scaffold
phaphola *n* फफोला bleb
phaphola *n* फफोला blister
phaphundi *n* फफूंदी mould
pharhana *v.t.* फाड़ना rip
pharhna *v.t.* फाड़ना tear
pharhpharhahat *n* फड़फड़ाहट flutter
pharhpharhana *v.t* फड़फड़ाना flutter
phasal *n* फ़सल crop
phatan *n.* फटन rift
phatehal *a.* फटेहाल shabby
phatkaar *n.* फटकार rebuke
phatkar bhara bhashan *n.* फटकार भरा
  भाषण tirade
phatkarna *v.t.* फटकारना rebuke
phatkarna *v.t* फटकारना upbraid
phatta *n.* पत्ता lath
phavrhe se khodna *v.t.* फावड़े से खोदना
  spade
phenk *n.* फेंक throw
phenkana *v.t* फेंकना fling
phenkana *v.t.* फेंकना pitch
phenkna *v.t.* फेंकना throw
phentana *v.t.* फेंटना whip
phentani *n* फेंटनी whisk
pheri lagana *v* फेरी लगना peddle
pheri wala *n* फेरीवाला hawker
phir *adv.* फिर anew
phir bhi *adv.* फिर भी nonetheless
phir se *adv.* फिर से again
phir se bharna *v.t.* फिर से भरना replenish
phisalna *v.i.* फिसलना skid

**phisalna** *v.i.* फिसलना slip

**phislan wala** *a.* फिसलन वाला slippery

**phiton se bandhana** *v.t.* फ़ीतों से बांधना lace

**phool bikrita** *n* फूल विक्रेता florist

**phool ki pankhuri** *n.* फूल की पंखुरी petal

**phoolgobhi** *n.* फूलगोभी broccoli

**phora** *n* फोड़ा sore

**phorha** *n* फोड़ा boil

**phorhna** *v. i.* फोड़ना burst

**photo** *n* फ़ोटो photo

**photo** *n.* फ़ोटो shot

**photo khinchne ki kala** *n.* फ़ोटो खींचने की कला photography

**photo lena** *v.t.* फ़ोटो लेना snap

**photo sambandhi** *a.* फ़ोटो संबंधी photographic

**photo utarna** *v.t.* फ़ोटो उतारना photograph

**photo utarnay wala** *n.* फ़ोटो उतारने वाला photographer

**phudakna** *v.i.* फुदकना skip

**phuhar** *a.* फूहड slatternly

**phuhar** *n.* फुहार spray

**phuhar istri** *n.* फूहड स्त्री slattern

**phuhar parhna** *n* फुहार drizzle

**phuhar parhna** *v. i* फुहार पड़ना drizzle

**phuhariya** *a.* फूहड़िया slipshod

**phulna** *v. i* फूलना cockle

**phunkarna** *v.i.* फुंकारना, फुफकारना snort

**phunsi** *n.* फुंसी pock

**phuphusa kar kehna** *v.t.* फुसफुसा कर कहना whisper

**phursat** *a* फ़ुर्सत leisure

**phurti** *n.* फुरती alacrity

**phurtila** *a.* फुर्तीला agile

**phurtila** *a.* फुरतीला alert

**phurtila** *a.* फुर्तीला smart

**phurtila khasta** *a* फुर्तीला खस्ता crisp

**phurtilapan** *n.* फुरतीलापन alertness

**phuslana** *v.t.* फुसलाना wheedle

**phus-phus** *n* फुसफुस whisper

**phut nikalna** *v.i.* फूट निकलना, spurt

**phutkar bikri** *v.t.* फुटकर बिक्री retail

**phutkar vikreta** *n.* फुटकर विक्रेता retailer

**piche ya dur jana** *v.i.* पीछे या दूर जाना recede

**pichha** *n.* पीछा chase

**pichha karna** *v. t.* पीछा करना chase

**pichhla** *a.* पिछला latter

**pichkari** *n.* पिचकारी syringe

**pichla bhag** *n.* पिछला भाग back

**pichla bhag** *n.* पिछला भाग rear

**pichli taraph** *adv.* पिछली तरफ़ back

**pichrha hua** *a.* पिछड़ा हुआ backward

**pida** *n.* पीड़ा pain

**pighal jana** *v.t.* पिघल जाना fuse

**pighalna** *v.t.* पिघलाना smelt

**pighalna** *v.i* पिघलना thaw

**pighalna** *n* पिघलन thaw

**pila nargis** *n.* पीला नरगिस daffodil

**piliya** *n.* पीलिया jaundice

**pilla** *n.* पिल्ला puppy

**pilla** *n.* पिल्ला whelp

**pind** *n.* पिंड lump

**pind** *n.* पिंड mass

**pindak** *n.* पिंडक lobe

**pindali** *n.* पिंडली calf

**pinjra** *n.* पिंजरा cage

**pipa** *n* पीपा barrel

**pipa** *n* पीपा cask

**pira hona** *v.t.* पीड़ा होना pain

**pira rahit** पीड़ा रहित painless

**piramid** *n.* पिरामिड pyramid

**pirhadayak** *a* पीड़ादायक bitter

**pirhadayak** *a.* पीड़ादायक sore

**pishach nivas** *n.* पिशाच निवास pandemonium

**pisi hui cheez** *v.t.* पिसी हुई चीज़ mince

**pisna** *v.i.* पिसना grind

**pisne ka upkaran** *n.* पीसने का उपकरण grinder

**pissu** *n.* पिस्सू flea

pistol *n.* पिस्तौल pistol

pit *n* पित्त bile

pita *n* पिता dad, daddy

pita *n* पिता father

pitar *n.* पितर manes

pithika *n.* पीठिका pedestal

pitna *v.t* पीटना flog

pitna *v.t.* पीटना thrash

pitpiti *n.* पिटपिटी wren

pitratava *adg* पितृत्व paternity

pitritva *n.* पितृत्व parentage

piyakkad *n* पियक्क्ड़ bibber

piyanovadak *n.* पियानोवादक pianist

plate *n.* प्लेट plate

pokhar *n.* पोखर puddle

police *n.* पुलिस police

police ka sipahi *n.* पुलिस का सिपाही policeman

polki *n.* पोलकी opal

ponchan *n.* पोंछन wipe

ponchna *v.t.* पोंछना wipe

poochhna *v.t.* पूछना ask

poonch *n.* पूंछ tail

pop sambandhi *a.* पोप संबंधी popal

poshaak *n.* पोशाक costume

poshak *n* पोशाक dress

poshak *a.* पोषक nutritious

poshak *n.* पोषक patron

poshan *n.* पोषण aliment

poshan *n.* पोषण nourishment

poshan *n.* पोषण nutrition

poshan karna *v.t.* पोषण करना foster

poshan karna *v.t.* पोषण करना nourish

poshan sambandhi *a.* पोषण-संबंधी nutritive

poshana *v. t.* पोसना cherish

potana *v. t.* पोतना daub

potarohan karna *v. t* पोतारोहण करना embark

potash *n* पोटास alkali

potash *n.* पोटाश potash

potassium yukt *n.* पोटैशियम युक्त potassium

potavashesh *n.* पोतावशेष wreckage

potbhang *n.* पोतभंग wreck

potbhar *n.* पोतभार cargo

potwahak *n.* पोतवाहक mariner

powder *n.* पाउडर powder

prabal *adj.* प्रबल cogent

prabal *a.* प्रबल potent

prabal *a.* प्रबल predominant

prabal *v.i.* प्रबल preponderate

prabal *a.* प्रबल prevalent

prabalta *n.* प्रबलता predominance

prabandh *n.* प्रबंध monograph

prabandh *n.* प्रबंध treatise

prabandh karna *v.t.* प्रबंध करना administer

prabandh karna *v.t.* प्रबंध करना manage

prabandh se sambandhit *a.* प्रबंध से संबंधित managerial

prabandhak *n.* प्रबंधक manager

prabandhak *n.* प्रबंधक steward

prabandhak *n.* प्रबंधक superintendent

prabandhakarta *n.* प्रबंधकर्त्ता regulator

prabandhan *n.* प्रबंधन administration

prabandhan *n.* प्रबंधन management

prabandhkarini samiti *n.* प्रबंधकारिणी समिति senate

prabandhniya *n* प्रबन्धियां organizable

prabha mandal *n.* प्रभा मंडल nimbus

prabhat *n* प्रभात dawn

prabhav *n* प्रभाव effect

prabhav *n.* प्रभाव impact

prabhav *n.* प्रभाव imprint

prabhav *n.* प्रभाव influence

prabhav *n.* प्रभाव pull

prabhav *n* प्रभाव sway

prabhav dalna *v.t.* प्रभाव डालना influence

prabhav puran *a.* प्रभाव पूर्ण operative

prabhavi *a* प्रभावी emphatic

prabhavit karna *v.t.* प्रभावित करना affect

**prabhavit karna** *v.t.* प्रभावित करना impress

**prabhavotpadakta** *n* प्रभावोत्पादकता efficacy

**prabhavshali** *a* प्रभावशाली effective

**prabhavshali** *a.* प्रभावशाली imposing

**prabhavshali** *a.* प्रभावशाली impressive

**prabhavshali** *a.* प्रभावशाली influential

**prabhusatta** *n.* प्रभुसत्ता majesty

**prabhusatta** *n.* प्रभुसत्ता sovereignty

**prabhutwa** *n.* प्रभुत्व mastery

**prabodhak** *a.* प्रबोधक monitory

**prachalak** *n.* प्रचालक operator

**prachalan** *n.* प्रचलन prevalence

**prachalit** *a* प्रचलित current

**prachand** *a* प्रचंड fierce

**prachand** *n.* प्रचंड impetuosity

**prachand** *a.* प्रचंड vehement

**prachand dhara** *n.* प्रचंड धारा torrent

**prachand dhara jaisa** *a.* प्रचंड धारा जैसा torrential

**prachand tufan** *n.* प्रचंड तूफान typhoon

**prachar** *n.* प्रचार propaganda

**prachar** *n.* प्रचार publicity

**pracharak** *n.* प्रचारक propagandist

**pracharit karna** *v. t* प्रचारित करना broadcast

**pracharit karna** *v.t.* प्रचारित करना publicize

**prachepaastra** *n.* प्रक्षेपास्त्र missile

**prachin** *a.* प्राचीन ancient

**prachin** *a.* प्राचीन antiquated

**prachin kaal mein** *prep.* प्राचीन काल में afore

**prachinkaal** *n.* प्राचीनकाल antiquity

**prachinkaal-sambandhi** *a* प्राचीनकाल-संबंधी classical

**prachlan** *n.* प्रचलन vogue

**prachlit mulya** *n.* प्रचलित मूल्य quotation

**prachur** *a* प्रचुर abundant

**prachur** *a.* प्रचुर ample

**prachur** *a* प्रचुर bountiful

**prachur** *a.* प्रचुर generous

**prachur** *a* प्रचुर gross

**prachur** *a.* प्रचुर lavish

**prachur** *a.* प्रचुर luxuriant

**prachur** *a.* प्रचुर profuse

**prachur matra** *adv.* प्रचुर मात्रा galore

**prachur matra mein** *adv.* प्रचुर मात्रा में thick

**prachurata mein hona** *v.i.* प्रचुरता में होना teem

**prachurta** *n* प्रचुरता abundance

**prachurta** *n.* प्रचुरता adequacy

**prachurta** *n.* प्रचुरता fullness

**prachurta** *n.* प्रचुरता luxuriance

**prachurta** *n.* प्रचुरता opulence

**prachurta** *n.* प्रचुरता plenty

**prachurta** *n.* प्रचुरता profusion

**prachurta** *n.* प्रचुरता spate

**prachurta, bahutayat** *n* प्रचुरता,बहुतायत glut

**prachya** *a.* प्राच्य oriental

**pradaan karna** *v. t* प्रदान करना bless

**pradaan karna** *v.t.* प्रदान करना supply

**pradan karna** *v.t.* प्रदान करना award

**pradan karna** *v. t* प्रदान करना bestow

**pradan karna** *v. i* प्रदान करना confer

**pradan karna** *v. t* प्रदान करना endow

**pradan karna** *v.t.* प्रदान करना grant

**pradarshak** *a.* प्रदर्शक representative

**pradarshan** *n.* प्रदर्शन demonstration

**pradarshan** *n* प्रदर्शन display

**pradarshan** *n.* प्रदर्शन performance

**pradarshan** *n.* प्रदर्शन show

**pradarshan karna** *v. t* प्रदर्शन करना demonstrate

**pradarshan karne wala** *n.* प्रदर्शन करने वाला performer

**pradarshini** *n.* प्रदर्शनी exhibition

**pradarshit karna** *v. t* प्रदर्शित करना display

pradarshit karna *v.t.* प्रदर्शित करना wear
pradarsiniya wastu *n.* प्रदर्शनीय वस्तु exhibit
pradayak *n.* प्रदायक supplier
pradesh *n* प्रदेश canton
pradesh *n.* प्रदेश county
pradhan *a* प्रधान arch
pradhan *a.* प्रधान cardinal
pradhan *a* प्रधान main
pradhan *a.* प्रधान primary
pradhan devdut *n* प्रधान देवदूत archangel
pradhan girjaghar *n.* प्रधान गिरजाघर cathedral
pradhan nyayalaya *n* प्रधान न्यायालय chancery
pradhan vyakti *n.* प्रधान व्यक्ति principal
pradhanmantri *n* प्रधानमंत्री premier
pradhikar *n* प्राधिकार charter
pradhikrit karna *v.t.* प्राधिकृत करना authorize
pradhinta *n* पराधीनता dependence
pradhyapak *n.* प्राध्यापक professor
pradushan *n.* प्रदूषण pollution
prafull *a.* प्रफुल्ल jolly
prafull karna *v. t* प्रफुल्ल करना enrapture
prafullta *n.* प्रफुल्लता hilarity
prafulta *n.* प्रफुल्लता gaiety
pragati *n.* प्रगति advancement
pragati *n.* प्रगति process
pragati *n.* प्रगति progress
pragati karna *v.i.* प्रगति करना progress
pragatikaar *n.* प्रगीतकार lyricist
pragatishil *a.* प्रगतिशील progressive
pragatiwadi vyakti *n* प्रगतिवादी व्यक्ति leftist
pragetihasik *a.* प्रागैतिहासिक prehistoric
pragya *n.* प्रज्ञा intellect
pragya *n.* प्रज्ञा intelligence
prahaar karna *v.t.* प्रहार करना hit
prahar *n* प्रहार cut
prahar *n* प्रहार hit

prahar *n.* प्रहार stroke
prahar karna *v.t.* प्रहार करना whack
prahasan *n.* प्रहसन comedy
prahasan *n.* प्रहसन mime
prahasan *n.* प्रहसन skit
prairet karna *v.t.* प्रेरित करना prick
prairet karna *v.t.* प्रेरित करना prompt
prairit karna *v.t* प्रेरित करना goad
prairit karna *v.t.* प्रेरित करना induce
prait *n.* प्रेत demon
prait *n* प्रेत fiend
praja *n.* प्रजा subject
prajatantra *n* प्रजातंत्र democracy
prajatantra rajya *n.* प्रजातंत्र राज्य republic
prajatantratmak *a* प्रजातंत्रात्मक democratic
prajnan *n* प्रजनन reproduction
prajwalan *n.* प्रज्वलन inflammation
prajwalankar *a.* प्रज्वलनकार inflammatory
prakaar *n* प्रकार make
prakar *n* प्रकार form
prakar *n.* प्रकार kind
prakar *n.* प्रकार sort
prakaran *n.* प्रकरण paragraph
prakartik was *n.* प्राकृतिक वास habitat
prakash *n.* प्रकाश illumination
prakash *n.* प्रकाश light
prakash stambh *n.* प्रकाश स्तम्भ light house
prakashan *n.* प्रकाशन publication
prakashan *n* प्रकाशन release
prakashit hona *v.t.* प्रकाशित होना light
prakashit karna *v.t.* प्रकाशित करना publish
prakashman *a.* प्रकाशमान luminous
prakash-rahit *a* प्रकाश-रहित black
prakash-rasayan *n.* प्रकाश-रसायन photochemistry

**prakasit karna** *v.i.* प्रकाशित करना irradiate

**prakat hona** *v. i.* प्रकट होना dawn

**prakat hona** *v. i* प्रकट होना emerge

**prakat karna** *v.t.* प्रकट करना betray

**prakat karna** *v. t.* प्रकट करना declare

**prakat karna** *v. t* प्रकट करना disclose

**prakat karna** *v. t* प्रकट करना divulge

**prakat karna** *v. t* प्रकट करना expose

**prakat karna** *v.t.* प्रकट करना manifest

**prakatan** *n.* प्रकटन revelation

**prakirtik drishya sthal** *n.* प्राकृतिक दर्शय स्थल landscape

**prakop** *n.* प्रकोप outbreak

**prakopak** *a.* प्रकोपक irritant

**prakriti** *n.* प्रकृति nature

**prakriti** *n.* प्रकृति temperament

**prakritik** *a.* प्राकृतिक natural

**prakritik rup se** *adv.* प्रकृति रूप से naturally

**prakriti-vad** *a* प्रकृति-वाद naturalism

**prakritivigyani** *n.* प्रकृतिविज्ञानी naturalist

**prakshepanastra** *n.* प्रक्षेपणास्त्र projectile

**prakshepitr** *n.* प्रक्षेपित्र projector

**prakshepya** *a* प्रक्षेप्य projectile

**pralobhan** *n* प्रलोभन allurement

**pralobhan** *n* प्रलोभन bait

**pralobhan** *n.* प्रलोभन lure

**pralobhan** *n.* प्रलोभन temptation

**pralobhit karna** *v.t.* प्रलोभित करना lure

**pramaan** *n.* प्रमाण proof

**pramaanit karna** *v.t.* प्रमाणित करना argue

**praman** *n* प्रमाण evidence

**praman dena** *v.i.* प्रमाण देना testify

**praman patra** *n* प्रमाण पत्र diploma

**pramanik** *a.* प्रामाणिक authentic

**pramanik** *a* प्रामाणिक credible

**pramanikaran** *n* प्रमाणीकरण confirmation

**pramanikaran** *n.* प्रमाणीकरण substantiation

**pramanit karna** *v.t.* प्रमाणित करना attest

**pramanit karna** *v. t.* प्रमाणित करना certify

**pramanit karna** *v.t.* प्रमाणित करना corroborate

**pramanit karna** *v.t.* प्रमाणित करना prove

**pramanit karna** *v.t.* प्रमाणित करना substantiate

**pramanpatra** *n.* प्रमाण पत्र certificate

**pramanpatra** *n.* प्रमाणपत्र testimonial

**pramapak** *n.* प्रमापक logarithm

**pramay** *n.* प्रमेय theorem

**pramodkaal** *n.* प्रमोदकाल honeymoon

**pramukh** *a* प्रमुख dominant

**pramukh** *a* प्रमुख first

**pramukh** *a.* प्रमुख premier

**pramukh hona** *v.i.* प्रमुख होना predominate

**pramukh padri** *n.* प्रमुख पादरी archbishop

**pramukhta** *n* प्रमुखता emphasis

**pramukhta** *n.* प्रमुखता preponderance

**pran ghatak** *a.* प्राणघातक murderous

**pranadhar** *a.* प्राणाधार vital

**pranay nivedan** *n.* प्रणय निवेदन courtship

**pranaya** *n* प्रणय love

**pranaya karna** *v.t.* प्रणय करना woo

**pranghatak** *a.* प्राणघातक lethal

**prani** *n.* प्राणी animal

**prani** *n* प्राणी being

**prani** *n* प्राणी creature

**prani** *n.* प्राणी wight

**prani vigyan** *n.* प्राणि विज्ञान zoology

**prani vigyan vishayak** *a.* प्राणि विज्ञान विषयक zoological

**prani vigyani** *n.* प्राणि विज्ञानी zoologist

**prant** *n.* प्रांत province

**prant** *n.* प्रांत shire

**prantiya** *a.* प्रान्तीय provincial

**prapak** *n.* प्रापक recipient

**prapaya** *a.* प्राप्य obtainable

**praphul** *adj.* प्रफुल्ल convivial

**prapt karna** *v.t.* प्राप्त करना acquire

**prapt karna** *v. t.* प्राप्त करना derive

**prapt karna** *v.t* प्राप्त करना find

**prapt karna** *v.t.* प्राप्त करना gain

**prapt karna** *v.t.* प्राप्त करना get

**prapt karna** *v.t.* प्राप्त करना have

**prapt karna** *v.t.* प्राप्त करना obtain

**prapt karna** *v.t.* प्राप्त करना procure

**prapt karna** *v.t.* प्राप्त करना reach

**prapt karna** *v.t.* प्राप्त करना win

**prapti** *n.* प्राप्ति acquirement

**prapti** *n.* प्राप्ति procurement

**prarambh** *n.* प्रांरभ outset

**prarambh** *n* प्रारंभ start

**prarambh** *n.* प्रारंभ beginning

**prarambh karna** *n* प्रारंभ करना begin

**prarambh karna** *v.t.* प्रारंभ करना start

**prarambha** *n* प्रारंभ commencement

**prarambha karna** *v. t* प्रांरभ करना commence

**prarambhik** *a.* प्रारंभिक inaugural

**prarambhik** *a.* प्रारंभिक preparatory

**prarambhik muul** *a.* प्रारंभिक मूल rudimentary

**prarmbhik** *a.* प्रारंभिक initial

**prarmbhik karyavahi** *n* प्रारंभिक कार्यवाही preliminary

**prarthana karna** *v.t.* प्रार्थना करना implore

**prarthi** *n.* प्रार्थी applicant

**prarthi** *n.* प्रार्थी suitor

**prarup hona** *v.t.* प्रारूप होना typify

**prarup taiyar karna** *v. t* प्रारूप तैयार करना draft

**prarup taiyar karna** *n* प्रारूप तैयार करना draught

**prarupik vishisht** *a.* प्रारूपिक विशिष्ट typical

**prasaan karna** *v.t.* प्रसन्न करना gladden

**prasang** *n* प्रसंग context

**prasangik** *a.* प्रासंगिक relevant

**prasangikta** *n.* प्रासंगिकता relevance

**prasann** *a.* प्रसन्न happy

**prasann** *a.* प्रसन्न cheerful

**prasann karna** *v. t* प्रसन्न करना enchant

**prasann karna** *v.t.* प्रसन्न करना please

**prasanna hona** *v.i.* प्रसन्न होना rejoice

**prasannata** *n.* प्रसन्नता cheer

**prasansa karna** *v.t.* प्रशंसा करना magnify

**prasanta** *n.* प्रसन्नता frolic

**prasaran** *n* प्रसारण broadcast

**prasaran** *n* प्रसारण circulation

**prasaran** *n.* प्रसारण propagation

**prasaran** *n.* प्रसारण radiation

**prasaran kaksh** *n.* प्रसारण कक्ष studio

**prasarit karana** *v.t.* प्रसारित करना relay

**prasarit karna** *v. i.* प्रसारित करना circulate

**prasarit karna** *v.t.* प्रसारित करना radiate

**prashan** *n* प्रश्न query

**prashan karna** *v.t.* प्रश्न करना interrogate

**prashan karna** *v.t* प्रश्न करना query

**prashan puchna** *v.t.* प्रश्न पूछना quiz

**prashanatmak** *a.* प्रश्त्मक interrogative

**prashanmaala** *n.* प्रश्नमाला questionnaire

**prashansa** *n* प्रशंसा acclamation

**prashansa** *n.* प्रशंसा admiration

**prashansa** *n.* प्रशंसा applause

**prashansa** *n.* प्रशंसा appreciation

**prashansa** *n* प्रशंसा commendation

**prashansa** *n.* प्रशंसा compliment

**prashansa** *n* प्रशंसा laud

**prashansa** *n.* प्रशंसा praise

**prashansa** *v.t.* प्रशंसा करना recommend

**prashansa karna** *v.t.* प्रशंसा करना admire

**prashansa karna** *v.t.* प्रशंसा करना applaud

**prashansa karna** *v. t* प्रशंसा करना commend

**prashansa karna** *v. t* प्रशंसा करना compliment

prashansa karna v. t. प्रशंसा करना extol

prashansa karna v.t. प्रशंसा करना laud

prashansa karna v.t. प्रशंसा करना praise

prashansniya a. प्रशंसनीय admirable

prashansniya a. प्रशंसनीय commendable

prashansniya a. प्रशंसनीय laudable

prashanvachak shabd n प्रश्नवाचक शब्द interrogative

prashasak n. प्रशासक administrator

prashasan n. प्रशासन regime

prashasan-sambandhi a. प्रशासन-संबंधी administrative

prashasti n. प्रशस्ति glorification

prashikshan n. प्रशिक्षण training

prashikshan dena v.t. प्रशिक्षण देना train

prashikshanarthi n. प्रशिक्षणार्थी trainee

prashikshu n. प्रशिक्षु apprentice

prashitan n. प्रशीतन refrigeration

prashiti yantra n. प्रशीतियंत्र fridge

prashititr n. प्रशीतित्र refrigerator

prasiddh a. प्रसिद्ध legendary

prasiddh banana v.t. प्रसिद्ध बनाना popularize

prasiddh vyakti n प्रसिद्ध व्यक्ति celebrity

prasiddhi n. प्रसिद्धि notability

prasiddhi n. प्रसिद्धि popularity

prasidh a. प्रसिद्ध famous

prasidh a. प्रसिद्ध renowned

prasidhi n प्रसिद्धि credit

prasphotan n. प्रस्फोटन outburst

prasphutit hona v. i प्रस्फुटित होना erupt

prastav n. प्रस्ताव motion

prastav n. प्रस्ताव suggestion

prastavak n. प्रस्तावक mover

prastavana n. प्रस्तावना preface

prastavit karna v.t. प्रस्तावित करना propound

prastavit karna v.t. प्रस्तावित करना suggest

prastavit karna v.t. प्रस्तावित करना propose

prasthan n. प्रस्थान exit

prastut karna v.t. प्रस्तुत करना adduce

prastut karna v.t. प्रस्तुत करना offer

prastut karna v.t. प्रस्तुत करना present

prastut karna v.t. प्रस्तुत करना submit

prastut karna v.t. प्रस्तुत करना table

prastut karna v.t. प्रस्तुत करना tender

prastutikaran v.i. प्रस्तुतिकरण pose

prasuti vidya n. प्रसूती विद्या midwifery

prasv peerha n. प्रसव पीड़ा labour

prataha kalin prarthana n. प्रातःकालीन प्रार्थना morning prayer

prataya-karan n. प्रयत्न-करना persuasion

pratha n. प्रथा convention

pratha n. प्रथा custom

prathagat a प्रथागत customary

pratham a प्रथम maiden

pratham a प्रथम principal

pratham dristiya adv. प्रथम द्रष्टया prima facie

pratham pradarshan n. प्रथम प्रदर्शन premiere

pratham sthan n प्रथम स्थान first

prathamik a. प्राथमिक preliminary

prathamta n. प्रथमता priority

prathana n. प्रार्थना prayer

prathana karna v.i. प्रार्थना करना pray

pratharna n प्रार्थना request

pratharna karna v.t. प्रार्थना करना request

prati prep. प्रति per

prati sainkrha adv. प्रति सैकड़ा per cent

pratibandh n. प्रतिबंध ban

pratibandh lagana v.t प्रतिबंध लगाना outlaw

pratibandhak a. प्रतिबंधक restrictive

pratibandhatmak a प्रतिबंधात्मक conditional

pratibandhith karna v.t प्रतिबंधित करना ban

pratibembit karna v.t. प्रतिबिंबित करना mirror

pratibha *n.* प्रतिभा talent

pratibha *n.* प्रतिभा genius

pratibha sampannata *n.* संपन्नता versatility

pratibhashali *a* प्रतिभाशाली brilliant

pratibhuti *n.* प्रतिभूति assurance

pratichhed *n.* प्रतिच्छेद intersection

pratidhvani *n* प्रतिध्वनि echo

pratidhvani *n.* प्रतिध्वनि repercussion

pratidin *adv.* प्रतिदिन daily

pratidwandi hona *v.t.* प्रतिद्वंद्वी होना rival

pratifal dena *v.t.* प्रतिफल देना recompense

pratigan *n.* प्रतिगान antiphony

pratigya karna *v. t.* प्रतिज्ञा करना commit

pratigya patra *n.* प्रतिज्ञा पत्र covenant

pratigyatmak *a.* प्रतिज्ञात्मक promissory

pratihastaksharit karna *v. t.* प्रतिहस्ताक्षरित करना countersign

pratik *n* प्रतीक emblem

pratik *n.* प्रतीक token

pratik hona *v.t.* प्रतीक होना symbolize

pratikar *n.* प्रतिकार retaliation

pratikar *n.* प्रतिकार revenge

pratikar karna *v.i.* प्रतिकार करना react

pratikar karna *v.i.* प्रतिकार करना retaliate

pratikarak *a.* प्रतिकारक repulsive

pratikatmak *a.* प्रतीकात्मक symbolic

pratikirti *n* प्रतिकृति fax

pratikrati *n.* प्रतिकृति replica

pratiksha *n.* प्रतीक्षा wait

pratiksha karna *v.i.* प्रतीक्षा करना wait

pratikshepak *n.* प्रतिक्षेपक reflector

pratikshipt hona *v.i.* प्रतिक्षिप्त होना rebound

pratikul aadesh dena *v.t.* प्रतिकूल आदेश देना countermand

pratikvad *n.* प्रतीकवाद symbolism

pratilipi *n* प्रतिलिपि copy

pratilipi *n* प्रतिलिपि duplicate

pratilipi banana *v. t* प्रतिलिपि बनाना duplicate

pratilipi lekhan *n.* प्रतिलिपि लेखन transcription

pratilom *n.* प्रतिलोम antipodes

pratimaah *adv* प्रतिमाह monthly

pratinidhan *n* प्रतिनिधान delegation

pratinidhi *n* प्रतिनिधि agent

pratinidhi *n.* प्रतिनिधि attorney

pratinidhi *n* प्रतिनिधि delegate

pratinidhi *n* प्रतिनिधि deputy

pratinidhi *n.* प्रतिनिधि representative

pratipadak *n* प्रतिपादक exponent

pratirakshit *a.* प्रतिरक्षित immune

pratirakshit karna *v.t.* प्रतिरक्षित करना immunize

pratirodh devi *n.* प्रतिरोध देवी nemesis

pratiroop *n.* प्रतिरूप pattern

pratiropit karna *v.t.* प्रतिरोपित करना transplant

pratirup *n* प्रतिरूप double

pratirup *a.* प्रतिरूप negative

pratisanvedi *a* प्रतिसंवेदी amenable

pratishat *n.* प्रतिशत percentage

pratishedh *n.* प्रतिषेध refusal

pratishodh *n.* प्रतिशोध vengeance

pratishodh lena *v.t.* प्रतिशोध लेना avenge

pratishodhi *a.* प्रतिशोधी revengeful

pratishtha *n.* प्रतिष्टता glory

pratishtha *n.* प्रतिष्ठा prestige

pratishtha sambandhi *a.* प्रतिष्ठा संबंधी prestigious

pratishtith *a* प्रतिष्ठित eminent

pratispardha *n.* प्रतिस्पर्धा rivalry

pratispardha karna *v. i* प्रतिस्पर्धा करना compete

pratispardhi *n.* प्रतिस्पर्धी rival

pratistha karna *v.t.* प्रतिष्ठा करना consecrate

pratisthapan *n.* प्रतिस्थापन replacement

pratisthapan *n.* प्रतिस्थापन substitution

pratit hona *v.i.* प्रतीत होना appear

pratiti samochan *n* प्रतीती सामोचान parole

prativad *n* प्रतिवाद contradiction

prativad *v.i.* प्रतिवाद करना protest

prativadi *n* प्रतिवादी defendant

prativadi *n.* प्रतिवादी respondent

prativarsh *adv.* प्रतिवर्ष yearly

prativastu *n.* प्रतिवस्तु counterpart

prativesh *n.* प्रतिवेश surroundings

pratiwaad karna *v.t.* प्रतिवाद करना gainsay

pratiyogi *a* प्रतियोगी competitive

pratiyogita *n.* प्रतियोगिता competition

pratiyogita *n.* प्रतियोगिता contest

pratyaksh *a.* प्रत्यक्ष apparent

pratyaksh darshak *n.* प्रत्यक्ष दर्शक witness

pratyaksh gyanshil *a.* प्रत्यक्ष ज्ञानशील perceptive

pratyavartit vykati *n* प्रत्यावर्तित व्यक्ति repatriate

pratyaya *n.* प्रत्यय suffix

pratyek *pron.* प्रत्येक each

pratyek *a* प्रत्येक every

pratyek saptah *adv.* प्रत्येक सप्ताह weekly

pratyuttar *n.* प्रत्युत्तर rejoinder

pratyuttar dena *v.t.* प्रत्युत्तर देना rejoin

praudyogiki *n.* प्रौद्योगिकी technology

praudyogikivad *n.* प्रौद्योगिकीविद् technologist

praudyogikiya *a.* प्रौद्योगिकीय technological

pravaasi *n.* प्रवासी migrant

pravachan *n* प्रवचन discourse

pravachan manch *a.* प्रवचन मंच pulpit

pravah *n* प्रवाह flush

pravah yukt *a* प्रवाह युक्त fluent

pravah-hin *a.* प्रभाव-हीन laboured

pravakta *n.* प्रवक्ता lecturer

pravakta *n.* प्रवक्ता spokesman

pravardhan *n* प्रवर्धन amplification

pravarjan *n.* प्रव्रजन migration

pravarjan karna *v.i.* प्रव्रजन करना migrate

pravesh *n* प्रवेश access

pravesh *n.* प्रवेश admission

pravesh *n.* प्रवेश admittance

pravesh *n* प्रवेश entrance

pravesh *n* प्रवेश entry

pravesh *n.* प्रवेश manhole

pravesh karna *v. t* प्रवेश करना enter

pravesh ki anumati dena *v.t.* प्रवेश की अनुमति देना admit

pravesh marg *n* प्रवेश मार्ग door

praveshak *n.* प्रवेशक usher

pravhu *n.* प्रभु lord

pravidhi *n.* प्रविधि technique

pravidhikta *n.* प्राविधिकता technicality

pravin *a* प्रवीण conversant

pravin *a.* प्रवीण proficient

pravin *a.* प्रवीण versed

pravishika *n.* प्रवेशिका primer

pravrat hona *v.i.* प्रवृत्त होना tend

pravrati *n.* प्रवृत्ति trend

pravriti *n.* प्रवृत्ति instinct

pravritimulak *a.* प्रवृत्तिमूलक instinctive

prawah *n* प्रवाह flow

prawah *n.* प्रवाह onrush

prawartak *n.* प्रवर्तक innovator

praya *adv.* प्राय oft

prayaan karna *v. i.* प्रयाण करना depart

prayas *n.* प्रयास attempt

prayas *n* प्रयास effort

prayas *n* प्रयास endeavour

prayashchit *n.* प्रायश्चित atonement

prayashchit karna *v.i.* प्रायश्चित करना atone

prayatan *n* प्रयत्न bid

prayatna *n* प्रयत्न try

prayatna karna *v.t.* प्रयत्न करना attempt

prayog *n.* प्रयोग exercise

**prayog** *n.* प्रयोग usage
**prayog karna** *v. t* प्रयोग करना exercise
**prayog karna** *v.t* प्रयोग करना harness
**prayog karna** *v.t.* प्रयोग करना utilize
**prayog mein laana** *v.t.* प्रयोग में लाना wield
**prayog yogya** *a.* प्रयोग योग्य applicable
**prayogsala** *n.* प्रयोगशाला laboratory
**prayojak** *n.* प्रायोजक sponsor
**prayojit karna** *v.t.* प्रयोजित करना sponsor
**praytan karna** *v.i* प्रयत्न करना endeavour
**prem** *n* प्रेम amour
**prem karna** *v. t.* प्रेम करना court
**prem karna** *v.t.* प्रेम करना love
**prem leela** *n.* प्रेम लीला romance
**prem prasangyukt** *a.* प्रेम प्रसंगयुक्त romantic
**prematur** *a.* प्रेमातुर amorous
**premi** *n.* प्रेमी lover
**premika** *n.* प्रेमिका paramour
**prempatra** *a.* प्रेमपात्र amiable
**prempatra** *n* प्रेमपात्र favourite
**prerak padarth** *n.* प्रेरक पदार्थ stimulant
**prerit karna** *v.t.* प्रेरित करना inspire
**prerit karna** *v* प्रेरित करना motivate
**prerna** *n.* प्रेरणा inspiration
**prerna** *n.* प्रेरणा motivation
**prerna** *n.* प्रेरणा stimulus
**preshak** *n.* प्रेषक transmitter
**preshan** *n.* प्रेषण remittance
**preshit karna** *v.t.* प्रेषित करना transmit
**preshit maal** *n.* प्रेषित माल consignment
**pret** *n.* प्रेत phantom
**pret** *n.* प्रेत wraith
**prethak karna** *v.t.* पृथक् करना insulate
**prethakaran** *n.* पृथक्करण insulation
**prishth** *n.* प्रसिद्ध page
**prishthbhumi** *n.* पृष्ठभूमि background
**prithak ho jana** *v.i.* पृथक् हो जाना secede
**prithak karna** *v.t.* पृथक् करना isolate
**prithak karna** *v.t.* पृथक् करना segregate

**prithakaran** *n.* पृथक्करण separation
**prithakari** *n.* पृथक्कारी insulator
**prithivi mandal** *n.* पृथ्वी मंडल orb
**prithvi** *n* पृथ्वी earth
**prithvi** *n.* पृथ्वी globe
**prithvi** *n.* पृथ्वी ground
**priti** *n.* प्रीति endearment
**pritibhoj** *n* प्रीतिभोज feast
**pritikar** *a.* प्रीतिकर lovable
**pritrihatya** *n.* पितृहत्या patricide
**priya** *a* प्रिय acceptable
**priya, pyara** *a.* प्रिय, प्यारा dear
**priyatam** *n* प्रियतम beloved
**priyatam** *n* प्रियतम darling
**protein** *n.* प्रोटीन protein
**protsaahan** *n.* प्रोत्साहन incentive
**protsahit karna** *v. t.* प्रोत्साहित करना embolden
**protsahit karna** *v. t* प्रोत्साहित करना encourage
**pryatna karna** *v.i.* प्रयत्न करना try
**puchaltara** *n* पुच्छलतारा comet
**puchkaarna** *v. t.* पुचकारना caress
**puchkarna** *v.t* पुचकारना fondle
**puchtach** *n.* पूछताछ interrogation
**puchtach** *n.* पूछताछ query
**pudding** *n.* पुडिंग pudding
**pudina** *n.* पुदीना mint
**puja** *n.* पूजा worship
**puja karna** *v.t.* पूजा करना adore
**puja karna** *v.t.* पूजा करना, worship
**pujari,upasak** *n.* पुजारी, उपासक worshipper
**pujarin** *n.* पुजारिन priestess
**pujasthal** *n.* पूजास्थल chapel
**pukaar** *n.* पुकार call
**pukaarna** *v. t.* पुकारना call
**pukar** *n* पुकार yell
**pukarna** *v. t* पुकारना evoke
**pukarna** *v.t.* पुकारना term
**pukhraj** *n.* पुखराज topaz

**pulaa** *n.* पूला sheaf
**pulak** *n.* पुलक thrill
**pulinda** *n* पुलिंदा bundle
**pulinda** *n.* पुलिंदा package
**puling** *a.* पुलिंग male
**puling** *a.* पुंलिंग masculine
**pulkit karna** *v.t.* पुलकित करना thrill
**pull** *n* पुल bridge
**pump** *n.* पंप pump
**pump se uthana** *v.t.* पंप से उठाना pump
**puna mudrit karna** *v.t.* पुन: मुद्रित करना reprint
**puna sthapit karna** *v.t.* पुन: स्थापित करना replace
**puna vishwas dilana** *v.t.* पुन: विश्वास दिलाना reassure
**punar mudran** *n.* पुनर्मुद्रण reprint
**punargrahan** *n.* पुनर्ग्रहण resumption
**punarjanam** *n.* पुनर्जन्म renaissance
**punarjanm** *n.* पुनर्जन्म rebirth
**punarjivit hona** *v.i.* पुनर्जीवित होना revive
**punarnirveshan** *n.* पुनर्निवेशन rehabilitation
**punarparikshan** *n* पुनर्परीक्षण review
**punarvichar karna** *v.t.* पुनर्विचार करना review
**punh jail bhejna** *v.t.* पुन: जेल भेजना remand
**punh prapt karna** *v.t.* पुन: प्राप्त करना retrieve
**punji** *n* पूंजी capital
**punji lagana** *v.t.* पूंजी लगाना invest
**punji nivesh** *n.* पूंजी निवेश investment
**punjipati** *n.* पूंजीपति capitalist
**punragaman** *n.* पुनरागमन recurrence
**punravrati** *n.* पुनरावृत्ति reiteration
**punravrati hona** *v.i.* पुनरावृत्ति होना recur
**punruthanshil** *a.* पुनरुत्थानशील resurgent
**punrutpadan** *a.* पुनरुत्पादक reproductive
**punyaatma** *a.* पुण्यात्मा saintly
**pura bharna** *v.t* पूरा भरना fill

**pura karna** *v. t* पूरा करना complete
**pura karna** *v.t* पूरा करना finish
**pura karna** *v.t.* पूरा करना supplement
**puraa karna** *v.t.* पूरा करना meet
**purak** *n* पूरक complement
**purak** *a.* पूरक supplementary
**puran asafalta.** *n* पूर्ण असफलता fiasco
**puran rup se** *a* पूर्ण रूप से outright
**purana** *a.* पुराना chronic
**purana** *a.* पुराना old
**purana** *a.* पुराना outdated
**purana** *a.* पुराना outmoded
**purana mitr** *n* पुराना मित्र chum
**purana sangrah** *n.* पुराण संग्रह mythology
**purankatha sambandhi** *a.* पुराणकथा संबंधी mythical
**puraskaar** *n.* पुरस्कार award
**puraskar** *n.* पुरस्कार prize
**puraskar** *n.* पुरस्कार remuneration
**puraskar** *n.* पुरस्कार trophy
**puratan** *a.* पुरातन primitive
**puratatvaveta** *n* पुरातत्ववेत्ता antiquarian
**puratatva-vishayak** *a.* पुरातत्व-विषयक antiquarian
**pure marammat** *n.* पूरी मरम्मत overhaul
**puri murammat karna** *v.t.* पुरानी मरम्मत करना overhaul
**puri tarah se** *adv* पूरी तरह से downright
**purna** *a* पूर्ण absolute
**purna** *a* पूर्ण complete
**purna** *a* पूर्ण thorough
**purna** *a* पूर्ण utter
**purna karna** *v.t.* पूर्ण करना accomplish
**purna karna** *v.t.* पूर्ण करना fulfil
**purna matra** *n.* पूर्ण मात्रा total
**purna rup se** *adv* पूर्ण रूप से absolutely
**purna rup se** *adv.* पूर्णरूप से altogether
**purna rup se** *adv.* पूर्ण रूप से fully
**purna rup se** *adv.* पूर्णरूप से wide
**purnataya** *adv.* पूर्णतया all
**purnataya** *adv.* पूर्णतया utterly

purntaya *adv.* पूर्णतया wholly
purohit *n.* पुरोहित priest
purohit *n.* पुरोहित vicar
purohit varg *n.* पुरोहित वर्ग priesthood
purruthan *n.* पुररुत्थान resurgence
purruthan *n.* पुररुत्थान revival
purti *adj.* पूर्ति completion
purti *n.* पूर्ति fulfilment
purti karna *v.t.* पूर्ति करना produce
purti, *n.* पूर्ति, पूतिता sepsis
purushochit *a.* पुरुषोचित manlike
purushochit *a.* पुरुषोचित manly
puruskar *n.* पुरस्कार recompense
purustwa *n.* पुरुषत्व manhood
purv janam ka smaran *n* पूर्व जन्म का स्मरण anamnesis
purv prayog *n.* पूर्व प्रयोग rehearsal
purva *n.* पूर्व orient
purva agman *n.* पूर्व आगमन precedence
purva awastha *v.t.* पूर्व अवस्था में लाना rehabilitate
purva chetawani dena *v.t* पूर्व चेतावनी देना forewarn
purva dharna *n.* पूर्व धारणा assumption
purva disha *n* पूर्व दिशा east
purva nishchit bhent *n.* पूर्व निश्चित भेंट tryst
purvabodh *n.* पूर्वबोध prescience
purvachintan *n.* पूर्वचिंतन premeditation
purvadharna *n.* पूर्वधारणा prejudice
purvadharna *n.* पूर्वधारणा presupposition
purvadhikari *n.* पूर्वाधिकारी predecessor
purvagami *n.* पूर्वगामी antecedent
purvagyan *n.* पूर्वज्ञान foreknowledge
purvaj *n.* पूर्वज ancestor
purvaniyati *n.* पूर्वनियति predestination
purvanuman hona *v.t.* पूर्वानुमान होना anticipate
purvapeksha *n* पूर्वापेक्षा prerequisite
purvapekshit *a.* पूर्वापेक्षित prerequisite
purvasarg *n.* पूर्वसर्ग preposition

purvasnatak *n.* पूर्वस्नातक undergraduate
purvasuchna *n.* पूर्वसूचना warning
purvavarti *a.* पूर्ववर्ती antecedent
purvavarti *a.* पूर्ववर्ती prior
purvavbodh *n.* पूर्वबोध premonition
purvawasi *n* पूर्ववासी oriental
purvayojan karna *v.t.* पूर्वयोजन करना premeditate
purvokt *pron* पूर्वोक्त former
purvprabhavi *a.* पूर्वप्रभावी retrospective
purv-suchna dena *v.t.* पूर्वसूचना देना portend
purwa wichar *n* पूर्व विचार forethought
purwaanuman *n.* पूर्वानुमान anticipation
purwahan *n* पूर्वाह्न forenoon
purwaj *n* पूर्वज forefather
purwanuman *n* पूर्वानुमान forecast
purwanuman karna *v.t* पूर्वानुमान करना forecast
pushp *n* पुष्प flower
pushti karna *v. t* पुष्टि करना confirm
pushti karna *v.t.* पुष्टि करना ratify
pushtikaran *n* पुष्टीकरण affirmation
pustak *n* पुस्तक book
pustak bechne wala *n* पुस्तक बेचने वाला book-seller
pustak ka naam *n.* पुस्तक का नाम title
pustakalaya. *n.* पुस्तकालय library
pustakalayadhayaksh *n.* पुस्तकालयाध्यक्ष librarian
pustika *n* पुस्तिका booklet
pustika *n.* पुस्तिका handbook
pustika *n.* पुस्तिका leaflet
pustika *n* पुस्तिका tract
putayee *n.* पुताई daub
putla *n* पुतला effigy
putlaa *n.* पुतला mannequin
putli *n.* पुतली pupil
putr *n.* पुत्र son
putri *n* पुत्री daughter
puttho mai dard *n.* पुट्ठों में दर्द myalgia

**puviya** *a* पूर्वीय eastern
**pyaaz jaisi sabzi** *n.* प्याज़ जैसी सब्ज़ी leek
**pyala** *n.* प्याला cup
**pyala** *n.* पहला goblet
**pyar** *n.* प्यार affection
**pyar karna** *v.t.* प्यार करना pet
**pyara** *a.* प्यारा affectionate
**pyara** *a* प्यारा darling
**pyara banana** *v.t* प्यारा बनाना endear
**pyas** *n.* प्यास thirst
**pyas bujhana** *v.t.* प्यास बुझाना slake
**pyasa** *adj.* प्यासा athirst
**pyasa** *a.* प्यासा thirsty
**pyasa hona** *v.i.* प्यासा होना thirst

**qabza dhari** *n.* कब्जा धारी occupant
**qabza karna** *v.t.* कब्ज़ा करना occupy
**qanoon** *n.* कानून law
**qanoon ke anusar** *a.* कानून के अनुसार
  lawfulness
**qilla** *n.* किला fort
**qilla** *n.* किला fortress
**qimti patharl ghoda** *n.* जीमती पथरी घोडा
  jade

**raag** *n.* राग melody
**raajhse** *a.* राजसी majestic
**raasta badalna** *v.t. & i.* रास्ता बदलना
  deflect
**raat bhar** *prep.* रात भर night long
**raat ka** *adv.* रात का nightly
**raat ka** *a.* रात का nocturnal
**raat kai samai** *adv.* रात के समय
  overnight
**rabar ka pipe** *n.* रबर का पाइप hose

**rachna** *n* रचना build
**rachna** *n* रचना composition
**rachna** *n* रचना creation
**radd** *n* रद्द cancellation
**radd karana** *v.t.* रद्द करना revoke
**radd karna** *v. t.* रद्द करना abrogate
**radd karna** *v. t.* रद्द करना cancel
**radd karna** *v. t* रद्द करना discard
**radd karna** *v.t.* रद्द करना overrule
**radd karna** *v.t.* रद्द करना void
**raddh karna** *v.t.* रद्द करना nullify
**raddi** *n.* रद्दी scrap
**radhya karna** *v.t.* रद्द करना annul
**radio** *n* रेडियो wireless
**radium dhatu** *n.* रेडियम धातु radium
**rafuchakar** *v.i* रफूचक्कर होना flee
**ragarna, ghisna** *v.t.* रगड़ना rub
**rahasmay** *a.* रहस्यमय mysterious
**rahasya** *n.* रहस्य mystery
**rahasyamaya** *a.* रहस्यमय uncanny
**rahasywad** *n.* रहस्यवाद mysticism
**rahasywadi** *n* रहस्यवादी mystic
**rahi** *n.* राही wayfarer
**rahit** *prep.* रहित without
**rahit** *a* रहित devoid
**rahne yogya** *a.* रहने योग्य habitable
**rail garhi ka dibba** *n.* रेलगाड़ी का डिब्बा
  compartment
**railgarhi** *n.* रेलगाड़ी train
**railgarhi ka dabba** *n* रेलगाड़ी का डिब्बा
  coach
**railmarg** *n.* रेलमार्ग rail
**railpath** *n.* रेलपथ railway
**railway shakha** *n.* रेलवे शाखा loop
**raj bhakt** *n.* राजभक्त royalist
**raja** *n* राजा duke
**raja** *n.* राजा king
**raja** *n.* राजा monarch
**rajasi** *a.* राजसी royal
**rajbhakt** *n.* राजभक्त loyalist
**rajdand** *n.* राजदंड sceptre

**rajdhani** *n.* राजधानी capital

**rajdoot** *n.* राजदूत ambassador

**rajdroh karna** *v.i.* राजद्रोह करना revolt

**rajgaddi** *n.* राजगद्दी throne

**rajgaddi par bithana** *v.t.* राजगद्दी पर बिठाना throne

**rajgeer** *n.* राजगीर mason

**rajgire** *n.* राजगीरी masonry

**rajhanta** *n.* राजहंता regicide

**rajkiya** *n* राजकीय official

**rajkiya** *a.* राजकीय regal

**rajkumar** *n.* राजकुमार prince

**rajkumari** *n.* राजकुमारी princess

**rajmukut** *n* राजमुकुट crown

**rajnayik** *n* राजनयिक diplomat

**rajneta** *n.* राजनेता statesman

**rajniti shastra** *n* राजनीति शास्त्र political science

**rajnitigya** *n.* राजनीतिज्ञ politician

**rajnitik** *a.* राजनीतिक political

**rajnitishastra** *n.* राजनीतिशास्त्र politics

**rajoniwirti** *n.* रजोनिवृत्ति menopause

**rajpath** *n.* राजपथ highway

**rajpatra** *n.* राजपत्र gazette

**rajtantra** *n.* राजतंत्र polity

**raj-tantra** *n.* राज-तंत्र monarchy

**rajvansh** *n* राजवंश dynasty

**rajya** *a.* राज्य realm

**rajya karna** *v.i.* राज्य करना reign

**rajyabhishek** *n* राज्याभिषेक coronation

**rajyakal** *n* राज्यकाल reign

**rajyapaal** *n.* राज्यपाल governor

**rakab** *n.* रकाब stirrup

**rakashak** *n.* प्रकाशक publisher

**rakhel** *n.* रखैल mistress

**rakhna** *v.t.* रखना lay

**rakhna** *v.t.* रखना lodge

**rakhna** *v.t.* रखना put

**rakhwali** रखवाली guard

**rakhwali** *n.* रखवाली vigil

**raksha karna** *v. t* रक्षा करना defend

**raksha karna** *v.t* रक्षा करना fend

**raksha karna** *vt.* रक्षा करना safeguard

**raksha karna** *v.t.* रक्षा करना ward

**rakshak** *n.* रक्षक protector

**rakshak** *n.* रक्षक saviour

**raksharth sath jana** *v. t* रक्षार्थ साथ जाना escort

**rakshas** *n.* राक्षस monster

**rakshit mrit sharir** *n* रक्षित मृत शरीर mummy

**rakt varna ka** *a.* रक्त वर्ण का sanguine

**raktapaat** *n* रक्तपात bloodshed

**ram baan** *n.* रामबाण nostrum

**ramaniya** *adj* रमणीय elegant

**ramaniya** *a.* रमणीय sightly

**rambhahat** *n.* रंभाहट low

**rambhana** *v.i.* रंभाना low

**rambhana** *v.i* रंभाना moo

**randi ka ghar** *n* रंडी का घर brothel

**rang** *n* रंग colour

**rang** *n* रंग dye

**rang** *n.* रंग paint

**rang** *n.* रंग tint

**rang urhna** *v.i* रंग उड़ना fade

**rang bhumi** *n* रंगभूमि amphitheatre

**rang ke the** *n* रंग की तह coating

**rangin khadiya** *n.* रंगीन खड़िया pastel

**rangna** *v. t* रंगना dye

**rangna** *v.t.* रंगना tint

**rangraliayan** *n.* रंगरलियां revelry

**rangroot** *n.* रंगरूट recruit

**ranniti** *n.* रणनीति tactics

**rannitigya** *n.* रणनीतिज्ञ tactician

**rasad** *n.* रसद ration

**rasatal** *n* रसातल abyss

**rasayan shastra** *n.* रसायन-शास्त्र chemistry

**rasayanik padarth** *n.* रासायनिक पदार्थ chemical

**rasayan-sambandhi** *a.* रसायन-संबंधी chemical

**rasdaar** *a.* रसदार juicy

**raseed** *n.* रसीद acknowledgement

**rashi panewala** *n.* राशि पानेवाला payee

**rashichakra** *n* राशिचक्र zodiac

**rashtra** *n.* राष्ट्र nation

**rashtraprem** *n.* राष्ट्रप्रेम nationalism

**rashtriya** *a.* राष्ट्रीय national

**rashtriya banana** *v.t.* राष्ट्रीय बनाना nationalize

**rashtriyakaran** *n.* राष्ट्रीयकरण nationalization

**rashtriyata** *n.* राष्ट्रीयता nationality

**rashtriyawadi** *n.* राष्ट्रवादी nationalist

**rashtr-mandal** *n.* राष्ट्रमंडल commonwealth

**rasila** *a.* रसीला lush

**rasoi ghar** *n.* रसोईघर kitchen

**rasoiyaa** *n* रसोइया cook

**rass** *n* रस juice

**rassa** *n.* डोरी cable

**rassi** *n.* रस्सी rope

**rassi** *n.* रस्सी string

**rassi** *n.* रस्सी tether

**rasta** *n* रास्ता pass

**ratan** *n* रत्न gem

**rath** *n* रथ chariot

**ratna** *v. t* रटना cram

**ratnabhushan** *n.* रत्नाभूषण jewellery

**ratranmandith karna** *v.t.* रत्नमंडित करना jewel

**ratri** *n.* रात्रि night

**ratri bhar** *a* रात्रि भर overnight

**ratri ka bhojan** *n.* रात्रि का भोजन supper

**raund dalna** *v.t* रौंद डालना overrun

**raviwar** *n.* रविवार sunday

**raye** *n.* राई rye

**razamandi** *n.* रज़ामंदी acquiescence

**razi hona** *v.i.* राज़ी होना acquiesce

**reader** *n.* रीडर reader

**rean ka chihan** *n* ऋण का चिह्न minus

**rechak aushadhi** *n.* रेचक औषधि laxative

**rechan** *n.* रेचन laxity

**redi ka tel** *n.* रेंडी का तेल castor oil

**reel** *n.* रील reel

**registan** *n* रेगिस्तान desert

**rehna** *v. i* रहना dwell

**rehna** *v.i.* रहना remain

**rehna** *v.i.* रहना stay

**rehne wala** *n* रहने वाला resident

**rekha** *n.* रेखा line

**rekha ganitiya** *a.* रेखा गणितीय geometrical

**rekhachitra** *n.* रेखाचित्र graph

**rekhachitra** *n.* रेखाचित्र profile

**rekhaganit** *n.* रेखागणित geometry

**rekhankit karna** *v.t.* रेखांकित करना underline

**rekhapath** *n.* रेखापथ locus

**rengna** *v.i.* रेंगना snake

**rengna** *v.i.* रेंगना wriggle

**rengne ki kriya** *n* रेंगने की क्रिया wriggle

**rengne wala jantu** *n.* रेंगनेवाला जंतु reptile

**renkna** *v. i* रेंकना bray

**resham** *n.* रेशम silk

**resham jaisa** *a.* रेशम जैसा silky

**resham ka patla feeta** *n.* रेशम का पतला फीता ribbon

**reshami** *a.* रेशमी silken

**ret** *n.* रेत sand

**reti** *n* रेती file

**reti lagana** *v.t* रेती लगाना file

**retila** *a.* रेतीला sandy

**revolver** *n.* रिवाल्वर revolver

**ridh** *n.* रीढ़ spine

**rifal** *n* राइफ़ल rifle

**riha karna** *v.t.* रिहा करना loosen

**rihayee** *n.* रिहाई ransom

**rijka** *n.* रिजका lucerne

**riksha** *n.* रिक्शा rickshaw

**rikt** *a.* रिक्त void

**rikt pad** *n.* रिक्त पद vacancy

**rikt sthan** *n* रिक्त स्थान blank

**rinankan karna** *v. t* ऋणांकन करना debit
**rinch** *n.* रिंच spanner
**rindata** *n* ऋणदाता creditor
**rinshodh kshamta** *n.* ऋणशोध क्षमता solvency
**rinshodhksham** *a.* ऋणशोधक्षम् solvent
**ririyana** *v.i.* रिरियाना whimper
**risan** *n.* रिसन leakage
**rishi** *n.* ऋषि sage
**rishtedar** *n.* रिश्तेदार kith
**rishtedar** *n.* रिश्तेदार relative
**rishvat dena** *v. t.* रिश्वत देना bribe
**risna** *v.i.* रिसना seep
**risnaa** *v.i.* रिसना leak
**riti** *n.* रीति modality
**riti riwaaj** *n.* रीति रिवाज manner
**ritu** *n.* ऋतु season
**ritustrav** *n.* ऋतुस्राव menses
**ritu-strav** *n.* ऋतुस्राव menstruation
**ritu-strav vishayak** *a.* ऋतुस्राव विषयक menstrual
**rituwigyani** *n.* ऋतुविज्ञानी meteorologist
**riwaaz,adat** *n* रिवाज, आदत wont
**rocket** *n.* राकेट rocket
**rodi** *n.* रोड़ी metal
**rog** *n.* रोग illness
**rogan** *n.* रोगन varnish
**rogan karna** *v.t.* रोगन करना varnish
**roganurodhak** *a.* रोगाणुरोधक antiseptic
**roganurodhak aushadhi** *n.* रोगाणुरोधक औषधि antiseptic
**rogatmak** *n* रोगात्मक pathological
**rogi** *n* रोगी patient
**rogi-vahan** *n.* रोगी-वाहन ambulance
**rognivarak** *a* रोगनिवारक curative
**rok rakhna** *v.t.* रोक रखना retain
**rok rakhna** *v.t.* रोक रखना withhold
**rokana** *v.t.* रोकना rebuff
**rokana** *v.t.* रोकना rein
**roke rakhna** *v. t* रोके रखना detain
**rokna** *v.t.* रोकना arrest

**rokna** *v.t.* रोकना avert
**rokna** *v.t* रोकना bar
**rokna** *v. t.* रोकना halt
**rokna** *v.t.* रोकना inhibit
**rokna** *v.t.* रोकना repress
**rokna** *v.t.* रोकना resist
**rokna** *v.t.* रोकना stop
**rokna** *v.t.* रोकना thwart
**roktham karna** *v.t* रोकथाम करना forestall
**roler** *n.* रोलर roller
**rome ka bada paadari** *n.* रोम का बड़ा पादरी pope
**romkup** *n.* रोमकूप pore
**rona** *v. i* रोना cry
**rona** *v.i.* रोना weep
**rona chilana** *v.i.* रोना चिल्लाना whine
**rooprekha** *n.* रूपरेखा outline
**roos ki mudra** *n.* रूस की मुद्रा, रूबल rouble
**roosi** *n* रूसी dandruff
**rootha hua** *a.* रूठा हुआ sullen
**roshni vala bulb** *n.* रोशनी वाला बल्ब bulb
**roti** *n* रोटी bread
**rubber** *n.* रबड़ rubber
**rubber chadha tyre** *n.* रबर चढ़ा टायर retread
**ruchi lene wala** *a.* रुचि लेने वाला interested
**ruchikar** *a.* रुचिकर interesting
**ruchikar** *a.* रुचिकर spicy
**ruchikar** *a.* रुचिकर tasteful
**ruchikar ghatna** *n.* रुचिकर घटना anecdote
**rudankari** *a.* रुदनकारी lachrymose
**rudhivadi** *a.* रूढ़िवादी orthodox
**rudhivaditha** *n.* रूढ़िवादिता orthodoxy
**ruganta** *n* रुग्णता morbidity
**rujhan** *n* रूझान bent
**rukaav** *n* रुकाव halt
**rukawat** *n* रुकावट stoppage
**rukha** *a.* रूखा mawkish
**rukha** *a.* रूखा rough

**rukhapan** *n* रूखापन acrimony
**rumaal** *n.* रूमाल handkerchief
**rumal** *n.* रूमाल kerchief
**rumal** *n.* रूमाल napkin
**rup** *a* रूप look
**rup badal dena** *v. t* रूप बदल देना colour
**rup badal dena** *v.* रूप बदल देना transform
**rup dena** *v.t.* रूप देना model
**rup rekha** *n* रूपरेखा contour
**rupak** *n.* रूपक metaphor
**rupantaran** *n.* रूपांतरण transfiguration
**rupantaran** *n.* रूपांतरण transformation
**rupantarit karna** *v. t* रूपांतरित करना
  convert
**rupantarit karna** *v.t.* रूपांतरित करना
  transfigure
**rupantran** *n* रूपांतरण conversion
**rupantran** *n.* रूपांतरण metamorphosis
**ruperekha** *n.* रूपरेखा synopsis
**rupiya** *n.* रुपया rupee
**ruprekha** *n.* रूपरेखा conspectus
**ruprekha** *n.* रूपरेखा design
**rurhivadi vyakti** *n* रूढ़िवादी व्यक्ति
  conservative

# S

**saada** *a.* सादा simple
**saadagi** *n.* सादगी simplicity
**saadhak** *adj.* साधक component
**saadhan** *n.* साधन mean
**saadharan** *a.* साधारण common
**saadharan** *a.* साधारण general
**saadharan** *a.* साधारण middling
**saaf** *a.* साफ़ clean
**saaf karna** *v. t* साफ़ करना clear
**saaf rakhna** *v. t* साफ़ करना clean
**saaf safai** *n.* साफ़ सफ़ाई sweep
**saaf-suthara** *a* साफ़-सुथरा clear
**saagar** *n.* सागर ocean

**saahas** *n.* साहस courage
**saahasi** *a.* साहसि courageous
**saaj saaman** *n* साज़ सामान equipment
**saaj sajja** *n.* साज सज्जा harness
**saaj samaan** *n.* साज सामान furniture
**saaj saman** *n.* साज़ सामान kit
**saakar rakhna** *v.t.* साकार रखना incarnate
**saakh** *n.* साख goodwill
**saakshatakaar karna** *v.t.* साक्षात्कार करना
  interview
**saakshatkar** *n.* साक्षात्कार interview
**saamaan** *n* सामान goods
**saamanjasyapurna** *a.* सामंजस्यपूर्ण
  harmonious
**saamant** *n.* सामंत feud
**saamanti** *a* सामंती feudal
**saamanya** *a.* सामान्य mediocre
**saamanya avastha** *n.* सामान्य अवस्था
  mediocrity
**saamiyvad** *n* साम्यवाद communism
**saamney** *adv.* सामने before
**saana huwa aata** *n.* साना हुआ आटा paste
**saandar** *a.* शानदार magnificent
**saangitik** *a.* सांगीतिक musical
**saans ghutanai wali ek gas** *n* साँस घुटाने
  वाली एक गैस chlorine
**saans ki rukawat** *n* साँस की रुकावट
  apnoea
**saans lena** *v.i.* सांस लेना inhale
**saans lena** *v.i.* सांस लेना respire
**saansarik** *a* सांसारिक earthly
**saanwala** *n.* सानवाला mulatto
**saar** *n* सार essence
**saar** *n* सार extract
**saar** *n.* सार gist
**saar** *n.* सार kernel
**saar, sanksep** *n.* सार, संक्षेप resume
**saarang** *n* सारंगी fiddle
**saarangi bajana** *v.i* सारंगी बजाना fiddle
**saarhinta** *n.* सारहीनता vanity
**saarhna** *vt* सड़न decay

saat *a* सात seven

saat ki sankhya *n.* सात की संख्या seven

saath *n.* साथ company

saath *prep.* साथ with

saath dena *v.t.* साथ देना accompany

saath he *adv* साथ ही besides

saath he *adv.* साथ ही also

saath may *adv.* साथ में along

saath saath *adv.* साथ साथ together

saathwan *a.* साठवां sixtieth

saatth *n., a.* साठ sixty

saayak nadi *n.* सहायक नदी tributary

saaz saaman *n. pl* साज़ सामान paraphernalia

sab *pron.* सब all

sab se bura *a* सब से बुरा worst

sabaq *n.* सबक lesson

sabha *n* सभा conference

sabha *n.* सभा meeting

sabha karna *v.i* सभा करना parley

sabha sthal *n.* सभा स्थल venue

sabhapati *n* सभापति chairman

sabhapati hona *v.i.* सभापति होना preside

sabha-sad *n.* सभासद councillor

sabhya banana *v. t* सभ्य बनाना civilize

sabhyta *n.* सभ्यता civilization

sabkuchh *n.* सबकुछ all

sabse adhik *a.* सबसे अधिक most

sabse buri baat *n.* सबसे बुरी बात worst

sabun *n.* साबुन soap

sabun jaisa *a.* साबुन जैसा soapy

sabun lagana *v.t.* साबुन लगाना soap

sabzi *n.* साग vegetable

sach manana *v.t.* सच मानना accredit

sach sidh karna *v.t.* सच सिद्ध करना vindicate

sachait *a* सचेत awake

sachait *a* सचेत careful

sachait hona *v.t.* सचेत होना awake

sachayee *n.* सच्चाई sincerity

sachchayee *n.* सच्चाई veracity

sachet karna *v.t.* सचेत करना warn

sachetan *a* सचेतन conscious

sachitra *a.* सचित्र pictorial

sachitra banana *v.t.* सचित्र बनाना illustrate

sachiv *n.* सचिव secretary

sachivalaya *n.* सचिवालय secretariat (e)

sachmuch *adv.* सचमुच yes

sad bhavpurna *a* सद् भावपूर्ण bonafide

sad bhavpurwak *adv* सद् भावपूर्वक bonafide

sada *a.* सादा sober

sada *a.* सादा workaday

sadabahar *a* सदाबहार evergreen

sadabahar lata *n* सदाबहार लता ivy

sadachaar purna *a.* सदाचार पूर्ण moral

sadachhar *n.* सदाचार morality

sadaiv ke leya *adv* सदैव के लिए forever

sadak *n.* सड़क road

sadan *n.* सदन chamber

sadar darwaza *n.* सदर दरवाज़ा portal

sadasyata *n.* सदस्य membership

sadgun *n.* सद् गुण merit

sadha hua *adj* सड़ा हुआ addle

sadhan *n.* साधन artifice

sadhan *n* साधन means

sadhan *n.* साधन resource

sadharan log *n.* साधारण लोग populace

sadharan vykati *n.* साधारण व्यक्ति layman

sadharanta *adv.* साधारणत ordinarily

sadhyata *n.* साध्यता practicability

sadna *v.i.* सड़ना perish

sadrishya *a.* सदृश similar

sadrishya hona *n.* सादृश्य होना resemblance

saf suthra *a.* साफ़ सुथरा trim

safaai *n* सफाई clarity

safai ka brush *n* सफाई का ब्रश brush

safai karamchari *n.* सफ़ाई कर्मचारी scavenger

safal *a.* सफल prosperous
safal hona *v.i.* सफल होना prevail
safal hona *v.i.* सफल होन prosper
safalta *n.* सफलता achievement
safalta *n.* सफलता prosperity
saga *n.* सगा akin
sagar *n.* सागर sea
sagariya *a.* सागरीय oceanic
saghan *a.* सघन intensive
saghna *a* सघन dense
saghnata *n* सघनता density
sagrahagaar *n* संग्रहागार depot
sahabhagi *n* सहभागी co-partner
sahabhagi hona *v.t.* सहभागी होना share
sahad *n.* शहद honey
sahaj *a.* सहज inborn
sahakari *a* सहकारी co-operative
sahakarita *n* सहकारिता co-operation
sahakarmi *n* सहकर्मी colleague
sahamaat *n* शहमात mate
sahamat *a.* सहमत agreeable
sahamat hona *v.i.* सहमत होना assent
sahamat hona *v. i* सहमत होना coincide
sahamat hona *v. i* सहमत होना consent
sahamat karna *v.t.* सहमत करना accord
sahamati *n* सहमति accession
sahamati *n.* सहमति agreement
sahamiti *n.* सहमति consent
sahan karna *v.t.* सहन करना endure
sahana *v. t* सहना bide
sahaniya *a* सहनीय endurable
sahaniya *a.* सहनीय tolerable
sahanshilta *n.* सहनशीलता endurance
sahanshilta *n.* सहनशीलता patience
sahanshilta *n.* सहनशीलता tolerance
sahanubhuti *n* सहानुभूति compassion
sahanubhuti *n.* सहानुभूति sympathy
sahanubhuti rakhna *v.i.* सहानुभूति रखना
  sympathize
sahanubhuti-purna *a.* सहानुभूतिपूर्ण
  sympathetic

sahara *n* सहारा boost
sahara *n.* सहारा support
sahara *v.t.* सहारा support
sahara dena *v.t.* सहारा देना prop
sahara lena *v.i.* सहारा लेना resort
sahas karna *v.t.* साहस करना presume
sahas karna *v.t.* साहस करना venture
sahashiksha *n.* सहशिक्षा co-education
sahasi *adj.* साहसी hardy
sahasi *a.* साहसी mettlesome
sahasi *a.* साहसी venturous
sahasik karya *n* साहसिक कार्य adventure
sahasik karya *n* साहसिक कार्य feat
sahasikta *n.* साहसिकता hardihood
sah-astitva *n* सहअस्तित्व co-existence
sahavarti hona *v. i* सहवर्ती होना co-exist
sahawas karna *v. t* सहवास करना cohabit
sahayak *n* सहायक aid
sahayak *n.* सहायक assistant
sahayak *a.* सहायक auxiliary
sahayak *a.* सहायक helpful
sahayak *n.* सहायक helpmate
sahayak *a.* सहायक instrumental
sahayak *a.* सहायक subservient
sahayak *a.* सहायक subsidiary
sahayak *a.* सहायक tributary
sahayak kriya *n.* सहायक क्रिया auxiliary
sahayata *n* सहायता aid
sahayata *n.* सहायता assistance
sahayata *n* सहायता help
sahayata dena *v.t* सहायता देना aid
sahayata dena *v.t.* सहायता देना patronize
sahayata karna *v.t.* सहायता करना assist
sahayog *n* सहयोग collaboration
sahayog karna *v. i* सहयोग करना
  collaborate
sahayta karna *v.t.* सहायता करना help
sahchaari *adj* सहचारी cohesive
sahi *a.* सही right
sahi karna *v.i.* सही करना rectify
sahishnu *a.* सहिष्णु tolerant

**sahitiya** *n.* साहित्य literature
**sahitiyik** *a.* साहित्यिक literary
**sahitiyik vyakti** *n.* साहित्यिक व्यक्ति litterateur
**sahmat hona** *v.i.* सहमत होना agree
**sahmati** *n.* सहमति accord
**sahpalan karna** *v. i* सहपलायन करना elope
**sahsambandhi banana** *v.t.* सहसंबंधी बनाना correlate
**sahsrabdi** *n.* सहस्राब्दी millennium
**sahyog karna** *v. i* सहयोग करना cooperate
**saidhantik** *a.* सैद्घांतिक theoretical
**saidhantik gyan** *n.* सैद्घांतिक ज्ञान theory
**saina ka afsar** *n.* सेना का अफ़सर lieutenant
**saina ka sadasya** *n.* सेना का सदस्य legionary
**sainanayak** *n* सेनानायक commandant
**sainapati** *n* सेनापति marshal
**sainavas** *n.* सेनावास barrack
**sainik** *n.* सैनिक soldier
**sainik chhatra** *n.* सैनिक छात्र cadet
**sainik dhang se** *a.* सैनिक ढंग से militarily
**sainik namavali** *n* सैनिक नामावली muster
**sainya nikaya** *n* सैन्य निकाय corps
**sainyadal** *n.* सैन्यदल regiment
**sainyikaran** *n* युद्घकर्त्ता militarization
**sair** *n.* सैर trip
**sair sapaata** *n.* सैर सपाटा outing
**sajaana** *v.t.* सजाना adorn
**sajaana** *v. t* सजाना deck
**sajaana** *v. t* सजाना decorate
**sajaana** *v.t.* साजाना furnish
**sajaatiya** *a.* सजातीय homogeneous
**sajaavat** *n* सजावट decoration
**sajana** *v. t* सजाना beautify
**sajana** *v.t.* सजाना bedight
**sajawat** *n.* सजावट ornamentation
**sajha** *n.* साझा partnership

**sajiv** *a.* सजीव vivid
**sajiv karna** *v. t.* सजीव करना enliven
**sajivta** *n* सजीवता animation
**sajja** *n.* सजा outfit
**sajja** *n* सज्जा trim
**sajjit** *v. t* सज्जित equip
**sajjit karna** *v.t* सज्जित करना outfit
**sakaratmak** *a* सकारात्मक affirmative
**sakaratmak** *a.* साकारत्माक positive
**sakarin** *n.* सैकरिन saccharin
**sakarmak** *n.* सकर्मक क्रिया transitive
**sakht** *a.* सख्त severe
**sakhti** *n.* सख्ती stringency
**sakirna banana** *v.t.* संकीर्ण बनाना straiten
**sakriya** *a.* सक्रिय lively
**sakriya sthiti mein** *adv.* सक्रिय स्थिति में afoot
**sakshar** *a.* साक्षर literate
**saksharta** *n.* साक्षरता literacy
**sakshya** *n.* साक्ष्य testimony
**saktihin baykti** *n.* शक्तिहीन व्यक्ति laggard
**salaahkaar** *n.* सलाहकार mentor
**salad** *n.* सलाद salad
**salahakar** *n.* सलाहकार counsellor
**sam karna** *v. t* सम करना even
**samaadhaan** *n.* समाधान rectification
**samaaj** *n.* समाज community
**samaan hona** *v. t* कसमान होना equal
**samaan hona** *v.i.* समान होना match
**samaan manana** *v. t* समान मानना equate
**samaanatar karna** *v.t.* समानांतर करना parallel
**samaantar** *a.* समानांतर parallel
**samaantar chaturvurj** *n.* समानांतर चतुर्भुज parallelogram
**samaapati** *n.* समाप्ति subversion
**samaarohapurna** *a.* समारोहपूर्ण ceremonial
**samaas** *n* समास compound

**samaayojan karna** *v. t* समायोजन करना co-ordinate

**samachar** *n.* समाचार message

**samachar** *n. pl.* समाचार tidings

**samadhaan** *n* समाधान answer

**samadhan** *n.* समाधान resolution

**samadhan** *n.* समाधान solution

**samadhey** *a.* समाधेय soluble

**samadhi** *n.* समाधि sepulchre

**samadhilekh** *n* समाधिलेख epitaph

**samai bitan** *v.t. & i.* समय बितान delay

**samaj** *n.* समाज society

**samaj shastra** *n.* समाजशास्त्र sociology

**samajhana** *v.t.* समझना understand

**samajhdaar** *a.* समझदार mellow

**samajhdar** *a.* समझदार sagacious

**samajhdar** *a.* समझदार sensible

**samajhdari** *n* समझदारी discretion

**samajhdari** *n.* समझदारी wisdom

**samajhna** *v. t* समझना comprehend

**samajhna** *v.t.* समझना perceive

**samajik** *n.* सामाजिक social

**samajsevi** *n.* समाजसेवी philanthropist

**samajvad** *n* समाजवाद socialism

**samajvadi** *n,a* समाजवादी socialist

**samakalin** *a* समकालीन contemporary

**samalochak** *n* समालोचक critic

**saman** *a.* समान alike

**saman** *conj.* समान as

**saman** *a* समान equal

**saman** *n.* सामान luggage

**saman** *a.* समान tantamount

**saman prakarti vala** *a.* समान प्रकृति वाला akin

**saman rup se** *adv* समान रूप से alike

**saman rup se** *conj* समान रूप से both

**samana karna** *v.t.* (सामना करना withstand

**samanantar** *prep.* समानांतर along

**samanarthi** *a* समानार्थी equivalent

**samanata** *n.* समानता conformity

**samanata** *n* समानता equality

**samanayata** *n.* सामान्यता normalcy

**samaney** *a* सामने front

**samaney hona** *v.t* सामने होना front

**samaniya bhasha** *n.* सामान्य भाषा lingua franca

**samaniya se bada** *a.* सामान्य से बड़ा outsize

**samaniya vaykti** *n.* सामान्य व्यक्ति commoner

**samaniyat** *adv.* सामान्यत: generally

**samanjasya** *n.* सामंजस्य concord

**samanjasya** *n.* सामंजस्य consistency

**samanjasya** *n.* सामंजस्य unison

**samanta** *n* समानता affinity

**samanta** *n.* समानता correspondence

**samanta** *n.* समानता parallelism

**samanta** *n.* समानता parity

**samanta** *n.* समानता similarity

**samanta** *n.* समानता similitude

**samanupatan karna** *v.t.* समानुपातन करना proportion

**samanupati** *a.* समानुपाती proportionate

**samanupatik** *a.* समानुपातिक proportional

**samanya** *a.* सामान्य commonplace

**samanya** *a* सामान्य elementary

**samanya** *n.* सामान्य infinitive

**samanya** *a* सामान्य standard

**samanya** *a.* सामान्य usual

**samanya bhasha** *n.* सामान्य भाषा vernacular

**samapak** *a* समापक finite

**samapan** *n.* समापन closure

**samapan** *n.* अंजाम end

**samapan karna** *v. t* समापन करना conclude

**samapati** *n.* समाप्ति termination

**samapt hona** *v.t.* समाप्त होना terminate

**samapt karna** *v. t.* समाप्त करना demolish

**samapt karna** *v. t* समाप्त करना end

**samapya** *a.* समाप्य terminable

**samaroh manana** *v.t.* समारोह मनाना solemnize

**samarpan** *n* समर्पण dedication

**samarpan** *n* समर्पण devotion

**samarpan** *n.* समर्पण submission

**samarpan karna** *v. t.* समर्पण करना dedicate

**samarpit vyakti** *n* समर्पित व्यक्ति devotee

**samarth** *a.* समर्थ competent

**samarthan** *n.* समर्थन countenance

**samarthan karna** *v. t.* समर्थन करना champion

**samarthan karna** *v. t.* समर्थन करना endorse

**samarthan karna** *v.t* समर्थन करना favour

**samarthniya** *a.* समर्थनीय tenable

**samarthya** *n.* सामर्थ्य capability

**samarthya** *n* सामर्थ्य competence

**samast** *a.* समस्त all

**samasya** *n.* समस्या problem

**samasyatmak** *a.* समस्यात्मक problematic

**samawesh** *n.* समावेश inclusion

**samay** *n* समय date

**samay** *n.* समय period

**samay** *n.* समय time

**samay** *n.* समय while

**samay gawana** *v.t.* समय गंवाना while

**samay ka paband** *a.* समय का पाबंद punctual

**samay ki pabandi** *n.* समय की पाबंदी punctuality

**samay se purva** *adv* समय से पूर्व early

**samay se purva ghatit hona** *v.t.* समय से पूर्व घटित होना antecede

**samayanukul** *a.* समयानुकूल well-timed

**samayik** *a.* सामयिक topical

**samayojan** *n* समायोजन co-ordination

**sambaah** *a* समबाह equilateral

**sambadh karna** *v.t.* संबद्घ करना annex

**sambandh** *n* संबंध connection

**sambandh** *n.* संबंध relation

**sambandh** *n.pl.* सम्बन्ध term

**sambandh viched** *n.* संबंध विच्छेद rupture

**sambandhi** *adj* सम्बन्धी cognate

**sambhalna** *v.t.* संभालना poise

**sambhalna** *v.t* संभालना uphold

**sambhav** *a* संभव feasible

**sambhav hona** *v.* संभव होना can

**sambhavana** *v* संभावना may

**sambhavana** *n.* संभावना possibility

**sambhavana** *a.* संभव possible

**sambhavana** *n.* संभावना probability

**sambhavayata** *adv.* संभवतया probably

**sambhavit** *a.* संभावित probable

**sambhavya** *a* संभाव्य subject

**sambhavyata** *n.* संभव्यता likelihood

**sambhawana** *n.* संभावना potentiality

**sambhodan karna** *v.t.* निवेदन करना address

**sambhog** *n.* संभोग intercourse

**sambhrant jan** *n.* संभांत जन personage

**samdaab rekha** *n.* समदाब रेखा isobar

**same** *n.* सेम bean

**samgrata** *n.* समग्रता integrity

**samikaran** *n* समीकरण assimilation

**samikaran** *n.* समीकरण equation

**samip** *a.* समीप approximate

**samipvarti** *a.* समीपवर्ती adjacent

**samir** *n* समीर breeze

**samiti** *n* समिति committee

**samiti sadasya** *n.* समिति सदस्य senator

**samjhana** *v. t.* समझाना enlighten

**samjhana** *v.t* समझाना urge

**samjhauta** *n.* समझौता settlement

**samjhota** *n* समझौता compromise

**samjhota karna** *v. t* समझौता करना compromise

**samkaksh** *a.* समकक्ष co-ordinate

**samkalik** *a.* समकालिक simultaneous

**samkonik rekha** *n.* समकोणिक रेखा perpendicular

**sammaan karna** *v.t.* सम्मान करना revere

sammalit *a.* सम्मिलित inclusive

samman *n* सम्मान deference

sammanarth *a.* सम्मानार्थ honorary

sammanit karna *v. t* सम्मानित करना honour

sammelan *n* सम्मेलन congress

sammilit karna *v.t.* सम्मिलित करना include

sammilit karna *vt.* सम्मिलित करना incorporate

sammishran *n.* सम्मिश्रण infusion

sammit *a.* सममित symmetrical

sammohan *n.* सम्मोहन hypnotism

sammohan *n.* सम्मोहन mesmerism

sammohit karna *v.t.* सम्मोहित करना hypnotize

samney *prep. & adv.* सामने afore

sampaan banana *v. t* संपन्न बनाना enrich

sampadak *n* संपादक editor

sampadan *n.* स्पंदन throb

sampadan *n.* संपादन transaction

sampadan karna *v. t* संपादन करना edit

sampadit hona *v.i.* स्पंदित होना pulse

sampadit karna *v.t.* संपादित करना transact

sampadkiya *a* संपादकीय editorial

sampann *a.* संपन्न well-to-do

sampannata *n.* संपन्नता affluence

sampark *n.* संपर्क affiliation

sampark *n.* संपर्क contact

sampark *n.* सम्पर्क liaison

sampark mein ana *v.t.* संपर्क में आना touch

sampark sthapit karna *v. t* संपर्क स्थापित करना contact

sampatti *n.* संपत्ति asset

sampatti *n.* संपत्ति mammon

sampatti-bhagi *n.* संपत्ति-भागी assignee

sampradayik *a* सांप्रदायिक communal

sampurna *a* संपूर्ण entire

sampurna *a.* संपूर्ण, समूचा total

sampurna *a.* संपूर्ण whole

sampurna *n* संपूर्ण whole

sampurnata *adv* संपूर्णत: entirely

sampurnata *n.* संपूर्णता totality

samraat *n* सम्राट emperor

samrajya *n* साम्राज्य empire

samrajya *n.* साम्राज्य kingdom

samrajyawad *n.* साम्राज्यवाद imperialism

samsvarit karna *v.t.* समस्वरित करना tune

samtal *a* समतल even

samtal *a* समतल level

sam-tal *v.t.* सम-तल plane

samtal karna *v.t.* समतल करना level

samuchi yojana *n.* समूची योजना strategy

samudari ghoda *n.* समुद्री घोड़ा walrus

samudari kachchap *n.* समुद्री कच्छप turtle

samudra ke shakha *a* समुद्र की शाखा armlet

samudra mein yatra karna *v.i.* समुद्र में यात्रा करना cruise

samudra tat *n* समुद्र-तट beach

samudra tat *n.* समुद्रतट shore

samudra tat *n* समुद्र तट strand

samudra yatra *n.* समुद्र यात्रा voyage

samudra yatra karna *v.i.* समुद्र यात्रा करना voyage

samudra yatri *n.* समुद्र यात्री voyager

samudra-tat *n* समुद्र-तट coast

samudri daketi *n.* समुद्री डकैती piracy

samudri daku *n.* समुद्री डाकू pirate

samudri shaiwal *n.* समुद्री शैवाल wrack

samudri tatiya *a.* समुद्री तटीय maritime

samudri vigyan sambandhi *n* सुमद्री विज्ञान संबन्धी oceanographic

samudrik *a.* समुद्रिक nautical

samudritar se bhejna *v. t.* समुद्रीतार से भेजना cable

samuh *n.* समूह group

samuh *n.* समूह multitude

samuhbadh hona *v. i.* समूहबद्घ होना cluster

samuhik *a* सामूहिक collective

samuhik *a* सामूहिक molar

samvadata *n.* संवाददाता correspondent

samvaddata *n.* संवाददाता reporter

samvedanatamak *a.* संवेदनात्मक sensational

samvedansheel *a.* संवेदनशील sensitive

samvedansheelta *n.* संवेदनशीलता sensibility

samyochit *a.* समयोचित timely

sanak *n.* सनक caprice

sanak *n* सनक fad

sanak *n.* सनक vagary

sanak *n.* सनक whim

sanand *a* सानंद merry

sanatak *n* स्नातक graduate

sanatak hona *v.i.* स्नातक होना graduate

sanatan सनातन eternal

sancha *n.* सांचा mould

sanchalan *n* संचालन drive

sanchalan *n.* संचालन superintendence

sanchalan karna *v. t* संचालन करना direct

sanchalan karna *v.t.* संचालन करना superintend

sanchalit karna *v.t.* संचालित करना mobilize

sancharan karna *n.* संचारण transmission

sanchar-saadhan *n* संचार-साधन medium

sanchay karna *v.t* संचय करना heap

sanchika *n* संचिका file

sanchit karna *v.t.* संचित करना aggregate

sanchit karna *v.t.* संचित करना treasure

sanchit vastu *n* संचित वस्तु collection

sand *n* सांड bull

sandeh *n.* संदेह suspicion

sandeh karna *v.t.* संदेह करना question

sandeh karna *v.t.* संदेह करना suspect

sandeh shunya *adj.* सन्देह शून्य credulity

sandehwadi *n.* संदेहवादी sceptic

sandehyukt *a.* संदेहयुक्त questionable

sandesh *n* संदेश errand

sandesh patra *n.* लिखित संदेश missive

sandeshvahak *n.* संदेशवाहक courier

sandeswahak *n.* संदेशवाहक messenger

sandheh *n.* संदेह misgiving

sandhi *n.* संधि alliance

sandhi *n.* संधि junction

sandhi *n.* संधि pact

sandhi *n.* संधि treaty

sandhi prastav *n.* संधि प्रस्ताव overture

sandhya *n* संध्या dusk

sandhya *n* संध्या evening

sandigadhata *n.* संदिग्धता ambiguity

sandigdh vyakti *n* संदिग्ध व्यक्ति suspect

sandighdh *a.* संदिग्ध suspect

sanduk *n* संदूक box

sanduk *n.* संदूक case

sandwich *n.* सैंडविच sandwich

sangalan karna *v. t* संग्लन करना enclose

sangam *n* संगम confluence

sangam *n.* संगम juncture

sangat *n* संगत accompaniment

sangat *a.* संगत apposite

sangathan *n* संगठन combination

sangathit *a.* संगठित organic

sangathit hona *v. t.* संघटित करना consolidate

sangathit karna *v.t.* संगठित करना regiment

sangati *n.* संगति association

sangeet gosthi *n.* संगीत गोष्ठी concert

sangh *n* संघ federation

sangh *n.* संघ guild

sangh *n.* संघ league

sangharsh *n.* संघर्ष clash

sangharsh *n.* संघर्ष conflict

sangharsh *n* संघर्ष struggle

sangharsh *n.* संघर्ष tussle

sangharsh karna *v. i* संघर्ष करना conflict

sangharsh karna *v. t* संघर्ष करना contest

sangharsh karna *v.i.* संघर्ष करना strive

sangharsh karna *v.i.* संघर्ष करना tussle

sanghatan *n.* संघटन organization

sanghatit karna *v.t.* संघटित करना organize

sanghiya *a* संघीय federal

sanghwadi *n.* संघवादी unionist

sangin *n* संगीन bayonet

sangit *n.* संगीत music

sangit natak *n.* संगीत नाटक opera

sangitkaar *n.* संगीतकार musician

sangmarmar *n.* संगमरमर marble

sangraam *n.* संग्राम warfare

sangrah *n.* संग्रह digest

sangrah *n.* संग्रह heap

sangrah karna *v. t* संग्रह करना compile

sangram *n* संग्राम combat

sangreh *n* संग्रह accumulation

sangreh karna *v. t* संग्रह करना collect

sangya *n.* संज्ञा noun

sanhar *n* संहार carnage

sanhita *n* संहिता code

sankaitak *n* संकेतक beacon

sankalp shakti *n.* संकल्प शक्ति volition

sankalpana *n* संकल्पना concept

sankalpshakti *n.* संकल्पशक्ति will

sankar *n* संकर cross

sankar *n* संकर hybrid

sankar jati ka *a.* संकर जाति का hybrid

sankar jatiya *a* संकर जाति mongrel

sankara karna *v.t.* संकरा करना narrow

sankat *n.* संकट danger

sankat kal *n* संकटकाल crisis

sankat mai dalna *v.t* संकट में डालना hazard

sankat mein dalna *v.t.* संकट में डालना imperil

sankat puran *n.* संकट पूरण peril

sankatmai *a.* संकटमय perilous

sankatpurna *a* संकटपूर्ण critical

sankatpurna *a* संकटपूर्ण disastrous

sankaya *n* संकाय faculty

sanket *n* संकेत allusion

sanket *n* संकेत clue

sanket *n* संकेत cue

sanket *n.* संकेत gesture

sanket *n.* संकेत hint

sanket *n.* संकेत indication

sanket *n.* संकेत sign

sanket *n.* संकेत signal

sanket *n.* संकेत tip

sanket karna *v.t.* संकेत करना beckon

sanket karna *v.t.* संकेत करना indicate

sanket karna *v.t.* संकेत करना signal

sanket karna *v.t.* संकेत करना spell

sanket lipi *n.* संकेत लिपि code

sanketik *a.* सांकेतिक allusive

sankhiya *n* संखिया arsenic

sankhya *n.* संख्या count

sankhya *n.* संख्याँ number

sankhyatmak *a.* संख्यात्मक numerical

sankhyiki *n.* सांख्यिकी statistics

sankhyikivid *n.* सांख्यिकीविद् statistician

sankhyikiya *a.* सांख्यिकीय statistical

sanki *a* सनकी crazy

sankirnata *n.* संकीर्णता provincialism

sankirnatapurna *a.* संकीर्णतापूर्ण suburban

sankoch *n.* संकोच hesitation

sankoch *n* संकोच modesty

sankoch karna *v.i.* संकोच करना hesitate

sankochi *a.* संकोची bashful

sankochi *adj.* संकोची compliant

sankochi *a.* संकोची sheepish

sankochi *n.* संकोची shy

sankraamak *a.* संक्रमणक infectious

sankramak *a* संक्रामक contagious

sankraman *n.* संक्रमण infection

sankshaleshan *n.* संश्लेषण synthesis

sankshaleshanatmak *a.* संश्लेषणात्मक synthetic

sankshep *n* संक्षेप abridgement

sankshep *n.* संक्षेप precis
sankshep karna *v.t* संक्षेप करना abridge
sankshipt *a.* संक्षिप्त brief
sankshipt *a* संक्षिप्त concise
sankshipt *a.* संक्षिप्त laconic
sankshipt *n.* संक्षिप्त वर्णन sketch
sankshipt *a.* संक्षिप्त, अधूरा sketchy
sankshipt *a* संक्षिप्त summary
sankshipt *a.* संक्षिप्त terse
sankshipt karna *v.t.* संक्षिप्त करना abbreviate
sankshipt karna *v.t.* संक्षिप्त करना summarize
sankshipt vivran *n.* संक्षिप्त विवरण summary
sankshiptata *n* संक्षिप्तता brevity
sankshiptikaran *n* संक्षिप्तीकरण abbreviation
sankuchit *a.* संकुचित limited
sankuchit marg *n.* संकुचित मार्ग defile
sanlaganak *n.* संलग्नक appendage
sanlagna *n.* संलग्न attachment
sanlagna karna *v.t.* संलग्न करना append
sanlagna karna *v.t.* संलग्न करना tag
sannivesh *n.* सन्निवेश insertion
sannivisht karna *v.t.* सन्निविष्ट करना insert
sanrakshak *n* संरक्षक custodian
sanrakshan *n.* संस्करण patronage
sanrakshi *a.* संरक्षी protective
sans lena *v. i.* सांस लेना breathe
sansaarik *a.* सांसारिक mundane
sansad *n.* संसद parliament
sansad sadasya *n.* संसद सदस्य parliamentarian
sansadiya *a.* संसदीय parliamentary
sansanana *v.i.* सनसनाना whiz
sansani khez *a.* सनसनीखेज़ melodramatic
sansarik anand *n.* सांसारिक आनंद worldling
sanshayatmak *a.* संशयात्मक sceptical

sanshayatmakta *n.* संशयात्मकता scepticism
sanshay-sheel *a.* संशयशील hesitant
sanshodhan *n* संशोधन alteration
sanshodhan karna *v.t.* संशोधन करना amend
sanshodhan karna *v. t* संशोधन करना correct
sanskaran *n* संस्करण edition
sanskritik *a* सांस्कृतिक cultural
sanstha *n.* संस्था institute/institution
sansthapak *n.* संस्थापक founder
sanstuti *n.* संस्तुति recommendation
sant *n.* संत saint
santan *n.* संतान progeny
santara *n.* संतरा orange
santari *n.* संतरी sentinel
santari *n.* संतरी sentry
santati *n.* संतति offspring
santosh *n* संतोष contentment
santosh *n.* संतोष gratification
santosh *n.* संतोष satisfaction
santoshjanak *a.* संतोषजनक satisfactory
santra *n.* संतरा kino
santras *n.* संत्रास intimidation
santulan *n.* संतुलन balance
santulan *n* संतुलन equation
santulan *n* संतुलन poise
santulan *n.* संतुलन symmetry
santulan *n.* संतुलन moderation
santulit karna *v.t.* संतुलित करना balance
santusht *adj.* सन्तुष्ट complacent
santusht *a.* संतुष्ट content
santusht karna *v.t.* संतुष्ट करना pamper
santusht karna *v.t.* संतुष्ट करना satisfy
santushti *n* संतुष्टि content
santushti pradan karna *v. t* संतुष्टि प्रदान करना| content
santushtii *n.* संतुष्टि saturation
santvana *n.* सांत्वना solace
santvana dena *v.t.* सांत्वना देना solace

santwana *n* सांत्वना consolation
santwana dena *v. t* सांत्वना देना console
sanvad *n* संवाद dialogue
sanvala *a.* सांवला swarthy
sanvedansheel *a.* संवेदनशील sentient
sanvida *n.* संविदा compact
sanvida *n* संविदा contract
sanvidhan nirmankari *adj.* संविधान निर्माणकारी constituent
sanwad *n* संवाद conversation
sanwasi *n.* संवासी inmate
sanyaasbhav *n* संन्यासभाव monasticism
sanyasi *n.* संन्यासी hermit
sanyog *n.* संयोग chance
sanyog *v.i.* संयोग coincide
sanyog *n.* संयोग hazard
sanyojak *n* संयोजक convener
sanyojan *n* संयोजन annexation
sanyojan *n.* संयोजन incorporation
sanyojana *v. t* संजोना enshrine
sanyukt *adj.* संयुक्त conjunct
sanyukt *adj.* संयुक्त corporate
sanyukt karna *v.t.* संयुक्त करना associate
sapath *n.* शपथ oath
sapeksh *a.* सापेक्ष relative
saphal *a* सफल successful
saphal hona *v.i.* सफल होना succeed
saphalta *n.* सफलता success
saphed *a.* सफ़ेद white
saphed karana *v. t* सफ़ेद करना bleach
saphed karna *v.t.* सफ़ेद करना whiten
saphed rang *n* सफेद रंग white
saphed sa *a.* सफ़ेद सा whitish
saphed saras pakshi *n* सफेद सारस पक्षी aigrette
saphedi *n.* सफ़ेदी whitewash
saphedi karna *v.t.* सफ़ेदी करना whitewash
saptah *n.* सप्ताह week
saptahik *a.* साप्ताहिक weekly
saptahik *n.* साप्ताहिक weekly
sar *n.* सिर head

sar kai bal *adv.* सिर के बल headlong
saraab banana *n.* शराब बनाना malt
sarabor kar dena *v. t* सराबोर कर देना drench
sarahana karna *v. t* सराहना करना exalt
sarai *n.* सराय inn
sarakna *v.i.* सरकाना slide
saral *a.* सरल austere
saral *a* सरल easy
saral *a* सरल light
saral banana *v.t.* सरल बनाना simplify
saranchana *n.* संरचना structure
saranchanatamak *a.* संरचनात्मक structural
saransh *n* सारांश abstract
saras *n.* सारस stork
sarasar *adv.* सरासर stark
saraswati(Hindu goddess) *n* सरस्वती muse
sarawsri *n.* सर्वश्री Messrs
sarbotam samay *n.* सर्वोत्तम समय heyday
sardal *n.* सरदल lintel
sardi *n* सर्दी cold
sares *n.* सरेस glue
sarhak ki patri *n.* सड़क की पटरी pavement
sarhan *n.* सड़न decomposition
sarhana *v.i.* सड़ना rot
sarhane yogya *a.* सराहने योग्य praiseworthy
sarhna *v. t* सड़ना decompose
sarjan karna *v. t* सर्जन करना create
sarjent *n.* सारजेंट sergeant
sarkaari vigyapati *n.* सरकारी विज्ञप्ति communiqué
sarkana *v.t.* सरकना glide
sarkas *n.* सर्कस circus
sarlikaran *n.* सरलीकरण simplification
sarniyak *n.* सारणीयक tabulator
sarniyan *n.* सारणीयन tabulation

sarp *n.* सर्प serpent

sarp *n.* सर्प snake

sarpat daurna *v.t.* सरपट दौड़ाना gallop

sarpil aakar *n.* सर्पिल आकार spiral

sarsari *a* सरसरी cursory

sarson *n.* सरसों mustard

sarthak *a.* सार्थक meaningful

sarvada *adv* सर्वदा always

sarvadhik matra mai *adv.* सर्वाधिक मात्रा में most

sarvagy *a.* सर्वज्ञ omniscient

sarvagyata *n.* सर्वज्ञता omniscience

sarvajanik *a.* सार्वजनिक public

sarvakshama *n.* सर्वक्षमा amnesty

sarvanaam *n.* सर्वनाम pronoun

sarvanash *n.* सर्वनाश holocaust

sarvasammat *a.* सर्वसम्मत unanimous

sarvasammati *n.* सर्वसम्मति unanimity

sarvashaktiman *a.* सर्वशक्तिमान almighty

sarvashaktiman *a.* सर्वशक्तिमान omnipotent

sarvashaktimata *n.* सर्वशक्तिमत्ता omnipotence

sarva-shreshth *a* सर्वश्रेष्ठ sovereign

sarvatra *adv.* सर्वत्र throughout

sarvavadit *a.* सर्वविदित proverbial

sarva-vyapakta *n.* सर्वव्यापकता omnipresence

sarvaypi *a.* सर्वव्यापी omnipresent

sarvekshan *n.* सर्वेक्षण survey

sarvoch *a.* सर्वोच्च supreme

sarvotkrist kriti *n.* सर्वोत्कृष्ट कृति masterpiece

sarvottam *n.* सर्वोत्तम paramount

sarwatam *a* सर्वोत्तम foremost

sasharir *adv.* सशरीर bodily

sashodhan *n.* संशोधन revision

sashodhan *n* संशोधन correction

sasta *a.* सस्ता frugal

sasta *a* सस्ता cheap

sasta karna *v. t.* सस्ता करना cheapen

sasural *n.* ससुराल in-laws

satah *n.* सतह side

satah *n.* सतह surface

satana *v.t.* सताना afflict

satana *v. t* सताना bedevil

satark *a.* सतर्क attentive

satark *a.* सतर्क vigilant

satark *a.* सतर्क wary

satark *a.* सतर्क watchful

satarkh *a.* सतर्क cautious

sath dena *v.t.* साथ देना associate

sath hona *v.t.* साथ होना attend

sath ugna *v.t.* साथ उगना accrete

sathi *n.* साथी associate

sathi *n.* साथी companion

sathi *n.* साथी comrade

sathi *n.* साथी consort

sathi *n* साथी fellow

sathi *n.* साथी mate

sathi *n.* साथी partner

satitva haran *n.* सतीत्व हरण seduction

satkaar karne wala *a.* सत्कार करने वाला hospitable

satrah *n., a* सत्रह seventeen

satrehwan *a.* सत्रहवां seventeenth

satta *n* सत्ता entity

sattar *n., a* सत्तर seventy

sattarwan *a.* सत्तरवां seventieth

satwan *a.* सातवां seventh

satya *n.* सत्य certainty

satyabhas *n.* सत्याभास verisimilitude

satyapan *n.* प्रमाणन verification

satyavadi *a.* सत्यवादी truthful

sau *n* सौ cent

sau *n.* सौ hundred

sau anshon mein vibhajit *a.* सौ अंशों में विभाजित centigrade

sau varsh ka samay *n.* सौ वर्ष का समय centenary

saubhagya *n* सौभाग्य felicity

**saubhagya se** *adv.* सौभाग्य से luckily
**sauda** *n.* सौदा bargain
**sauda** *n.* सौदा merchandise
**sauda karna** *v.t.* सौदा करना bargain
**sauda karna** *v.t.* सौदा करना negotiate
**saudebaji karna** *v.i.* सौदेबाज़ी करना haggle
**saugunna** *n. & adj* सौगुना centuple
**saujanya** *n.* सौजन्य courtesy
**saumya** *n.* सौम्य amiable
**saumyata** *n.* सौम्यता urbanity
**saundariya** *n* सौंदर्य beauty
**saundarya vardhak** *a.* सौंदर्यवर्धक cosmetic
**saundryashastra** *n.pl.* सौंदर्यशास्त्र aesthetics
**saunf ka beej** *n* सौंफ का बीज aniseed
**saunpana** *v. t* सौंपना entrust
**saur** *a.* सौर solar
**sauvin varshaganth** *adj.* सौवीं वर्षगाँठ centennial
**savdhan** *n.* सावधान attention
**savdhan** *adj.* सावधान circumspect
**savdhan** *a.* सावधान mindful
**savdhan** *a.* सावधान particular
**savdhani** *n.* सावधानी prudence
**sawaar** *n.* सवार rider
**sawaar hona** *v.t.* सवार होना mount
**sawar hona** *v.t.* सवार होना board
**sawari** *n* सवारी conveyance
**sawari karna** *v.t.* सवारी करना ride
**sawdhan** *a.* सावधान observant
**scooter** *n.* स्कूटर scooter
**scotland ka niwasi** *n.* स्कॉटलैंड का निवासी Scot
**scotland niwasi** *n.* स्कॉटलैंड निवासी scotch
**se** *prep.* से from
**se baad mein** *prep* से बाद में behind
**se bachna** *v.t.* से बचना avoid
**se neechay** *prep* से नीचे below
**se sambandhit** *v.i.* से सम्बधित pertain

**se upar** *prep.* से ऊपर beyond
**seb** *n.* सेब apple
**seedh nirdharan** *n.* सीध निर्धारण alignment
**seedha** *a.* सीधा upright
**seedha karna** *v.t.* सीधा करना straighten
**seekh** *n.* सीख moral
**seekhna** *v.i.* सीखना learn
**seema** *n.* सीमा bound
**seema** *n.* सीमा limit
**seema** *n.* सीमा restriction
**seema** *n.* सीमा span
**seema rekha** *n* सीमारेखा boundary
**seema shulk** *n.* सीमा शुल्क tariff
**seemant** *n* किनारी border
**seemit karna** *v.i.* सीमित करना qualify
**seengh** *n.* सींग horn
**seer hilana** *v.i.* सिर हिलाना nod
**seer katna** *v. t.* सिर काटना behead
**seeti bajana** *v.i.* सीटी बजाना whistle
**seeti ki awaaz** *n* सीटी की आवाज़ whistle
**seetkaar sahith bholna** *v.* सीत्कार सहित बोलना assibilate
**seetnindra** *n.* शीतनिद्रा hibernation
**sena** *n.* सेना army
**sena** *n* सेना military
**sena ka pradarshan** *n.* सेना का प्रदर्शन tattoo
**senavas** *n* सेनावास bunker
**senkna** *v.t.* सेंकना bake
**senkna** *v.t* सेंकना foment
**service** *n.* सर्विस serve
**setambar** *n.* सितंबर September
**setu** *n.* सेतु weir
**sevak** *n.* सेवक attendant
**sevak** *n* सेवक tender
**sewa karna** *v.i.* सेवा करना minister
**sewak** *n* सेवक menial
**sewak** *a.* सेवक ministrant
**sewak** *n.* सेवक servant
**seyaar** *n.* सियार jackal

shaabdik *a.* शाब्दिक verbatim

shaan *n.* शान grandeur

shaandar jhankian *n.* शानदार झांकियां pageant

shaant *n* शांत still

shaanti *n.* शांति quiet

shaaririk *a.* शरीरिक physical

shabadkosh *n.* शब्दकोश lexicon

shabd *n.* शब्द word

shabd chayan *n* शब्द चयन diction

shabd soochi *n.* शब्द सूची vocabulary

shabdabahul *a.* शब्दबहुल verbose

shabdabahulata *n.* शब्दबहुलता verbosity

shabdadambarpurna *a.* शब्दाडंबरपूर्ण wordy

shabdakosh *n* शब्दकोश dictionary

shabdandpurna *a.* शब्दाडंबरपूर्ण rhetorical

shabdashah *adv.* शब्दश: verbatim

shabdawali *n.* शब्दावली glossary

shabdh *n.* शब्द term

shabdik *a.* शाब्दिक literal

shadi *n.* शादी marriage

shadi karna *v.t.* शादी करना marry

shadyantra *n.* षड्यंत्र conspiracy

shadyantra *n.* षड्यंत्रकर्त्ता conspirator

shadyantra *n* षड्यंत्र intrigue

shadyantra karna *v.t.* षड्यंत्र करना intrigue

shahad ki madira *n.* शहद की मदिरा mead

shahamat *n* शहमात checkmate

shahatut *n.* शहतूत mulberry

shah-balut *n.* शाहबलूत oak

shahd aur sirka ka sharbat *n* शहद और सिरका का शरबत oxymel

shahi *a.* शाही imperial

shahid *n.* शहीद martyr

shahmaat dena *v.t.* शहमात देना mate

shahteer *n.* शहतीर girder

shaidayi संन्धि nympholept

shaishav *n.* शैशव childhood

shaitan *n* शैतान devil

shaitan *n.* शैतान satan

shakahari *n.* शाकाहारी vegetarian

shakha *n.* शाखा agency

shakha *n* शाखा bough

shakha *n* शाखा branch

shakha *n.* शाखा limb

shakki *a.* शक्की suspicious

shakti *n* शक्ति force

shakti *n.* शक्ति potency

shakti *n.* शक्ति power

shakti *n.* शक्ति sap

shakti *n.* शक्ति strength

shakti barhana *v.t.* शक्ति बढ़ाना activate

shakti jutaana *v.t.* शक्ति जुटाना rally

shakti puran *a* शक्ति-पुरण forcible

shakti ya adhikar *n.* शक्ति या अधिकार authority

shaktiheen karna *v.t.* शक्तिहीन करना sap

shaktihin *a.* शक्तिहीन lethargic

shaktihin *a.* शक्तिहीन nerveless

shaktishali *a* शक्तिशाली energetic

shaktishali *a.* शक्तिशाली muscular

shaktishali *a.* शक्तिशाली powerful

shaktishali *a.* शक्तिशाली strong

shaktishali *a.* शक्तिशाली vigorous

shaktishali *a.* शक्तिशाली virile

shakun wichar *n.* शकुन विचार auspice

shakya *a.* शक्य potential

shalinta *n* शालीनता decency

shaljam *n.* शलजम turnip

shalya chikitsa *n.* शल्य चिकित्सा operation

shalya chikitsa *n.* शल्य चिकित्सा surgery

shalya chikitsak *n.* शल्य चिकित्सक surgeon

shamak *a.* शामक sedative

shamak aushadh *n* शामक औषध sedative

shamiz *n* शमीज़ chemise

shan *n.* शान stateliness

shandaar *a.* शानदार sumptuous

shandar *a.* शानदार princely

shandar *a.* शानदार splendid

shaniwar *n.* शनिवार Saturday

shanka *n* शंका doubt

shanka karna *v. i* शंका करना doubt

shankh *n.* शंख conch

shanku *n.* शंकु cone

shant *n.* शांत calm

shant *a.* शांत pacific

shant *a.* शांत peaceful

shant *a.* शांत placid

shant *a.* शांत serene

shant *a.* शांत silent

shant *a.* शांत tranquil

shant hona *v.i* शांत होना hush ·

shant karna *v.t.* शांत करना allay

shant karna *v.t.* शांत करना appease

shant karna *v. t.* शांत करना calm

shant karna *v.t.* शान्त करना conciliate

shant karna *v.t.* शांत करना pacify

shant karna *v.t.* शांत करना quench

shant karna *v.t.* शांत करना soothe

shant karna *v.t.* शांत करना tranquillize

shanti *n.* शांति calm

shanti *n.* शान्ति composure

shanti *n.* शांति peace

shanti *n.* शांति repose

shanti *n.* शांति serenity

shanti *n.* शांति silence

shanti *n.* शांति tranquillity

shanti kaal *n.* शांति काल lull

shanti lane wali *adj* शान्ति लाने वाली calmative

shantpriya *a.* शांतिप्रिय peaceable

shap dena *v. t.* शाप देना damn

shapath *n* शपथ adjuration

shapathpatra *n* शपथपत्र affidavit

sharab *n* शराब ale

sharab *n* शराब drink

sharab *n.* शराब rum

sharab *n.* शराब whisky

sharab banana *v. t.* शराब बनाना brew

sharabi *n* शराबी drunkard

sharam *n.* शरम shame

sharan *n.* शरण refuge

sharan dena *v.t* शरण देना harbour

sharanarthi *n.* शरणार्थी refugee

sharansthal *n.* शरणस्थल shelter

sharan-sthal *n* शरण-स्थल asylum

shararat *n* शरारत mischief

sharbat *n.* शरबत syrup

shareer rachna vigyan *n.* शरीर-रचना विज्ञान anatomy

sharir rachna *n.* शरीर रचना organism

sharir rachna *n.* शरीर रचना physique

sharirik *a* शारीरिक bodily

sharm shodhak *n.* चर्म शोधक tanner

sharm shodhanshala *n.* चर्म शोधनशाला tannery

sharm-naak *a.* शर्मनाक ignoble

shart *n* शर्त bet

shart *n* शर्त condition

shart *n.* शर्त proviso

shart *n.* शर्त wager

shart lagana *v.i* शर्त लगाना bet

shart lagana *v.t.* शर्त लगाना stipulate

shasak *n.* शासक ruler

shasan *n* शासन domination

shasan *n.* शासन governance

shasan *n.* शासन government

shasan karna *v. t* शासन करना dominate

shasan karna *v.t.* शासन करना rule

shasan kshetra *n* शासन क्षेत्र domain

shasit karna *v.t.* शासित करना govern

shastragar *n.* शास्त्रागार armoury

shatak *n.* शतक century

shatayu vyakti *n* शतायु व्यक्ति centenarian

shatranj *n.* शतरंज chess

shatranj mein zich *n.* शतरंज में ज़िच stalemate

shatru *n* शत्रु enemy

shatru *n* शत्रु foe

shatruta *n* शत्रुता enmity
shauchalaya *n.* शौचालय latrine
shauchalya *n.* शौचालय lavatory
shauchghar *n.* शौचघर toilet
shauk *n.* शौक hobby
shaul *n.* शॉल shawl
shaurya *n.* शौर्य valour
shauryavan *a.* शौर्यवान chivalrous
shav *n* शव corpse
shav pariksha *n.* शव परीक्षा post-mortem
shav yatra *n.* शव यात्रा funeral
shavlep karna *v. t* शवलेप करना embalm
shayan saamagri *n.* शयन सामग्री bedding
shayanika *n.* शयनिका sleeper
shayika *n* शायिका berth
sheera *n* शीरा molasses
sheeshi *n.* शीशी vial
sheet ritu *n.* शीत ऋतु winter
sheetal *a* शीतल cold
sheetal *a* शीतल cool
sheetal karna *v.t.* शीतल करना refrigerate
sheetoshna *a.* शीतोष्ण temperate
sher *n* शेर lion
sherni *n.* शेरनी lioness
shesh *n.* शेष remainder
shesh bhag *a.* शेष (भाग) residual
shesh sangreh *n.* शेष संग्रह appendix
sheshtama jvar *n.* श्लेष्मा ज्वर influenza
shighra *adv.* शीघ्र anon
shighra grahankari *a.* शीघ्र ग्रहणकारी
    receptive
shighra hi *adv.* शीघ्र ही shortly
shighrah *adv.* शीघ्र presently
shighrata *n.* शीघ्रता haste
shigrahta se *adv.* शीघ्रता से apace
shigrata *n* शीघ्रता hurry
shikaar *n.* शिकार prey
shikaar *n* शिकार shoot
shikaar karna *v.t.* शिकार करना hunt
shikaar karna *v.i.* शिकार करना prey
shikanja *n* शिकंजा clamp

shikanja *n.* शिकंजा rack
shikanji *n.* शिकंजी lemonade
shikar *n.* शिकार victim
shikar karna *v.t.* शिकार करना deprecate
shikari *n.* शिकारी hunter
shikari kutta *n.* शिकारी कुत्ता greyhound
shikari kutta *n.* शिकारी कुत्ता hound
shikayat *n.* शिकायत complaint
shikayat *n.* शिकायत grievance
shikayat karna *v. i* शिकायत करना
    complain
shikhar *n.* शिखर apex
shikhar *n.* शिखर climax
shikhar *n.* शिखर pinnacle
shiksha *n* शिक्षा education
shiksha *n.* शिक्षा learning
shiksha dena *v. t* शिक्षा देना educate
shiksha dena *v.t.* सिखा देना inculcate
shiksha dena *v.t.* शिक्षा देना teach
shikshak *n.* शिक्षक instructor
shikshak *n.* शिक्षक teacher
shikshakiya *a.* शिक्षकीय tutorial
shikshan shastra *n.* शिक्षणशास्त्र
    pedagogy
shilp *n.* शिल्प workmanship
shilpi *n.* शिल्पी artisan
shilpi *n* शिल्पी craftsman
shira *n.* शिरा vein
shirovastra *n.* शिरोवस्त्र wimple
shirshak *n.* शीर्षक caption
shirstraan *n.* शिरस्त्राण helmet
shisha lagana *v.t.* शीशा लगाना glaze
shisht *a.* शिष्ट courteous
shisht mandal *n* शिष्टमंडल deputation
shisht mandal *n.* शिष्ट मंडल mission
shishtachar *n* शिष्टाचार decorum
shishtachar *n* शिष्टाचार etiquette
shishtachar *n.* शिष्टाचार nicety
shishtata *n.* शिष्टता chivalry
shishu *n.* शिशु baby

shishudhani jeev *n.* शिशुधानी जीव marsupial

shishu-sadan *n.* शिशु-सदन nursery

shishuvadh *n.* शिशुवध infanticide

shishya *n.* शिष्य learner

shithil karna *v.t.* शिथिल करना relax

shithil karna *v.t.* शिथिल करना remit

shithilta *n.* शिथिलता relaxation

shivir *n.* शिविर camp

shoak bhar *n.* शोक भार load

shobha *n.* शोभा grace

shobha badhana *v.t.* शोभा बढ़ाना grace

shobha yukt *a.* शोभायुक्त glorious

shobhayukt karna *v.t* शोभायुक्त करना dignify

shobh-niya *a.* शोभनीय decent

shodh granth *n.* शोध ग्रंथ thesis

shodhak *a* शोधक purgative

shok *n* शोक condolence

shok *n.* शोक grief

shok *n.* विषाद woe

shok janak *a.* शोक जनक grievous

shok manana *v. t* शोक मनाना bewail

shok manana *v.t.* शोक मनाना grieve

shok prakat karna *v. i.* शोक प्रकट करना condole

shokakul *n.* शोकाकुल mournful

shokgeet *n* शोकगीत elegy

shokgeet *n.* शोकगीत monody

shokpurna *n.* शोकपूर्ण woeful

shorba *n* शोरबा broth

shorba *n.* शोरबा soup

shorgul *n* शोरगुल commotion

shraddha *n.* श्रद्धा homage

shraddha *n.* श्रद्धा veneration

shraddhapurna *a.* श्रद्धापूर्ण reverential

shradhalu *a.* श्रद्धालु respectful

shradhalu *a.* श्रद्धालु reverent

shradhapurna naman *n.* श्रद्धापूर्ण नमन obeisance

shramik *n.* श्रमिक labourer

shravan sambandhi *adj.* श्रवण सम्बन्धी auditive

shravya *a* श्रव्य audible

shreni *n.* श्रेणी category

shreni *n.* श्रेणी gradation

shreni *n.* श्रेणी type

shrenibadh karna *v.t.* श्रेणीबद्ध करना align

shreshtha *a.* श्रेष्ठ perfect

shreshthata *n.* श्रेष्ठता superiority

shreshthatasuchak *a.* श्रेष्ठतासूचक superlative

shriman *n.* श्रीमान sir

shrota *n.* श्रोता listener

shrotagan *n.* श्रोतागण audience

shrotakaksh *n.* श्रोताकक्ष auditorium

shubh *a.* शुभ providential

shubhsuchak *a.* शुभसूचक auspicious

shuchita *n.* शुचिता purity

shuchita *n.* शुचिता virginity

shudh karna *v. t* शुद्ध करना distil

shudh karna *v.t.* शुद्ध करना refine

shudhata *n.* शुद्धता accuracy

shudhata *n.* शुद्धता refinement

shudhi ka sthan *n.* शुद्धि का स्थान purgatory

shudhikaran *n.* शुद्धिकरण purification

shudhivadi *n.* शुद्धिवादी purist

shudhta *n.* शुद्धता chastity

shukar-mans *n.* शूकर- मांस bacon

shukranu *n.* शुक्राणु sperm

shukrawar *n.* शुक्रवार Friday

shulk *n* शुल्क fee

shulk se mukt शुल्क से मुक्त exempt

shunya *n.* शून्य void

shunya *n.* शून्य zero

shunya ka ank *n.* शून्य का अंक cipher, cypher

shunya,nirvat *n.* शून्य, निर्वात vacuum

shushkan *n.* शुष्कन soak

shuturmurg *n.* शुतुरमुर्ग ostrich

**shvas avrodhan** *n.* श्वास अवरोधन strangulation

**shvasan** *n* श्वसन breath

**shwasan** *n.* श्वसन respiration

**shwet** *n.* श्वेत muscovite

**shwet saar** *n.* श्वेत सार starch

**siddhant** *n.* सिद्घांत tenet

**siddhant sthapit karna** *v.i.* सिद्घांत स्थापित करना theorize

**siddhantshastri** *n.* सिद्घांतशास्त्री theorist

**sidha** *a.* सीधा artless

**sidha** *a* सीधा direct

**sidha** *a.* सीधा plain

**sidha** *a.* सीधा, straight

**sidha sada** *a.* सीधा सादा straightforward

**sidhant** *n* सिद्घांत doctrine

**sidhant vadi** *n.* सिद्घांत वादी nestorian

**sidhantheen** *a.* सिद्घांतहीन unprincipled

**sidhe** *n.* सीढ़ी ladder

**sidhi ka danda** *n.* सीढ़ी का डंडा rung

**sidhpurush** *n.* सिद्घपुरुष seer

**sigaar** *n* सिगार cheroot

**sigaar** *n.* सिगार cigar

**sikhar** *n.* शिखर peak

**sikka** *n* सिक्का coin

**sikka** *n* सिक्का coinage

**sikurh jana** *v.i.* सिकुड़ जाना wince

**sikurhan** *n.* सिकुड़न shrinkage

**sikurhna** *v.i* सिकुड़ना shrink

**silayee se jodna** *v.t.* सिलाई से जोड़ना seam

**silencer** *n.* साइलेंसर silencer

**silna** *v.t.* सिलना sew

**silna** *v.t.* सिलना stitch

**silwat dalna** *v.t.* सिलवट डालना wrinkle

**sima nirdharan** *n.* सीमा निर्धारण demarcation

**simaant** *n* सीमांत march

**simant** *n.* सीमांत frontier

**simit karna** *v.t.* सीमित करना limit

**sinchai** *n.* सिंचाई irrigation

**sinchna** *v.t.* सींचना irrigate

**sindur** *n* सिन्दूर cinnabar

**sinha jaisa** *a* सिंह जैसा leonine

**sinha rashi** *n.* सिंह राशि Leo

**sinhasanarurh karna** *v. t* सिंहासनारूढ़ करना enthrone

**sinhavalokan** *n.* सिंहावलोकन retrospection

**sipahi** *n* सिपाही constable

**sira** *n* सिरा terminal

**sirdard** *n.* सिरदर्द headache

**sirka** *n.* सिरका vinegar

**sirka banana** *v.* सिरका बनाना acetify

**sirsak** *n.* शीर्षक heading

**sisa** *n.* सीसा lead

**siskari** *n* सिसकारी hiss

**sista** *a.* शिष्ट mannerly

**sisu** *a.* शिशु infantile

**sitakani lagana** *v. t* सिटकनी लगाना bolt

**sivandar** *a.* सीवनदार seamy

**siwan** *n.* सीवन stitch

**siwaya** *prep* सिवाय save

**skait** *n.* स्केट skate

**skaiton par phisalna** *v.t.* स्केटों पर फिसलना skate

**slate** *n.* स्लेट slate

**smaarak** *n.* स्मारक monument

**smarak** *n.* स्मारक memorial

**smarak** *n.* स्मारक remembrance

**smaran** *n.* स्मरण reminiscence

**smaran** *n.* स्मरण recollection

**smaran karna** *v.t.* स्मरण करना recollect

**smaran karna** *v.t.* स्मरण रखना remember

**smaran patar** *n.* स्मरणपत्र reminder

**smaran patra** *n* स्मरण पत्र memorandum

**smaran vishayak** *a* स्मरण विषयक memorial

**smaranotsava** *n.* स्मरणोत्सव commemoration

**smarkiya** *a.* स्मारकीय monumental

**smarniya** *a.* स्मरणीय memorable

**smirtihin** *a.* स्मृतिहीन oblivious

smriti chinha *n.* स्मृतिचिन्ह keepsake
smritichinh *n.* स्मृतिचिह्न memento
snaan *n* स्नान bath
snaan karna *v. t* स्नान करना bathe
snayu rog *n.* स्नायु रोग neurosis
snehan *n.* स्नेहन lubrication
soak prakat karna *v.i.* शोक प्रकट करना lament
soar *n.* शोर noise
sobhakaari *a.* शोभाकारी ornamental
soch lena *v. t* सोच लेना devise
soch-vichar *n* सोच विचार thought
sofa *n.* सोफ़ा couch
sofa *n.* सोफ़ा sofa
sokhna *v.t* सोखना absorb
solaha *n., a.* सोलह sixteen
solahawan *a.* सोलहवां sixteenth
somvaar *n.* सोमवार Monday
sona *n.* सोना gold
sona *v.i.* सोना sleep
sona *v.i.* सोना slumber
sone ke liye patri *n* सोने के लिये पटरी bunk
soodkhor *n.* सूदखोर usurer
soodkhori *n.* सूदखोरी usury
sookha *n* सूखा drought
sookhi ghaas *n.* सूखी घास hay
soonghna *v.t.* सूंघना smell
sota hua *adv.* सोता हुआ asleep
spain ka *a.* स्पेन का Spanish
spain ka nivasi *n.* स्पेन का निवासी Spaniard
spain ki bhasha *n.* स्पेन की भाषा Spanish
spanj *n.* स्पंज sponge
sparsh *n* स्पर्श touch
sparsh karna *v.t.* स्पर्श करना touch
sparsh yogya *a.* स्पर्श योग्य tactile
sparshaniya *a.* स्पर्शनीय palpable
sparshjya *n.* स्पर्शज्या tangent
sparshniya *a.* स्पर्शनीय tangible

spash+D3379twadi *a* स्पष्टवादी downright
spasht *a.* स्पष्ट articulate
spasht *a.* स्पष्ट obvious
spasht *a.* स्पष्ट patent
spasht karna *v. t* स्पष्ट करना clarify
spasht rup se *adv* स्पष्ट रूप से clearly
spashta karna *v. t* स्पष्ट करना elucidate
spashtikaran *n* स्पष्टीकरण clarification
spashti-karan *n* स्पष्ट करना explanation
spast roop se *adv.* स्पष्ट रूप से outright
spastwadi *a.* स्पष्टवादी outspoken
squadran *n.* स्क्वाड्रन squadron
srimaan *n.* श्रीमान mister
stabdha karna *v. t* स्तब्ध करना daze
stabdhata *n* स्तब्धता daze
stambh *n.* स्तंभ column
stanagra *n.* स्तनाग्र nipple
stanagra *n.* स्तनाग्र teat
stanpan karana *v.t.* स्तनपान कराना suckle
station *n.* स्टेशन station
stethoscope *n.* स्टैथौस्कोप stethoscope
sthagan *n.* स्थगन adjournment
sthagan *n.* स्थगन postponener
sthagit karna *v.t.* स्थगित करना adjourn
sthaitiki *n.* स्थैतिकी statics
sthal *n.* स्थल place
sthalakriti *n.* स्थलाकृति topography
sthalakriti visheshagya *n.* स्थलाकृति विशेषज्ञ topographer
sthalakritik *a.* स्थलाकृतिक topographical
sthan *n.* स्थान locality
sthan *n.* स्थान location
sthan *n.* स्थान position
sthan *n.* स्थान quarter
sthan *n.* स्थान site
sthan lena *v.t.* स्थान लेना supersede
sthan rakhna *v.t.* स्थान रखना rank
sthan se jodna *v.t.* स्थान से जोड़ना locate
sthan vishayak *a.* स्थान विषयक spatial

sthananataran *n.* स्थानांतरण transfer

sthanantaraniya *a.* स्थानांतरणीय transferable

sthanantarit karana *v.t.* स्थानांतरित करना shift

sthanantarit karna *v.t.* स्थानांतरित करना transfer

sthanapann *n.* स्थानापन्न substitute

sthanapann *a.* स्थानापन्न vicarious

sthaniya *a.* स्थानीय local

sthaniya banana *v.t.* स्थानीय बनाना localize

sthanpaye *n.* स्तनपायी mammal

sthansambandhi *a.* स्तन संबंधी mammary

sthapana *n* स्थापना establishment

sthapit karna *v. t.* स्थापित करना establish

sthayitva *n.* स्थायित्व stability

sthir *a* स्थिर constant

sthir *a.* स्थिर stable

sthir *a.* स्थिर stagnant

sthir *n.* स्थिर static

sthir *a.* स्थिर stationary

sthir *a.* स्थिर still

sthir banana *v.t.* स्थिर बनाना stabilize

sthir hona *v.i.* स्थिर होना rest

sthir kaal se purve ka samay *n* स्थिर काल से पूर्व का समय antedate

sthir karna *vt* स्थिर करना fix

sthir karna *v.t.* स्थिर करना peg

sthir karna *v.t.* स्थिर करना quiet

sthirikaran *n.* स्थिरीकरण stabilization

sthirta *n.* स्थिरता permanence

sthirta *n.* स्थिरता stillness

sthulkaya *a.* स्थूलकाय stout

stool *n.* स्टूल stool

stotra sangreh *n.* स्तोत्र संग्रह breviary

stove *n.* स्टोव stove

strav *n.* स्त्राव secretion

stravit karna *v.t.* स्त्रावित करना secrete

stri jati *a* स्त्री जाति female

stri-jatiya *a* स्त्री-जाति feminine

stuti *n.* स्तुति hymn

suar *n* सूअर boar

suar *n.* सूअर swine

suar ka mans *n.* सुअर का मांस pork

suar ki charbi *n.* सुअर की चरबी lard

suawsar *n.* सुअवसर opportunity

subah *n.* सुबह morning

subakna *v.i.* सुबकना sob

subhankar tabiz *n.* शुभंकर ताबीज़ mascot

subki *n* सुबकी sob

subodh *a.* सुबोध intelligible

suchak *n.* सूचक indicator

suchana *n.* सूचना intimation

suchana dena *v.t.* सूचना देना intimate

suchi *n.* सूची index

suchibadh karna *v.t.* सूचीबद्ध करना list

suchipatra *n.* सूचीपत्र catalogue

suchipatra *n.* सूचीपत्र list

suchit karna *v.t.* सूचित करना apprise

suchit karna *v. t* सूचित करना communicate

suchit karna *v. t.* सूचित करना convey

suchna *n.* सूचना communication

suchna *n.* सूचना note

suchna *a.* सूचना notice

suchna dena *v.t.* सूचना देना inform

suchna dena *v.t.* सूचना देना notify

suchnapurna *a.* सूचनापूर्ण informative

sudhaar *n* सुधार redress

sudhaar *n.* सुधार reform

sudhaar *n.* सुधार reformation

sudhaarna *v. t* सुधारना better

sudhar *n.* सुधार amelioration

sudhar *n.* सुधार amendment

sudhar *n* सुधार betterment

sudhar *n.* सुधार improvement

sudhar *n* सुधार reclamation

sudhar *n.* सुधार regeneration

sudhar *n* सुधार uplift

sudhar greha *n.* सुधार गृह reformatory

sudharak *n.* सुधारक reformer

sudharana *v.t.* सुधारना reclaim

sudharatmak *a* सुधारात्मक reformatory

sudharna *v.t.* सुधारना ameliorate

sudharna *v.t.* सुधारना improve

sudharna *v.t.* सुधारना meliorate

sudharna *v.t.* सुधारना reform

sudharna *v.t.* सुधारना regenerate

sudhridhikaran *n.* सुदृढ़ीकरण
reinforcement

sudridh banana *v.t.* सुदृढ़ बनाना reinforce

sugam *a* सुगम facile

sugandh *n* सुगंध flavour

sugandh *n.* सुगंध incense

sugandh *n.* सुगंध perfume

sugandh *n.* सुगंध scent

sugandhi *a.* सुगंधि odorous

sugandhit *a.* सुगंधित fragrant

sugandhit karna *v.t.* सुगंधित करना
incense

sugandith karna *v.t.* सुगंधित करना
perfume

sugharh *a.* सुघड़ shapely

sui lagana *n.* सूई लगाना injection

sujhao *n.* सुझाव proposal

sukh kar सुखकर cosy

sukh se *adv.* सुख से readily

sukha *a* सूखा dry

sukha angur *n.* सूखा अंगूर currant

sukha rog *n.* सूखा रोग rickets

sukha rogi *a.* सूखा रोगी rickety

sukhad *a.* सुखद welcome

sukhane ka karya *n* सुखाने का कार्य
rarefaction

sukhna *v. i.* सूखना dry

suksham tarang *n.* सूक्ष्म तरंग microwave

sukshamdarshi yantra *n.* सूक्ष्मदर्शी यंत्र
microscope

sukshm janch *n.* सूक्ष्म जांच scrutiny

sukshm parikshan karna *v.t.* सूक्ष्म
परीक्षण करना scan

sulagna *v.i.* सुलगना smoulder

sumirani *n.* सुमिरनी rosary

sunamya *a.* सुनम्य supple

sunana *v.t.* सुनाना recite

sundar *a* सुंदर beautiful

sundar *adj* सुन्दर celestial

sundar *a* सुंदर fair

sundar *a.* सुंदर gallant

sundar *a.* सुंदर handsome

sundar *a.* सुंदर lovely

sundar *a* सुंदर pretty

sundari *n* सुंदरी belle

sundarta *n.* सुंदरता prettiness

sunderta *n* सुन्दरता elegance

sunghana *v.* सूंघाना nuzzle

sunghani *n.* सूंघनी snuff

sunhara *a.* सुनहरा gilt

sunhara *a.* सुनहरा golden

sunishchit *a.* सुनिश्चित categorical

sunishchit karna सुनिश्चित करना ensure

sunishchit karna *v.t.* सुनिश्चित करना
insure

sunn *a.* सुन्न numb

supari ka vriksh *n* सुपारी का वृक्ष areca

suparichit *a.* सुपरिचित well-known

supathya *a.* सुपाठ्य legible

supathya rup mein *adv.* सुपाठ्य रूप में
legibly

supurd karna *v. t.* सुपुर्द करना consign

suraag *n.* सुराग़ clew, clue

suraakh *n* सूराख eyelet

surag pa lena *v.t.* सुराग़ पा लेना trace

suragaya, chamar *n.* सुरागाय, चमर yak

surahi *n* सुराही flask

suraksha *n.* सुरक्षा safety

suraksha *n.* सुरक्षा security

surakshatmak *adv.* सुरक्षात्मक defensive

surakshit *a.* सुरक्षित safe

surakshit *a.* सुरक्षित scot-free

surakshit *a.* सुरक्षित secure

surakshit karna *v.t.* सुरक्षित करना secure

**surakshit rakhna** *v. t* सुरक्षित रखना conserve

**surakshit rakhna** *v.t.* सुरक्षित रखना save

**surang** *n.* सुरंग tunnel

**surang banana** *v.t.* सुरंग बनाना undermine

**surang banana** *v.i.* सुरंग बनाना tunnel

**sureela** *a.* सुरीला melodious

**surhak** *n* सुड़क sniff

**surilapan** *n.* सुरीलापन symphony

**surya** *n.* सूर्य sun

**susabhya** *a.* सुसभ्य urbane

**susangat** *a* सुसंगत coherent

**sushil** *adj.* सुशील complaisant

**sushilta** *n.* सुशीलता amiability

**sushri** *n..* सुश्री missus

**suspasht** *a.* सुस्पष्ट evident

**suspasht** *a.* सुस्पष्ट explicit

**sust** *n.* सुस्ती lethargy

**sust** *n.* सुस्त sluggard

**sust rehna** *v.i.* सुस्त रहना laze

**su-svabhav** *a.* सु-सुभाव nice

**suswad** *a.* सुस्वाद luscious

**sut** *n.* सूत yarn

**sutrabadh karna** *v.t* सूत्रबद्घ करना formulate

**sutrapaat karna** *v.t.* सूत्रपात करना initiate

**suuksmmaape** *n.* सूक्ष्ममापी micrometer

**suvas** *n.* सुवास fragrance

**suvidha** *n.* सुविधा convenience

**suvidha** *n* सुविधा facility

**suvidha dena** *v. t* सुविधा देना ease

**suvidha janak** *a* सुविधा जनक convenient

**suvidhajanak** *a.* सुविधाजनक handy

**suvyavastha** *n.* सुव्यवस्था harmony

**suvyavasthit** *a.* सुव्यवस्थित tidy

**suvyavasthit karna** *v.t.* सुव्यवस्थित करना systematize

**suvyavasthit karna** *v.t.* सुव्यवस्थित करना tidy

**suvyavstha** *n.* सर्वश्रेष्ठा orderly

**suwaywasthit** *a.* सुव्यवस्थित methodical

**svabhavik** *a.* स्वाभाविक temperamental

**svabhavikta** *n.* स्वाभाविकता spontaneity

**svachata** *n.* स्वच्छता, सुव्यवस्था tidiness

**svachhata** *n* स्वच्छता cleanliness

**svad** *n.* स्वाद taste

**svadisht** *a* स्वादिष्ट delicious

**svadisht** *a.* स्वादिष्ट tasty

**svadisht** *a.* स्वादिष्ट toothsome

**svadisht khadya** *n.* स्वादिष्ट खाद्य dainty

**svadosh svikar** *n.* स्वदोष-स्वीकार apology

**svagat kaksh** *n.* स्वागत कक्ष saloon

**svagat karna** *v.t* स्वागत करना welcome

**svaicha se** *adv.* स्वेच्छा से voluntarily

**svaichik** *a.* स्वैच्छिक spontaneous

**svaichik** *a.* स्वैच्छिक voluntary

**svang bharna** *v.i* स्वांग भरना mime

**svapan** *n* स्वप्न dream

**svapan dekhna** *v. i.* स्वप्न देखना dream

**svapan drishta** *n.* स्वप्न दृष्टा visionary

**svar** *n* स्वर accent

**svar** *n.* स्वर tone

**svar** *n.* स्वर vowel

**svarn shuddhta ka map** *n.* स्वर्ण शुद्धता का माप carat

**svarnapind** *n.* स्वर्णपिंड nugget

**svarochaaran karna** *v.t* स्वरोच्चारण करना accent

**svasthavardhak aushadhi** *n.* स्वास्थ्यवर्धक औषधि tonic

**svasthya sambandhi** *a.* स्वास्थ्य संबंधी hygienic

**svasthya vigyaan** *n.* स्वास्थ्य विज्ञान hygiene

**svayamsevak** *n.* स्वयंसेवक volunteer

**svayat** *a* स्वायत्त autonomous

**svayattikaran** *n.* स्वायत्ती करण appropriation

**svecha se dena** *v.t.* स्वेच्छा से देना volunteer

**svechachari** *a.* स्वेच्छाचारी headstrong

sveekar karna *v.t.* स्वीकार करना accept
svikar karna स्वीकार करना admit
svikar karna *v. t.* स्वीकार करना confess
svikar karna *v.t.* स्वीकार करना consent
svikarya *a.* स्वीकार्य admissible
svikriti *n* स्वीकृति acceptance
swaad *n.* स्वाद smack
swad *n* स्वाद relish
swad *n.* स्वाद savour
swad lena *v.t.* स्वाद लेना relish
swadesh bhejna *v.t.* स्वदेश भेजना repatriate
swadeshya *a.* सोद्देश्य intentional
swadhhinta *n.* स्वादहीनता insipidity
swadisht *a.* स्वादिष्ट palatable
swadisht hona *v.t.* स्वादिष्ट होना savour
swagat *n.* स्वागत reception
swagat *n.* स्वगत soliloquy
swami *n.* स्वामी owner
swami *n.* स्वामी proprietor
swami *n.* स्वामी master
swamijnochit *a.* स्वामिजनोचित masterly
swamitwa *n.* स्वामित्व ownership
swar *n.* स्वर organ
swar shastra *n.* स्वर शास्त्र phonetics
swarg *n.* स्वर्ग heaven
swarnakar *n.* स्वर्णकार goldsmith
swarthi *a.* स्वार्थी selfish
swarth-rahit *a.* स्वार्थरहित selfless
swasth *v.t* स्वस्थ fit
swasth chit ka *a.* स्वस्थ चित्त का sane
swastha *a.* स्वस्थ healthy
swastha *a.* स्वस्थ well
swatantra *a.* स्वतंत्र independent
swatantrata *n.* स्वतंत्रता freedom
swatantrata *n.* स्वतंत्रता liberty
swayam *pron.* स्वयं myself
sweater *n.* स्वेटर sweater
swikaar karna *v.t.* स्वीकार करना receive
swikriti *n* स्वीकृति placet
switch *n.* स्विच switch

switzerland ka nivasi *n.* स्विट्ज़रलैंड का निवासी Swiss
swtantrata *n.* स्वतंत्रता independence
syahi *n.* स्याही ink

# T

taabut *n* ताबूत coffin
taak jhaank karna *v.i.* ताक झांक करना pry
taak par rakhana *v.t.* ताक पर रखना shelve
taakna *v.t.* ताकना ogle
taal *b.* ताल rhythm
taal dena *v.t.* तल देना parry
taal matol *n* टाल मटोल evasion
taalbadh *a.* तालबद्ध rhythmic
taalmatol *n.* टालमटोल procrastination
taal-matol *n.* छेकान parry
taalmatol karna *v.i.* टालमटोल करना procrastinate
taalna *v. t* टालना elude
taalu *n.* तालु palate
taalu sambandhi *a.* तालु संबंधी palatal
taan vishayak *a.* तान विषयक tonic
taanbadh karna *v.t.* तानबद्ध करना tone
taand *n.* टांड shelf
taang *n.* तंग leg
taapman *n.* तापमान temperature
taapman ka maap *n.* तापमान का माप calorie
taapmapi *n.* तापमापी thermometer
taar *n.* तार chord
taar *n.* तार wire
taar dwara bhejana *v.t.* तार द्वारा भेजना telegraph
taar dwara preshit *a.* तार द्वारा प्रेषित telegraphic
taar sandesh *n.* तार संदेश telegram

**taar yantra** *n.* तार यंत्र telegraph
**taar yantrik** *n.* तार यांत्रिक telegraphist
**taarak chinha** *n.* तारक चिन्ह asterisk
**taarkoal** *n.* तारकोल pitch
**taarpin** *n.* तारपीन turpentine
**taarsanchar** *n.* तारसंचार telegraphy
**taash ka ikka** *n* ताश का इक्का ace
**taash ka patta** *n.* ताश का पत्ता card
**taaza** *a.* ताज़ा recent
**tab se ab tak** *adv.* तब से अब तक since
**tabeez** *n.* ताबीज़ amulet
**tadantar** *adv.* तदंनतर thereafter
**tadanusar** *adv.* तद् नुसार accordingly
**taha ka nisan** *n* तह का निशान crease
**tahakhana** *n.* तहख़ाना basement
**tahakhana** *n* तहख़ाना cellar
**tahakhana** *n.* तहख़ाना vault
**tahalna** *v.i.* टहलना stroll
**tahani** *n* टहनी shoot
**tahani** *n.* टहनी sprig
**tahani** *n.* टहनी twig
**tahas nahas karna** *v.t.* तहस नहस करना ravage
**tainaat karna** *v.t.* तैनात करना station
**tairak** *n.* तैराक swimmer
**tairaki** *n* तैराकी swim
**tairana** *v.i.* तैरना swim
**tairane wala** *a* तैरने वाला natant
**taiyar** *a.* तैयार ready
**taiyari karna** *v.i.* तैयारी करना provide
**taiyyar karna** *v.t.* तैयार करना prepare
**tak** *prep.* तक until
**takha** *n.* ताखा corbel
**takhna** *n.* टखना ankle
**takht** *n.* तख़्त board
**takhta palat** *n.* ताकता पलट coup
**takhta ulat jana** *v.t.* तख़्ता उलट देना overthrow
**takhte lagana** *v.t.* तख़्ते लगाना plank
**taki** *adv.* ताकि that
**takiya** *n* तकिया pillow

**takiya lagana** *v.t.* तकिया लगाना pillow
**takkar maarna** *v.t.* टक्कर मारना ram
**takla** *n.* तकला spindle
**takneek jananevala** *n.* तकनीक जाननेवाला technician
**takniki** *n.* तकनीकी technical
**taksaal** *n* टकसाल mint
**taktaki** *n* टकटकी gaze
**taktaki** *n.* टकटकी stare
**tala hua** *n* टाला हुआ fry
**tala lagana** *v.t* ताला लगाना lock
**talaak** *n* तलाक divorce
**talaak dena** *v. t* तलाक देना divorce
**talash karna** *v.i* तलाश करना fish
**talash karna** *vt* तलाश करना fossick
**talashna** *v.t.* तलाशना grope
**talchat** *n.* तलछट sediment
**taledaar almarhi** *n.* तालेदार अलमारी locker
**tali bajana** *v. i.* ताली बजाना clap
**talika badh** *a.* तालिकाबद्घ tabular
**talikabadh karna** *v.t.* तालिकाबद्घ करना tabulate
**talla** *n.* तल्ला sole
**talla lagana** *v.t* तल्ला लगाना sole
**tallin karna** *v.t.* तल्लीन करना preoccupy
**talna** *v. t* टालना evade
**talna** *v.t.* टालना postpone
**talwar** *n* तलवार brand
**talwar** *n.* तलवार sabre
**talwar** *n.* तलवार sword
**talwar ghopna** *v.i* तलवार घोंपना lunge
**talwar ka war** *n.* तलवार का वार lunge
**tamacha** *n* तमाचा cuff
**tamacha maarana** *v.t.* तमाचा मारना slap
**tamacha maarna** *v. t* तमाचा मारना cuff
**tamasha** *n* तमाशा farce
**tamatar** *n.* टमाटर tomato
**tamba** *n* तांबा copper
**tambaku** *n.* तंबाकू tobacco
**tambu** *n.* तंबू lodge

**tambu** *n.* तंबू tent
**tamchini** *n* तामचीनी enamel
**tan** *n.* टन ton
**tana** *n* ताना gibe
**tana** *n.* ताना scoff
**tana** *n* ताना taunt
**tana maarna** *v.t.* ताना मारना taunt
**tana marna** *v.i.* ताना मारना gibe
**tanashah** *n.* तानाशाह tyrant
**tanashaha** *n* तानाशाह dictator
**tanashahi** *n.* तानाशाही tyranny
**tandrik jvar** *n.* तंद्रिक ज्वर typhus
**tang** *a.* तंग narrow
**tang karna** *v.t.* तंग करना bait
**tang karna** *v.t.* तंग करना harass
**tang karna** *v.t.* तंग करना molest
**tang karna** *v.t.* तंग करना oppress
**tang karna** *v.t.* तंग करना vex
**tanka** *n.* टांका solder
**tankak** *n.* टंकक typist
**tanke se jodna** *v.t.* टांके से जोड़ना solder
**tanki** *n.* टंकी tank
**tankit karna** *v.t.* टंकित करना type
**tanmaya** *a.* तन्मय rapt
**tantra** *n.* तंत्र mechanism
**tantra** *n.* तंत्र network
**tantrika vigyan** *n.* तंत्रिका विज्ञान neurology
**tantrika vigyani** *n.* तंत्रिका विज्ञानी neurologist
**tantu bandh** *n.* संयोजिका commissure
**tapakna** *v.i.* टपकना, trickle
**tapasvi** *n.* तपस्वी ascetic
**tapasyapurna** *a.* तपस्यापूर्ण ascetic
**tapkan** *n* टपकन drip
**tapkana** *v. i* टपकना drip
**tapkana** *v. i* टपकना drop
**tapkana** *v.t.* टपकाना instill
**tapu** *n.* टापू island
**tapu** *n.* टापू isle
**tar karna** *v.t.* तर करना steep

**tara** *n.* तारा star
**taral** *a* तरल fluid
**taral** *a.* तरल liquid
**taramaya** *a.* तारामय starry
**taras khana** *v.t.* तरस खाना pity
**tarazoo mein tolana** *v.t.* तराज़ू में तोलना scale
**tarbooj** *n.* तरबूज़ melon
**tarbooz** *n.* तरबूज़ water-melon
**tarhak** *n* तड़क snap
**tarjani** *n* तर्जनी forefinger
**tark** *n* तर्क contention
**tark karna** *v.i.* तर्क करना reason
**tark prastut karna** *n.* तर्क प्रस्तुत करना argue
**tarkas** *n.* तरकस quiver
**tarkasheel** *a.* तर्कशील reasonable
**tarkol** *n.* तारकोल tar
**tarkol potna** *v.t.* तारकोल पोतना tar
**tarksammat** *a.* तर्कसम्मत logical
**tarksangat** *a.* तर्कसंगत justifiable
**tarksastri** *n.* तर्कशास्त्री logician
**tarkshakti** *n.* तर्कशक्ति rationality
**tarkshastra** *n.* तर्कशास्त्र logic
**tarkshunya** *a.* तर्कशून्य irrational
**tarkwirodh** *a.* तर्कविरूद्घ illogical
**tarsana** *v.t.* तरसाना tantalize
**tarunya** *n.* तारुण्य puberty
**tash ka rami khel** *n.* ताश का रमी खेल rummy
**tashtari** *n* तश्तरी dish
**tashtari** *n.* तश्तरी saucer
**taskar** *n.* तस्कर smuggler
**taskari karna** *v.t.* तस्करी करना smuggle
**tatasthu** *interj.* तथास्तु amen
**tatbandhan** *n* तटबंधन embankment
**tathapi** *conj* तथापि however
**tathapi** *adv.* तथापि though
**tathapi** *conj.* तथापि yet
**tathasth banana** *v.t.* तटस्थ बनाना neutralize

tathyatmak *a.* तथ्यात्मक true

tatitya leharain *n.* तटीय लहरें surf

tatiya *n.* ततैया wasp

tatkaleen *a* तत्कालीन then

tatkalik *a.* तात्कालिक instantaneous

tatpar *a.* तत्पर prompt

tatpar *a.* तत्पर willing

tatparta *n.* तत्परता willingness

tattu *n.* टट्टू nag

tatwamimansa *n.* तत्वमीमांसा metaphysics

tatwarti *a.* तटवर्ती littoral

tauliya *n.* तौलिया towel

tauliye se paunchna *v.t.* तौलिये से पोंछना towel

taveez *n.* तावीज़ talisman

taxi *n.* टैक्सी cab

taxi *n.* टैक्सी taxi

taxi mein jaana *v.i.* टैक्सी में जाना taxi

tay karna *v. t* तय करना determine

taza *a.* ताज़ा new

tedha *a.* टेढ़ा wry

tedha medha *a.* टेढ़ा मेढ़ा sinuous

tedha medha *a.* टेढ़ा मेढ़ा tortuous

tedha medha *a.* टेढ़ा मेढ़ा zigzag

teeka dravya *n.* टीका द्रव्य vaccine

teeka lagana *v.t.* टीका लगाना vaccinate

teeka lagane wala *n.* टीका लगाने वाला vaccinator

teekakaran *n.* टीकाकरण vaccination

teekha *a.* तीखा caustic

teekha *a.* तीखा piquant

teela *n.* टीला hill

teela *n.* टीला hillock

teela *n.* टीला mound

teen *a* तीन three

teen baar *adv.* तीन बार thrice

teen ki sankhya *n.* तीन की संख्या three

teen taaron ka chinha *n.* तीन तारों का चिन्ह asterism

teer *n* तीर arrow

tees *n* तीस smart

tees *a* तीस thirty

tees ki sankhya *n.* तीस की संख्या thirty

tees lagna *v.i* टीस लगना smart

teesra *a.* तीसरा third

teesre sthan par *adv.* तीसरे स्थान पर thirdly

teesvan *a.* तीसवां thirtieth

teesvan bhag *n* तीसवां भाग thirtieth

teh *n* तह bottom

tej daurhna *v.t.* तेज़ दौड़ना outrun

teji se *adv* तेज़ी से fast

tel *n.* तेल oil

tel lagana *v.t* तेल लगाना oil

tel pot *n.* तेल पोत tanker

telephone *n.* टेलिफोन phone

tendua *n.* तेंदुआ leopard

tenis ka balla *n.* टेनिस का बल्ला racket

tennis *n.* टैनिस tennis

terah *a* तेरह thirteen

terah ki sankhya *n.* तेरह की संख्या thirteen

terahawan *a.* तेरहवां thirteenth

tevar *n.* तेवर frown

tez *a.* तेज़ keen

tez daurh *n* तेज़ दौड़ scamper

tez daurhana *v.i* तेज़ दौड़ना race

tez hawa *n.* तेज़ हवा gale

tez karana *v.t.* तेज़ करना sharpen

tez karana *v.t.* तेज़ करना whet

tez raftar *adh* तेज़ रफ्तार outspeed

tez udharv udan *n.* तेज़ ऊर्ध्व उड़ान zoom

tezab *n* तेज़ाब acid

tezi *n.* तेज़ी speed

tezi se bahar nikalna *v.i.* तेज़ी से बाहर निकलना spout

tezi se chalna *v.i.* तेज़ी से चलना speed

tezi se daurana *v.i.* तेज़ी से दौड़ना sprint

tezi se le jana *v.t.* तेज़ी से ले जाना rush

thag *n.* ठग cheat

thag *n.* ठग sharper

thag *n.* झांसिया, ठग swindler

thagana *v.t.* ठगना rook

thagi *n.* ठगी, झांसा swindle

thagna *v. t.* ठगना cheat

thagna *v.t.* ठगना swindle

thah lena *v.t* थाह लेना fathom

thaharav *n.* ठहराव visit

thaharna *v.i.* ठहरना pause

thahrana *v.i.* ठहरना sojourn

thahrav *n.* ठहराव abeyance

thahrav *n* ठहराव sojourn

thahrav *n.* ठहराव stand

thahrav *n* ठहराव stay

thaila *n.* थैला bag

thaila *n.* झोला satchel

thaile *n.* थैली pouch

thaili *n.* थैली wallet

thaka dena *v. t.* थका देना exhaust

thaka jana *v.t.* थक जाना tire

thaka manda *a.* थका मांदा haggard

thaka manda *a.* थका मांदा weary

thakaana *v.t.* थकाना weary

thakan *n* थकान fatigue

thakana *v.t* थकाना fatigue

thakana *v.t. & i* थकना weary

thakau *a.* थकाऊ tiresome

thakka *n.* थक्का clot

thakka banana *v. t* थक्का बनाना clot

than par rakhna *v.t.* थान पर रखना stall

thand *n.* ठंड chill

thanda *a* ठंडा chilly

thanda *a.* ठंडा frigid

thanda *a.* ठंडा wintry

thanda hona *v. i.* ठंडा होना cool

thapki *n* थपकी pat

thapthapna *v.t.* थपथपाना pat

tharmas *n.* थर्मस thermos (flask)

thasathas bhar dena *v.t.* ठसाठस भर देना throng

thathera *n.* ठठेरा tinker

theek *a.* ठीक accurate

theek *a* ठीक exact

theek hona *v.i.* ठीक होना heal

theek karna *v.t.* ठीक करना mend

theek karna *v.t.* ठीक करना modulate

theek prakar se *adv.* ठीक प्रकार से aright

theek samay se *adv.* ठीक समय से sharp

thekedar *n* ठेकेदार contractor

thela *n.* ठेला lorry

thela *n.* ठेला, धक्का shove

thelna *v.t.* ठेलना propel

thik karana *v.t* ठीक करना remedy

thikaana *n* ठिकाना nest

thoda *a.* थोड़ा meagre

thok bikri *n.* थोक बिक्री wholesale

thok mein *adv.* थोक में wholesale

thok sambandhi *a* थोक संबंधी wholesale

thok vyapari *n.* थोक व्यापारी wholesaler

thokar *n.* ठोकर kick

thokar *n.* ठोकर stumble

thokar khana *v.i.* ठोकर खाना stumble

thokare marna *v.t.* ठोकर मारना kick

thopna *v.t.* थोपना inflict

thora se *adv.* थोड़ा सा little

thorha *a.* थोड़ा slight

thorhe se *a* थोड़े से few

thorhi *n.* ठोड़ी chin

thos *a.* ठोस compact

thos *a* ठोस concrete

thos *a.* ठोस solid

thos *a.* ठोस substantial

thos padarth *n* ठोस पदार्थ solid

thos rup dena *v. t* ठोस रूप देना concrete

thuk *n* थूक spit

thuk *n* थूक spittle

thuk *n.* थूक sputum

thukara dena *v.t.* ठुकरा देना spurn

thukna *v.i.* थूकना spit

thuni *n.* थूनी prop

thunskar bharna 2 *v.t.* ठूंसकर भरना stuff

thuthan *n.* थूथन snout

tibra iccha *n.* तीव्र इच्छा longing

**ticket** *n.* टिकट ticket

**ticket sangrahi** *adj* टिकट संग्रहरी philatelist

**tiddi** *n.* टिड्डी locust

**tie** *n* टाई tie

**tiguna** *a.* तिगुना triple

**tiguna** *a.* तिगुना triplicate

**tiguna karna** *v.t.* तिगुना करना triplicate

**tiguna karna** *adj* तिगुना करना triple

**tihayee bhag** *n.* तिहाई भाग third

**tijori** *n* तिजोरी ark

**tijori** *n.* तिजोरी safe

**tik tik karna** *v.i.* टिक टिक करना tick

**tik tik ki dhwani** *n.* टिक टिक की ध्वनि tick

**tika lagana** *v.t.* टीका लगाना inoculate

**tikakaran** *n.* टीकाकरण inoculation

**tika-tippani** *n* टीका टिप्पणी commentary

**tikau** *a* टिकाऊ durable

**tikau** *a.* टिकाऊ lasting

**tikau** *a.* टिकाऊ permanent

**tikha** *a.* तीखा poignant

**tikhapan** *n.* तीखापन poignancy

**tikhapan** *n.* तीखापन pungency

**tikna** *v.i.* टिकना last

**tikshna awaz** *a.* तीक्ष्ण आवाज़ shrill

**tilchatta** *n* तिलचट्टा cockroach

**tilli** *n.* तिल्ली spleen

**timtimahat** *v. t. & i* टिमटिमाहट blink

**timtimahat** *n* टिमटिमाहट flicker

**timtimana** *v.t* टिमटिमाना flicker

**tin** *n.* टिन tin

**tin ka dabba** *n.* टिन का डिब्बा tin

**tin saman dhatu** *n* टीन समान धातु cadmium

**tipahiya cycle** *n.* तिपहिया साइकिल tricycle

**tipayee** *n.* तिपाई tripod

**tippani** *n* टिप्पणी comment

**tippani** *n.* टिप्पणी remark

**tippni** *n.* टिप्पणी observation

**tippni karna** *v. i* टिप्पणी करना comment

**tiranga** *a.* तिरंगा tricolour

**tiraskaar** *n.* तिरस्कार repudiation

**tiraskaarpurna** *a* तिरस्कारपूर्ण contemptuous

**tiraskar** *n.* तिरस्कार scorn

**tiraskar** *n* तिरस्कार sneer

**tircha** *a* तिरछा cross

**tircha** *a.* तिरछा italic

**tircha** *a.* तिरछा oblique

**tircha karna** *v.t.* तिरछा करना slant

**tircha mudran** *n.* तिरछा मुद्रण italics

**tirth mandir** *n.* तीर्थ मंदिर oracle

**tirth sthal** *n.* तीर्थ pilgrimage

**tirthyatri** *n.* तीर्थयात्री pilgrim

**tis par bhi** *conj.* तिस पर भी nevertheless

**tithyankit karna** *v. t* तिथ्यंकित करना date

**titli** *n* तितली butterfly

**tivra** *a.* तीव्र pungent

**tivra** *a.* तीव्र rapid

**tivra** *a.* तीव्र speedy

**tivra** *a.* तीव्र violent

**tivra dhalan wala** *a.* तीव्र ढलान वाला steep

**tivra ichcha** *n* तीव्र इच्छा urge

**tivra kolahal** *n.* तीव्र कोलाहल tumult

**tivra peerha** *n.* तीव्र पीड़ा throe

**tivra prakash** *n.* तीव्र प्रकाश limelight

**tivra vridhi** *n.* तीव्र बृद्घि proliferation

**tivra, tatper** *a.* तीव्र, तत्पर swift

**tivrata** *n.* तीव्रता rapidity

**tivrata** *n.* तीव्रता tenacity

**tivrata** *n.* तीव्रता vehemence

**todna,** *v.t.* तोड़ना rupture

**toffee** *n.* टॉफी toffee

**tokari** *n.* टोकरी basket

**tolan** *v.t.* तोलन weigh

**toli** *n.* टोली team

**toli** *n.* टोली troop

**toli mein chalna** *v.i* टोली में चलना troop

**tonsil** *n.* टॉन्सिल tonsil

**tonti** *n.* टोंटी nozzle

tonti *n.* टोंटी tap
toofan *n.* तूफ़ान storm
toofan *n.* तूफ़ान tempest
toofan *n.* तूफ़ान tornado
toofani *a.* तूफ़ानी stormy
toofani *a.* तूफ़ानी tempestuous
tooshak ki kholi *n.* तोषक की खोली quilt
top *n.* तोप cannon
top *n.* टोप hood
top gola *n.* तोप गोला canon
top khana *n.* तोपखाना ordnance
tope *n.* टोप hat
topi *n.* टोपी cap
topi *n* टोपी coif
topi pahanana *v. t.* टोपी पहनाना cap
topkhana *n.* तोपखाना artillery
topkhana *n* तोपखाना battery
tor phor *n.* तोड़फोड़ sabotage
tor phor karna *v.t.* सतोड़ फोड़ करना sabotage
toran *n.* तोरण arch
torh marorh *v. t* तोड़ मरोड़ देना distort
torhna *v. i* तोड़ना crack
torhna *v.t* तोड़ना fracture
torhna *v.t.* तोड़ना pluck
torhne ki kriya *n* तोड़ने की क्रिया breakage
tota *n.* तोता parrot
tractor *n.* ट्रैक्टर tractor
tramgarhi *n.* ट्रामगाड़ी tram
trasadikar *n.* त्रासदीकार tragedian
tray *n.* ट्रे tray
tribhuj *n.* त्रिभुज triangle
tribhujakar *a.* त्रिभुजाकार triangular
trigunan *n.* त्रिगुणन triplication
trijya *n.* त्रिज्या radius
trik *n.* त्रिक trinity
trik *n.* त्रिक trio
trinbhumi *n.* तृणभूमि turf
trin-bhumi *n.* तृणभूमि sod
tripakshiya *a.* त्रिपक्षीय tripartite
tript *a.* तृप्त satiable

tript kar dena *v.t.* तृप्त कर देना satiate
tripti aghav *n.* तृप्ति अघाव satiety
truck *n.* ट्रक truck
tub *n.* टब tub
tufani *a.* तूफ़ानी windy
tuk *n.* तुक rhyme
tukbandi ka khel *n.* तुकबंदी का खेल crambo
tukkarh *n.* तुक्कड़ poetaster
tukra *n* टुकड़ा bit
tukrha *n* टुकड़ा crumb
tukrha *n.* टुकड़ा stump
tukrhe tukrhe karna *v. t* टुकड़े टुकड़े करना crumble
tulna karna *v. t* तुलना करना compare
tulna karna *v.t.* तुलना करना liken
tulnaatmak *a* तुलनात्मक comparative
tulsi *n.* तुलसी basil
turahi *n.* तुरही trumpet
turahi *n.* तुरही clarion
turahi banana *v.i.* तुरही बजाना trumpet
turant *adv.* तुरंत forthwith
turant *a* तुरंत immediate
turant *adv.* तुरंत instantly
turant *adv.* तुरंत straightway
turant *adv.* तुरंत summarily
turbine *n.* टरबाइन turbine
turup *n.* तुरुप trump
tushar *n.* तुषार frost
tutlahat *n* तुतलाहट lisp
tutlana *v.t.* तुतलाना lisp
tutne-yogya *a.* टूटने-योग्य brittle
tvacha *n.* त्वचा skin
tyag *n* त्याग abnegation
tyag dena *v.t.* त्याग देना abandon
tyag dena *v.t* त्याग देना forgo
tyag dena *v.t.* त्याग देना forsake
tyag dena *v.t.* त्याग देना relinquish
tyag karna *v. t* त्याग करना abnegate
tyagna *v.t,* त्यागना abdicate
tyori chadhna *v.i.* त्योरी चढ़ाना scowl
tyre *n.* टायर tyre

# U

ubalna *v.i.* उबलना simmer

ubalna *v.i.* उबलना boil

ubalna *v.i.* उबलना seethe

ubane ya thakane wala *a.* उबाऊ या उकताने वाला tedious

ubarh khabarh *a.* ऊबड़खाबड़ rough

ubharana *v.t.* उभारना stimulate

uccha *a.* उच्च superior

ucchalana *v.t.* उछालना hurl

ucchalkud karna *v.i.* उछलकूद करना frolic

uccharan *n.* उच्चारण pronunciation

ucchata *n* उच्चता eminence

ucchit *a.* उचित good

ucchit *a.* उचित just

ucchit *a.* उचित proper

ucchit pramanit karna *v.t.* उचित प्रमाणित करना justify

ucchit rup mein *adv.* उचित रूप में justly

uchaal *n* उछाल skip

uchakankshi vyakti *n.* उच्चाकांक्षी व्यक्ति aspirant

uchakka *n* उचक्का sneak

uchal *n* उछाल spring

uchal kud *n.* उछल कूद romp

uchalana *n.* उच्छलन rebound

ucharan ikayee *n.* उच्चारण इकाई syllable

uchayee *n.* ऊँचाई altitude

uchchal *n* उछाल toss

uchchata *n.* उच्चता supremacy

uchhal wala *adj* उछाल वाला bumpy

uchhalna *v.i.* उछलना spring

uchit *a.* उचित advisable

uchit *a* उचित due

uchit *a.* उचित opportune

uchit *a.* उचित pertinence

uchit *a.* उचित suitable

uchit *adv* उचित pat

uchit riti se *adv* उचित रीति से appositely

uchit riti se *adv* उचित रीति से aright

uchit,vaidh *a.* उचित, वैध valid

udaar *a.* उदार large

udaar *a.* उधार liberal

udaar *a.* उदार philanthropic

udaarta *n.* उदारता lenience, leniency

udaas *a.* उदास moody

udaas *a.* उदास morose

udaas hona *v.i.* उदास होना mope

udaat banana *v. t.* उदात्त बनाना ennoble

udaatt *a.* उदात्त sublime

udaharan *n* उदाहरण example

udar *a.* उदार chivalrous

udarhridayata *n.* उदारहृदयता magnanimity

udarta *n.* उदारता generosity

udarta *n.* उदारता liberality

udarta *n.* उदारता prodigality

udarvad *n.* उदारवाद liberalism

udas *a* उदास cheerless

udas *a* उदास dull

udas *a.* उदास gloomy

udas *a.* उदास woebegone

udas karna *v. t* उदास करना depress

udashin *a.* उदासीन listless

udasi *n* उदासी depression

udasi *n.* उदासी gloom

udasin *a.* उदासीन indifferent

udasinta *n.* उदासीनता apathy

udasinta *n.* उदासीनता indifference

udasinta *n.* उदासीनता nonchalance

udattata *n.* उदात्तता sublimity

udattikaran karna *v.t.* उदात्तीकरण करना sublimate

uday *n* उदय appearance

uday *n.* उदय rise

uddarta *n.* उदारता goodness

uddeshya rakhna *v.t.* उद्देश्य रखना purpose

uddhami *a.* उद्यमी painstaking

uddhar *n.* उधार loan

uddhar dena *v.t.* उधार देना loan

udeshyahin *a.* उदेश्यहीन wanton

udgam *n.* उद्गम source

udghatan *n.* उद्घाटन inauguration

udha dena *v.t.* उड़ा देना squander

udhaar *n.* उधार advance

udhahran *n.* उदाहरण illustration

udhar *n* उधार debt

udhar *n* उधार due

udhar dena *v.t.* उधार देना lend

udhar lena *v. t* उधार लेना borrow

udhbilaav *n.* ऊदबिलाव otter

udhghoshak *n.* उद्घोषक herald

udjan *n.* उदजन hydrogen

udna *v.i* उड़ना fly

udyaan *n.* उद्यान garden

udyaan *n* उद्यान park

udyg *n.* उद्योग industry

ugaana *v.t.* उगाना grow

ugra *a.* उग्र furious

ugra krantikari *a* उग्र क्रांतिकारी extreme

ugrata *n.* उग्रता turbulence

ukhadana *v.t.* उखाड़ना pull

ukharhna *v.t.* उखाड़ना uproot

uksaana *v.t.* उकसाना irritate

uksaav *n.* उकसाव abetment

uksana *v.t.* उकसाना abet

uksana *v.t.* उकसाना instigate

uksana *v.t.* उकसाना persuade

uktti *n.* उक्ति maxim

ulanghan *n.* उल्लंघन violation

ulanghan karna *v.t.* उल्लंघन करना infringe

ulat dena *v.t.* उलट देना subvert

ulat jaana *v.i.* उलट जाना topple

ulat jana *v. i.* उलट जाना capsize

ulat pulat sthiti mein *adv* उलट पुलट स्थिति में topsy turvy

ulatna *v.t.* उलटना upset

ulekhaniya *a.* उल्लेखनीय signal

uljalul bate karna *v.i.* ऊलजलूल बातें करना gabble

uljhan *n.* उलझन complication

uljhan *n.* उलझन labyrinth

uljhan *n.* उलझन puzzle

uljhan *n.* उलझन tangle

uljhan may dalna *v. t* उलझन में डालना bewilder

uljhana *v. t* उलझाना complicate

uljhana *v.t.* उलझाना tangle

uljhav *n.* उलझाव implication

ulka *n.* उल्का meteor

ullasamai *a* उल्लासमय festive

ullasit *a.* उल्लसित hilarious

ullasit *a.* उल्लसित jubilant

ullasit hona *v. i* उल्लसित होना exult

ullaspurna *a.* उल्लासपूर्ण jovial

ullekh *n.* उल्लेख mention

ullekhaniya *a.* उल्लेखनीय appreciable

ullekhniya *a.* उल्लेखनीय notable

ullekhniya *a.* उल्लेखनीय noteworthy

ullu *n.* उल्लू owl

ullu ki boli *n.* उल्लू की बोली hoot

ultaav *n.* उल्टाव reversal

umarhna *v.i.* उमड़ना teem

umarna *v.i* उमड़ना flow

umasdar *a.* उमसदार sultry

uncha *a.* ऊँचा high

uncha karna *v.t.* ऊंचा करना heighten

uncha uthna *v.i.* ऊंचा उठना tower

unchai *n.* ऊँचाई height

unchayee *n* ऊंचाई elevation

unchi awaz may *adv.* ऊँची आवाज़ में aloud

unchi urhaan bharna *v.i.* ऊंची उड़ान भरना soar

unghana *v. i* ऊँघना doze

ungli *n* उंगली digit

ungli *n* उंगली finger

ungliyo se chuna *v.t* उंगलियों से छूना finger

**uni kaprha** *n* ऊनी कपड़ा flannel
**unidrapan** *n.* उनींदापन narcosis
**uninda** *a.* उनींदा sleepy
**unka** *a.* उनका their
**unka** *pron.* उनका theirs
**unko** *pron.* उनको them
**unmaad** *n.* उन्माद frenzy
**unmaad** *n.* उन्माद hysteria
**unmat** *a.* उन्मत्त
hysterical
**unmulan** *v* उन्मूलन abolition
**unmulan karna** *v.t* उन्मूलन करना abolish
**unmulan karna** *v. t* उन्मूलन करना
eradicate
**unnis** *n.* उन्नीस nineteen
**unnisvan** *a.* उन्नीसवां nineteenth
**unt** *n.* ऊँट camel
**untkataara** *n.* ऊंटकटारा thistle
**up patni** *n* उपपत्नी concubine
**upadhik** *a.* औपाधिक titular
**upahar** *n.* उपहार largess
**upahas karna** *v.i.* उपहास करना scoff
**upaj** *n* उपज yield
**upantika** *n.* उपांतिका lobby
**upantrashool** *n.* उपांत्रशूल appendicitis
**upar** *adv* ऊपर above
**upar** *prep.* ऊपर over
**upar chadhna** *v.i.* ऊपर चढ़ना scramble
**upar faila hona** *v.t.* ऊपर फैला होना span
**upar jana** *v.t.* ऊपर जाना ascend
**upar ki aur** *adv.* ऊपर की ओर up
**upar ki aur** *adv.* ऊपर की ओर upwards
**upar uthana** *v.i.* ऊपर उठना arise
**upar uthana** *v.t.* ऊपर उठाना hoist
**upar wala** *a.* ऊपर वाला upper
**uparjan karna** *v. t* अर्जन करना earn
**upasthith** *n.* उपस्थिति attendance
**upasthiti** *n.* उपस्थिति presence
**upaya** *n.* उपाय remedy
**upaya karna** *v.t.* उपाय करना redress
**upaya kushal** *a.* उपाय कुशल resourceful

**upbhasha** *n* उपभाषा dialect
**upbhawan** *n.* उपभवन outhouse
**upchaari** *a.* उपचारी remedial
**upchar karna** *v. t.* उपचार करना cure
**up-chunav** *n* उप-चुनाव by-election
**updaan** *n.* उपदान gratuity
**updesh** *n.* उपदेश precept
**updeshatmak** *a* उपदेशात्मक didactic
**updeshpurna kahani** *n* उपदेशपूर्ण कहानी
apologue
**updrava** *n.* उपद्रव uprising
**updravi** *a.* उपद्रवी unruly
**upekchha karna** *v.t.* उपेक्षा करना neglect
**upeksha** *n* उपेक्षा neglect
**upeksha** *n.* उपेक्षा negligence
**upeksha karna** *v. t* उपेक्षा करना disregard
**upeksha karna** *v.t.* उपेक्षा करना ignore
**upgreha** *n.* उपग्रह satellite
**uphaas** *n.* उपहास ridicule
**uphar** *n* उपहार bounty
**uphar** *n.* उपहार gift
**uphar** *n.* उपहार offering
**uphar pradan karna** *n.* उपहार प्रदान
करना presentation
**uphas karna** *v.t.* उपहास करना ridicule
**upkaar** *n.* उपकार benefaction
**upkaran** *n.* उपकरण apparatus
**upkaran** *n.* उपकरण appliance
**upkaran** *n.* उपकरण implement
**upkram** *n* उपक्रम enterprise
**upmaa** *n.* उपमा simile
**upmarg** *n* उपमार्ग bypass
**upnaam** *n.* उपनाम alias
**upnaam** *n.* उपनाम nickname
**upnagariya** *a.* उपनगरीय suburban
**upnagariya kshetra** *n.* उपनगरीय क्षेत्र
suburb
**upnam dena** *v.t.* उपनाम देना nickname
**upnayas** *n* उपन्यास novel
**upnayaskar** *n.* उपन्यासकार novelist
**upnivesh** *n* उपनिवेश colony

upnivesh n उपनिवेश dominion
upniveshak a औपनिवेशिक colonial
upniveshi n. उपनिवेशी settler
upniyam n उपनियम bye-law
uppar aana v.i ऊपर आना surface
uppar ke aur adv ऊपर की ओर over
uppar se dekhna v.t. ऊपर से देखना
  overlook
uppar uthna v.t. ऊपर उठाना uplift
uppari a. ऊपरी outward
uprayukt a. अप्रयुक्त fresh
uprodhak n. उपरोधक throttle
upsadhan n उपसाधन accessory
upsanhaar n उपसंहार epilogue
upsarga n. उपसर्ग prefix
upsarga lagana v.t. उपसर्ग लगाना prefix
up-shakha n. उप शाखा offshoot
uptopadan n उपोत्पादन by-product
upwas n उपवास fast
upwas karna v.i उपवास करना fast
upyog n उपयोग consumption
upyog n. उपयोग utilization
upyogi a. उपयोगी practical
upyogi a. उपयोगी useful
upyogi a. उपयोगी utilitarian
upyogi a. उपयोगी valuable
upyogi hona v.t. उपयोगी होना avail
upyogita n. उपयोगिता subservience
upyogita n. उपयोगिता value
upyogita n. उपयोगिता worth
upyukt a. उपयुक्त appropriate
upyukt a उपयुक्त becoming
upyukt a उपयुक्त eligible
upyukt a उपयुक्त expedient
upyukt उपयुक्त fit
upyukt a. उपयुक्त likely
upyukt a. उपयुक्त seemly
upyukt banana v.t. उपयुक्त बनाना suit
upyuktata n. उपयुक्तता propriety
upyuktata n. उपयुक्तता suitability
urdhvarvagaami a. उर्ध्वगामी upward

urhati gend par maar v.t. उड़ती गेंद पर
  मार volley
urja n. ऊर्जा energy
urwarta n उर्वरता fertility
us (istri)ka a उस (स्री)का her
us aur, vahan ko adv. उस ओर, वहां को
  thither
us samay adv. उस समय then
ushmiya a. ऊष्मीय thermal
usi tarah adv. उसी तरह likewise
uska pron. उसका his
uske atirikt prep उसके अतिरिक्त but
uske baad adv उसके बाद after
uske baad jab conj. उसके बाद जब after
uske dwara adv. उसके द्वारा thereby
usko pron. उसको him
usne dem. pron. उसने that
ustara n. उस्तरा razor
utaar n. उतार descent
utar jana v. i उतर जाना ebb
utaridhruva-sambandhi n उत्तरीध्रुव-
  संबंधी Arctic
utejit karna v. t उत्तेजित करना excite
utejna adj उत्तेजना gadfly
uthaana v.t. उठाना pick
uthal puthal n. उथल पुथल upheaval
uthana v. t. उठाना carry
uthana v.i. उठाना heave
uthana v. उठना rise
uthkrisht a. उत्कृष्ट pre-eminent
uthkrishta n. उत्कृष्टता pre-eminence
uthla a. उथला shallow
uthpadak a. उत्पादक productive
uthpadakta n. उत्पादकता productivity
uthsahi a उत्साही fervent
utkanthit a. उत्कंठित wistful
utkat ichcha adv. उत्कट इच्छा avidity
utkatata n. उत्कटता intensity
utkeerna karna v. t उत्कीर्ण करना engrave
utkhanan n. उत्खनन excavation
utkrisht a उत्कृष्ट classic

utkrisht *a.* उत्कृष्ट excellent
utkrisht kriti *n* उत्कृष्ट कृति classic
utkrishta *a* उत्कृष्ट fabulous
utkrishtata *n.* उत्कृष्टता excellence
utpaadak *n.* उत्पादक grower
utpaadak *n* उत्पादक manufacturer
utpaat *n.* उत्पाद nuisance
utpadak *adj.* उत्पादक creative
utpadak *n.* उत्पादक generator
utpadan *n.* उत्पादन generation
utpadan *n.* उत्पादन output
utpadan *n.* उत्पादन production
utpadan shulk *n* उत्पादन शुल्क excise
utpatti se purv *adj.* उत्पत्ति से पूर्व antenatal
utpeeran *n.* उत्पीड़न persecution
utradhikaar *n.* उत्तराधिकार inheritance
utradhikar mai pana *v.t.* उत्तराधिकार में पाना inherit
utradhikari *n.* उत्तराधिकारी heir
utsa *n.* उत्साह zeal
utsah *n* उत्साह enthusiasm
utsah *n.* उत्साह mettle
utsah *n.* उत्साह verve
utsah *n.* उत्साह zest
utsah dena *v.t.* उत्साह देना galvanize
utsahi *a.* उत्साही ardent
utsahi *a* उत्साही enthusiastic
utsahi *a.* उत्साही spirited
utsahi *a.* उत्साही zealous
utsahpurna *a.* उत्साहपूर्ण sprightly
utsav *n.* उत्सव celebration
utsav *n.* उत्सव function
utsav gaan *n.* उत्सवगान wassail
utsav manana *v. t. & i.* उत्सव मनाना celebrate
utsuk *adj.* उत्सुक avid
utsukta *n.* उत्सुकता keenness
utsukta se *adv* उत्सुकता से avidly
utsvaagni *n* उत्सवाग्नि bonfire
uttam *a.* उत्तम noble

uttam *a.* उत्तम superb
uttar *n.* उत्तर north
uttar *n* उत्तर reply
uttar *n.* उत्तर response
uttar dena *v.i.* उत्तर देना reply
uttar dena *v.i.* उत्तर देना respond
uttar ki or *adv.* उत्तर की ओर northwards
uttar ki ore ka *adv.* उत्तर की ओर northerly
uttar pashankalin *a.* उत्तर पाषाणकालीन neolithic
uttardayi *a* उत्तरदायी accountable
uttardayi *a.* उत्तरदायी answerable
uttardayi *a.* उत्तरदायी responsible
uttardayitva *n.* उत्तरदायित्व responsibility
uttari *a* उत्तरी north
uttari *a.* उत्तरी northerly
uttari *a.* उत्तरी northern
uttarjeevita *n.* उत्तरजीविता survival
uttejak *a.* उत्तेजक provocative
uttejak padarth *a.* उत्तेजक पदार्थ irritant
uttejana *n* उत्तेजना fermentation
uttejana *n.* उत्तेजना stew
uttejet karna *v. t* उत्तेजित करना commove
uttejit *a.* उत्तेजित frantic
uttejit karna *v.t.* उत्तेजित करना agitate
uttejit karna *v.t.* उत्तेजित करना incite
uttejit karna *v.t.* उत्तेजित करना inflame
uttejit karna *v.i.* उत्तेजित करना rouse
utterdinankit karna *v.t.* उत्तरदिनांकित करना post-date
uttolak *n.* उत्तोलक lever
uttolok ki sakti *n.* उत्तोलक की शक्ति leverage
uttradhikari *n.* उत्तराधिकारी successor
uun *n* ऊन fleece
uunat karna *v. t* उन्नत करना elevate
uwar banana *v.t* उर्वर बनाना fertilize

# V

vaadi *n.* वादी plaintiff

vaad-vivad *n.* वाद-विवाद argument

vaagdan *v. t* वाग्दान करना betroth

vaagdan *n.* वाग्दान betrothal

vaakpatuta *n.* वाक्पटुता rhetoric

vaas karna *v.t.* वास करना inhabit

vaastukar *n.* वास्तुकार architect

vachak *n.* वाचक narrator

vachan *n* वचन aphorism

vachan *n.* वाचन perusal

vachan dena *v.t* वचन देना promise

vachan dena *v.t.* वचन देना undertake

vada *n* वादा promise

vadakvrind *n.* वादकवृंद orchestra

vadh karna *v.t.* वध करना slaughter

vadh karna *v.t.* वध करना slay

vadyavrind rachna *n.* वाद्यवृंद रचना symphony

vadyavrindiya *a.* वाद्यवृंदीय orchestral

vagvidagdh *a.* वाग्विदग्ध witty

vah *a.* वह that

vahak *n.* वाहक carrier

vahan *adv.* वहां there

vahan *n.* वाहन vehicle

vahan ka *a.* वहाँ का yonder

vahan se *adv.* वहां से thence

vahi *a.* वही same

vahi *a.* वही very

vahini *n* वाहिनी battalion

vahini *n.* वाहिनी brigade

vaidh *a.* वैध legitimate

vaidh adhikaar *n.* वैध अधिकार lien

vaidhanik *a.* वैधानिक statutory

vaidhata *n.* वैधता legality

vaidhata *n.* वैधता legitimacy

vaidhata *n.* वैधता validity

vaidhsalla *n.* वैधशाला observatory

vaigyanik *a.* वैज्ञानिक scientific

vaigyanik *n.* वैज्ञानिक scientist

vaikalpik *a.* वैकल्पिक alternative

vaikalpik *a.* वैकल्पिक optional

vair *n* वैर animosity

vairagi *n.* वैरागी stoic

vaishya *n.* वेश्या courtesan

vaishya *n.* वेश्या whore

vaitan *n* वेतन pay

vaivahik *a* वैवाहिक conjugal

vaivahik *a.* वैवाहिक matrimonial

vaivahik *a.* वैवाहिक nuptial

vakalat *n.* वकालत advocacy

vakalat karna *v.i.* वकालत करना plead

vakhtarband sena *n.* वख्तरबंद सेना cavalry

vakil *n* वकील advocate

vakil *n.* वकील barrister

vakil *n.* वकील lawyer

vakil *n.* वकील pleader

vakpatuta *n* वाक्पटुता eloquence

vakra *n* वक्र curve

vakrchal *n.* वाक्छल quibble

vakrchal karna *v.i.* वाक्छल करना quibble

vakrotipurna *a.* वक्रोक्तिपूर्ण ironical

vakya rachna *n.* वाक्य रचना syntax

vakya vigreh *n.* वाक्य-विग्रह analysis

vakyaansh *n.* वाक्यांश parenthesis

vakya-shaili *n.* वाक्य-शैली phraseology

valve *n.* वाल्व valve

vaman kriya *n* वमन क्रिया vomit

van lagana *v.t.* वन लगाना afforest

van sanjali *n.* वन संजली hawthorn

vanar-sadrish *a.* वानर-सदृश apish

vanaspati *n* वनस्पति flora

vanaspati jagat *v.t.* वनस्पति जगत plant

vanchaniya *a* वांछनीय desirable

vanchit karna *v. t.* वंचित करना bereave

vanchit karna *v. t* वंचित करना deprive

vandana *n.* वंदना invocation

vani *n.* वाणी speech

vaniki *n* वानिकी forestry
vanmaanush *n.* वनमानुष chimpanzee
vanmanush *n.* वनमानुष gorilla
vanpal *n.* वनपाल ranger
vanrakshak *n* वनरक्षक forester
vansavali *n.* वंशावली pedigree
vansh *n.* वंश posterity
vansh *n.* वंश race
vanshagat *a.* वंशागत heritable
vanshaj *n* वंशज descendant
vanshanugat *n.* वंशानुगत hereditary
vanshavali *n.* वंशावली ancestry
vansthali *n.* वनस्थली woodland
van-vihar manoranjan *n.* वन-विहार
   मनोरंजन picnic
vapas bulaana *n.* वापस बुलाना recall
vapas karna *v.t.* वापस करना repay
vapas nikal jana *v.i.* वापस निकल जाना
   recoil
vapasi *n.* वापसी recession
vapasi *adv.* वापसी recoil
vapasi *n.* वापसी repayment
vapasi *n.* वापसी return
vapasi *n.* वापसी withdrawal
vapis pana *v.t.* वापिस पाना recover
vardaan *n.* वरदान godsend
vardan *n* वरदान benison
vardan *n* वरदान boon
varg *n.* वर्ग square
varg dambh *n.* वर्गदंभ snobbery
varg dambhi *n.* वर्गदंभी snob
vargakar banana *v.t.* वर्गाकार बनाना
   square
vargikaran *n* वर्गीकरण classification
vargikaran karna *v.t.* वर्गीकरण करना
   assort
vargikaran karna *v.t* वर्गीकरण करना
   grade
vargikrit karna *v. t* वर्गीकृत करना classify
vargikrit karna *v.t.* वर्गीकृत करना group
variyata *n.* वरीयता seniority

varjit karna *v. t.* वर्जित करना debar
varnakramanusari *a.* वर्णक्रमानुसारी
   alphabetical
varnamala *n.* वर्णमाला alphabet
varnan *n.* वर्णन narrative
varnan karna *v. t.* वर्णन करना depict
varnan karna *v. t* वर्णन करना describe
varnan karna *v.t.* वर्णन करना portray
varnan karna *v.t.* वर्णन करना represent
varnatmak *a* वर्णनात्मक descriptive
varsh *n.* वर्ष year
varsh ganth *n.* वर्षगांठ jubilee
varsha *n* वर्षा rain
varsha hona *v.i.* वर्षा होना rain
varsh-bhar rahne wali *a.* वर्ष-भर रहने
   वाली perennial
varshik *a.* वार्षिक annual
varshik *a.* वार्षिक yearly
varshik anudaan *n.* वार्षिक अनुदान
   annuity
varshik vrintant *n.pl.* वार्षिक वृत्तांत
   annals
varshwala *a.* वर्षावाला rainy
varta *n.* वार्ता negotiation
varta yogya *a.* वार्ता योग्य negotiable
vartakaar *a.* वार्ताकार negotiator
vartaman *n.* वर्तमान present
vasantik *a.* वासंतिक vernal
vaseline *n.* वैसलीन vaseline
vash mein karna *v.t.* वश में करना quell
vash mein karna *v.t.* वश में करना subdue
vashibhut karna *v.t.* वशीभूत करना master
vashp *n.* वाष्प vapour
vashp jaisa *a.* वाष्प जैसा vaporous
vashp mein badal jaana *v.t.* वाष्प में बदल
   जाना vaporize
vasiyat *n.* वसीयत legacy
vasiyat *n.* वसीयत testament
vasiyat mein dena *v. t.* वसीयत में देना
   bequeath
vaskat *n.* वास्कट waistcoat

vasool karna *v.t.* वसूल करना realize

vastav mein *adv.* वास्तव में indeed

vastav mein *adv.* वास्तव में really

vastavik *n.* वास्तविक objective

vastr *n.* वस्त्र apparel

vastr *n* वस्त्र dressing

vastr pehenana *v.t.* वस्त्र पहनना apparel

vastr vikreta *n* वस्त्र विक्रेता draper

vastra *n* वस्त्र textile

vastra *n.* वस्त्र wardrobe

vastra pahanaana *v.t.* वस्त्र पहनाना attire

vastrkhand *n.* वस्त्रखंड rag

vastu *n.* वस्तु article

vastu *n.* वस्तु object

vastu *n.* वस्तु thing

vastuen *n.* वस्तुएं ware

vastuteh *adv.* वस्तुत: actually

vastvik *a* वास्तविक virtual

vastvik sach *a.* वास्तविक सच्चा veritable

vastvikta *n.* वास्तविकता reality

vastvikta *n.* वास्तविकता truth

vasul karna *v.t.* वसूल करना levy

vasul karnewala *n* वसूल करनेवाला collector

vasuli *n.* वसूली realization

vasuli *n.* वसूली recovery

vatapurti *n.* वातापूर्ति हवादारी ventilation

vaykt *a.* व्यक्त manifest

vayngya karna *v.i.* व्यंग्य करना jest

vayovridh *a.* वयोवृद्घ senior

vayo-vridh *a* वयो-वृद्ध elderly

vayu kay saman *adj.* वायु के समान aeriform

vayumandal *n* वायुमण्डल air

vayumandal *n.* वायुमंडल atmosphere

vayu-sambandhi *a.* वायु- संबंधी airy

vayuyan *n* वायुयान plane

vayuyan mein chalak kaksha *n.* वायुयान में चालक-कक्ष cock-pit

vazan *n.* वज़न weight

vazan kam karna *v.i.* वज़न कम करना slim

vazifa *n.* वज़ीफ़ा stipend

vedna *n.* वेदना pang

veena *n.* वीणा harp

veerta *n.* वीरता heroism

veh (stri) *pron.* वह (स्त्री) she

veri banana *v.t.* वैरी बनाना antagonize

vesh badalana *v. t* वेश बदलना disguise

veshya *n.* वेश्या prostitute

veshya *n.* वेश्या strumpet

veshyagaman karna, *v.t.* वेश्यागमन करना womanise

veshyapan *n.* वेश्यापन concubinage

vetan *n.* वेतन salary

vhagyasali *a.* भाग्यशाली lucky

vhisan aakraman *n.* भीषण आक्रमण onslaught

vhramansil *a.* भ्रमणशील nomadic

vibhaag *n* विभाग department

vibhajan *n* विभाजन division

vibhajan *n* विभाजन split

vibhajit karana *v. t* विभाजित करना dissect

vibhajit karna *v.t.* विभाजित करना segment

vibhakt *a.* विभक्त separate

vibhedan kshamata *n* विभेदन क्षमता discrimination

vibhin prakar ka *a.* विभिन्न प्रकार के multifarious

vibhin rang *n.* पच्चीकारी mosaic

vibhinn *a.* विभिन्न miscellaneous

vibhinn *a.* विभिन्न sundry

vibhinn *a.* विभिन्न varied

vibhinn *a.* various

vichaar karna *v. t* विचार करना conceive

vichalan *n* विचलन departure

vichalan *n* विचलन deviation

vichalit hona *n.* विचलित होना aberrance

vichar *n* विचार consideration

vichar *n.* विचार idea
vichar *n.* विचार impression
vichar *n.* विचार notion
vichar goshthi *n.* विचार गोष्ठी symposium
vichar karna *v.t.* विचार करना account
vichar karna *v. t* विचार करना consider
vichar karna *v. t* विचार करना contemplate
vichar karna *v.t.* विचार करना meditate
vichar karna *v.t.* विचार करना ponder
vichar karte huye *prep.* विचार करते हुए
  considering
vichar vimarsh *n* विचार विमर्श
  deliberation
vichar vinimaya karna *v. t.* विचार
  विनिमय करना discuss
vicharadhin *a* विचाराधीन pending
vicharak *n.* विचारक thinker
vicharna *v.i.* विचारना deem
vicharna *v. i* विचारना deliberate
vicharniya *a* विचारणीय considerable
vicharotejak *a.* विचारोत्तेजक suggestive
viched *n* विच्छेद breach
vichhed *n.* विच्छेद severance
vichitra *n.* विचित्र oddish
vichitra *a.* विचित्र quaint
vicrit ang wala *adj* विकृत अंग वाला
  anamorphous
vida *n* विदा farewell
vidagdhokti *n* विदग्धोक्ति epigram
vidambana *n.* विडंबना irony
vidayee *n.* विदाई adieu
vidayee *n.* विदाई conge
videsh *adv* विदेश abroad
videsh *a* विदेश foreign
videshi bhasha *n.* विदेशी भाषा lingo
videshi vyakti *n* विदेशी व्यक्ति foreigner
vidha *n.* विद्या lore
vidhan *n* विधान constitution
vidhan *n.* विधान legislation
vidhanmandal *n.* विधानमंडल legislature
vidhaya *n.* विधेय predicate

vidhayi *a.* विधायी legislative
vidhi *n.* विधि approach
vidhi *n.* विधि method
vidhi *n.* विधि mode
vidhi vicharadhin *a.* विधि विचाराधीन
  sub-judice
vidhivat *adv* विधिवत् duly
vidhur *n.* विधुर widower
vidhva *n.* विधवा widow
vidhva banana *v.t.* विधवा बनाना widow
vidhvans *n.* विध्वंस havoc
vidhwans *n.* विध्वंस ravage
vidroh *n.* विद्रोह insurrection
vidroh karna *v.i.* विद्रोह करना rebel
vidroha *n.* विद्रोह sedition
vidrohi *a.* विद्रोही insurgent
vidrohi vyakti *n.* विद्रोही व्यक्ति insurgent
vidroohi *n.* विद्रोही rebel
vidushak *n* विदूषक clown
vidvaan *a.* विद्वान learned
vidvan *a.* विद्वान well-read
vidvatapurna *a.* विद्वत्तापूर्ण scholarly
vidyadambar *n.* विद्याडंबर pedantry
vidyadambari *n.* विद्याडंबरी pedant
vidyalaya *n.* विद्यालय school
vidyaman *a.* विद्यमान present
vidyamulak *a* विद्यामूलक academic
vidyan *n.* विद्वान् scholar
vidyan sambandhi *a.* विद्वान् संबंधी
  scholastic
vidyarthi *n.* विद्यार्थी student
vidyashi *a.* विद्वेषी malicious
vidyesh *n.* विद्वेष malignancy
vidyut *n* विद्युत् electricity
vidyut dhara ki ekayee *n* विद्युत् धारा की
  इकाई ampere
vidyut kan *n.* विद्युत कण neutron
vidyut sanket *n.* विद्युत संकेत neonsign
vidyut seerhi *n.* विद्युत सीढ़ी lift
vidyut shakti yantra *n* विद्युत् शक्ति यंत्र
  dynamo

**vidyutikaran karna** *v. t* विद्युतीकरण करना electrify

**vidyutiya** *a* विद्युतीय electric

**vifal hona** *v.i.* विफल होना miscarry

**vifal kar dena** *v. t.* विफल कर देना baffle

**vig** *n.* विग wig

**vigyan** *n.* विज्ञान science

**vigyapan** *n* विज्ञापन advertisement

**vigyapan karna** *v.t.* विज्ञापन करना advertise

**vigyapan patra** *n.* विज्ञापन पत्र placard

**vigyapati** *n* विज्ञप्ति bulletin

**vigyapna patra** *n.* विज्ञापन पत्र pamphlet

**vihar** *n.* विहार sally

**vijay** *n* विजय conquest

**vijay** *n.* विजय triumph

**vijay** *n.* विजय victory

**vijay** *n* विजय win

**vijay prapt karna** *v.i.* विजय प्राप्त करना triumph

**vijay pana** *v.t.* विजय पाना surmount

**vijay sambandhi** *a.* विजय संबंधी triumphal

**vijayayi** *a.* विजयी triumphant

**vijayi** *a.* विजयी victorious

**vijeta** *n.* विजेता champion

**vijeta** *n.* विजेता victor

**vijeta** *n.* विजेता winner

**vikalp** *n.* विकल्प alternative

**vikarshak** *a.* विकर्षक repellent

**vikarshak vastu** *n* विकर्षक वस्तु repellent

**vikas** *n.* विकास development

**vikas** *n* विकास evolution

**vikas** *n.* विकास growth

**vikas** *n.* विकास promotion

**vikas rokna** *v.t.* विकास रोकना stunt

**viklang** *a* विकलांग disabled

**viklang banana** *v. t* विकलांग बनाना disable

**viklang vyakti** *n* विकलांग व्यक्ति cripple

**viklangata** *n* विकलांगता disability

**vikray** *a.* विक्रय saleable

**vikreta** *n.* विक्रेता salesman

**vikreta** *n.* विक्रेता seller

**vikreta** *n.* विक्रेता vendor

**vikreya** *a.* विक्रेय marketable

**vikrit** *a.* विकृत perverse

**vikrit karna** *v.t.* विकृत करना mangle

**vikriti** *n.* विकृति perversion

**viksit hona** *v.i* विकसित होना mature

**viksit karna** *v. t.* विकसित करना develop

**viksit karna** *v.t* विकसित करना evolve

**vilaap** *n.* विलाप moan

**vilaap karna** *v.i.* विलाप करना moan

**vilakshan** *a* विलक्षण fantastic

**vilakshan** *a* विलक्षण rum

**vilamb karna** *v.i.* विलम्ब करना dawdle

**vilamb karna** *v.i.* विलंब करना linger

**vilamb shulk** *adv.* विलम्ब शुल्क late fee

**vilambit** *a.* विलंबित overdue

**vilap** *n.* विलाप lamentation

**vilap** *n* विलाप wail

**vilap karna** *v.i.* विलाप करना mourn

**vilap karna** *v.i.* विलाप करना wail

**vilap karnewala** *n.* विलाप करनेवाला mourner

**vilasita** *n.* विलासिता luxury

**vilasmaya** *a.* विलासमय luxurious

**vilayak drav** *n* विलायक द्रव solvent

**vilayan** *n.* विलयन fusion

**vilom** *n.* विलोम antonym

**vilomatah** *adv.* विलोमतः vice-versa

**viman** *n.* विमान aircraft

**viman chalak** *n.* विमान चालक pilot

**viman chalan-vigyan** *n.pl.* विमान चालन-विज्ञान aeronautics

**viman-bhedi** *a.* विमान-भेदी anti-aircraft

**vimanchalak** *n.* विमानचालन aviation

**vimanchalak** *n.* विमानचालक aviator

**vimukh** *pref.* विमुख contra

**vina** *n.* वीणा lute

**vinamra** *a* विनम्र docile

vinamra *a.* विनम्र humble
vinamra *a.* विनम्र meek
vinamra *a.* विनम्र modest
vinamrata *n.* विनमता humility
vinash *n* विनाश destruction
vinash *n* विनाश doom
vinash *n* विनाश fall
vinash *n.* विनाश obliteration
vinash *n* विनाश overthrow
vinashkaari *a.* विनाशकारी subversive
vinashkari *a.* विनाशकारी wasteful
vinast karna *v.t.* विनष्ट करना obliterate
vinay *n.* विनय politeness
vinayshil *a.* विनयशील lowly
vineet *adj.* विनीत bland
vinimaya *n.* विनिमय barter
vinimaya karna *v. t* विनिमय करना exchange
vinit *a.* विनीत polite
vinod puran *a.* विनोदपूर्ण humorous
vinodi *n.* विनोदी humorist
vinti *n.* विनती entreaty
vinti *n.* विनती solicitation
vinti karna *v.t.* विनती करना appeal
vinti karna *v.t.* विनती करना solicit
violin *n.* वायलिन violin
violin vadak *n.* वायलिन वादक violinist
vipakshi *n.* विपक्षी antagonist
viparit *a.* विपरीत averse
viparyaya *n* विपर्यय reverse
vipatti *n.* विपत्ति scourge
vipatti *n.* विपत्ति calamity
vipatti mai dalna *v. t.* विपत्ति में डालना endanger
vipatti mein daalna *v.t.* विपत्ति में डालना peril
viplavkari *a.* विप्लवकारी seditious
viprit *a.* विपरीत reverse
viraam *n.* विराम standstill
viraasat *n.* विरासत heritage
viral *a.* विरल rare

viram *n.* विराम pause
viram *n* विराम stop
viram chihn vidhan *n.* विराम चिह्न विधान punctuation
virasat *n.* विरासत patrimony
virechek padarth *n.* विरेचक पदार्थ purgative
virechen *n.* विरेचन purgation
virodh *n.* विरोध antipathy
virodh *n.* विरोध antithesis
virodh *n.* विरोध confrontation
virodh *n* विरोध contrast
virodh *n.* विरोध hostility
virodh *n.* विरोध negation
virodh *n.* विरोध protest
virodh *n.* विरोध protestation
virodh *n.* विरोध resistance
virodh hona *v. t.* विरोध होना clash
virodh karna *v. t.* विरोध करना combat
virodh karna *v. i* विरोध करना contend
virodh karna *v. t* विरोध करना contradict
virodh karna *v. t* विरोध करना counter
virodh karna *v. t* विरोध करना cross
virodh karna *v.t.* विरोध करना object
virodh karna *v.t.* विरोध करना oppose
virodh mein *prep.* विरोध में against
virodh patr *n.* विरोध पत्र representation
virodhabhasaatmak *a.* विरोधाभासात्मक paradoxical
virodhatmak *a* विरोधत्माक contrary
virodhi *a.* विरोधी hostile
virodhi *a.* विरोधी inimical
virodhi *n.* विरोधी opponent
virodhi *a.* विरोधी opposite
virodhi dal *n.* विरोधी दल opposition
virodhi par kabu *n.* विरोधी पर काबू tackle
virta *n.* वीरता prowess
virtapurna *a.* वीरतापूर्ण quixotic
virudh kriya *n.* विरूद्घ क्रिया reaction
virya *n.* वीर्य semen
virya sambandhi *a.* वीर्य संबधी seminal

visangat *a.* विसंगत irrelevant

vish *n.* विष poison

vish *n.* विष venom

vishaad rog *n.* विषाद रोग melancholia

vishaadgrast *a.* विषादग्रस्त melancholic

vishaal *a.* विशाल immense

vishaalkaaya *a* विशालकाय mammoth

vishaalkaaya haathi *n.* विशालकाय हाथी mammoth

vishaila *a.* विषैला poisonous

vishaila *a.* विषैला venomous

vishaila sanp *n* विषैला साँप cobra

vishaishadhikar *n.* विशेषाधिकार privilege

vishakt *a.* विषाक्त septic

vishakt *a.* विषाक्त virulent

vishakt tatva *n.* विषाक्त तत्व virus

vishal *a.* विशाल capacious

vishal *a* विशाल enormous

vishal *a* विशाल great

vishal *a.* विशाल huge

vishal *a.* विशाल massive

vishal *a.* विशाल roomy

vishal *a.* विशाल sizable

vishal *a.* विशाल stupendous

vishal *a.* विशाल titanic

vishal *a.* विशाल tremendous

vishal *a.* विशाल vast

vishal *a.* विशाल voluminous

vishal granth *n.* विशाल ग्रंथ tome

vishal hridya *a.* विशाल हृदय magnanimous

vishal sankhya *n.* विशाल संख्या legion

vishal sankhya *n.* विशाल संख्या myriad

vishal vhawan *n.* विशाल भवन mansion

vishal-kaaya *n.* विशालकाय monstrous

vishalta *n.* विशालता immensity

visham *a.* विषम odd

vishamta dikhana *v. t* विषमता दिखाना contrast

vishay *n.* विषय theme

vishay *n.* विषय topic

vishay mein *prep* विषय में about

vishay soochi *n.* विषय सूची content

vishaygat *a.* विषयगत thematic

vishayi *n* विषयी debauchee

vishayvastu *n.* विषयवस्तु subject

visheshagya *a* विशेषज्ञ expert

visheshagya *n.* विशेषज्ञ specialist

visheshagya banana *v.i.* विशेषज्ञ बनना specialize

visheshan *n.* विशेषण adjective

visheshta *n.* विशेषता peculiarity

visheshta *n.* विशेषता speciality

visheshta *n.* विशेषता trait

vishishit *a.* विशिष्ट prominent

vishishita *a.* विशिष्ट conspicuous

vishishitata *n.* विशिष्टता prominence

vishisht nirdeshan *n.* विशिष्ट निर्देशन specification

vishisht vyakti *n.* विशिष्ट व्यक्ति somebody

vishishtikaran *n.* विशिष्टीकरण specialization

vishleshan *n* विश्लेषण dissection

vishleshan karna *v.t.* विश्लेषण करना resolve

vishleshan karta *n* विश्लेषणकर्ता analyst

vishleshanaatmak *a* विश्लेषणात्मक analytical

vishuvat rekha *n* विषुवत् रेखा equator

vishv *n.* विश्व world

vishv vidyalaya *n.* विश्वविद्यालय university

vishvakosh *n.* विश्वकोश encyclopaedia

vishvas *n.* विश्वास trust

vishvas dilana *v. t* विश्वास दिलाना convince

vishvas na rakhna *v. t.* विश्वास न रखना distrust

vishvasaniya *a.* विश्वसनीय reliable

vishvasghat *n.* विश्वासघात perfidy

vishvasghat *n.* विश्वासघात treason

vishvasghat *n* विश्वासघात betrayal

vishvasghat karna *vt.* विश्वासघात करना betray

vishvasghati *a* विश्वासघाती disloyal

vishvasghati *n.* विश्वासघाती traitor

vishvasi *a.* विश्वासी trustful

vishvasniya *a.* विश्वसनीय staunch

vishvaspatra *n* विश्वासपात्र confidant

vishvast *n* विश्वास confidence

vishva-vyapi *a.* विश्व-व्यापी global

vishwa *n.* विश्व universe

vishwas *n.* विश्वास belief

vishwasniya anuchar *n.* विश्वसनीय अनुचर henchman

vishwayopakata *n.* विश्वव्योपकता universality

vishyai *n.* विषय item

vishyasakt *n.* विषयासक्त voluptuary

vismaran *n.* विस्मरण oblivion

vismay *n.* विस्मय amazement

vismaya *n.* विस्मय astonishment

vismaya *n.* विस्मय awe

vismayodgaar *n* विस्मयोद्गार exclamation

vismit ho jana *v.i* विस्मित हो जाना marvel

vismit karna *v.t.* विस्मित करना amaze

vismit karna *v.t.* विस्मित करना astonish

vismyadibodhak *n.* विस्मयादिबोधक interjection

visphot *n* विस्फोट burst

visphot *n* विस्फोट eruption

vistaar *n.* विस्तार expansion

vistaar *n.* विस्तार quantity

vistar *n.* विस्तार continuation

vistar *n* विस्तार increase

vistar *n.* चादर sheet

vistar *n.* विस्तार spread

vistar karna *v. t* विस्तार करना enlarge

vistar se kahana *v. t* विस्तार से कहना elaborate

visthapit karna *v. t* विस्थापित करना displace

vistrit *a* विस्तृत elaborate

vistrit *a.* विस्तृत spacious

vistrit bhubhag *n.* विस्तृत भूभाग tract

vistrit varnan *n.* विस्तृत वर्णन particular

viswavyapi *a.* विश्वव्यापी universal

vitamin *n.* विटामिन vitamin

vitaran *n* वितरण distribution

vitt varsh वित्त वर्ष fiscal year

vivaadgrast sammelan *n.* विवादग्रस्त सम्मेलन parley

vivad *v. i. & n* विवाद brawl

vivad *n* विवाद controversy

vivad *n.* विवाद debate

vivad *n* विवाद dispute

vivad karna *v. t* विवाद करना bicker

vivad karna *v. i* विवाद करना dispute

vivah *n.* विवाह spousal

vivah *n.* विवाह wedlock

vivah karna *v.t. & i.* विवाह करना conjugate

vivah karna *v.t.* विवाह करना wed

vivah sambandhi *n.* विवाह संबंधी nuptials

vivah se purva hone wala *adj.* विवाह से पूर्व होने वाला ante nuptial

vivah se purva ka *a.* विवाह से पूर्व का premarital

vivah virodhi *n* विवाह विरोधी agamist

vivah yogya *a.* विवाह योग्य marriageable

vivahutsav *n.* विवाहोत्सव wedding

vivaran *v. t* विवरण detail

vivaran dena *v. t.* विवरण देना explain

vivek *n* विवेक conscience

vivek *a.* विवेक prudent

vivekhin *adj* विवेकहीन absurd

vivekpurna *a.* विवेकपूर्ण prudential

viveksheel *a.* विवेकशील rational

vivekshil *a.* विवेकशील judicious

vividh *a* विविध diverse

vividh *a.* विविध manifold

**vividh** *a.* बहुप्रसवा multifarious

**vividh,vibhinn** *a.* विविध, विभिन्न various

**vividhata** *n.* विविधता variety

**vividhkala vidhaylaya** *n.* विविधकला विद्यालय polytechnic

**vividhtapurna sangrah** *n.* विविधतापूर्ण संग्रह miscellany

**vivran** *n.* विवरण report

**vivran pustika** *n.* विवरण पुस्तिका prospectus

**vivranika** *n* विवरणिका brochure

**viyog** *n* वियोग bereavement

**viyojit karna** *v. t* वियोजित करना disconnect

**viyojya** *a.* वियोज्य separable

**voh** *pron.* वह he

**volt** *n.* वोल्ट volt

**voltata** *n.* वोल्टता voltage

**vote mangana** *v. t.* वोट मांगना canvass

**vraniya, vranyukt** *a.* व्रणीय, व्रणयुक्त ulcerous

**vrat** *n.* व्रत vow

**vrat lena** *v.t.* व्रत लेना vow

**vriddhi** *n.* वृद्धि increment

**vridh** *a.* वृद्ध aged

**vridhavastha sambandhi** *a.* वृद्घावस्था संबंधी senile

**vridhi** *n.* वृद्धि aggravation

**vridhi** *n.* वृद्धि augmentation

**vridhi hona** *v.i.* वृद्धि होना accrue

**vrikshiya** *a.* वृक्षीय sylvan

**vrish hanta** *n .* वृषहंता matador

**vrit** *n.* वृत circle

**vyabhichar** *n.* व्यभिचार adultery

**vyabhichari** *n.* व्यभिचारी libertine

**vyabhicharini stri ka pati** *n.* व्यभिचारिणी स्त्री का पति cuckold

**vyabhicharita** *n* व्यभिचारिता debauchery

**vyagra** *a* व्यग्र eager

**vyaiktikata** *n.* वैयक्तिकता individuality

**vyakaran** *n.* व्याकरण grammar

**vyakaranweta** *n.* व्याकरणवेत्ता grammarian

**vyakatitva** *n.* व्यक्तित्व personality

**vyakhayan** *n.* व्याकरण lecture

**vyakhya** *n.* व्याकरण gloss

**vyakhya karna** *v.t.* व्याख्या करन interpret

**vyakhyan** *n.* व्याख्यान say

**vyakti** *n.* व्यक्ति person

**vyaktigat** *a.* व्यक्तिगत individual

**vyaktigat maal-asbaab** *n.* व्यक्तिगत माल-असबाब belongings

**vyaktigat vartalap** *n.* व्यक्तिगत वार्तालाप tete-a-tete

**vyaktivad** *n.* व्यक्तिवाद individualism

**vyakul karna** *v.t.* व्याकुल करना perplex

**vyakul karna** *v.t.* व्याकुल करना perturb

**vyang-kavita likhna** *v.t.* वियोग-कविता लिखना parody

**vyangya** *n.* व्यंग्य satire

**vyangya chitr** *n.* व्यंग्य-चित्र caricature

**vyangya karna** *v.t.* व्यंग्य करना lampoon

**vyangya karna** *v.t.* व्यंग्य करना satirize

**vyangya kathan** *n.* व्यंग्य कथन sarcasm

**vyangya lekhak** *n.* व्यंग्य लेखक satirist

**vyangya ukti** *n.* व्यंग्य उक्ति repartee

**vyangyapurna** *a.* व्यंग्यपूर्ण sarcastic

**vyangyapurna** *a.* व्यंग्यपूर्ण satirical

**vyanjan** *n.* व्यंजन consonant

**vyapaari** *n.* व्यापारी merchant

**vyapak** *a* व्यापक comprehensive

**vyapak** *a.* व्यापक widespread

**vyapar** *n* व्यापार business

**vyapar** *n.* व्यापार trade

**vyapar karna** *v.i* व्यापार करना trade

**vyapar sambandh** *n.* व्यापार संबंध dealing

**vyapari** *n* व्यापारी businessman

**vyapari** *n.* व्यापारी dealer

**vyapari** *n.* व्यापारी trader

**vyaparik chinh** *n.* व्यापारिक चिन्ह brand

**vyapt hona** *v.t.* व्याप्त होना pervade

**vyarth** *a.* व्यर्थ worthless

vyartha *a.* व्यर्थ vain
vyartha *adv.* व्यर्थ vainly
vyartha *a.* व्यर्थ waste
vyas *n* व्यास diameter
vyasak *a* वयस्क adult
vyasak vyakti *n.* वयस्क व्यक्ति adult
vyasan *n.* व्यसन vice
vyast *a* व्यस्त busy
vyast rakhna *v.t* व्यस्त रखना engross
vyastata व्यवस्था engagement
vyastata ka samay *n.* व्यस्तता का समय
  rush
vyavahar *n.* व्यवहार treatment
vyavaharmulak *a.* व्यवहारमूलक
  pragmatic
vyavaharya *a.* व्यवहार्य viable
vyavaharya *a.* व्यवहार्य workable
vyavasay sambandhi *a.* व्यवसाय संबंधी
  professional
vyavasaya sangh *n.* व्यवसाय-संघ firm
vyavasayee *n.* व्यवसायी practitioner
vyavasayi *n.* व्यवसायी monger
vyavasayik *a* व्यवसायिक commercial
vyavasayik kshetra *n.* व्यावसायिक क्षेत्र
  sector
vyavdhan *n.* व्यवधान trouble
vyaya *v.t.* व्यय retrench
vyaya karna *v.t.* व्यय करना spend
vyaya ki rasid *n.* व्यय की रसीद voucher
vyaya mein kami *n.* व्यय में कमी
  retrenchment
vyayam sambandhi *a.* व्यायाम संबंधी
  gymnastic
vyayam vidha *n.* व्यायाम विद्या
  gymnastics
vyayami *n.* व्यायामी gymnast
vyom *n* व्योम ether
vyovridh vyakati *n.* वयोवृद्ध व्यक्ति
  senior
vyutpatishastra *n.* व्युत्पत्तिशास्त्र etymology
vyvahar kaushal *n.* व्यवहार कौशल tact

vyvasaya *n.* व्यवसाय career
vyvasaya *n.* व्यवसाय vocation
vyvasaya *n.* व्यवसाय work
vyvastha *n.* व्यवस्था ruling
vyvasthapan *n.* व्यवस्थापन regulation
vyvasthata *n.* व्यवस्था stipulation

wadak *n.* वादक instrumentalist
wafaadar *a* वफ़ादार faithful
wahan *adv.* वहाँ yonder
wakta *n.* वक्ता speaker
wakya *n.* वाक्य sentence
wanijaya *n* वाणिज्य commerce
wanijya-sambandhi *a.* वाणिज्य- संबंधी
  mercantile
wanshavali *n.* वंशावली lineage
warden *n.* वार्डन warden
warn *n* वर्ण complexion
warnan karna *v. t.* वर्णन करना express
washer *n.* वाशर washer
watt *n.* वाट watt
wayrth *a.* व्यर्थ futile
wayudaabmapi *n* वायुदाबमापी barometer
whale *n.* वेल whale
whale machali ki haddi *n.* ह्वेल मछली की
  हड्डी baleen
wilaap *n* विलाप lament
williyan *n.* विलयन merger
wisfot karna *v. t.* विस्फोट करना explode
wisfotak *a* विस्फोटक explosive
wisfotak padarth *n.* विस्फोटक पदार्थ
  explosive
wishisht *a* विशिष्ट especial
wishishta *n.* विशिष्टता forte
wishishtata chinha *n.* विशिष्टता चिन्ह
  hallmark
wishmarak aushadhi *n.* विषमारक औषध
  antidote

**Y**

yaad dilaana *v.t.* याद दिलाना remind
yaadgaar *n.* यादगार memory
yaajkiya *a* याजकीय clerical
yaanshala *n.* यानशाला garage
yaantrik *a* यांत्रिक mechanic
yaantrik *a.* यांत्रिक mechanical
yaantrika *n.* यांत्रिकी mechanics
yaapasi *n.* वापसी restoration
yachika *n.* याचिका petition
yachna karna *v.t.* याचना करना crave
yada kada *adv.* यदा कदा seldom
yada kada *adv.* यदा कदा occasionally
yadgar *n.* यादगार souvenir
yadi *conj.* यदि if
yadi *conj.* यदि whether
yadi nahin *conj.* यदि नहीं unless
yadyapi *conj.* यद्यपि although
yadyapi *conj.* यद्यपि though
yahan यहां here
yahan se *adv.* यहां से hence
yahi *a.* यही very
yahudi *n.* यहूदी Jew
yamak *n.* यमक pun
yantr manav *n.* यंत्र मानव robot
yantra *n* यंत्र engine
yantrana *n.* यंत्रणा agony
yantrana dena *v.t.* यंत्रणादेना lacerate
yanyukt *a.* यानयुक्त vehicular
yash *n.* यश renown
yash *n.* यश reputation
yatayaat *n.* यातायात traffic
yathapi *conj.* यद्यपि notwithstanding
yatharth *a.* यथार्थ actual
yatharth *n* यथार्थ fact
yatharth *n.* यथार्थ precise
yatharth *n.* यथार्थ realism
yatharthavadi *n.* यथार्थवादी realist
yatharthavadi *a.* यथार्थवादी realistic
yatharthta *n.* यथार्थता precision
yathesht *a* यथेष्ट enough
yathopari *n.* यथोपरि ditto
yatna *n.* यातना affliction
yatna *n.* यातना torment
yatna *n.* यातना torture
yatna dena *v.t.* यातना देना torment
yatna dena *v.t.* यातना देना torture
yatra *n.* यात्रा journey
yatra *n* यात्रा travel
yatra karna *v.i.* यात्रा करना journey
yatra karna *v.i.* यात्रा करना travel
yatri *n.* यात्री passenger
yatri *n.* यात्री traveller
yatri-saman *n.* यात्री- सामान baggage
yaun kriya *n.* यौन क्रिया sex
yauvan *n* यौवन bloom
yauvan *n.* यौवन youth
yavsura nirmansala *n* यवसुरा निर्माणशाला brewery
yayawar *a.* व्यवहार migrator
yeh *pron.* यह it
yeh din *n.* यह दिन today
yodha *n* योद्घा agonist
yodha *n* योद्घा combatant
yodha *n.* योद्घा knight
yodha *a.* योद्धा militant
yodha *a.* योद्घा warrior
yog *n* योग amount
yog dena *v. t* योग देना contribute
yogdaan *n* योगदान contribution
yogik *a* यौगिक compound
yogya *a* योग्य able
yogya *adj* योग्य apposite
yogya *a.* योग्य apt
yogya *a.* योग्य capable
yogya *a.* योग्य meritorious
yogya *a.* योग्य, सम्मान्य worthy
yogya banana *v. t* योग्य बनाना enable
yogya hona *v.t* योग्य होना merit

yogya hona *v. t.* योग्य होना deserve
yogyata *n* योग्यता ability
yojak *n.* योजक joiner
yojana *n* योजना device
yojana *n.* योजना plan
yojana *n.* योजना programme
yojana *n.* योजना project
yojana banana *v. t.* योजना बनाना design
yojana banana *v.t.* योजना बनाना plan
yojana banana *v.i.* योजना बनाना scheme
yojna *n.* योजना measure
yojna *n.* योजना system
yoni *n.* योनि vagina
yuddh *n.* युद्घ war
yudh *n* युद्घ battle
yudh karna *v.i.* युद्घ करना militate
yudh ke liye taiyar karna *v.t.* युद्घ के लिए तैयारी करना arm
yudh ladna *v. i.* युद्घ लड़ना battle
yudh saamagri *n.* युद्घ सामग्री munition
yudhapriyata *n* युद्घप्रियता belligerency
yudhniti vishayak *a.* युद्घनीति विषयक strategic
yudhnitigya *n.* युद्घनीतिज्ञ strategist
yudhpot *n* युद्घपोत cruiser
yudhpoton ka berha *n.* युद्घपोतों का बेड़ा armada
yudhpriya *a.* युद्घप्रिय warlike
yudhrat *a* युद्घरत belligerent
yudhrat rajya *n* युद्घरत राज्य belligerent
yudh-saamagri *n.* युद्घ-सामग्री armament
yudhshil *a.* युद्घशील combatant
yudhviram *n.* युद्घविराम armistice
yudhviram *n.* युद्घविराम truce
yug *n* युग epoch
yugmit karna *v.t.* युग्मित करना yoke
yunani bhasha *n.* युनानी भाषा greek
yuva *a.* युवा youthful
yuvan *n.* यौवन prime

**Z**

zabt *n* ज़ब्त forfeit
zabt ho jana *v.t* ज़ब्त हो जाना forfeit
zabti *n* ज़ब्ती confiscation
zahar dena *v.t.* ज़हर देना poison
zaitoon *n.* जैतून olive
zamanat *n.* जमानत guarantee
zamanat *n.* ज़मानत bail
zameen se sat jana *v. i.* ज़मीन से सट जाना crouch
zamindar *n.* जमींदार squire
zanzir ki kadi *n.* ज़ंजीर की कड़ी link
zaridar kapda *n* ज़रीदार कपड़ा brocade
zebra *n.* ज़ेबरा zebra
zimma lena *v.t.* जिम्मा लेना warrant
zimmedaar *a.* ज़िम्मेदार liable
zinda *a* ज़िंदा alive
zinda-dil *a.* जिंदादिल gay
zindadili *n.* जिंदादिली joviality
zip *n.* जिप zip
zor dena *v.t.* ज़ोर देना push
zor se band karna *v.t.* ज़ोर से बंद करना slam
zor se khinchna *v.t.* ज़ोर से खींचना tug
zordaar *a.* ज़ोरदार strenuous
zordaar dhakka *n* ज़ोरदार धक्का thrust